PORSCHE
DATA BOOK

Dedicated to Ferdinand Alexander Porsche

PORSCHE

DATA BOOK

THE DEFINITIVE REFERENCE TO SPECIFICATIONS AND STATISTICS

MARC BONGERS

First published in Germany in 2004
by Motorbuch Verlag

This English-language edition published in 2006
by Haynes Publishing

A catalogue record for this book is available
from the British Library

ISBN 1 84425 316 3

Library of Congress catalog card no 2005935249

Translation by Peter L. Albrecht, California

Published by Haynes Publishing,
Sparkford, Yeovil, Somerset BA22 7JJ, UK
Tel: 01963 442030 Fax: 01963 440001
Int. tel: +44 1963 442030
Int. fax: +44 1963 440001
E-mail: sales@haynes.co.uk
Website: www.haynes.co.uk

Haynes North America Inc.,
861 Lawrence Drive, Newbury Park,
California 91320, USA

Printed and bound in the Czech Republic

Contents

Acknowledgements

The author's grateful thanks and appreciation go out to the following people and organisations who provided invaluable assistance in the creation of this book:

Dr Ing. h.c. F. Porsche AG, Zuffenhausen and Ludwigsburg
Klaus Parr, Jens Torner, Dieter Gross, Klaus Boizo, Günther Scheithauer, Wolfgang Karger, Hans Baisch and Yvonne Knotek

Porsche Zentrum Oberschwaben, Weingarten
Max Lang, Wilhelm Lang, Michael Stahlbaumer, Gerda Theuer, Markus Ardemani and Willy Silmen

Porsche Club Biberach e.V., Biberach/Riss
Heinz Miller, Hermann Heck and Thomas Hepp

Porsche Automuseum Helmut Pfeifhofer, Gmünd/Carinthia, Austria
Helmut Pfeifhofer

RUF-Automobile GmbH, Pfaffenhausen
Alois Ruf, Estonia Ruf, H.-P. Lieb, Hans Lampert, Josef Waltenberger and Robert Besl

and Jörg Austen, Weissach

Foreword

Porsche cars have, since 1948, captivated sports car enthusiasts throughout the world. For more than 50 years Porsche has satisfied the demanding standards of its worldwide customers with its unique combination of handcrafted quality, the brilliance of its engineers and painstaking, individual vehicle assembly. No other automobile marque has been more successful in motorsport, and Porsche consistently applies the hard-won lessons of racing to its production cars. A Porsche sports car combines high performance, a sports driving experience, individuality, active and passive safety and environmental responsibility with complete everyday utility.

This book is a comprehensive reference, chronicling the development of every Porsche production model, from the first Porsche 356 built in Gmünd, in the Austrian province of Carinthia, through the classic rear-engined models (the 356 and 911) and the transaxle models with four or eight cylinders, to mid-engined cars such as the Porsche 914 and the current Porsche Boxster. The two latest Porsche models, the Leipzig-built off-road-capable Porsche Cayenne and the high-end Carrera GT sports car, are presented in detail. Special models, built in limited series, are also described. In short, all air-cooled and water-cooled Porsche production models are presented in a complete and concise manner.

This book is a worldwide first in that it also includes a history of all models produced by RUF Automobile GmbH, based on the outstanding technical foundation provided by Porsche. The story of the RUF firm is closely bound to that of Porsche. For more than 40 years the Pfaffenhausen-based company has been maintaining, repairing and restoring Porsche cars, and for nearly 30 years RUF has been building its own complete cars. (Since 1981 RUF has been registered as an independent vehicle manufacturer by the German Federal Bureau of Motor Vehicles.) RUF has contributed to the development of the 911 with significant engineering innovations which are sometimes just a step ahead of the Porsche factory itself. 'You can hardly see the difference, but you can really feel it!'

RUF offers Porsche connoisseurs throughout the world the same engineering excellence and quality craftsmanship as Porsche itself, and a book covering all Porsche production cars would not be complete without a dedicated chapter covering RUF Porsches.

Marc Bongers
Biberach/Riss

Introduction

By the time Ferdinand Porsche decided, at the end of 1930, to start his own company, he had already made a name for himself in the automobile industry.

On 25 April 1931 his company, Dr Ing. h.c. F. Porsche Gesellschaft mit beschränkter Haftung, Konstruktionen und Beratungen für Motoren- und Fahrzeugbau [Dr Ing. h.c. F. Porsche Ltd., Engine and Vehicle Design and Consultancy], based at Kronenstrasse 24, Stuttgart, was entered in the commercial register. There followed designs such as the Auto Union Grand Prix cars and the original Volkswagen Beetle.

In June 1938 the design office moved to Stuttgart-Zuffenhausen, in Spitalwaldstrasse (today, Otto-Dürr-Strasse). The Reutter coachbuilding plant was located directly across the street. In the same year the company was transformed from a limited company to a limited partnership. In 1939 three aluminium-bodied streamlined coupés with performance-modified Volkswagen engines were built to take part in the long-distance Berlin-Rome rally, but because of the outbreak of war the road race did not take place.

In the autumn of 1944, to avoid Allied bombing, the company moved to Gmünd in the Austrian province of Carinthia. There, in July 1947 under the direction of Ferry Porsche, the first drawings of a sports car bearing the Porsche name were made. On 6 June 1948 Porsche was issued a road use permit by the Carinthian provincial government. The 356/1 would remain a one-off. Beginning with the second car, the 356/2, the engine was relocated behind the rear axle. In all, 53 examples were hand-built in Gmünd.

In November 1949, Reutter in Stuttgart was contracted to build 500 Porsche 356 bodies in steel. The very first Stuttgart-built Porsche 356 coupé was completed on the Thursday before Easter in 1950. The 500th Porsche 356 was built on 2 March 1951. At the 1953 Paris salon, Porsche showed its 550 Spyder with its Ernst Fuhrmann-designed four-cam engine. At the beginning of December 1955 Porsche's Werk I was returned to the company by the American occupation forces. Simultaneously, Werk II, designed by architect Rolf Gutbrod, was completed. In March 1956 Porsche celebrated its 25th anniversary as a company, as well as the completion of the 10,000th Porsche. Just two years later the 25,000th car rolled out of the workshops.

In 1961 Ferdinand Alexander Porsche took charge of the design studio and the design of the 356 successor. Immediately after completing his studies at the Swiss Federal Institute of Technology, in April 1963, Ferdinand Piëch joined the company.

In autumn 1963 Porsche presented its new Porsche 901 to the public at the Frankfurt International Automobile Show. In March 1964 Porsche took over body assembly from Reutter, and on 14 September that year the first Porsche 901 rolled off the assembly line. A short time later the model was renamed 911, because Peugeot had patented all three-digit model designations with a central zero. Assembly of the new 911 and the 356 continued in parallel for several months. On 28 April 1965 the last production 356 left the assembly line. In May 1966 Porsche laid on one more limited-production run of ten white 356s for the Dutch police, the Rijkspolitie. In the spring of 1965 Porsche began production of the affordable 912, powered by a four-cylinder engine, as the 911 had grown too expensive for many former Porsche customers. In autumn 1966 the 911 and 912 were available in Targa form, with a removable hood and folding plastic rear window. In that same year the 100,000th Porsche, a 912 Targa, was delivered to the police. Beginning in 1968, Ferdinand Piëch was placed in charge of all development activities at Porsche. The 912 was discontinued in 1969. In that same year the Porsche 914 was exhibited at the Frankfurt IAA as a joint venture with Volkswagen. The 'Porsche-VW Vertriebsgesellschaft mbH' was formed to market the 914. Bodies for the 914 were built by Karmann in Osnabrück. Final assembly of the 914/4 was done by Karmann itself, while the 914/6 was assembled by Porsche in Zuffenhausen.

In October 1971 Porsche opened its Weissach Development Centre, with 500 employees. In 1972 the firm was transformed into a joint stock company, and Porsche and Piëch family members withdrew from management. Dr Ernst Fuhrmann was made spokesman for the Board of Directors.

In the autumn of 1972 Porsche began production of the 911 Carrera RS. Assembly of the 911 turbo began in the spring of 1975. From mid-1975 Porsche began using two-side hot-dip galvanized steel body panels, and provided a warranty against rust-through for all structural parts. Production of the Porsche 924 began in January 1976 at the Audi plant in Neckarsulm. Production of the 914 ended in the same year. In November 1976 Dr Ernst Fuhrmann was appointed Chairman of the Board. In 1977 Porsche built its 250,000th car; production of the Porsche 928 began in the autumn. A year later, a jury of European automobile journalists chose the 928 as the first, and to date only, sports car to be named 'Car of the Year'. In early 1979 the 924 turbo rounded out the four-cylinder model range.

From the 1981 model year Porsche extended its warranty against rust-through to cover the entire body. On 1 January 1981 Peter W. Schutz assumed his duties as Chairman of the Board. The year 1981 was one of celebration for Porsche: 50 years of Porsche; in the spring the 100,000th Porsche 924 rolled off the line; September saw the 200,000th 911 and 300,000th Zuffenhausen-built Porsche. The Porsche 944 was introduced to the market in early 1982. In January 1983 Porsche's long period without a Cabriolet ended with the start of 911 SC Cabriolet production. In the spring of 1984 Porsche increased its capitalization and issued non-voting preferred stock. Beginning with the 1985 model year, all Porsche models were fitted with side-impact protection. In late January 1985 the 944 turbo was introduced to the international motoring press. The Porsche 959, first shown in autumn 1985 at the Frankfurt IAA, went into limited production in 1987. On 1 January 1988 Heinz Branitzki was named Chairman of the Board. Production of the Porsche 924 model line ended in autumn 1988, just as assembly of the 944 S2 Cabriolet began at ASC in Weinsberg. In Zuffenhausen, the first model of the new 964 series, the 911 Carrera 4, began rolling off the production line. The summer of 1989 saw completion of the last examples of the torsion-bar 911 Carrera series as the old Reutter body plant was wound up. A new body plant, Werk V, began operation with production of the 911 Carrera 2. As of autumn 1989 all Porsche vehicles have been equipped with anti-lock brakes as standard equipment. Prof. Dr Ferry Porsche retired from the Supervisory Board in March 1990, and was named Honorary Chairman; he was succeeded by Ferdinand Alexander Porsche. At the same time, Arno Bohn, a Board member since January 1990, was named Chairman of the Board. The 964 turbo, shown at the Geneva salon in early 1990, entered production later that autumn. From 1 February 1991 Porsche became the world's first auto-manufacturer to equip all left-hand-drive models with driver and front passenger airbags as standard equipment. Restructuring of Porsche marketing operations in Germany was completed; of the original 220 Porsche dealerships, 80 remained as Porsche Centres. In April 1991 the last Neckarsulm-produced Porsche 944 left the assembly line; thereafter, until the end of the year, 944 S2 production continued in Zuffenhausen. In the autumn, production of the 968 began in Zuffenhausen. Dr Wendelin Wiedeking was appointed spokesman for the Board of Directors in October 1992. In January 1993 the Porsche Boxster styling study was exhibited at the Detroit Motor Show. In March 1993 Prof. Dr Ferry Porsche relinquished his duties as a member of the Supervisory Board, and Prof. Dr Helmut Sihler was appointed successor to Ferdinand Alexander Porsche as Chairman of the Supervisory Board. The Supervisory Board made Dr Wendelin Wiedeking Chairman of the Board of Directors with effect from 1 August 1993. In autumn 1993 the 993 Carrera was presented at the Frankfurt IAA and was simultaneously introduced to the market. In April 1995 the all-wheel-drive 993 turbo was introduced. In the summer of 1995 production of the transaxle models, the 968 and 928, was terminated. Porsche's high degree of competence in the field of emissions was recognized with the founding, in January 1996, of the ADA (Abgaszentrum der Automobilindustrie – the Automotive Industry Exhaust Emissions Centre) at Porsche's Weissach development centre. Founding members of the ADA were Audi, BMW, Mercedes-Benz, Volkswagen and Porsche.

On 15 July 1996 the one-millionth Porsche vehicle, a 993 Carrera Coupé with Tiptronic S, was delivered to the Autobahnpolizei in Stuttgart in a festive ceremony.

Beginning in the autumn of 1996 the Porsche Boxster (a two-seat roadster with a newly-developed, water-cooled six-cylinder boxer engine) rolled off the assembly line. Demand for the Boxster was so great that Porsche had to look for additional production capacity, which it found with Valmet, a Finnish company. Valmet primarily built vehicles for overseas export. At the 1997 Frankfurt International Automobile Exposition, Porsche presented its successor to the air-cooled 911 model line.

The Porsche 996 Carrera was equipped with a water-cooled six-cylinder boxer engine. The 996 and Boxster were built using a cost-saving shared-parts concept. On 27 March 1998 Prof. Dr Ferry Porsche passed away in Zell am See, Austria, at the age of 88. He did not live to see the end of air-cooled 911 production four days later. In the late 1990s, Porsche continued to expand its 996 and Boxster model lines. The 996 was produced in an unprecedented variety of models. Porsche now sought to extend its market beyond sports cars, and in autumn 2002 the company ventured into unexplored territory with its off-road-capable Cayenne. This was Porsche's entry into the growing Sports Utility Vehicle (SUV) market. A year later, Porsche's high-end sports car, the Carrera GT, with production limited to 1,500, went into production. While the Cayenne and Carrera GT began production in a new Porsche plant in Leipzig, Porsche was already thinking about a potential fourth model line.

Porsche 356

The Gmünd-built Porsche Type 356

After establishing his independent engineering design company in 1931, Ferdinand Porsche worked primarily for outside clients. His best-known design contract was the original Volkswagen Beetle (Porsche Type 60), of which about 21,520,000 examples were built by the time production ceased in the summer of 2003. Even as he worked on outside design contracts, Porsche's thoughts often turned to the idea of producing his own small sports car.

The Berlin-Rome car (Type 64), based on Volkswagen mechanicals, may be regarded as the immediate ancestor of the first car to bear the Porsche name. Only three examples of this 40hp (29kW) streamliner were built, but these anticipated a number of engineering and styling features of later Porsches.

In 1944, in the midst of the turmoil of war, Porsche relocated its design office to Gmünd, in the Austrian province of Carinthia (Kärnten). The first drawings of an open sports car were created under the direction of Ferry Porsche in mid-June, 1947. During development, its designers deliberately drew on Volkswagen components, including engine, transmission and suspension parts.

The first Porsche was issued its road-use permit on 8 June 1948. The car was a two-seat roadster with a rudimentary top and with its engine installed ahead of the rear axle – a true mid-engined sports car. While the air-cooled, four-cylinder horizontally-opposed ('boxer') Volkswagen engine of the day managed 24.5hp (18kW) out of its 1131cc displacement, Porsche, by means of classic engine tuning techniques, raised this to all of 35hp (26kW) at 4000rpm. This was sufficient to accelerate the aluminium-bodied, tubular-framed 356/1 Roadster to a top speed of 135kph (84mph). Its four drum brakes were cable actuated. The car was soon sold to a Swiss car dealer, Rupprecht von Senger of Zürich, for 7000 Swiss Francs; he sold it to the first Porsche customer for 7500 Francs. Porsche used the sale proceeds to obtain materials to build more cars.

Beginning with the second car, a coupé, the engine was relocated behind the rear axle in order to provide more interior space for luggage or jump seats. The 356/2 was intended to provide greater comfort and everyday utility than the first car. Alongside the Coupé, Porsche also developed a convertible ('Cabriolet') version. Both variants employed a sheet-steel box frame. The aluminium bodywork was hand-formed over wooden formers, and the bumpers were mounted flush against the bodywork. The windscreen was split by a central brace, and on the Coupé small quarterlights were mounted on the doors.

Suspension was by means of crank arms, sprung by enclosed transverse torsion bars. At the rear, swing axles were located by trailing arms and transverse torsion bars. The four-cylinder boxer engine was fitted with overhead valves. Its 1131cc displacement and 7:1 compression yielded 40hp (29kW) at 4000rpm. Carburation was by means of a pair of Solex 26 VFI downdraught carburettors, topped by two dry-element air cleaners. Maximum torque of 64Nm (47lb ft) was developed at 2600rpm. Weighing only 680kg (1500lb), fuel consumption was a very economical 35 to 40mpg. With an eye to motorsport applications, engine displacement was reduced to 1086cc, while maintaining power output. The first four vehicles with this new engine were built before the end of 1948.

A total of 52 vehicles were built in Gmünd. The last Gmünd-built Porsche 356 was delivered on 20 March 1951. Porsche retained five Gmünd Coupés for its own racing purposes.

356/1 Roadster Gmünd 1948

Engine

Engine design:	4-cylinder horizontally-opposed
Installation:	Mid-engine
Cooling system:	Air-cooled
Engine type:	VW
Displacement (cc):	1131
Bore x stroke (mm):	75 x 64
Engine output DIN (kW/hp):	26/35 at 4000rpm
Maximum torque (Nm/lb ft):	69/51 at 2600rpm
Output per litre(kW/l/hp/l):	23.0 / 30.9
Compression ratio:	7.0 : 1
Valve operation & camshaft drive:	ohv, cam driven by gears, 2 valves per cylinder
Carburation:	1 downdraught carburettor Solex 26 VFI
Ignition system:	Battery coil ignition
Firing order:	1 - 4 - 3 - 2
Crankshaft bearing:	4 slide bearings
Engine lubrication:	Full pressure oil lubrication
Engine oil total (l):	3.0*
*Filling new assembled engine, oil change 2.5	

Transmission

Drive configuration:	Rear-axle drive
Manual gearbox:	4-speed
Transmission type:	VW
Transmission ratios:	
1st gear:	3.60
2nd gear:	2.07
3rd gear:	1.25
4th gear:	0.80
Reverse gear:	6.60
Drive ratio:	4.43

Body, chassis, suspension, brakes, wheels

Body design:	Aluminium Roadster body, 2 doors, 2 seats, fixed on a steel grid frame, split windscreen, bumpers fixed close to body, single layer Roadster top
Suspension, front:	Two independent parallel arms, torsion rods, hydraulic single-action shock absorbers
Suspension, rear:	Oscillating half through spring stays, torsion rods, hydraulic double-action shock absorbers

Brakes, front/rear (Size (mm)):	Brake drums Simplex (230 x 30) / Brake drums Simplex (230 x 30)
Wheels, front/rear:	3.00 D x 16 / 3.00 D x 16
Tyres, front/rear:	5.00-16 / 5.00-16

Electrical system

Alternator (W):	130
Battery (V/Ah):	6 / 75

Dimensions and weight

Track, front/rear (mm):	1290 / 1250
Wheelbase (mm):	2150
Length x width x height (mm):	3860 x 1670 x 1250
Kerb weight (kg):	585
Permissible gross weight (kg):	785
Fuel tank capacity (l):	50, including 5 reserve
C_w x A (m²):	0.46 x 1.41 = 0.648*
Power/weight ratio (kg/kW/kg/hp):	22.50 / 16.71
*open top with driver and passenger	

Fuel consumption

(mpg / l/100km):	35-40 / 7-8; 74-80 RON normal leaded

Performance, production, prices

Acceleration 0-62mph/100kph (s):	23.0
Maximum speed (mph / kph):	84 / 135 (with covered passenger seat: 87 / 140)
Production, total number:	1
Purchase price to dealer:	sFr 7,000
Purchase price to customer:	sFr 7,500

356/2 Coupé Gmünd
356/2 Cabriolet Gmünd 1948–1950

Engine

Engine design:	4-cylinder horizontally-opposed
Installation:	Rear-engine
Cooling system:	Air-cooled
Engine type:	VW
1949-1950:	369*
Displacement (cc):	1131
1949-1950:	1086*
Bore x stroke (mm):	75 x 64
1949-1950:	73.5 x 64*
Engine output DIN (kW/hp):	29/40 at 4000rpm
Maximum torque (Nm/lb ft):	69/51 at 2600rpm
1949-1950:	64/47 at 3300rpm*
Output per litre(kW/l / hp/l):	25.6 / 35.4
1949-1950:	26.7 / 36.8*
Compression ratio:	7.0 : 1
Valve operation & camshaft drive:	ohv, cam driven by gears, 2 valves per cylinder
Carburation:	2 downdraught carburettors Solex 26 VFI
Ignition system:	Battery coil ignition
Firing order:	1 - 4 - 3 - 2
Crankshaft bearing:	4 slide bearings
Engine lubrication:	Full pressure oil lubrication
Engine oil total (l):	3.0**

*In year 1948 already four cars with engine-type 369
**Filling new assembled engine, oil change 2.5

Transmission

Drive configuration:	Rear axle drive
Manual gearbox:	4-speed
Transmission type:	VW
Transmission ratios:	
1st gear:	3.60
2nd gear:	2.07
3rd gear:	1.25
4th gear:	0.80
Reverse gear:	6.60
Drive ratio:	4.43

Body, chassis, suspension, brakes, wheels

Body design:	Aluminium body, 2 doors, 2 seats, pressed and welded steel frame, split windscreen, single grille on rear lid, bumpers fixed close to body
Coupé:	Fixed aluminium roof
Cabriolet:	Multi-layer hood with small glass rear window
Suspension, front:	Two independent parallel arms, torsion rods, hydraulic single-action shock absorbers
Suspension, rear:	Oscillating half through spring stays, torsion rods, hydraulic double-action shock absorbers
Brakes, front/rear (Size (mm)):	Brake drums Simplex (230 x 30) / Brake drums Simplex (230 x 30)
Wheels, front/rear:	3.00 D x 16 / 3.00 D x 16
Tyres, front/rear:	5.00-16 / 5.00-16

Electrical system

Alternator (W):	130
Battery (V/Ah):	6 / 75

Dimensions and weight

Track, front/rear (mm):	1290 / 1250
Wheelbase (mm):	2100
Length x width x height (mm):	3870 x 1660 x 1300
Kerb weight (kg):	680*
Permissible gross weight (kg):	880**
Fuel tank capacity (l):	50, including 5 reserve
C_w x A (m^2) Coupé:	0.29 x 1.62 = 0.469
Power/weight ratio (kg/kW/ kg/hp):	23.44 / 17.00

*in the first sales leaflet: 600 kg
**in the first sales leaflet: 800 kg

Fuel consumption

(mpg / l/100km):	35-40 / 7-8; 74-80 RON normal leaded

Performance, production, prices

Acceleration 0-62mph/100kph (s):	23.5
Maximum speed (mph/kph):	87 / 140
Production, total number:	52
Purchase prices:	
Coupé:	sFr 14,500
Cabriolet:	sFr 16,500

The Stuttgart cars
Porsche 356

The early Porsche 356s

In late 1949, Porsche contracted the Reutter coachworks of Stuttgart to build 500 bodies. Production in Stuttgart-Zuffenhausen began in the spring of 1950. The very first Zuffenhausen-built Porsche 356 Coupé was completed on the Thursday before Easter.

Model year 1950

The steel bodywork of Stuttgart-built 356s was welded to the box-section frame. Front and rear bumpers were flush-mounted to the bodywork. The Sekurit windscreen was split by a vertical brace. A slim chromium handle graced the front boot lid, and a chromium-plated grille was inset into the engine lid. Small round indicators were mounted below the headlamps at the front, and below the rectangular tail lamps at the rear. Brake lamps and number plate illumination were incorporated in a single chromium housing below the number plate. Compared to the Gmünd coupés, the Stuttgart cars showed more smoothly-flowing lines in the roof area, the flanks were curved more strongly and the door vent windows were deleted. The doors were fitted with winding windows. At cd = 0.296, the 356 Coupés enjoyed a very low drag coefficient. Thanks to its tight-fitting front bumper, the car had aerodynamic downforce on the front axle. As well as the Coupé, Porsche also offered a convertible version.

An air-cooled four-cylinder boxer engine, derived from the Volkswagen power unit, performed its duties at the rear. Its cylinder bore and stroke dimensions of 73.5mm x 64mm yielded a displacement of 1086cc; with a 7:1 compression ratio, power output was 40hp (29kW) at 4200rpm. Two Solex 32 PBI downdraught carburettors supplied the correct air-fuel mixture. Angled overhead valves were actuated by pushrods and rocker arms. A tubular oil cooler mounted in the cooling air stream inside the engine blower housing ensured acceptable oil temperatures for the pressurized oil lubrication system.

The 16-inch steel wheels, 3.00 D x 16, were as yet devoid of cooling air openings and carried 4.75-16 or 5.00-16 tyres. Hubcaps were from Volkswagen, but without emblems. At the front, each wheel was attached to a pair of crank arms on transverse torsion bars. The front shock absorbers were double-acting, the rears single-acting. A Porsche worm-and-peg steering box actuated the steering linkage. The four brake drums had an inside diameter of 230mm, and 30mm wide shoes.

The sheet-steel dashboard was painted in body colour, and devoid of any upholstery. Inset behind the white three-spoke steering wheel were two round instruments, a speedometer and a clock. A rectangular cut-out at the centre of the dash served to house an optional radio. In the 356, the ignition lock was located to the left of the steering column. Driver and passenger sat on an undivided bench seat. As an option, two individual seats could be installed. There were as yet no jump seats in the rear, although an additional passenger might be accommodated in the back.

Power was transmitted through a single-plate dry clutch and four-speed manual transmission to the spiral-bevel gear final drive at the rear axle. Top speed was 87mph (140kph), zero to 62mph (100kph) took 23.5 seconds.

Model year 1951

On 21 March 1951 Porsche celebrated a milestone as the 500th Porsche rolled off the assembly line. At the IAA (International Automobil-Ausstellung – International Automobile Show) in Frankfurt am Main, which in the early 1950s was still held in the spring, Porsche presented its new model year line-up, featuring further development of the 356. The IAA also saw the introduction of a new 1.3-litre engine.

On the 1.3 litre the bore of the aluminium-alloy cylinders was increased to 80mm. These were matched to aluminium-alloy domed pistons with a nose-like projection into the combustion chamber. At 6.5:1 compression, the engine developed 44hp (32kW) at 4200rpm. The two Solex Type 32 PBI downdraught carburettors were equipped with a different jet package. Pushrods were modified in keeping with the other engine changes.

The Volkswagen four-speed manual transmission continued its service. The first two gears were still straight-cut, while third and fourth gear employed helical gears for reduced noise.

For improved ventilation, the rear side-windows of the Coupé could be swung out. Porsche conducted tests in an effort to reduce body resonance and improve sound insulation. In May 1951, thought was given to producing right-hand-drive vehicles for the British and Commonwealth markets. Other matters under consideration included special bumpers for the American market.

As of April 1951, the previously used rear lever-action shock absorbers were replaced by telescopic versions, and their axle mounting points altered accordingly. For improved cooling, the brakes were fitted with finned aluminium drums.

As an option, a tachometer could be installed in place of the large clock next to the speedometer. An extended steering column was available for drivers of shorter stature. Porsche drivers were now better able to announce their presence with a new two-tone horn.

Performance of the new 1.3-litre model was somewhat better than that of the 1.1-litre variant. In a spring 1951 road test, the German motoring magazine *Auto, Motor und Sport* measured 0-62mph (100kph) acceleration at 19 seconds. Repeated speed tests yielded a true average of 96mph (155kph). This particular car performed better than Porsche's own factory claims. Tester and magazine publisher Paul Pietsch was so enthusiastic about the car that he bought the Coupé right after the test.

Model year 1952

For 1952, the most obvious change in the 356 bodywork was the introduction of a one-piece windscreen with a vertical crease at the centre line, the so-called 'bent window'. The first right-hand-drive cars became available in October 1951.

The most powerful engine in the 356 model line-up was the new 1488cc power unit, developing 60hp (44kW) at 5000rpm, and maximum torque was an impressive 102Nm (75lb ft) at 3000rpm. The crankshaft was mounted in roller bearings.

An early Stuttgart-built, split-windscreen 356 Coupé

Apart from the single-piece bent windscreen, the most noticeable style change was the bumpers which projected away from the bodywork. The front bonnet handle was somewhat larger, and perforated for better grip.

In the rear seat area, the floorpan was lowered to provide space for upholstery and a folding rear backrest, which also served as a luggage shelf. A tachometer was now standard equipment, along with instruments with green markings and small 'eyebrows' to prevent unwanted reflections.

The steel wheels now had ventilation holes for improved brake cooling. The front brakes were of duplex (dual wheel cylinder) configuration.

By early 1950s standards, the 356 powered by the 1500 engine provided remarkable performance. Top speed was about 107mph (170kph). In 1952, there were virtually no other German cars with higher top speed. Acceleration to 62mph (100kph) was accomplished in just 15.5 seconds.

A limited-production Roadster was built for the American market – the 'America Roadster' – with aluminium open-top bodywork fitted with a collapsible hood and side curtains, and lightweight bucket seats. This made it appreciably lighter than the Coupé, and with a 70hp (51kW) 1.5-litre engine it had a respectable performance.

Model year 1953

The engine range was extended to include two new 1.5-litre power units. A 55hp (40kW) engine replaced the erstwhile 60hp (44kW) unit. The new top of the line was called the 356 1500 Super; thanks to higher compression and larger carburettors, this produced all of 70hp (51kW) at 5000rpm. Maximum torque of 108Nm (80lb ft) was developed at 3600rpm. All models were fitted with a full-synchromesh manual transmission, using Porsche's patented synchronizing system.

The improved brake system was an important new feature for increased safety. The inside diameter of the brake drums was increased from 230mm to 280mm, and brake shoe width was increased from 30mm to 40mm.

Bumpers were reworked yet again; they were now mounted even further away from the bodywork, and fitted with over-riders. The front indicators were moved to directly below the headlamps. Two large round tail lamps incorporated indicators, brake lights and back lights. The Cabriolet had a larger, flexible plastic rear window.

A new two-spoke steering wheel carried the newly introduced Porsche crest on its horn button.

The gear lever was moved forward by 120mm, and angled rearward. Two-speed windscreen wipers were available as an option.

Thanks to outstanding aerodynamics, well run-in 356 1500 Supers could top 112mph (180kph). Acceleration from a standstill to 62mph (100kph) took just 14.0 seconds.

Model year 1954

The proven 1.1-litre engine entered its last year of production. Porsche presented a new engine in the form of the 1300 Super, with a roller-bearing Hirth crankshaft, providing 60hp (44kW) from its 1290cc displacement. This 1.3-litre power unit developed its maximum torque of 88Nm (65lb ft) at 3600rpm.

The 356 1300 Super topped out at 99mph (160kph). Acceleration to 62mph (100kph) was achieved in just over 17 seconds.

At the front, small chromium-plated horn grilles were mounted towards the centre line, inward of the round indicators. Behind these grilles were new Bosch horns. As of 1 June 1954, a manual sliding sunroof, made by Golde, became available for Coupés. The noise level inside the cars was reduced thanks to improved body sound deadening.

The inner door panels had newly designed storage pockets, a pneumatic fuel gauge and two coat hooks permitting clothing articles to hang wrinkle-free. For the front passenger, the dashboard now included a grab handle. A horn ring was integrated in the lower segment of the steering wheel, allowing the driver to sound the horn without removing hands from the wheel. For a greater range of seat-back adjustment, the front seats were fitted with reclining seat mechanisms.

Model year 1955

Further improvements were made to comfort and safety, but this year's 356 was heavier than its predecessor. In the autumn of 1954, Porsche presented its 356 Speedster, a basically equipped, open-top car, put on sale at the instigation of Max Hoffman, Porsche's American importer. While the Cabriolet might be regarded as a car which can also be driven with the top down, the Speedster was one which, if necessary, could be driven with its minimalist top raised. The Speedster, built primarily for the US market, was offered at a price of $2995.

The 1955 model year was the last for the 1.5-litre pushrod engines. As of September 1954, all

356 'bent window' Cabriolet

power units were based on three-piece crankcases, finally replacing the Volkswagen-sourced cases. The 1.3 litre engines were fitted with crankshafts made by Alfing. The Speedster was only available with either of the 1500cc engines.

Porsche offered another open-top variant in the form of the Speedster. The chromium-plated frame of its low-cut windscreen, with large radius upper corners, was bolted to the bodywork. When raised, the lightweight, unpadded and rudimentary top provided less headroom than the Cabriolet.

Instead of winding windows in the doors, the Speedster had side curtains. Door height was 35mm lower than that of its siblings. Chromium-plated trim strips at door-handle height graced its flanks, with gold-coloured 'Speedster' script attached just above the strip on the front wings.

Like the other 356 models, the Speedster rolled on 16-inch wheels. Fifteen-inch wheels would be introduced with the later 356 A.

The Speedster had a newly-designed instrument panel. Mounted below a padded, arched cover were three round instruments – two large, and one smaller one set slightly higher in the centre. The ignition lock was located to the right of the steering column, alongside 'Porsche' script and two trim strips. There was no glove compartment. The bucket seats provided good side support, even in turns taken at speed. There were two elongated holes through each seat back.

Given identical engines, the Speedster could out-accelerate a Coupé, but not match it for top speed.

Of these early models (1948-1954), Porsche built a total of 9100 examples of all body types.

356 1100 Coupé / 356 1100 Cabriolet
MY 1950–MY 1954

Engine
Engine design:	4-cylinder horizontally-opposed
Installation:	Rear-engine
Cooling system:	Air-cooled
Engine type:	369
Displacement (cc):	1086
Bore x stroke (mm):	73.5 x 64
Engine output DIN (kW/hp):	29/40 at 4200rpm
Maximum torque (Nm/ft lb):	70/52 at 2800rpm
Output per litre(kW/l / hp/l):	26.7 / 36.8
Compression ratio:	7.0:1
Valve operation & camshaft drive:	ohv, cam driven by gears, 2 valves per cylinder
Carburation:	2 downdraught carburettors Solex 32 PBI
Ignition system:	Battery coil ignition
Firing order:	1 - 4 - 3 - 2
Crankshaft bearing:	4 slide bearings
Engine lubrication:	Full pressure oil lubrication
Engine oil total (l):	3.0*
*Filling new assembled engine, oil change 2.5	

Transmission
Drive configuration:	Rear-axle drive
Manual gearbox:	4-speed
Transmission type:	VW (519)*
Transmission ratios:	
1st gear:	3.60 (3.182)
2nd gear:	2.07 (1.765)
3rd gear:	1.25 (1.130)
4th gear:	0.80 (0.815)
Reverse gear:	6.60 (3.560)
Drive ratio:	4.43 (4.375)
*MY 1953 - MY 1954	

Body, chassis, suspension, brakes, wheels
Body design:	Steel body, 2 doors, 2 seats, pressed and welded steel frame, split windscreen, one grille in engine lid, bumpers fixed close to body
MY 1953 - MY 1954:	2 + 2 seats, bent single-piece windscreen, bumpers project away from body with over-riders
Coupé:	Fixed steel roof
Option June 1954:	Manual sunroof
Cabriolet:	Multi-layer hood with small glass rear window
Cabriolet April 1953 - MY 1954:	Bigger flexible plastic rear window
Suspension, front:	2 independent parallel arms, 2 continuous square laminated torsion rods, the upper with 6, the lower with 5 leaves, telescopic type hydraulic double-action shock absorbers
Suspension, rear:	Oscillating half axles through spring stays, independently sprung with a round individual torsion rod on each wheel, lever type shock absorbers

April 1951 - MY 1954:	telescopic type hydraulic double-action shock absorbers
Brakes, front/rear (Size (mm)):	Brake drums Simplex (230 x 30) / Brake drums Simplex (230 x 30)
MY 1952:	Brake drums Duplex (230 x 30) / Brake drums Simplex (230 x 30)
MY 1953 - MY 1954:	Brake drums Duplex (280 x 40) / Brake drums Simplex (280 x 40)
Wheels, front/rear:	3.00 D x 16 / 3.00 D x 16
Tyres, front/rear:	5.00-16 / 5.00-16

Electrical system
Alternator (W):	130
Battery (V/Ah):	6 / 75

Dimensions and weight
Track, front/rear (mm):	1290 / 1250
Wheelbase (mm):	2100
Length x width x height (mm):	3850 x 1660 x 1300
MY 1953 - MY 1954:	3950 x 1660 x 1300
Kerb weight (kg):	770
MY 1953 - MY 1954:	810
Permissible gross weight (kg):	1100
MY 1953 - MY 1954:	1200
Fuel tank capacity (l):	52, including 5 reserve
C_w x A (m²) Coupé - MY 1952:	0.296 x 1.677 = 0.496
C_w x A (m²) Coupé MY 1953 -:	0.365 x 1.692 = 0.618
Power/weight ratio (kg/kW/ kg/hp):	24.06 / 17.50
MY 1953 - MY 1954:	25.31 / 18.40

Fuel consumption
(mpg):	40; 76 - 80 RON normal leaded

Performance, production, prices
Acceleration 0-62mph/100kph (s):	23.5
Maximum speed (mph / kph):	87 / 140
Production, total number:	
356 Coupé:*	6,252
356 Cabriolet:*	1,593
davon 356 Cabriolet Heuer:*	237
*Total number all engine versions	
Purchase prices:	
05/1950 Coupé:	DM 10,200
Cabriolet:	DM 12,200
04/1951 Coupé:	DM 10,200
Cabriolet:	DM 12,200
04/1952 Coupé:	DM 10,200
Cabriolet:	DM 12,200
10/1952 Coupé:	DM 11,400
Cabriolet:	DM 13,400
10/1953 Coupé:	DM 11,400
Cabriolet:	DM 13,400
01/1954 Coupé:	DM 11,400
Cabriolet:	DM 13,400

356 1300 Coupé / 356 1300 Cabriolet MY 1951–MY 1953

Engine
Engine design:	4-cylinder horizontally-opposed
Installation:	Rear-engine
Cooling system:	Air-cooled
Engine type:	506
Displacement (cc):	1286
Bore x stroke (mm):	80 x 64
Engine output DIN (kW/hp):	32/44 at 4200rpm
Maximum torque (Nm/ft lb):	81/60 at 2800rpm
Output per litre(kW/l / hp/l):	24.9 / 34.2
Compression ratio:	6.5 : 1
Valve operation & camshaft drive:	ohv, cam driven by gears, 2 valves per cylinder
Carburation:	2 downdraught carburettors Solex 32 PBI
Ignition system:	Battery coil ignition
Firing order:	1 - 4 - 3 - 2
Crankshaft bearing:	4 slide bearings
Engine lubrication:	Full pressure oil lubrication
Engine oil total (l):	3.0*
*Filling new assembled engine, oil change 2.5	

Transmission
Drive configuration:	Rear-axle drive
Manual gearbox:	4-speed
Transmission type:	VW (519)*
Transmission ratios:	
1st gear:	3.60 (3.182)
2nd gear:	2.07 (1.765)
3rd gear:	1.25 (1.130)
4th gear:	0.80 (0.815)
Reverse gear:	6.60 (3.560)
Drive ratio:	4.43 (4.375)
*MY 1953	

Body, chassis, suspension, brakes, wheels
Body design:	Steel body, 2 doors, 2 seats, pressed and welded steel frame, split windscreen, one grille in engine lid, bumpers fixed close to body
MY 1953:	2 + 2 seats, bent single-piece windscreen, bumpers project away from body with over-riders
Coupé:	Fixed steel roof
Cabriolet:	Multi-layer hood with small glass rear window
April 1953:	Bigger flexible plastic rear window
Suspension, front:	2 independent parallel arms, 2 continuous square laminated torsion rods, the upper with 6, the lower with 5 leaves, telescopic type hydraulic double-action shock absorbers
Suspension, rear:	Oscillating half axles through spring stays, independently sprung with a round individual torsion rod on each wheel, lever type shock absorbers
April 1951 - MY 1953:	telescopic type hydraulic double-action shock absorbers
Brakes, front/rear (Size (mm)):	Brake drums Duplex (230 x 30) / Brake drums Simplex (230 x 30)
MY 1953:	Brake drums Duplex (280 x 40) / Brake drums Simplex (280 x 40)
Wheels, front/rear:	3.00 D x 16 / 3.00 D x 16
Tyres, front/rear:	5.00-16 / 5.00-16

Electrical system
Alternator (W):	130
Battery (V/Ah):	6 / 75

Dimensions and weight
Track, front/rear (mm):	1290 / 1250
Wheelbase (mm):	2100
Length x width x height (mm):	3850 x 1660 x 1300
MY 1953:	3950 x 1660 x 1300
Kerb weight (kg):	770
MY 1953:	810
Permissible gross weight (kg):	1100
MY 1953:	1200
Fuel tank capacity (l):	52, including 5 reserve
C_w x A (m^2) Coupé - MY 1952:	0.296 x 1.677 = 0.496
C_w x A (m^2) Coupé MY 1953:	0.365 x 1.692 = 0.618
Power/weight ratio (kg/kW/kg/hp):	24.06 / 17.50
MY 1953:	25.31 / 18.40

Fuel consumption
(mpg):	38.75; 76 - 80 RON normal leaded

Performance, production, prices
Acceleration 0-62mph/100kph (s):	22.0
Maximum speed (mph / kph):	90 / 145

Production, total number:	
356 Coupé:*	6,252
356 Cabriolet:*	1,593
davon 356 Cabriolet Heuer:*	237
*Total number all engine versions	

Purchase prices:	
04/1951 Coupé:	DM 10,200
Cabriolet:	DM 12,200
04/1952 Coupé:	DM 10,200
Cabriolet:	DM 12,200
01/1952 Coupé:	DM 11,400
Cabriolet:	DM 13,400
10/1953 Coupé:	DM 11,400
Cabriolet:	DM 13,400
01/1954 Coupé:	DM 11,400
Cabriolet:	DM 13,400
10/1954 Coupé:	DM 11,400
Cabriolet:	DM 13,400

356 1500 Coupé / 356 1500 Cabriolet
MY 1952

Engine

Engine design:	4-cylinder horizontally-opposed
Installation:	Rear-engine
Cooling system:	Air-cooled
Engine type:	527
Displacement (cc):	1488
Bore x stroke (mm):	80 x 74
Engine output DIN (kW/hp):	44/60 at 5000rpm
Maximum torque (Nm/lb ft):	102/75 at 3000rpm
Output per litre(kW/l / hp/l):	29.6 / 40.3
Compression ratio:	7.0 : 1
Valve operation & camshaft drive:	ohv, cam driven by gears, 2 valves per cylinder
Carburation:	2 downdraught carburettors Solex 40 PBIC
Ignition system:	Battery coil ignition
Firing order:	1 - 4 - 3 - 2
Crankshaft bearing:	4 slide bearings
Engine lubrication:	Full pressure oil lubrication
Engine oil total (l):	3.0*
*Filling new assembled engine, oil change 2.5	

Transmission

Drive configuration:	Rear-axle drive
Manual gearbox:	4-speed
Transmission type:	VW
Transmission ratios:	
1st gear:	3.60
2nd gear:	2.07
3rd gear:	1.25
4th gear:	0.80
Reverse gear:	6.60
Drive ratio:	4.43

Body, chassis, suspension, brakes, wheels

Body design:	Steel body, 2 doors, 2 seats, pressed and welded steel frame, split windscreen, one grille in engine lid, bumpers fixed close to body
Coupé:	Fixed steel roof
Cabriolet:	Multi-layer hood with small glass rear window
Suspension, front:	2 independent parallel arms, 2 continuous square laminated torsion rods, the upper with 6, the lower with 5 leaves, telescopic type hydraulic double-action shock absorbers
Suspension, rear:	Oscillating half axles through spring stays, independently sprung with a round individual torsion rod on each wheel, telescopic type hydraulic double-action shock absorbers
Brakes, front/rear (Size (mm)):	Brake drums Duplex (230 x 30) / Brake drums Simplex (230 x 30)
Wheels, front/rear:	3.25 D x 16 / 3.25 D x 16
Tyres, front/rear:	5.00-16 / 5.00-16

Electrical system

Alternator (W):	130
Battery (V/Ah):	6 / 75

Dimensions and weight

Track, front/rear (mm):	1290 / 1250
Wheelbase (mm):	2100
Length x width x height (mm):	3850 x 1660 x 1300
Kerb weight (kg):	770
Permissible gross weight (kg):	1100
Fuel tank capacity (l):	52, including 5 reserve
C_w x A (m^2) Coupé:	0.296 x 1.677 = 0.496
Power/weight ratio (kg/kW / kg/hp):	17.50 / 12.83

Fuel consumption

(mpg):	32.6; 76 - 80 RON normal leaded

Performance, production, prices

Acceleration 0-62mph/100kph (s):	15.5
Maximum speed (mph / kph):	105 / 170
Production, total number:	
356 Coupé:*	6,252
356 Cabriolet:*	1,593
davon 356 Cabriolet Heuer:*	237
*Total number all engine versions	
Purchase prices:	
04/1952 Coupé:	DM 12,700
Cabriolet:	DM 14,700

356 1500 America Roadster (Type 540) MY 1952–MY 1953

Engine
Engine design:	4-cylinder horizontally-opposed
Installation:	Rear-engine
Cooling system:	Air-cooled
Engine type:	528
Displacement (cc):	1488
Bore x stroke (mm):	80 x 74
Engine output DIN (kW/hp):	51/70 at 5000rpm
Maximum torque (Nm/lb ft):	80/108 at 3600rpm
Output per litre(kW/l / hp/l):	34.3 / 47.0
Compression ratio:	8.2 : 1
Valve operation & camshaft drive:	ohv, cam driven by gears, 2 valves per cylinder
Carburation:	2 downdraught carburettors Solex 40 PBIC
Ignition system:	Battery coil ignition
Firing order:	1 - 4 - 3 - 2
Crankshaft bearing:	4 slide bearings
Engine lubrication:	Full pressure oil lubrication
Engine oil total (l):	3.0*

*Filling new assembled engine, oil change 2.5

Transmission
Drive configuration:	Rear-axle drive
Manual gearbox:	4-speed
Transmission type:	VW (519)*
Transmission ratios:	
1st gear:	3.60 (3.182)
2nd gear:	2.07 (1.765)
3rd gear:	1.25 (1.130)
4th gear:	0.80 (0.815)
Reverse gear:	6.60 (3.560)
Drive ratio:	4.43 (4.375)

*MY 1953

Body, chassis, suspension, brakes, wheels
Body design:	Aluminium Roadster body, 2 doors, 2 seats, pressed and welded steel frame, split windscreen, twin grille in engine lid, bumpers project away from body with over-riders, single-layer hood with flexible plastic rear window, side curtains at doors
Suspension, front:	2 independent parallel arms, 2 continuous square laminated torsion rods, the upper with 6, the lower with 5 leaves, telescopic type hydraulic double-action shock absorbers
Suspension, rear:	Oscillating half axles through spring stays, independently sprung with a round individual torsion rod on each wheel, telescopic type hydraulic double-action shock absorbers
Brakes, front/rear (Size (mm)):	Brake drums Duplex (230 x 30) / Brake drums Simplex (230 x 30)
MY 1953:	Brake drums Duplex (280 x 40) / Brake drums Simplex (280 x 40)
Wheels, front/rear:	3.25 D x 16 / 3.25 D x 16
Tyres, front/rear:	5.25-16 / 5.25-16

Electrical system
Alternator (W):	130
Battery (V/Ah):	6 / 75

Dimensions and weight
Track, front/rear (mm):	1306 / 1248
Wheelbase (mm):	2100
Length x width x height (mm):	3850 x 1660 x 1250*
Kerb weight (kg):	605
Permissible gross weight (kg):	n/a
Fuel tank capacity (l):	52, including 5 reserve
C_w x A (m^2):	n/a
Power/weight ratio (kg/kW/kg/hp):	11.86 / 8.64

*with closed top

Fuel consumption
Standard consumption (mpg):	37; 76 - 80 RON normal leaded

Performance, production, prices
Acceleration 0-62mph/100kph (s):	approx. 10.0
Maximum speed (mph / kph):	112 / 180
Production, total number:	21*

*other sources: 16 cars, of these one steel body

Purchase price:	US$ 4,600

356 1500 Coupé / 356 1500 Cabriolet
MY 1953–MY 1955

Engine

Engine design:	4-cylinder horizontally-opposed
Installation:	Rear-engine
Cooling system:	Air-cooled
Engine type:	546
MY 1955:	546/2
Displacement (cc):	1488
Bore x stroke (mm):	80 x 74
Engine output DIN (kW/hp):	40/55 at 4400rpm
Maximum torque (Nm/lb ft):	106/78 at 2800rpm
Output per litre(kW/l / hp/l):	26.9 / 37.0
Compression ratio:	7.0 : 1
Valve operation & camshaft drive:	ohv, cam driven by gears, 2 valves per cylinder
Carburation:	2 downdraught carburettors Solex 32 PBI
Ignition system:	Battery coil ignition
Firing order:	1 - 4 - 3 - 2
Crankshaft bearing:	4 slide bearings
Engine lubrication:	Full pressure oil lubrication
Engine oil total (l):	3.0*
MY 1955:	5.0**

*Filling new assembled engine, oil change 2.5
**Filling new assembled engine, oil change 4.0

Transmission

Drive configuration:	Rear-axle drive
Manual gearbox:	4-speed
Transmission type:	519
Transmission ratios:	
1st gear:	3.182
2nd gear:	1.765
3rd gear:	1.130
4th gear:	0.815
Reverse gear:	3.560
Drive ratio:	4.375

Body, chassis, suspension, brakes, wheels

Body design:	Steel body, 2 doors, 2 + 2 seats, pressed and welded steel frame, bent single-piece windscreen, one grille in engine lid, bumpers project away from body with over-riders
Coupé:	Fixed steel roof
Option June 1954 - MY 1955:	Manual sunroof
Cabriolet:	Multi-layer hood with small glass rear window
April 1953 - MY 1955:	Bigger flexible plastic rear window
Suspension, front:	2 independent parallel arms, 2 continuous square laminated torsion rods, the upper with 6, the lower with 5 leaves, telescopic type hydraulic double-action shock absorbers
Suspension, rear:	Oscillating half axles through spring stays, independently sprung with a round individual torsion rod on each wheel, telescopic type hydraulic double-action shock absorbers
Brakes, front/rear (Size (mm)):	Brake drums Duplex (280 x 40) / Brake drums Simplex (280 x 40)
Wheels, front/rear:	3.25 D x 16 / 3.25 D x 16
Tyres, front/rear:	5.00-16 Sport / 5.00-16 Sport

Electrical system

Alternator (W):	130
Battery (V/Ah):	6 / 75

Dimensions and weight

Track, front/rear (mm):	1290 / 1250
Wheelbase (mm):	2100
Length x width x height (mm):	3950 x 1660 x 1300
Kerb weight (kg):	810
MY 1955:	830
Permissible gross weight (kg):	1200
Fuel tank capacity (l):	52, including 5 reserve
C_w x A (m²) Coupé:	0.365 x 1.692 = 0.618
Power/weight ratio (kg/kW/kg/hp):	20.25 / 14.72
MY 1955:	20.75 / 15.09

Fuel consumption

Standard consumption (mpg):	38.75; 76 - 80 RON normal leaded

Performance, production, prices

Acceleration 0-62mph/100kph (s):	17.0
Maximum speed (mph / kph):	99 / 160
Production, total number:	
356 Coupé:*	6,252
356 Cabriolet:*	1,593
*Total number all engine versions	
Purchase prices:	
10/1952 Coupé:	DM 12,700
Cabriolet:	DM 14,700
10/1953 Coupé:	DM 12,700
Cabriolet:	DM 14,700
01/1954 Coupé:	DM 12,700
Cabriolet:	DM 14,700
10/1954 Coupé:	DM 12,700
Cabriolet:	DM 14,700

356 1500 Super Coupé
356 1500 Super Cabriolet
MY 1953–MY 1955

Engine

Engine design:	4-cylinder horizontally-opposed
Installation:	Rear-engine
Cooling system:	Air-cooled
Engine type:	528
MY 1955:	528/2
Displacement (cc):	1488
Bore x stroke (mm):	80 x 74
Engine output DIN (kW/hp):	51/70 at 5000rpm
Maximum torque (Nm/lb ft):	108/80 at 3600rpm
Output per litre(kW/l / hp/l):	34.3 / 47.0
Compression ratio:	8.2 : 1
Valve operation & camshaft drive:	ohv, cam driven by gears, 2 valves per cylinder
Carburation:	2 downdraught carburettors Solex 40 PBIC
Ignition system:	Battery coil ignition
Firing order:	1 - 4 - 3 - 2
Crankshaft bearing:	4 slide bearings
Engine lubrication:	Full pressure oil lubrication
Engine oil total (l):	3.0*
MY 1955:	5.0**

*Filling new assembled engine, oil change 2.5
**Filling new assembled engine, oil change 4.0

Transmission

Drive configuration:	Rear-axle drive
Manual gearbox:	4-speed
Transmission type:	519
Transmission ratios:	
1st gear:	3.182
2nd gear:	1.765
3rd gear:	1.130
4th gear:	0.815
Reverse gear:	3.560
Drive ratio:	4.375

Body, chassis, suspension, brakes, wheels

Body design:	Steel body, 2 doors, 2 + 2 seats, pressed and welded steel frame, bent single-piece windscreen, one grille in engine lid, bumpers project away from body with over-riders
Coupé:	Fixed steel roof
Option June 1954 - MY 1955:	Manual sunroof
Cabriolet:	Multi-layer hood with small glass rear window
April 1953 - MY 1955:	Bigger flexible plastic rear window
Suspension, front:	2 independent parallel arms, 2 continuous square laminated torsion rods, the upper with 6, the lower with 5 leaves, telescopic type hydraulic double-action shock absorbers

Suspension, rear:	Oscillating half axles through spring stays, independently spring with a round individual torsion rod on each wheel, telescopic type hydraulic double-action shock absorbers
Brakes, front/rear (Size (mm)):	Brake drums Duplex (280 x 40) / Brake drums Simplex (280 x 40)
Wheels, front/rear:	3.25 D x 16 / 3.25 D x 16
Tyres, front/rear:	5.00-16 Sport / 5.00-16 Sport

Electrical system

Alternator (W):	130
Battery (V/Ah):	6 / 75

Dimensions and weight

Track, front/rear (mm):	1290 / 1250
Wheelbase (mm):	2100
Length x width x height (mm):	3950 x 1660 x 1300
Kerb weight (kg):	810
MY 1955:	830
Permissible gross weight (kg):	1200
Fuel tank capacity (l):	52, including 5 reserve
C_w x A (m^2) Coupé:	0.365 x 1.692 = 0.618
Power/weight ratio (kg/kW/kg/hp):	15.88 / 11.57
MY 1955:	16.27 / 11.85

Fuel consumption

Standard consumption (mpg):	36.5; 76 - 80 RON normal leaded

Performance, production, prices

Acceleration 0-62mph/100kph (s):	13.5
Maximum speed (mph / kph):	108.5 / 175
Production, total number:	
356 Coupé:*	6,252
356 Cabriolet:*	1,593
*Total number all engine versions	
Purchase prices:	
10/1952 Coupé:	DM 13,800
Cabriolet:	DM 15,800
10/1953 Coupé:	DM 13,800
Cabriolet:	DM 15,800
01/1954 Coupé:	DM 13,800
Cabriolet:	DM 15,800
10/1954 Coupé:	DM 13,800
Cabriolet:	DM 15,800

356 1300 Coupé / 356 1300 Cabriolet MY 1954–MY 1955

Engine
Engine design:	4-cylinder horizontally-opposed
Installation:	Rear-engine
Cooling system:	Air-cooled
Engine type:	506/2
Displacement (cc):	1290
Bore x stroke (mm):	74.5 x 74
Engine output DIN (kW/hp):	32/44 at 420rpm
Maximum torque (Nm/lb ft):	81/60 at 2800rpm
Output per litre(kW/l / hp/l):	24.8 / 34.1
Compression ratio:	6.5 : 1
Valve operation & camshaft drive:	ohv, cam driven by gears, 2 valves per cylinder
Carburation:	2 downdraught carburettors Solex 32 PBI
Ignition system:	Battery coil ignition
Firing order:	1 - 4 - 3 - 2
Crankshaft bearing:	4 slide bearings
Engine lubrication:	Full pressure oil lubrication
Engine oil total (l):	5.0*

*Filling new assembled engine, oil change 4.0

Transmission
Drive configuration:	Rear-axle drive
Manual gearbox:	4-speed
Transmission type:	519
Transmission ratios:	
1st gear:	3.182
2nd gear:	1.765
3rd gear:	1.130
4th gear:	0.815
Reverse gear:	3.560
Drive ratio:	4.375

Body, chassis, suspension, brakes, wheels
Body design:	Steel body, 2 doors, 2 + 2 seats, pressed and welded steel frame, bent single-piece windscreen, one grille in engine lid, bumpers project away from body with over-riders
Coupé:	Fixed steel roof
Option June 1954 - MY 1955:	Manual sunroof
Cabriolet:	Multi-layer hood with flexible plastic rear window
Suspension, front:	2 independent parallel arms, 2 continuous square laminated torsion rods, the upper with 6, the lower with 5 leaves, telescopic type hydraulic double-action shock absorbers
Suspension, rear:	Oscillating half axles through spring stays, independently sprung with a round individual torsion rod on each wheel, telescopic type hydraulic double-action shock absorbers
Brakes, front/rear (Size (mm)):	Brake drums Duplex (280 x 40) / Brake drums Simplex (280 x 40)
Wheels, front/rear:	3.25 D x 16 / 3.25 D x 16
Tyres, front/rear:	5.00-16 Sport / 5.00-16 Sport

Electrical system
Alternator (W):	130
Battery (V/Ah):	6 / 75

Dimensions and weight
Track, front/rear (mm):	1290 / 1250
Wheelbase (mm):	2100
Length x width x height (mm):	3950 x 1660 x 1300
Kerb weight (kg):	810
MY 1955:	830
Permissible gross weight (kg):	1200
Fuel tank capacity (l):	52, including 5 reserve
C_w x A (m^2) Coupé:	0.365 x 1.692 = 0.618
Power/weight ratio (kg/kW/kg/hp):	25.31 / 18.40
MY 1955:	25.93 / 18.86

Fuel consumption
Standard consumption (mpg):	42; 76 - 80 RON normal leaded

Performance, production, prices
Acceleration 0-62mph/100kph (s):	22.0
Maximum speed (mph / kph):	90 / 145
Production, total number:	
356 Coupé:*	6,252
356 Cabriolet:*	1,593

*Total number all engine versions

Purchase prices:	
10/1953 Coupé:	DM 11,400
Cabriolet:	DM 13,400
01/1954 Coupé:	DM 11,400
Cabriolet:	DM 13,400
10/1954 Coupé:	DM 11,400
Cabriolet:	DM 13,400

356 1300 Super Coupé
356 1300 Super Cabriolet
MY 1954–MY 1955

Engine
Engine design:	4-cylinder horizontally-opposed
Installation:	Rear-engine
Cooling system:	Air-cooled
Engine type:	589
MY 1955:	589/2
Displacement (cc):	1290
Bore x stroke (mm):	74.5 x 74
Engine output DIN (kW/hp):	44/60 at 5500rpm
Maximum torque (Nm/lb ft):	88/65 at 3600rpm
Output per litre(kW/l / hp/l):	34.1 / 46.5
Compression ratio:	8.2 : 1
Valve operation & camshaft drive:	ohv, cam driven by gears, 2 valves per cylinder
Carburation:	2 downdraught carburettors Solex 32 PBI
MY 1955:	32 PBIC and 40 PICB
Ignition system:	Battery coil ignition
Firing order:	1 - 4 - 3 - 2
Crankshaft bearing:	4 slide bearings
Engine lubrication:	Full pressure oil lubrication
Engine oil total (l):	3.0*
MY 1955:	5.0**

*Filling new assembled engine, oil change 2.5
**Filling new assembled engine, oil change 4.0

Transmission
Drive configuration:	Rear-axle drive
Manual gearbox:	4-speed
Transmission type:	519/2
Transmission ratios:	
1st gear:	3.182
2nd gear:	1.765
3rd gear:	1.227
4th gear:	0.885
Reverse gear:	3.560
Drive ratio:	4.375

Body, chassis, suspension, brakes, wheels
Body design:	Steel body, 2 doors, 2 + 2 seats, pressed and welded steel frame, bent single-piece windscreen, one grille in engine lid, bumpers project away from body with over-riders
Coupé:	Fixed steel roof
Option June 1954 - MY 1955:	Manual sunroof
Cabriolet:	Multi-layer hood with flexible plastic rear window
Suspension, front:	2 independent parallel arms, 2 continuous square laminated torsion rods, the upper with 6, the lower with 5 leaves, telescopic type hydraulic double-action shock absorbers
Suspension, rear:	Oscillating half axles through spring stays, independently sprung with a round individual torsion rod on each wheel, telescopic type hydraulic double-action shock absorbers
Brakes, front/rear (Size (mm)):	Brake drums Duplex (280 x 40) / Brake drums Simplex (280 x 40)
Wheels, front/rear:	3.25 D x 16 / 3.25 D x 16
Tyres, front/rear:	5.00-16 Sport / 5.00-16 Sport

Electrical system
Alternator (W):	130
Battery (V/Ah):	6 / 75

Dimensions and weight
Track, front/rear (mm):	1290 / 1250
Wheelbase (mm):	2100
Length x width x height (mm):	3950 x 1660 x 1300
Kerb weight (kg):	810
MY 1955:	830
Permissible gross weight (kg):	1200
Fuel tank capacity (l):	52, including 5 reserve
C_w x A (m^2) Coupé:	0.365 x 1.692 = 0.618
Power/weight ratio (kg/kW/kg/hp):	18.40 / 13.50
MY 1955:	18.86 / 13.83

Fuel consumption
Standard consumption (mpg):	38.75; 76 - 80 RON normal leaded

Performance, production, prices
Acceleration 0-62mph/100kph (s):	17.0
Maximum speed (mph / kph):	99 / 160
Production, total number:	
356 Coupé:*	6,252
356 Cabriolet:*	1,593
*Total number all engine versions	
Purchase prices:	
10/1953 Coupé:	DM 13,500
Cabriolet:	DM 15,500
01/1954 Coupé:	DM 13,500
Cabriolet:	DM 15,500
10/1954 Coupé:	DM 13,500
Cabriolet:	DM 15,500

356 1500 Speedster MY 1955

Engine
Engine design:	4-cylinder horizontally-opposed
Installation:	Rear-engine
Cooling system:	Air-cooled
Engine type:	546/2
Displacement (cc):	1488
Bore x stroke (mm):	80 x 74
Engine output DIN (kW/hp):	40/55 at 4400rpm
Maximum torque (Nm/lb ft):	106 at 2800rpm
Output per litre(kW/l / hp/l):	26.9 / 37.0
Compression ratio:	7.0 : 1
Valve operation & camshaft drive:	ohv, cam driven by gears, 2 valves per cylinder
Carburation:	2 downdraught carburettors Solex 32 PBI
Ignition system:	Battery coil ignition
Firing order:	1 - 4 - 3 - 2
Crankshaft bearing:	4 slide bearings
Engine lubrication:	Full pressure oil lubrication
Engine oil total (l):	5.0*
*Filling new assembled engine, oil change 4.0	

Transmission
Drive configuration:	Rear-axle drive
Manual gearbox:	4-speed
Transmission type:	519/2
Transmission ratios:	
1st gear:	3.182
2nd gear:	1.765
3rd gear:	1.227
4th gear:	0.885
Reverse gear:	3.560
Drive ratio:	4.375

Body, chassis, suspension, brakes, wheels
Body design:	Steel body, 2 doors, 2 seats, pressed and welded steel frame, curved single-piece windscreen, corners with large radius, one grille on Rear-engine lid, bumpers project away from body with over-riders, single-layer hood with flexible plastic rear window, side curtains on doors
Suspension, front:	2 independent parallel arms, 2 continuous square laminated torsion rods, the upper with 6, the lower with 5 leaves, telescopic type hydraulic double-action shock absorbers
Suspension, rear:	Oscillating half axles through spring stays, independently sprung with a round individual torsion rod on each wheel, telescopic type hydraulic double-action shock absorbers
Brakes, front/rear (Size (mm)):	Brake drums Duplex (280 x 40) / Brake drums Simplex (280 x 40)
Wheels, front/rear:	3.25 D x 16 / 3.25 D x 16
Tyres, front/rear:	5.00-16 Sport / 5.00-16 Sport
Option:	5.25-16 / 5.25-16

Electrical system
Alternator (W):	130
Battery (V/Ah):	6 / 75

Dimensions and weight
Track, front/rear (mm):	1290 / 1250
Wheelbase (mm):	2100
Length x width x height (mm):	3950 x 1660 x 1220*
Kerb weight (kg):	760
Permissible gross weight (kg):	1100
Fuel tank capacity (l):	52, including 5 reserve
C_w x A (m²):	0.377 x 1.640 = 0.618
Power/weight ratio (kg/kW / kg/hp):	19.00 / 13.81
*with closed top	

Fuel consumption
Standard consumption (mpg):	38.75; 76 - 80 RON normal leaded

Performance, production, prices
Acceleration 0-62mph/100kph (s):	17.0
Maximum speed (mph / kph):	99 / 160
Production, total number:	
356 Speedster:*	1,234
*Total number all engine versions	
Purchase price:	
10/1954 Speedster:	DM 12,200

356 1500 Super Speedster MY 1955

Engine
Engine design:	4-cylinder horizontally-opposed
Installation:	Rear-engine
Cooling system:	Air-cooled
Engine type:	528/2
Displacement (cc):	1488
Bore x stroke (mm):	80 x 74
Engine output DIN (kW/hp):	51/70 at 5000rpm
Maximum torque (Nm/lb ft):	108 at 3600rpm
Output per litre(kW/l / hp/l):	34.3 / 47.0
Compression ratio:	8.2 : 1
Valve operation & camshaft drive:	ohv, cam driven by gears, 2 valves per cylinder
Carburation:	2 downdraught carburettors Solex 40 PBIC
Ignition system:	Battery coil ignition
Firing order:	1 - 4 - 3 - 2
Crankshaft bearing:	4 slide bearings
Engine lubrication:	Full pressure oil lubrication
Engine oil total (l):	5.0*
*Filling new assembled engine, oil change 4.0	

Transmission
Drive configuration:	Rear-axle drive
Manual gearbox:	4-speed
Transmission type:	519/2
Transmission ratios:	
1st gear:	3.182
2nd gear:	1.765
3rd gear:	1.227
4th gear:	0.885
Reverse gear:	3.560
Drive ratio:	4.375

Body, chassis, suspension, brakes, wheels
Body design:	Steel body, 2 doors, 2 seats, pressed and welded steel frame, curved single-piece windscreen, corners with large radius, one grille on Rear-engine lid, bumpers project away from body with over-riders, single layer hood with flexible plastic rear window, side curtains on doors

Suspension, front:	2 independent parallel arms, 2 continuous square laminated torsion rods, the upper with 6, the lower with 5 leaves, telescopic type hydraulic double-action shock absorbers
Suspension, rear:	Oscillating half axles through spring stays, independently sprung with a round individual torsion rod on each wheel, telescopic type hydraulic double-action shock absorbers
Brakes, front/rear (Size (mm)):	Brake drums Duplex (280 x 40) / Brake drums Simplex (280 x 40)
Wheels, front/rear:	3.25 D x 16 / 3.25 D x 16
Tyres, front/rear:	5.00-16 Sport / 5.00-16 Sport

Electrical system
Alternator (W):	130
Battery (V/Ah):	6 / 75

Dimensions and weight
Track, front/rear (mm):	1290 / 1250
Wheelbase (mm):	2100
Length x width x height (mm):	3950 x 1660 x 1220*
Kerb weight DIN (kg):	760
Permissible gross weight (kg):	1100
Fuel tank capacity (l):	52, including 5 reserve
C_w x A (m²):	0.377 x 1.640 = 0.618
Power/weight ratio (kg/kW/kg/hp):	14.90 / 10.85
*with closed top	

Fuel consumption
Standard consumption (mpg):	36.5; 76 - 80 RON normal leaded

Performance, production, prices
Acceleration 0-62mph/100kph (s):	13.5
Maximum speed (mph / kph):	108.5 / 175
Production, total number:	
356 Speedster:*	1,234
*Total number all engine versions	
Purchase price:	
10/1954 Speedster:	DM 13,300

Porsche 356 A

In the autumn of 1955 the 356 A, a more highly developed model, replaced the original 356. The 356 A was available in Coupé, Cabriolet and Speedster variants. Engines of 1.6-litre displacement superseded the 1.5-litre engines. On 12 March 1956, the staff celebrated the company's 25th anniversary. On this occasion, the company presented the 10,000th Porsche, a 356 A. In that same year, Porsche moved back to its pre-war facilities in Werk I, which had been appropriated by occupation forces after the end of the war. Werk I housed design offices, experimental, repair and accounting departments.

Model year 1956

At its introduction the 356 A was offered with five different engine options:
356 A 1300 with 44hp (32kW) at 4200rpm;
356 A 1300 Super with 60hp (44kW) at 5500rpm;
356 A 1600 with 60hp (44kW) at 4500rpm;
356 A 1600 Super with 75hp (55kW) at 5000rpm;
356 A Carrera 1500 GS with 100hp (74kW) at 6200rpm.

All engines had cast-aluminium-alloy crankcases, cylinder heads and cylinder barrels. Cylinder bores were chrome plated. The pushrod (i.e. non-Carrera) engines had a central camshaft, pushrods and rocker arms. The crankshaft was mounted in roller bearings. Pressure lubrication was provided by a gear pump. Individual gears of the full-synchromesh four-speed transmission were engaged through a single-plate dry clutch.

The all-steel body of the 356 A formed a self-supporting structure with the platform frame. The 'panorama' windscreen was of a single, curved piece. Front indicators were integrated with the horn grilles. All models were given a redesigned bonnet handle with inset Porsche crest. Sliding vents allowed partial or full opening of the heating air ducts. The windscreen-washer system was worked by a foot-operated pump.

Two full-width square-section leaf-spring bundles and longitudinal crank arms provided front springing and suspension. At the front, all 356 As were given reinforced spindles and an anti-roll bar

for improved stability when cornering. The rear wheels were carried by swing-axles located by trailing arms, sprung by a round torsion bar on each side. Springs and shock absorbers were retuned, torsion bar mounting points were adjustable and trailing arms were mounted on needle bearings. The hydraulic brake system employed four 280mm brake drums made by Teves. Wheel size was reduced, from 16 to 15 inches. Sport tyres, 5.60 x 15, were mounted to 4.5 J x 15 steel rims. Steering was by means of a Porsche worm-and-peg system.

The top of the instrument panel was covered by padded leatherette. Three large, identically-sized instruments were mounted behind the two-spoke steering wheel: a speedometer at the left, a tachometer in the centre and a combination instrument on the right. The dashboard included an electric cigarette lighter, ashtray and radio fascia. A grab handle for the passenger was mounted to the right of the glove compartment. The handbrake was located to the left of the steering column, and heater controls were on the central tunnel behind the gear lever. The front seats were fitted with recliner mechanisms, while folding down the rear seat-back provided a larger, flat luggage area. The front footwell side panels, interior door sills and rear seating area were trimmed with bouclé carpet.

Even the simple instrument panel of the Speedster was given three equal-sized instruments, with the tachometer moved upwards. On the Speedster, the ignition lock remained to the right of the steering column.

Performance of the 356 A 1300 was roughly equal to that of its predecessor. The 356 A 1300 Super and the 356 A 1600, also known as the 'Dame' ('Lady') in Germany or the 'Normal' in the USA, compared to the 356 1300 Super in terms of acceleration and top speed. In tests, a 356 A 1600 Super reached 62mph (100kph) in 14.2 seconds, and a top speed of 113mph (182kph).

One of the quintessential dream cars of the 1950s was unveiled at the IAA in the autumn of 1955 – a Porsche 356 powered by a pure-bred racing power unit, as the 356 A 1500 GS (Grand Sport) Carrera was presented to the public for the first time. The Carrera was available as a Coupé, Cabriolet or Speedster. 'Carrera' is Spanish for 'race', made popular by the Carrera Panamericana, a well-known Mexican road race. With 100hp (74kW) at 6200rpm, the 1.5-litre Carrera engine provided all of 25 more horsepower (18kW) than Porsche's most powerful pushrod engine to date. This power unit virtually demanded to be driven at high rpm; its shrill engine note imparted pure racing atmosphere. The Carrera engine was developed by Ernst Fuhrmann, who later described it as his 'youthful indiscretion'. It employed a built-up, roller-bearing Hirth crankshaft. Two overhead camshafts per cylinder head were driven by quill shafts and spiral-bevel gearing. Oil supply was by means of a dry sump lubrication system with a separate oil tank, ensuring the best possible lubrication even in extended, high-speed corners. A dual ignition system with twin sparkplugs per cylinder, and a pair of twin-choke carburettors, transformed the air-fuel mixture to usable power. The car approached 124mph (200kph) and acceleration to 62mph (100kph) took just 12 seconds. Visually, the Carrera was distinguished from its siblings by somewhat wider tyres, 'Carrera' script on the front wings and engine lid, a somewhat larger wood-rimmed steering wheel, modified instruments with a speedometer marked to 250kph and tachometer ranging to 8000rpm, as well as bucket seats for driver and passenger.

Gearing in the top two gears was higher. For the dedicated private driver the Carrera provided the ultimate in racing equipment.

Model year 1957

The 1957 model year was the last in which the 1300 engines were offered.

In the course of model development, the Speedster was given an altered top for more headroom. The Cabriolet and Speedster tops were fitted with larger rear windows. In March of 1957, all models had their speedometers and combination instruments switch places: the speedometer was moved to the right of the tachometer, the combi instrument to the left. The ashtray was enlarged and mounted below the dashboard. In the transmission department, a tunnel case replaced the erstwhile split-transmission case.

The 356 Carrera was available in an even more powerful, more agile version: the 356 A 1500 Carrera GS/GT ('Grand Tourisme') was only available as a Coupé or Speedster. Its engine developed 110hp (81kW) at 6400rpm. For weight reduction, it had aluminium doors, bonnet and engine lid. At the

Paul-Ernst Strähle of Schorndorf's well-known 356 A Carrera, number plate 'WN-V2', in the wind tunnel

rear, on either side of the chromium-plated grille, the Carrera was given additional cooling louvres. In the Coupé the rear seat was discontinued, and lightweight Plexiglas was used for the rear and side quarterlights. On top of this, the over-riders were deleted from all Carrera models in the interests of weight reduction.

Model year 1958 (T2)

For the 1958 model year the 356 line carried the Porsche internal designation 'Technical Program II', or T2. The 356 A 1300 and 356 A 1300 Super were deleted from the model line-up. Of the pushrod engines, only the 1600 'Normal' ('Dame') and 1600 Super remained in the model list. The Super and Normal were fitted with pairs of new Zenith twin-choke carburettors, which provided each cylinder with its own venturi. A new crankcase improved oil circulation and distribution, with higher oil pressure at low engine speeds. On the Super engine, the Hirth roller-bearing crank was abandoned in favour of a journal-bearing crankshaft. The Normal was fitted with cast-iron cylinder barrels.

A new diaphragm pressure plate made for easier clutch engagement on the Normal model.

New body variants were the Hardtop-Coupé, built by Karmann in Osnabrück, with its hard top rigidly welded to the lower body, and the Hardtop/Cabriolet, with a removable hard top.

The tailpipes of the 1600 pushrod engines were rerouted to exit through the over-riders, thereby providing greater ground clearance. In Carrera models, the exhausts exited the car near the centreline. New teardrop-shaped tail lamps, introduced in March 1957, incorporated indicators, brake and tail lights in a single unit. Number plate illumination and reversing lamps were mounted below the number plate. Cabriolets and Speedsters could be ordered with an optional hard top for winter use. A towing eye was located under the front of the car. Reinforcements for seat-belt mounting points were welded to the floorpan. The doors were given new locks, a stop to keep the doors from swinging shut even on hills and an altered window-winder mechanism. The Cabriolet was given front quarterlights for better ventilation; these could also be installed on the Coupé. The Coupé was equipped with two interior lamps.

Chromium wheels with Rudge knock-off hubs were available as an option. Super models had flatter hubcaps with Porsche crests in their centres. The Normal version continued to be fitted with 'baby moon' hubcaps. A new Ross steering system, made by

356 A Carrera 1600 GS Cabriolet

A right-hand-drive 356 A Speedster

ZF, replaced the Porsche worm-and-peg steering box. New anatomically-revised seats provided a better fit for the occupants.

For the 1958 model year, the more luxuriously equipped, but heavier, 356 A 1500 GS Carrera de Luxe replaced the erstwhile 356 A 1500 GS Carrera. The Carrera de Luxe was available in all body variants. Standard equipment included a petrol-fuelled heater in place of the engine-dependent heating system.

Model year 1959

1959 marked the end of the 356 A model line. All 356 A models were given reinforced spindles. The Speedster was deleted from the programme, replaced by the Convertible D. The 'D' represented the Drauz coachbuilding firm of Heilbronn, which provided the bodies for this model.

The Convertible D was differentiated from its predecessor, the Speedster, by its larger windscreen, winding side windows, and larger rear window in its convertible top. Chromium trim strips were also mounted to the flanks of the Convertible D. Although the Convertible D weighed 40kg more than the Speedster, it provided more comfortable appointments. Only the first 14 examples of the Convertible D carried 'Speedster D' script on the front wings.

The Convertible D had the exact same instrument panel as the Speedster, with ignition lock to the right of the steering column. The Speedster's bucket seats were replaced by normal padded seats. At the rear, two padded jump seats with a folding backrest were available. In addition, the Convertible D was given a windscreen washer system.

For the 1959 model, the displacement of the Carrera engine was raised to 1.6 litres. Porsche offered the Carrera in two different equipment levels. The 356 A 1600 GS Carrera de Luxe was intended for the pampered driver of public roads, with 105hp (77kW) and Solex twin-choke carburettors, in Coupé, Cabriolet, Hardtop-Coupé and Hardtop/Cabriolet versions, while drivers with racing ambitions could choose the lighter 356 A 1600 GS/GT Carrera, with 115hp (85kW) and Weber twin-choke carburettors, available only as a Coupé. Both Carrera engines had roller-bearing crankshafts, and for the first time both Carrera variants were available with an optional 12-volt electrical system.

The GT bodies showed many changes. Bumpers were fitted without guards, while doors and lids were of aluminium. Six louvres were cut into the engine lid on either side of the air-inlet grille. Rear and side windows were of lighter Plexiglas.

Only 686 of the 356 A Carrera were built. In all, 20,541 356 As rolled out of Porsche's factory.

356 A 1300 Coupé
356 A 1300 Cabriolet
MY 1956–MY 1957

Engine

Engine design:	4-cylinder horizontally-opposed
Installation:	Rear-engine
Cooling system:	Air-cooled
Engine type:	506/2
Displacement (cc):	1290
Bore x stroke (mm):	74.5 x 74
Engine output DIN (kW/hp):	32/44 at 4200rpm
Maximum torque (Nm/lb ft):	81/60 at 2800rpm
Output per litre(kW/l / hp/l):	24.8 / 34.1
Compression ratio:	6.5 : 1
Valve operation & camshaft drive:	ohv, cam driven by gears, 2 valves per cylinder
Carburation:	2 downdraught carburettors Solex 32 PBIC also 32 PBI
Ignition system:	Battery coil ignition
Firing order:	1 - 4 - 3 - 2
Crankshaft bearing:	4 slide bearings
Engine lubrication:	Full pressure oil lubrication
Engine oil total (l):	5.0*
*Filling new assembled engine, oil change 4.0	

Transmission

Drive configuration:	Rear-axle drive
Manual gearbox:	4-speed
Transmission type:	644
Transmission ratios:	
1st gear:	3.182
2nd gear:	1.765
3rd gear:	1.130
4th gear:	0.815
Reverse gear:	3.560
Drive ratio:	4.428

Body, chassis, suspension, brakes, wheels

Body design:	Steel body, 2 doors, 2 + 2 seats, pressed and welded steel-sheet sections, one unit with body, curved single-piece windscreen, one grille in engine lid, bumpers project away from body with over-riders
Coupé:	Fixed steel roof
Option:	Manual sunroof
Cabriolet:	Multi-layer hood with flexible plastic rear window
Option MY 1957 - MY 1959:	Hardtop

Suspension, front:	2 longitudinal swinging arms (suspension arms), 2 transverse, square torsion bars of laminated construction, adjustable, anti-roll bars, hydraulic telescopic double-action shock absorbers
Suspension, rear:	Oscillating half axles and radius arms, (longitudinal swinging arms), one round torsion bar on each side, hydraulic telescopic double-action shock absorbers
Brakes, front/rear (Size (mm)):	Brake drums Duplex (280 x 40) / Brake drums Simplex (280 x 40)
Wheels, front/rear:	4.5 J x 15 / 4.5 J x 15
Tyres, front/rear:	5.60-15 Sport / 5.60-15 Sport

Electrical system

Alternator (W):	160
Battery (V/Ah):	6 / 84

Dimensions and weight

Track, front/rear (mm):	1306 / 1272
Wheelbase (mm):	2100
Length x width x height (mm):	3950 x 1670 x 1310
Kerb weight DIN (kg):	850
Permissible gross weight (kg):	1200
Fuel tank capacity (l):	52, including 5 reserve
Cw x A (m2) Coupé:	0.365 x 1.692 = 0.618
Power/weight ratio (kg/kW / kg/hp):	26.56 / 19.31

Fuel consumption

DIN 70 030 (mpg):	36.7; 86 RON normal leaded
Performance, production, prices	
Acceleration 0-62mph/100kph (s):	22.0
Maximum speed (mph / kph):	90 / 145

Production, total number:

356 A Coupé:*	13,016
356 A Cabriolet:*	3,285
*Total number all engine versions	
Purchase prices:	
09/1955 Coupé:	DM 11,400
Cabriolet:	DM 12,600
09/1956 Coupé:	DM 11,400
Cabriolet:	DM 12,600

356 A 1300 Super Coupé
356 A 1300 Super Cabriolet
MY 1956–MY 1957

Engine

Engine design:	4-cylinder horizontally-opposed
Installation:	Rear-engine
Cooling system:	Air-cooled
Engine type:	589/2
Displacement (cc):	1290
Bore x stroke (mm):	74.5 x 74
Engine output DIN (kW/hp):	44/60 at 5500rpm
Maximum torque (Nm/lb ft):	88/65 at 3600rpm
Output per litre(kW/l / hp/l):	34.1 / 46.5
Compression ratio:	7.5 : 1
Valve operation & camshaft drive:	ohv, cam driven by gears, 2 valves per cylinder
Carburation:	2 downdraught carburettors Solex 32 PBIC also 40 PICB
Ignition system:	Battery coil ignition
Firing order:	1 - 4 - 3 - 2
Crankshaft bearing:	4 slide bearings
Engine lubrication:	Full pressure oil lubrication
Engine oil total (l):	5.0*
*Filling new assembled engine, oil change 4.0	

Transmission

Drive configuration:	Rear-axle drive
Manual gearbox:	4-speed
Transmission type:	644
Transmission ratios:	
1st gear:	3.182
2nd gear:	1.765
3rd gear:	1.227
4th gear:	0.885
Reverse gear:	3.560
Drive ratio:	4.428

Body, chassis, suspension, brakes, wheels

Body design:	Steel body, 2 doors, 2 + 2 seats, pressed and welded steel-sheet sections, one unit with body, curved single-piece windscreen, one grille in engine lid, bumpers project away from body with over-riders
Coupé:	Fixed steel roof
Option:	Manual sunroof
Cabriolet:	Multi-layer hood with flexible plastic rear window
Option MY 1957:	Hardtop

Suspension, front:	2 longitudinal swinging arms (suspension arms), 2 transverse, square torsion bars of laminated construction, adjustable, anti-roll bars, hydraulic telescopic double-action shock absorbers
Suspension, rear:	Oscillating half axles and radius arms, (longitudinal swinging arms), one round torsion bar on each side, hydraulic telescopic double-action shock absorbers
Brakes, front/rear (Size (mm)):	Brake drums Duplex (280 x 40) / Brake drums Simplex (280 x 40)
Wheels, front/rear:	4.5 J x 15 / 4.5 J x 15
Tyres, front/rear:	5.60-15 Sport / 5.60-15 Sport

Electrical system

Alternator (W):	160
Battery (V/Ah):	6 / 84

Dimensions and weight

Track, front/rear (mm):	1306 / 1272
Wheelbase (mm):	2100
Length x width x height (mm):	3950 x 1670 x 1310
Kerb weight DIN (kg):	850
Permissible gross weight (kg):	1200
Fuel tank capacity (l):	52, including 5 reserve
Cw x A (m2) Coupé:	0.365 x 1.692 = 0.618
Power/weight ratio (kg/kW/ kg/hp):	19.31 / 14.16

Fuel consumption

DIN 70 030 (mpg):	36.5; 86 RON normal leaded

Performance, production, prices

Acceleration 0-62mph/100kph (s):	17.0
Maximum speed (mph / kph):	99 / 160
Production, total number:	
356 A Coupé:*	13,016
356 A Cabriolet:*	3,285
*Total number all engine versions	
Purchase prices:	
09/1955 Coupé:	DM 13,500
Cabriolet:	DM 14,700
09/1956 Coupé:	DM 13,500
Cabriolet:	DM 14,700

356 A 1600 Coupé
356 A 1600 Cabriolet
MY 1956–MY 1959

Engine

Engine design:	4-cylinder horizontally-opposed
Installation:	Rear-engine
Cooling system:	Air-cooled
Engine type:	616/1
Displacement (cc):	1582
Bore x stroke (mm):	82.5 x 74
Engine output DIN (kW/hp):	44/60 at 4500rpm
Maximum torque (Nm/lb ft):	110/81 at 2800rpm
Output per litre(kW/l / hp/l):	27.8 / 37.9
Compression ratio:	7.5 : 1
Valve operation & camshaft drive:	ohv, cam driven by gears, 2 valves per cylinder
Carburation:	2 downdraught carburettors Solex 32 PBIC
MY 1958 - MY 1959:	Zenith 32 NDIX
Ignition system:	Battery coil ignition
Firing order:	1 - 4 - 3 - 2
Crankshaft bearing:	4 slide bearings
Engine lubrication:	Full pressure oil lubrication
Engine oil total (l):	5.0*
*Filling new assembled engine, oil change 4.0	

Transmission

Drive configuration:	Rear-axle drive
Manual gearbox:	4-speed
Transmission type:	644
Transmission ratios:	
1st gear:	3.182
2nd gear:	1.765
3rd gear:	1.130
4th gear:	0.815
Reverse gear:	3.560
Drive ratio:	4.428

Body, chassis, suspension, brakes, wheels

Body design:	Steel body, 2 doors, 2 + 2 seats, pressed and welded steel-sheet sections, one unit with body, curved single-piece windscreen, one grille in engine lid, bumpers project away from body with over-riders
MY 1958 - MY 1959:	tailpipes go through over-riders
Coupé:	Fixed steel roof
Option:	Manual sunroof
Cabriolet:	Multi-layer hood with flexible plastic rear window
Option MY 1957 - MY 1959:	Hardtop
Suspension, front:	2 longitudinal swinging arms (suspension arms), 2 transverse, square torsion bars of laminated construction, adjustable, anti-roll bars, hydraulic telescopic double-action shock absorbers

Suspension, rear:	Oscillating half axles and radius arms, (longitudinal swinging arms), one round torsion bar on each side, hydraulic telescopic double-action shock absorbers
Brakes, front/rear (Size (mm)):	Brake drums Duplex (280 x 40) / Brake drums Simplex (280 x 40)
Wheels, front/rear:	4.5 J x 15 / 4.5 J x 15
Tyres, front/rear:	5.60-15 Sport / 5.60-15 Sport

Electrical system

Alternator (W):	160
Battery (V/Ah):	6 / 84

Dimensions and weight

Track, front/rear (mm):	1306 / 1272
Wheelbase (mm):	2100
Length x width x height (mm):	3950 x 1670 x 1310
Kerb weight DIN (kg):	850
MY 1959:	885
Permissible gross weight (kg):	1200
MY 1959:	1250
Fuel tank capacity (l):	52, including 5 reserve
Cw x A (m2) Coupé:	0.365 x 1.692 = 0.618
Power/weight ratio (kg/kW/kg/hp):	19.31 / 14.16
MY 1959:	20.11 / 14.75

Fuel consumption

DIN 70 030 (mpg):	37; 86 RON normal leaded

Performance, production, prices

Acceleration 0-62mph/100kph (s):	16.5
Maximum speed (mph / kph):	99 / 160
Production, total number:	
356 A Coupé:*	13,016
356 A Cabriolet:*	3,285
*Total number all engine versions	
Purchase prices:	
09/1955 Coupé:	DM 12,700
Cabriolet:	DM 13,900
09/1956 Coupé:	DM 12,700
Cabriolet:	DM 13,900
09/1957 Coupé:	DM 12,700
Cabriolet:	DM 13,900
08/1958 Coupé:	DM 12,700
Cabriolet:	DM 13,900

356 A 1600 Hardtop-Coupé
356 A 1600 Hardtop/Cabriolet
MY 1958–MY 1959

Engine

Engine design:	4-cylinder horizontally-opposed
Installation:	Rear-engine
Cooling system:	Air-cooled
Engine type:	616/1
Displacement (cc):	1582
Bore x stroke (mm):	82.5 x 74
Engine output DIN (kW/hp):	44/60 at 4500rpm
Maximum torque (Nm/lb ft):	110/81 at 2800rpm
Output per litre(kW/l / hp/l):	27.8 / 37.9
Compression ratio:	7.5 : 1
Valve operation & camshaft drive:	ohv, cam driven by gears, 2 valves per cylinder
Carburation:	2 downdraught carburettors Solex 32 PBIC
MY 1958 - MY 1959:	Zenith 32 NDIX
Ignition system:	Battery coil ignition
Firing order:	1 - 4 - 3 - 2
Crankshaft bearing:	4 slide bearings
Engine lubrication:	Full pressure oil lubrication
Engine oil total (l):	5.0*
*Filling new assembled engine, oil change 4.0	

Transmission

Drive configuration:	Rear-axle drive
Manual gearbox:	4-speed
Transmission type:	644
Transmission ratios:	
1st gear:	3.182
2nd gear:	1.765
3rd gear:	1.130
4th gear:	0.815
Reverse gear:	3.560
Drive ratio:	4.428

Body, chassis, suspension, brakes, wheels

Body design:	Steel body, 2 doors, 2 + 2 seats, pressed and welded steel-sheet sections, one unit with body, curved single-piece windscreen, one grille in engine lid, bumpers project away from body with over-riders, tailpipes go through over-riders
Hardtop-Coupé:	Fixed hardtop
Hardtop/Cabriolet:	Removable hardtop
Suspension, front:	2 longitudinal swinging arms (suspension arms), 2 transverse, square torsion bars of

	laminated construction, adjustable, anti-roll bars, hydraulic telescopic double-action shock absorbers
Suspension, rear:	Oscillating half axles and radius arms, (longitudinal swinging arms), one round torsion bar on each side, hydraulic telescopic double-action shock absorbers
Brakes, front/rear (Size (mm)):	Brake drums Duplex (280 x 40) / Brake drums Simplex (280 x 40)
Wheels, front/rear:	4.5 J x 15 / 4.5 J x 15
Tyres, front/rear:	5.60-15 Sport / 5.60-15 Sport

Electrical system

Alternator (W):	160
Battery (V/Ah):	6 / 84

Dimensions and weight

Track, front/rear (mm):	1306 / 1272
Wheelbase (mm):	2100
Length x width x height (mm):	3950 x 1670 x 1290
Kerb weight DIN (kg):	850
MY 1959:	885
Permissible gross weight (kg):	1200
MY 1959:	1250
Fuel tank capacity (l):	52, including 5 reserve
Cw x A (m2) Coupé:	0.365 x 1.692 = 0.618
Power/weight ratio (kg/kW/kg/hp):	19.31 / 14.16
MY 1959:	20.11 / 14.75

Fuel consumption

DIN 70 030 (mpg):	37; 86 RON normal leaded

Performance, production, prices

Acceleration 0-62mph/100kph (s):	16.5
Maximum speed (mph / kph):	99 / 160
Production, total number:	
356 A Coupé:*	13,016
356 A Cabriolet:*	3,285
*Total number all engine versions	
Purchase prices:	
09/1957 Hardtop-Coupé:	DM 13,600
Hardtop/Cabriolet:	DM 14,960
08/1958 Hardtop-Coupé:	DM 13,600
Hardtop/Cabriolet:	DM 14,960

356 A 1600 Speedster
MY 1956–MY 1958

Engine

Engine design:	4-cylinder horizontally-opposed
Installation:	Rear-engine
Cooling system:	Air-cooled
Engine type:	616/1
Displacement (cc):	1582
Bore x stroke (mm):	82.5 x 74
Engine output DIN (kW/hp):	44/60 at 4500rpm
Maximum torque (Nm/lb ft):	110/81 at 2800rpm
Output per litre(kW/l / hp/l):	27.8 / 37.9
Compression ratio:	7.5 : 1
Valve operation & camshaft drive:	ohv, cam driven by gears, 2 valves per cylinder
Carburation:	2 downdraught carburettors Solex 32 PBIC
MY 1958 - MY 1959:	Zenith 32 NDIX
Ignition system:	Battery coil ignition
Firing order:	1 - 4 - 3 - 2
Crankshaft bearing:	4 slide bearings
Engine lubrication:	Full pressure oil lubrication
Engine oil total (l):	5.0*
*Filling new assembled engine, oil change 4.0	

Transmission

Drive configuration:	Rear-axle drive
Manual gearbox:	4-speed
Transmission type:	644
Transmission ratios:	
1st gear:	3.182
2nd gear:	1.765
3rd gear:	1.227
4th gear:	0.885
Reverse gear:	3.560
Drive ratio:	4.428

Body, chassis, suspension, brakes, wheels

Body design:	Steel body, 2 doors, 2 seats, pressed and welded steel frame, curved single-piece windscreen, corners with large radius, one grille on rear hood, bumpers project away from body with over-riders, single layer hood with flexible plastic rear window, side curtains on doors
MY 1958:	tailpipes go through over-riders
Option MY 1957 - MY 1958:	Hardtop
Suspension, front:	2 longitudinal swinging arms (suspension arms), 2 transverse, square torsion bars of

	laminated construction, adjustable, anti-roll bars, hydraulic telescopic double-action shock absorbers
Suspension, rear:	Oscillating half axles and radius arms, (longitudinal swinging arms), one round torsion bar on each side, hydraulic telescopic double-action shock absorbers
Brakes, front/rear (Size (mm)):	Brake drums Duplex (280 x 40) / Brake drums Simplex (280 x 40)
Wheels, front/rear:	4.5 J x 15 / 4.5 J x 15
Tyres, front/rear:	5.60-15 Sport / 5.60-15 Sport

Electrical system

Alternator (W):	160
Battery (V/Ah):	6 / 84

Dimensions and weight

Track, front/rear (mm):	1306 / 1272
Wheelbase (mm):	2100
Length x width x height (mm):	3950 x 1670 x 1220*
Kerb weight DIN (kg):	760
Permissible gross weight (kg):	1100
Fuel tank capacity (l):	52, including 5 reserve
C_w x A (m^2):	0.377 x 1.640 = 0.618
Power/weight ratio (kg/kW/ kg/hp):	17.27 / 12.66
*with closed top	

Fuel consumption

DIN 70 030 (mpg):	37; 86 RON normal leaded

Performance, production, prices

Acceleration 0-62mph/100kph (s):	16.5
Maximum speed (mph / kph):	99 / 160
Production, total number:	
356 A Speedster:*	2,910
*Total number all engine versions	
Purchase prices:	
09/1955 Speedster:	DM 11,900
09/1956 Speedster:	DM 11,900
09/1957 Speedster:	DM 11,500

356 A 1600 Super Coupé
356 A 1600 Super Cabriolet
MY 1956–MY 1959

Engine

Engine design:	4-cylinder horizontally-opposed
Installation:	Rear-engine
Cooling system:	Air-cooled
Engine type:	616/2
Displacement (cc):	1582
Bore x stroke (mm):	82.5 x 74
Engine output DIN (kW/hp):	55/75 at 5000rpm
Maximum torque (Nm/lb ft/lb ft):	117/86 at 3700rpm
Output per litre(kW/l / hp/l):	34.8 / 47.4
Compression ratio:	8.5 : 1
Valve operation & camshaft drive:	ohv, cam driven by gears, 2 valves per cylinder
Carburation:	2 downdraught carburettors Solex 40 PICB
MY 1958 - MY 1959:	Zenith 32 NDIX
Ignition system:	Battery coil ignition
Firing order:	1 - 4 - 3 - 2
Crankshaft bearing:	4 slide bearings
Engine lubrication:	Full pressure oil lubrication
Engine oil total (l):	5.0*
*Filling new assembled engine, oil change 4.0	

Transmission

Drive configuration:	Rear-axle drive
Manual gearbox:	4-speed
Transmission type:	644
Transmission ratios:	
1st gear:	3.182
2nd gear:	1.765
3rd gear:	1.130
4th gear:	0.815
Reverse gear:	3.560
Drive ratio:	4.428

Body, chassis, suspension, brakes, wheels

Body design:	Steel body, 2 doors, 2 + 2 seats, pressed and welded steel-sheet sections, one unit with body, curved single-piece windscreen, one grille in engine lid, bumpers project away from body with over-riders
MY 1958 - MY 1959:	tailpipes go through over-riders
Coupé:	Fixed steel roof
Option:	Manual sunroof
Cabriolet:	Multi-layer hood with flexible plastic rear window
Option MY 1957 - MY 1959:	Hardtop
Suspension, front:	2 longitudinal swinging arms (suspension arms), 2 transverse, square torsion bars of laminated construction, adjustable, anti-roll bars, hydraulic telescopic double-action shock absorbers
Suspension, rear:	Oscillating half axles and radius arms, (longitudinal swinging arms), one round torsion bar on each side, hydraulic telescopic double-action shock absorbers
Brakes, front/rear (Size (mm)):	Brake drums Duplex (280 x 40) / Brake drums Simplex (280 x 40)
Wheels, front/rear:	4.5 J x 15 / 4.5 J x 15
Tyres, front/rear:	5.60-15 Sport / 5.60-15 Sport
Option:	5.90-15 Sport / 5.90-15 Sport

Electrical system

Alternator (W):	160
Battery (V/Ah):	6 / 84

Dimensions and weight

Track, front/rear (mm):	1306 / 1272
Wheelbase (mm):	2100
Length x width x height (mm):	3950 x 1670 x 1310
Kerb weight DIN (kg):	850
MY 1959:	885
Permissible gross weight (kg):	1200
MY 1959:	1250
Fuel tank capacity (l):	52, including 5 reserve
Cw x A (m2) Coupé:	0.365 x 1.692 = 0.618
Power/weight ratio (kg/kW/kg/hp):	15.45 / 11.33
MY 1959:	16.09 / 11.80

Fuel consumption

DIN 70 030 (mpg):	34; 86 RON normal leaded

Performance, production, prices

Acceleration 0-62mph/100kph (s):	14.5
Maximum speed (mph / kph):	108.5 / 175
Production, total number:	
356 A Coupé:*	13,016
356 A Cabriolet:*	3,285
*Total number all engine versions	
Purchase prices:	
09/1955 Coupé:	DM 13,800
Cabriolet:	DM 15,000
09/1956 Coupé:	DM 13,800
Cabriolet:	DM 15,000
09/1957 Coupé:	DM 13,800
Cabriolet:	DM 15,000
08/1958 Coupé:	DM 13,800
Cabriolet:	DM 15,000

356 A 1600 Super Hardtop-Coupé
356 A 1600 Super Hardtop/Cabriolet
MY 1958–MY 1959

Engine

Engine design:	4-cylinder horizontally-opposed
Installation:	Rear-engine
Cooling system:	Air-cooled
Engine type:	616/2
Displacement (cc):	1582
Bore x stroke (mm):	82.5 x 74
Engine output DIN (kW/hp):	55/75 at 5000rpm
Maximum torque (Nm/lb ft):	117/86 at 3700rpm
Output per litre(kW/l / hp/l):	34.8 / 47.4
Compression ratio:	8,5 : 1
Valve operation & camshaft drive:	ohv, cam driven by gears, 2 valves per cylinder
Carburation:	2 downdraught carburettors Solex 40 PICB
MY 1958 - MY 1959:	Zenith 32 NDIX
Ignition system:	Battery coil ignition
Firing order:	1 - 4 - 3 - 2
Crankshaft bearing:	4 slide bearings
Engine lubrication:	Full pressure oil lubrication
Engine oil total (l):	5.0*
*Filling new assembled engine, oil change 4.0	

Transmission

Drive configuration:	Rear-axle drive
Manual gearbox:	4-speed
Transmission type:	644
Transmission ratios:	
1st gear:	3.182
2nd gear:	1.765
3rd gear:	1.130
4th gear:	0.815
Reverse gear:	3.560
Drive ratio:	4.428

Body, chassis, suspension, brakes, wheels

Body design:	Steel body, 2 doors, 2 + 2 seats, pressed and welded steel-sheet sections, one unit with body, curved single-piece windscreen, one grille in engine lid, bumpers project away from body with over-riders, tailpipes go through over-riders
Hardtop-Coupé:	Fixed hardtop
Hardtop/Cabriolet:	Removable hardtop
Suspension, front:	2 longitudinal swinging arms (suspension arms), 2 transverse, square torsion bars of laminated construction, adjustable, anti-roll

	bars, hydraulic telescopic double-action shock absorbers
Suspension, rear:	Oscillating half axles and radius arms, (longitudinal swinging arms), one round torsion bar on each side, hydraulic telescopic double-action shock absorbers
Brakes, front/rear (Size (mm)):	Brake drums Duplex (280 x 40) / Brake drums Simplex (280 x 40)
Wheels, front/rear:	4.5 J x 15 / 4.5 J x 15
Tyres, front/rear:	5.60-15 Sport / 5.60-15 Sport
Option:	5.90-15 Sport / 5.90-15 Sport

Electrical system

Alternator (W):	160
Battery (V/Ah):	6 / 84

Dimensions and weight

Track, front/rear (mm):	1306 / 1272
Wheelbase (mm):	2100
Length x width x height (mm):	3950 x 1670 x 1290
Kerb weight DIN (kg):	850
MY 1959:	885
Permissible gross weight (kg):	1200
MY 1959:	1250
Fuel tank capacity (l):	52, including 5 reserve
Cw x A (m2) Coupé:	0.365 x 1.692 = 0.618
Power/weight ratio (kg/kW/kg/hp):	15.45 / 11.33
MY 1959:	16.09 / 11.80

Fuel consumption

DIN 70 030 (mpg):	34; 86 RON normal leaded

Performance, production, prices

Acceleration 0-62mph/100kph (s):	14.5
Maximum speed (mph / kph):	108.5 / 175
Production, total number:	
356 A Coupé:*	13,016
356 A Cabriolet:*	3,285
*Total number all engine versions	
Purchase prices:	
09/1957 Hardtop-Coupé:	DM 14,700
Hardtop/Cabriolet:	DM 15,750
08/1958 Hardtop-Coupé:	DM 14,700
Hardtop/Cabriolet:	DM 15,750

356 A 1600 Super Speedster
MY 1956–MY 1958

Engine

Engine design:	4-cylinder horizontally-opposed
Installation:	Rear-engine
Cooling system:	Air-cooled
Engine type:	616/2
Displacement (cc):	1582
Bore x stroke (mm):	82.5 x 74
Engine output DIN (kW/hp):	55/75 at 5000rpm
Maximum torque (Nm/lb ft):	117/86 at 3700rpm
Output per litre(kW/l / hp/l):	34.8 / 47.4
Compression ratio:	8.5 : 1
Valve operation & camshaft drive:	ohv, cam driven by gears, 2 valves per cylinder
Carburation:	2 downdraught carburettors Solex 32 PBIC
MY 1958:	Zenith 32 NDIX
Ignition system:	Battery coil ignition
Firing order:	1 - 4 - 3 - 2
Crankshaft bearing:	4 slide bearings
Engine lubrication:	Full pressure oil lubrication
Engine oil total (l):	5.0*
*Filling new assembled engine, oil change 4.0	

Transmission

Drive configuration:	Rear-axle drive
Manual gearbox:	4-speed
Transmission type:	644
Transmission ratios:	
1st gear:	3.182
2nd gear:	1.765
3rd gear:	1.227
4th gear:	0.885
Reverse gear:	3.560
Drive ratio:	4.428

Body, chassis, suspension, brakes, wheels

Body design:	Steel body, 2 doors, 2 seats, pressed and welded steel frame, curved single-piece windscreen, corners with large radius, one grille in engine lid, bumpers project away from body with over-riders, single layer hood with flexible plastic rear window, side curtains on doors
MY 1958:	tailpipes go through over-riders
Option MY 1957 - MY 1958:	Hardtop

Suspension, front:	2 longitudinal swinging arms (suspension arms), 2 transverse, square torsion bars of laminated construction, adjustable, anti-roll bars, hydraulic telescopic double-action shock absorbers
Suspension, rear:	Oscillating half axles and radius arms, (longitudinal swinging arms), one round torsion bar on each side, hydraulic telescopic double-action shock absorbers
Brakes, front/rear (Size (mm)):	Brake drums Duplex (280 x 40) / Brake drums Simplex (280 x 40)
Wheels, front/rear:	4.5 J x 15 / 4.5 J x 15
Tyres, front/rear:	5.60-15 Sport / 5.60-15 Sport
Option:	5.90-15 Sport / 5.90-15 Sport

Electrical system

Alternator (W):	160
Battery (V/Ah):	6 / 84

Dimensions and weight

Track, front/rear (mm):	1306 / 1272
Wheelbase (mm):	2100
Length x width x height (mm):	3950 x 1670 x 1220*
Kerb weight DIN (kg):	760
Permissible gross weight (kg):	1100
Fuel tank capacity (l):	52, including 5 reserve
C_w x A (m²):	0.377 x 1.640 = 0.618
Power/weight ratio (kg/kW/kg/hp):	13.81 / 10.13
*with closed top	

Fuel consumption

DIN 70 030 (mpg):	34; 86 RON normal leaded

Performance, production, prices

Acceleration 0-62mph/100kph (s):	14.5
Maximum speed (mph / kph):	108.5 / 175
Production, total number:	
356 A Speedster:*	2,910
*Total number all engine versions	
Purchase prices:	
09/1955 Speedster:	DM 13,000
09/1956 Speedster:	DM 13,000
09/1957 Speedster:	DM 12,600

356 A 1600 Convertible D
MY 1959

Engine

Engine design:	4-cylinder horizontally-opposed
Installation:	Rear-engine
Cooling system:	Air-cooled
Engine type:	616/1
Displacement (cc):	1582
Bore x stroke (mm):	82.5 x 74
Engine output DIN (kW/hp):	44/60 at 4500rpm
Maximum torque (Nm/lb ft):	110/81 at 2800rpm
Output per litre(kW/l / hp/l):	27.8 / 37.9
Compression ratio:	7.5 : 1
Valve operation & camshaft drive:	ohv, cam driven by gears, 2 valves per cylinder
Carburation:	2 downdraught carburettors Zenith 32 NDIX
Ignition system:	Battery coil ignition
Firing order:	1 - 4 - 3 - 2
Crankshaft bearing:	4 slide bearings
Engine lubrication:	Full pressure oil lubrication
Engine oil total (l):	5.0*
*Filling new assembled engine, oil change 4.0	

Transmission

Drive configuration:	Rear-axle drive
Manual gearbox:	4-speed
Transmission type:	716/0
Transmission ratios:	
1st gear:	3.091
2nd gear:	1.765
3rd gear:	1.130
4th gear:	0.815
Reverse gear:	3.560
Drive ratio:	4.428

Body, chassis, suspension, brakes, wheels

Body design:	Steel body, 2 doors, 2 + 2 seats, pressed and welded steel frame, curved single-piece windscreen, one grille in engine lid, bumpers project away from body with over-riders, tailpipes go through over-riders, single layer hood with flexible plastic rear window, winding windows in doors
Option:	Hardtop

Suspension, front:	2 longitudinal swinging arms (suspension arms), 2 transverse, square torsion bars of laminated construction, adjustable, anti-roll bars, hydraulic telescopic double-action shock absorbers
Suspension, rear:	Oscillating half axles and radius arms, (longitudinal swinging arms), one round torsion bar on each side, hydraulic telescopic double-action shock absorbers
Brakes, front/rear (Size (mm)):	Brake drums Duplex (280 x 40) / Brake drums Simplex (280 x 40)
Wheels, front/rear:	4.5 J x 15 / 4.5 J x 15
Tyres, front/rear:	5.60-15 Sport / 5.60-15 Sport

Electrical system

Alternator (W):	160
Battery (V/Ah):	6 / 84

Dimensions and weight

Track, front/rear (mm):	1306 / 1272
Wheelbase (mm):	2100
Length x width x height (mm):	3950 x 1670 x 1220*
Kerb weight DIN (kg):	855
Permissible gross weight (kg):	1250
Fuel tank capacity (l):	52, including 5 reserve
C_w x A (m²):	0.377 x 1.640 = 0.618
Power/weight ratio (kg/kW/kg/hp):	19.43 / 14.25
*with closed top	

Fuel consumption

DIN 70 030 (mpg):	37; 86 RON normal leaded

Performance, production, prices

Acceleration 0-62mph/100kph (s):	16.5
Maximum speed (mph / kph):	99 / 160
Production, total number:	
356 A Convertible D:*	1,330
*Total number all engine versions	
Purchase price:	
08/1958 Convertible D:	DM 12,650

356 A 1600 Super Convertible D MY 1959

Engine

Engine design:	4-cylinder horizontally-opposed
Installation:	Rear-engine
Cooling system:	Air-cooled
Engine type:	616/2
Displacement (cc):	1582
Bore x stroke (mm):	82.5 x 74
Engine output DIN (kW/hp):	55/75 at 5000rpm
Maximum torque (Nm/lb ft):	117/86 at 3700rpm
Output per litre(kW/l / hp/l):	34.8 / 47.4
Verdichtung:	8.5 : 1
Valve operation & camshaft drive:	ohv, cam driven by gears, 2 valves per cylinder
Carburation:	2 downdraught carburettors Solex Zenith 32 NDIX
Ignition system:	Battery coil ignition
Firing order:	1 - 4 - 3 - 2
Crankshaft bearing:	4 slide bearings
Engine lubrication:	Full pressure oil lubrication
Engine oil total (l):	5.0*
*Filling new assembled engine, oil change 4.0	

Transmission

Drive configuration:	Rear-axle drive
Manual gearbox:	4-speed
Transmission type:	716/0
Transmission ratios:	
1st gear:	3.091
2nd gear:	1.765
3rd gear:	1.130
4th gear:	0.815
Reverse gear:	3.560
Drive ratio:	4.428

Body, chassis, suspension, brakes, wheels

Body design:	Steel body, 2 doors, 2 + 2 seats, pressed and welded steel frame, curved single-piece windscreen, one grille in engine lid, bumpers project away from body with over-riders, tailpipes go through over-riders, single layer hood with flexible plastic rear window, winding windows in doors
Option:	Hardtop

Suspension, front:	2 longitudinal swinging arms (suspension arms), 2 transverse, square torsion bars of laminated construction, adjustable, anti-roll bars, hydraulic telescopic double-action shock absorbers
Suspension, rear:	Oscillating half axles and radius arms, (longitudinal swinging arms), one round torsion bar on each side, hydraulic telescopic double-action shock absorbers
Brakes, front/rear (Size (mm)):	Brake drums Duplex (280 x 40) / Brake drums Simplex (280 x 40)
Wheels, front/rear:	4.5 J x 15 / 4.5 J x 15
Tyres, front/rear:	5.60-15 Sport / 5.60-15 Sport
Option:	5.90-15 Sport / 5.90-15 Sport

Electrical system

Alternator (W):	160
Battery (V/Ah):	6 / 84

Dimensions and weight

Track, front/rear (mm):	1306 / 1272
Wheelbase (mm):	2100
Length x width x height (mm):	3950 x 1670 x 1220*
Kerb weight DIN (kg):	855
Permissible gross weight (kg):	1250
Fuel tank capacity (l):	52, including 5 reserve
C_w x A (m²):	0.377 x 1.640 = 0.618
Power/weight ratio (kg/kW/kg/hp):	15.54 / 11.40
*with closed top	

Fuel consumption

DIN 70 030 (mpg):	34; 86 RON normal leaded

Performance, production, prices

Acceleration 0-62mph/100kph (s):	14.5
Maximum speed (mph / kph):	108.5 / 175
Production, total number:	
356 A Convertible D:*	1,330
*Total number all engine versions	
Purchase prices:	
08/1958 Convertible D:	DM 13,750

356 A 1500 GS Carrera Coupé
356 A 1500 GS Carrera Cabriolet
MY 1956–MY 1957

Engine
Engine design:	4-cylinder horizontally-opposed
Installation:	Rear-engine
Cooling system:	Air-cooled
Engine type:	547/1
Displacement (cc):	1498
Bore x stroke (mm):	85 x 66
Engine output DIN (kW/hp):	74/100 at 6200rpm
Maximum torque (Nm/lb ft):	119/88 at 5200rpm
Output per litre(kW/l / hp/l):	49.4 / 66.8
Compression ratio:	9.0: 1
Valve operation & camshaft drive:	dohc, two vertical shafts, 2 valves per cylinder
Carburation:	2 dual throat downdraught carburettors Solex 40 PII
Ignition system:	Battery coil dual ignition
Firing order:	1 - 4 - 3 - 2
Crankshaft bearing:	4 roller bearings
Engine lubrication:	Dry sump
Engine oil total (l):	8.0

Transmission
Drive configuration:	Rear-axle drive
Manual gearbox:	4-speed
Transmission type:	644 Carrera
Transmission ratios:	
1st gear:	3.182
2nd gear:	1.765
3rd gear:	1.227
4th gear:	0.960
Reverse gear:	3.560
Drive ratio:	4.428

Body, chassis, suspension, brakes, wheels
Body design:	Steel body, 2 doors, 2 + 2 seats, pressed and welded steel-sheet sections, one unit with body, curved single-piece windscreen, one grille in engine lid, bumpers project away from body with over-riders
Coupé:	Fixed steel roof
Option:	Manual sunroof
Cabriolet:	Multi-layer hood with flexible plastic rear window

Option MY 1957:	Hardtop
Suspension, front:	2 longitudinal swinging arms (suspension arms), 2 transverse, square torsion bars of laminated construction, adjustable, anti-roll bars, hydraulic telescopic double-action shock absorbers
Suspension, rear:	Oscillating half axles and radius arms, (longitudinal swinging arms), one round torsion bar on each side, hydraulic telescopic double-action shock absorbers
Brakes, front/rear (Size (mm)):	Brake drums Duplex (280 x 40) / Brake drums Simplex (280 x 40)
Wheels, front/rear:	4.5 J x 15 / 4.5 J x 15
Tyres, front/rear:	5.90-15 Supersport / 5.90-15 Supersport

Electrical system
Alternator (W):	160
Battery (V/Ah):	6 / 84

Dimensions and weight
Track, front/rear (mm):	1306 / 1272
Wheelbase (mm):	2100
Length x width x height (mm):	3950 x 1670 x 1310
Hardtop-Coupé:	3950 x 1670 x 1290
Hardtop/Cabriolet:	3950 x 1670 x 1290
Kerb weight DIN (kg):	850
Permissible gross weight (kg):	1200
Fuel tank capacity (l):	52, including 5 reserve
Cw x A (m2) Coupé:	0.365 x 1.692 = 0.618
Power/weight ratio (kg/kW/kg/hp):	11.48 / 8.50

Fuel consumption
DIN 70 030 (mpg):	30; 86 RON normal leaded

Performance, production, prices
Acceleration 0-62mph/100kph (s):	12.0
Maximum speed (mph / kph):	124 / 200
Prod., 356 A 1500 GS total no.:	447
Purchase prices:	
09/1955 Coupé:	DM 18,500
Cabriolet:	DM 19,700
09/1956 Coupé:	DM 18,500
Cabriolet:	DM 19,700

356 A 1500 GS Carrera Speedster
My 1956–MY 1957

Engine
Engine design:	4-cylinder horizontally-opposed
Installation:	Rear-engine
Cooling system:	Air-cooled
Engine type:	547/1
Displacement (cc):	1498
Bore x stroke (mm):	85 x 66
Engine output DIN (kW/hp):	74/100 at 6200rpm
Maximum torque (Nm/lb ft):	119/88 at 5200rpm
Output per litre(kW/l / hp/l):	49.4 / 66.8
Compression ratio:	9.0: 1
Valve operation & camshaft drive:	dohc, two vertical shafts, 2 valves per cylinder
Carburation:	2 twin-choke downdraught carburettors Solex 40 PII
Ignition system:	Battery coil dual ignition
Firing order:	1 - 4 - 3 - 2
Crankshaft bearing:	4 roller bearings
Engine lubrication:	Dry sump
Engine oil total (l):	8.0

Transmission
Drive configuration:	Rear-axle drive
Manual gearbox:	4-speed
Transmission type:	644 Carrera
Transmission ratios:	
1st gear:	3.182
2nd gear:	1.765
3rd gear:	1.227
4th gear:	0.960
Reverse gear:	3.560
Drive ratio:	4.428

Body, chassis, suspension, brakes, wheels
Body design:	Steel body, 2 doors, 2 seats, pressed and welded steel frame, curved single-piece windscreen, corners with large radius, one grille in engine lid, bumpers project away from body with over-riders, single layer hood with flexible plastic rear window, side curtains on doors
Option MY 1957:	Hardtop

Suspension, front:	2 longitudinal swinging arms (suspension arms), 2 transverse, square torsion bars of laminated construction, adjustable, anti-roll bars, hydraulic telescopic double-action shock absorbers
Suspension, rear:	Oscillating half axles and radius arms, (longitudinal swinging arms), one round torsion bar on each side, hydraulic telescopic double-action shock absorbers
Brakes, front/rear (Size (mm)):	Brake drums Duplex (280 x 40) / Brake drums Simplex (280 x 40)
Wheels, front/rear:	4.5 J x 15 / 4.5 J x 15
Tyres, front/rear:	5.90-15 Supersport / 5.90-15 Supersport

Electrical system
Alternator (W):	160
Battery (V/Ah):	6 / 84

Dimensions and weight
Track, front/rear (mm):	1306 / 1272
Wheelbase (mm):	2100
Length x width x height (mm):	3950 x 1670 x 1220*
Kerb weight DIN (kg):	790
Permissible gross weight (kg):	1100
Fuel tank capacity (l):	52, including 5 reserve
C_w x A (m^2):	0.377 x 1.640 = 0.618
Power/weight ratio (kg/kW/kg/hp):	10.67 / 7.90
*with closed top	

Fuel consumption
DIN 70 030 (mpg):	30; 86 RON normal leaded

Performance, production, prices
Acceleration 0-62mph/100kph (s):	12.0
Maximum speed (mph / kph):	124 / 200
Prod., 356 A 1500 GS total no.:	447
356 A 1500 GS & GT Speedster:	167
Purchase prices:	
09/1955 Speedster:	DM 17,700
09/1956 Speedster:	DM 17,700

356 A 1500 GS Carrera GT Coupé
MY 1957–MY 1958

Engine
Engine design:	4-cylinder horizontally-opposed
Installation:	Rear-engine
Cooling system:	Air-cooled
Engine type:	
Engine-No. P91001 - P92021:	692/0
Engine-No. P92001 - P92014:	692/1
Displacement (cc):	1498
Bore x stroke (mm):	85 x 66
Engine output DIN (kW/hp):	81/110 at 6400rpm
Maximum torque (Nm/lb ft):	124/91 at 5200rpm
Output per litre(kW/l / hp/l):	54.1 / 73.4
Compression ratio:	9.0 : 1
Valve operation & camshaft drive:	dohc, two vertical shafts, 2 valves per cylinder
Carburation:	2 twin-choke downdraught carburettors Solex 40 PII-4
Ignition system:	Battery coil dual ignition
Firing order:	1 - 4 - 3 - 2
Crankshaft bearing 692/0:	4 roller bearings
Crankshaft bearing 692/1:	3 slide bearings
Engine lubrication:	Dry sump
Engine oil total (l):	8.0

Transmission
Drive configuration:	Rear-axle drive
Manual gearbox:	4-speed
Transmission type:	716/1
Transmission ratios:	
1st gear:	3.091
2nd gear:	1.765
3rd gear:	1.227
4th gear:	0.960
Reverse gear:	3.560
Drive ratio:	4.428

Body, chassis, suspension, brakes, wheels
Body design:	Steel body, 2 doors, 2 seats, pressed and welded steel-sheet sections, one unit with body, curved single-piece windscreen, one grille in engine lid additional slots left and right, bumpers in higher position, two air intakes, bumpers project away from body without over-riders, aluminium doors and lids, Plexiglas rear and side windows

Suspension, front:	2 longitudinal swinging arms (suspension arms), 2 transverse, square torsion bars of laminated construction, adjustable, anti-roll bars, hydraulic telescopic double-action shock absorbers
Suspension, rear:	Oscillating half axles and radius arms, (longitudinal swinging arms), one round torsion bar on each side, hydraulic telescopic double-action shock absorbers
Brakes, front/rear (Size (mm)):	Brake drums Duplex (280 x 60) / Brake drums Simplex (280 x 40)
Wheels, front/rear:	4.5 J x 15 / 4.5 J x 15
Tyres, front/rear:	5.90-15 Supersport / 5.90-15 Supersport

Electrical system
Alternator (W):	160
Battery (V/Ah):	6 / 84

Dimensions and weight
Track, front/rear (mm):	1306 / 1272
Wheelbase (mm):	2100
Length x width x height (mm):	3950 x 1670 x 1310
Kerb weight DIN (kg):	865
Permissible gross weight (kg):	1225
Fuel tank capacity (l):	80, including 15 reserve
Cw x A (m2) Coupé:	0.365 x 1.692 = 0.618
Power/weight ratio (kg/kW / kg/hp):	10.67 / 7.86

Fuel consumption
DIN 70 030 (mpg):	30; 86 RON normal leaded

Performance, production, prices
Acceleration 0-62mph/100kph (s):	11.0
Maximum speed (mph / kph):	124 / 200
Prod., 356 A 1500 GS/GT total no.:	35
Purchase prices:	
09/1956 Coupé:	DM 18,500
09/1957 Coupé:	DM 18,500

356 A 1500 GS Carrera GT Speedster
MY 1957–MY 1958

Engine

Engine design:	4-cylinder horizontally-opposed
Installation:	Rear-engine
Cooling system:	Air-cooled
Engine type:	
Engine-No. P91001 - P92021:	692/0
Engine-No. P92001 - P92014:	692/1
Displacement (cc):	1498
Bore x stroke (mm):	85 x 66
Engine output DIN (kW/hp):	81/110 at 6400rpm
Maximum torque (Nm/lb ft):	124/91 at 5200rpm
Output per litre(kW/l / hp/l):	54.1 / 73.4
Compression ratio:	9.0 : 1
Valve operation & camshaft drive:	dohc, two vertical shafts, 2 valves per cylinder
Carburation:	2 twin-choke downdraught carburettors Solex 40 PII-4
Ignition system:	Battery coil dual ignition
Firing order:	1 - 4 - 3 - 2
Crankshaft bearing 692/0:	4 roller bearings
Crankshaft bearing 692/1:	3 slide bearings
Engine lubrication:	Dry sump
Engine oil total (l):	8.0

Transmission

Drive configuration:	Rear-axle drive
Manual gearbox:	4-speed
Transmission type:	
Transmission ratios:	
1st gear:	3.180
2nd gear:	1.765
3rd gear:	1.130
4th gear:	0.815
Reverse gear:	3.560
Drive ratio:	4.429

Body, chassis, suspension, brakes, wheels

Body design:	Steel body, 2 doors, 2 seats, pressed and welded steel frame, curved single-piece windscreen, corners with large radius, one grille in engine lid additional slots left and right, bumpers project away from body with over-riders, aluminium doors and lids, single layer hood with flexible plastic rear window, side curtains on doors
Option:	Hardtop

Suspension, front:	2 longitudinal swinging arms (suspension arms), 2 transverse, square torsion bars of laminated construction, adjustable, anti-roll bars, hydraulic telescopic double-action shock absorbers
Suspension, rear:	Oscillating half axles and radius arms, (longitudinal swinging arms), one round torsion bar on each side, hydraulic telescopic double-action shock absorbers
Brakes, front/rear (Size (mm)):	Brake drums Duplex (280 x 60) / Brake drums Simplex (280 x 40)
Wheels, front/rear:	4.5 J x 15 / 4.5 J x 15
Tyres, front/rear:	5.90-15 Supersport / 5.90-15 Supersport

Electrical system

Alternator (W):	160
Battery (V/Ah):	6 / 84

Dimensions and weight

Track, front/rear (mm):	1306 / 1272
Wheelbase (mm):	2100
Length x width x height (mm):	3950 x 1670 x 1220*
Kerb weight DIN (kg):	840
Permissible gross weight (kg):	1180
Fuel tank capacity (l):	80, including 15 reserve
C_w x A (m²):	0.377 x 1.640 = 0.618
Power/weight ratio (kg/kW/kg/hp):	10.37 / 7.63
*with closed top	

Fuel consumption

DIN 70 030 (mpg):	30; 86 RON normal leaded

Performance, production, prices	
Acceleration 0-62mph/100kph (s):	11.0
Maximum speed (mph / kph):	124 / 200

Prod., 356 A 1500 GS/GT total no.:	35
356 A 1500 GS & GT Speedster:	167

Purchase prices:	
09/1956 Speedster:	DM 17,700
09/1957 Speedster:	DM 17,300

356 A 1500 GS Carrera de Luxe Coupé
356 A 1500 GS Carrera de Luxe Cabriolet
356 A 1500 GS Carrera de Luxe Hardtop-Coupé
356 A 1500 GS Carrera de Luxe Hardtop/Cabriolet MY 1958

Engine

Engine design:	4-cylinder horizontally-opposed
Installation:	Rear-engine
Cooling system:	Air-cooled
Engine type:	547/1
Displacement (cc):	1498
Bore x stroke (mm):	85 x 66
Engine output DIN (kW/hp):	74/100 at 6200rpm
Maximum torque (Nm/lb ft):	119/88 at 5200rpm
Output per litre(kW/l / hp/l):	49.4 / 66.8
Compression ratio:	9.0 : 1
Valve operation & camshaft drive:	dohc, two vertical shafts, 2 valves per cylinder
Carburation:	2 twin-choke downdraught carburettors Solex 40 PII-4
Ignition system:	Battery coil dual ignition
Firing order:	1 - 4 - 3 - 2
Crankshaft bearing:	4 roller bearings
Engine lubrication:	Dry sump
Engine oil total (l):	8.0

Transmission

Drive configuration:	Rear-axle drive
Manual gearbox:	4-speed
Transmission type:	644 Carrera
Transmission ratios:	
1st gear:	3.182
2nd gear:	1.765
3rd gear:	1.227
4th gear:	0.960
Reverse gear:	3.560
Drive ratio:	4.428

Body, chassis, suspension, brakes, wheels

Body design:	Steel body, 2 doors, 2 + 2 seats, pressed and welded steel-sheet sections, one unit with body, curved single-piece windscreen, one grille in engine lid, bumpers project away from body with over-riders
Coupé:	Fixed steel roof
Option:	Manual sunroof
Cabriolet:	Multi-layer hood with flexible plastic rear window
Option:	Hardtop
Hardtop-Coupé:	Fixed hardtop
Hardtop/Cabriolet:	Removable hardtop
Suspension, front:	2 longitudinal swinging arms (suspension arms), 2 transverse, square torsion bars of laminated construction, adjustable, anti-roll bars, hydraulic telescopic double-action shock absorbers
Suspension, rear:	Oscillating half axles and radius arms, (longitudinal swinging arms), one round torsion bar on each side, hydraulic telescopic double-action shock absorbers
Brakes, front/rear (Size (mm)):	Brake drums Duplex (280 x 40) / Brake drums Simplex (280 x 40)
Wheels, front/rear:	4.5 J x 15 / 4.5 J x 15
Tyres, front/rear:	5.90-15 Supersport / 5.90-15 Supersport

Electrical system

Alternator (W):	160
Battery (V/Ah):	6 / 84

Dimensions and weight

Track, front/rear (mm):	1306 / 1272
Wheelbase (mm):	2100
Length x width x height (mm):	3950 x 1670 x 1310
Hardtop-Coupé:	3950 x 1670 x 1290
Hardtop/Cabriolet:	3950 x 1670 x 1290
Kerb weight DIN (kg):	930
Permissible gross weight (kg):	1225
Fuel tank capacity (l):	52, including 5 reserve
Cw x A (m2) Coupé:	0.365 x 1.692 = 0.618
Power/weight ratio (kg/kW/ kg/hp):	12.56 / 9.30

Fuel consumption

DIN 70 030 (mpg):	30; 86 RON normal leaded

Performance, production, prices	
Acceleration 0-62mph/100kph (s):	12.0
Maximum speed (mph / kph):	124 / 200
Prod., 356 A 1500 GS total no.:	447
Purchase prices:	
09/1957 Coupé:	DM 18,500
Cabriolet:	DM 19,700
Hardtop-Coupé:	DM 19,400
Hardtop/Cabriolet:	DM 20,490

356 A 1500 GS Carrera de Luxe Speedster MY 1958

Engine
Engine design:	4-cylinder horizontally-opposed
Installation:	Rear-engine
Cooling system:	Air-cooled
Engine type:	547/1
Displacement (cc):	1498
Bore x stroke (mm):	85 x 66
Engine output DIN (kW/hp):	74/100 at 6200rpm
Maximum torque (Nm/lb ft):	119/88 at 5200rpm
Output per litre(kW/l / hp/l):	49.4 / 66.8
Compression ratio:	9.0 : 1
Valve operation & camshaft drive:	dohc, two vertical shafts, 2 valves per cylinder
Carburation:	2 twin-choke downdraught carburettors Solex 40 PII-4
Ignition system:	Battery coil dual ignition
Firing order:	1 - 4 - 3 - 2
Crankshaft bearing:	4 roller bearings
Engine lubrication:	Dry sump
Engine oil total (l):	8.0

Transmission
Drive configuration:	Rear-axle drive
Manual gearbox:	4-speed
Transmission type:	644 Carrera
Transmission ratios:	
1st gear:	3.182
2nd gear:	1.765
3rd gear:	1.227
4th gear:	0.960
Reverse gear:	3.560
Drive ratio:	4.428

Body, chassis, suspension, brakes, wheels
Body design:	Steel body, 2 doors, 2 seats, pressed and welded steel frame, curved single-piece windscreen, corners with large radius, one grille in engine lid, bumpers project away from body with over-riders, single layer hood with flexible plastic rear window, side curtains on doors
Option:	Hardtop
Suspension, front:	2 longitudinal swinging arms (suspension arms), 2 transverse, square torsion bars of laminated construction, adjustable, anti-roll bars, hydraulic telescopic double-action shock absorbers
Suspension, rear:	Oscillating half axles and radius arms, (longitudinal swinging arms), one round torsion bar on each side, hydraulic telescopic double-action shock absorbers
Brakes, front/rear (Size (mm)):	Brake drums Duplex (280 x 40) / Brake drums Simplex (280 x 40)
Wheels, front/rear:	4.5 J x 15 / 4.5 J x 15
Tyres, front/rear:	5.90-15 Supersport / 5.90-15 Supersport

Electrical system
Alternator (W):	160
Battery (V/Ah):	6 / 84

Dimensions and weight
Track, front/rear (mm):	1306 / 1272
Wheelbase (mm):	2100
Length x width x height (mm):	3950 x 1670 x 1220*
Kerb weight DIN (kg):	885
Permissible gross weight (kg):	1180
Fuel tank capacity (l):	52, including 5 reserve
C_w x A (m²):	0.377 x 1.640 = 0.618
Power/weight ratio (kg/kW/kg/hp):	11.95 / 8.85
*with closed top	

Fuel consumption
DIN 70 030 (mpg):	30; 86 RON normal leaded

Performance, production, prices
Acceleration 0-62mph/100kph (s):	12.0
Maximum speed (mph / kph):	124 / 200
Prod., 356 A 1500 GS total no.:	447
356 A 1500 GS & GT Speedster:	167
Purchase price:	
09/1957 Speedster:	DM 17,300

356 A 1600 GS Carrera de Luxe Coupé
[356 A 1600 GS Carrera GT Coupé]
356 A 1600 GS Carrera de Luxe Cabriolet
356 A 1600 GS Carrera de Luxe Hardtop-Coupé
356 A 1600 GS Carrera de Luxe Hardtop/Cabriolet MY 1959

Engine

Engine design:	4-cylinder horizontally-opposed
Installation:	Rear-engine
Cooling system:	Air-cooled
Engine type:	692/2 [692/3]
Displacement (cc):	1588
Bore x stroke (mm):	87.5 x 66
Engine output DIN (kW/hp):	77/105 [85/115] at 6500rpm
Maximum torque (Nm/lb ft):	121/89 [135/99] at 5000 [5500]rpm
Output per litre(kW/l / hp/l):	48.5 [53.5] / 66.1 [72.4]
Compression ratio:	9.5: 1 [9.8: 1]
Valve operation & camshaft drive:	dohc, two vertical shafts, 2 valves per cylinder
Carburation:	2 twin-choke downdraught carburettors Solex 40 PII-4 [2 twin-choke downdraught carburettors Weber 40 DCM 1]
Ignition system:	Battery coil dual ignition
Firing order:	1 - 4 - 3 - 2
Crankshaft bearing:	3 slide bearings
Engine lubrication:	Dry sump
Engine oil total (l):	8.0

Transmission

Drive configuration:	Rear-axle drive
Manual gearbox:	4-speed
Transmission type:	741/3 [716/5]
Transmission ratios:	
1st gear:	3.091 [3.091]
2nd gear:	1.938 [1.938]
3rd gear:	1.350 [1.350]
4th gear:	0.960 [0.885]
Reverse gear:	3.560 [3.560]
Drive ratio:	4.428 [4.428]

Body, chassis, suspension, brakes, wheels

Body design:	Steel body, 2 doors, 2 + 2 seats, pressed and welded steel-sheet sections, one unit with body, curved single-piece windscreen, one grille in engine lid, bumpers project away from body with over-riders
Coupé:	Fixed steel roof
Option:	Manual sunroof
Cabriolet:	Multi-layer hood with flexible plastic rear window
Hardtop-Coupé:	Fixed hardtop
Hardtop/Cabriolet:	Removable hardtop
Coupé GT:	Steel body, 2 doors, 2 seats, pressed and welded steel-sheet sections, one unit with body, curved single-piece windscreen, one grille in engine lid additional slots left and right, bumpers in higher position, two air-intakes, bumpers project away from body without over-riders, aluminium doors and lids, Plexiglas rear and side windows
Suspension, front:	2 longitudinal swinging arms (suspension arms), 2 transverse, square torsion bars of laminated construction, adjustable, anti-roll bars, hydraulic telescopic double-action shock absorbers
Suspension, rear:	Oscillating half axles and radius arms, (longitudinal swinging arms), one round torsion bar on each side, hydraulic telescopic double-action shock absorbers
Brakes, front/rear (Size (mm)):	Brake drums Duplex (280 x 40 [60]) / Brake drums Simplex (280 x 40)
Wheels, front/rear:	4.5 J x 15 / 4.5 J x 15
Tyres, front/rear:	5.90-15 Supersport / 5.90-15 Supersport

Electrical system

Alternator (W):	160
Battery (V/Ah):	6 / 84
Option:	12 / 50

Dimensions and weight

Track, front/rear (mm):	1306 / 1272
Wheelbase (mm):	2100
Length x width x height (mm):	3950 x 1670 x 1310
Hardtop-Coupé:	3950 x 1670 x 1290
Hardtop/Cabriolet:	3950 x 1670 x 1290

Hardtop/Cabriolet:	3950 x 1670 x 1290
Kerb weight DIN (kg):	950 [870]
Permissible gross weight (kg):	1250 [1250]
Fuel tank capacity (l):	52 [80], including 5 [15] reserve
Cw x A (m2) Coupé:	0.365 x 1.692 = 0.618
Power/weight ratio (kg/kW/kg/hp):	12.33 [10.23] / 9.04 [7.56]

Fuel consumption

| DIN 70 030 (mpg): | 29.5 [29]; 88 RON normal leaded |

Performance, production, prices

Acceleration 0-62mph/100kph (s):	11.0 [10.0]
Maximum speed (mph / kph):	124 / 200 [124 / 200]
Prod., 356 A 1600 GS total no.:	101 [103]
Purchase prices:	
09/1958 Coupé:	DM 18,500 [DM 18,500]
Cabriolet:	DM 19,700
Hardtop-Coupé:	DM 19,400
Hardtop/Cabriolet:	DM 20,490

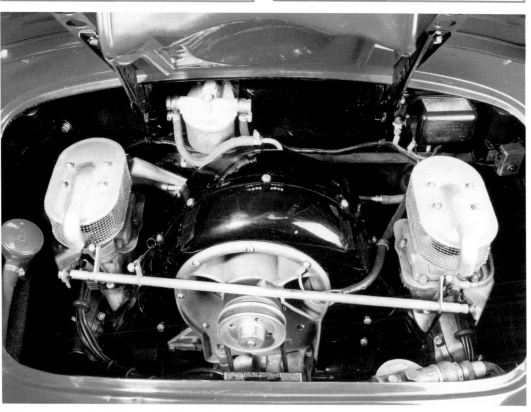

A Carrera power unit, with four shaft-driven overhead cams

Porsche 356 B

The autumn of 1959 saw the launch of Porsche's fully redesigned 356 B. This model was known internally as the T5 ('Technical Programme V'). All pushrod engines displaced 1.6 litres, and the 356 B was available in four body variations: Coupé, Cabriolet, Roadster, and the Hardtop-Coupé. Coupé and Cabriolet bodies were built by Reutter in Stuttgart, while Hardtop-Coupé bodies, with their welded-on tops, were built by Karmann in Osnabrück, and Roadsters were built by Drauz in Heilbronn. The Roadster was equipped with an unpadded top and winding windows in the doors.

Model year 1960 (T5)

The 356 B body was recognizable by the raised level of its headlamps, and the resulting higher line of the front wings. The front bumper was 95mm higher, and fitted with larger over-riders. At the front, slightly larger indicators protruded further, and the adjacent horn grilles were longer and flatter. Below the bumper, the lower valance was given two oval air inlets with decorative grilles, for better brake cooling.

Fog lamps could be mounted below the bumper. The front number plate was fastened to the lower part of the bumper. A wide, chromium-plated handle was fixed to the bonnet. The rear bumper was mounted 105mm higher. Two tailpipes exited through reshaped over-riders. Two number plate lamps were mounted in the bumper, and a reversing lamp at the centre below the bumper.

New transverse cooling fins on the brake drums promised improved cooling. Hubcaps on the more powerful Super and Super 90 models adopted the shape of the 356 A Super hubcaps, with attached Porsche crest. Only the entry level model carried the convex 'baby moon' hubcaps, minus crest. The 356 B Super 90 and Carrera were fitted with a compensating spring at the rear axle, braced against the transmission case; its intended purpose was to force the lightly loaded, inner wheel against the road during cornering.

For the first time, the model range included a 1600 Normal engine of 60hp (44kW) and the 1600 Super power unit of 75hp (55kW). Both engines incorporated revised valve springs and reinforced valve spring seats. The most powerful engine in the line-up was the Super 90, available from the spring of 1960. With a displacement of 1582cc and 9:1 compression, it developed 90hp (66kW) at 5500rpm. The Super 90 power unit achieved its maximum torque of 121Nm (89lb ft) at 4300rpm.

The thrust ring was deleted from the diaphragm clutch, and the transmission installed lower, with the gearbox mechanism modified accordingly. Another new transmission detail was use of Porsche's patented blocking synchromesh.

Inside, the most obvious change was the new, black, three-spoke deeply-dished steering wheel. Detail changes were made to the dashboard. The gear lever was shortened by 40mm. Front seats were reworked for increased comfort, the rear seat-backs were split to fold individually, and the rear seat wells deepened by 60mm. In the Coupé, adjustable front quarterlights admitted fresh air to the interior. The rear window was kept mist free by warm air vents connected to the heating system.

The Roadster retained its purist dashboard, with its high-mounted tachometer and ignition lock to the right of the steering column.

In the spring of 1960 the German magazine *Auto, Motor und Sport* tested three Coupés in all available engine versions. The Normal accelerated to 62mph (100kph) in 15.4 seconds, with a top speed of 102mph (164kph). The 356 B 1600 Super took 14.6 seconds to reach 62mph, and attained a top speed of 109mph (175kph). The top of the pushrod engine line, 356 B Super 90, sprinted to 62mph in just 13.6 seconds, and achieved a measured top speed of 117mph (188kph).

For the 1960 and 1961 model years, the 356 B 1600 Carrera GS/GT (Grand Tourisme) was Porsche's top model. No luxuriously equipped Carrera variant was offered. The Reutter coachworks of Stuttgart-Zuffenhausen produced forty lightweight 356 B (T5) bodies. This variation, built only as Coupés, used a steel box-section frame and main body structure.

To save weight, doors and lids were of aluminium. Even the seat shells were made of aluminium, and Plexiglas was used for rear and side windows. Six louvres were cut into the engine lid on either side of the air inlet grille. Also, the over-riders were deleted for the sake of weight reduction.

Fitted with a pair of Weber twin-choke downdraught carburettors, the 1.6-litre Carrera engine produced 115hp (85kW) at 6500rpm, giving it a top speed of 124mph (200kph). More transmission gear ratios were available, and a 12-volt electrical system was standard.

Model year 1961

Roadster production at Drauz of Heilbronn ended in February 1961. Thereafter, production continued at D'leteren in Brussels, Belgium. Karmann of Osnabrück continued building Cabriolets with welded-on hardtops – the Hardtop-Coupés.

Model year 1962 (T6)

Production of the 356 B T6 (Technical Programme VI) began in September 1961. Many bodywork details were optimized. The boot opening was enlarged, and the corners of the bonnet were somewhat more angular. A new flatter fuel tank resulted in increased boot capacity, and a new fuel filler flap in the front right wing permitted refuelling of the 356 B without need to open the boot lid. A fresh air inlet grille was located just forward of the windscreen for better interior ventilation. Adjustable flaps distributed air to the defroster vents or to the footwells. The larger engine lid was fitted with two vertically oriented grilles ('twin grille'). Bigger

windows in the Coupé made for a brighter interior, and a sliding steel sunroof was available as an option. The windscreen-wiper system offered continuously-variable speeds, and was combined with a new washer-fluid reservoir.

The inside rear-view mirror now had a day/night selector, seat rails were more precisely guided, and seat hardware incorporated a backrest catch (except on the Roadster). An electric clock was also standard equipment on all models.

The wire-mesh grille on the engine-fan shroud air-inlet was deleted. Fuel lines and throttle linkage were altered. The 1600 Super engine was fitted with improved piston rings running in cast-iron cylinders, composite steel/aluminium pushrods and an improved oil cooler.

The Super 90 was equipped with a 200mm diaphragm clutch and a new flywheel.

Spring 1962 saw the launch of the 356 B 2000 GS Carrera 2 (first shown in late 1961), with its 2-litre overhead-cam engine. Its 1966cc displacement developed 130hp (96kW) at 6200rpm in the comfortable road version. In the lightweight GT version, 140hp (103kW) was on tap at 6200rpm, and with the racing exhaust, as much as 155hp (114kW) at 6600rpm. Bodywork, suspension and equipment were carried over from the predecessor 356 B 1600 GS Carrera, although the Carrera 2 made use of the new T6 body. Externally, the Carrera 2 was recognizable by its lack of over-riders and no horn grilles alongside the front indicators.

The two tailpipes exited below the rear bumper, through a steel valance panel bolted to the bottom of the bodywork and pierced with vertical slots. The

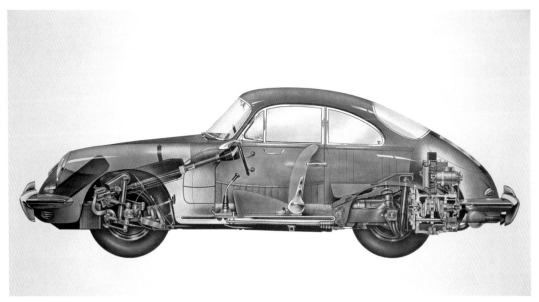

Cutaway drawing of the 356 B T6 Coupé body

most striking feature of the interior was the large wood-rimmed steering wheel. While the 356 B 2000 GS Carrera 2 drew heavily on the equipment of the more common 356 B, the GT version had aluminium doors and lids, as well as Plexiglas rear and side glazing.

For the 356 B 2000 GS Carrera 2, a transmission geared for the American market was available alongside the standard gearing. In the GT version, four different transmission packages were available.

The first examples of the Carrera 2 were delivered with drum brakes. Porsche began installing disc brakes in 356s in April 1962. These early examples consisted of Porsche's own brake concept, with callipers that grabbed the disc from the inside, rather than the more usual calliper position on the periphery of the disc. The advantage of this design was that it allowed the use of larger diameter discs without increasing wheel size. The disc was bolted to a star-shaped carrier. The handbrake also acted directly on the brake disc. In the 1962 racing season this design was used on Porsche's Formula 1 racers (Type 804).

In all, only 310 examples of the 356 B Carrera 2 were built. One hundred were needed for homologation in the GT racing class.

Model year 1963

Development of the 356 successor, the 901, proceeded at full speed. The 356 B remained in production without major changes. About 50 of the 356 B series were delivered with the new disc brakes that would be standard on the 356 C.

With a total of 31,440 examples built, the 356 B was highest production 356 model.

356 B 1600 Coupé
356 B 1600 Cabriolet
356 B 1600 Hardtop-Coupé
356 B 1600 Hardtop/Cabriolet
MY 1960–MY 1963

Engine

Engine design:	4-cylinder horizontally-opposed
Installation:	Rear-engine
Cooling system:	Air-cooled
Engine type:	616/1
Displacement (cc):	1582
Bore x stroke (mm):	82.5 x 74
Engine output DIN (kW/hp):	44/60 at 4500rpm
Maximum torque (Nm/lb ft):	110/81 at 2800rpm
Output per litre(kW/l / hp/l):	27.8 / 37.9
Compression ratio:	7.5 : 1
Valve operation & camshaft drive:	ohv, cam driven by gears, 2 valves per cylinder
Carburation:	2 downdraught carburettors Zenith 32 NDIX
Ignition system:	Battery coil ignition
Firing order:	1 - 4 - 3 - 2
Crankshaft bearing:	4 slide bearings
Engine lubrication:	Full pressure oil lubrication
Engine oil total (l):	5.0*
*Filling new assembled engine, oil change 4.0	

Transmission

Drive configuration:	Rear-axle drive
Manual gearbox:	4-speed
Transmission type:	741/0 A
Transmission ratios:	
1st gear:	3.091
2nd gear:	1.765
3rd gear:	1.130
4th gear:	0.815
Reverse gear:	3.560
Drive ratio:	4.428

Body, chassis, suspension, brakes, wheels

Body design:	Steel body, 2 doors, 2 + 2 seats, pressed and welded steel-sheet sections, one unit with body, curved single-piece windscreen, one grille in engine lid, bumpers in higher position, two air-intake grilles under the front bumpers, tailpipes go through over-riders
MY 1962 - MY 1963 (T 6):	Twin grille in engine lid, fuel filler flap in right front wing
Coupé:	Fixed steel roof
Option:	Manual sunroof
Option MY 1962 - MY 1963 (T 6):	Electric sunroof
Cabriolet:	Multi-layer hood with flexible plastic rear window
Hardtop-Coupé:	Fixed hardtop
Hardtop/Cabriolet:	Removable hardtop
Suspension, front:	2 longitudinal swinging arms (suspension arms), 2 transverse, square torsion bars of laminated construction, adjustable, anti-roll bars, hydraulic telescopic double-action shock absorbers
Suspension, rear:	Oscillating half axles and radius arms, (longitudinal swinging arms), one round torsion bar on each side, hydraulic telescopic double-action shock absorbers
Option:	Compensating spring acting as counter-stabilizer
Brakes, front/rear (Size (mm)):	Brake drums Duplex (280 x 40) / Brake drums Simplex (280 x 40)
Wheels, front/rear:	4.5 J x 15 / 4.5 J x 15
Tyres, front/rear:	5.60-15 Sport / 5.60-15 Sport
Option radial tyres:	165-15 Sport / 165-15 Sport

Electrical system

Alternator (W):	200
Battery (V/Ah):	6 / 84
Option MY 1962 - MY 1963 (T 6):	12 / 50

Dimensions and weight

Track, front/rear (mm):	1306 / 1272
Wheelbase (mm):	2100
Length x width x height (mm):	4010 x 1670 x 1330
Hardtop-Coupé	4010 x 1670 x 1315
Hardtop/Cabriolet:	4010 x 1670 x 1315
Kerb weight DIN (kg):	900
MY 1962 - MY 1963 (T 6):	935
Permissible gross weight (kg):	1250
Fuel tank capacity (l):	52, including 5 reserve
MY 1962 - MY 1963 (T 6):	50, including 6 reserve
Cw x A (m2) Coupé:	0.398 x 1.611 = 0.641
Power/weight ratio (kg/kW/kg/hp):	20.45 / 15.00
MY 1962 - MY 1963 (T 6):	21.25 / 15.58

Fuel consumption

DIN 70 030 (mpg):	37, 88 RON normal leaded

Performance, production, prices

Acceleration 0-62mph/100kph (s):	16.5
Maximum speed (mph / kph):	96 / 155
Production, total number:	
356 B Coupé total no.:*	20,597
356 B Coupé T 5:*	8,559
356 B Coupé T 6:*	12,038
356 B Cabriolet total no.:*	6,194
356 B Cabriolet T 5:*	3,094
356 B Cabriolet T 6:*	3,100
356 B Hardtop-Coupé total no.:*	1,747
356 B Hardtop-Coupé T 5:*	1,048
356 B Hardtop-Coupé T 6:*	699
*Total number all engine versions	
Purchase prices:	
09/1959 Coupé:	DM 12,700
Cabriolet:	DM 13,900
Hardtop-Coupé:	DM 13,600
Hardtop/Cabriolet:	DM 14,390
07/1960 Coupé:	DM 13,300
Cabriolet:	DM 14,500
Hardtop-Coupé:	DM 13,300
Hardtop/Cabriolet:	DM 15,290
09/1961 Coupé:	DM 13,850
Cabriolet:	DM 14,950
Hardtop-Coupé:	DM 13,850
Hardtop-Cabriolet:	DM 15,820
05/1962 Coupé:	DM 14,300
Cabriolet:	DM 15,400
Hardtop-Cabriolet:	DM 16,200
10/1962 Coupé:	DM 14,300
Cabriolet:	DM 15,400
Hardtop-Cabriolet:	DM 16,200

356 B 1600 Roadster
MY 1960–MY 1962

Engine

Engine design:	4-cylinder horizontally-opposed
Installation:	Rear-engine
Cooling system:	Air-cooled
Engine type:	616/1
Displacement (cc):	1582
Bore x stroke (mm):	82.5 x 74
Engine output DIN (kW/hp):	44/60 at 4500rpm
Maximum torque (Nm/lb ft):	110/81 at 2800rpm
Output per litre(kW/l / hp/l):	27.8 / 37.9
Compression ratio:	7.5 : 1
Valve operation & camshaft drive:	ohv, cam driven by gears, 2 valves per cylinder
Carburation:	2 downdraught carburettors Zenith 32 NDIX
Ignition system:	Battery coil ignition
Firing order:	1 - 4 - 3 - 2
Crankshaft bearing:	4 slide bearings
Engine lubrication:	Full pressure oil lubrication
Engine oil total (l):	5.0*
*Filling new assembled engine, oil change 4.0	

Transmission

Drive configuration:	Rear-axle drive
Manual gearbox:	4-speed
Transmission type:	741/2 A
Transmission ratios:	
1st gear:	3.091
2nd gear:	1.765
3rd gear:	1.130
4th gear:	0.852
Reverse gear:	3.560
Drive ratio:	4.428

Body, chassis, suspension, brakes, wheels

Body design:	Steel Roadster body, 2 doors, 2 seats, pressed and welded steel-sheet sections, one unit with body, curved single-piece windscreen, single layer hood with flexible plastic rear window, one grille in engine lid, bumpers in higher position, two air-intake grilles under the front bumpers, tailpipes go through over-riders
MY 1962 (T 6):	Twin grille in engine lid, fuel filler flap in right front wing
Suspension, front:	2 longitudinal swinging arms (suspension arms), 2 transverse, square torsion bars of laminated construction, adjustable, anti-roll

	bars, hydraulic telescopic double-action shock absorbers
Suspension, rear:	Oscillating half axles and radius arms, (longitudinal swinging arms), one round torsion bar on each side, hydraulic telescopic double-action shock absorbers
Option:	Compensating spring acting as counter-stabilizer
Brakes, front/rear (Size (mm)):	Brake drums Duplex (280 x 40) / Brake drums Simplex (280 x 40)
Wheels, front/rear:	4.5 J x 15 / 4.5 J x 15
Tyres, front/rear:	5.60-15 Sport / 5.60-15 Sport
Option radial tyres:	165-15 Sport / 165-15 Sport
Electrical system	
Alternator (W):	200
Battery (V/Ah):	6 / 84
Option MY 1962 (T 6):	12 / 50

Dimensions and weight

Track, front/rear (mm):	1306 / 1272
Wheelbase (mm):	2100
Length x width x height (mm):	4010 x 1670 x 1310*
Kerb weight DIN (kg):	870
Permissible gross weight (kg):	1250
Fuel tank capacity (l):	52, including 5 reserve
MY 1962 (T 6):	50, including 6 reserve
C_w x A (m²):	0.386 x 1.599 = 0.617
Power/weight ratio (kg/kW/ kg/hp):	19.77 / 14.50
*with closed top	

Fuel consumption

DIN 70 030 (mpg):	37; 88 RON normal leaded

Performance, production, prices

Acceleration 0-62mph/100kph (s):	16.5
Maximum speed (mph / kph):	96 / 155
Prod., 356 B Roadster total no.:*	2,902
356 B Roadster T 5:	2,653
356 B Roadster T 6:	249
*Total number all engine versions	
Purchase prices:	
09/1959 Roadster:	DM 12,650
07/1960 Roadster:	DM 13,200

356 B 1600 Super Coupé
356 B 1600 Super Cabriolet
356 B 1600 Super Hardtop-Coupé
356 B 1600 Super Hardtop/Cabriolet
MY 1960–MY 1963

Engine

Engine design:	4-cylinder horizontally-opposed
Installation:	Rear-engine
Cooling system:	Air-cooled
Engine type:	616/2
Displacement (cc):	1582
Bore x stroke (mm):	82.5 x 74
Engine output DIN (kW/hp):	55/75 at 5000rpm
Maximum torque (Nm/lb ft):	117/86 at 3700rpm
Output per litre(kW/l / hp/l):	34.8 / 47.4
Compression ratio:	8.5 : 1
Valve operation & camshaft drive:	ohv, cam driven by gears, 2 valves per cylinder
Carburation:	2 downdraught carburettors Zenith 32 NDIX
Ignition system:	Battery coil ignition
Firing order:	1 - 4 - 3 - 2
Crankshaft bearing:	4 slide bearings
Engine lubrication:	Full pressure oil lubrication
Engine oil total (l):	5.0*
*Filling new assembled engine, oil change 4.0	

Transmission

Drive configuration:	Rear-axle drive
Manual gearbox:	4-speed
Transmission type:	741/0 A
Transmission ratios:	
1st gear:	3.091
2nd gear:	1.765
3rd gear:	1.130
4th gear:	0.815
Reverse gear:	3.560
Drive ratio:	4.428

Body, chassis, suspension, brakes, wheels

Body design:	Steel body, 2 doors, 2 + 2 seats, pressed and welded steel-sheet sections, one unit with body, curved single-piece windscreen, one grille in engine lid, bumpers in higher position, two air-intake grilles under the front bumpers, tailpipes go through over-riders
MY 1962 - MY 1963 (T 6):	Twin grille in engine lid, fuel filler flap in right front wing
Coupé:	Fixed steel roof
Option:	Manual sunroof
Option MY 1962 - MY 1963 (T 6):	Electric sunroof
Cabriolet:	Multi-layer hood with flexible plastic rear window
Hardtop-Coupé:	Fixed hardtop
Hardtop/Cabriolet:	Removable hardtop
Suspension, front:	2 longitudinal swinging arms (suspension arms), 2 transverse, square torsion bars of laminated construction, adjustable, anti-roll bars, hydraulic telescopic double-action shock absorbers
Suspension, rear:	Oscillating half axles and radius arms, (longitudinal swinging arms), one round torsion bar on each side, hydraulic telescopic double-action shock absorbers
Option:	Compensating spring acting as counter-stabilizer
Brakes, front/rear (Size (mm)):	Brake drums Duplex (280 x 40) / Brake drums Simplex (280 x 40)
Wheels, front/rear:	4.5 J x 15 / 4.5 J x 15
Tyres, front/rear:	5.60-15 Sport / 5.60-15 Sport
Option radial tyres:	165-15 Sport / 165-15 Sport

Electrical system

Alternator (W):	200
Battery (V/Ah):	6 / 84
Option MY 1962 - MY 1963 (T 6):	12 / 50

Dimensions and weight

Track, front/rear (mm):	1306 / 1272
Wheelbase (mm):	2100
Length x width x height (mm):	4010 x 1670 x 1330
Hardtop-Coupé:	4010 x 1670 x 1315
Hardtop/Cabriolet:	4010 x 1670 x 1315
Kerb weight DIN (kg):	900
MY 1962 - MY 1963 (T 6):	935
Permissible gross weight (kg):	1250
Fuel tank capacity (l):	52, including 5 reserve
MY 1962 - MY 1963 (T 6):	50, including 6 reserve
Cw x A (m2) Coupé:	0.398 x 1.611 = 0.641
Power/weight ratio (kg/kW/kg/hp):	16.36 / 12.00
MY 1962 - MY 1963 (T 6):	17.00 / 12.46

Fuel consumption

DIN 70 030 (mpg):	34; 94 RON super leaded

Performance, production, prices

Acceleration 0-62mph/100kph (s):	15.0
Maximum speed (mph / kph):	108.5 / 175
Production, total number:	
356 B Coupé total no.:*	20,597
356 B Coupé T 5:*	8,559
356 B Coupé T 6:*	12,038
356 B Cabriolet total no.:*	6,194
356 B Cabriolet T 5:*	3,094
356 B Cabriolet T 6:*	3,100
356 B Hardtop-Coupé total no.:*	1,747
356 B Hardtop-Coupé T 5:*	1,048
356 B Hardtop-Coupé T 6:*	699
*Total number all engine versions	
Purchase prices:	
09/1959 Coupé:	DM 13,500
Cabriolet:	DM 14,700
Hardtop-Coupé:	DM 14,400
Hardtop/Cabriolet:	DM 15,190
07/1960 Coupé:	DM 14,100
Cabriolet:	DM 15,300
Hardtop-Coupé:	DM 15,000
Hardtop/Cabriolet:	DM 16,090
06/1961 Coupé:	DM 14,650
Cabriolet:	DM 15,750
Hardtop-Coupé:	DM 14,650
Hardtop/Cabriolet:	DM 16,620
05/1962 Coupé:	DM 14,950
Cabriolet:	DM 16,050
Hardtop/Cabriolet:	DM 16,950
10/1962 Coupé:	DM 14,950
Cabriolet:	DM 16,050
Hardtop/Cabriolet:	DM 16,950

356 B 1600 Super Roadster
MY 1960–MY 1962

Engine
Engine design:	4-cylinder horizontally-opposed
Installation:	Rear-engine
Cooling system:	Air-cooled
Engine type:	616/2
Displacement (cc):	1582
Bore x stroke (mm):	82,.5 x 74
Engine output DIN (kW/hp):	55/75 at 5000rpm
Maximum torque (Nm/lb ft):	117/86 at 3700rpm
Output per litre(kW/l / hp/l):	34.8 / 47.4
Compression ratio:	8.5 : 1
Valve operation & camshaft drive:	ohv, cam driven by gears, 2 valves per cylinder
Carburation:	2 downdraught carburettors Zenith 32 NDIX
Ignition system:	Battery coil ignition
Firing order:	1 - 4 - 3 - 2
Crankshaft bearing:	4 slide bearings
Engine lubrication:	Full pressure oil lubrication
Engine oil total (l):	5.0*
*Filling new assembled engine, oil change 4.0	

Transmission
Drive configuration:	Rear-axle drive
Manual gearbox:	4-speed
Transmission type:	741/2 A
Transmission ratios:	
1st gear:	3.091
2nd gear:	1.765
3rd gear:	1.130
4th gear:	0.852
Reverse gear:	3.560
Drive ratio:	4.428

Body, chassis, suspension, brakes, wheels
Body design:	Steel Roadster body, 2 doors, 2 seats, pressed and welded steel-sheet sections, one unit with body, curved single-piece windscreen, single layer hood with flexible plastic rear window, one grille in engine lid, bumpers in higher position, two air-intake grilles under the front bumpers, tailpipes go through over-riders
MY 1962 (T 6):	Twin grille in engine lid, fuel filler flap in right front wing
Suspension, front:	2 longitudinal swinging arms (suspension arms), 2 transverse, square torsion bars of laminated construction, adjustable, anti-roll bars, hydraulic telescopic double-action shock absorbers
Suspension, rear:	Oscillating half axles and radius arms, (longitudinal swinging arms), one round torsion bar on each side, hydraulic telescopic double-action shock absorbers
Option:	Compensating spring acting as counter-stabilizer
Brakes, front/rear (Size (mm)):	Brake drums Duplex (280 x 40) / Brake drums Simplex (280 x 40)
Wheels, front/rear:	4.5 J x 15 / 4.5 J x 15
Tyres, front/rear:	5.60-15 Sport / 5.60-15 Sport
Option radial tyres:	165-15 Sport / 165-15 Sport

Electrical system
Alternator (W):	200
Battery (V/Ah):	6 / 84
Option MY 1962 (T 6):	12 / 50

Dimensions and weight
Track, front/rear (mm):	1306 / 1272
Wheelbase (mm):	2100
Length x width x height (mm):	4010 x 1670 x 1310*
Kerb weight DIN (kg):	870
Permissible gross weight (kg):	1250
Fuel tank capacity (l):	52, including 5 reserve
MY 1962 (T 6):	50, including 6 reserve
C_w x A (m^2):	0.386 x 1.599 = 0.617
Power/weight ratio (kg/kW/kg/hp):	15.81 / 11.60
*with closed top	

Fuel consumption
DIN 70 030 (mpg):	34; 94 RON super leaded

Performance, production, prices
Acceleration 0-62mph/100kph (s):	15.0
Maximum speed (mph / kph):	108.5 / 175
Prod., 356 B Roadster total no.:*	2,902
356 B Roadster T 5:	2,653
356 B Roadster T 6:	249
*Total number all engine versions	
Purchase prices:	
09/1959 Roadster:	DM 13,450
07/1960 Roadster:	DM 14,000

356 B 1600 Super 90 Coupé
356 B 1600 Super 90 Cabriolet
356 B 1600 Super 90 Hardtop-Coupé
356 B 1600 Super 90 Hardtop/Cabriolet
MY 1960–MY 1963

Engine

Engine design:	4-cylinder horizontally-opposed
Installation:	Rear-engine
Cooling system:	Air-cooled
Engine type:	616/7
Displacement (cc):	1582
Bore x stroke (mm):	82.5 x 74
Engine output DIN (kW/hp):	66/90 at 5500rpm
Maximum torque (Nm/lb ft):	121/89 at 4300rpm
Output per litre(kW/l / hp/l):	41.7 / 56.9
Compression ratio:	9.0 : 1
Valve operation & camshaft drive:	ohv, cam driven by gears, 2 valves per cylinder
Carburation:	2 twin-choke downdraught carburettors Solex 40 PII-4
Ignition system:	Battery coil ignition
Firing order:	1 - 4 - 3 - 2
Crankshaft bearing:	4 slide bearings
Engine lubrication:	Full pressure oil lubrication
Engine oil total (l):	5.0*
*Filling new assembled engine, oil change 4.0	

Transmission

Drive configuration:	Rear-axle drive
Manual gearbox:	4-speed
Transmission type:	741/2 A
Transmission ratios:	
1st gear:	3.091
2nd gear:	1.765
3rd gear:	1.130
4th gear:	0.852
Reverse gear:	3.560
Drive ratio:	4.428

Body, chassis, suspension, brakes, wheels

Body design:	Steel body, 2 doors, 2 + 2 seats, pressed and welded steel-sheet sections, one unit with body, curved single-piece windscreen, one grille in engine lid, bumpers in higher position, two air-intake grilles under the front bumpers, tailpipes go through over-riders
MY 1962 - MY 1963 (T 6):	Twin grille in engine lid, fuel filler flap in right front wing
Coupé:	Fixed steel roof
Option:	Manual sunroof
Option MY 1962 - MY 1963 (T 6):	Electric sunroof
Cabriolet:	Multi-layer hood with flexible plastic rear window
Hardtop-Coupé:	Fixed hardtop
Hardtop/Cabriolet:	Removable hardtop
Suspension, front:	2 longitudinal swinging arms (suspension arms), 2 transverse, square torsion bars of laminated construction, adjustable, anti-roll bars, hydraulic telescopic double-action shock absorbers
Suspension, rear:	Oscillating half axles and radius arms, (longitudinal swinging arms), one round torsion bar on each side, compensating spring acting as counter-stabilizer, hydraulic telescopic double-action shock absorbers
Brakes, front/rear (Size (mm)):	Brake drums Duplex (280 x 40) / Brake drums Simplex (280 x 40)
Wheels, front/rear:	4.5 J x 15 / 4.5 J x 15
Tyres, front/rear:	5.90-15 Sport / 5.90-15 Sport
Option radial tyres:	165-15 Sport / 165-15 Sport

Electrical system

Alternator (W):	200
Battery (V/Ah):	6 / 84
Option MY 1962 - MY 1963 (T 6):	12 / 50

Dimensions and weight

Track, front/rear (mm):	1306 / 1272
Wheelbase (mm):	2100
Length x width x height (mm):	4010 x 1670 x 1330
Hardtop-Coupé:	4010 x 1670 x 1315
Hardtop/Cabriolet:	4010 x 1670 x 1315
Kerb weight DIN (kg):	900
MY 1962 - MY 1963 (T 6):	935
Permissible gross weight (kg):	1250
Fuel tank capacity (l):	52, including 5 reserve
MY 1962 - MY 1963 (T 6):	50, including 6 reserve
Cw x A (m2) Coupé:	0.398 x 1.611 = 0.641
Power/weight ratio (kg/kW/kg/hp):	13.63 / 10.00
MY 1962 - MY 1963 (T 6):	14.16 / 10.38

Fuel consumption

DIN 70 030 (mpg):	32.6; 96 RON super leaded

Performance, production, prices

Acceleration 0-62mph/100kph (s):	13.5
Maximum speed (mph / kph):	112 / 180
Production, total number:	
356 B Coupé total no.:*	20,597
356 B Coupé T 5:*	8,559
356 B Coupé T 6:*	12,038
356 B Cabriolet total no.:*	6,194
356 B Cabriolet T 5:*	3,094
356 B Cabriolet T 6:*	3,100
356 B Hardtop-Coupé total no.:*	1,747
356 B Hardtop-Coupé T 5:*	1,048
356 B Hardtop-Coupé T 6:*	699
*Total number all engine versions	

Purchase prices:	
09/1959 Coupé:	DM 14,500
Cabriolet:	DM 15,700
Hardtop-Coupé:	DM 15,400
Hardtop/Cabriolet:	DM 16,190
07/1960 Coupé:	DM 15,300
Cabriolet:	DM 16,500
Hardtop-Coupé:	DM 15,300
Hardtop/Cabriolet:	DM 17,290
09/1961 Coupé:	DM 15,850
Cabriolet:	DM 16,950
Hardtop-Coupé:	DM 15,850
Hardtop/Cabriolet:	DM 17,820
05/1962 Coupé:	DM 16,450
Cabriolet:	DM 17,550
Hardtop/Cabriolet:	DM 18,450
10/1962 Coupé:	DM 16,450
Cabriolet:	DM 17,550
Hardtop/Cabriolet:	DM 18,450

356 B 1600 Super 90 Roadster
MY 1960–MY 1962

Engine

Engine design:	4-cylinder horizontally-opposed
Installation:	Rear-engine
Cooling system:	Air-cooled
Engine type:	616/7
Displacement (cc):	1582
Bore x stroke (mm):	82.5 x 74
Engine output DIN (kW/hp):	66/90 at 5500rpm
Maximum torque (Nm/lb ft):	121/89 at 4300rpm
Output per litre(kW/l / hp/l):	41.7 / 56.9
Compression ratio:	9.0 : 1
Valve operation & camshaft drive:	ohv, cam driven by gears, 2 valves per cylinder
Carburation:	2 twin-choke downdraught carburettors Solex 40 PII-4
Ignition system:	Battery coil ignition
Firing order:	1 - 4 - 3 - 2
Crankshaft bearing:	4 slide bearings
Engine lubrication:	Full pressure oil lubrication
Engine oil total (l):	5.0*
*Filling new assembled engine, oil change 4.0	

Transmission

Drive configuration:	Rear-axle drive
Manual gearbox:	4-speed
Transmission type:	741/2 A
Transmission ratios:	
1st gear:	3.091
2nd gear:	1.765
3rd gear:	1.130
4th gear:	0.852
Reverse gear:	3.560
Drive ratio:	4.428

Body, chassis, suspension, brakes, wheels

Body design:	Steel Roadster body, 2 doors, 2 seats, pressed and welded steel-sheet sections, one unit with body, curved single-piece windscreen, single layer hood with flexible plastic rear window, one grille in engine lid, bumpers in higher position, two air-intake grilles under the front bumpers, tailpipes go through over-riders
MY 1962 (T 6):	Twin grille in engine lid, fuel filler flap in right front wing
Suspension, front:	2 longitudinal swinging arms (suspension arms), 2 transverse, square torsion bars of

laminated construction, adjustable, anti-roll bars, hydraulic telescopic double-action shock absorbers

Suspension, rear:	Oscillating half axles and radius arms, (longitudinal swinging arms), one round torsion bar on each side, compensating spring acting as counter-stabilizer, hydraulic telescopic double-action shock absorbers
Brakes, front/rear (Size (mm)):	Brake drums Duplex (280 x 40) / Brake drums Simplex (280 x 40)
Wheels, front/rear:	4.5 J x 15 / 4.5 J x 15
Tyres, front/rear:	5.90-15 Sport / 5.90-15 Sport
Option radial tyres:	165-15 Sport / 165-15 Sport

Electrical system

Alternator (W):	200
Battery (V/Ah):	6 / 84
Option MY 1962 (T 6):	12 / 50

Dimensions and weight

Track, front/rear (mm):	1306 / 1272
Wheelbase (mm):	2100
Length x width x height (mm):	4010 x 1670 x 1310*
Kerb weight DIN (kg):	870
Permissible gross weight (kg):	1250
Fuel tank capacity (l):	52, including 5 reserve
MY 1962 (T 6):	50, including 6 reserve
C_w x A (m²):	0.386 x 1.599 = 0.617
Power/weight ratio (kg/kW/kg/hp):	13.18 / 9.66
*with closed top	

Fuel consumption

DIN 70 030 (mpg):	32.6; 96 RON super leaded

Performance, production, prices

Acceleration 0-62mph/100kph (s):	13.5
Maximum speed (mph / kph):	112 / 180
Prod., 356 B Roadster total no.:*	2,902
356 B Roadster T 5:*	2,653
356 B Roadster T 6:*	249
*Total number all engine versions	
Purchase prices:	
09/1959 Roadster:	DM 14,450
07/1960 Roadster:	DM 15,200

356 B 1600 GS Carrera GT Coupé
MY 1960–MY 1961

Engine

Engine design:	4-cylinder horizontally-opposed
Installation:	Rear-engine
Cooling system:	Air-cooled
Engine type:	692/3
Displacement (cc):	1588
Bore x stroke (mm):	87.5 x 66
Engine output DIN (kW/hp):	85/115 at 6500rpm
with sports exhaust I:	94/128 at 6700rpm
with sports exhaust II:	99/135 at 7400rpm
Maximum torque (Nm/lb ft):	135/99 at 5500rpm
with sports exhaust I:	139/102 at 6000rpm
with sports exhaust II:	145/107 at 5900rpm
Output per litre(kW/l / hp/l):	53.5 / 72.4
with sports exhaust I:	59.2 / 80.6
with sports exhaust II:	62.3 / 85.0
Compression ratio:	9.8: 1
Valve operation & camshaft drive:	dohc, two vertical shafts, 2 valves per cylinder
Carburation:	2 twin-choke downdraught carburettors Weber 40 DCM 2
Ignition system:	Battery coil dual ignition
Firing order:	1 - 4 - 3 - 2
Crankshaft bearing:	3 slide bearings
Engine lubrication:	Dry sump
Engine oil total (l):	8.0

Transmission

Drive configuration:	Rear-axle drive
Manual gearbox:	4-speed
Transmission type:	741/1
Transmission ratios:	
1st gear:	3.091
2nd gear:	1.765
3rd gear:	1.227
4th gear:	0.960
Reverse gear:	3.560
Drive ratio:	4.429
Option:	Limited-slip differential

Body, chassis, suspension, brakes, wheels

Body design:	Steel body, 2 doors, 2 seats, pressed and welded steel-sheet sections, one unit with body, curved single-piece windscreen, one grille and additional slots left and right in engine lid, bumpers in higher position, two air-intake grilles under the front bumpers, no horn grilles over the front bumpers, aluminium doors and lids, Plexiglas rear and side windows
Suspension, front:	2 longitudinal swinging arms (suspension arms), 2 transverse, square torsion bars of laminated construction, adjustable, anti-roll bars, hydraulic telescopic double-action shock absorbers
Suspension, rear:	Oscillating half axles and radius arms, (longitudinal swinging arms), one round torsion bar on each side, compensating spring acting as counter-stabilizer, hydraulic telescopic double-action shock absorbers
Brakes, front/rear (Size (mm)):	Brake drums Duplex (280 x 60) / Brake drums Simplex (280 x 40)
Wheels, front/rear:	4.5 J x 15 / 4.5 J x 15
Tyres, front/rear:	5.90-15 Supersport / 5.90-15 Supersport
Option:	165 x 15 radial / 165 x 15 radial

Electrical system

Alternator (W):	200/300
Battery (V/Ah):	12 / 50

Dimensions and weight

Track, front/rear (mm):	1306 / 1272
Wheelbase (mm):	2100
Length x width x height (mm):	3980* x 1670 x 1320
Kerb weight DIN (kg):	845
Permissible gross weight (kg):	1250
Fuel tank capacity (l):	80, including 15 reserve
Cw x A (m2) Coupé:	0.398 x 1.611 = 0.641
Power/weight ratio (kg/kW/kg/hp):	9.94 / 7.34
with sports exhaust I:	8.98 / 6.60
with sports exhaust II:	8.53 / 6.25
*length without bumpers 3810	

Fuel consumption

DIN 70 030 (mpg):	29.5; 96 RON super leaded

Performance, production, prices

Acceleration 0-62mph/100kph (s):	10.5*
Maximum speed (mph / kph):	124 / 200*
*with standard exhaust	
Production, total number:	40
Purchase prices:	
09/1959 Coupé:	DM 21,500
07/1960 Coupé:	DM 21,500

356 B 2000 GS Carrera 2 Coupé
[356 B 2000 GS-GT Carrera 2 Coupé]
356 B 2000 GS Carrera 2 Cabriolet
356 B 2000 GS Carrera 2 Hardtop/ Cabriolet
MY 1962–MY 1963

Engine

Engine design:	4-cylinder horizontally-opposed
Installation:	Rear-engine
Cooling system:	Air-cooled
Engine type::	587/1 [587/2]
Displacement (cc):	1966
Bore x stroke (mm):	92 x 74
Engine output DIN (kW/hp):	96/130 [102/140] at 6200rpm
GT with sports exhaust:	[114/155 at 6600rpm]
Maximum torque (Nm/lb ft):	162/119 [174/128] at 4600[4700]rpm
GT with sports exhaust:	[196/144 at 5000rpm]
Output per litre(kW/l / hp/l):	48.8 [51.9] / 66.1 [71.2]
GT with sports exhaust:	[58.0 / 78.8]
Compression ratio:	9.5 : 1 [9.8 : 1]
Valve operation & camshaft drive:	dohc, two vertical shafts, 2 valves per cylinder
Carburation:	2 twin-choke downdraught carburettors Solex 40 PII-4 [2 twin-choke downdraught carburettors Weber 46 IDM 2]
Ignition system:	Battery coil dual ignition
Firing order:	1 - 4 - 3 - 2
Crankshaft bearing:	3 slide bearings
Engine lubrication:	Dry sump
Engine oil total (l):	8.0

Transmission

Drive configuration:	Rear-axle drive
Manual gearbox:	4-speed
Transmission type:	741/2 A [741/9 A]
Transmission ratios:	
1st gear:	3.091 [3.091] [2.750]* [3.091]** [3.091]² [3.091]³
2nd gear:	1.765 [1.765] [1.611]* [1.938]** [1.765]² [1.611]³
3rd gear:	1.130 [1.227] [1.130]* [1.611]** [1.350]² [1.130]³
4th gear:	0.852 [0.855] [0.885]* [1.227]** [1.227]² [1.042]³
Reverse gear:	3.560 [3.560] [3.560]* [3.560]** [3.560]² [3.560]³
Drive ratio:	4.428 [4.428] [4.428]* [4.428]** [4.428]² [4.428]³
Option:	Limited-slip differential
*Nürburgring transmission	
**Hill climb transmission	
²Airfield transmission	
³Le Mans transmission	

Body, chassis, suspension, brakes, wheels

Body design:	Steel body, 2 doors, 2 + 2 seats, pressed and welded steel-sheet sections, one unit with body, curved single-piece windscreen, twin grille in engine lid, bumpers in higher position, two air-intake grilles under the front bumpers, no horn grilles over the front bumpers, tailpipes go through additional valance panel, fuel filler flap in right front wing
Option:	Over-riders front and rear
Coupé:	Fixed steel roof
Option:	Electric sunroof
Cabriolet:	Multi-layer hood with flexible plastic rear window
Hardtop/Cabriolet:	Removable hardtop
Coupé GT:	Steel body, 2 doors, 2 + 2 seats, pressed and welded steel-sheet sections, one unit with body, curved single-piece windscreen, twin grille in engine lid, bumpers in higher position, two air-intake grilles under the front bumpers, no horn grilles over the front bumpers, tailpipes go through additional valance panel, fuel filler flap in the middle of the front lid, aluminium doors and lids, Plexiglas rear and side windows

Suspension, front:	2 longitudinal swinging arms (suspension arms), 2 transverse, square torsion bars of laminated construction, adjustable, anti-roll bars, hydraulic telescopic double-action shock absorbers
Suspension, rear:	Oscillating half axles and radius arms, (longitudinal swinging arms), one round torsion bar on each side, compensating spring acting as counter-stabilizer, hydraulic telescopic double-action shock absorbers
Brakes, front/rear (Size (mm)):	Brake drums Duplex (280 x 60) / Brake drums Simplex (280 x 40)
April 1962 - MY 1963:	innenumfassende brake discs (297 x 10) / innenumfassende brake discs (297 x 10) / Aluminium brake callipers / Aluminium brake callipers
Wheels, front/rear:	4.5 J x 15 / 4.5 J x 15
Tyres, front/rear:	165 x 15 radial / 165 x 15 radial [165 R 15 / 165 R 15]

Electrical system

Alternator (W):	200/300
Battery (V/Ah):	12 / 50

Dimensions and weight

Track, front/rear (mm):	1306 / 1272
Wheelbase (mm):	2100
Length x width x height (mm):	3980*≈ x 1670 x 1320
Hardtop/Cabriolet:	3980* x 1670 x 1305
Kerb weight DIN (kg):	1010 [850]
Permissible gross weight (kg):	1360 [1250]
Fuel tank capacity (l):	50 [110], including 6 [6] reserve
Cw x A (m2) Coupé:	0.398 x 1.611 = 0.641
Power/weight ratio (kg/kW/ kg/hp):	10.52 [8.33] / 7.76 [6.07]
GT with sports exhaust:	[7.45 / 5.48]
*with over-riders 4010	
≈GT length without bumpers 3810	

Fuel consumption

DIN 70 030 (mpg):	29; 96 RON super leaded

Performance, production, prices

Acceleration 0-62mph/100kph (s):	9.0 [ca. 8.0]
Maximum speed (mph / kph):	124 / 200 [130 / 210]*
*dependent on gear ratios	
Prod., 356 B Carrera 2 total no.:	310
Purchase prices:	
09/1961 Coupé:	DM 23,700 [DM 23,700]
Cabriolet:	DM 24,850
Hardtop/Cabriolet:	DM 25,750
05/1962 Coupé:	DM 23,700 [DM 23,700]
Cabriolet:	DM 24,850
Hardtop/Cabriolet:	DM 25,750
10/1962 Coupé:	DM 23,700 [DM 23,700]
Cabriolet:	DM 24,850
Hardtop/Cabriolet:	DM 25,750

Porsche 356 B Carrera GTL-Abarth (Type 756)

Over the years, the 356 Carrera became ever more luxurious, and therefore heavier. In racing, this is a distinct disadvantage. Porsche therefore decided to build a lightweight, aerodynamic race car. Between January and June of 1960, Carlo Abarth of Turin built 21 aluminium bodies for Porsche. This limited-edition 356 B Carrera GTL Abarth was in extremely high demand and quickly sold out at a price of 25,000 Deutschmarks.

In terms of aerodynamics, the Carrera GTL (L for light) was superior to the Reutter-bodied production 356 B. Overall, it had a longer, lower appearance, even though window sizes were increased for better outward visibility. The interior was spartan and functional for weight-saving purposes. The power

unit for the Carrera GTL was the 1.6 litre Carrera engine with shaft-driven overhead cams, available in three power levels: with standard exhaust, for 115hp (85kW) at 6500rpm; with sport exhaust, for 128hp (94kW) at 6700rpm; and with the Sebring exhaust, for 135hp (99kW) at 7400rpm. Adjustment of the pair of Weber 40 DCM 2 twin-choke carburettors was specific for each exhaust variant. The most powerful version clocked 0-62mph (100kph) in just 8.8 seconds, and a top speed of more than 137mph (220kph).

The most famous 356 B Carrera GTL Abarth is most certainly the example owned by Paul-Ernst Strähle of Schorndorf, near Stuttgart, with its well-known number plate, WN-V1.

The Fuhrmann engine, with shaft-driven cams, at the rear of a 356 B 1600 GS Carrera GTL Abarth Coupé

356 B 1600 GS Carrera GTL Abarth Coupé (Typ 756) 1960

Engine

Engine design:	4-cylinder horizontally-opposed
Installation:	Rear-engine
Cooling system:	Air-cooled
Engine type:	692/3 and 692/3A
Displacement (cc):	1588
Bore x stroke (mm):	87.5 x 66
Engine output DIN (kW/hp):	85/115 at 6500rpm
With sports exhaust:	94/128 at 6700rpm
With Sebring exhaust:	99/135 at 7400rpm
Maximum torque (Nm/lb ft):	135/99 at 5500rpm
With sports exhaust:	139/102 at 6000rpm
With Sebring exhaust:	146/108 at 5800rpm
Output per litre(kW/l / hp/l):	53.5 / 72.4
with sports exhaust I:	59.2 / 80.6
with sports exhaust II:	62.3 / 85.0
Compression ratio:	9.8 : 1
Valve operation & camshaft drive:	dohc, two vertical shafts, 2 valves per cylinder
Carburation:	2 twin-choke downdraught carburettors Weber 40 DCM 2
Ignition system:	Battery coil dual ignition
Firing order:	1 - 4 - 3 - 2
Engine lubrication:	Dry sump
Engine oil total (l):	8.0

Transmission

Drive configuration:	Rear-axle drive
Manual gearbox:	4-speed
Transmission type:	741/1
Transmission ratios:	
1st gear:	3.091
2nd gear:	1.765
3rd gear:	1.227
4th gear:	0.960
Reverse gear:	3.560
Standard:	Limited-slip differential

Body, chassis, suspension, brakes, wheels

Body design:	Aluminium body, 2 doors, 2 seats, pressed and welded steel-sheet frame, flap in engine lid for better cooling, later cars with additional slots left and right

Suspension, front:	2 longitudinal swinging arms (suspension arms), 2 transverse, square torsion bars of laminated construction, adjustable, anti-roll bars, hydraulic telescopic double-action shock absorbers
Suspension, rear:	Oscillating half axles and radius arms, (longitudinal swinging arms), one round torsion bar on each side, compensating spring acting as counter-stabilizer, hydraulic telescopic double-action shock absorbers
Brakes, front/rear (Size (mm)):	Brake drums Duplex (280 x 60) / Brake drums Simplex (280 x 40)
Wheels, front/rear:	4.5 J x 15 / 4.5 J x 15
Tyres, front/rear:	5.90-15 Supersport / 5.90-15 Supersport
Option:	165 R 15 / 165 R 15

Electrical system

Alternator (W):	200/300
Battery (V/Ah):	12 / 50

Dimensions and weight

Track, front/rear (mm):	1306 / 1272
Wheelbase (mm):	2100
Length x width x height (mm):	3980* x 1550 x 1200
Kerb weight DIN (kg):	845
Permissible gross weight (kg):	n/a
Fuel tank capacity (l):	80
Cw x A (m2) Coupé:	0.389 x 1.495 = 0.581
Power/weight ratio (kg/kW/kg/hp):	9.94 / 7.35
With sports exhaust:	8.99 / 6.60
With Sebring exhaust:	8.54 / 6.26

Fuel consumption

DIN 70 030 (mpg):	29.5; 96 RON super leaded
Performance, production, prices	
Acceleration 0-62mph/100kph (s):	8.8*
Maximum speed (mph / kph):	more than 136 / 220*
*with Sebring exhaust	
Production, total number:	21
Purchase prices:	
1960 Coupé:	DM 25,000

Porsche 356 C

As the new Porsche 901 was being readied for the autumn 1963 International Automobile Show, Porsche began production of the final 356 model.

Model year 1964

The 356 C replaced the 356 B. Externally, the newly-designed wheels with their flat hubcaps were a key recognition feature. The two pushrod-engined versions were named 356 C and 356 SC, available as Coupé and Cabriolet. Both bodies were identical to the final version of the T6 body used in the 356 B. On the Cabriolet, the plastic rear window could be unzipped from inside or outside, and folded down. This provided yet another open-air motoring mode. As before, the Cabriolet was also available with a removable hardtop.

The 60hp Normal engine was removed from the line-up. Compared to the 356 B power units, the remaining 1.6 litre engines featured numerous detail revisions. Both variations had identical valves: 38mm intake valves and 34mm exhaust valves. While the 356 C engine was tuned for torque and long life, the heart of the 356 SC was a traditional sports car engine with a throaty intake note; it demanded high

revs for brisk performance, and the driver was expected to keep it within its optimum speed range – at least 2500rpm for good torque, and to preserve the crankshaft bearings, no sustained revs over 5500rpm. Detail changes included valve timing, machining of the crankshaft and its main bearings, intake and exhaust ports, and the shape of the piston crown.

The highly reliable 356 C power unit developed 75hp (55kW) at 5200rpm, with maximum torque of 123Nm (91lb ft) at 3600rpm. The most powerful of all pushrod 356 engines, the 356 SC produced 95hp (70kW) at 5800rpm. Maximum torque of 124Nm (91lb ft) was available at 4200rpm. While the pistons of the 75hp engine ran in cast-iron cylinders, the SC engine was fitted with Ferral-coated aluminium cylinders.

The 356 C 2000 GS Carrera 2 engine was continued without any significant change; only generator output was raised to 450 Watts.

Both pushrod engines were fitted with a 200mm clutch. Synchro rings of the four-speed transmission were reinforced for greater durability. A limited-slip differential was available as an option.

The 356 C was able to reach the 62mph (100kph) mark in 14 seconds, and had a top speed of 109mph (175kph). The even sportier 356 SC had

Engine compartment of a 356 C 2000 GS Carrera 2

the best acceleration of any pushrod 356 ever, reaching 62mph in 11.5 seconds and with a top speed of 115mph (185 kph).

All cars in the 356 C line were fitted with a four-disc brake system by Ate, following Dunlop brake practice. Accordingly, the wheels were of a new design, with a smaller (130mm) bolt circle and flatter hubcaps. The 356 Carrera 2 also received this new brake system. Wheel and tyre sizes remained unchanged. Roadholding was improved by a 1mm thicker front anti-roll bar. At the rear, torsion bars were softer, and preloaded. Shock absorber mounts were altered in keeping with the new brake system. Boge supplied dampers for the 356 C, Koni for the SC. The rear compensating spring was deleted for all models, although it could still be ordered as an option. Only the Carrera 2 kept the compensator as standard equipment. As a result of alterations to the connection between steering column and steering box, the steering column was slightly shorter.

Inside, the centre of the dashboard was extended downward. This caused the gear lever to be s hortened. Switches for windscreen wipers, headlamps, and cigarette lighter were located to the right of the steering column. Heating and ventilation controls were redesigned. A lever now controlled the flow of warm air from the engine compartment. In the Coupé a reading lamp was installed for the passenger. A warning lamp in the combination instrument indicated parking brake application. Two warm-air ducts kept the rear window free of condensation. The lower cushions of the front seat were reshaped. At the rear, a raised edge on the folded-down rear seat-backs prevented luggage from sliding forward. An armrest on the inner door panels improved comfort and served as a door handle.

Model year 1965

The bodywork, suspension and equipment of the 356 C remained unchanged for its final model year. On the 356 SC engine, Ferral-coated cylinders were replaced by Biral cylinders, the cast-iron liners of which were combined with a finned aluminium jacket.

After only 126 had been built, the 356 C Carrera 2 was dropped from the model line-up. In terms of performance, its place was taken by the new, more affordable Porsche 901.

On 14 September 1964, the new Porsche 901 began rolling off the assembly line. At first, the factory produced just five 901s, against 40 356 Cs and SCs per day. On 28 April 1965, a flower-bedecked 356 C Cabriolet left the assembly line – the last series-built 356.

1966

The very last 356 was delivered on 26 May 1966. During that month, Porsche manufactured a special run of ten white Cabriolets with black tops for the Dutch police.

Production of 356 C models totalled 16,685.

The total number of all 356 models built, from 1950 to 1966, added up to 77,766 vehicles.

356 C 1600 Coupé
356 C 1600 Cabriolet
356 C 1600 Hardtop/Cabriolet
MY 1964–MY 1965

Engine

Engine design:	4-cylinder horizontally-opposed
Installation:	Rear-engine
Cooling system:	Air-cooled
Engine type:	616/15
Displacement (cc):	1582
Bore x stroke (mm):	82.5 x 74
Engine output DIN (kW/hp):	55/75 at 5200rpm
Maximum torque (Nm/lb ft):	123/91 at 3600rpm
Output per litre(kW/l / hp/l):	34.8 / 47.4
Compression ratio:	8.5 : 1
Valve operation & camshaft drive:	ohv, cam driven by gears, 2 valves per cylinder
Carburation:	2 twin-choke downdraught carburettors Zenith 32 NDIX
Ignition system:	Battery coil ignition
Firing order:	1 - 4 - 3 - 2
Crankshaft bearing:	4 slide bearings
Engine lubrication:	Full pressure oil lubrication
Engine oil total (l):	5.0*
*Filling new assembled engine, oil change 4.0	

Transmission

Drive configuration:	Rear-axle drive
Manual gearbox:	4-speed
Transmission type:	741/0 A
Transmission ratios:	
1st gear:	3.091
2nd gear:	1.765
3rd gear:	1.130
4th gear:	0.815
Reverse gear:	3.560
Drive ratio:	4.428
Option:	Limited-slip differential

Body, chassis, suspension, brakes, wheels

Body design:	Steel body, 2 doors, 2 + 2 seats, pressed and welded steel-sheet sections, one unit with body, curved single-piece windscreen, twin grille in engine lid, bumpers in higher position, two air-intake grilles under the front bumpers, tailpipes go through over-riders, fuel filler flap in right front wing
Coupé:	Fixed steel roof
Option:	Electric sunroof
Cabriolet:	Multi-layer hood with flexible plastic rear window
Hardtop/Cabriolet:	Removable hardtop

Suspension, front:	2 longitudinal swinging arms (suspension arms), 2 transverse, square torsion bars of laminated construction, adjustable, anti-roll bars, hydraulic telescopic double-action shock absorbers
Suspension, rear:	Oscillating half axles and radius arms, (longitudinal swinging arms), one round torsion bar on each side, hydraulic telescopic double-action shock absorbers
Option:	Compensating spring acting as counter-stabilizer
Brakes, front/rear (Size (mm)):	Brake discs (274.5 x 10.5) / Brake discs (285 x 10) 2-piston cast-iron fixed callipers / 2-piston cast-iron fixed callipers
Wheels, front/rear:	4.5 J x 15 / 4.5 J x 15
Tyres, front/rear:	5.60-15 Sport / 5.60-15 Sport

Electrical system

Alternator (W):	200/300
Battery (V/Ah):	6 / 84
Option:	12 / 50

Dimensions and weight

Track, front/rear (mm):	1306 / 1272
Wheelbase (mm):	2100
Length x width x height (mm):	4010 x 1670 x 1315
Hardtop/Cabriolet:	4010 x 1670 x 1300
Kerb weight DIN (kg):	935
Permissible gross weight (kg):	1250
Fuel tank capacity (l):	50, including 6 reserve
Cw x A (m2) Coupé:	0.398 x 1.611 = 0.641
Power/weight ratio (kg/kW/kg/hp):	17.0 / 12.46

Fuel consumption

DIN 70 030 (mph):	34; 94 RON super leaded

Performance, production, prices

Acceleration 0-62mph/100kph (s):	14.0
Maximum speed (mph / kph):	108.5 / 175
Production, total number:	
356 C Coupé:*	13,510
356 C Cabriolet:*	3,175
*Total number all engine versions	
Purchase prices:	
07/1963 Coupé:	DM 14,950
Cabriolet:	DM 15,950
Hardtop/Cabriolet:	DM 16,900
04/1965 Coupé:	DM 14,950
Cabriolet:	DM 15,950
Hardtop/Cabriolet:	DM 16,900

356 C 1600 SC Coupé
356 C 1600 SC Cabriolet
356 C 1600 SC Hardtop/Cabriolet
MY 1964–MY1965

Engine

Engine design:	4-cylinder horizontally-opposed
Installation:	Rear-engine
Cooling system:	Air-cooled
Engine type:	616/16
Displacement (cc):	1582
Bore x stroke (mm):	82.5 x 74
Engine output DIN (kW/hp):	70/95 at 5800rpm
Maximum torque (Nm/lb ft):	124/91 at 4200rpm
Output per litre(kW/l / hp/l):	44.2 / 60.0
Compression ratio:	9.5 : 1
Valve operation & camshaft drive:	ohv, cam driven by gears, 2 valves per cylinder
Carburation:	2 twin-choke downdraught carburettors Solex 40 PII-4
Ignition system:	Battery coil ignition
Firing order:	1 - 4 - 3 - 2
Crankshaft bearing:	4 slide bearings
Engine lubrication:	Full pressure oil lubrication
Engine oil total (l):	5.0*
*Filling new assembled engine, oil change 4.0	

Transmission

Drive configuration:	Rear-axle drive
Manual gearbox:	4-speed
Transmission type:	741/2 A
Transmission ratios:	
1st gear:	3.091
2nd gear:	1.765
3rd gear:	1.130
4th gear:	0.852
Reverse gear:	3.560
Drive ratio:	4.428
Option:	Limited-slip differential

Body, chassis, suspension, brakes, wheels

Body design:	Steel body, 2 doors, 2 + 2 seats, pressed and welded steel-sheet sections, one unit with body, curved single-piece windscreen, twin grille in engine lid, bumpers in higher position, two air-intake grilles under the front bumpers, tailpipes go through over-riders, fuel filler flap in right front wing
Coupé:	Fixed steel roof
Option:	Electric sunroof
Cabriolet:	Multi-layer hood with flexible plastic rear window
Hardtop/Cabriolet:	Removable hardtop

Suspension, front:	2 longitudinal swinging arms (suspension arms), 2 transverse, square torsion bars of laminated construction, adjustable, anti-roll bars, hydraulic telescopic double-action shock absorbers
Suspension, rear:	Oscillating half axles and radius arms, (longitudinal swinging arms), one round torsion bar on each side, hydraulic telescopic double-action shock absorbers
Option:	Compensating spring acting as counter-stabilizer
Brakes, front/rear (Size (mm)):	Brake discs (274.5 x 10.5) / Brake discs (285 x 10) 2-piston cast-iron fixed callipers / 2-piston cast-iron fixed callipers
Wheels, front/rear:	4.5 J x 15 / 4.5 J x 15
Tyres, front/rear:	165-15 radial / 165-15 radial

Electrical system

Alternator (W):	200/300
Battery (V/Ah):	6 / 84
Option:	12 / 50

Dimensions and weight

Track, front/rear (mm):	1306 / 1272
Wheelbase (mm):	2100
Length x width x height (mm):	4010 x 1670 x 1315
Hardtop/Cabriolet:	4010 x 1670 x 1300
Kerb weight DIN (kg):	935
Permissible gross weight (kg):	1250
Fuel tank capacity (l):	50, including 6 reserve
Cw x A (m2) Coupé:	0.398 x 1.611 = 0.641
Power/weight ratio (kg/kW/ kg/hp):	13.35 / 9.84

Fuel consumption

DIN 70 030 (mpg):	33; 96 RON super leaded

Performance, production, prices

Acceleration 0-62mph/100kph (s):	11.5
Maximum speed (mph / kph):	115 / 185
Production, total number:	
356 C Coupé:*	13,510
356 C Cabriolet:*	3,175
*Total number all engine versions	
Purchase prices:	
07/1963 Coupé:	DM 16,450
Cabriolet:	DM 17,450
Hardtop/Cabriolet:	DM 18,400
04/1965 Coupé:	DM 16,450
Cabriolet:	DM 17,450
Hardtop/Cabriolet:	DM 18,400

356 C 2000 GS Carrera 2 Coupé
356 C 2000 GS Carrera 2 Cabriolet
356 C 2000 GS Carrera 2 Hardtop/
Cabriolet MY 1964

Engine

Engine design:	4-cylinder horizontally-opposed
Installation:	Rear-engine
Cooling system:	Air-cooled
Engine type:	587/1
Displacement (cc):	1966
Bore x stroke (mm):	92 x 74
Engine output DIN (kW/hp):	96/130 at 6200rpm
Maximum torque (Nm/lb ft):	162/119 at 4600rpm
Output per litre(kW/l / hp/l):	48.8 / 66.1
Compression ratio:	9.5 : 1
Valve operation & camshaft drive:	dohc, two vertical shafts, 2 valves per cylinder
Carburation:	2 twin-choke downdraught carburettors Solex 40 PII-4
Ignition system:	Battery coil dual ignition
Firing order:	1 - 4 - 3 - 2
Crankshaft bearing:	3 slide bearings
Engine lubrication:	Dry sump
Engine oil total (l):	8.0

Transmission

Drive configuration:	Rear-axle drive
Manual gearbox:	4-speed
Transmission type:	741/20 C
Transmission ratios:	
1st gear:	3.091
2nd gear:	1.765
3rd gear:	1.130
4th gear:	0.852
Reverse gear:	3.560
Drive ratio:	4.428
Option:	Limited-slip differential

Body, chassis, suspension, brakes, wheels

Body design:	Steel body, 2 doors, 2 + 2 seats, pressed and welded steel-sheet sections, one unit with body, curved single-piece windscreen, twin grille in engine lid, bumpers in higher position, two air-intake grilles under the front bumpers, no horn grilles over the front bumpers, tailpipes go through additional valance panel, fuel filler flap in right front wing
Option:	Over-riders front and rear
Coupé:	Fixed steel roof
Option:	Electric sunroof
Cabriolet:	Multi-layer hood with flexible plastic rear window
Hardtop/Cabriolet:	Removable hardtop
Suspension, front:	2 longitudinal swinging arms (suspension arms), 2 transverse, square torsion bars of laminated construction, adjustable, anti-roll bars, hydraulic telescopic double-action shock absorbers
Suspension, rear:	Oscillating half axles and radius arms, (longitudinal swinging arms), one round torsion bar on each side, compensating spring acting as counter-stabilizer, hydraulic telescopic double-action shock absorbers
Brakes, front/rear (Size (mm)):	Brake discs (274.5 x 10.5) / Brake discs (285 x 10) 2-piston cast-iron fixed callipers / 2-piston cast-iron fixed callipers
Wheels, front/rear:	4.5 J x 15 / 4.5 J x 15
Tyres, front/rear:	165 x 15 radial / 165 x 15 radial

Electrical system

Alternator (W):	450
Battery (V/Ah):	12 / 50

Dimensions and weight

Track, front/rear (mm):	1306 / 1272
Wheelbase (mm):	2100
Length x width x height (mm):	3980* x 1670 x 1320
Kerb weight DIN (kg):	1010
Permissible gross weight (kg):	1360
Fuel tank capacity (l):	50, including 6 reserve
Cw x A (m2) Coupé:	0.398 x 1.611 = 0.641
Power/weight ratio (kg/kW/kg/hp):	10.52 / 7.76
*with over-riders 4010	

Fuel consumption

DIN 70 030 (mpg):	29; 96 RON super leaded

Performance, production, prices

Acceleration 0-62mph/100kph (s):	9.0
Maximum speed (mph / kph):	124 / 200
Production, total number:	126
Purchase prices:	
07/1963 Coupé:	DM 23,700
Cabriolet:	DM 24,700
Hardtop/Cabriolet:	DM 25,650

Porsche 550

Porsche 550 1500 RS Spyder

As early as 1950, privateers such as Walter Glöckler of Frankfurt entered in races home-made, open-top Spyders based on Porsche mechanicals. (Although 'Spider' is written with an 'i' in Italy, the Porsche style is to use a 'y'). In the winter of 1952, Porsche engineers at Zuffenhausen began building their own Spyder, and at the same time work started under the direction of Dr Ernst Fuhrmann on a completely new engine. The result was a power unit with four shaft-driven overhead camshafts, a design that would go down in Porsche history as the Carrera engine. The first two 550 Spyders, built in 1953, could be driven in open-top form, or with a closed, coupé hardtop. The closed version had aerodynamic advantages. Propulsion was still by means of a performance-tuned 1.5-litre pushrod engine of 78hp (57kW).

Bodywork of the 550 1500 RS Spyder was of aluminium. This was mounted on a ladder-frame of welded steel tubes. Its aluminium doors were fitted with locks. The windscreen was of curved laminated safety glass, and could be quickly and easily removed from the car. A simple tonneau or coupé hardtop could be attached to the windscreen frame. The doors were topped by side curtains. The Spyder was delivered with a simple emergency top, but it could also be ordered with just a small windscreen for the driver, and a tonneau cover. The entire rear section of the bodywork hinged rearward. Two chromium-plated grilles were set into the rear lid. The front lid covered a 65-litre fuel tank with a quick-release filler cap. As an option, for long-distance races this could be replaced by a 90-litre tank. The 550 1500 RS Spyders tipped the scales with an empty weight of 685kg. For the 1955 model year, the front and rear bodywork around the lamps was shaped slightly flatter.

The welded-in dashboard acted as a load-bearing member of the body structure, and its facing surface was covered with leatherette. The instrument panel contained three round gauges, switches for windscreen wipers, instrument illumination and headlamps, as well as warning lamps for the charging system, oil pressure and undipped headlamps. In addition, the dash carried the ignition lock, starter button and an electrical accessory socket. For heating, warm air was regulated by a flap, ducted to the vehicle interior through the longitudinal frame members, and could be closed off by sliding vents at the sides of the cockpit.

The two bucket seats were adjustable for reach. Door panels were of leatherette-covered cardboard. The Spyders had independent suspension on all four wheels, damped by telescopic shock absorbers. Front suspension was by longitudinal crank arms, two transverse, square-leaf spring bundles and an anti-roll bar. Rear suspension was by half-shafts (swing-axles) located by trailing arms and sprung by round, transverse torsion bars. The hydraulic brake system acted on four drum brakes. Size 3.50 D x 16 wheels were shod with 5.00-16 tyres at the front and 5.25-16 at the rear.

The power unit was mounted amidships, behind the driver and ahead of the rear axle. The engine developed 110hp (81kW) at 6200rpm, with maximum torque of 119Nm (88lb ft) at 5000rpm. Its four overhead cams were driven by quill shafts and spiral-bevel gearing. Crankcase, cylinders and cylinder heads were of cast aluminium-alloy. Two Solex twin-choke downdraught carburettors, Type 40 PII, provided fuel-air mixture. Its dual ignition consisted of two sparkplugs per cylinder, two ignition distributors and two ignition coils. Initially, the distributors were driven by an extension from two camshafts; later, this was changed to a V-shaped arrangement driven directly from the crankshaft. Engine cooling was provided by an upright blower. The dry sump lubrication system included a separate oil tank with a capacity of eight litres. Electrical power was supplied by a 6-volt system. A four-speed manual transmission was hung behind the rear axle. The final drive included a ZF limited-slip differential.

From a standstill, the 550 1500 RS Spyder could reach 62mph (100kph) in 10 seconds; and its top speed was 136mph (220kph).

550 1500 RS Spyder
1954–1956

Engine

Engine design:	4 cylinder horizontally opposed
Installation:	Mid-engine
Cooling system:	Air-cooled
Engine type:	547/1
Displacement (cc):	1498
Bore x stroke (mm):	85 x 66
Engine output DIN (kW/hp):	81/110 at 6200rpm
Maximum torque (Nm/lb ft):	129/95 at 5300rpm
Output per litre (kW/l / hp/l):	54.1 / 73.4
Compression ratio:	9.5 : 1
Valve operation & camshaft drive:	dohc, two vertical shafts, 2 valves per cylinder
Carburation:	2 twin-choke downdraught carburettors Solex 40 PII
Alternative:	2 twin-choke downdraught carburettors Weber 40 DCM
Ignition system:	Battery coil dual ignition
Firing order:	1 - 4 - 3 - 2
Engine lubrication:	Dry sump
Engine oil total (l):	8.0

Transmission

Drive configuration:	Rear-axle drive
Manual gearbox:	4-speed
Transmission type:	550
Transmission ratios:	
1st gear:	3.182 [3.182] [3.182]
2nd gear:	1.765 [1.938] [1.611]
3rd gear:	1.130 [1.227] [1.042]
4th gear:	0.815 [0.960] [0.885]
Reverse gear:	3.560 [3.560] [3.560]
Drive ratio:	4.375 [4.429] [4.576]
Sandard:	Limited-slip differential

Body, chassis, suspension, brakes, wheels

Body design:	Open aluminium body, 2 doors, 2 seats, single-layer soft-top, steel frame, front lid and rear part can be opened
Suspension, front:	2 longitudinal swinging arms (suspension arms), 2 transverse, square torsion bars of laminated construction, adjustable, anti-roll bar, hydraulic telescopic double-action shock absorbers
Suspension, rear:	Oscillating half axles and radius arms, (longitudinal swinging arms), one round torsion bar on each side, compensating spring acting as counter-stabilizer, hydraulic telescopic double-action shock absorbers
Brakes, front/rear (Size (mm)):	Brake drums Duplex (280 x 40) / Brake drums Simplex (280 x 40)
Wheels, front/rear:	3.50 D x 16 / 3.50 D x 16
Tyres, front/rear:	5.00-16 / 5.25-16

Electrical system

Alternator (W):	160
Battery (V/Ah):	6 / 70

Dimensions and weight

Track, front/rear (mm):	1290 / 1250
Wheelbase (mm):	2100
Length x width x height (mm):	3600 x 1550 x 1015
Kerb weight DIN (kg):	685
Permissible gross weight (kg):	900
Fuel tank capacity (l):	65, without reserve
Option:	90, without reserve
C_w x A (m^2) Coupé:	n/a
Power/weight ratio (kg/kW/kg/hp):	8.47 / 6.23

Fuel consumption

DIN 70 030 (mpg):	30; 86 RON normal leaded

Performance, production, prices

Acceleration 0-62mph/100kph (s):	app. 10.0
Maximum speed (mph / kph):	136 / 220
Production, total number:	
550 1500 RS Spyder:	90
Purchase prices:	
Spyder:	DM 24,600

Porsche 904 Carrera GTS

With its presentation of the 904 Carrera GTS in November 1963, at the Solitude Palace on the heights overlooking its factory, Porsche presented not only one of its most beautiful racing cars, but also a new construction method. Its design, the inspiration of Ferdinand Alexander ('Butzi') Porsche, was a composite construction, combining a steel box-section ladder frame joined to a fibreglass body. The frame, weighing about 50kg (110lb) was spot-welded, making it easy to build and repair. The body was moulded by Heinkel Flugzeugbau GmbH in Speyer, as a 2mm thick hand lay-up. Using these small-volume production methods, Heinkel turned out just two bodies per day. Frame and body were bonded together, and also bolted at key points. This new composite construction method resulted in a light yet rigid car. At just over 1.4 square meters (15sq ft), the frontal area of the 904 was extremely small and assisted the low-slung (1065mm/42in) coupé in achieving outstandingly low aerodynamic drag figures. For easier entry, the doors were cut partway into the roof, and were fitted with sliding Plexiglas windows. The steering column was designed as a safety column, with two universal joints. Steering wheel and pedal cluster were longitudinally adjustable, as the thinly padded seats were rigidly bolted to the body.

Interior equipment was limited to only the basics needed for driving. The spare tyre and 110-litre fuel tank were located in the nose of the car. The familiar four-cylinder power unit with its shaft-driven overhead cams was positioned amidships,

immediately behind the driver. Fitted with the 'Sport Exhaust III' in the 904 Carrera GTS, it developed 180hp (132kW) at 7200rpm from a displacement of 1966cc. Thanks to good aerodynamics, the 904 could reach 163mph (263kph). Weighing only 740kg (1631lb), the 904 could accelerate to 62mph in just 5.5 seconds.

The hydraulically actuated dual-circuit disc brake system was a modified version of the 911 system. Bias-belted or racing tyres could be mounted on 15 inch rims, optionally 5 to 7 inches wide. Front and rear suspension was by coil springs, rubber-mounted A-arms, and anti-roll bar. A newly designed five-speed manual transmission with a rigid tunnel case transmitted engine power to the road through a ZF Limited-slip differential. On 31 March 1964, Porsche officially completed the 100 examples necessary for racing homologation in the GT class. In all, 106 examples were built with the Carrera engine. Porsche also built four more cars for racing purposes, powered by a 210hp (154kW) six-cylinder based on the 911 engine, and two more vehicles with the eight-cylinder of the Type 718, developing 240hp (176kW). Priced at 29,700 Deutschmarks, the 904 Carrera GTS was licensed for use on public roads, but could also be entered in races. In early prototype testing on the Nürburgring north circuit, a 904 Carrera GTS powered by the 155hp (114kW) engine and stock exhaust broke the magic 10 minute barrier, with a lap time of 9:55.3. An improved version shaved another ten seconds off that time.

904 Carrera GTS Coupé
1964–1965

Engine

Engine design:	4 cylinder horizontally opposed
Installation:	Mid-engine
Cooling system:	Air-cooled
Engine type::	587/3
Displacement (cc):	1966
Bore x stroke (mm):	92 x 74
Engine output DIN (kW/hp):	114/155 at 6900rpm
with sports exhaust III:	132/180 at 7200rpm
Maximum torque (Nm/lb ft):	169/125 at 5000rpm
with sports exhaust III:	196/144 at 5000rpm
Output per litre (kW/l / hp/l):	58.0 / 78.8
with sports exhaust III:	67.1 / 91.6
Compression ratio:	9.8 : 1
Valve operation & camshaft drive:	dohc, two vertical shafts, 2 valves per cylinder
Carburation:	2 twin-choke downdraught carburettors Weber 46 IDA 2/3*
26th - 106th vehicle:	2 twin-choke downdraught carburettors Solex 44 PII-4
Ignition system:	Battery coil dual ignition
Firing order:	1 - 4 - 3 - 2
Engine lubrication:	Dry sump
Engine oil total (l):	10.0

Transmission

Drive configuration:	Rear-axle drive
Manual gearbox:	4-speed
Transmission type:	904/0 [904/1] [904/2] [904/3]
Transmission ratios:	
1st gear:	2.643 [2,833] [2.643]* [2.643]**
2nd gear:	1.684 [2.000] [1.833]* [1.550]**
3rd gear:	1.318 [1.476] [1.364]* [1.125]**
4th gear:	1.040 [1.217] [1.125]* [0.889]**
5th gear:	0.821 [1.040] [0.962]* [0.759]**
Reverse gear:	2.690 [2.690] [2.690]* [2.690]**
Drive ratio:	4.428 [4.428] [4.428]* [4.428]**
Standard:	Limited-slip differential
Standard or Nürburgring transmission	
[Hill climb transmission]	
*[Airfield transmission]	
**[Transmission for fast tracks]	

Body, chassis, suspension, brakes, wheels

Body design:	Plastic body, 2 doors, 2 seats, pressed and welded steel-sheet frame, fixed plastic roof, front lid and rear lid removable
Suspension, front:	Individually suspended on double wishbones, coil springs in combination with shock absorbers, hydraulic telescopic double-action shock absorbers, anti-roll bar
Suspension, rear:	Individually suspended on double wishbones, coil springs in combination with shock absorbers, hydraulic telescopic double-action hock absorbers, anti-roll bar
Brakes, front/rear (Size (mm)):	Discs (274.5 x 12.7) / Discs (285 x 10)
1965:	Discs (282 x 12.7) / Discs (288 x 10) 2-piston fixed cast-iron callipers / 2-piston fixed cast-iron callipers
Wheels, front/rear:	5.0 JK x 15 / 5.0 JK x 15
Option:	5.0 JK x 15 / 6.0 JK x 15
Option August 1965:	6.0 K x 15 / 7.0 K x 15
Tyres, front/rear:	165 HR 15 Dunlop Sp CB 59 / 165 HR 15 Dunlop Sp CB 59
Option:	Dunlop Racing 5.50 L 15 R 6 D 12 / Dunlop Racing 5.50 L 15 R 6 D 12

Electrical system

Alternator (W):	450
Battery (V/Ah):	12 / 50

Dimensions and weight

Track, front/rear (mm):	1316 / 1312
6.0 K x 15 / 7.0 K x 15:	1328 / 1352
Wheelbase (mm):	2300
Length x width x height (mm):	4090 x 1540 x 1065
Kerb weight DIN (kg):	740
Permissible gross weight (kg):	n/a
Fuel tank capacity (l):	110, no reserve
C_w x A (m²):	0.383 x 1.401 = 0.536
Power/weight ratio (kg/kW/ kg/hp):	6.49 / 4.77
with sports exhaust III:	5.61 / 4.11

Fuel consumption

DIN 70 030 (mpg):	29; 96 RON super leaded

Performance, production, prices

Acceleration 0-62mph/100kph (s):	5.5
with sports exhaust III:	5.4
Maximum speed (mph / kph):	156 / 252
with sports exhaust III:	164 / 263
Production, total number:	
904 Carrera GTS:	106
Purchase price:	
1964 Coupé:	DM 29,700

Porsche 911

The early Porsche 911 and Porsche 912

As early as the mid-1950s, Porsche began to consider which aspects of the 356 could be improved. In many areas these improvements exceeded the scope of mere model development, and their implementation would require designing a completely new vehicle. In the late 1950s these plans began their transformation into reality. The new Porsche would offer occupants more space, along with a boot designed to give sufficient space for a set of golf clubs. Performance was targeted at the level of the 356 Carrera 2, with 130hp (96kW), while matching the refinement of the 60hp (44kW) 356 'Normal'. The basic layout of an air-cooled rear-mounted engine was to be retained, as was the world-renowned Porsche shape, but customers were to be given somewhat more comfort. Ferdinand Alexander Porsche, eldest son of Ferry Porsche, was responsible for the design. During testing, Porsche even experimented with a four-seater (Type 745 T7); and the front of the car closely resembled the final form of the eventual new model. A fastback model remained the favoured solution, however, and they stayed with the 2+2 concept; in Ferry Porsche's view, the company did not need to compete with Mercedes-Benz, and one should stick to what one did best. Various engine design concepts were also tried for the new car.

Finally, the design designated Type 901 with an air-cooled six-cylinder boxer engine, was approved as the 356's successor.

The new Porsche 901 was first presented to the public at the IAA (International Automobile Exhibition) in Frankfurt am Main on 12 September 1963. The price was set at 23,900 Deutschmarks; this was about 9000DM more than the lowest-priced 356 model. After some initial reluctance, public reaction soon turned to enthusiasm. Before long, Porsche's road-testing department had 13 prototype 901s in operation; two of these were designated Type 902 (later renamed Type 912). In October 1964, Porsche displayed the 901 at the Paris Auto Show. Peugeot took note of the model designation, with its central '0', and invoked its power of veto, as it had trademarked all model designations with a '0' in the middle for the French

market. Porsche reacted quickly, and renamed the car the 911.

The first production 901, with chassis number 300.007, rolled off the assembly line on 14 September 1964. A total of 82 Type 901s were built before the type number was changed to 911 in production. The new Porsche was priced at 21,900DM, below the initial price target announced in 1963. At that time the 356 continued in production. Porsche production goes by model year; a model year generally begins on 1 August of the previous year, and ends on the following 31 July.

Model year 1965

The unit body structure of the Porsche 911 was made of sheet steel. Initially, the car was only available as a coupé and there was no sunroof option, but it retained the classic Porsche silhouette. For economical repairs, the front wings were now bolted to the body structure. Bumpers, painted in body colour, were supplemented by chromium-plated over-riders (as yet without rubber inserts). A chromium-plated trim strip was mounted below the doors. At the front, small chromium-plated grilles were mounted above the bumper and between the indicators and front edge of the bonnet. Chromium-plated wiper arms were parked on the right side. Window trim, headlamp bezels, and round wing mirrors were also chromium-plated. A matt-black painted border could be seen beneath the brightwork air inlet grille on the engine lid. Gold-coloured 'PORSCHE' script was attached below the grille, and the '911' emblem was mounted at an angle to its right. The windscreen was made of laminated safety glass. The spare tyre and 62-litre (13.5-gallon) fuel tank were located in the boot at the front.

The 911 power unit was a completely new design. The six-cylinder horizontally-opposed ('boxer') engine was conceived as a short-stroke unit, making the engine very rev happy. A bore of 80mm and stroke of 66mm gave a displacement of 1991cc. Cylinder spacing of 118mm was retained through all succeeding 911 engine generations. With a 9:1 compression ratio, the engine developed

130hp (96kW) at 6100rpm. Maximum torque of 174Nm (128lb ft) was reached at 4200rpm. In this classical boxer engine, each connecting rod was seated on its own crankpin. The forged crankshaft spun in eight journal bearings. Crankcase and cylinder heads were made of an aluminium alloy; the Biral cylinders consisted of a cast-iron liner surrounded by an aluminium alloy jacket and cooling fins. The overhead valves were inclined to the cylinder centreline. Each cylinder head contained a camshaft, driven by a double roller chain, which actuated one intake and one exhaust valve per cylinder through rocker arms. Cooling was accomplished by a vertical V-belt-driven blower mounted on the alternator shaft. Oil was supplied by a dry sump system with a separate oil tank. Carburation was by six Solex Type 40 PI overflow carburettors, fed by an electric fuel pump. Conventional battery ignition fired the cylinders in the order 1 - 6 - 2 - 4 - 3 - 5.

The 911 was delivered with a five-speed manual transmission. Transmission and differential were co-located in a single housing. Drive to the rear wheels was through Nadella-jointed halfshafts.

The 901's front wheels were independently suspended. Each wheel was located by a transverse link, combined with a hydraulic shock absorber which included a progressively acting hollow rubber bumper. Springing was by means of one adjustable, longitudinally-mounted torsion bar on each side. Rear wheels were located by semi-trailing arms. Each rear wheel was sprung by a transverse torsion bar. The rear telescopic shock absorbers also incorporated progressive hollow rubber bumpers. The hydraulic single-circuit brake system acted on four brake discs. Drums for the parking brake were integrated in the rear discs. Steel wheels, size 4.5J x 15, were painted silver, or optionally chromium-plated. Each wheel had ten slots for brake ventilation. Wheels were fastened to hubs by five wheelnuts on a 130mm bolt circle. Tyre size was 165 HR 15. Steering was by a ZF rack-and-pinion unit, with a double-jointed safety steering column. The original 911 wheelbase was 2211mm.

Initially, the 911 exhibited very unbalanced handling and was difficult to manage. As a result, even in the first model year, beginning with vehicle number 301340, heavy cast-iron weights were added in the corners of the front bumper. The resulting higher front axle loading made for noticeably improved handling.

Five round gauges were mounted in the instrument panel. The large tachometer had a dominant, central position, flanked to its left by the

An early Porsche 902. At the wheel: Thora Hornung, of the Porsche press department

combined oil temperature and pressure gauge, and at the far left the combined fuel level gauge with reserve indicator and oil level gauge. The speedometer was mounted to the right of the tach, and finally a clock to the far right. The top and bottom of the dashboard was padded. The dash fascia of exotic wood carried silver '911' script at the right, on the door of the lockable glove compartment. Integrated in the wood fascia was the ignition lock to the left of the steering column, a cigarette lighter, ashtray and radio faceplate at the centre. The four-spoke steering wheel included an exotic wood rim. Pockets were built into the inner door panels. The reclining seats were anatomically shaped. Rear seat-backs were individually foldable for added luggage space. The body included anchor points for seat belts. The passenger-side sun visor incorporated a make-up mirror. The windscreen washer system operated electrically, with three-speed wipers. The rear window was electrically-heatable. Other equipment included dual horns and a petrol-fired Webasto heater.

The first 911 boasted respectable performance figures: 0-62mph (100kph) in 9.1 seconds, and a top speed of 130mph (210kph).

The Porsche 912 was presented to the public in April 1965. This was powered by a 1.6 litre four-cylinder engine derived from the 356 SC, and was fitted with a slightly reduced level of trim and equipment. The reason for introducing a model below the 911 was that the 911 had become too expensive for many former customers. The 912 was priced more than 5500DM below the 911.

Body, suspension, brakes and wheels of the Porsche 912 were largely identical to those of the 911. In handling, the 912 was more forgiving than the 911, as the car was less tail-happy thanks to its lighter four-cylinder engine.

The 1.6 litre engine of the 912 was derived from the four-cylinder power unit of the 356 SC. Power was throttled from 95hp (70kW) to 90hp (66kW) at 5800rpm in order to tune the engine for more torque and greater durability. The pushrod engine employed pressure lubrication and a pair of twin-choke Solex PII-4 downdraught carburettors.

The 912 was offered with a four-speed manual transmission, but most buyers opted for the five-speed manual at additional cost. The 912, like the 911, was driven by the rear wheels.

Equipment and interior trim of the Porsche 912 were also somewhat simpler than those of the 911. For example, the 912 had only three round instruments as standard equipment: the large, central tachometer, speedometer on the right, combination instrument with fuel level and oil temperature on the left. Two additional instruments

were available as an option. On the first 912s, the instrument panel was painted in body colour as on the 356. Thereafter, the dashboard was trimmed with a metal fascia.

In acceleration, the 912 took all of 13.5 seconds to reach 62mph (100kph). A top speed of up to 115mph (185kph) was possible.

Model year 1966

At the Frankfurt International Automobile Exhibition in the autumn of 1965, Porsche presented a 'safety convertible', the 911 Targa, with a fixed roll bar, removable folding top and flexible, fold-down plastic rear window. This was Porsche's reaction to stricter safety requirements for open-top cars in the American market, and was a response to those who would ban convertibles entirely from American roads for reasons of rollover safety. The name 'Targa' was taken from the Italian, and not only means 'shield', but also recalls the Targa Florio, a Sicilian road race in which Porsche had always been very successful.

The 911 Coupé benefited from minor product development for the 1966 model year. Carburation was switched to Weber 40 IDA 3l and 3C1, which were easier to adjust than the Solex carburettors used in its first year. Simultaneously, a more powerful 490 watt alternator was installed, and modified brake callipers were fitted. Externally, the 1966 model could be recognized by its straight (as opposed to angled) '911' script.

The inside was marked by a new, leather-covered steering wheel as standard equipment, replacing the wood-rimmed wheel. The wooden dashboard trim was replaced by black leatherette.

Model year 1967

In the autumn of 1966, Porsche presented a revised, more powerful engine in the 911 S. In addition, the 911 Targa expanded the model line as a second body variation. Porsche offered the 912, 911 and 911 S in Coupé and Targa form.

The 911 Targa was a 'safety convertible', so named because of its rigidly-mounted stainless-steel roll bar. The centre section of the roof could be removed, folded and stowed in the luggage compartment. The flexible plastic rear window could be folded downwards. The Targa combined the safety of a coupé with the open-air motoring of a convertible, and could be driven in four different configurations: completely open, with open roof but closed rear window, with roof installed but open rear window, or completely closed.

Beginning with the 1967 model year, the inside rear view mirror of all models was cemented to the windscreen. The ashtray and glove compartment knobs were altered. An obvious external change was rubber inserts for the over-riders. Rubber inserts for the below-door side trim and bumper trim strips were modified. The 912 was given a five-speed manual transmission as standard equipment, since most customers had ordered this as an option in the previous model year.

The 911 S engine had a compression ratio of 9.8:1, and was fitted with forged-aluminium pistons, altered cam profiles, and bigger valves. These modifications raised power to 160hp (118kW) at 6600rpm, and torque to 179Nm (132lb ft) at 5200rpm. Redline was set at 7200rpm. The Weber carburettors were matched to the higher power output. The 911 S was fitted with a five-speed manual transmission. Four additional transmissions, with different gear packages, were available as options.

The suspension of the 911 S was optimized with anti-roll bars at both ends and Koni shock absorbers. It was the first Porsche to be fitted with front and rear ventilated brake discs. Also standard were 4.5J x 15 forged-aluminium wheels, made by Fuchs, and taking 165 VR 15 tyres.

The 911 S cockpit was equipped with a grippy leather-covered steering wheel and woven-texture dashboard trim.

The 911 S offered first-class performance, with 0-62mph (100kph) acceleration of 7.6 seconds and a top speed of 140mph (225kph), limited by aerodynamic drag.

Model year 1968 (A Series)

For 1968, Porsche again expanded the 911 model range. The 911 T (Touring) was offered as a new entry-level six-cylinder model. The normal 911 was now designated 911 L. All 911s could be ordered with the semi-automatic 'Sportomatic' transmission as an option. The Sportomatic was a 'manual' transmission fitted with a torque converter and clutch, but minus a clutch pedal. When the gear lever was moved to a different gear, a vacuum-operated servo actuated the clutch. For driving off from standstill, the torque converter provided the necessary slip.

The 911 T was equipped like the 912. On the 912 and 911 T, script on the engine lid was in silver, while the 911 S had gold script. For improved crash safety, the ashtray was given a rubber knob. A new generation of instruments was introduced: a simpler design with black-trim rings and white lettering. The 911 T and 912 had identical instrumentation with five round gauges, but without oil pressure and oil level indicators.

The 911 T engine represented the basic level of Porsche six-cylinder power. Developing 110hp (81kW), the boxer engine was fitted with cast-iron cylinder barrels and achieved its rated power at 5800rpm. Compression was reduced to 8.6:1. Porsche's most basic six-cylinder achieved its maximum torque of 157Nm (116lb ft) at 4200rpm. Mixture was supplied by a pair of Weber triple-choke carburettors.

All 911 models, with the exception of the 911 T, were fitted with a five-speed manual transmission as standard equipment. The 912 reverted to a four-speed shared with the 911 T.

The windscreen wipers now parked on the left side, so that the area immediately in front of the driver could be cleared more quickly. The wiper arms were given a matt-black finish to eliminate reflections. External door-handle buttons were recessed. The modified exterior door handles had ridges above and below the lock cylinder pushbutton; these were intended to prevent the button from being actuated, thereby opening the door, in a rollover accident. The body was fitted with anchor points for rear seat-belts. Targa models could be ordered with an optional, permanently-fitted, heated safety-glass rear window.

Except for the 911 S Coupé, all 911 and 912 models were equipped with Boge shock absorbers; the 911 S Coupé continued to use Koni shock absorbers. All 911 models were given a dual-circuit brake system. For improved handling, wider wheels were fitted – 5.5J x 15. The 911 L was given an 11mm front anti-roll bar, while the 911 S had 15mm anti-roll bars at both ends. The 911 L was equipped with the ventilated discs of the 911 S.

The 911 T was the slowest accelerating 911, taking ten seconds to reach 62mph (100kph). Its top speed was exactly 124mph (200kph). Vehicles equipped with the Sportomatic transmission generally gave up 3mph (5kph) in top speed.

Model year 1969 (B Series)

For 1969, the 912 entered its last year of production, and the 911 its last year powered by the 2-litre engine.

Engines for the 911 E (which replaced the 911 L

in the model line-up) and the 911 S were now fitted with a mechanical twin-row Bosch fuel injection pump. This change increased engine output by 10hp (7kW). At 6500rpm, drivers of the 911 E could call on 140hp (103kW). The boxer engine of the 911 S developed 170hp (125kW) at 6800rpm; with 85hp per litre, this represented the highest specific output of all (including all future) air-cooled production normally-aspirated engines. Maximum torque of 182Nm (134lb ft) was available at a sporty high engine speed of 5500rpm, and the engine could be revved to 7200rpm. Of the six-cylinder engines, only the 911 T retained the two Weber triple-choke downdraught carburettors. All injected engines were fitted with capacitive-discharge ignition systems. Clutch pressure was increased in the 911 S.

The wheelbase of the 911 and 912 models was increased by 57mm, from 2211mm to 2268mm. The 911 E and 911 S were fitted with 6J x 15 alloy wheels, carrying 185/70 VR 15 tyres, as standard equipment. The 911 T and 911 E models, when equipped with the Sportomatic transmission, were also available with more comfort-oriented 185 HR 14 tyres on 5.5 J x 14 rims. Because the maximum speed of these Sportomatic vehicles was less than 130mph (210kph), they could use H-rated tyres. The

911 E was equipped with front hydropneumatic struts as standard equipment; these were self-levelling and further improved ride comfort. Hydropneumatic struts were available as an option on the 911 T and 911 S Coupé models. Both front brake effective disc diameter and brake pad area were increased.

The wings of all 911 and 912 models were flared to provide space for new six-inch wheels. Front indicators were enlarged, and horn grilles accordingly reduced in size. The Targa was now only available with the rigidly-attached, heated safety-glass rear window. The stainless-steel Targa roll bar was given vent slots on both sides. For improved handling, the erstwhile single 45 amp-hour battery was replaced by two smaller batteries, each rated at 36Ah. The batteries were mounted in corners at the left and right sides of the luggage compartment, ahead of the front wheels. Thanks to the resulting improved front-end weight distribution, the cast-iron weights could now be deleted from the corners of the front bumper.

Many interior details were improved as well. The new steering wheel was smaller in diameter, and fitted with a padded horn button. The inside rear view mirror had a day/night adjustment. The ashtray flipped downward from the lower dashboard padding. Interior door panels were fitted with a

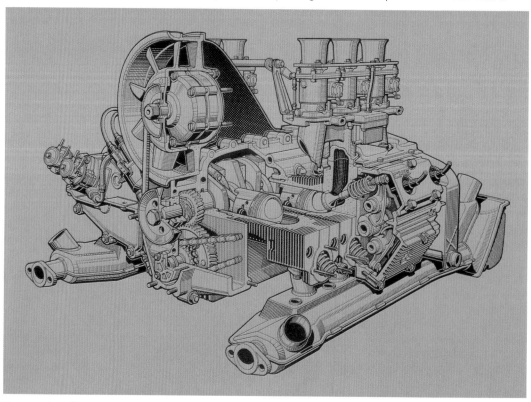

Cutaway view of a Porsche 911 2-litre carburated engine

door release integrated in the armrest, and larger storage compartments. Front seat latches were also improved.

Performance of vehicles equipped with fuel-injected engines was comparable to that of the earlier carburated models.

Model year 1970 (C Series)

The year 1970 marked the first model year in which 911 engine displacement was increased for improved performance. The 912 was deleted from the model line-up.

By increasing cylinder bore to 84mm, displacement of all 911 engines was enlarged to 2.2 litres. To save weight, crankcases were of cast magnesium. Crankshafts were of forged steel, pistons of aluminium-alloy cast in permanent moulds, except for the 911 S which had forged pistons. The 911 E and 911 S engines were fitted with Biral cylinders. Cylinder heads were given larger valves: 46mm intakes and 40mm exhausts. All engines were equipped with a Bosch breakerless high-tension capacitive-discharge ignition system. The 911 T engine was fitted with two triple-choke downdraught carburettors, while fuel for the E and S power units was metered by a Bosch two-row mechanical injection pump. The T engine, with 8.6:1 compression, developed 125hp (92kW) at 5800rpm; maximum torque of 176Nm (130lb ft) was available at 4200rpm. With 9.1:1 compression, the fuel-injected 911 E produced 155hp (114kW) at 6200rpm, and 191Nm (141lb ft) at 4500rpm. The top-of-the-range 911 S mobilized all of 180hp (132kW) at 6500rpm. With a compression ratio of 9.8:1, this sports-oriented engine had the highest compression of the Porsche range, and also the highest output torque – 199Nm (147lb ft) at a lofty 5200rpm.

All models were given a 225mm diameter clutch. The 911 T had a four-speed manual transmission as standard equipment, while the 911 E and 911 S had five-speeds. The four-speed Sportomatic was only available as an option on the 911 T and 911 E.

The entire floorpan of the 911 was made of galvanized steel. All vehicles were protected by sprayed-on PVC undercoating. On the 911 E and 911 S, engine lid and tail centre section were made of aluminium for weight-saving. New 'pistol grip' exterior door handles were fitted, actuated by a lever on their inner surfaces.

The 911 T was now also fitted with ventilated brake discs. The 911 E continued to use front hydropneumatic struts as standard equipment.

Instruments were now installed from the interior side, and held in place by a rubber ring. Interior ventilation was by means of a forced-air system, combined with a three-stage blower. The interior used 'Skai'-pattern leatherette. A two-stage heated windscreen was available as an option. The 911 S was also fitted with a petrol-electric auxiliary heater as standard equipment.

The 911 T could reach exactly 124mph (200kph). The 62mph (100 kph) mark was achieved in 9.5 seconds. At 134mph (215kph), the 911 E was slightly faster, and took only 9.0 seconds to reach 62mph. The 911 S accelerated to 62mph in just 7.0 seconds; available power and aerodynamic drag reached stalemate at 140 mph (225kph).

Model year 1971 (D Series)

The 911 line-up underwent only minor modifications for the 1971 model year. The 911 S was given over-riders with rubber inlays, and its petrol-electric auxiliary heater was dropped; it was engine-heated like the other 911 models.

Instead of two wiper speeds and an interval setting, the wiper system now had three speed ranges.

More stringent exhaust emissions standards in various export destinations resulted in changes to the fuel-injection system. Pressure sensor, ignition distributor, throttle body, and control unit were modified accordingly.

Compared to the previous year, all 911 models added about 3mph (5kph) to their top speed, but were slightly slower in acceleration.

Model year 1972 (E Series)

More stringent exhaust emissions rules in the United States demanded the generation of a new engine. In several export markets, high-octane fuel with a high level of tetraethyl lead was no longer available. To enable the use of regular-grade petrol, Porsche lowered the compression ratio for the new 2.4-litre engine series. Nevertheless, Porsche's engineers were able to raise engine power, acceleration and performance levels. A newly-designed crankshaft with a 70.4mm stroke resulted in a displacement of 2341cc. The crankshaft had one counterweight per cylinder. Fitted with new Solex-Zenith carburettors, the 911 T developed 130hp (96kW) at 5600rpm, the same output as the original 911 of 1964. Yet with 196Nm (145lb ft) of torque at 4000rpm, this engine provided considerably better acceleration across the rev range. The other boxer engines were fitted with mechanical fuel injection. The 911 E engine developed 165hp (121kW) at 6200rpm and 206Nm (152lb ft) at 4500rpm. The most powerful engine in the line-up was the 911 S, with 190hp (140kW) at 6500rpm. Its torque curve peaked at 5200rpm, with 216Nm (159lb ft).

Also new for 1972 was the Type 915 manual transmission generation, designed to cope with the higher torque of the 2.4-litre engines. The gear change pattern was altered; putting first and second gear in a single plane, with first to the left and forward. This new arrangement had advantages when racing and rallying in situations where tight curves required changing down to first. All 911 models were fitted with a four-speed manual transmission as standard equipment. A five-speed manual and four-speed Sportomatic were available as options.

One obvious feature of the 1972 models was an external filler lid for the oil tank, on the right rear wing. For better weight distribution, the oil tank was relocated ahead of the rear axle. The 911 S was fitted with a plastic front valance shaped to act as a spoiler. This resulted in reduced front-end lift at high speeds. The front over-riders were deleted, but bright trim strips were added to the sills of the 911 S. The air-inlet grille on the engine lid was now black, with chromium '2.4' script on the right side. Script on the rear lid was black anodized. For the 911 T and 911 E models, the front spoiler was available as an option.

The wheelbase of all 911 models was increased by 3mm to 2271mm. Front hydropneumatic struts were deleted from the 911 E, but remained available for all 911 models as an option. All vehicles were fitted with somewhat softer Boge shock absorbers. While the 911 T and 911 E had to make do without anti-roll bars, the 911 S was fitted with 15mm bars front and rear.

Instead of forged-aluminium wheels, the 911 E was fitted with painted 6J x 15 steel wheels. The alloy wheels remained available as an option.

Interior door panels and dashboard insert of all 911s were in the same colour as the rest of the interior. Interior equipment of the 911 E matched that of the 911 T.

With a top speed of 127mph (205kph), the entry level 911 now topped the 124mph (200kph) barrier. In acceleration, with a 0-62mph (100kph) time of 9.5 seconds, it was well inside the 10-second mark. The 911 E sprinted to 62mph in only 7.9 seconds, with a top speed of 137mph (220kph), while the top-of-the-range 911 S took just 7.0 seconds to reach 62mph from standstill. Its top speed was a respectable 143mph (230kph).

Model year 1973 (F Series)

With the 911 Carrera RS, a new star was born. It marked the first appearance of the legendary Carrera name in the 911 model line. The suffix 'RS' stood for 'Rennsport' – racing sports. This 911 was not only the ultimate sports machine, but in many respects also represented the watershed between the early 911 and the so-called 'G Series' introduced in the autumn of 1973. A total of 1580 of the Carrera RS were built. Originally, 'optimistic' estimates called for only 500 examples to meet minimum homologation requirements for the GT sports car racing class, but as it turned out Porsche's own marketing planners' estimates were wide of the mark.

In keeping with its racing aspirations, the body of the 911 Carrera RS consistently employed lightweight design elements. Thin-gauge sheetmetal was employed wherever structurally feasible. The windscreen and rear quarterlights were of thin glass made by Belgian supplier Glaverbel. Rear glass and door windows were supplied by Sekurit. The most obvious body feature was the plastic engine lid with its integral rear spoiler, soon dubbed 'ducktail' by fans and the press. The purpose of this aerodynamic aid was to reduce aerodynamic lift over the rear axle. With the aid of this and the plastic front spoiler, the Carrera RS was more stable at speed, achieved higher cornering speeds, and even reached about 3mph (5kph) higher top speed. To provide room for wider rims, the rear wings were widened by 21mm. The Carrera RS was offered in a sports and a touring version. The sports version was even lighter; its rear bumper was made of plastic, and deco trim consisted of tape appliqués. The touring version had a steel rear bumper, rubber trim strips and bright aluminium sill trim. Another visual hallmark was unique 'Carrera' script applied to the sides. This script was in black for all body colours except Grand Prix White, in which the script could be ordered in red, blue or green.

Matching the Carrera script were the wheels. For cars with black Carrera script, the wheel centres were black with polished rims. For red, blue, or green script, the wheel centres were painted in the same colour, with the rims in matt-aluminium finish. For the first time on any production vehicle, front and rear axles carried different wheel widths. The front carried forged Fuchs alloys in the familiar 6 J x 15 size with 185/70 VR 15 tyres, and at the rear were 7 J x 15 wheels with 215/60 VR 15 tyres. This significantly increased maximum lateral acceleration. The suspension was tuned with Bilstein shock absorbers and anti-roll bars.

The Carrera RS was lighter and about 20hp more powerful than the 911 S. New Nikasil-coated aluminium cylinders increased the bore to 90mm, and the displacement to 2687cc. Crankshaft, connecting rods, compression ratio and valve timing were the same as the 911 S. Like the S, the Carrera RS engine ran happily on regular-grade petrol. Maximum output of 210hp (154kW) was available at 6300rpm. Thanks to the increase in the displacement, maximum torque rose to 255Nm (188lb ft) at 5100rpm.

The five-speed transmission was modified especially for the Carrera RS: fourth and fifth gears were slightly higher. For cooling, most Carrera RSs were fitted with a transmission oil cooler. The gear lever was also modified for quicker changes.

While the touring version drew heavily on the interior equipment of the 911 S, the sports version was remarkably spartan. Driver and passenger sat in adjustable racing bucket seats. Inner door panels were extremely simple, with only a window winder, a door release strap and door handle. Rear seats and trim were deleted entirely. Even the clock and glove compartment door were sacrificed on the altar of weight reduction.

By early 1970s standards, the lightweight Carrera RS offered breathtaking acceleration. The 62mph (100kph) mark was reached in only 5.8 seconds,

performance that could leave any of the much more expensive and powerful Italian exotics in its dust in this classic performance test. The Carrera RS's maximum speed was 152mph (245kph).

Development continued for the other 911 models as well. For all 911s, the small front horn grilles, indicator surrounds, and rear light units were made of black plastic. On the 2.4-litre model, wing mirrors were no longer round but rather rectangular. The oil tank was again relocated to its former position behind the rear axle, and the outside oil filler lid was eliminated, because pump attendants often confused this with the fuel tank filler and filled the oil tank with petrol. An 85-litre (18.5-gallon) plastic fuel tank and space-saver spare wheel were standard equipment on the 911 E, 911 S and Carrera RS. For the 911 T, this fuel tank was available as an option. Porsche took another step towards the 'long term car' with the fitting of stainless-steel silencers.

The 911 E was equipped with cast-alloy, silver-painted 6J x 15 wheels made by ATS. For the 911 T, these were available as an option.

In the United States, the 911 T was delivered with a 140hp (103kW) 2.4-litre engine fitted with a Bosch K-Jetronic fuel-injection system.

Through the 1973 model year, Porsche produced a total of 80,100 examples of the early 911 series.

901 Coupé 1964

Engine
Engine design:	6-cylinder horizontally-opposed
Installation:	Rear-engine
Cooling system:	Air-cooled
Number & form of blower blades:	11, straight
Blower outside diameter (mm):	245
Engine type:	901/01
Displacement (cc):	1991
Bore x stroke (mm):	80 x 66
Engine output DIN (kW/hp):	96/130 at 6100rpm
Maximum torque (Nm/lb ft):	174/128 at 4200rpm
Output per litre (kW/l / hp/l):	48.2 / 65.3
Compression ratio:	9.0 : 1
Valve operation & camshaft drive:	ohc, cams driven by double chain, 2 valves per cylinder
Carburation:	Solex overflow carburettors 40 PI
Ignition system:	Battery coil ignition
Firing order:	1 - 6 - 2 - 4 - 3 - 5
Engine lubrication:	Dry sump
Engine oil total (l):	9.0

Transmission
Drive configuration:	Rear-axle drive
Manual gearbox:	5-speed
Transmission type:	901/0
Transmission ratios:	
1st gear:	2.833
2nd gear:	1.778
3rd gear:	1.217
4th gear:	0.962
5th gear:	0.821
Reverse gear:	3.127
Drive ratio:	4.428

Body, chassis, suspension, brakes, wheels
Body design:	Steel coupé body, 2 doors, 2 + 2 seats, welded assembly, sheet metal box-section, unitized with body, bumpers fixed close to body, chromium-plated horn grilles near indicators, engine lid with chromium grille, round, chromium wing mirror
Suspension, front:	Independent suspension with wishbones and McPherson struts, one round, longitudinal torsion bar per wheel, hydraulic double-action shock absorbers
Suspension, rear:	Independent suspension with semi-trailing arms, one round, transverse torsion bar per wheel, hydraulic double-action shock absorbers
Brakes, front/rear (Size (mm)):	Discs (282 x 12.7) / Discs (285 x 10) 2-piston fixed cast-iron callipers / 2-piston fixed cast-iron callipers
Wheels, front/rear:	4.5 J x 15 / 4.5 J x 15
Tyres, front/rear:	165-15 radial / 165-15 radial

Electrical system
Alternator (W/A):	490 / 30
Battery (V/Ah):	12 / 45

Dimensions and weight
Track, front/rear (mm):	1337 / 1317
Wheelbase (mm):	2211
Length x width x height (mm):	4163 x 1610 x 1320
Kerb weight DIN (kg):	1080
Permissible gross weight (kg):	1400
Luggage compartment (l):	200
Luggage volume interior (l)*:	250
Fuel tank capacity (l):	62, including 6 reserve
C_w x A (m²):	0.363 x 1.685 = 0.612
Power/weight ratio (kg/kW / kg/hp):	11.25 / 8.30
*on folded-down rear seat-backs	

Fuel consumption
DIN 70 030 (mpg):	29.5; 98 RON super leaded

Performance, production, prices
Acceleration 0-62mph/100kph (s):	9.1
Maximum speed (mph / kph):	130 / 210
Production, total number:	82
Purchase price:	DM 21,900

911 Coupé
MY 1965–MY 1967

Engine

Engine design:	6-cylinder horizontally-opposed
Installation:	Rear-engine
Cooling system:	Air-cooled
Number & form of blower blades:	11, straight
Blower outside diameter (mm):	245
Engine type:	901/01
February - October 1966:	901/05
November 1966 - MY 1967:	901/06
Displacement (cc):	1991
Bore x stroke (mm):	80 x 66
Engine output DIN (kW/hp):	96/130 at 6100rpm
Maximum torque (Nm/lb ft):	174/128 at 4200rpm
Output per litre (kW/l / hp/l):	48.2 / 65.3
Compression ratio:	9.0 : 1
Valve operation & camshaft drive:	ohc, cams driven by double chain, 2 valves per cylinder
Carburation:	Solex overflow carburettors 40 PI
February 1966 - MY 1967:	Weber carburettor 40 IDA 3L or 3C1
Ignition system:	Battery coil ignition
Firing order:	1 - 6 - 2 - 4 - 3 - 5
Engine lubrication:	Dry sump
Engine oil total (l):	9.0

Transmission

Drive configuration:	Rear-axle drive
Manual gearbox:	5-speed
Transmission type:	901/0 (901/02)*
Transmission ratios:	
1st gear:	2.833 (3.091)*
2nd gear:	1.778 (1.889)*
3rd gear:	1.217 (1.318)*
4th gear:	0.962 (1.004)*
5th gear:	0.821 (0.793)*
Reverse gear:	3.127 (3.127)*
Drive ratio:	4.428 (4.428)*
Option:	Limited-slip differential
*MY 1966 - MY 1967	

Body, chassis, suspension, brakes, wheels

Body design:	Steel coupé body, 2 doors, 2 + 2 seats, welded assembly, sheet metal box-section, unitized with body, bumpers fixed close to body, chromium-plated horn grilles near indicators, engine lid with chromium grille, round, chromium wing mirror
Option:	Electric sunroof
Suspension, front:	Independent suspension with wishbones and McPherson struts, one round, longitudinal torsion bar per wheel, hydraulic double-action shock absorbers
Option:	Anti-roll bar
Suspension, rear:	Independent suspension with semi-trailing arms, one round, transverse torsion bar per wheel, hydraulic double-action shock absorbers
Option:	Anti-roll bar
Brakes, front/rear (Size (mm)):	Discs (282 x 12.7) / Discs (285 x 10) 2-piston fixed cast-iron callipers / 2-piston fixed cast-iron callipers
Wheels, front/rear:	4.5 J x 15 / 4.5 J x 15
Tyres, front/rear:	165-15 radial / 165-15 radial

Electrical system

Alternator (W/A):	490 / 30
Battery (V/Ah):	12 / 45

Dimensions and weight

Track, front/rear (mm):	1337 / 1317
MY 1967:	1353 / 1321
Wheelbase (mm):	2211
Length x width x height (mm):	4163 x 1610 x 1320
Kerb weight DIN (kg):	1080
Permissible gross weight (kg):	1400
Luggage compartment (l):	200
Luggage volume interior (l)*:	250
Fuel tank capacity (l):	62, including 6 reserve
C_w x A (m²):	0.363 x 1.685 = 0.612
Power/weight ratio (kg/kW/kg/hp):	11.25 / 8.30
*on folded-down rear seat-backs	

Fuel consumption

DIN 70 030 (mpg):	29.5; 98 RON super leaded

Performance, production, prices

Acceleration 0-62mph/100kph (s):	9.1
Maximum speed (mph / kph):	130 / 210
Production, total number:	6,607
Purchase prices:	
04/1965:	DM 21,900
08/1965:	DM 22,900
07/1966:	DM 20,980
10/1966:	DM 20,980

912 Coupé
April 1965–MY 1969
912 Targa
MJ 1967–MY 1969

Motor

Engine design:	4-cylinder horizontally-opposed
Installation:	Rear-engine
Cooling system:	Air-cooled
Engine type:	616/36
Displacement (cc):	1582
Bore x stroke (mm):	82.5 x 74
Engine output DIN (kW/hp):	66/90 at 5800rpm
Maximum torque (Nm/lb ft):	122/90 at 3500rpm
Output per litre (kW/l / hp/l):	41.7 / 56.9
Compression ratio:	9.3 : 1
Valve operation & camshaft drive:	ohv, driven by gears, 2 valves per cylinder
Carburation:	2 twin-choke downdraught carburettors Solex 40 PII-4
Ignition system:	Battery coil ignition
Firing order:	1 - 4 - 3 - 2
Engine lubrication:	Full-pressure oil lubrication
Engine oil total (l):	4.0

Transmission

Drive configuration:	Rear-axle drive
Manual gearbox:	4-speed (5-speed)*
Transmission type:	616/36 (902/1)
Transmission ratios:	
1st gear:	3.091 (3.091)
2nd gear:	1.684 (1.889)
3rd gear:	1.125 (1.318)
4th gear:	0.857 (1.040)
5th gear:	(0.857)
Reverse gear:	3.127 (3.127)
Drive ratio:	4.429 (4.429)
Option:	Limited-slip differential

*Option, only MY 1966 and MY 1967 standard

Body, chassis, suspension, brakes, wheels

Body design:	Steel body, 2 doors, 2 + 2 seats, welded assembly, sheet metal box-section, unitized with body, bumpers fixed close to body, chromium-plated horn grilles near indicators, engine lid with chromium grille, round, chromium wing mirror
Coupé:	Fixed steel roof
Option:	Electric sunroof
Targa:	Removable, foldable Targa top, fixed stainless-steel Targa roll bar, turn-down flexible plastic rear window
Option MY 1968, MY 1969 stand.:	Fixed glass rear window
Suspension, front:	Independent suspension with wishbones and McPherson struts, one round, longitudinal torsion bar per wheel, hydraulic double-action shock absorbers
Suspension, rear:	Independent suspension with semi-trailing arms, one round, transverse torsion bar per wheel, hydraulic double-action shock absorbers
Brakes, front/rear (Size (mm)):	Discs (282 x 12.7) / Discs (285 x 10) 2-piston fixed cast-iron callipers / 2-piston fixed cast-iron callipers
Wheels, front/rear:	4.5 J x 15 / 4.5 J x 15
MY 1968 - MY 1969:	5.5 J x 15 / 5.5 J x 15
Tyres, front/rear:	6.95 H 15 / 6.95 H 15
Option:	165 HR 15 / 165 HR 15

Electrical system

Alternator (W/A):	300
MY 1968 - MY 1969:	420
Battery (V/Ah):	12 / 45

Dimensions and weight

Track, front/rear (mm):	1337 / 1317
MY 1967:	1353 / 1321
MY 1968:	1367 / 1335
MY 1969:	1362 / 1343
Wheelbase (mm):	2211
MY 1969:	2268

Length x width x height (mm):	4163 x 1610 x 1320
Kerb weight DIN (kg):	970
MY 1969:	950
Permissible gross weight (kg):	1290
MY 1969:	1300
Luggage compartment (l):	200
Luggage volume interior (l)*:	250
Fuel tank capacity (l):	62, including 6 reserve
C_w x A (m²):	0.363 x 1.685 = 0.612
MY 1968:	0.38 x 1.685 = 0.640
MY 1969:	0.408 x 1.71 = 0.697
Power/weight ratio (kg/kW / kg/hp):	14.69 / 10.77
MY 1969:	14.39 / 10.55

*on folded-down rear seat-backs

Fuel consumption

DIN 70 030 (mpg):	32.5; 96 RON super leaded

Performance, production, prices

Acceleration 0-62mph/100kph (s):	13.5
Maximum speed (mph / kph):	115 / 185
Production, total number:	
Coupé:	28,333
Targa:	2,562
Purchase prices:	
04/1965 Coupé:	DM 16,250
08/1965 Coupé:	DM 17,590
07/1966 Coupé:	DM 17,590
Targa:	DM 18,990
10/1966 Coupé:	DM 17,590
Targa:	DM 18,990
09/1967 Coupé:	DM 16,980
Targa:	DM 18,380
03/1968 Coupé:	DM 16,995
Targa:	DM 18,425
07/1968 Coupé:	DM 17,150
Targa:	DM 18,593
10/1968 Coupé:	DM 17,538
Targa:	DM 19,314

911 Targa MY 1967

Engine

Engine design:	6-cylinder horizontally-opposed
Installation:	Rear-engine
Cooling system:	Air-cooled
Number & form of blower blades:	11, straight
Blower outside diameter (mm):	245
Engine type:	901/06
Displacement (cc):	1991
Bore x stroke (mm):	80 x 66
Engine output DIN (kW/hp):	96/130 at 6100rpm
Maximum torque (Nm/lb ft):	174/128 at 4200rpm
Output per litre (kW/l / hp/l):	48.2 / 65.3
Compression ratio:	9.0 : 1
Valve operation & camshaft drive:	ohc, cams driven by double chain, 2 valves per cylinder
Carburation:	Weber carburettors 40 IDA 3L and 3C1
Ignition system:	Battery coil ignition
Firing order:	1 - 6 - 2 - 4 - 3 - 5
Engine lubrication:	Dry sump
Engine oil total (l):	9.0

Transmission

Drive configuration:	Rear-axle drive
Manual gearbox:	5-speed
Transmission type:	901/02
Transmission ratios:	
1st gear:	3.091
2nd gear:	1.889
3rd gear:	1.318
4th gear:	1.004
5th gear:	0.793
Reverse gear:	3.127
Drive ratio:	4.428
Option:	Limited-slip differential

Body, chassis, suspension, brakes, wheels

Body design:	Steel Targa body, 2 doors, 2 + 2 seats, welded assembly, sheet metal box-section, unitized with body, bumpers close to body, chromium-plated horn grilles near indicators, engine lid with chromium grille, round, chromium wing mirror, removable, foldable Targa top, fixed stainless-steel Targa roll bar, turn-down flexible plastic rear window

Suspension, front:	Independent suspension with wishbones and McPherson struts, one round, longitudinal torsion bar per wheel, hydraulic double-action shock absorbers
Option:	Anti-roll bar
Suspension, rear:	Independent suspension with semi-trailing arms, one round, transverse torsion bar per wheel, hydraulic double-action shock absorbers
Option:	Anti-roll bar
Brakes, front/rear (Size (mm)):	Discs (282 x 12.7) / Discs (285 x 10) 2-piston fixed cast-iron callipers / 2-piston fixed cast-iron callipers
Wheels, front/rear:	4.5 J x 15 / 4.5 J x 15
Tyres, front/rear:	165-15 radial / 165-15 radial

Electrical system

Alternator (W/A):	490 / 30
Battery (V/Ah):	12 / 45

Dimensions and weight

Track, front/rear (mm):	1353 / 1321
Wheelbase (mm):	2211
Length x width x height (mm):	4163 x 1610 x 1320
Kerb weight DIN (kg):	1080
Permissible gross weight (kg):	1400
Luggage compartment (l):	200
Luggage volume interior (l)*:	250
Fuel tank capacity (l):	62, including 6 reserve
C_w x A (m^2):	0.363 x 1.685 = 0.612
Power/weight ratio (kg/kW/kg/hp):	11.25 / 8.30
*on folded-down rear seat-backs	

Fuel consumption

DIN 70 030 (mpg):	29.5; 98 RON super leaded

Performance, production, prices

Acceleration 0-62mph/100kph (s):	9.1
Maximum speed (mph / kph):	130 / 210
Production, total number:	236
Purchase prices:	
07/1966:	DM 22,380
10/1966:	DM 22,380

911 S Coupé [Sportomatic]
911 S Targa [Sportomatic]
MY 1967–MY 1968

Engine
Engine design:	6-cylinder horizontally-opposed
Installation:	Rear-engine
Cooling system:	Air-cooled
Number & form of blower blades:	11, straight
Blower outside diameter (mm):	245
Engine type:	901/02 [901/08]
Displacement (cc):	1991
Bore x stroke (mm):	80 x 66
Engine output DIN (kW/hp):	118/160 at 6600rpm
Maximum torque (Nm/lb ft):	179/132 at 5200rpm
Output per litre (kW/l / hp/l):	59.3 / 80.4
Compression ratio:	9.8 : 1
Valve operation & camshaft drive:	ohc, cams driven by double chain, 2 valves per cylinder
Carburation:	Weber carburettors 40 IDS
Ignition system:	Battery coil ignition
Firing order:	1 - 6 - 2 - 4 - 3 - 5
Engine lubrication:	Dry sump
Engine oil total (l):	9.0 [11.5]

Transmission
Drive configuration:	Rear-axle drive
Manual gearbox:	5-speed
Option Sportomatic MY 1968:	[4-speed]
Transmission type:	901/03 [905/01]
Transmission ratios:	
1st gear:	3.091 [2.400]
2nd gear:	1.889 [1.631]
3rd gear:	1.318 [1.217]
4th gear:	1.004 [0.926]
5th gear:	0.793
Reverse gear:	3.127 [3.127]
Drive ratio:	4.428 [3.857]
Option:	Limited-slip differential

Body, chassis, suspension, brakes, wheels
Body design:	Steel body, 2 doors, 2 + 2 seats, welded assembly, sheet metal box-section, unitized with body, bumpers close to body, chromium-plated horn grilles near indicators, engine lid with chromium grille, round, chromium wing mirror
Coupé:	Fixed steel roof
Option:	Electric sunroof
Targa:	Removable, foldable Targa top, fixed stainless-steel Targa roll bar, turn-down flexible plastic rear window
Option MY 1968:	Fixed glass rear window
Suspension, front:	Independent suspension with wishbones and
Suspension, rear:	McPherson struts, one round, longitudinal torsion bar per wheel, hydraulic double-action shock absorbers, anti-roll bar Independent suspension with semi-trailing arms, one round, transverse torsion bar per wheel, hydraulic double-action shock absorbers, anti-roll bar
Brakes, front/rear (Size (mm)):	Ventilated discs (282 x 20) / Ventilated discs (285 x 20) 2-piston fixed cast-iron callipers / 2-piston fixed cast-iron callipers
Wheels, front/rear:	4.5 J x 15 / 4.5 J x 15
Tyres, front/rear:	165-15 radial / 165-15 radial
MY 1968:	5.5 J x 15 / 5.5 J x 15
	165 VR 15 / 165 VR 15

Electrical system
Alternator (W/A):	490 / 30
Battery (V/Ah):	12 / 45

Dimensions and weight
Track, front/rear (mm):	1353 / 1325.4
MY 1968:	1367 / 1339
Wheelbase (mm):	2211
Length x width x height (mm):	4163 x 1610 x 1320
Kerb weight DIN (kg):	1030
Permissible gross weight (kg):	1400
Luggage compartment (l):	200
Luggage volume interior (l)*:	250
Fuel tank capacity (l):	62, including 6 reserve
C_w x A (m²):	0.363 x 1.685 = 0.612
MY 1968:	0.38 x 1.685 = 0.640
Power/weight ratio (kg/kW/ kg/hp):	8.72/ 6.43
*on folded-down rear seat-backs	

Fuel consumption
DIN 70 030 (mpg):	27.5; 96 RON super leaded

Performance, production, prices
Acceleration 0-62mph/100kph (s):	7.6 [7.6]
Maximum speed (mph / kph):	139.5 / 225 [136.5 / 220]
Production, total number:	
Coupé:	3,573
Targa:	925
Purchase prices:	
07/1966 Coupé:	DM 24.480
Targa:	DM 25.880
10/1966 Coupé:	DM 24.480
Targa:	DM 25.880
09/1967 Coupé:	DM 24.480 [DM 25,470]
Targa:	DM 25.880 [DM 26,870]
03/1968 Coupé:	DM 24.970 [DM 25,960]
Targa:	DM 26.400 [DM 27,390]

911 T Coupé [Sportomatic]
911 T Targa [Sportomatic] MJ 1968

Engine

Engine design:	6-cylinder horizontally-opposed
Installation:	Rear-engine
Cooling system:	Air-cooled
Number & form of blower blades:	11, straight
Blower outside diameter (mm):	245
Engine type:	901/03 [901/13]
Displacement (cc):	1991
Bore x stroke (mm):	80 x 66
Engine output DIN (kW/hp):	81/110 at 5800rpm
Maximum torque (Nm/lb ft):	157/116 at 4200rpm
Output per litre (kW/l / hp/l):	40.7 / 55.2
Compression ratio:	8.6 : 1
Valve operation & camshaft drive:	ohc, cams driven by double chain, 2 valves per cylinder
Carburation:	Weber carburettors 40 IDT P
Ignition system:	Battery coil ignition
Firing order:	1 - 6 - 2 - 4 - 3 - 5
Engine lubrication:	Dry sump
Engine oil total (l):	9.0 [11.5]

Transmission

Drive configuration:	Rear-axle drive
Manual gearbox:	4-speed (5-speed)*
Option Sportomatic:	[4-speed]
Transmission type:	901/10 (901/03) [905/01]
Transmission ratios:	
1st gear:	3.091 (3.091) [2.400]
2nd gear:	1.631 (1.889) [1.613]
3rd gear:	1.040 (1.318) [1.217]
4th gear:	0.793 (1.004) [0.926]
5th gear:	(0.793)
Reverse gear:	3.127 (3.127) [3.127]
Drive ratio:	4.428 (4.428) [3.857]
Option:	Limited-slip differential
*Option	

Body, chassis, suspension, brakes, wheels

Body design:	Steel body, 2 doors, 2 + 2 seats, welded assembly, sheet metal box-section, unitized with body, bumpers fixed close to body, chromium-plated horn grilles near indicators, engine lid with chromium grille, round, chromium wing mirror
Coupé:	Fixed steel roof
Option:	Electric sunroof
Targa:	Removable, foldable Targa top, fixed stainless-steel Targa roll bar, turn down flexible plastic rear window

Option MY 1968:	Fixed glass rear window
Suspension, front:	Independent suspension with wishbones and McPherson struts, one round, longitudinal torsion bar per wheel, hydraulic double-action shock absorbers
Option:	Anti-roll bar
Suspension, rear:	Independent suspension with semi-trailing arms, one round, transverse torsion bar per wheel, hydraulic double-action shock absorbers
Option:	Anti-roll bar
Brakes, front/rear (Size (mm)):	Discs (282 x 12.7) / Discs (285 x 10)
Sportomatic:	[Ventilated discs (282 x 20)] / [Ventilated discs (285 x 20)] 2-piston fixed cast-iron callipers / 2-piston fixed cast-iron callipers
Wheels, front/rear:	5.5 J x 15 / 5.5 J x 15
Tyres, front/rear:	165 HR 15 / 165 HR 15

Electrical system

Alternator (W/A):	490 / 30
Battery (V/Ah):	12 / 45

Dimensions and weight

Track, front/rear (mm):	1367 / 1335
Wheelbase (mm):	2211
Length x width x height (mm):	4163 x 1610 x 1320
Kerb weight DIN (kg):	1080
Permissible gross weight (kg):	1400
Luggage compartment (l):	200
Luggage volume interior (l)*:	250
Fuel tank capacity (l):	62, including 6 reserve
C_w x A (m²):	0.38 x 1.685 = 0.640
Power/weight ratio (kg/kW/kg/hp):	13.33 / 9.81
*on folded-down rear seat-backs	

Fuel consumption

DIN 70 030 (mpg):	31; 98 RON super leaded

Performance, production, prices

Acceleration 0-62mph/100kph (s):	10.0 [10.0]
Maximum speed (mph / kph):	124 / 200 [121 / 195]
Production, total number:	
Coupé:	1,611
Targa:	789
Purchase prices:	
09/1967 Coupé:	DM 18,980 [DM 19,970]
Targa:	DM 20,380 [DM 21,370]
03/1968 Coupé:	DM 19,305 [DM 20,295]
Targa:	DM 20,735 [DM 21,725]

911 L Coupé [Sportomatic]
911 L Targa [Sportomatic]
MY 1968

Engine

Engine design:	6-cylinder horizontally-opposed
Installation:	Rear-engine
Cooling system:	Air-cooled
Number & form of blower blades:	11, straight
Blower outside diameter (mm):	245
Engine type:	901/06 [901/07]
Displacement (cc):	1991
Bore x stroke (mm):	80 x 66
Engine output DIN (kW/hp):	96/130 at 6100rpm
Maximum torque (Nm/lb ft):	174/128 at 4600rpm
Output per litre (kW/l / hp/l):	48.2 / 65.3
Compression ratio:	9.0 : 1
Valve operation & camshaft drive:	ohc, cams driven by double chain, 2 valves per cylinder
Carburation:	Weber carburettors 40 IDA
Ignition system:	Battery coil ignition
Firing order:	1 - 6 - 2 - 4 - 3 - 5
Engine lubrication:	Dry sump
Engine oil total (l):	9.0 [11.5]

Transmission

Drive configuration:	Rear-axle drive
Manual gearbox:	5-speed
Option Sportomatic:	[4-speed]
Transmission type:	902/1 [905/00]
Transmission ratios:	
1st gear:	3.091 [2.400]
2nd gear:	1.889 [1.631]
3rd gear:	1.318 [1.217]
4th gear:	1.004 [0.961]
5th gear:	0.857
Reverse gear:	3.127 [3.127]
Drive ratio:	4.428 [3.857]
Option:	Limited-slip differential

Body, chassis, suspension, brakes, wheels

Body design:	Steel body, 2 doors, 2 + 2 seats, welded assembly, sheet metal box-section, unitized with body, bumpers fixed close to body, chromium-plated horn grilles near indicators, engine lid with chromium grille, round, chromium wing mirror
Coupé:	Fixed steel roof
Option:	Electric sunroof
Targa:	Removable, foldable Targa top, fixed

	stainless-steel Targa roll bar, turn down flexible plastic rear window
Option MY 1968:	Fixed glass rear window
Suspension, front:	Independent suspension with wishbones and McPherson struts, one round, longitudinal torsion bar per wheel, hydraulic double-action shock absorbers, anti-roll bar
Suspension, rear:	Independent suspension with semi-trailing arms, one round, transverse torsion bar per wheel, hydraulic double-action shock absorbers
Option:	Anti-roll bar
Brakes, front/rear (Size (mm)):	Ventilated discs (282 x 20) / Ventilated discs (285 x 20) 2-piston fixed cast-iron callipers / 2-piston fixed cast-iron callipers
Wheels, front/rear:	5.5 J x 15 / 5.5 J x 15
Tyres, front/rear:	165 HR 15 / 165 HR 15

Electrical system

Alternator (W/A):	490 / 30
Battery (V/Ah):	12 / 45

Dimensions and weight

Track, front/rear (mm):	1367 / 1339
Wheelbase (mm):	2211
Length x width x height (mm):	4163 x 1610 x 1320
Kerb weight DIN (kg):	1080
Permissible gross weight (kg):	1400
Luggage compartment (l):	200
Luggage volume interior (l)*:	250
Fuel tank capacity (l):	62, including 6 reserve
C_w x A (m^2):	0.38 x 1.685 = 0.640
Power/weight ratio (kg/kW/ kg/hp):	11.25 / 8.30
*on folded-down rear seat-backs	

Fuel consumption

DIN 70 030 (mpg):	29.5; 98 RON super leaded

Performance, production, prices

Acceleration 0-62mph/100kph (s):	9.1 [9.1]
Maximum speed (mph / kph):	130 / 210 [127 / 205]
Production, total number:	
Coupé:	1,169
Targa:	444
Purchase prices:	
09/1967 Coupé:	DM 20,980 [DM 21,970]
Targa:	DM 22,380 [DM 23,370]
03/1968 Coupé:	DM 21,450 [DM 22,440]
Targa:	DM 28,880 [DM 29,870]

911 T Coupé [Sportomatic]
911 T Targa [Sportomatic] MY 1969

Engine

Engine design:	6-cylinder horizontally-opposed
Installation:	Rear-engine
Cooling system:	Air-cooled
Number & form of blower blades:	11, straight
Blower outside diameter (mm):	245
Engine type:	901/03 [901/13]
Displacement (cc):	1991
Bore x stroke (mm):	80 x 66
Engine output DIN (kW/hp):	81/110 at 5800rpm
Maximum torque (Nm/lb ft):	116/157 at 4200rpm
Output per litre (kW/l / hp/l):	40.7 / 55.2
Compression ratio:	8.6 : 1
Valve operation & camshaft drive:	ohc, cams driven by double chain, 2 valves per cylinder
Carburation:	Weber carburettors 40 IDT P
Ignition system:	Battery coil ignition
Firing order:	1 - 6 - 2 - 4 - 3 - 5
Engine lubrication:	Dry sump
Engine oil total (l):	9.0 [11.5]

Transmission

Drive configuration:	Rear-axle drive
Manual gearbox:	4-speed (5-speed)*
Option Sportomatic:	[4-speed]
Transmission type:	901/06 (901/13) [905/13]
Transmission ratios:	
1st gear:	3.091 (3.091) [2.400]
2nd gear:	1.631 (1.889) [1.613]
3rd gear:	1.040 (1.318) [1.217]
4th gear:	0.793 (1.004) [0.926]
5th gear:	(0.793)
Reverse gear:	3.127 (3.127) [3.127]
Drive ratios:	4.428 (4.428) [3.857]
Option:	Limited-slip differential
*Option	

Body, chassis, suspension, brakes, wheels

Body design:	Steel body, 2 doors, 2 + 2 seats, welded assembly, sheet metal box-section, unitized with body, wing flares, bumpers fixed close to body, chromium-plated horn grilles near indicators, engine lid with chromium grille, round, chromium wing mirror
Coupé:	Fixed steel roof
Option:	Electric sunroof
Targa:	Removable, foldable Targa top, fixed stainless-steel Targa roll bar, fixed glass rear window
Suspension, front:	Independent suspension with wishbones and McPherson struts, one round, longitudinal torsion bar per wheel, hydraulic double-action shock absorbers
Option:	Anti-roll bar

Option Coupé only:	Hydropneumatic struts
Suspension, rear:	Independent suspension with semi-trailing arms, one round, transverse torsion bar per wheel, hydraulic double-action shock absorbers
Option:	Anti-roll bar
Brakes, front/rear (Size (mm)):	Discs (282 x 12.7) / Discs (285 x 10)
Sportomatic:	[Ventilated discs (282 x 20)] / [Ventilated discs (285 x 20)] 2-piston fixed cast-iron callipers / 2-piston fixed cast-iron callipers
Wheels, front/rear:	5.5 J x 15 / 5.5 J x 15
Tyres, front/rear:	165 HR 15 / 165 HR 15
Option:	6 J x 15 / 6 J x 15 185/70 HR 15 / 185/70 HR 15
Option:	5.5 J x 14 / 5.5 J x 14 185 HR 14 / 185 HR 14

Electrical system

Alternator (W/A):	770 / 55
Battery (V/Ah):	2 x 12 / 36

Dimensions and weight

Track, front/rear (mm):	1362 / 1343
6 J x 15 / 6 J x 15:	1374 / 1355
5.5 J x 14 / 5.5 J x 14:	1364 / 1345
Wheelbase (mm):	2268
Length x width x height (mm):	4163 x 1610 x 1320
Kerb weight DIN (kg):	1020
Permissible gross weight (kg):	1400
Luggage compartment (l):	200
Luggage volume interior (l)*:	250
Fuel tank capacity (l):	62, including 6 reserve
C_w x A (m²):	0.408 x 1.71 = 0.697
Power/weight ratio (kg/kW/ kg/hp):	13.33 / 9.81
*on folded-down rear seat-backs	

Fuel consumption

DIN 70 030 (mpg):	31; 96 RON super leaded

Performance, production, prices

Acceleration 0-62mph/100kph (s):	10.0 [10.0]
Maximum speed (mph / kph):	124 / 200 [121 / 195]
Production, total number:	
Coupé:	1,611
Targa:	789
Purchase prices:	
07/1968 Coupé:	DM 19,481 [DM 20,471]
Targa:	DM 20,924 [DM 21,914]
10/1968 Coupé:	DM 19,969 [DM 20,959]
Targa:	DM 21,745 [DM 22,735]

911 E Coupé [Sportomatic]
911 E Targa [Sportomatic] MY 1969

Engine

Engine design:	6-cylinder horizontally-opposed
Installation:	Rear-engine
Cooling system:	Air-cooled
Number & form of blower blades:	11, straight
Blower outside diameter (mm):	245
Engine type:	901/09 [901/11]
Displacement (cc):	1991
Bore x stroke (mm):	80 x 66
Engine output DIN (kW/hp):	103/140 at 6500rpm
Maximum torque (Nm/lb ft):	175/129 at 4500rpm
Output per litre (kW/l / hp/l):	51.7 / 70.3
Compression ratio:	9.1 : 1
Valve operation & camshaft drive:	ohc, cams driven by double chain, 2 valves per cylinder
Carburation:	6-plunger, twin-row, mechanical Bosch injection pump, manifold injection
Ignition system:	Battery, capacitive-discharge system
Firing order:	1 - 6 - 2 - 4 - 3 - 5
Engine lubrication:	Dry sump
Engine oil total (l):	9.0 [11.5]

Transmission

Drive configuration:	Rear-axle drive
Manual gearbox:	5-speed
Option Sportomatic:	[4-speed]
Transmission type:	901/07 [905/13]
Transmission ratios:	
1st gear:	3.091 [2.400]
2nd gear:	1.889 [1.631]
3rd gear:	1.318 [1.217]
4th gear:	1.004 [0.926]
5th gear:	0.793
Reverse gear:	3.127 [3.127]
Drive ratio:	4.428 [3.857]
Option:	Limited-slip differential

Body, chassis, suspension, brakes, wheels

Body design:	Steel body, 2 doors, 2 + 2 seats, welded assembly, sheet metal box-section, unitized with body, wing flares, bumpers fixed close to body, chromium-plated horn grilles near indicators, engine lid with chromium grille, round, chromium wing mirror
Coupé:	Fixed steel roof
Option:	Electric sunroof
Targa:	Removable, foldable Targa top, fixed stainless-steel Targa roll bar, fixed glass rear window
Suspension, front:	Independent suspension with wishbones and hydropneumatic struts
Option:	Anti-roll bar
Suspension, rear:	Independent suspension with semi-trailing arms, one round, transverse torsion bar per wheel, hydraulic double-action shock absorbers
Option:	Anti-roll bar
Brakes, front/rear (Size (mm)):	Ventilated discs (282 x 20) / Ventilated discs (285 x 20) 2-piston fixed cast-iron callipers / 2-piston fixed cast-iron callipers
Wheels, front/rear:	6 J x 15 / 6 J x 15
Tyres, front/rear:	185/70 VR 15 / 185/70 VR 15

Electrical system

Alternator (W/A):	770 / 55
Battery (V/Ah):	2 x 12 / 36

Dimensions and weight

Track, front/rear (mm):	1374 / 1355
Wheelbase (mm):	2268
Length x width x height (mm):	4163 x 1610 x 1320
Kerb weight DIN (kg):	1020
Permissible gross weight (kg):	1400
Luggage compartment (l):	200
Luggage volume interior (l)*:	250
Fuel tank capacity (l):	62, including 6 reserve
C_w x A (m²):	0.408 x 1.71 = 0.697
Power/weight ratio (kg/kW/kg/hp):	9.90/ 7.28
*on folded-down rear seat-backs	

Fuel consumption

DIN 70 030 (mpg):	29.5; 98 RON super leaded

Performance, production, prices

Acceleration 0-62mph/100kph (s):	9.0 [9.0]
Maximum speed (mph / kph):	133 / 215 [130 / 210]
Production, total number:	
Coupé:	1,968
Targa:	858
Purchase prices:	
07/1968 Coupé:	DM 21,645 [DM 22,635]
Targa:	DM 23,088 [DM 24,078]
10/1968 Coupé:	DM 24,698 [DM 25,688]
Targa:	DM 26,474 [DM 27,464]

911 S Coupé
911 S Targa MY 1969

Engine

Engine design:	6-cylinder horizontally-opposed
Installation:	Rear-engine
Cooling system:	Air-cooled
Number & form of blower blades:	11, straight
Blower outside diameter (mm):	245
Engine type:	901/10
Displacement (cc):	1991
Bore x stroke (mm):	80 x 66
Engine output DIN (kW/hp):	125/170 at 6800rpm
Maximum torque (Nm/lb ft):	182/134 at 5500rpm
Output per litre (kW/l / hp/l):	62.8 / 85.4
Compression ratio:	9.8 : 1
Valve operation & camshaft drive:	ohc, cams driven by double chain, 2 valves per cylinder
Carburation:	6-plunger, twin-row, mechanical Bosch injection pump, manifold injection
Ignition system:	Battery, capacitive-discharge system
Firing order:	1 - 6 - 2 - 4 - 3 - 5
Engine lubrication:	Dry sump
Engine oil total (l):	10.0

Transmission

Drive configuration:	Rear-axle drive
Manual gearbox:	5-speed
Transmission type:	901/07
Transmission ratios:	
1st gear:	3.091
2nd gear:	1.889
3rd gear:	1.318
4th gear:	1.004
5th gear:	0.793
Reverse gear:	3.127
Drive ratio:	4.428
Option:	Limited-slip differential

Body, chassis, suspension, brakes, wheels

Body design:	Steel body, 2 doors, 2 + 2 seats, welded assembly, sheet metal box-section, unitized with body, wing flares, bumpers fixed close to body, chromium-plated horn grilles near indicators, engine lid with chromium grille, round, chromium wing mirror
Coupé:	Fixed steel roof
Option:	Electric sunroof
Targa:	Removable, foldable Targa top, fixed stainless-steel Targa roll bar, fixed glass rear window
Suspension, front:	Independent suspension with wishbones and McPherson struts, one round, longitudinal torsion bar per wheel, hydraulic double-action shock absorbers, anti-roll bar
Option Coupé only:	Hydropneumatic struts
Suspension, rear:	Independent suspension with semi-trailing arms, one round, transverse torsion bar per wheel, hydraulic double-action shock absorbers, anti-roll bar
Brakes, front/rear (Size (mm)):	Ventilated discs (282 x 20) / Ventilated discs (285 x 20) 2-piston fixed aluminium callipers / 2-piston fixed cast-iron callipers
Wheels, front/rear:	6 J x 15 / 6 J x 15
Tyres, front/rear:	185/70 VR 15 / 185/70 VR 15

Electrical system

Alternator (W/A):	770 / 55
Battery (V/Ah):	2 x 12 / 36

Dimensions and weight

Track, front/rear (mm):	1374 / 1355
Wheelbase (mm):	2268
Length x width x height (mm):	4163 x 1610 x 1320
Kerb weight DIN (kg):	1020
Permissible gross weight (kg):	1400
Luggage compartment (l):	200
Luggage volume interior (l)*:	250
Fuel tank capacity (l):	62, including 6 reserve
C_w x A (m^2):	0.408 x 1.71 = 0.697
Power/weight ratio (kg/kW / kg/hp):	8.16 / 6.37
*on folded-down rear seat-backs	

Fuel consumption

DIN 70 030 (mpg):	27.5; 98 RON super leaded

Performance, production, prices

Acceleration 0-62mph/100kph (s):	8.0
Maximum speed (mph / kph):	140 / 225
Production, total number:	
Coupé:	1,492
Targa:	614
Purchase prices:	
07/1968 Coupé:	DM 25,197
Targa:	DM 26,640
10/1968 Coupé:	DM 26,918
Targa:	DM 28,694

911 T Coupé [Sportomatic]
911 T Targa [Sportomatic]
MY 1970–MY 1971

Engine

Engine design:	6-cylinder horizontally-opposed
Installation:	Rear-engine
Cooling system:	Air-cooled
Number & form of blower blades:	11, straight
Blower outside diameter (mm):	245
Engine type:	911/03 [911/06]
Displacement (cc):	2195
Bore x stroke (mm):	84 x 66
Engine output DIN (kW/hp):	92/125 at 5800rpm
Maximum torque (Nm/lb ft):	176/130 at 4200rpm
Output per litre (kW/l / hp/l):	41.9 / 56.9
Compression ratio:	8.6 : 1
Valve operation & camshaft drive:	ohc, cams driven by double chain, 2 valves per cylinder
Carburation:	Weber carburettors 40 IDT 3C
Ignition system:	Battery, capacitive-discharge system
Firing order:	1 - 6 - 2 - 4 - 3 - 5
Engine lubrication:	Dry sump
Engine oil total (l):	9.0 [11.5]

Transmission

Drive configuration:	Rear-axle drive
Manual gearbox:	4-speed (5-speed)*
Option Sportomatic:	[4-speed]
Transmission type:	911/00 (911/01) [905/20]
Transmission ratios:	
1st gear:	3.091 (3.091) [2.400]
2nd gear:	1.631 (1.778) [1.550]
3rd gear:	1.040 (1.217) [1.125]
4th gear:	0.758 (0.926) [0.857]
5th gear:	(0.758)
Reverse gear:	3.127 (3.127) [3.127]
Drive ratio:	4.428 (4.428) [3.857]
Option:	Limited-slip differential
*Option	

Body, chassis, suspension, brakes, wheels

Body design:	Steel body, 2 doors, 2 + 2 seats, welded assembly, sheet metal box-section, unitized with body, galvanized floorpanel, wing flares, bumpers fixed close to body, chromium-plated horn grilles near indicators, engine lid with chromium grille, round, chromium wing mirror
Coupé:	Fixed steel roof
Option:	Electric sunroof
Targa:	Removable, foldable Targa top, fixed stainless-steel Targa roll bar, fixed glass rear window
Suspension, front:	Independent suspension with wishbones and McPherson struts, one round, longitudinal torsion bar per wheel, hydraulic double-action shock absorbers
Option:	Anti-roll bar
Option Coupé only:	Hydropneumatic struts
Suspension, rear:	Independent suspension with semi-trailing arms, one round, transverse torsion bar per wheel, hydraulic double-action shock absorbers
Option:	Anti-roll bar
Brakes, front/rear (Size (mm)):	Ventilated discs (282,5 x 20) / Ventilated discs (290 x 20) 2-piston fixed cast-iron callipers / 2-piston fixed cast-iron callipers
Wheels, front/rear:	5,5 J x 15 / 5,5 J x 15
Tyres, front/rear:	165 HR 15 / 165 HR 15
Option:	6 J x 15 / 6 J x 15 185/70 HR 15 / 185/70 HR 15
Option:	5,5 J x 14 / 5,5 J x 14 185 HR 14 / 185 HR 14

Electrical system

Alternator (W/A):	770 / 55
Battery (V/Ah):	2 x 12 / 36

Dimensions and weight

Track, front/rear (mm):	1362 / 1343
6 J x 15 / 6 J x 15:	1374 / 1355
5.5 J x 14 / 5.5 J x 14:	1364 / 1345
Wheelbase (mm):	2268
Length x width x height (mm):	4163 x 1610 x 1320
Kerb weight DIN (kg):	1020
Permissible gross weight (kg):	1400
Luggage compartment (l):	200
Luggage volume interior (l)*:	250
Fuel tank capacity (l):	62, including 6 reserve
C_w x A (m²):	0.408 x 1.71 = 0.697
Power/weight ratio (kg/kW/kg/hp):	11.08 / 8.16
*on folded-down rear seat-backs	

Fuel consumption

DIN 70 030 (mpg):	31; 96 RON super leaded

Performance, production, prices

Acceleration 0-62mph/100kph (s):	10.0 [10.0]
Maximum speed (mph / kph):	127 / 205 [124 / 200]
Production, total number:	
Coupé:	11,019
Targa:	6,000
Purchase prices:	
10/1969 Coupé:	DM 19,969 [DM 20,959]
Targa:	DM 21,911 [DM 22,901]
01/1970 Coupé:	DM 20,979 [DM 21,969]
Targa:	DM 23,199 [DM 24,189]
09/1970 Coupé:	DM 20,979 [DM 21,969]
Targa:	DM 23,199 [DM 24,189]
01/1971 Coupé:	DM 21,980 [DM 22,970]
Targa:	DM 24,200 [DM 25,190]

911 E Coupé [Sportomatic]
911 E Targa [Sportomatic]
MY 1970–MY 1971

Engine

Engine design:	6-cylinder horizontally-opposed
Installation:	Rear-engine
Cooling system:	Air-cooled
Number & form of blower blades:	11, straight
Blower outside diameter (mm):	245
Engine type:	911/01 [911/04]
Displacement (cc):	2195
Bore x stroke (mm):	84 x 66
Engine output DIN (kW/hp):	114/155 at 6200rpm
Maximum torque (Nm/lb ft):	191/141 at 4500rpm
Output per litre (kW/l / hp/l):	51.9 / 70.6
Compression ratio:	9.1 : 1
Valve operation & camshaft drive:	ohc, cams driven by double chain, 2 valves per cylinder
Carburation:	6-plunger, twin-row, mechanical Bosch injection pump, manifold injection
Ignition system:	Battery, capacitive-discharge system
Firing order:	1 - 6 - 2 - 4 - 3 - 5
Engine lubrication:	Dry sump
Engine oil total (l):	9.0 [11.5]

Transmission

Drive configuration:	Rear-axle drive
Manual gearbox:	5-speed
Option Sportomatic:	[4-speed]
Transmission type:	911/01 [905/20]
Transmission ratios:	
1st gear:	3.091 [2.400]
2nd gear:	1.778 [1.550]
3rd gear:	1.217 [1.125]
4th gear:	0.926 [0.857]
5th gear:	0.758
Reverse gear:	3.127 [3.127]
Drive ratios:	4.428 [3.857]
Option:	Limited-slip differential

Body, chassis, suspension, brakes, wheels

Body design:	Steel body, 2 doors, 2 + 2 seats, welded assembly, sheet metal box-section, unitized with body, galvanized floorpanel, wing flares, bumpers fixed close to body, chromium-plated horn grilles near indicators, aluminium engine lid with chromium grille, aluminium rear panel, round, chromium wing mirror
Coupé:	Fixed steel roof
Option:	Electric sunroof
Targa:	Removable, foldable Targa top, fixed stainless-steel Targa roll bar, fixed glass rear window

Suspension, front:	Independent suspension with wishbones and hydropneumatic struts
Option:	Anti-roll bar
Suspension, rear:	Independent suspension with semi-trailing arms, one round, transverse torsion bar per wheel, hydraulic double-action shock absorbers
Option:	Anti-roll bar
Brakes, front/rear (Size (mm)):	Ventilated discs (282.5 x 20) / Ventilated discs (290 x 20) 2-piston fixed cast-iron callipers / 2-piston fixed cast-iron callipers
Wheels, front/rear:	6 J x 15 / 6 J x 15
Tyres, front/rear:	185/70 VR 15 / 185/70 VR 15

Electrical system

Alternator (W/A):	770 / 55
Battery (V/Ah):	2 x 12 / 36

Dimensions and weight

Track, front/rear (mm):	1374 / 1355
Wheelbase (mm):	2268
Length x width x height (mm):	4163 x 1610 x 1320
Kerb weight DIN (kg):	1020
Permissible gross weight (kg):	1400
Luggage compartment (l):	200
Luggage volume interior (l)*:	250
Fuel tank capacity (l):	62, including 6 reserve
C_w x A (m²):	0.408 x 1.71 = 0.697
Power/weight ratio (kg/kW/kg/hp):	8.94 / 6.58
*on folded-down rear seat-backs	

Fuel consumption

DIN 70 030 (mpg):	9.5; 96 RON super leaded

Performance, production, prices

Acceleration 0-62mph/100kph (s):	8.0 [8.0]
Maximum speed (mph / kph):	220 [215]
Production, total number:	
Coupé:	3,028
Targa:	1,848
Purchase prices:	
10/1969 Coupé:	DM 24,975 [DM 25,965]
Targa:	DM 26,918 [DM 27,908]
01/1970 Coupé:	DM 26,473 [DM 27,463]
Targa:	DM 28,694 [DM 29,684]
09/1970 Coupé:	DM 26,473 [DM 27,463]
Targa:	DM 28,694 [DM 29,684]
01/1971 Coupé:	DM 26,980 [DM 27,970]
Targa:	DM 29,200 [DM 30,190]

911 S Coupé
911 S Targa
MY 1970–MY 1971

Engine

Engine design:	6-cylinder horizontally-opposed
Installation:	Rear-engine
Cooling system:	Air-cooled
Number & form of blower blades:	11, straight
Blower outside diameter (mm):	245
Engine type:	911/02
Displacement (cc):	2195
Bore x stroke (mm):	84 x 66
Engine output DIN (kW/hp):	132/180 at 6500rpm
Maximum torque (Nm/lb ft):	199/147 at 5200rpm
Output per litre (kW/l / hp/l):	60.1 / 82.0
Compression ratio:	9.8 : 1
Valve operation & camshaft drive:	ohc, cams driven by double chain, 2 valves per cylinder
Carburation:	6-plunger, twin-row, mechanical Bosch injection pump, manifold injection
Ignition system:	Battery, capacitive-discharge system
Firing order:	1 - 6 - 2 - 4 - 3 - 5
Engine lubrication:	Dry sump
Engine oil total (l):	10.0

Transmission

Drive configuration:	Rear-axle drive
Manual gearbox:	5-speed
Transmission type:	911/01
Transmission ratios:	
1st gear:	3.091
2nd gear:	1.778
3rd gear:	1.217
4th gear:	0.926
5th gear:	0.758
Reverse gear:	3.127
Drive ratio:	4.428
Option:	Limited-slip differential

Body, chassis, suspension, brakes, wheels

Body design:	Steel body, 2 doors, 2 + 2 seats, welded assembly, sheet metal box-section, unitized with body, galvanized floorpanel, wing flares, bumpers fixed close to body, chromium-plated horn grilles near indicators, aluminium engine lid with chromium grille, aluminium rear panel, round, chromium wing mirror
Coupé:	Fixed steel roof
Option:	Electric sunroof
Targa:	Removable, foldable Targa top, fixed stainless-steel Targa roll bar, fixed glass rear window

Suspension, front:	Independent suspension with wishbones and McPherson struts, one round, longitudinal torsion bar per wheel, hydraulic double-action shock absorbers, anti-roll bar
Option Coupé only:	Hydropneumatic struts
Suspension, rear:	Independent suspension with semi-trailing arms, one round, transverse torsion bar per wheel, hydraulic double-action shock absorbers, anti-roll bar
Brakes, front/rear (Size (mm)):	Ventilated discs (282.5 x 20) / Ventilated discs (290 x 20) 2-piston fixed aluminium callipers / 2-piston fixed cast-iron callipers
Wheels, front/rear:	6 J x 15 / 6 J x 15
Tyres, front/rear:	185/70 VR 15 / 185/70 VR 15

Electrical system

Alternator (W/A):	770 / 55
Battery (V/Ah):	2 x 12 / 36

Dimensions and weight

Track, front/rear (mm):	1374 / 1355
Wheelbase (mm):	2268
Length x width x height (mm):	4163 x 1610 x 1320
Kerb weight DIN (kg):	1020
Permissible gross weight (kg):	1400
Luggage compartment (l):	200
Luggage volume interior (l)*:	250
Fuel tank capacity (l):	62, including 6 reserve
C_w x A (m²):	0.408 x 1.71 = 0.697
Power/weight ratio (kg/kW/kg/hp):	7.27 / 5.66
*on folded-down rear seat-backs	

Fuel consumption

DIN 70 030 (mpg):	27.5; 98 RON super leaded

Performance, production, prices

Acceleration 0-62mph/100kph (s):	7.5
Maximum speed (mph / kph):	143 / 230
Production, total number:	
Coupé:	3,154
Targa:	1,496
Purchase prices:	
10/1969 Coupé:	DM 27,139
Targa:	DM 29,193
01/1970 Coupé:	DM 28,749
Targa:	DM 31,080
09/1970 Coupé:	DM 28,749
Targa:	DM 31,080
01/1971 Coupé:	DM 29,980
Targa:	DM 32,200

911 T Coupé [Sportomatic]
911 T Targa [Sportomatic]
MY 1972–MY 1973

Engine

Engine design:	6-cylinder horizontally-opposed
Installation:	Rear-engine
Cooling system:	Air-cooled
Number & form of blower blades:	11, straight
Blower outside diameter (mm):	245
Engine type:	911/57 [911/67]
Displacement (cc):	2341
Bore x stroke (mm):	84 x 70.4
Engine output DIN (kW/hp):	96/130 at 5600rpm
Maximum torque (Nm/lb ft):	196/144 at 4000rpm
Output per litre (kW/l / hp/l):	41.0 / 55.5
Compression ratio:	7.5 : 1
Valve operation & camshaft drive:	ohc, cams driven by double chain, 2 valves per cylinder
Carburation:	Solex-Zenith carburettors 40 TIN
Ignition system:	Battery, capacitive-discharge system
Firing order:	1 - 6 - 2 - 4 - 3 - 5
Engine lubrication:	Dry sump
Engine oil total (l):	8.0 [10.0]
MY 1973:	10.5 [13.0]

Transmission

Drive configuration:	Rear-axle drive
Manual gearbox:	4-speed (5-speed)*
Option Sportomatic:	[4-speed]
Transmission type:	915/12 (915/03) [905/21]
Transmission ratios:	
1st gear:	3.182 (3.182) [2.400]
2nd gear:	1.778 (1.833) [1.550]
3rd gear:	1.125 (1.261) [1.125]
4th gear:	0.821 (0.962) [0.857]
5th gear:	(0.759)
Reverse gear:	3.325 (3.325) [2.553]
Drive ratio:	4.428 (4.428) [3.857]
Option:	Limited-slip differential 80%
*Option	

Body, chassis, suspension, brakes, wheels

Body design:	Steel body, 2 doors, 2 + 2 seats, welded assembly, sheet metal box-section, unitized with body, galvanized floorpanel, wing flares, bumpers fixed close to body, chromium-plated horn grilles near indicators, engine lid with black grille, round, chromium wing mirror
MY 1972:	Filler lid for oil tank on right rear wing
Option:	Plastic front spoiler
MY 1973:	Black horn grilles near indicators, chromium-plated rectangular wing mirror
Coupé:	Fixed steel roof
Option:	Electric sunroof
Targa:	Removable, foldable Targa top, fixed stainless-steel Targa roll bar, fixed glass rear window
Suspension, front:	Independent suspension with wishbones and McPherson struts, one round, longitudinal torsion bar per wheel, hydraulic double-action shock absorbers
Option:	Anti-roll bar
Option:	Hydropneumatic struts
Suspension, rear:	Independent suspension with semi-trailing arms, one round, transverse torsion bar per wheel, hydraulic double-action shock absorbers
Option:	Anti-roll bar
Brakes, front/rear (Size (mm)):	Ventilated discs (282.5 x 20) / Ventilated discs (290 x 20) 2-piston fixed cast-iron callipers / 2-piston fixed cast-iron callipers
Wheels, front/rear:	5.5 J x 15 / 5.5 J x 15
Tyres, front/rear:	165 HR 15 / 165 HR 15
Option:	6 J x 15 / 6 J x 15
	185/70 HR 15 / 185/70 HR 15

Electrical system

Alternator (W/A):	770 / 55
Battery (V/Ah):	2 x 12 / 36

Dimensions and weight

Track, front/rear (mm):	1366 / 1342
6 J x 15 / 6 J x 15:	1372 / 1354
Wheelbase (mm):	2271
Length x width x height (mm):	4127 x 1610 x 1320
Kerb weight DIN (kg):	1050 [1065]
Permissible gross weight (kg):	1400 [1400]
Luggage compartment (l):	200
Luggage volume interior (l)*:	250
Fuel tank capacity (l):	62, including 6 reserve
Option, MY 1973:	85, including 9 reserve
C_w x A (m²):	0.408 x 1.71 = 0.697
Power/weight ratio (kg/kW/kg/hp):	10.93 [11.09] / 8.07 [8.19]
*on folded-down rear seat-backs	

Fuel consumption

DIN 70 030 (mpg):	31; 91 RON normal leaded

Performance, production, prices

Acceleration 0-62mph/100kph (s):	9.5 [9.5]
Maximum speed (mph / kph):	127 / 205 [124 / 200]
Production, total number:	
Coupé:	10,173
Targa:	7,147
Purchase prices:	
09/1971 Coupé:	DM 22,980 [DM 23,980]
Targa:	DM 25,200 [DM 26,200]
03/1972 Coupé:	DM 23,480 [DM 24,480]
Targa:	DM 25,700 [DM 26,700]
08/1972 Coupé:	DM 23,480 [DM 24,480]
Targa:	DM 25,700 [DM 26,700]
03/1973 Coupé:	DM 24,480 [DM 25,480]
Targa:	DM 26,700 [DM 27,700]

911 E Coupé [Sportomatic]
911 E Targa [Sportomatic]
MY 1972–MY 1973

Engine

Engine design:	6-cylinder horizontally-opposed
Installation:	Rear-engine
Cooling system:	Air-cooled
Number & form of blower blades:	11, straight
Blower outside diameter (mm):	245
Engine type:	911/52 [911/62]
Displacement (cc):	2341
Bore x stroke (mm):	84 x 70.4
Engine output DIN (kW/hp):	121/165 at 6200rpm
Maximum torque (Nm/lb ft):	206/152 at 4500rpm
Output per litre (kW/l / hp/l):	51.7 / 70.5
Compression ratio:	8.0 : 1
Valve operation & camshaft drive:	ohc, cams driven by double chain, 2 valves per cylinder
Carburation:	6-plunger, twin-row, mechanical Bosch injection pump, manifold injection
Ignition system:	Battery, capacitive-discharge system
Firing order:	1 - 6 - 2 - 4 - 3 - 5
Engine lubrication:	Dry sump
Engine oil total (l):	8.0 [10.0]
MY 1973:	10.5 [13.0]

Transmission

Drive configuration:	Rear-axle drive
Manual gearbox:	4-speed (5-speed)*
Option Sportomatic:	[4-speed]
Transmission type:	915/12 (915/03) [925/00]
Transmission ratios:	
1st gear:	3.182 (3.182) [2.400]
2nd gear:	1.778 (1.833) [1.550]
3rd gear:	1.125 (1.261) [1.125]
4th gear:	0.821 (0.962) [0.857]
5th gear:	(0.759)
Reverse gear:	3.325 (3.325) [2.533]
Drive ratio:	4.428 (4.428) [3.857]
Option:	Limited-slip differential 80%
*Option	

Body, chassis, suspension, brakes, wheels

Body design:	Steel body, 2 doors, 2 + 2 seats, welded assembly, sheet metal box-section, unitized with body, galvanized floorpanel, wing flares, bumpers fixed close to body, chromium-plated horn grilles near indicators, aluminium engine lid with black grille, aluminium rear panel, round, chromium wing mirror
MY 1972:	Filler lid for oil tank on right rear wing
Option MY 1972:	Plastic front spoiler
MY 1973:	Plastic front spoiler, black horn grilles near indicators, chromium-plated rectangular wing mirror
Coupé:	Fixed steel roof
Option:	Electric sunroof
Targa:	Removable, foldable Targa top, fixed stainless-steel Targa roll bar, fixed glass rear window
Suspension, front:	Independent suspension with wishbones and McPherson struts, one round, longitudinal torsion bar per wheel, hydraulic double-action shock absorbers
Option:	Anti-roll bar
Option:	Hydropneumatic struts
Suspension, rear:	Independent suspension with semi-trailing arms, one round, transverse torsion bar per wheel, hydraulic double-action shock absorbers
Option:	Anti-roll bar
Brakes, front/rear (Size (mm)):	Ventilated discs (282.5 x 20) / Ventilated discs (290 x 20) 2-piston fixed cast-iron callipers / 2-piston fixed cast-iron callipers
Wheels, front/rear:	6 J x 15 / 6 J x 15
Tyres, front/rear:	185/70 VR 15 / 185/70 VR 15

Electrical system

Alternator (W/A):	770 / 55
Battery (V/Ah):	2 x 12 / 36

Dimensions and weight

Track, front/rear (mm):	1372 / 1354
Wheelbase (mm):	2271
Length x width x height (mm):	4127 x 1610 x 1320
Kerb weight DIN (kg):	1075 [1090]
Permissible gross weight (kg):	1400 [1400]
Luggage compartment (l):	200
Luggage volume interior (l)*:	250
Fuel tank capacity (l):	62, including 6 reserve
MY 1973:	85, including 9 reserve
C_w x A (m²):	0.408 x 1.71 = 0.697
Power/weight ratio (kg/kW/ kg/hp):	8.88 [9.00] / 6.51 [6.60]
*on folded-down rear seat-backs	

Fuel consumption

DIN 70 030 (mpg):	29.5; 91 RON normal leaded

Performance, production, prices

Acceleration 0-62mph/100kph (s):	7.9 [7.9]
Maximum speed (mph / kph):	136 / 220 [133 / 215]
Production, total number:	
Coupé:	2,470
Targa:	1,896
Purchase prices:	
09/1971 Coupé:	DM 25,980 [DM 26,980]
Targa:	DM 28,200 [DM 29,200]
03/1972 Coupé:	DM 26,480 [DM 27,480]
Targa:	DM 28,700 [DM 29,700]
08/1972 Coupé:	DM 27,775 [DM 28,775]
Targa:	DM 29,995 [DM 30,995]
02/1973 Coupé:	DM 28,780 [DM 29,780]
Targa:	DM 31,000 [DM 32,000]

911 S Coupé [Sportomatic]
911 S Targa [Sportomatic]
MY 1972–MY 1973

Engine

Engine design:	6-cylinder horizontally-opposed
Installation:	Rear-engine
Cooling system:	Air-cooled
Number & form of blower blades:	11, straight
Blower outside diameter (mm):	245
Engine type:	911/53 [911/63]
Displacement (cc):	2341
Bore x stroke (mm):	84 x 70.4
Engine output DIN (kW/hp):	140/190 at 6500rpm
Maximum torque (Nm/lb ft):	216/159 at 5200rpm
Output per litre (kW/l / hp/l):	59.8 / 81.2
Compression ratio:	8.5 : 1
Valve operation & camshaft drive:	ohc, cams driven by double chain, 2 valves per cylinder
Carburation:	6-plunger, twin-row, mechanical Bosch injection pump, manifold injection
Ignition system:	Battery, capacitive-discharge system
Firing order:	1 - 6 - 2 - 4 - 3 - 5
Engine lubrication:	Dry sump
Engine oil total (l):	9.0 [11.0]
MY 1973:	13.0 [15.5]

Transmission

Drive configuration:	Rear-axle drive
Manual gearbox:	4-speed (5-speed)*
Option Sportomatic:	[4-speed]
Transmission type:	915/12 (915/03) [925/01]
Transmission ratios:	
1st gear:	3.182 (3.182) [2.400]
2nd gear:	1.778 (1.833) [1.550]
3rd gear:	1.125 (1.261) [1.125]
4th gear:	0.821 (0.926) [0.857]
5th gear:	(0.759)
Reverse gear:	3.325 (3.325) [2533]
Drive ratio:	4.428 (4.428) [3.857]
Option:	Limited-slip differential 80%
*Option	

Body, chassis, suspension, brakes, wheels

Body design:	Steel body, 2 doors, 2 + 2 seats, welded assembly, sheet metal box-section, unitized with body, galvanized floorpanel, wing flares, bumpers fixed close to body, plastic front spoiler, chromium-plated horn grilles near indicators, aluminium engine lid with black grille, aluminium rear panel, round, chromium wing mirror
MY 1972:	Filler lid for oil tank on right rear wing
MY 1973:	Black horn grilles near indicators, chromium-plated rectangular wing mirror
Coupé:	Fixed steel roof
Option:	Electric sunroof

Targa:	Removable, foldable Targa top, fixed stainless-steel Targa roll bar, fixed glass rear window
Suspension, front:	Independent suspension with wishbones and McPherson struts, one round, longitudinal torsion bar per wheel, hydraulic double-action shock absorbers, anti-roll bar
Option:	Hydropneumatic struts
Suspension, rear:	Independent suspension with semi-trailing arms, one round, transverse torsion bar per wheel, hydraulic double-action shock absorbers, anti-roll bar
Brakes, front/rear (Size (mm)):	Ventilated discs (282.5 x 20) / Ventilated discs (290 x 20) 2-piston fixed aluminium callipers / 2-piston fixed cast-iron callipers
Wheels, front/rear:	6 J x 15 / 6 J x 15
Tyres, front/rear:	185/70 VR 15 / 185/70 VR 15

Electrical system

Alternator (W/A):	770 / 55
Battery (V/Ah):	2 x 12 / 36

Dimensions and weight

Track, front/rear (mm):	1372 / 1354
Wheelbase (mm):	2271
Length x width x height (mm):	4147 x 1610 x 1320
Kerb weight DIN (kg):	1075 [1090]
Permissible gross weight (kg):	1400 [1400]
Luggage compartment (l):	200
Luggage volume interior (l)*:	250
Fuel tank capacity (l):	62, including 6 reserve
MY 1973:	85, including 9 reserve
C_w x A (m²):	0.408 x 1.71 = 0.697
Power/weight ratio (kg/kW/kg/hp):	7.67 [7.73] / 5.65 [5.73]
*on folded-down rear seat-backs	

Fuel consumption

DIN 70 030 (mpg):	27.5; 91 RON normal leaded

Performance, production, prices

Acceleration 0-62mph/100kph (s):	7.0 [7.0]
Maximum speed (mph / kph):	143 / 230 [140 / 225]
Production, total number:	
Coupé:	3,160
Targa:	1,894
Purchase prices:	
09/1971 Coupé:	DM 30,680 [DM 31,680]
Targa:	DM 32,900 [DM 33,900]
03/1972 Coupé:	DM 31,180 [DM 32,180]
Targa:	DM 33,400 [DM 34,400]
08/1972 Coupé:	DM 31,500 [DM 32,500]
Targa:	DM 33,720 [DM 34,720]
02/1973 Coupé:	DM 32,480 [DM 33,480]
Targa:	DM 34,700 [DM 35,700]

911 Carrera RS Coupé Touring
MY 1973

Engine

Engine design:	6-cylinder horizontally-opposed
Installation:	Rear-engine
Cooling system:	Air-cooled
Number & form of blower blades:	11, straight
Blower outside diameter (mm):	245
Engine type:	911/83
Displacement (cc):	2687
Bore x stroke (mm):	90 x 70.4
Engine output DIN (kW/hp):	154/210 at 6300rpm
Maximum torque (Nm/lb ft):	255/188 at 5100rpm
Output per litre (kW/l / hp/l):	57.3 / 78.2
Compression ratio:	8.5 : 1
Valve operation & camshaft drive:	ohc, cams driven by double chain, 2 valves per cylinder
Carburation:	6-plunger, twin-row, mechanical Bosch injection pump, manifold injection
Ignition system:	Battery, capacitive-discharge system
Firing order:	1 - 6 - 2 - 4 - 3 - 5
Engine lubrication:	Dry sump
Engine oil total (l):	13.0

Transmission

Drive configuration:	Rear-axle drive
Manual gearbox:	5-speed
Transmission type:	915/08
Transmission ratios:	
1st gear:	3.182
2nd gaer:	1.834
3rd gear:	1.261
4th gear:	0.925
5th gear:	0.724
Reverse gear:	3.325
Drive ratio:	4.429
Option:	Limited-slip differential 80%

Body, chassis, suspension, brakes, wheels

Body design:	Steel Coupé body, 2 doors, 2 + 2 seats, welded assembly, sheet metal box-section, unitized with body, thin-gauge sheet metal parts, galvanized floorpanel, wing flares, wider rear wings, bumpers fixed close to body, plastic front spoiler, black horn grilles near indicators, plastic engine lid with rear spoiler (ducktail) and black grille, aluminium rear panel, thin glass, chromium rectangular wing mirror, 'Carrera' script on sides
Option:	Electric sunroof

Suspension, front:	Independent suspension with wishbones and McPherson struts, one round, longitudinal torsion bar per wheel, hydraulic double-action shock absorbers, anti-roll bar
Suspension, rear:	Independent suspension with semi-trailing arms, one round, transverse torsion bar per wheel, hydraulic double-action shock absorbers, anti-roll bar
Brakes, front/rear (Size (mm)):	Ventilated discs (282.5 x 20) / Ventilated discs (290 x 20) 2-piston fixed aluminium callipers / 2-piston fixed cast-iron callipers
Wheels, front/rear:	6 J x 15 / 7 J x 15
Tyres, front/rear:	185/70 VR 15 / 215/60 VR 15

Electrical system

Alternator (W/A):	770 / 55
Battery (V/Ah):	12 / 36

Dimensions and weight

Track, front/rear (mm):	1372 / 1394
Wheelbase (mm):	2271
Length x width x height (mm):	4147 x 1652 x 1320
Kerb weight DIN (kg):	1075
Permissible gross weight (kg):	1400
Luggage compartment (l):	200
Luggage volume interior (l)*:	250
Fuel tank capacity (l):	85, including 9 reserve
C_w x A (m²):	0.397 x 1.73 = 0.686
Power/weight ratio (kg/kW/ kg/hp):	6.98/ 5.11
*on folded-down rear seat-backs	

Fuel consumption

DIN 70 030 (mpg):	26; 91 RON normal leaded

Performance, production, prices

Acceleration 0-62mph/100kph (s):	6.3
Maximum speed (mph / kph):	149 / 240
Production, total number:	
Touring (M 472):	1,308
Purchase prices:	
08/1972:	DM 34,000
incl. M 472:	DM 36,500
02/1973:	DM 34,000
incl. M 472:	DM 36,500

911 Carrera RS Coupé sports version MY 1973

Engine

Engine design:	6-cylinder horizontally-opposed
Installation:	Rear-engine
Cooling system:	Air-cooled
Number & form of blower blades:	11, straight
Blower outside diameter (mm):	245
Engine type:	911/83
Displacement (cc):	2687
Bore x stroke (mm):	90 x 70.4
Engine output DIN (kW/hp):	154/210 at 6300rpm
Maximum torque (Nm/lb ft):	255/188 at 5100rpm
Output per litre (kW/l / hp/l):	57.3 / 78.2
Compression ratio:	8.5 : 1
Valve operation & camshaft drive:	ohc, cams driven by double chain, 2 valves per cylinder
Carburation:	6-plunger, twin-row, mechanical Bosch injection pump, manifold injection
Ignition system:	Battery, capacitive-discharge system
Firing order:	1 - 6 - 2 - 4 - 3 - 5
Engine lubrication:	Dry sump
Engine oil total (l):	13.0

Transmission

Drive configuration:	Rear-axle drive
Manual gearbox:	5-speed
Transmission type:	915/08
Transmission ratios:	
1st gear:	3.182
2nd gaer:	1.834
3rd gear:	1.261
4th gear:	0.925
5th gear:	0.724
Reverse gear:	3.325
Drive ratio:	4.429
Option:	Limited-slip differential 80%

Body, chassis, suspension, brakes, wheels

Body design:	Steel coupé body, 2 doors, 2 seats, welded assembly, sheet metal box-section, unitized with body, thin-gauge sheet-metal parts, galvanized floorpanel, wing flares, wider rear wings, bumpers fixed close to body, plastic front spoiler, black horn grilles near indicators, plastic engine lid with rear spoiler (ducktail) and black grille, aluminium rear panel, thin glass, chromium rectangular wing mirror, 'Carrera' script on sides
Suspension, front:	Independent suspension with wishbones and McPherson struts, one round, longitudinal torsion bar per wheel, hydraulic double-action shock absorbers, anti-roll bar
Suspension, rear:	Independent suspension with semi-trailing arms, one round, transverse torsion bar per wheel, hydraulic double-action shock absorbers, anti-roll bar
Brakes, front/rear (Size (mm)):	Ventilated discs (282.5 x 20) / Ventilated discs (290 x 20) 2-piston fixed aluminium callipers / 2-piston fixed cast-iron callipers
Wheels, front/rear:	6 J x 15 / 7 J x 15
Tyres, front/rear:	185/70 VR 15 / 215/60 VR 15

Electrical system

Alternator (W/A):	770 / 55
Battery (V/Ah):	12 / 36

Dimensions and weight

Track, front/rear (mm):	1372 / 1394
Wheelbase (mm):	2271
Length x width x height (mm):	4102 x 1652 x 1320
Kerb weight DIN (kg):	960
Permissible gross weight (kg):	1400
Luggage compartment (l):	200
Fuel tank capacity (l):	85, including 9 reserve
C_w x A (m²):	0.397 x 1.73 = 0.686
Power/weight ratio (kg/kW/kg/hp):	6.23 / 4.57

Fuel consumption

DIN 70 030 (mpg):	26; 91 RON normal leaded

Performance, production, prices

Acceleration 0-62mph/100kph (s):	5.8
Maximum speed (mph / kph):	152 / 245
Production, total number:	
Sportsversion (M 471):	200
plus homologation vehicles:	17
Purchase prices:	
08/1972:	DM 34,000
incl. M 471:	DM 34,700
02/1973:	DM 34,000
incl. M 471:	DM 34,700

Porsche 911 ('G Series') and Porsche 912 E

Model year 1974 (G Series)

For the first time in its history, the bodywork of the 911 underwent fundamental modification. New laws in the United States demanded higher-mounted bumpers capable of withstanding 5mph impacts without body damage. The new model range included the 911, 911 S and 911 Carrera. A new top-of-the-range model, the 911 turbo, was presented at the Paris Auto Show.

Immediately obvious on the restyled 911 body were the new, boxy bumpers with black bellows at their corners. These could withstand impacts at speeds up to 5mph/8kph without body damage. The front grilles were deleted, and indicators were integrated in the bumpers. Between the tail lamps was a red non-reflecting valance with 'PORSCHE' script. The rear number plate was mounted directly to the bumper, between two rubber over-riders and integral number plate illumination. A thick black rubber trim strip was attached to the sills. On the 911 and 911 S, trim strips around windows, door handles, wing mirrors and headlamps were executed in brightwork, while the Carrera used black window frames and door handles. Carrera bodywork featured discreetly widened rear wings. All 911 models were also available as Targas. The 911 Targa was fitted with a rigid, removable plastic roof panel. This version of the Targa top was available from the beginning of the model year. As an added-cost option, the familiar folding top was also available. Subsequently, the folding top once again became standard equipment. A space-saver spare wheel was nestled in a well in the 80-litre (17.5-gallon) fuel tank; in the event of a flat tyre, this could be inflated with a supplied electric compressor. A high-pressure headlamp-cleaning system was available as an option.

All engines had identical displacement of 2.7 litres, and were tuned to use regular-grade petrol. The Nikasil-coated aluminium cylinders had a bore of 90mm. Carreras used forged pistons, while the slipper-skirt pistons of the other two models were cast. Valves, rocker arms, and camshaft drive remained unchanged. The 911 and 911 S models were given different valve timing. While the power units of the base and S models were equipped with Bosch K-Jetronic injection systems, the Carrera engine continued to use the mechanical manifold-injection system of the Carrera RS. Because of the altered rear valance panels, exhaust systems were modified. The base 911 engine developed 150hp (110kW) at 5700rpm and a maximum torque of 235Nm (173lb ft) at 3800rpm. The 911 S produced 175hp (129kW) at 5800rpm and a peak torque of 235Nm (173lb ft) at 4000rpm. Engine output of the 911 Carrera was identical to that of the previous year's 911 Carrera RS.

All models were equipped with a four-speed manual transmission as standard equipment. As an option, all could be had with a five-speed manual, a limited-slip differential, and, for the 911 and 911 S, a Sportomatic transmission.

The front axles were now equipped with self-centering hubs. The rear suspension employed aluminium semi-trailing arms with larger wheel bearings. The 911 and 911 S used a 16mm front anti-roll bar, while the Carrera used a 20mm bar. The Carrera also used an 18mm rear anti-roll bar, which could also be fitted to the 911 and 911 S as an option. The 911 rolled on 5.5J x 15 steel disc wheels and 165 HR 15 rubber. On the 911 S, standard ATS cast wheels, size 6J x 15, carried 185/70 VR 15 tyres. The Carrera was equipped with the same wheel and tyre package as the previous year's Carrera RS.

Vehicle interiors were reworked for increased safety. New seats, with integrated headrests, were combined with automatic safety-belts. Side defroster vents were added to the dashboard, and knobs and buttons were padded. The new inner door panels incorporated lidded storage pockets. The steering wheel surrounded a large padded hub. The Carrera was given a three-spoke steering wheel. On the Carrera Coupé, electric windows were standard.

The 911 topped out at 130mph (210 kph) and sped through the 62mph (100 kph) mark in 8.5 seconds. In the sprint to 62mph, the 911 S was somewhat quicker at 7.6 seconds, and reached a top speed of 140mph (225kph). The top of the line, the

911 Carrera, could reach 149mph (240kph) and accelerated to 62mph (100kph) in just 6.3 seconds.

To keep the 911 Carrera RS competitive on the race track, Porsche modified this model to reflect development of the regular production cars. The 911 Carrera RS 3.0 was designed for racing, but could also be licensed for road use. Porsche's Zuffenhausen plant initiated limited production of the RS 3.0 in the autumn of 1973. In all, 110 examples were built, of which 50 were converted to Carrera RSR form. The first 15 examples went to the United States, ordered by Roger Penske, who used them in his International Race of Champions (IROC) racing series. The Carrera RS 3.0 was entered in races by customer teams, but not by Porsche itself.

Externally, the most obvious feature was the RSR's extremely wide wings. At the front, these covered Pirelli CN 36 tyres, size 215/60 VR 15, on 9-inch aluminium-alloy rims. At the rear, 235/60 VR 15 tyres rode on 9-inch wheels. The larger, higher-mounted bumpers, the front bumper with its oil-cooler duct, the bonnet and the engine lid, with its new integrated flat rear wing and black polyurethane surround, were made of fibreglass. Thin-gauge components for doors, roof, rear seat pans and dashboard shaved several kilograms off vehicle kerb weight. The windscreen was a regular production item, but the remaining glazing was made of thinner-gauge glass. Headlamp bezels were painted in body colour. Wing mirrors and window frames were black anodized. Like its predecessor, the interior was kept spartan. The headliner was of black felt. The driver's seat was a Recaro lightweight shell, while the passenger got a Recaro racing seat.

The engine developed 230hp (169kW) at 6200rpm and a maximum torque of 275Nm (203lb ft) from a displacement of 2994cc. For added strength, the crankcase was an aluminium-alloy casting. Its dry-sump lubrication system contained 16 litres (3.5 gallons) of oil. The five-speed manual transmission had its own oil cooler and a limited-slip differential with an 80 per cent lock-up factor. Only the clutch was carried over from regular production.

In most respects, the suspension was identical to that of the 1973 Carrera RSR 2.8, but was reinforced at numerous key points. If desired, coil springs were available for the rear suspension. For the 911 Carrera RS 3.0, Porsche reached into its racing parts bins for the proven brake system of the Type 917. Four-piston fixed callipers wrapped around cross-drilled, ventilated rotors. Despite their larger diameter, the 300mm brake discs were lighter than regular production rotors. In terms of handling, the 911 Carrera RS 3.0 was superior to its predecessor. Weighing in at 1060kg (2337lb), the car was priced at 64,980 Deutschmarks.

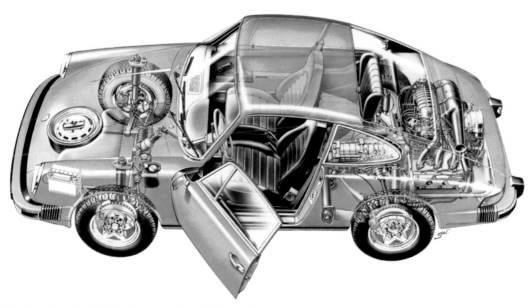

Phantom view of a 911 Coupé powered by a 2.7-litre engine

Model year 1975 (H Series)

In 1975, Porsche had been building cars in Stuttgart-Zuffenhausen for a quarter century. The company celebrated this anniversary with a special edition, silver with blue-black leatherette interior and a dash plaque on the glove-compartment lid bearing the signature of Ferry Porsche. Four hundred examples of this special model were built, available as a 911, 911 S and 911 Carrera. In the spring of 1975, Porsche introduced its new flagship, the 911 turbo, to the market, powered by a turbocharged 3-litre engine. The turbo was the fastest German production car of the time.

The 911 turbo, known internally as the 930, was distinguished by its wide bodywork, about 12cm (nearly 5 inches) wider than the 911 Carrera. Front and rear wings were significantly wider. At the front the turbo carried a distinctive black polyurethane spoiler. At the rear, a flat, polyurethane-rimmed rear wing sprouted from the plastic engine lid. Mirror and headlamp bezels were painted body colour. Window frames and door handles were black.

With cylinder bore expanded to 95mm, engine displacement grew to 2994cc. Beginning with the 3-litre engines, the crankcase was once again made of a sturdy aluminium alloy. Compression was reduced to 6.5:1 using special forged-aluminium alloy pistons. With the help of a Type KKK 3 LDZ turbocharger, made by Kühnle, Kopp & Kausch of Frankenthal, Germany, the engine developed 260hp

(191kW) at only 5500rpm, and 343Nm (253lb ft) of torque at 4000rpm. At full boost, air was fed to the combustion chambers at 0.8bar above atmospheric pressure, with the turbocharger turning at 90,000rpm. Premium-grade petrol was metered by a Bosch K-Jetronic fuel-injection system. Ignition was by a Bosch capacitive-discharge system. To ensure continuity of fuel supply even at high engine speeds, two electric fuel pumps were installed in series, a principle that had already been proven on the turbocharged 917 racing engines. The 911 turbo was teamed solely with a four-speed manual transmission; for years, Porsche would hold fast to the opinion that with so much torque available, four speeds were plenty. A limited-slip differential was available as an option.

The suspension was completely reworked for the turbo. Front transverse links and cast-aluminium rear semi-trailing arms were newly-designed components. Front and rear anti-roll bars were 18mm in diameter. Bilstein provided gas-pressure shock absorbers. The front two-piston callipers of the dual-circuit brake system were of aluminium, while the rears were cast iron. All four brake rotors were ventilated. Fuchs forged-alloy wheels, 7 J x 15 at the front, carried 185/70 VR 15 tyres, while 8-inch rear wheels carried 215/60 VR 15 rubber. The wheel centres were painted black, and the rims were bare aluminium. For wider track, spacer rings were installed, 21mm at the front and 28mm at the rear.

The turbo left little to be desired in terms of standard equipment, which included a four-speaker stereo system, air-conditioning, rear wiper, electric windows, 66Ah battery, 980-watt alternator, automatic heating control, the Carrera's three-spoke sports steering wheel, and all-leather upholstery, which could be combined with plaid inserts.

All normally-aspirated 911 models were given improved sound insulation. The base model was now fitted with the 6 J x 15 ATS aluminium wheels from the 911 S, with 185/70 VR 15 tyres. On the Carrera, headlamp bezels and wing mirrors were now painted body colour. The Carrera Targa was recognizable by its black Targa bar.

Acceleration of the 911 turbo could only be described as explosive: 62mph (100 kph) in just 5.5 seconds. Even Italian super sports cars had to admit defeat in this performance test. Top speed was in excess of 155mph (250kph).

A 3-litre turbo engine, without intercooler

Model year 1976 (J Series)

The model range was trimmed for 1976. The new base model was given a 165hp (121kW) 2.7-litre engine, replacing the earlier 150hp (110kW) and 175hp (129kW) motors. The 911 S was removed from the line-up, and the Carrera given a 3-litre engine with K-Jetronic fuel injection, developing 200hp (147kW). All six-cylinder engines were now fitted with K-Jetronic.

As of the autumn of 1975, all Porsche cars had hot-dip galvanized body panels and were assembled using the most modern corrosion-protection methods. All structural components were made of galvanized steel. Porsche provided a six-year warranty against floorpan rust-through.

For the 1976 model year only, Porsche offered the 912 E Coupé for the American market, priced at $10,845. This USA-only model had a brief run of only 2099 examples. The 912 E was powered by an air-cooled 2-litre four-cylinder boxer engine, derived from the 914 2.0 power unit. This yielded 86hp (62kW) and drove the 912 E to a top speed of 109mph (176kph) and acceleration to 62mph (100 kph) in 13.5 seconds.

The base 911's 2.7-litre engine enjoyed higher compression at 8.5:1. Power increased to 165hp (121kW) at 5800rpm. With the inclusion of the 3-litre normally-aspirated engine of the Carrera 3.0, all 911 engines were now fitted with K-Jetronic fuel injection. Along with increased displacement, the Carrera engine had larger valves. The new Carrera engine developed 200hp (147kW) at 6000rpm; at 255Nm (188lb ft) its peak torque was identical to that of the 2.7-litre Carrera, but was reached at a lower speed, 4200rpm. Both normally-aspirated engines were fitted with an altered, higher-speed cooling blower with just five fan blades (previously, all 911 blowers had 11 blades). The outside diameter of the blower was reduced from 245mm to 226mm. These measures also gave the engines a different sound. The turbo engine was fitted with an auxiliary air valve and air injection to reduce exhaust emissions.

Gear ratios were matched to the characteristics of the normally-aspirated engines. Only four-speeds were offered as standard equipment, although five-speed transmissions were optional. A Sportomatic transmission was optional on the 911 and 911 Carrera 3.0; on the Carrera 3.0 it could be ordered at no extra charge.

The turbo's forged-aluminium wheels were now fitted with low-profile tyres – front 205/50 VR 15, and rear 225/50 VR 15. If desired, the previous year's tyre sizes could be provided. The turbo's final drive ratio was altered in keeping with the lower-profile tyres.

Externally, the 1976 911 models could be recognized by their electrically-adjustable, heated, body-colour wing mirrors. A headlamp-washer system was standard on the 911 Carrera 3.0 and 911 turbo.

Door panels of the Carrera 3.0 and turbo had stitched decorative pleats. Storage pockets in the doors were trimmed with carpeting. The 911 and 911 Carrera 3.0 were fitted with an electronic speedometer, and one audio speaker was installed in each door panel. Cruise control was available as an option. Automatic heat control, standard on the Carrera 3.0 and turbo, could be ordered as an option on the 911.

Performance of the base 911 was slightly better than that of the previous year's model. The Carrera 3.0 accelerated more strongly than the 2.7-litre Carrera, but its top speed of 143mph (230 kph) was somewhat lower.

Model year 1977 (K Series)

All three 911 models entered their last model year. New emissions regulations in the United States, Canada and Japan necessitated secondary air injection and thermal reactors, a rudimentary form of catalytic converter. New, more powerful fuel pumps generated less noise. Improvements to the clutch system made clutch operation more comfortable on the Carrera 3.0 and turbo; these models were also fitted with a vacuum brake booster as standard equipment. When equipped with a Sportomatic transmission, the base 911 was also given a brake booster.

The Carrera 3.0 was now equipped with ATS cast-aluminium wheels as standard equipment. The 911 turbo was the first 911 model to be fitted with 16-inch forged wheels. The front wheels carried 205/55 VR 16 tyres on 7 J x 16 rims, the rear 8 J x 16s carried 225/50 VR 16 rubber. The turbo's front anti-roll bar diameter grew to 20 mm.

On the turbo, black decals were applied just ahead of the rear wheel cut-outs to protect the bodywork against rock nicks. On the Targa, the opening front quarterlights were deleted in order to better protect the vehicle against theft. The Carrera 3.0 had a rear wiper fitted as standard equipment.

For 1977 the interior was marked by several improvements. For better ventilation and climate control, two additional, individually-adjustable air vents were installed in the centre of the dashboard. Ventilation controls were now illuminated at night.

The instrument panel included a large red safety-belt warning lamp. Rotary knobs for locking and unlocking the doors were set into the inner door panels, for better anti-theft protection. The door-locking push-buttons now fully retracted into the door in their locked position, to prevent unlocking by means of a wire or coathanger slipped through the window. Pinstripe seat upholstery was available as an option. The 911 turbo tachometer included an analog boost-pressure gauge.

Model year 1978 (L Series)

The 911 line-up was trimmed to only two models for 1978. The 911 SC (S for Super and C for Carrera) was the only normally-aspirated version, with performance falling between that of the earlier 911 S and Carrera models. Available in Coupé and Targa form, the 911 SC was powered by a 3-litre engine. The 911 turbo was now fitted with a new, 3.3-litre turbocharged power unit.

The 911 SC had somewhat wider bodywork than the earlier Carrera. Window frames, door handles and headlamp bezels were chromium-plated. The turbo had a steel engine lid, on which was mounted a larger plastic rear wing with an upturned, wrap-around polyurethane lip. The intercooler was mounted below the new wing. The front spoiler was modified slightly. Rear quarterlights were now fixed in place.

The 911 SC suspension had anti-roll bars fitted as standard equipment, 20mm at the front and 18mm at the rear. A brake booster made for decreased brake pedal effort. Standard equipment included ATS cast-aluminium wheels, 6 J x 15 at the front and 7 J x 15 at the rear, carrying 185/70 and 215/60 VR 15 tyres, respectively. Sixteen-inch Fuchs forged-alloys were available as an option.

The turbo was fitted with a new brake system, derived from that of the 917 race car. For better response in wet conditions, the internally-vented rotors were cross-drilled. For the first time on a production vehicle, Porsche installed four-piston fixed alloy callipers of its own design. The 3.3-litre turbo rolled on 16-inch forged-alloy wheels.

Mounted in the rear of the 911 SC was a 3-litre power unit developing 180hp (132kW) at 5500rpm. A low compression ratio of 8.5:1 permitted continued use of regular-grade petrol. Because its engine was tuned for greater across-the-board torque, the SC gave up 20hp to the earlier Carrera 3.0, but its maximum torque of 265Nm (195lb ft) at 4200rpm exceeded that of the Carrera 3.0. The crankshaft was reinforced, main-bearing diameter increased to 60mm and connecting rods were

redesigned to match the new crankshaft. The blower once again used 11 blades, but retained the smaller, 226mm outside diameter.

By increasing cylinder bore to 97mm and installing a new crankshaft with 74.4mm stroke, displacement of the turbo engine increased to 3299cc. Pistons were altered accordingly, compression ratio raised to 7.0:1, and a charge-air intercooler installed. These measures boosted the turbo to 300hp (221kW) at 5500rpm, making it the most powerful production Porsche to date. Torque, too, achieved a new high – 412Nm (304lb ft) at 4000rpm. The new engine demanded premium fuel, with a Research Octane Number of 98. For the United States, Canada and Japan, the engine was designed to operate with unleaded fuel, and was fitted with secondary air-injection, thermal reactors and exhaust gas recirculation. These emissions measures reduced power output to 265hp (195kW) in the affected markets.

While the 911 SC was available with the standard five-speed manual or optional three-speed Sportomatic transmission, the 911 turbo could only be ordered with a four-speed manual, now with a higher fourth gear.

The combination instrument scaling was changed. The tachometer now bore markings up to 7000rpm. The speedometer of the 3.3 turbo ranged up to 186mph (300kph), and the boost-pressure gauge was improved.

The 911 SC hit 62mph (100kph) in 7 seconds, with a top speed of 140mph (225kph). The 911 turbo could sprint to 62mph in just 5.4 seconds, and topped out at 162mph (260kph).

Model year 1979 (M Series)

Few changes were noted for the 1979 model year. Headlamp bezels for the 911 SC were now painted in body colour, exterior door handles and window frames were black anodized. On the Targa the roll bar was now black.

The interior featured new short-pile carpeting. The turbo had green-tinted glass all round, but the standard radio was deleted.

Model year 1980 (A Programme)

After the M Series of 1979, Porsche introduced a new internal model year designation. The 911 SC was given a minor horsepower increase of about 8hp (6kW). The 1980 model year 911 turbo was

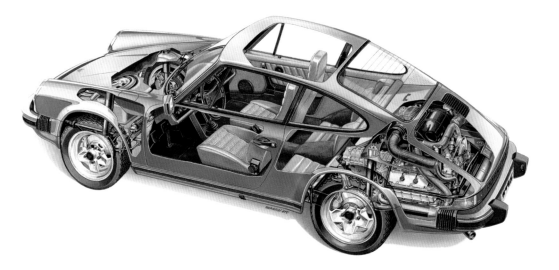

Phantom view of a 911 SC Coupé with its 3-litre engine

recognizable by its new twin-outlet exhaust system. For the US market Porsche built its first engines fitted with catalytic converters and oxygen sensors.

All engines had new, ribbed valve covers and improved valve cover gaskets. The SC engines reverted to a larger 245mm blower, and crankcase oil scavenging was improved. Power increased to 188hp (138kW). Torque and performance, however, remained unchanged. The Sportomatic transmission was no longer listed as an option.

All Porsche models were fitted with standardized safety-belts. Speedometers were marked in 20kph increments. The 911 SC was fitted with the three-spoke steering wheel as standard equipment, a centre console and electric windows. The engine compartment was now illuminated, and an alarm system was offered as an option.

Model year 1981 (B Programme)

Porsche's long-term warranty against rust-through was extended to seven years and applied to the entire body, which was now made entirely of hot-dip galvanized steel. One recognition feature of the new model year (for non-US market cars) was side-mounted indicators on the front wings, just ahead of the doors. The small headlamp-washer snorkels were replaced by flush-mounted nozzles.

In the early 1970s, in the interest of environmental protection, Porsche's normally-aspirated engines were tuned to run on lower-lead regular-grade petrol. In the early 1980s, engine development emphasis shifted to improved fuel economy. Compression ratios of 9.8:1 and altered valve timing again necessitated premium petrol. As a pleasant side-effect of these fuel economy measures, the engine developed even more power: 204hp (150kW) at 5900rpm, and slightly higher peak torque of 267Nm (197lb ft) at 4300rpm. The 911 SC clutch disc was also improved.

To prevent actuation errors at night, illuminated pull knobs were installed on the dashboard. As an option, seats could be ordered with 'Berber' upholstery, and new sports seats were available.

Performance of the 911 SC was noticeably improved. Top speed was about 146mph (235kph), and the 62mph (100 kph) mark was reached in 6.8 seconds.

Model year 1982 (C Programme)

In August 1981, Porsche celebrated its 50th anniversary with a special edition, painted Meteor Metallic. Only 200 examples were built, as 911 SC Coupés and Targas. One unique feature was the special edition's burgundy leather and fabric interior. Seating surfaces, door and rear side-panels were covered in burgundy fabric with silver pinstripes; steering wheel and seat side-bolsters were covered in burgundy leather. The headrests had embroidered

'F. Porsche' signatures. The special edition cars were also fitted with rear wipers, green-tinted glass and 15-inch forged-alloy rims, 7 inches at the front and 8 inches at the rear. Tyres were the same as those used in regular production.

In the autumn of 1981, at the Frankfurt International Automobile Show, Porsche displayed an all-wheel-drive 911 turbo Cabriolet study. As Porsche cognoscenti know, both a 911 Cabriolet and all-wheel-drive technology would one day be regular production items.

A new Porsche roof carrier-system was introduced to enable 911 Coupés to carry additional loads of up to 75kg (165lb).

As an option, the 911 SC could be ordered with the front spoiler and rear wing of the 911 turbo. The headlamp-washer system became standard equipment for the 911 SC. The side-vents on the dashboard now also delivered warm air with the aim of preventing condensation on the side windows. The oil temperature gauge was revised, with different scaling.

All six-cylinder engines were fitted with a more powerful 1050-watt, 75-amp alternator. The 911 was given a reinforced differential. ATS cast wheels were given a bright treatment at their rims, and had black-painted centres, echoing the visual appearance of the more attractive forged alloys.

Model year 1983 (D Programme)

In the spring of 1983, Porsche's long spell without a convertible came to an end. After 18 years a Cabriolet rejoined the model line-up. The 911 SC Cabriolet, one of the world's fastest convertibles, became available in all Porsche markets worldwide, even as the 911 SC entered its last model year.

The basic body of the new 911 Cabriolet was derived from that of the Targa. The 911 SC hood incorporated sheet-steel structural shapes; 50 per cent of the hood consisted of rigid components. This permitted high-speed motoring in closed configuration without having the hood 'inflate'. In the event of a rollover accident, this design also offered the best possible protection for the occupants. Hood operation was very simple and could be accomplished manually. The flexible rear window could be opened by means of a zipper. For better outward visibility, the Cabriolet was equipped with two electrically adjustable and heatable wing mirrors.

Floorpan reinforcements made the open-top 911 one of the most torsionally rigid convertibles in existence. Later, a removable hardtop would become available.

Beginning with the 1983 model year, Porsche's repair department offered the so-called 'flat nose' or

Engine compartment of a 911 SC, with 3-litre engine and secondary air pump

'slant nose' conversion for the wide turbo body. On newly-ordered vehicles this conversion was performed on the raw body shell, thereby retaining Porsche's anti-corrosion warranty. The 'slant nose' included flatter front wings with flip-up headlamps from the Porsche 944, and a front spoiler with integral oil cooler. Additionally, many customers chose special sill extensions and air inlets in the rear wings. These provided better rear brake cooling.

All 911s were fitted with static two-point rear seat-belts. Porsche presented a new generation of radios in the form of the Blaupunkt Köln. The 911 SC Coupé and Targa were equipped with automatic heat control, while the Cabriolet retained manual controls; in open-top driving, automatic controls would make erroneous heat control adjustments. The Cabriolet was equipped with leather seats as standard equipment. Two extra heating blowers were installed on the turbo, to provide more warm air to the cabin during the engine's warm-up phase.

A new exhaust pre-silencer was adapted to the 911 SC exhaust system. Vehicles for the Swiss market were fitted with a special silencer.

For the turbo engine, detail engineering improved the K-Jetronic fuel-injection system and ignition system. The main exhaust silencer was modified. The turbo-boost bypass system now exhausted through a separate, small silencer. These measures resulted in slight fuel economy improvements. Torque rose to 430Nm (317lb ft) at the same engine speed. For Switzerland, turbos were fitted with an altered transmission having a higher second gear, lowering engine rpm (and thereby reducing noise level) at a specific road speed in order to meet that nation's drive-by noise standard.

Beginning with the 1983 model year, Porsche's repair department offered a performance boost for the 911 turbo, officially yielding 330hp. Porsche took advantage of the legally-permitted five per cent 'window' in officially-stated power output by means of a larger turbocharger, four-pipe exhaust system and optimized intercooler.

Performance of the modified turbo was markedly faster, sprinting to 62mph (100kph) in just 5.2 seconds. Top speed was about 168mph (270kph), indeed 171mph (275kph) for the flat-nose conversion.

Model year 1984 (E Programme)

As of the autumn of 1983, the 911 SC was replaced by the 911 Carrera, with its 3.2-litre engine. For racing, Porsche built a limited series of 20 cars, the 911 SC/RS. At the Frankfurt International Automobile Show, Porsche displayed its design study for the Porsche 959.

The most important new feature of the 911 Carrera was its 3.2-litre boxer engine. By increasing stroke to 74.4mm and retaining a 95mm bore, displacement grew to 3164cc. Fuel-injection and map-ignition were controlled by a Digital Motor Electronics (DME) unit, with overrun fuel cut-off and idle compensation. The injection system was based on the familiar L-Jetronic, with a mass-airflow meter. For better cylinder filling at high engine speeds, a resonance induction system was fitted. With 10.3:1 compression, the engine developed 231hp (170kW) at 5900rpm, and maximum torque of 284Nm (209lb ft) at 4800rpm.

A different engine version was developed for the United States and Japanese export markets. With compression lowered to 9.5:1, this engine could operate on 91-octane regular unleaded petrol. Power output was decidedly lower: 207hp (152kW) at 5900rpm. Torque was also reduced to 260Nm (192lb ft) at 4800rpm. The DME unit for this engine was equipped with a heated oxygen sensor for mixture control.

The crankcase for all 3.2-litre engines was reinforced and fitted with improved chain tensioners connected to the oil-circulation system. This eliminated the boxer engine's most significant weakness.

A more powerful 90-amp alternator was teamed with a 66Ah battery and delivered 1260 watts for the Carrera and turbo. All 911 models were fitted with an auxiliary oil cooler in the right front wheel well to keep engine oil temperatures within acceptable limits even at high engine speeds.

Like the turbo transmission, the five-speed manual transmission of the Carrera was fitted with a speed-dependent transmission oil pump and a finned oil-cooler mounted on the transmission housing. As an option, the Carrera and turbo could be ordered with a limited-slip differential providing a 40% locking factor.

The new 911 Carrera could be ordered in the familiar Coupé, Targa and Cabriolet body variations. Optionally, these models could be fitted with a polyurethane front spoiler and a flat rear wing, developed especially for the Carrera, with polyurethane edging. These reduced front and rear lift at high speeds, making the car more stable and even raising top speed slightly. All 911s were fitted with fog lamps integrated in the front valance as standard equipment. The 911 Coupé could be ordered with the 'turbo look' option; along with the turbo's wide body and spoilers. This included the turbo suspension, four-piston fixed callipers, cross-drilled rotors, 16-inch forged-alloy rims and low-profile tyres.

Standard on the Carrera were 15-inch cast-alloy 'telephone design' wheels, 6 inches wide at the front and 7 inches at the rear, with 185/70 and 215/60 VR 15 tyres respectively. Optionally, these tyre sizes could be ordered with inch-wider Fuchs forged alloys. Also optional were 16-inch forged wheels in the same widths. The Carrera's already uprated brake system was once again improved with a brake force regulator, ejector vacuum pump and larger brake booster. All 911s were equipped with brake-pad wear sensors. Front and rear anti-roll bars were standard. Coupé and Targa buyers could opt for sports shock absorbers.

All Carrera models were well-equipped with green-tinted rear window, electric windows, electrically adjustable and heatable wing mirror (two in the case of the Cabriolet), high-pressure headlamp-washer system, and leather-covered steering wheel. The Coupé and Targa had automatic heater control and a two-stage heatable rear window as standard. On the Cabriolet, heating was manually adjustable with separate left and right controls. Leather seats were standard in the Cabriolet. New in the line-up was seat fabric with embroidered 'PORSCHE' script in a matching shade.

The Carrera accelerated to 62mph (100kph) in 6.1 seconds, with a published top speed of 152mph (245 kph). Well run-in examples with the optional spoiler package could exceed 155mph (250 kph).

In late 1983 Porsche produced an evolution series of 20 cars to meet homologation requirements for Group B competition. Because the Carrera 3.2 was already rolling off the Zuffenhausen assembly line, the new competition car, which would primarily be used in rallies, was named the 911 SC/RS, and not Carrera, as its technology was based on the 3-litre 911 SC engine.

Bodywork, suspension, wheels and brakes were taken from the regular production 911 turbo, and were combined with many lightweight components: plastic bumpers, aluminium parts and thinner glass. Inside, the glove compartment lid, rear interior trim, rear seats and clock were deleted. Comfortable stock seats were replaced by thinly-padded racing seats.

The normally-aspirated engine was given a significant power increase through higher 10.3:1 compression, forged pistons, cylinder heads from the racing 935 with increased valve lift and Bosch-Kugelfischer mechanical fuel injection. This resulted in 250hp (184kW) at 7000rpm. Fully-fuelled, the 911 SC/RS tipped the scales at just 1057kg (2330lb). For displacement below 3 litres, racing rules allowed further weight reduction to 960kg (2116lb). In accelerating to 99mph (160kph) in just 11.7 seconds, the 911 SC/RS left in its wake just about anything that could be considered street legal, including the more powerful but heavier 911 turbo. Still, at a price of 188,100 Deutschmarks, one was unlikely to encounter it on public roads.

Model year 1985 (F Programme)

Porsche expanded the range of Carrera model choices. The 'turbo look' body was made available for Targa and Cabriolet as well. All models were fitted with side-impact beams in the doors as standard equipment, to better protect occupants in the event of an accident.

Targa and Cabriolet models with turbo-look bodywork needed extra body reinforcement, since the turbo suspension could generate higher forces.

The 911 turbo suspension was recalibrated. Anti-roll bar diameter grew by 2mm; front bars were now 22mm, rears 20mm. The forged-alloy wheels could now be ordered with their centres painted Grand Prix White or White Gold Metallic.

The 911 was fitted with a new seat design which was somewhat slimmer. Standard seats in all Carrera models had fabric seating surfaces, with leather side-panels. The driver's seat had independent front and rear electric rake and height adjustments. Optional sports seats had the same electrical adjustment feature. Also optional were 'comfort seats' with electric reach and seat-back rake adjustments. The four-spoke leather-covered steering wheel could be ordered in the same colour as the interior trim. The gear lever boot was leather. Windscreen-washer nozzles were electrically heated. A radio installation kit with an antenna embedded in the windscreen, four speakers and fader rounded out the equipment package. As an option, an especially rigid Sekuriflex windscreen could be ordered. On the 911 turbo, standard equipment now included air-conditioning and central door-locking activated from the centre console.

Porsche's patented synchromesh was reworked for reduced gear forces. Altered gear lever geometry provided shorter, sportier gear changes.

Model year 1986 (G Programme)

Porsche greatly expanded its warranty coverage. The long-term warranty against rust-through was extended to ten years, the paint warranty to three years, and the overall vehicle warranty to two years and unlimited mileage. Porsche provided a one-year warranty on genuine Porsche replacement parts. Porsche was the first manufacturer to provide a ten-year rust-through warranty. The Carrera turbo look could also be ordered in spoilerless form. For a cleaner environment, the non-USA Carrera could be ordered with an optional catalytic converter package; catalytic converters were already required equipment in the United States.

Suspension tuning of the Carrera models was improved by thicker anti-roll bars, 22mm at the front, 21mm at the rear, and larger rear torsion bars, going from 24mm to 25mm in diameter. As an option, sports shock absorbers were now available for the Cabriolet as well. The rear axle of the turbo now carried 9 J x 16 rims with 245/45 VR 16 tyres.

In the interior, obvious changes included a redesigned dashboard with larger air vents and altered switches. All vehicles were fitted with an intensive windscreen-washer system and sliding make-up mirror covers in the sun visors. The front seats were lowered by 20mm, giving tall drivers more headroom. The heating system was equipped with a new interior temperature sensor, which enabled the Carrera Cabriolet to be equipped with automatic heat control.

For the first time in the German market, Porsche offered a catalytic-converter-equipped engine tuned to produce 207hp (152kW) on unleaded regular (91 octane) petrol. The catalyst-equipped Carrera models were given a reinforced transmission housing, minus the transmission oil cooler. The US version of the turbo had modified ignition and mixture control, a three-way catalytic converter, oxygen sensor and secondary air injection. This engine developed 282hp (207kW) at 5500rpm. Peak torque was at the same engine speed as before, but 40Nm (30lb ft) lower.

Performance of the catalyst-equipped Carrera was slower than that of the unregulated version; catalyst Carreras needed 6.5 seconds to reach 62mph, and top speed was 146mph (235kph).

Model year 1987 (H Programme)

In the spring of 1987 the 911 turbo became available in Targa and Cabriolet form. Like the 911 Carrera, the turbo was now available in all three body variations.

The Carrera's catalytic-converter engine was reworked for unleaded 95 octane Euro Super fuel. This raised output to 217hp (160kW) at 5900rpm. Maximum torque also climbed slightly, to 265Nm (195lb ft) at 4800rpm.

Carrera models were fitted with the new G50 manual transmission. This was reinforced and easier to use, thanks to new Borg-Warner synchromesh. The fully-synchromesh reverse gear was now located forward and to the left, giving a total of four gear change planes, and the Carrera clutch was hydraulically actuated. Because of the new transmission, a new rear axle tube was installed. The rear torsion bars had finer-pitch splines. At the front the Carrera carried 195/65 VR 15 tyres.

The 1987 model year 911 showed only minor external modifications. The red tail-light band now included two integrated rear fog lamps. The torsion bar modifications necessitated larger round covers in the sills ahead of the rear wheels. An added-cost option on the Carrera Cabriolet was an electric convertible top; this was a no-cost option on the turbo Cabriolet.

As an exception, for the 1987 model year, intensive windscreen-washers and headlamp-washers were not included as standard equipment. The rear glass had only single-stage heating.

Actuation of the electrically adjustable wing mirrors was changed. The control knob was leather covered to match the rest of the interior. The 911 turbo was fitted with fully electrically-adjustable seats as standard equipment.

Performance of cars with the more powerful catalytic converter engine was improved slightly, but still could not match the unregulated version above 4000rpm. Acceleration to 62mph (100kph) took 6.3 seconds, and top speed was 149mph (240kph).

Model year 1988 (J Programme)

The 250,000th Porsche 911 rolled off the assembly line in the summer of 1987. Porsche celebrated this event with a special limited edition of 875 examples. Of these, 250 were sold in Germany, 300 went to the United States and the remaining 325 to other export markets.

Available in all three body variations, the special edition was painted Diamond Blue Metallic. A sunroof was standard on the Coupé, and an electric convertible top was standard on the Cabriolet. The centres of the 15-inch Fuchs forged-alloys were painted in body colour. Interior trim included silver-blue partial-crushed leather, with the 'F. Porsche' signature embroidered in the headrests. Steering wheel and shortened gear lever were covered with the same leather. The interior and boot were lined with especially-luxurious velour carpeting, and a plaque was affixed to the glove compartment door. At the autumn 1987 Frankfurt International

Automobile Exhibition, Porsche presented the 911 Speedster with narrow Carrera bodywork.

In place of 'telephone design' cast-alloy wheels, standard equipment on 911 Carreras now consisted of Fuchs forged-alloys, 7 J x 15 at the front and 8 J x 15 rear. Clutch linings of all 911 models were asbestos-free, and for Scandinavian markets all vehicles used asbestos-free brake pads.

Gas struts supporting the lids of all 911s were modified. The black anodized trim strip around the windscreen was replaced by plastic. A second wing mirror, intensive windscreen-washers and a headlamp-washer system were reintroduced as standard equipment.

The steering wheel pad, which also served as the horn button, now included an embossed horn symbol, as required by US regulations. The passenger seat was fitted with the same electric adjustments as the driver's seat. Central-locking, with the locking button on the centre console, was standard equipment on all Carrera models.

Porsche offered a lighter weight, especially sporty coupé in the form of the 911 Carrera Clubsport, which was externally identifiable by its standard spoiler, lack of fog lamps and 'Clubsport' decal on its left front wing.

As well as its reduced equipment package, the Clubsport was trimmed for even more sporty performance. On the principle of 'less is more', the rear seats, side and rear trim, sound-insulation material, electric heating control, passenger-side sun visor, door-pocket lids, radio-installation kit, power windows and coathooks were all deleted. Compared to a well-equipped 'normal' Carrera, the Clubsport weighed a good 100kg (220lb) less.

With 231hp (170kW) at 5900rpm on tap, the Clubsport engine had the same nominal power output as the regular production Carrera. However, thanks to lighter intake valves and a rev limit bumped from 6520rpm to 6840rpm, the Clubsport engine was much more rev-happy. The 911 Clubsport suspension also benefited from firmer tuning.

The Clubsport Carrera accelerated noticeably faster, and pulled more strongly, than the production Carrera, but its top speed was identical.

Model year 1989 (K Programme)

The Carrera and turbo models entered their last year of production. The Carrera was now available as a Speedster. The Speedster was an instant classic, a collectible in its own time. The turbo was finally granted a long-awaited five-speed transmission. But the most important news was the 911 Carrera 4 (Type 964) with all-wheel drive, ABS brakes, new 3.6-litre engine, new suspension and major aerodynamic body improvements.

The 911 Speedster's stock equipment included spoilerless turbo-look bodywork, with 911 turbo suspension, brakes and wheels. Genuine rarities were the 171 narrow-bodied examples built for export. The cut-down windscreen, with its rounded upper corners, was set in an aluminium frame and could be removed from the body. Door windows were modified accordingly. The basic, manually-operated top was stowed under a tilt-up plastic hatch with two fairings behind the seats. An electrically-operated top system would not have been 'intelligent' enough to cope with the mechanics involved in raising or lowering the top. Speedster equipment was more rudimentary than that of the Carrera; windows were raised and lowered by hand-operated winders. In the German market the Speedster's 3.2-litre engine was available with or without catalytic converters.

Standard on the final 911 Carrera were Fuchs forged-alloy wheels, 6 J x 16 front and 8 J x 16 rear, carrying 205/55 and 225/50 ZR 16 tyres. Additionally, a new alarm system with light-emitting diode (LED) indicators in the door buttons was standard equipment.

The 911 turbo was equipped with a reinforced five-speed manual transmission and hydraulically actuated clutch. In the suspension department, the turbo had 22mm front and 18mm rear anti-roll bars.

With the five-speed transmission, the 911 turbo passed the 62mph (100kph) mark in just 5.2 seconds. Top speed remained unchanged at 162mph (260kph).

Porsche built a total of 196,392 examples of 'G Series' 911 models.

911 Coupé [Sportomatic]
911 Targa [Sportomatic]
MY 1974–MY 1975

Engine

Engine design:	6-cylinder horizontally-opposed
Installation:	Rear-engine
Cooling system:	Air-cooled
Number & form of blower blades:	11, straight
Blower outside diameter (mm):	245
Engine type:	911/92 [911/97]
Displacement (cc):	2687
Bore x stroke (mm):	90 x 70.4
Engine output DIN (kW/hp):	110/150 at 5700rpm
Maximum torque (Nm/lb ft):	235/173 at 3800rpm
Output per litre (kW/l / hp/l):	40.9 / 55.8
Compression ratio:	8.0 : 1
Valve operation & camshaft drive:	ohc, cams driven by double chain, 2 valves per cylinder
Carburation:	Bosch K-Jetronic injection
Ignition system:	Battery, capacitive-discharge system
Firing order:	1 - 6 - 2 - 4 - 3 - 5
Engine lubrication:	Dry sump
Engine oil total (l):	11.0 [13.0]

Transmission

Drive configuration:	Rear-axle drive
Manual gearbox:	4-speed (5-speed)*
Option Sportomatic:	[4-speed]
Transmission type:	915/16 (915/06) [925/02]
Transmission ratios:	
1st gear:	3.182 (3.182) [2.400]
2nd gear:	1.600 (1.883) [1.550]
3rd gear:	1.104 (1.261) [1.125]
4th gear:	0.724 (0.926) [0.821]
5th gear:	(0.724)
Reverse gear:	3.325 (3.325) [2.533]
Drive ratio:	4.428 (4.428) [3.857]
Option:	Limited-slip differential 40%
*Option	

Body, chassis, suspension, brakes, wheels

Body design:	Steel body, 2 doors, 2 + 2 seats, welded assembly, sheet metal box-section, unitized with body, galvanized floorpan, boxy bumpers with black bellows, engine lid with black grille, red non-reflecting valance, bigger chromium-plated rectangular wing mirror
MY 1975:	Wing mirror painted
Coupé:	Fixed steel roof
Option:	Electric sunroof
Targa:	Removable solid Targa top, fixed stainless-steel Targa roll bar, fixed glass rear window
Option:	Foldable Targa roof
Suspension, front:	Independent suspension with wishbones and McPherson struts, one round, longitudinal torsion bar per wheel, hydraulic double-action shock absorbers, anti-roll bar

Suspension, rear:	Independent suspension with light-alloy semi-trailing arms, one round, transverse torsion bar per wheel, hydraulic double-action shock absorbers
Option:	Anti-roll bar
Brakes, front/rear (Size (mm)):	Ventilated discs (282.5 x 20) / Ventilated discs (290 x 20) 2-piston fixed cast-iron callipers / 2-piston fixed cast-iron callipers
Wheels, front/rear:	5.5 J x 15 / 5.5 J x 15
Tyres, front/rear:	165 HR 15 / 165 HR 15
Option, MY 1975 standard:	6 J x 15 / 6 J x 15 185/70 VR 15 / 185/70 VR 15

Electrical sytem

Alternator (W/A):	770 / 55
MY 1975:	980 / 70
Battery (V/Ah):	12 / 66
Option:	12 / 88

Dimensions and weight

Track, front/rear (mm):	1360 / 1342
6 J x 15 / 6 J x 15:	1372 / 1354
Wheelbase (mm):	2271
Length x width x height (mm):	4291 x 1610 x 1320
Kerb weight DIN (kg):	1075 [1090]
Permissible gross weight (kg):	1440
Luggage compartment (l):	200
Luggage compartment VDA (l):	130
Luggage volume interior*:	175
Fuel tank capacity (l):	80, including 8 reserve
C_w x A (m²):	0.39 x 1.76 = 0.686
Power/weight ratio (kg/kW/ kg/hp):	9.77 [9.90] / 7.16 [7.26]
*on folded down rear seat-backs	

Fuel consumption

DIN 70 030 (mpg):	30; 91 RON normal leaded

Performance, production, prices

Acceleration 0-62mph/100kph (s):	8.5 [8.5]
Maximum speed (mph / kph):	130 / 210 [127 / 205]
Production, total number:	
Coupé:	5,232
Targa:	4,088
Purchase prices:	
08/1973 Coupé:	DM 26,980 [DM 27,980]
Targa:	DM 28,980 [DM 29,980]
03/1974 Coupé:	DM 29,250 [DM 30,250]
Targa:	DM 31,740 [DM 32,740]
08/1974 Coupé:	DM 29,950 [DM 30,950]
Targa:	DM 31,950 [DM 32,950]
01/1975 Coupé:	DM 32,350 [DM 33,350]
Targa:	DM 34,510 [DM 35,510]

911 S Coupé [Sportomatic]
911 S Targa [Sportomatic]
MY 1974–MY 1975

Engine
Engine design:	6-cylinder horizontally-opposed
Installation:	Rear-engine
Cooling system:	Air-cooled
Number & form of blower blades:	11, straight
Blower outside diameter (mm):	245
Engine type:	911/93 [911/98]
Displacement (cc):	2687
Bore x stroke (mm):	90 x 70.4
Engine output DIN (kW/hp):	129/175 at 5800rpm
Maximum torque (Nm/lb ft):	235/173 at 4000rpm
Output per litre (kW/l / hp/l):	48.0 / 65.1
Compression ratio:	8.5 : 1
Valve operation & camshaft drive:	ohc, cams driven by double chain, 2 valves per cylinder
Carburation:	Bosch K-Jetronic injection
Ignition system:	Battery, capacitive-discharge system
Firing order:	1 - 6 - 2 - 4 - 3 - 5
Engine lubrication:	Dry sump
Engine oil total (l):	13.0 [15.0]

Transmission
Drive configuration:	Rear-axle drive
Manual gearbox:	4-speed (5-speed)*
Option Sportomatic:	[4-speed]
Transmission :	915/16 (915/06) [925/02]
Transmission ratio:	
1st gear:	3.182 (3.182) [2.400]
2nd gear:	1.600 (1.833) [1.550]
3rd gear:	1.104 (1.261) [1.125]
4th gear:	0.724 (0.926) [0.821]
5th gear:	(0.724)
Reverse gear:	3.325 (3.325) [2.533]
Drive ratio:	4.428 (4.428) [3.857]
Option:	Limited-slip differential 40%
*Option	

Body, chassis, suspension, brakes, wheels
Body design:	Steel body, 2 doors, 2 + 2 seats, welded assembly, sheet metal box-section, unitized with body, galvanized floorpan, boxy bumpers with black bellows, engine lid with black grille, red non-reflecting valance, bigger chromium-plated rectangular wing mirror
MY 1975:	Wing mirror painted
Coupé:	Fixed steel roof
Option:	Electric sunroof
Targa:	Removable solid Targa top, fixed stainless-steel Targa roll bar, fixed glass rear window
Option:	Foldable Targa roof

Suspension, front:	Independent suspension with wishbones and McPherson struts, one round, longitudinal torsion bar per wheel, hydraulic double-action shock absorbers, anti-roll bar
Suspension, rear:	Independent suspension with light-alloy semi-trailing arms, one round, transverse torsion bar per wheel, hydraulic double-action shock absorbers
Option:	Anti-roll bar
Brakes, front/rear (Size (mm)):	Ventilated discs (282.5 x 20) / Ventilated discs (290 x 20) 2-piston fixed cast-iron callipers / 2-piston fixed cast-iron callipers
Wheels, front/rear:	6 J x 15 / 6 J x 15
Tyres, front/rear:	185/70 VR 15 / 185/70 VR 15

Electrical system
Alternator (W/A):	770 / 55
MY 1975:	980 / 70
Battery (V/Ah):	12 / 66
Option:	12 / 88

Dimensions and weight
Track, front/rear (mm):	1372 / 1354
Wheelbase (mm):	2271
Lenght x width x height (mm):	4291 x 1610 x 1320
Kerb weight DIN (kg):	1075 [1090]
Permissible gross weight (kg):	1440
Luggage compartment (l):	200
Luggage compartment VDA (l):	130
Luggage volume interior*:	175
Fuel tank capacity (l):	80, including 8 reserve
C_w x A (m²):	0.39 x 1.76 = 0.686
Power/weight ratio (kg/kW/kg/hp):	8.33 [8.44] / 6.14 [6.22]
*on folded down rear seat-backs	

Fuel consumption
DIN 70 030 (mpg):	30; 91 RON normal leaded

Performance, production, prices
Acceleration 0-62mph/100kph (s):	7.6 [7.6]
Maximum speed (mph / kph):	140 / 225 [136 / 220]
Production, total number:	
Coupé:	4,927
Targa:	3,051
Purchase price:	
08/1973 Coupé:	DM 30,980 [DM 31,980]
Targa:	DM 32,980 [DM 33,980]
03/1974 Coupé:	DM 32,950 [DM 33,950]
Targa:	DM 35,440 [DM 36,440]
08/1974 Coupé:	DM 33,450 [DM 34,450]
Targa:	DM 35,450 [DM 36,450]
01/1975 Coupé:	DM 36,130 [DM 37,130]
Targa:	DM 38,290 [DM 39,290]

911 Carrera Coupé
911 Carrera Targa
MY 1974–MY 1975

Engine
Engine design:	6-cylinder horizontally-opposed
Installation:	Rear-engine
Cooling system:	Air-cooled
Number & form of blower blades:	11, straight
Blower outside diameter (mm):	245
Engine type:	911/83
Displacement (cc):	2687
Bore x stroke (mm):	90 x 70.4
Engine output DIN (kW/hp):	154/210 at 6300rpm
Maximum torque (Nm/lb ft):	255/188 at 5100rpm
Output per litre (kW/l / hp/l):	57.3 / 78.2
Compression ratio:	8.5 : 1
Valve operation & camshaft drive:	ohc, cams driven by double chain, 2 valves per cylinder
Carburation:	6-plunger, twin-row, mechanical Bosch injection pump, manifold injection
Ignition system:	Battery, capacitive-discharge system
Firing order:	1 - 6 - 2 - 4 - 3 - 5
Engine lubrication:	Dry sump
Engine oil total (l):	13.0

Transmission
Drive configuration:	Rear-axle drive
Manual gearbox:	4-speed (5-speed)*
Transmission type:	915/16 (915/06)
Transmission ratios:	
1st gear:	3.182 (3.182)
2nd gear:	1.600 (1.833)
3rd gear:	1.104 (1.261)
4th gear:	0.724 (0.926)
5th gear:	(0.724)
Reverse gear:	3.325 (3.325)
Drive ratio:	4.428 (4.428)
Option:	Limited-slip differential 40%
*Option	

Body, chassis, suspension, brakes, wheels
Body design:	Steel body, 2 doors, 2 + 2 seats, welded assembly, sheet metal box-section, unitized with body, galvanized floorpan, wider rear wings, boxy bumpers with black bellows, engine lid with black grille, red non-reflecting valance, painted wing mirror
Coupé:	Fixed steel roof
Option:	Electric sunroof
Targa:	Removable solid Targa top, fixed stainless-steel Targa roll bar, fixed glass rear window
Option without extra charge:	Foldable Targa roof

Suspension, front:	Independent suspension with wishbones and McPherson struts, one round, longitudinal torsion bar per wheel, hydraulic double-action shock absorbers, anti-roll bar
Suspension, rear:	Independent suspension with light-alloy semi-trailing arms, one round, transverse torsion bar per wheel, hydraulic double-action shock absorbers, anti-roll bar
Brakes, front/rear (Size (mm)):	Ventilated discs (282.5 x 20) / Ventilated discs (290 x 20) 2-piston fixed cast-iron callipers / 2-piston fixed cast-iron callipers
Wheels, front/rear:	6 J x 15 / 7 J x 15
Tyres, front/rear:	185/70 VR 15 / 215/60 VR 15

Electrical system
Alternator (W):	770 / 55
MY 1975:	980 / 70
Battery (V/Ah):	12 / 66
Option:	12 / 88

Dimensions and weight
Track, front/rear (mm):	1372 / 1380
Wheelbase (mm):	2271
Length x width x height (mm):	4291 x 1652 x 1320
Kerb weight DIN (kg):	1075
Permissible gross weight (kg):	1400
Luggage compartment (l):	200
Luggage compartment VDA (l):	130
Luggage volume interior*:	175
Fuel tank capacity (l):	80, including 8 reserve
C_w x A (m^2):	0.40 x 1.77 = 0.708
Power/weight ratio (kg/kW/kg/hp):	6.98 / 5.11
*on folded down rear seat-backs	

Fuel comsumption
DIN 70 030 (mpg):	26; 91 RON normal leaded

Performance, production, prices
Acceleration 0-62mph/100kph (s):	6.3
Maximum speed (mph / kph):	149 / 240

Production, total number:
Coupé:	1,534
Targa:	610
Purchase prices:	
08/1973 Coupé:	DM 37,980
Targa:	DM 39,980
03/1974 Coupé:	DM 39,950
Targa:	DM 41,950
08/1974 Coupé:	DM 40,950
Targa:	DM 42,950
03/1975 Coupé:	DM 44,230
Targa:	DM 46,390

911 Carrera RS 3.0 Coupé MY 1974

Engine

Engine design:	6-cylinder horizontally-opposed
Installation:	Rear-engine
Cooling system:	Air-cooled
Number & form of blower blades:	11, straight
Blower outside diameter (mm):	245
Engine type:	911/77
Displacement (cc):	2994
Bore x stroke (mm):	95 x 70.4
Engine output DIN (kW/hp):	169/230 at 6200rpm
Maximum torque (Nm/lb ft):	275/203 at 5000rpm
Output per litre (kW/l / hp/l):	56.4 / 76.8
Compression ratio:	9.8 : 1
Valve operation & camshaft drive:	ohc, cams driven by double chain, 2 valves per cylinder
Carburation:	6-plunger, twin-row, mechanical Bosch injection pump, manifold injection
Ignition system:	Battery, capacitive-discharge system
Firing order:	1 - 6 - 2 - 4 - 3 - 5
Engine lubrication:	Dry sump
Engine oil total (l):	13.0

Transmission

Drive configuration:	Rear-axle drive
Manual gearbox:	5-speed
Transmission type:	915
Transmission ratios:	
1st gear:	3.182
2nd gear:	1.833
3rd gear:	1.261
4th gear:	0.926
5th gear:	0.724
Reverse gear:	3.325
Drive ratio:	4.429
Standard:	Limited-slip differential 80%

Body, chassis, suspension, brakes, wheels

Body design:	Steel coupé body, 2 doors, 2 seats, welded assembly, sheet metal box-section, unitized with body, thin-gauge sheet metal parts for roof and doors, galvanized floorpan, wide wing flares for 9" wheels front and 11" wheels rear, plastic bumpers, plastic front spoiler with integrated oil cooler, fibreglass front lid, fibreglass engine lid with flat rear wing with black polyurethane surround, red non-reflecting valance, thin glass rear and side windows, black wing mirror, 'Carrera' script on sides
Suspension, front:	Independent suspension with wishbones and McPherson struts, one round, longitudinal torsion bar per wheel, hydraulic shock absorbers, anti-roll bar
Suspension, rear:	Independent suspension with light-alloy semi-trailing arms, one round, transverse torsion bar per wheel, hydraulic shock absorbers, anti-roll bar
Option:	Coil springs
Brakes, front/rear (Size (mm)):	Ventilated and drilled discs (304 x 32) Ventilated and drilled discs (309 x 28) Black 4-piston fixed aluminium callipers / Black 4-piston fixed aluminium callipers
Wheels, front/rear:	8 J x 15 / 9 J x 15
Tyres, front/rear:	215/60 VR 15 / 235/60 VR 15

Electrical system

Alternator (W/A):	770 / 55
Battery (V/Ah):	12 / 36

Dimensions and weight

Track, front/rear (mm):	1437 / 1462
Wheelbase (mm):	2271
Length x width x height (mm):	4235 x 1775 x 1320
Kerb weight DIN (kg):	1060
Permissible gross weight (kg):	1400
Luggage compartment (l):	200
Luggage compartment VDA (l):	130
Fuel tank capacity (l):	80, including 8 reserve
C_w x A (m^2):	n.a.
Power/weight ratio (kg/kW/kg/hp):	5.32 / 3.91

Fuel consumption

(mpg):	app. 17; 98 RON super leaded

Performance, production, prices

Acceleration 0-62mph/100kph (s):	5.3
0-124mph/200kph (s):	21.1
Maximum speed (mph / kph):	152 / 245
Production, total number: (incl. IROC and RSR):	110
Purchase price:	DM 64,980

911 turbo Coupé
MY 1975–MY 1977

Engine

Engine design:	6-cylinder horizontally-opposed, turbo charger
Installation:	Rear-engine
Cooling system:	Air-cooled
Number & form of blower blades:	11, straight
Blower outside diameter (mm):	245
Engine type:	930/50
MY 1977:	930/52
Displacement (cc):	2994
Bore x stroke (mm):	95 x 70.4
Engine output DIN (kW/hp):	191/260 at 5500rpm
Maximum torque (Nm/lb ft):	343/253 at 4000rpm
Output per litre (kW/l / hp/l):	63.8 / 86.8
Compression atio:	6.5 : 1
Valve operation & camshaft drive:	ohc, cams driven by double chain, 2 valves per cylinder
Carburation:	Bosch K-Jetronic injection
Ignition system:	Battery, capacitive-discharge system, without contact
Firing order:	1 - 6 - 2 - 4 - 3 - 5
Engine lubrication:	Dry sump
Engine oil total (l):	13.0

Transmission

Drive configuration:	Rear-axle drive
Manual gearbox:	4-speed
Transmission type:	930/30 (930/32)*
MY 1977:	930/33
Transmission ratios:	
1st gear:	2.250 (2.250)
2nd gear:	1.304 (1.304)
3rd gear:	0.893 (0.893)
4th gear:	0.656 (0.656)
Reverse gear:	2.438 (2.438)
Drive ratio:	4.222 (4.000)
Option:	Limited-slip differential 40%

*MY 1976 with tyres of 50ies series

Body, chassis, suspension, brakes, wheels

Body design:	Steel coupé body, 2 doors, 2 + 2 seats, welded assembly, sheet metal box-section, unitized with body with wider front and rear wings, galvanized floorpan, boxy bumpers with black bellows, black polyurethane front spoiler lip, fibreglass engine lid with flat rear wing with black polyurethane surround, red non-reflecting valance, painted wing mirror
MY 1976 - MY 1977:	Hot-dip galvanized body panels, painted electric wing mirror
Option:	Electric sunroof
Suspension, front:	Independent suspension with wishbones and McPherson struts, one round, longitudinal torsion bar per wheel, dual-tube gas-filled shock absorbers, anti-roll bar
Suspension, rear:	Independent suspension with semi-trailing arms, one round, transverse torsion bar per wheel, dual-tube gas-filled shock absorbers, anti-roll bar
Brakes, front/rear (Size (mm)):	Ventilated discs (282.5 x 20) / Ventilated discs (290 x 20) 2-piston fixed aluminium callipers / 2-piston fixed cast-iron callipers
Wheels, front/rear:	7 J x 15* / 8 J x 15*
Tyres, front/rear:	185/70 VR 15 / 215/60 VR 15
Option, Standard MY 1976:	205/50 VR 15 / 225/50 VR 15
Standard MY 1977:	7 J x 16* / 8 J x 16*
	205/55 VR 16 / 225/50 VR 16

*Spacers front 21 mm, rear 28 mm

Electrical system

Alternator (W/A):	980 / 70
Battery (V/Ah):	12 / 66
Option:	12 / 88

Dimensions and weight

Track, front/rear (mm):	1438 / 1511
Wheelbase (mm):	2272
Length x width x height (mm):	4291 x 1775 x 1320
Kerb weight DIN (kg):	1140
MY 1976 - MY 1977:	1195
Permissible gross weight (kg):	1470
MY 1976 - MY 1977:	1525
Luggage compartment (l):	200
MY 1977:	190
Luggage compartment VDA (l):	130
Luggage volume interior*:	175
Fuel tank capacity (l):	80, including 8 reserve
C_w x A (m²):	0.39 x 1.86 = 0.725
Power/weight ratio (kg/kW/kg/hp):	6.00 / 4.38
MY 1976 - MY 1977:	6.25 / 4.59

*on folded rear setbacks

Fuel consumption

DIN 70 030 (mpg):	26; 96 RON super leaded
MY 1977:	28

Performance, production, prices

Acceleration 0-62mph/100kph (s):	5.5
Maximum speed (mph / kph):	more than 155 / 250
Production, total number:	2,850
Purchase prices:	
08/1974:	DM 65,800
03/1975:	DM 65,800
08/1975:	DM 66,450
03/1976:	DM 67,850
08/1976:	DM 67,850
03/1977:	DM 70,000

912 E Coupé (USA only) MY 1976

Engine

Engine design:	4-cylinder horizontally-opposed
Installation:	Rear-engine
Cooling system:	Air-cooled
Engine type:	923/02
Displacement (cc):	1971
Bore x stroke (mm):	94 x 71
Engine output DIN (kW/hp):	64/86* at 4900rpm
Maximum torque (Nm/lb ft):	133/98* at 4000rpm
Output per litre (kW/l / hp/l):	32.5 / 43.6
Compression ratio:	7.6 : 1
Valve operation & camshaft drive:	ohv, cam driven by gears, 2 valves per cylinder
Carburation:	Bosch L-Jetronic injection
Ignition system:	Battery coil ignition
Firing order:	1 - 4 - 3 - 2
Engine lubrication:	Full-pressure oil lubrication
Engine oil total (l):	3.5
*SAE	

Transmission

Drive configuration:	Rear-axle drive
Manual gearbox:	5-speed
Transmission type:	923/02
Transmission ratios:	
1st gear:	3.181
2nd gear:	1.833
3rd gear:	1.261
4th gear:	0.962
5th gear:	0.724
Reverse gear:	3.325
Drive ratio:	4.428
Option:	Limited-slip differential 40%

Body, chassis, suspension, brakes, wheels

Body design:	Steel coupé body, 2 doors, 2 + 2 seats, welded assembly, sheet metal box-section, unitized with body, hot-dip galvanized body panels, boxy bumpers with black bellows, engine lid with black grille, red non-reflecting valance, bigger chromium-plated rectangular wing mirror
Option:	Electric sunroof

Suspension, front:	Independent suspension with wishbones and McPherson struts, one round, longitudinal torsion bar per wheel, hydraulic double-action shock absorbers, anti-roll bar
Suspension, rear:	Independent suspension with light-alloy semi-trailing arms, one round, transverse torsion bar per wheel, hydraulic double-action shock absorbers
Brakes, front/rear (Size (mm)):	Discs (282.5 x 12.7) / Discs (290 x 12.7) 2-piston fixed cast-iron callipers / 2-piston fixed cast-iron callipers
Wheels, front/rear:	5.5 J x 15 / 5.5 J x 15
Tyres, front/rear:	165 HR 15 / 165 HR 15
Option:	5.5 J x 14 / 5.5 J x 14 185 HR 14 / 185 HR 14

Electrical system

Alternator (W/A):	700 / 50
Battery (V/Ah):	12 / 44
Option:	12 / 66

Dimensions and weight

Track, front/rear (mm):	1349 / 1330
Wheelbase (mm):	2272
Length x width x height (mm):	4291 x 1610 x 1340
Kerb weight DIN (kg):	1160
Permissible gross weight (kg):	1400
Luggage compartment (l):	200
Luggage compartment VDA (l):	130
Luggage volume interior*:	175
Fuel tank capacity (l):	80, including 8 reserve
C_w x A (m²):	0.39 x 1.76 = 0.686
Power/weight ratio (kg/kW/ kg/hp):	18.12 / 13.48
*on folded down rear seat-backs	

Fuel consumption

(mpg):	app. 31; 91 RON normal leaded

Performance, production, prices

Acceleration 0-62mph/100kph (s):	13.5
Maximum speed (mph / kph):	109 / 176
Production, total number:	2,099
Purchase price:	US$ 10,845

911 Coupé [Sportomatic]
911 Targa [Sportomatic]
MY 1976–MY 1977

Engine
Engine design:	6-cylinder horizontally-opposed
Installation:	Rear-engine
Cooling system:	Air-cooled
Number & form of blower blades:	5, straight
Blower outside diameter (mm):	226
Engine type:	911/81 [911/86]
Displacement (cc):	2687
Bore x stroke (mm):	90 x 70.4
Engine output DIN (kW/hp):	121/165 at 5800rpm
Maximum torque (Nm/lb ft):	235/173 at 4000rpm
Output per litre (kW/l / hp/l):	45.0 / 61.4
Compression ratio:	8.5 : 1
Valve operation & camshaft drive:	ohc, cams driven by double chain, 2 valves per cylinder
Carburation:	Bosch K-Jetronic injection
Ignition system:	Battery, capacitive-discharge system
Firing order:	1 - 6 - 2 - 4 - 3 - 5
Engine lubrication:	Dry sump
Engine oil total (l):	13.0 [15.0]

Transmission
Drive configuration:	Rear-axle drive
Manual gearbox:	4-speed (5-speed)*
Option Sportomatic:	[3-speed]
Transmission type:	915/49 (915/44) [925/09]
Transmission ratios:	
1st gear:	3.182 (3.182) [2.400]
2nd gear:	1.600 (1.833) [1.429]
3rd gear:	1.080 (1.261) [0.926]
4th gear:	0.821 (1.000)
5th gear:	(0.821)
Reverse gear:	3.325 (3.325) [2.533]
Drive ratio:	3.875 (3.875) [3.375]
Option:	Limited-slip differential 40%
*Option	

Body, chassis, suspension, brakes, wheels
Body design:	Steel body, 2 doors, 2 + 2 seats, welded assembly, sheet metal box-section, unitized with body, hot-dip galvanized body panels, boxy bumpers with black bellows, engine lid with black grille, red non-reflecting valance, painted electric wing mirror
Coupé:	Fixed steel roof
Option:	Electric sunroof
Targa:	Removable, foldable Targa top, fixed stainless-steel Targa roll bar, fixed glass rear window
Suspension, front:	Independent suspension with wishbones and McPherson struts, one round, longitudinal torsion bar per wheel, hydraulic double-action shock absorbers, anti-roll bar

Suspension, rear:	Independent suspension with light-alloy semi-trailing arms, one round, transverse torsion bar per wheel, hydraulic double-action shock absorbers
Option:	Anti-roll bar
Brakes, front/rear (Size (mm)):	Ventilated discs (282.5 x 20) / Ventilated discs (290 x 20) 2-piston fixed cast-iron callipers / 2-piston fixed cast-iron callipers
Wheels, front/rear:	6 J x 15 / 6 J x 15
Tyres, front/rear:	185/70 VR 15 / 185/70 VR 15

Electrical system
Alternator (W/A):	980 / 70
Battery (V/Ah):	12 / 66
Option:	12 / 88

Dimensions and weight
Track, front/rear (mm):	1369 / 1354
Wheelbase (mm):	2272
Length x width x height (mm):	4291 x 1610 x 1320
Kerb weight DIN (kg):	1120
Permissible gross weight (kg):	1440
Luggage compartment (l):	200
Luggage compartment VDA (l):	130
Luggage volume interior*:	175
Fuel tank capacity (l):	80, including 8 reserve
C_w x A (m²):	0.39 x 1.76 = 0.686
Power/weight ratio (kg/kW/kg/hp):	9.25/ 6.78
*on folded down rear seat-backs	

Fuel consumption
DIN 70 030 (mpg):	91 RON normal leaded
At constant 56mph/90kph:	37.5 (37.5)* [34]
At constant 74mph/120kph:	29.5 (29.5)* [31]
Urban cycle:	16 (16)* [16]
1/3 mix:	25 (24)* [24]
*with 5-speed gearbox	

Performance, production, prices
Acceleration 0-62mph/100kph (s):	7.8 [7.8]
MY 1977:	7.5 [7.5]
Maximum speed (mph / kph):	more than 130 / 210 [130 / 210]
Production, total number:	
Coupé:	9,904
Targa:	8,182
Purchase prices:	
09/1975 Coupé:	DM 34,350 [DM 35,340]
Targa:	DM 36,850 [DM 37,840]
02/1976 Coupé:	DM 35,750 [DM 36,740]
Targa:	DM 38,250 [DM 39,240]
08/1976 Coupé:	DM 35,950 [DM 37,140]
Targa:	DM 38,450 [DM 39,640]
02/1977 Coupé:	DM 37,300 [DM 38,490]
Targa:	DM 39,800 [DM 40,990]

911 Carrera 3.0 Coupé [Sportomatic]
911 Carrera 3.0 Targa [Sportomatic]
MY 1976–MY 1977

Engine

Engine design:	6-cylinder horizontally-opposed
Installation:	Rear-engine
Cooling system:	Air-cooled
Number & form of blower blades:	5, straight
Blower outside diameter (mm):	226
Engine type:	930/02 [930/12]
Displacement (cc):	2994
Bore x stroke (mm):	95 x 70.4
Engine output DIN (kW/hp):	147/200 at 6000rpm
Maximum torque (Nm/lb ft):	255/188 at 4200rpm
Output per litre (kW/l / hp/l):	49.1 / 66.8
Compression ratio:	8.5 : 1
Valve operation & camshaft drive:	ohc, cams driven by double chain, 2 valves per cylinder
Carburation:	Bosch K-Jetronic injection
Ignition system:	Battery, capacitive-discharge system
Firing order:	1 - 6 - 2 - 4 - 3 - 5
Engine lubrication:	Dry sump
Engine oil total (l):	13.0 [15.0]

Transmission

Drive configuration:	Rear-axle drive
Manual gearbox:	4-speed (5-speed)*
Option Sportomatic:	[3-speed]
Transmission type:	915/49 (915/44) [925/13]
Transmission ratios:	
1st gear:	3.182 (3.182) [2.400]
2nd gear:	1.600 (1.833) [1.429]
3rd gear:	1.080 (1.261) [0.926]
4th gear:	0.821 (1.000)
5th gear:	(0.821)
Reverse gear:	3.325 (3.325) [2.533]
Drive ratio:	3.875 (3.875) [3.375]
Option:	Limited-slip differential 40%
*Option	

Body, chassis, suspension, brakes, wheels

Body design:	Steel body, 2 doors, 2 + 2 seats, welded assembly, sheet metal box-section, unitized with body, hot-dip galvanized body panels, wider rear wings, boxy bumpers with black bellows, engine lid with black grille, red non-reflecting valance, painted electric wing mirror
Coupé:	Fixed steel roof
Option:	Electric sunroof
Targa:	Removable, foldable Targa top, fixed stainless-steel Targa roll bar, fixed glass rear window
Suspension, front:	Independent suspension with wishbones and McPherson struts, one round, longitudinal torsion bar per wheel, hydraulic double-action shock absorbers, anti-roll bar
Suspension, rear:	Independent suspension with light-alloy semi-trailing arms, one round, transverse

	torsion bar per wheel, hydraulic double-action shock absorbers, anti-roll bar
Brakes, front/rear (Size (mm)):	Ventilated discs (282.5 x 20) / Ventilated discs (290 x 20) 2-piston fixed cast-iron callipers / 2-piston fixed cast-iron callipers
Wheels, front/rear:	6 J x 15 / 7 J x 15
Tyres, front/rear:	185/70 VR 15 / 215/60 VR 15
Option MY 1976:	7 J x 15 / 8 J x 15 205/50 VR 15 / 225/50 VR 15*
Option MY 1977:	6 J x 16 / 7 J x 16 205/55 VR 16 / 225/50 VR 16
*with adjusted speedometer	

Electrical system

Alternator (W/A):	980 / 70
Battery (V/Ah):	12 / 66
Option:	12 / 88

Dimensions and weight

Track, front/rear (mm):	1369 / 1380
Wheelbase (mm):	2272
Length x width x height (mm):	4291 x 1652 x 1320
Kerb weight DIN (kg):	1120
Permissible gross weight (kg):	1440
Luggage compartment (l):	200
MY 1977:	190
Luggage compartment VDA (l):	130
Luggage volume interior*:	175
Fuel tank capacity (l):	80, including 8 reserve
C_w x A (m^2):	0.40 x 1.77 = 0.708
Power/weight ratio (kg/kW/kg/hp):	7.61/ 5.6
*on folded down rear seat-backs	

Fuel consumption

DIN 70 030 (mpg):	91 RON normal leaded
At constant 56mph/90kph:	31 (31)* [30]
At constant 74mph/120kph:	27.5 (27.5)* [26.6]
Urban cycle:	15 (13.5)* [13]
1/3 mix:	22 (21)* [20]
*with 5-speed gearbox	

Performance, production, prices

Acceleration 0-62mph/100kph (s):	6.5 [6.5]
MY 1977:	6.3 [6.3]
Maximum speed (mph / kph):	more than 143 / 230 [143 / 230]
Production, total number:	
Coupé:	2,546
Targa:	1,105
Purchase prices:	
09/1975 Coupé:	DM 44,950 [DM 44,950]*
Targa:	DM 46,950 [DM 46,950]
02/1976 Coupé:	DM 46,350 [DM 46,350]
Targa:	DM 48,350 [DM 48,350]
08/1976 Coupé:	DM 46,350 [DM 46,350]
Targa:	DM 48,850 [DM 48,850]
02/1977 Coupé:	DM 47,700 [DM 47,700]
Targa:	DM 50,200 [DM 50,200]
*Sportomatic no extra charge	

911 SC Coupé [Sportomatic]
911 SC Targa [Sportomatic]
MY 1978–MY 1979

Engine
Engine design:	6-cylinder horizontally-opposed
Installation:	Rear-engine
Cooling system:	Air-cooled
Number & form of blower blades:	11, straight
Blower outside diameter (mm):	226
Engine type:	930/03 [930/13]
Displacement (cc):	2994
Bore x stroke (mm):	95 x 70.4
Engine output DIN (kW/hp):	132/180 at 5500rpm
Maximum torque (Nm/lb ft):	265/195 at 4200rpm
Output per litre (kW/l / hp/l):	44.1 / 60.1
Compression ratio:	8.5 : 1
Valve operation & camshaft drive:	ohc, cams driven by double chain, 2 valves per cylinder
Carburation:	Bosch K-Jetronic injection
Ignition system:	Battery, capacitive-discharge system
Firing order:	1 - 6 - 2 - 4 - 3 - 5
Engine lubrication:	Dry sump
Engine oil total (l):	13.0 [15.0]

Transmission
Drive configuration:	Rear-axle drive
Manual gearbox:	5-speed
Option Sportomatic:	[3-Gang]
Transmission type:	915/61 [925/16]
Transmission ratios:	
1st gear:	3.182 [2.400]
2nd gear:	1.833 [1.429]
3rd gear:	1.261 [0.926]
4th gear:	1.000
5th gear:	0.821
Reverse gear:	3.325 [2.533]
Drive ratio:	3.875 [3.375]
Option:	Limited-slip differential 40%

Body, chassis, suspension, brakes, wheels
Body design:	Steel body, 2 doors, 2 + 2 seats, welded assembly, sheet metal box-section, unitized with body, hot-dip galvanized body panels, wider rear wings, boxy bumpers with black bellows, engine lid with black grille, red non-reflecting valance, painted electric wing mirror
Coupé:	Fixed steel roof
Option:	Electric sunroof
Targa:	Removable, foldable Targa top, fixed stainless-steel Targa roll bar, fixed glass rear window
MY 1979:	Black Targa roll bar
Suspension, front:	Independent suspension with wishbones and McPherson struts, one round, longitudinal torsion bar per wheel, hydraulic double-action shock absorbers, anti-roll bar
Suspension, rear:	Independent suspension with light-alloy semi-trailing arms, one round, transverse torsion bar per wheel, hydraulic double-action shock absorbers, anti-roll bar
Brakes, front/rear (Size (mm)):	Ventilated discs (282.5 x 20) / Ventilated discs (290 x 20) 2-piston fixed cast-iron callipers / 2-piston fixed cast-iron callipers
Wheels, front/rear:	6 J x 15 / 7 J x 15
Tyres, front/rear:	185/70 VR 15 / 215/60 VR 15
Option:	6 J x 16 / 7 J x 16 205/55 VR 16 / 225/50 VR 16

Electrical system
Alternator (W/A):	980 / 70
Battery (V/Ah):	12 / 66
Option:	12 / 88

Dimension and weight
Track, front/rear (mm):	1369 / 1379
Wheelbase (mm):	2272
Length x width x height (mm):	4291 x 1652 x 1320
Kerb weight DIN (kg):	1160
Permissible gross weight (kg):	1500
Luggage compartment (l):	190
Luggage compartment VDA (l):	130
Luggage volume interior*:	175
Fuel tank capacity (l):	80, including 8 reserve
C_w x A (m^2):	0.40 x 1.77 = 0.708
Power/weight ratio (kg/kW/kg/hp):	8.78 / 6.44
*on folded down rear seat-backs	

Fuel consumption
DIN 70 030/1 (mpg):	91 RON normal leaded
At constant 56mph/90kph:	27.5 [28]
At constant 74mph/120kph:	22.5 [23]
EG-emission-urban cycle:	15.6 [15.7]
1/3 mix:	20.7 [21]

Performance, production, prices
Acceleration 0-62mph/100kph (s):	7.0 [7.0]
Maximum speed (mph / kph):	140 / 225 [140 / 225]
Production, total number:	
Coupé:	10,832
Targa:	8,108
Purchase prices:	
06/1977 Coupé:	DM 39,900 [DM 41,090]
Targa:	DM 42,700 [DM 43,890]
01/1978 Coupé:	DM 41,850 [DM 43,050.72]
Targa:	DM 44,790 [DM 45,990.72]
08/1978 Coupé:	DM 42,950 [DM 44,200]
Targa:	DM 45,890 [DM 47,140]
01/1979 Coupé:	DM 42,950 [DM 44,200]
Targa:	DM 45,890 [DM 47,140]
Coupé*:	DM 43,333.48 [DM 44,594.64]
Targa*:	DM 46,299.73 [DM 47,560.89]
*delivery after 30 June 1979	

911 turbo Coupé
MY 1978–MY 1988

Engine

Engine design:	6-cylinder horizontally-opposed, turbo charger, intercooler
Installation:	Rear-engine
Cooling system:	Air-cooled
Number & form of blower blades:	11, straight
Blower outside diameter (mm):	245
Engine type:	930/60
MY 1983 - MY 1988:	930/66
Displacement (cc):	3299
Bore x stroke (mm):	97 x 74.4
Engine output DIN (kW/hp):	221/300 at 5500rpm
Maximum torque (Nm/lb ft):	412/304 at 4000rpm
MY 1983 - MY 1988:	430/317 at 4000rpm
Output per litre (kW/l / hp/l):	68.4 / 92.9
Compression ratio:	7.0 : 1
Valve operation & camshaft drive:	ohc, cams driven by double chain, 2 valves per cylinder
Carburation:	Bosch K-Jetronic injection
Ignition system:	Battery, capacitive-discharge system, without contact
Firing order:	1 - 6 - 2 - 4 - 3 - 5
Engine lubrication:	Dry sump
Engine oil total (l):	13.0

Transmission

Drive configuration:	Rear-axle drive
Manual gearbox:	4-speed
Transmission type:	930/34
MY 1985 - MY 1988:	930/36
Transmission ratios:	
1st gear:	2.250
2nd gear:	1.304
3rd gear:	0.893
4th gear:	0.625
Reverse gear:	2.438
Drive ratio:	4.222
Option:	Limited-slip differential 40%

Body, chassis, suspension, brakes, wheels

Body design:	Steel coupé body, 2 doors, 2 + 2 seats, welded assembly, sheet metal box-section, unitized with body, hot-dip galvanized body panels with wider front and rear wings, boxy bumpers with black bellows, black polyurethane front spoiler lip, rear wing with black polyurethane surround on engine lid, red non-reflecting valance, painted electric wing mirror
MY 1981 - MY 1988:	Entirely hot-dip galvanized body, side indicators on front wings
MY 1984 - MY 1988:	Integrated front fog lamps
MY 1985 - MY 1988:	Side-impact protection beams in doors
MY 1987 - MY 1988:	Red non-reflecting valance with two integrated rear fog lamps
Option:	Electric sunroof
Suspension, front:	Independent suspension with wishbones and McPherson struts, one round, longitudinal torsion bar per wheel, dual-tube gas-filled shock absorbers, anti-roll bar
Suspension, rear:	Independent suspension with semi-trailing arms, one round, transverse torsion bar per wheel, dual-tube gas-filled shock absorbers, anti-roll bar
Brakes, front/rear (Size (mm)):	Ventilated and drilled discs (304 x 32) Ventilated and drilled discs (309 x 28) Black 4-piston fixed aluminium callipers / Black 4-piston fixed aluminium callipers
Wheels, front/rear:	7 J x 16 / 8 J x 16
Tyres, front/rear:	205/55 VR 16 / 225/50 VR 16
MY 1986 - MY 1988:	7 J x 16 / 9 J x 16 205/55 VR 16 / 245/45 VR 16

Electrical system

Alternator (W/A):	980 / 70
MY 1982 - MY 1983:	1050 / 75
MY 1984 - MY 1988:	1260 / 90
Battery (V/Ah):	12 / 66
Option:	12 / 88

Dimensions and weight

Track, front/rear (mm):	1432 / 1501
MY 1986 - MY 1988:	1432 / 1492
Wheelbase (mm):	2272
Length x width x height (mm):	4291 x 1775 x 1310
Kerb weight DIN (kg):	1300
MY 1986 - MY 1988:	1335
Permissible gross weight (kg):	1680
Luggage compartment (l):	190
Luggage compartment VDA (l):	130
Luggage volume interior*:	175
Fuel tank capacity (l):	80, including 8 reserve
c_w x A (m²):	0.39 X 1.86 = 0.725
Power/weight ratio (kg/kW/kg/hp):	5.88 / 4.33
MY 1986 - MY 1988:	6.04 / 4.45
*on folded down rear seat-backs	

Fuel consumption

DIN 70 030/1 (mpg):	98 RON super leaded
At constant 56mph/90kph:	8.1
At constant 74mph/120kph:	15.3
EG-emission-urban cycle:	20.0
1/3 mix:	14.5
MY 1983 - MY 1988:	
DIN 70 030/1 (mpg):	98 RON super leaded
At 56mph/90kph:	29
At 74mph/120kph:	24
EG-emission-urban cycle:	18
1/3 mix:	23

Performance, production, prices

Acceleration 0-62mph/100kph (s):	5,4
Maximum speed (mph / kph):	161 / 260
Production, total number:	14,476
Purchase prices:	
06/1977 Coupé:	DM 78,500
01/1978 Coupé:	DM 79,900
08/1978 Coupé:	DM 79,900
01/1979 Coupé:	DM 79,900
Delivery after 30 June 1979:	DM 80,613,40
08/1979 Coupé:	DM 82,950
03/1980 Coupé:	DM 85,950
08/1980 Coupé:	DM 85,950
03/1981 Coupé:	DM 88,450
08/1981 Coupé:	DM 89,800
03/1982 Coupé:	DM 92,800
08/1982 Coupé:	DM 96,400
03/1983 Coupé:	DM 99,800
08/1983 Coupé:	DM 102,000
02/1984 Coupé:	DM 105,300
08/1984 Coupé:	DM 111,000
02/1985 Coupé:	DM 114,000
08/1985 Coupé:	DM 119,000
03/1986 Coupé:	DM 119,000
08/1986 Coupé:	DM 125,000
03/1987 Coupé:	DM 127,850
08/1987 Coupé:	DM 131,000
04/1988 Coupé:	DM 133,500

911 SC Coupé
911 SC Targa MY 1980

Engine

Engine design:	6-cylinder horizontally-opposed
Installation:	Rear-engine
Cooling system:	Air-cooled
Number & form of blower blades:	11, straight
Blower outside diameter (mm):	245
Engine type:	930/09
Displacement (cc):	2994
Bore x stroke (mm):	95 x 70.4
Engine output DIN (kW/hp):	138/188 at 5500rpm
Maximum torque (Nm/lb ft):	265/195 at 4200rpm
Output per litre (kW/l / hp/l):	46.1 / 62.8
Compression ratio:	8.6 : 1
Valve operation & camshaft drive:	ohc, cams driven by double chain, 2 valves per cylinder
Carburation:	Bosch K-Jetronic injection
Ignition system:	Battery, capacitive-discharge system
Firing order:	1 - 6 - 2 - 4 - 3 - 5
Engine lubrication:	Dry sump
Engine oil total (l):	13.0

Transmission

Drive configuration:	Rear-axle drive
Manual gearbox:	5-speed
Transmission type:	915/62
Transmission ratios:	
1st gear:	3.182
2nd gear:	1.833
3rd gear:	1.261
4th gear:	1.000
5th gear:	0.786
Reverse gear:	3.325
Drive ratio:	3.875
Option:	Limited-slip differential 40%

Body, chassis, suspension, brakes, wheels

Body design:	Steel body, 2 doors, 2 + 2 seats, welded assembly, sheet metal box-section, unitized with body, hot-dip galvanized body panels, wider rear wings, boxy bumpers with black bellows, engine lid with black grille, red non-reflecting valance, painted electric wing mirror
Coupé:	Fixed steel roof
Option:	Electric sunroof
Targa:	Removable, foldable Targa top, fixed black Targa roll bar, fixed glass rear window
Suspension, front:	Independent suspension with wishbones and McPherson struts, one round, longitudinal torsion bar per wheel, hydraulic double-action shock absorbers, anti-roll bar
Suspension, rear:	Independent suspension with light-alloy semi-trailing arms, one round, transverse torsion bar per wheel, hydraulic double-action shock absorbers, anti-roll bar
Brakes, front/rear (Size (mm)):	Ventilated discs (282.5 x 20) / Ventilated discs (290 x 20) 2-piston fixed cast-iron callipers / 2-piston fixed cast-iron callipers
Wheels, front/rear:	6 J x 15 / 7 J x 15
Tyres, front/rear:	185/70 VR 15 / 215/60 VR 15
Option:	6 J x 16 / 7 J x 16 205/55 VR 16 / 225/50 VR 16

Electrical system

Alternator (W/A):	980 / 70
Battery (V/Ah):	12 / 66
Option:	12 / 88

Dimension and weight

Track, front/rear (mm):	1369 / 1379
Wheelbase (mm):	2272
Length x width x height (mm):	4291 x 1652 x 1320
Kerb weight DIN (kg):	1160
Permissible gross weight (kg):	1500
Luggage compartment (l):	190
Luggage compartment VDA (l):	130
Luggage volume interior*:	175
Fuel tank capacity (l):	80, including 8 reserve
C_w x A (m²):	0.40 x 1.77 = 0.708
Power/weight ratio (kg/kW/ kg/hp):	8.40 / 6.17
*on folded down rear seat-backs	

Fuel consumtion

DIN 70 030/1 (mpg):	91 RON normal leaded
At constant 56mph/90kph:	31
At constant 74mph/120kph:	25
EG-emission-urban cycle:	16
1/3 mix:	22

Performance, production, prices

Acceleration 0-62mph/100kph (s):	7.0
0-100mph/160kph (s):	17.8
Maximum speed (mph / kph):	140 / 225
Production, total number:	
Coupé:	5,010
Targa:	3,603
Purchase prices:	
08/1979 Coupé:	DM 46,950
Targa:	DM 49,950
04/1980 Coupé:	DM 48,750
Targa:	DM 51,750

911 SC Coupé
911 SC Targa MY 1981–MY 1983

Engine
Engine design:	6-cylinder horizontally-opposed
Installation:	Rear-engine
Cooling system:	Air-cooled
Number & form of blower blades:	11, straight
Blower outside diameter (mm):	245
Engine type:	930/10
Displacement (cc):	2994
Bore x stroke (mm):	95 x 70.4
Engine output DIN (kW/hp):	150/204 at 5900rpm
Maximum torque (Nm/lb ft):	267/197 at 4300rpm
Output per litre (kW/l / hp/l):	50.1 / 68.1
Compression ratio:	9.8 : 1
Valve operation & camshaft drive:	ohc, cams driven by double chain, 2 valves per cylinder
Carburation:	Bosch K-Jetronic injection
Ignition system:	Battery, capacitive-discharge system
Firing order:	1 - 6 - 2 - 4 - 3 - 5
Engine lubrication:	Dry sump
Engine oil total (l):	13.0

Transmission
Drive configuration:	Rear-axle drive
Manual gearbox:	5-speed
Transmission type:	915/62
Transmission ratios:	
1st gear:	3.182
2nd gear:	1.833
3rd gear:	1.261
4th gear:	1.000
5th gear:	0.786
Reverse gear:	3.325
Drive ratio:	3.875
Option:	Limited-slip differential 40%

Body, chassis, suspension, brakes, wheels
Body design:	Steel body, 2 doors, 2 + 2 seats, welded assembly, sheet metal box-section, unitized with body, entirely hot-dip galvanized body, wider rear wings, boxy bumpers with black bellows, engine lid with black grille, red non-reflecting valance, painted electric wing mirror, side indicators on front wings
Coupé:	Fixed steel roof
Option:	Electric sunroof
Targa:	Removable, foldable Targa top, fixed black Targa roll bar, fixed glass rear window
Suspension, front:	Independent suspension with wishbones and McPherson struts, one round, longitudinal torsion bar per wheel, hydraulic double-action shock absorbers, anti-roll bar
Suspension, rear:	Independent suspension with light-alloy semi-trailing arms, one round, transverse torsion bar per wheel, hydraulic double-action shock absorbers, anti-roll bar

Brakes, front/rear (Size (mm)):	Ventilated discs (282.5 x 20) / Ventilated discs (290 x 20) 2-piston fixed cast-iron callipers / 2-piston fixed cast-iron callipers
Wheels, front/rear:	6 J x 15 / 7 J x 15
Tyres, front/rear:	185/70 VR 15 / 215/60 VR 15
Option:	6 J x 16 / 7 J x 16 205/55 VR 16 / 225/50 VR 16

Electrical system
Alternator (W/A):	980 / 70
MY 1982 - MY 1983:	1050 / 75
Battery (V/Ah):	12 / 66
Option:	12 / 88

Dimension and weight
Track, front/rear (mm):	1369 / 1379
Wheelbase (mm):	2272
Length x width x height (mm):	4291 x 1652 x 1320
Kerb weight DIN (kg):	1160
Permissible gross weight (kg):	1500
Luggage compartment (l):	190
Luggage compartment VDA (l):	130
Luggage volume interior*:	175
Fuel tank capacity (l):	80, including 8 reserve
C_w x A (m²):	0.40 x 1.77 = 0.708
Power/weight ratio (kg/kW/ kg/hp):	7.73 / 5.68
*on folded down rear seat-backs	

Fuel consumption
DIN 70 030/1 (mpg):	98 RON super leaded
At constant 56mph/90kph:	38
At constant 74mph/120kph:	29
EG-emission-urban cycle:	21
1/3 mix:	27

Performance, production, prices
Acceleration 0-62mph/100kph (s):	6.8
Maximum speed (mph / kph):	146 / 235
Production, total number:	
Coupé:	16,099
Targa:	9,837
Purchase prices:	
08/1980 Coupé:	DM 49,900
Targa:	DM 52,900
03/1981 Coupé:	DM 51,350
Targa:	DM 54,350
08/1981 Coupé:	DM 51,850
Targa:	DM 54,850
03/1982 Coupé:	DM 53,600
Targa:	DM 56,700
08/1982 Coupé:	DM 55,690
Targa:	DM 58,910
03/1983 Coupé:	DM 57,800
Targa:	DM 60,620

911 SC Cabriolet MY 1983

Engine

Engine design:	6-cylinder horizontally-opposed
Installation:	Rear-engine
Cooling system:	Air-cooled
Number & form of blower blades:	11, straight
Blower outside diameter (mm):	245
Engine type:	930/10
Displacement (cc):	2994
Bore x stroke (mm):	95 x 70.4
Engine output DIN (kW/hp):	150/204 at 5900rpm
Maximum torque (Nm/lb ft):	267/197 at 4300rpm
Output per litre (kW/l / hp/l):	50.1 / 68.1
Compression ratio:	9.8 : 1
Valve operation & camshaft drive:	ohc, cams driven by double chain, 2 valves per cylinder
Carburation:	Bosch K-Jetronic injection
Ignition system:	Battery, capacitive-discharge system
Firing order:	1 - 6 - 2 - 4 - 3 - 5
Engine lubrication:	Dry sump
Engine oil total (l):	13.0

Transmission

Drive configuration:	Rear-axle drive
Manual gearbox:	5-speed
Transmission type:	915/62
Transmission ratios:	
1st gear:	3.182
2nd gear:	1.833
3rd gear:	1.261
4th gear:	1.000
5th gear:	0.786
Reverse gear:	3.325
Drive ratio:	3.875
Option:	Limited-slip differential 40%

Body, chassis, suspension, brakes, wheels

Body design:	Steel cabriolet body, 2 doors, 2 + 2 seats, welded assembly, sheet metal box-section, unitized with body, entirely hot-dip galvanized body, wider rear wings, boxy bumpers with black bellows, engine lid with black grille, red non-reflecting valance, painted electric wing mirror, side indicators on front wings, manual soft-top with flexible plastic rear window
Suspension, front:	Independent suspension with wishbones and McPherson struts, one round, longitudinal torsion bar per wheel, hydraulic double-action shock absorbers, anti-roll bar
Suspension, rear:	Independent suspension with light-alloy semi-trailing arms, one round, transverse torsion bar per wheel, hydraulic double-action shock absorbers, anti-roll bar
Brakes, front/rear (Size (mm)):	Ventilated discs (282.5 x 20) / Ventilated discs (290 x 20) 2-piston fixed cast-iron callipers / 2-piston fixed cast-iron callipers
Wheels, front/rear:	6 J x 15 / 7 J x 15
Tyres, front/rear:	185/70 VR 15 / 215/60 VR 15
Option:	6 J x 16 / 7 J x 16
	205/55 VR 16 / 225/50 VR 16

Electrical system

Alternator (W/A):	1050 / 75
Battery (V/Ah):	12 / 66
Option:	12 / 88

Dimension and weight

Track, front/rear (mm):	1369 / 1379
Wheelbase (mm):	2272
Length x width x height (mm):	4291 x 1652 x 1320
Kerb weight DIN (kg):	1160
Permissible gross weight (kg):	1500
Luggage compartment (l):	190
Luggage compartment VDA (l):	130
Luggage volume interior*:	175
Fuel tank capacity (l):	80, including 8 reserve
C_w x A (m^2):	0.40 x 1.77 = 0.708
Power/weight ratio (kg/kW/kg/hp):	7.73 / 5.68
*on folded down rear seat-backs	

Fuel consumption

DIN 70 030/1 (mpg):	98 RON super leaded
At constant 56mph/90kph:	35
At constant 74mph/120kph:	29
EG-emission-urban cycle:	21
1/3 mix:	27

Performance, production, prices

Acceleration 0-62mph/100kph (s):	6.8
Maximum speed (mph / kph):	146 / 235
Production, total number:	4,096
Purchase price:	
08/1982 Cabriolet:	DM 64,500
03/1983 Cabriolet:	DM 64,500

911 turbo Coupé 'slant nose'
with performance kit
MY 1983–MY 1989

Engine

Engine design:	6-cylinder horizontally-opposed, turbo charger, intercooler
Installation:	Rear-engine
Cooling system:	Air-cooled
Number & form of blower blades:	11, straight
Blower outside diameter (mm):	245
Engine type:	930/60 S
Displacement (cc):	3299
Bore x stroke (mm):	97 x 74,4
Engine output DIN (kW/hp):	243/330 at 5750rpm
Maximum torque (Nm/lb ft):	467/344 at 4000rpm
Output per litre (kW/l / hp/l):	75.2 / 102.1
Compression ratio:	7.0 : 1
Valve operation & camshaft drive:	ohc, cams driven by double chain, 2 valves per cylinder
Carburation:	Bosch K-Jetronic injection
Ignition system:	Battery, capacitive-discharge system, without contact
Firing order:	1 - 6 - 2 - 4 - 3 - 5
Engine lubrication:	Dry sump
Engine oil total (l):	13.0

Transmission

Drive configuration:	Rear-axle drive
Manual gearbox:	4-speed (5-speed)*
Transmission type:	930/36 (G 50/50)
Transmission ratios:	
1st gear:	2.250 (3.145)
2nd gear:	1.304 (1.789)
3rd gear:	0.893 (1.269)
4th gear:	0.625 (0.967)
5th gear:	(0.756)
Reverse gear:	2.438 (2.857)
Drive ratio:	4.222 (3.444)
Option:	Limited-slip differential 40%
*MY 1989	

Body, chassis, suspension, brakes, wheels

Body design:	Steel coupé body, 2 doors, 2 + 2 seats, welded assembly, sheet metal box-section, unitized with body, entirely hot-dip galvanized body, wider front and rear wings, air-intakes in rear wings, flat front wings with 944 headlamps, side-skirts, boxy bumpers with black bellows, 'Exclusive' front spoiler with integrated oil-cooler and fog lamps, rear wing with black polyurethane surround on engine lid, red non-reflecting valance, painted electric wing mirror, side indicators on front wings
MY 1985 - MY 1989:	Side-impact protection beams in doors
MY 1987 - MY 1989:	Red non-reflecting valance with two integrated rear fog lamps
Option:	Electric sunroof
Suspension, front:	Independent suspension with wishbones and McPherson struts, one round, longitudinal torsion bar per wheel, dual-tube gas-filled shock absorbers, anti-roll bar
Suspension, rear:	Independent suspension with light-alloy semi-trailing arms, one round, transverse torsion bar per wheel, dual-tube gas-filled shock absorbers, anti-roll bar
Brakes, front/rear (Size (mm)):	Ventilated and drilled discs (304 x 32) Ventilated and drilled discs (309 x 28) Black 4-piston fixed aluminium callipers / Black 4-piston fixed aluminium callipers
Wheels, front/rear:	7 J x 16 / 8 J x 16
Tyres, front/rear:	205/55 VR 16 / 225/50 VR 16
MY 1986 - MY 1989:	7 J x 16 / 9 J x 16
	205/55 VR 16 / 245/45 VR 16

Electrical system

Alternator (W/A):	980 / 70
MY 1982 - MY 1983:	1050 / 75
MY 1984 - MY 1989:	1260 / 90
Battery (V/Ah):	12 / 66
Option:	12 / 88

Dimension and weight

Track, front/rear (mm):	1432 / 1501
MY 1986 - MY 1989:	1432 / 1492
Wheelbase (mm):	2272
Length x width x height (mm):	4291 x 1775 x 1310
Kerb weight DIN (kg):	1300
MY 1986 - MY 1989:	1335
Permissible gross weight (kg):	1680
Luggage compartment (VDA (l)):	130
Luggage volume interior*:	175
Fuel tank capacity (l):	80, including 8 reserve
C_w x A (m²):	0.39 x 1.86 = 0.725
Power/weight ratio (kg/kW/kg/hp):	5.34 / 3.93
MY 1986 - MY 1989:	5.49 / 4.05
*on folded down rear seat-backs	

Fuel consumption

(mpg):	app. 14; 98 RON super leaded

Performance, production, prices

Acceleration 0-62mph/100kph (s):	5.2
MY 1989:	5.0
Maximum speed (mph / kph):	170 / 275*
*Performance kit in standard body	167mph / 270kph
*Slant nose with standard engine	164mph / 265kph
Production, total number: Slant nose	948
Conversion prices: 12/1984 (09/1986):	
Slant nose with 944 headlamps, front spoiler with oil cooler:	DM 38,340 (DM 39,810)
Side skirts left and right:	DM 3,137 (DM 3,300)
Air-intakes in rear wings:	DM 7,635 (DM 8,145)
Air-intakes on top of front wings:	DM 2,185 (DM 2,490)
Performance kit 330hp with exhaust with 4 tailpipes:	DM 20,975 (DM 23,585)
Purchase price complete car with equipment above:	DM 183,272 (DM 202,330)

911 SC/RS Coupé (Typ 954) MY 1984

Engine

Engine design:	6-cylinder horizontally-opposed
Installation:	Rear-engine
Cooling system:	Air-cooled
Number & form of blower blades:	11, straight
Blower outside diameter (mm):	245
Engine type:	930/18
Displacement (cc):	2994
Bore x stroke (mm):	95 x 70.4
Engine output DIN (kW/hp):	184/250 at 7000rpm
Maximum torque (Nm/lb ft):	250/184 at 6500rpm
Output per litre (kW/l / hp/l):	61.5 / 83.5
Compression ratio:	10.3 : 1
Valve operation & camshaft drive:	ohc, cams driven by double chain, 2 valves per cylinder
Carburation:	Bosch Kugelfischer injection
Ignition system:	Battery, capacitive-discharge system
Firing order:	1 - 6 - 2 - 4 - 3 - 5
Engine lubrication:	Dry sump
Engine oil total (l):	13.0

Transmission

Drive configuration:	Rear-axle drive
Manual gearbox:	5-speed
Transmission type:	915/71
Transmission ratios:	
1st gear:	3.182
2nd gear:	2.000
3rd gear:	1.381
4th gear:	1.080
5th gear:	0.888
Reverse gear:	3.325
Drive ratio:	3.875
Standard:	Limited-slip differential 40%

Body, chassis, suspension, brakes, wheels

Body design:	Steel coupé body, 2 doors, 2 seats, welded assembly, sheet metal box-section, unitized with body, entirely hot-dip galvanized body, wider front and rear wings, plastic bumpers (GfK), aluminium front lid and doors, black polyurethane front spoiler lip, rear wing with black polyurethane surround on engine lid, red non-reflecting valance, thin-glass rear and side windows, black wing mirror, side indicators on front wings
Option:	Roll cage
Suspension, front:	Independent suspension with wishbones and McPherson struts, one round, longitudinal torsion bar per wheel, dual-tube gas-filled shock absorbers, anti-roll bar
Suspension, rear:	Independent suspension with light-alloy semi-trailing arms, one round, transverse torsion bar per wheel, dual-tube gas-filled shock absorbers, anti-roll bar
Brakes, front/rear (Size (mm)):	Ventilated and drilled discs (304 x 32) Ventilated and drilled discs (309 x 28) Black 4-piston fixed aluminium callipers / Black 4-piston fixed aluminium callipers
Wheels, front/rear:	7 J x 16 / 8 J x 16
Tyres, front/rear:	205/55 VR 16 / 225/50 VR 16

Electrical system

Alternator (W/A):	980 / 70
Battery (V/Ah):	12 / 44

Dimensions and weight

Track, front/rear (mm):	1432 / 1501
Wheelbase (mm):	2272
Lenght x width x height (mm):	4235 x 1775 x 1290
Kerb weight DIN (kg):	1057
Permissible gross weight (kg):	1300
Luggage compartment (VDA (l)):	130
Fuel tank capacity (l):	80, including 8 reserve
C_w x A (m²):	0.39 x 1.86 = 0.725
Power/weight ratio (kg/kW/kg/hp):	5.74 / 4.22

Fuel consumption

(mpg):	app. 14; 98 RON super leaded

Performance, production, prices

Acceleration 0-62mph/100kph (s):	5.3
Maximum speed (mph / kph):	158 / 255
Production, total number:	20
Purchase price:	DM 188,100

911 Carrera Coupé [catalytic converter]
911 Carrera Targa [catalytic converter]
911 Carrera Cabriolet
[catalytic converter]
MY 1984–MY 1989
[MY 1986–MY 1989]

Engine

Engine design:	6-cylinder horizontally-opposed
Installation:	Rear-engine
Cooling system:	Air-cooled
Number & form of blower blades:	11, straight
Blower outside diameter (mm):	245
Engine type:	930/20
Displacement (cc):	3164
Bore x stroke (mm):	95 x 70.4
Engine output DIN (kW/hp):	170/231 [152/207] at 5900rpm
MY 1987 - MY 1989:	[160/217] at 5900 rpm
Maximum torque (Nm/lb ft):	284/209 [264/194.7] at 4800rpm
Output per litre (kW/l / hp/l):	53.7 [48.0] / 73.0 [65.4]
MY 1987 - MY 1989:	[50.6 / 68.6]
Compression ratio:	10.3 : 1 [9.5 : 1]
Valve operation & camshaft drive:	ohc, cams driven by double chain, 2 valves per cylinder
Carburation:	Bosch DME with L-Jetronic injection
Ignition system:	Bosch DME
Firing order:	1 - 6 - 2 - 4 - 3 - 5
Engine lubrication:	Dry sump
Engine oil total (l):	13.0

Transmission

Drive configuration:	Rear-axle drive
Manual gearbox:	5-speed
Transmission type:	915/67 (G 50/00)*
MY 1986:	915/72
Transmission ratios:	
1st gear:	3.182 (3.500)
2nd gear:	1.833 (2.059)
3rd gear:	1.261 (1.409)
4th gear:	0.965 (1.074)
5th gear:	0.763 (0.861)
Reverse gear:	3.325 (2.857)
Drive ratio:	3.875 (3.444)
Option:	Limited-slip differential 40%

*MY 1987 - MY 1989 gearbox type G 50

Body, chassis, suspension, brakes, wheels

Body design:	Steel body, 2 doors, 2 + 2 seats, welded assembly, sheet metal box-section, unitized with body, entirely hot-dip galvanized body, wider rear wings, boxy bumpers with black bellows, intregrated front fog lamps, engine lid with black grille, red non-reflecting valance, painted electric wing mirror, side indicators on front wings
MY 1985 - MY 1989:	Side-impact protection beams in doors
MY 1987 - MY 1989:	Red non-reflecting valance with two integrated rear fog lamps
Option:	Black polyurethane front spoiler lip, rear wing with black polyurethane surround on engine lid
Coupé:	Fixed steel roof
Option:	Electric sunroof
Targa:	Removable, foldable Targa top, fixed black Targa roll bar, fixed glass rear window
Cabriolet:	Manual soft-top with flexible plastic rear window
Option MY 1987 - MY 1989:	Electric soft-top with flexible plastic rear window
Suspension, front:	Independent suspension with wishbones and McPherson struts, one round, longitudinal torsion bar per wheel, dual-tube gas-filled shock absorbers, anti-roll bar
Suspension, rear:	Independent suspension with light-alloy semi-trailing arms, one round, transverse torsion bar per wheel, dual-tube gas-filled shock absorbers, anti-roll bar
Brakes, front/rear (Size (mm)):	Ventilated discs (282.5 x 24) / Ventilated discs (290 x 24) 2-piston fixed cast-iron callipers / 2-piston fixed cast-iron callipers
Wheels, front/rear:	6 J x 15 / 7 J x 15
Tyres, front/rear:	185/70 VR 15 / 215/60 VR 15
Option, MY 1988 standard:	7 J x 15 / 8 J x 15 195/65 VR 15 / 215/60 VR 15
Option until MY 1988:	6 J x 16 / 7 J x 16 205/55 VR 16 / 225/50 VR 16
MY 1989 standard:	6 J x 16 / 8 J x 16 205/55 VR 16 / 225/50 VR 16

Electrical system

Alternator (W/A):	1260 / 90
Battery (V/Ah):	12 / 66
Option:	12 / 88

Dimensions and weight

Track, front/rear (mm):	1372 / 1380
7 J x 15 / 8 J x 15:	1398 / 1405
6 J x 16 / 8 J x 16:	1372 / 1405
Wheelbase (mm):	2272
Length x width x height (mm):	4291 x 1652 x 1320
Kerb weight DIN (kg):	1160
MY 1986 - MY 1989:	1210
Permissible gross weight (kg):	1500
MY 1986 - MY 1989:	1530
Luggage compartment (VDA (l)):	130
Luggage volume interior*:	175
Fuel tank capacity (l):	80, including 8 reserve
C_w x A (m²):	0.39 x 1.77 = 0.690
With front- and rear spoiler:	0.38 x 1.77 = 0.672
Power/weight ratio (kg/kW/kg/hp):	6.82 / 5.02
MY 1986:	7.11 [7.96] / 5.23 [5.84]
MY 1987 - MY 1989:	[7.56 / 5.57]
*on folded down rear seat-backs	

Fuel consumption

DIN 70 030/1; MY 1985 - MY 1989
EG-Norm 80/1268 (mpg):

With catalytic converter:	98 RON super leaded
	91 RON normal unleaded
With catalytic converter MY 1987 -:	95 RON super unleaded
At constant 56mph/90kph:	42 [36] [36]*
At constant 74mph/120kph:	31 [29] [29]*
EG-emissions-urban cycle:	21 [18] [19]*
1/3 mix:	29 [25] [26]*
*MY 1987 - MY 1989	

Performance, production, prices

Acceleration 0-62mph/100kph (s):	6.1 [6.5] [6.3]*
Maximum speed (mph / kph):	152 / 245 [146 / 235] [149 / 240]*
*MY 1987 - MY 1989	

Production, total number
all Carrera 3.2*:

Coupé:	35,571
Targa:	18,468
Cabriolet:	19,987
*Carrera body and Turbolook	

Purchase prices:

08/1983 Coupé:	DM 61,950
Targa:	DM 64,950
Cabriolet:	DM 68,990
02/1984 Coupé:	DM 63,950
Targa:	DM 67,050
Cabriolet:	DM 71,200
08/1984 Coupé:	DM 66,950
Targa:	DM 69,980
Cabriolet:	DM 74,200
02/1985 Coupé:	DM 68,560
Targa:	DM 71,660
Cabriolet:	DM 75,980
08/1985 Coupé:	DM 72,000 [DM 74,190]
Targa:	DM 66,000 [DM 78,190]
Cabriolet:	DM 82,000 [DM 84,190]
03/1986 Coupé:	DM 73,800 [DM 75,990]
Targa:	DM 77,900 [DM 80,090]
Cabriolet:	DM 84,050 [DM 86,240]
08/1986 Coupé:	DM 75,250 [DM 76,825]
Targa:	DM 79,250 [DM 80,825]
Cabriolet:	DM 85,250 [DM 86,825]
03/1987 Coupé:	DM 76,880 [DM 78,455]
Targa:	DM 80,880 [DM 82,455]
Cabriolet:	DM 86,880 [DM 88,455]
08/1987 Coupé:	DM 80,500 [DM 82,075]
Targa:	DM 84,600 [DM 86,175]
Cabriolet:	DM 90,800 [DM 92,375]
04/1988 Coupé:	DM 82,000 [DM 83,575]
Targa:	DM 86,200 [DM 87,775]
Cabriolet:	DM 92,500 [DM 94,075]
08/1988 Coupé:	DM 83,700 [DM 85,275]
Targa:	DM 88,000 [DM 89,575]
Cabriolet:	DM 94,200 [DM 95,775]
04/1989 Coupé:	DM 86,000 [DM 87,575]
Targa:	DM 90,500 [DM 92,075]
Cabriolet:	DM 96,800 [DM 98,375]

911 Carrera Coupé Turbolook [catalytic converter] MY 1984– MY 1989 [MY 1986–MY 1989] 911 Carrera Targa Turbolook [catalytic converter] 911 Carrera Cabriolet Turbolook [catalytic converter] MY 1985–MY 1989 [MY 1986–MY 1989]

Engine

Engine design:	6-cylinder horizontally-opposed
Installation:	Rear-engine
Cooling system:	Air-cooled
Number & form of blower blades:	11, straight
Blower outside diameter (mm):	245
Engine type:	930/20
Displacement (cc):	3164
Bore x stroke (mm):	95 x 70.4
Engine output DIN (kW/hp):	170/231 [152/207] at 5900rpm
MY 1987 - MY 1989:	[160/217] at 5900rpm
Maximum torque (Nm/lb ft):	284/209 [264/195] at 4800rpm
Output per litre (kW/l / hp/l):	53.7 [48.0] / 73.0 [65.4]
MY 1987 - MY 1989:	[50.6 / 68.6]
Compression ratio:	10.3 : 1 [9.5 : 1]
Valve operation & camshaft drive:	ohc, cams driven by double chain, 2 valves per cylinder
Carburation:	Bosch DME with L-Jetronic injection
Ignition system:	Bosch DME
Firing order:	1 - 6 - 2 - 4 - 3 - 5
Engine lubrication:	Dry sump
Engine oil total (l):	13.0

Transmission

Drive configuration:	Rear-axle drive
Manual gearbox:	5-speed
Transmission type:	915/67 (G 50/00)*
MY 1986:	915/72
Transmission ratios:	
1st gear:	3.182 (3.500)
2nd gear:	1.833 (2.059)
3rd gear:	1.261 (1.409)
4th gear:	0.965 (1.074)
5th gear:	0.763 (0.861)
Reverse gear:	3.325 (2.857)
Drive ratio:	3.875 (3.444)

Option:	Limited-slip differential 40%

*MY 1987 - MY 1989 gearbox type G 50

Body, chassis, suspension, brakes, wheels

Body design:	Steel body, 2 doors, 2 + 2 seats, welded assembly, sheet metal box-section, unitized with body, entirely hot-dip galvanized body, wider front and rear wings, boxy bumpers with black bellows, intregrated front fog lamps, black polyurethane front spoiler lip, rear wing with black polyurethane surround on engine lid, red non-reflecting valance, painted electric wing mirror, side indicators on front wings
MY 1985 - MY 1989:	Side-impact protection beams in doors
MY 1987 - MY 1989:	Red non-reflecting valance with two integrated rear fog lamps
Alternative:	Turbolook without front spoiler and rear wing
Coupé:	Fixed steel roof
Option:	Electric sunroof
Targa:	Removable, foldable Targa top, fixed black Targa roll bar, fixed glass rear window
Cabriolet:	Manual soft-top with flexible plastic rear window
Option MY 1987 - MY 1989:	Electric soft-top with flexible plastic rear window
Suspension, front:	Independent suspension with wishbones and McPherson struts, one round, longitudinal torsion bar per wheel, dual-tube gas-filled shock absorbers, anti-roll bar
Suspension, rear:	Independent suspension with light-alloy semi-trailing arms, one round, transverse torsion bar per wheel, dual-tube gas-filled shock absorbers, anti-roll bar
Brakes, front/rear (Size (mm)):	Ventilated and drilled discs (304 x 32) Ventilated and drilled discs (309 x 28) Black 4-piston fixed aluminium callipers / Black 4-piston fixed aluminium callipers
Wheels, front/rear:	7 J x 16 / 8 J x 16
Tyres, front/rear:	205/55 VR 16 / 225/50 VR 16
MY 1986 - MY 1989:	7 J x 16 / 9 J x 16 205/55 VR 16 / 245/45 VR 16

Electrical system

Alternator (W/A):	1260 / 90
Battery (V/Ah):	12 / 66
Option:	12 / 88

Dimensions and weight

Track, front/rear (mm):	1432 / 1501
MY 1986 - MY 1989:	1432 / 1492
Wheelbase (mm):	2272
Length x width x height (mm):	4291 x 1775 x 1310
Kerb weight DIN (kg):	1210
MY 1986 - MY 1989:	1260
Permissible gross weight (kg):	1530
MY 1986 - MY 1989:	1580
Luggage compartment (VDA (l)):	130
Luggage volume interior*:	175
Fuel tank capacity (l):	80, including 8 reserve
C_w x A (m²)	
with front- and rear spoiler:	0.39 x 1.86 = 0.725
Power/weight ratio (kg/kW/kg/hp):	7.11 / 5.23
MY 1986:	7.41 [8.28] / 5.45 [6.08]
MY 1987 - MY 1989:	[7.87 / 5.80]
*on folded down rear seat-backs	

Fuel consumption

DIN 70 030/1; MY1985–MY1989	
EG-Norm 80/1268 (mpg):	98 RON super unleaded
With catalytic converter:	91 RON normal unleaded
With cat. converter from MY1987:	95 RON super unleaded
At constant 56mph/90kph:	36.3 [35.6] [35.6]*
At constant 74mph/120kph:	28 [29] [29]*
EG-emission-urban cycle:	20.7 [18] [19]*
1/3 mix:	26.8 [25.4] [25.8]*
*MY 1987 - MY 1989	

Performance, production, prices

Acceleration 0-62mph/100kph (s):	6.1 [6.5] [6.3]*
Maximum speed (mph / kph):	152 / 245 [146 / 235] [149 / 240]*
*MY 1987 - MY 1989	

Production, total number

all Carrera 3.2*:

Coupé:	35,571
Targa:	18,468
Cabriolet:	19,987

*Carrera body and Turbolook

Purchase prices incl. Turbolook with / w/o Spoiler MY 1986 - MY 1989:

08/1983 Coupé:	DM 86,850
02/1984 Coupé:	DM 88,850
08/1984 Coupé:	DM 92,900
Targa:	DM 95,930
Cabriolet:	DM 100,150
02/1985 Coupé:	DM 94,510
Targa:	DM 97,500
Cabriolet:	DM 101,930
08/1985 Coupé*:	DM 99,950 / DM 97,950
Targa*:	DM 103,950 / DM 101,950
Cabriolet*:	DM 109,950 / DM 107,950
03/1986 Coupé*:	DM 101,750 / DM 99,750
Targa*:	DM 105,850 / DM 103,850
Cabriolet*:	DM 112,000 / DM 110,000
08/1986 Coupé**:	DM 104,600 / DM 102,600
Targa**:	DM 108,600 / DM 106,600
Cabriolet**:	DM 114,600 / DM 112,600
03/1987 Coupé**:	DM 106,230 / DM 104,230
Targa**:	DM 110,230 / DM 108,230
Cabriolet**:	DM 116,230 / DM 114,230
08/1987 Coupé**:	DM 109,850 / DM 107,850
Targa**:	DM 113,950 / DM 111,950
Cabriolet**:	DM 120,150 / DM 118,150
04/1988 Coupé**:	DM 111,350 / DM 109,350
Targa**:	DM 115,550 / DM 113,550
Cabriolet**:	DM 121,850 / DM 119,850
08/1988 Coupé**:	DM 113,490 / DM 111,490
Targa**:	DM 117,790 / DM 115,790
Cabriolet**:	DM 123,990 / DM 121,990
04/1989 Coupé**:	DM 115,790 / DM 113,790
Targa**:	DM 120,290 / DM 118,290
Cabriolet**:	DM 126,590 / DM 124,590

*Price for catalytic converter MY 1986: DM 2,190

**Price for catalytic converter MY 1987 - MY 1989: DM 1,575

911 turbo Targa
911 turbo Cabriolet
MY 1987–MY 1988

Engine

Engine design:	6-cylinder horizontally-opposed, turbocharger, intercooler
Installation:	Rear-engine
Cooling system:	Air-cooled
Number & form of blower blades:	11, straight
Blower outside diameter (mm):	245
Engine type:	930/66
Displacement (cc):	3299
Bore x stroke (mm):	97 x 74.4
Engine output DIN (kW/hp):	221/300 at 5500rpm
Maximum torque (Nm/lb ft):	430/317 at 4000rpm
Output per litre (kW/l / hp/l):	68.4 / 92.9
Compression ratio:	7.0 : 1
Valve operation & camshaft drive:	ohc, cams driven by double chain, 2 valves per cylinder
Carburation:	Bosch K-Jetronic injection
Ignition system:	Battery, capacitive-discharge system, without contact
Firing order:	1 - 6 - 2 - 4 - 3 - 5
Engine lubrication:	Dry sump
Engine oil total (l):	13.0

Transmission

Drive configuration:	Rear-axle drive
Manual gearbox:	4-speed
Transmission type:	930/36
Transmission ratios:	
1st gear:	2.250
2nd gear:	1.304
3rd gear:	0.893
4th gear:	0.625
Reverse gear:	2.438
Drive ratio:	4.222
Option:	Limited-slip differential 40%

Body, chassis, suspension, brakes, wheels

Body design:	Steel body, 2 doors, 2 + 2 seats, welded assembly, sheet metal box-section, unitized with body, entirely hot-dip galvanized body, wider front and rear wings, side impact protection beams in doors, boxy bumpers with black bellows, intregrated front fog lamps, black polyurethane front spoiler lip, rear wing with black polyurethane surround on engine lid, red non-reflecting valance with two integrated rear fog lamps, painted electric wing mirror, side indicators on front wings
Targa:	Removable, foldable Targa top, fixed black Targa roll bar, fixed glass rear window
Cabriolet:	Manual soft-top with flexible plastic rear window
Option without extra charge:	Electric soft-top with flexible plastic rear window
Suspension, front:	Independent suspension with wishbones and McPherson struts, one round, longitudinal torsion bar per wheel, dual-tube gas-filled shock absorbers, anti-roll bar
Suspension, rear:	Independent suspension with light-alloy semi-trailing arms, one round, transverse torsion bar per wheel, dual-tube gas-filled shock absorbers, anti-roll bar
Brakes, front/rear (Size (mm)):	Ventilated and drilled discs (304 x 32) Ventilated and drilled discs (309 x 28) Black 4-piston fixed aluminium callipers / Black 4-piston fixed aluminium callipers
Wheels, front/rear:	7 J x 16 / 9 J x 16
Tyres, front/rear:	205/55 VR 16 / 245/45 VR 16

Electrical system

Alternator (W/A):	1260 / 90
Battery (V/Ah):	12 / 66
Option:	12 / 88

Dimensions and weight

Track, front/rear (mm):	1432 / 1492
Wheelbase (mm):	2272
Length x width x height (mm):	4291 x 1775 x 1310
Kerb weight DIN (kg):	1335
Permissible gross weight (kg):	1680
Luggage compartment (VDA (l)):	130
Luggage volume interior*:	175
Fuel tank capacity (l):	80, including 8 reserve
C_w x A (m²):	0.39 x 1.86 = 0.725
Power/weight ratio (kg/kW/kg/hp):	6.04 / 4.45
*on folded down rear seat-backs	

Fuel consumption

EG-Norm 80/1268 (mpg):	98 RON super leaded
At constant 56mph/90kph:	29
At constant 74mph/120kph:	24
EG-emission-urban cycle:	18
1/3 mix:	23

Performance, production, prices

Acceleration 0-62mph/100kph (s):	5.4
Maximum speed (mph / kph):	161 / 260
Production, total number:	
Targa:	193
Cabriolet:	918
Purchase prices:	
03/1987 Targa:	DM 134,850
Cabriolet:	DM 147,850
08/1987 Targa:	DM 138,000
Cabriolet:	DM 152,000
04/1988 Targa:	DM 140,500
Cabriolet:	DM 155,000

911 Carrera Clubsport Coupé
[catatytic converter]
911 Carrera Clubsport Targa
MY 1987–MY 1989

Engine

Engine design:	6-cylinder horizontally-opposed
Installation:	Rear-engine
Cooling system:	Air-cooled
Number & form of blower blades:	11, straight
Blower outside diameter (mm):	245
Engine type:	930/20 [930/25]
Displacement (cc):	3164
Bore x stroke (mm):	95 x 70.4
Engine output DIN (kW/hp):	170/231 [160/217] at 5900rpm
Maximum torque (Nm/lb ft):	284/209 [264/195] at 4800rpm
Output per litre (kW/l / hp/l):	53.7 [50.6] / 73.0 [68.6]
Compression ratio:	10.3 : 1 [9.5 : 1]
Valve operation & camshaft drive:	ohc, cams driven by double chain, 2 valves per cylinder
Carburation:	Bosch DME with L-Jetronic injection
Ignition system:	Bosch DME
Firing order:	1 - 6 - 2 - 4 - 3 - 5
Engine lubrication:	Dry sump
Engine oil total (l):	13.0

Transmission

Drive configuration:	Rear-axle drive
Manual gearbox:	5-speed
Transmission type:	G 50/00
Transmission ratios:	
1st gear:	3.500
2nd gear:	2.059
3rd gear:	1.409
4th gear:	1.074
5th gear:	0.861
Reverse gear:	2.857
Drive ratio:	3.444
Option:	Limited-slip differential 40%

Body, chassis, suspension, brakes, wheels

Body design:	Steel body, 2 doors, 2 seats, welded assembly, sheet metal box-section, unitized with body, entirely hot-dip galvanized body, wider rear wings, side-impact protection beams in doors, boxy bumpers with black bellows, black polyurethane front spoiler lip, rear wing with black polyurethane surround on engine lid, red non-reflecting valance with two integrated rear fog lamps, painted electric wing mirror, side indicators on front wings
Coupé:	Fixed steel roof
Targa:	Removable, foldable Targa top, fixed black Targa roll bar, fixed glass rear window

Suspension, front:	Independent suspension with wishbones and McPherson struts, one round, longitudinal torsion bar per wheel, dual-tube gas-filled shock absorbers, anti-roll bar
Suspension, rear:	Independent suspension with light-alloy semi-trailing arms, one round, transverse torsion bar per wheel, dual-tube gas-filled shock absorbers, anti-roll bar
Brakes, front/rear (Size (mm)):	Ventilated discs (282.5 x 24) / Ventilated discs (290 x 24) 2-piston fixed cast-iron callipers / 2-piston fixed cast-iron callipers
Wheels, front/rear:	7 J x 15 / 8 J x 15
Tyres, front/rear:	195/65 VR 15 / 215/60 VR 15
Option, MY 1989 standard:	6 J x 16 / 8 J x 16 205/55 VR 16 / 225/50 VR 16

Electrical system

Alternator (W/A):	1260 / 90
Battery (V/Ah):	12 / 66
Option:	12 / 88

Dimensions and weight

Track, front/rear (mm):	1398 / 1405
6 J x 16 / 8 J x 16:	1372 / 1405
Wheelbase (mm):	2272
Length x width x height (mm):	4291 x 1652 x 1320
Kerb weight DIN (kg):	1160
Permissible gross weight (kg):	1530
Luggage compartment (VDA (l)):	130
Fuel tank capacity (l):	80, including 8 reserve
C_w x A (m^2):	0.38 x 1.77 = 0.672
Power/weight ratio (kg/kW/ kg/hp):	6.82 [7.25] / 5.02 [5.34]

Fuel consumption

EG-Norm 80/1268 (mpg):	98 RON super leaded
With catalytic converter:	95 RON super unleaded
At constant 56mph/90kph:	42 [36]
At constant 74mph/120kph:	31 [29]
EG-emissions-urban cycle:	21 [19]
1/3 mix:	29 [26]

Performance, production, prices

Acceleration 0-62mph/100kph (s):	6.1 [6.3]
Maximum speed (mph / kph):	152 / 245 [149 / 240]
Production, total number:	
Coupé:	189
Targa:	1
Purchase prices:	
08/1987:	DM 80,500 [DM 82,075]
04/1988:	DM 82,000 [DM 83,575]
08/1988:	DM 83,700 [DM 85,275]

911 Carrera Speedster
[catalytic converter] MY 1989

Engine
Engine design:	6-cylinder horizontally-opposed
Installation:	Rear-engine
Cooling system:	Air-cooled
Number & form of blower blades:	11, straight
Blower outside diameter (mm):	245
Engine type:	930/20 [930/25]
Displacement (cc):	3164
Bore x stroke (mm):	95 x 70.4
Engine output DIN (kW/hp):	170/231 [160/217] at 5900rpm
Maximum torque (Nm/lb ft):	284/209 [264/195] at 4800rpm
Output per litre (kW/l / hp/l):	53.7 [50.6] / 73.0 [68.6]
Compression ratio:	10.3 : 1 [9.5 : 1]
Valve operation & camshaft drive:	ohc, cams driven by double chain, 2 valves per cylinder
Carburation:	Bosch DME with L-Jetronic injection
Ignition system:	Bosch DME
Firing order:	1 - 6 - 2 - 4 - 3 - 5
Engine lubrication:	Dry sump
Engine oil total (l):	13.0

Transmission
Drive configuration:	Rear-axle drive
Manual gearbox:	5-speed
Transmission type:	G 50/00
Transmission ratios:	
1st gear:	3.500
2nd gear:	2.059
3rd gear:	1.409
4th gear:	1.074
5th gear:	0.861
Reverse gear:	2.857
Drive ratio:	3.444
Option:	Limited-slip differential 40%

Body, chassis, suspension, brakes, wheels
Body design:	Steel Speedster body, 2 doors, 2 seats, welded assembly, sheet metal box-section, unitized with body, entirely hot-dip galvanized body, wider rear wings, small Speedster windscreen with black frame, side-impact protection beams in doors, boxy bumpers with black bellows, intregrated front fog lamps, engine lid with black grille, red non-reflecting valance with two integrated rear fog lamps, painted electric wing mirror, side indicators on front wings,

	manual soft-top with flexible plastic rear window, Speedster plastic hatch with two fairings
Suspension, front:	Independent suspension with wishbones and McPherson struts, one round, longitudinal torsion bar per wheel, dual-tube gas-filled shock absorbers, anti-roll bar
Suspension, rear:	Independent suspension with light-alloy semi-trailing arms, one round, transverse torsion bar per wheel, dual-tube gas-filled shock absorbers, anti-roll bar
Brakes, front/rear (Size (mm)):	Ventilated discs (282.5 x 24) / Ventilated discs (290 x 24) 2-piston fixed cast-iron callipers / 2-piston fixed cast-iron callipers
Wheels, front/rear:	6 J x 16 / 8 J x 16
Tyres, front/rear:	205/55 ZR 16 / 225/50 ZR 16

Electrical system
Alternator (W/A):	1260 / 90
Battery (V/Ah):	12 / 66
Option:	12 / 88

Dimensions and weight
Track, front/rear (mm):	1372 / 1405
Wheelbase (mm):	2272
Length x width x height (mm):	4291 x 1652 x 1220
Kerb weight DIN (kg):	1210
Permissible gross weight (kg):	1530
Luggage compartment (VDA (l)):	130
Fuel tank capacity (l):	80, including 8 reserve
C_w x A (m^2):	n/a
Power/weight ratio (kg/kW/kg/hp):	7.17 [7.62] / 5.28 [5.62]

Fuel consumption
EG-Norm 80/1268 (mpg):	98 RON super leaded
With catalytic converter:	95 RON super unleaded
At constant 56mph/90kph:	42 [36]
At constant 74mph/120kph:	31 [29]
EG-emissions-urban cycle:	21 [19]
1/3 mix:	29 [26]

Performance, production, prices
Acceleration 0-62mph/100kph (s):	6.1 [6.3]
Maximum speed (mph / kph):	152 / 245 [149 / 240]
Production, total number:	171
Purchase price:	Export only

911 Carrera Speedster Turbolook [catalytic converter] MY 1989

Engine

Engine design:	6-cylinder horizontally-opposed
Installation:	Rear-engine
Cooling system:	Air-cooled
Number & form of blower blades:	11, straight
Blower outside diameter (mm):	245
Engine type:	930/20 [930/25]
Displacement (cc):	3164
Bore x stroke (mm):	95 x 70.4
Engine output DIN (kW/hp):	170/231 [160/217] at 5900rpm
Maximum torque (Nm/lb ft):	284/209 [264/195] at 4800rpm
Output per litre (kW/l / hp/l):	53.7 [50.6] / 73.0 [68.6]
Compression ratio:	10.3 : 1 [9.5 : 1]
Valve operation & camshaft drive:	ohc, cams driven by double chain, 2 valves per cylinder
Carburation:	Bosch DME with L-Jetronic injection
Ignition system:	Bosch DME
Firing order:	1 - 6 - 2 - 4 - 3 - 5
Engine lubrication:	Dry sump
Engine oil total (l):	13.0

Transmission

Drive configuration:	Rear-axle drive
Manual gearbox:	5-speed
Transmission type:	G 50/00
Transmission ratios:	
1st gear:	3.500
2nd gear:	2.059
3rd gear:	1.409
4th gear:	1.074
5th gear:	0.861
Reverse gear:	2.857
Drive ratio:	3.444
Option:	Limited-slip differential 40%

Body, chassis, suspension, brakes, wheels

Body design:	Steel Speedster body, 2 doors, 2 seats, welded assembly, sheet metal box-section, unitized with body, entirely hot-dip galvanized body, wider front and rear wings, small Speedster windscreen with black frame, side-impact protection beams in doors, boxy bumpers with black bellows, intregrated front fog lamps, engine lid with black grille, red non-reflecting valance with two integrated rear fog lamps, painted electric wing mirror, side indicators on front wings, manual soft-top with flexible plastic rear window, Speedster plastic hatch with two fairings

Suspension, front:	Independent suspension with wishbones and McPherson struts, one round, longitudinal torsion bar per wheel, dual-tube gas-filled shock absorbers, anti-roll bar
Suspension, rear:	Independent suspension with light-alloy semi-trailing arms, one round, transverse torsion bar per wheel, dual-tube gas-filled shock absorbers, anti-roll bar
Brakes, front/rear (Size (mm)):	Ventilated and drilled discs (304 x 32) Ventilated and drilled discs (309 x 28) Black 4-piston fixed aluminium callipers / Black 4-piston fixed aluminium callipers
Wheels, front/rear:	7 J x 16 / 9 J x 16
Tyres, front/rear:	205/55 ZR 16 / 245/45 ZR 16

Electrical system

Alternator (W/A):	1260 / 90
Battery (V/Ah):	12 / 66
Option:	12 / 88

Dimensions and weight

Track, front/rear (mm):	1432 / 1492
Wheelbase (mm):	2272
Length x width x height (mm):	4291 x 1775 x 1220
Kerb weight DIN (kg):	1290
Permissible gross weight (kg):	1530
Luggage compartment (VDA (l)):	130
Fuel tank capacity (l):	80, including 8 reserve
C_w x A (m²):	n/a
Power/weight ratio (kg/kW/kg/hp):	7.58 [8.06] / 5.58 [5.94]

Fuel consumption

EG-Norm 80/1268 (mpg):	98 RON super leaded
With catalytic converter:	95 RON super unleaded
At constant 56mph/90kph:	42 [36]
At constant 74mph/120kph:	31 [29]
EG-emissions-urban cycle:	21 [19]
1/3 mix:	29 [26]

Performance, production, prices

Acceleration 0-62mph/100kph (s):	6.1 [6.3]
Maximum speed (mph / kph):	152 / 245 [149 / 240]
Production, total number:	2,103
Purchase prices:	
04/1989:	DM 110,000 [DM 111,575]

911 turbo Coupé
911 turbo Targa
911 turbo Cabriolet MY 1989

Engine

Engine design:	6-cylinder horizontally-opposed, turbo charger, intercooler
Installation:	Rear-engine
Cooling system:	Air-cooled
Number & form of blower blades:	11, straight
Blower outside diameter (mm):	245
Engine type:	930/66
Displacement (cc):	3299
Bore x stroke (mm):	97 x 74.4
Engine output DIN (kW/hp):	221/300 at 5500rpm
Maximum torque (Nm/lb ft):	430/317 at 4000rpm
Output per litre (kW/l / hp/l):	68.4 / 92.9
Compression ratio:	7.0 : 1
Valve operation & camshaft drive:	ohc, cams driven by double chain, 2 valves per cylinder
Carburation:	Bosch K-Jetronic injection
Ignition system:	Battery, capacitive-discharge system, without contact
Firing order:	1 - 6 - 2 - 4 - 3 - 5
Engine lubrication:	Dry sump
Engine oil total (l):	13.0

Transmission

Drive configuration:	Rear-axle drive
Manual gearbox:	5-speed
Transmission type:	G 50/50
Transmission ratios:	
1st gear:	3.154
2nd gear:	1.789
3rd gear:	1.269
4th gear:	0.967
5th gear:	0.756
Reverse gear:	2.857
Drive ratio:	3.444
Option:	Limited-slip differential 40%

Body, chassis, suspension, brakes, wheels

Body design:	Steel body, 2 doors, 2 + 2 seats, welded assembly, sheet metal box-section, unitized with body, entirely hot-dip galvanized body, wider front and rear wings, side-impact protection beams in doors, boxy bumpers with black bellows, intregrated front fog lamps, black polyurethane front spoiler lip, rear wing with black polyurethane surround on engine lid, red non-reflecting valance with two integrated rear fog lamps, painted electric wing mirror, side indicators on front wings
Coupé:	Fixed steel roof
Option:	Electric sunroof
Targa:	Removable, foldable Targa top, fixed black Targa roll bar, fixed glass rear window

Cabriolet:	Electric soft-top with flexible plastic rear window
Suspension, front:	Independent suspension with wishbones and McPherson struts, one round, longitudinal torsion bar per wheel, dual-tube gas-filled shock absorbers, anti-roll bar
Suspension, rear:	Independent suspension with light-alloy semi-trailing arms, one round, transverse torsion bar per wheel, dual-tube gas-filled shock absorbers, anti-roll bar
Brakes, front/rear (Size (mm)):	Ventilated and drilled discs (304 x 32) Ventilated and drilled discs (309 x 28) Black 4-piston fixed aluminium callipers / Black 4-piston fixed aluminium callipers
Wheels, front/rear:	7 J x 16 / 9 J x 16
Tyres, front/rear:	205/55 VR 16 / 245/45 VR 16

Electrical system

Alternator (W/A):	1260 / 90
Battery (V/Ah):	12 / 66
Option:	12 / 88

Dimension and weight

Track, front/rear (mm):	1432 / 1492
Wheelbase (mm):	2272
Length x width x height (mm):	4291 x 1775 x 1310
Kerb weight DIN (kg):	1335
Permissible gross weight (kg):	1680
Luggage compartment (VDA (l)):	130
Luggage volume interior*:	175
Fuel tank capacity (l):	80, including 8 reserve
C_w x A (m²):	0.39 x 1.86 = 0.725
Power/weight ratio (kg/kW/kg/hp):	6.04 / 4.45
*on folded down rear seat-backs	

Fuel consumption

EG-Norm 80/1268 (mpg):	98 RON super leaded
At constant 56mph/90kph:	26
At constant 74mph/120kph:	22
EG-emissions-urban cycle:	20
1/3 mix:	22

Performance, production, prices

Acceleration 0-62mph/100kph (s):	5.2
Maximum speed (mph / kph):	161 / 260
Production, total number:	
Coupé:	1,376
Targa:	104
Cabriolet:	724
Purchase prices:	
08/1988 Coupé:	DM 135,000
Targa:	DM 142,000
Cabriolet:	DM 156,500
04/1989 Coupé:	DM 138,800
Targa:	DM 146,000
Cabriolet:	DM 160,900

Porsche 911 (Type 964)

Model year 1989 (K Programme)

As the 'G Series' 911 Carrera and turbo models entered their last model year, the 911 Carrera 4 (Type 964), with all-wheel drive, ABS brakes, 3.6-litre engine, coil spring suspension and major aerodynamic improvements, ushered in the next generation of 911s. Although Porsche held to the classic body shape, 85 per cent of the 964's parts were new.

The 911 Carrera 4 body exhibited very important aerodynamic improvements. Its drag coefficient (cd) of 0.32 multiplied by a frontal area of $1.79m^2$ resulted in an overall drag product of only 0.57. This compared very favourably with the 0.59 recorded by the earlier 3.2 Carrera without spoiler. The new Carrera generation was the most slippery air-cooled production-911 yet built. Contributing to these improvements were aerodynamically-shaped, plastic nose and tail pieces, optimized rain gutters on the A-pillars, modified sill fairings, completely flat undertray and a rear spoiler which automatically deployed from the engine lid at speeds above 50mph (80kph). Once speed dropped to a walking pace, the spoiler automatically retracted back into the lid. Even at high speeds, rear axle lift was nearly non-existent, and at the front, the Carrera 4 even exhibited slight downforce. The nose-piece incorporated number plate, air-inlet vents, indicators and fog lamps. The rear cap carried the number plate and a cut-out for the tailpipe, now located at the right. The light band at the rear, and all-red rear light units met the bumper at a slight rake. The entire floorpan was a new design, necessary to mount the all-wheel-drive components. At its market introduction the 911 Carrera 4 was only available in coupé form.

The Carrera 4 was powered by a completely new 3.6-litre engine. This developed 250hp (184kW) at 6100rpm, and a maximum torque of 310Nm (229lb ft) at 4800rpm. A larger, 100mm cylinder bore and a new crankshaft with 76.4mm stroke raised displacement to exactly 3600cc. The crankshaft included a torsional vibration damper. The chain boxes were made of lighter, noise-suppressing magnesium. Duplex camshaft drive chains passed over two hydraulic chain tensioners and noise-reducing plastic tensioning and locating guides. With a very high compression ratio of 11.3:1, the engine was equipped with twin-plug ignition, taking advantage of the very large cylinder bore to optimize spark location. The second ignition distributor was driven by a small timing belt from the first distributor. Each cylinder's pair of spark plugs were fired simultaneously. Dual ignition, knock control, and fuel injection were handled by a Digital Motor Electronics (DME) system. A two-stage resonance-induction system provided optimum cylinder filling at high engine speeds. Tuned for operation with unleaded 95 octane Euro Super petrol, the boxer engine was usually paired with a catalytic converter; this was deleted only in response to specific customer request. Exhaust ports in the cylinder heads were formed by ceramic port-liners. Ceramic liners have the advantage of keeping exhaust gases as hot as possible on their way to the catalytic converter, and of better insulating the cylinder heads from that heat. A hollow alternator shaft permitted cooling-blower and alternator to be driven at different speeds. The Carrera 4 was the first car to be equipped with a controlled metal catalytic converter. The tailpipe of the new stainless-steel exhaust system now exited on the right side of the car.

The Carrera 4 was fitted with a five-speed manual transmission and electronically-controlled full-time all-wheel drive. The front differential received its power through a trans-axle system. In normal situations, 31 per cent of the drive torque was directed to the front axle, and 69 per cent to the rear. This torque split could be varied in response to driving situations. For starting off on particularly difficult, slippery surfaces, the driver could manually activate an integrated lock-up system by means of a knob on the centre console.

The Carrera 4 suspension represented a completely new development. For the first time, a production 911 was equipped with front and rear coil springs. At the front, MacPherson struts were attached to aluminium transverse links. Rear wheels were located by aluminium semi-trailing arms. Anti-roll bars rounded out the new suspension package. Four ventilated disc brakes were clamped by aluminium four-piston fixed callipers. The 964 marked the first-ever production 911 to be fitted with anti-lock brakes as standard equipment. The cast aluminium 'Design 90' wheels, 6 J x 16 at the front and 8 J x 16 rear, were shod with 205/55 and 225/50 ZR 16 tyres respectively. Another entirely new feature for a Porsche 911 was power-assisted steering, which made the 911 even more nimble.

The interior of the Carrera 4 benefited from continued development. Instruments were illuminated by new lighting technology. Integrated in the instrument package was a new warning system, which used indicator lamps to display vital information. A short gear lever sprouted from the uninterrupted centre console. The heating system was greatly improved, with much quicker response and outstanding heating capacity. This relegated yet another 911 weakness to the pages of history. Several switches were relocated. An alarm system was integrated in the central-locking system. Partial leather seats were electrically adjustable for height. Electric windows, radio installation package and headlamp-washer system rounded out the Carrera 4's equipment list.

Top speed of the new Carrera 4, at 162mph (260kph), matched the previous year's 911 turbo. In acceleration, too, the Carrera 4 approached the performance of the 930 turbo, reaching 62mph (100kph) in 5.7 seconds.

Model year 1990 (L Programme)

For 1990, the 911 was only available in the new 964 body. Bodies were all built in Porsche's new body plant, Werk V. Freshly welded bodies were automatically conveyed to the paint shop and final assembly by means of a bridge over Schwieberdinger Strasse, a main public road. New in the line-up was the rear-drive Carrera 2, available in Coupé, Targa, and Cabriolet bodies. As of spring 1990, the Carrera 2 could be ordered with the new 'Tiptronic' transmission, the first fully-automatic transmission offered in a Porsche 911. The 1990 model range did not include a turbo.

Carrera 2 and Carrera 4 bodies were largely identical. The Cabriolet was now fitted with the power-operated hood as standard equipment. The Carrera 2 also received the 3.6-litre engine introduced in the Carrera 4. In the German market, only catalyst-equipped engines were offered. The Carrera 2 and Carrera 4 also shared many suspension components. Differences could be found in brake systems: while the Carrera 4 had a high-pressure hydraulic brake booster, the Carrera 2 used a vacuum booster system. At the rear axle, the Carrera 2 had simpler two-piston fixed callipers.

Wheels and tyres for Carrera 2 and Carrera 4 were identical. Forged-alloy disc wheels were available as an option in the same sizes as the standard wheels.

The Carrera 2 could be ordered with the optional four-speed Tiptronic transmission. The Tiptronic could be driven like a conventional automatic transmission, with the added benefit of 'intelligent' gear-change programs which fine-tuned the automatic change process. Alternatively, by moving the gear lever into a second gate to the right of the main gate, the lever could be 'tipped' forward (+) for manual change-ups or back (–) for manual change-downs.

Equipment of the Carrera 2 and Carrera 4 was nearly identical. New for the Coupé and Targa were three-point automatic belts for rear-seat occupants. All vehicles were equipped with manual headlamp adjustment and a twist knob on the centre console to extend or retract the rear spoiler. On Tiptronic-equipped vehicles, the mechanical trip odometer within the speedometer was replaced by a gear indicator. The trip odometer function was moved to the standard-equipment on-board computer.

All Carrera 2 and Carrera 4 models equipped with the five-speed manual transmission were fitted with a dual-mass flywheel to reduce annoying transmission rattle at low engine rpm.

In terms of performance, the approximately 100kg (220lb) lighter Carrera 2 was at roughly the same high level as the Carrera 4. In high-speed acceleration, the Carrera 2 was slightly quicker. Fitted with the Tiptronic, the Carrera 2 showed somewhat less temperament and, with a top speed of 159mph (256kph), was slightly slower.

Model year 1991 (M Programme)

After a turbo-less year, the 911 turbo rejoined the line-up. As of February 1991, all left-hand-drive Porsches were equipped with driver and front passenger airbags as standard equipment.

The widened turbo bodywork was adapted to the visual appearance of the new Carrera generation by means of new front and rear ends and sill fairings. The turbo rear wing was slightly modified and fitted with a somewhat shorter black lip. Also new were more aerodynamically-shaped, oval 'Cup'-style wing mirrors.

The familiar 3.3-litre engine formed the basis for the new turbo power unit. By means of a larger turbocharger, the K-Jetronic injection system and oxygen sensor of the US model, electronic map ignition, larger intercooler and metal catalyst, output was raised to 320hp (235kW) at 5750rpm even as exhaust emissions were reduced. This 'clean' turbo achieved maximum torque of 450Nm (332lb ft) at 4500rpm. The turbo engine was fitted with single-plug ignition. The exhaust system had one oval tailpipe on each side of the car. The 911 turbo was only available in a rear-drive version with a five-speed manual transmission. A limited-slip differential, with different lock-up factors under load and coasting, was included as standard.

The turbo suspension was based on that of the Carrera 2, but was further refined and stiffened for the turbo. Front anti-roll bars were 21mm in diameter, rears 22mm. The turbo brake system was equipped with cross-drilled rotors and larger four-piston fixed callipers. The ABS (anti-lock brake system) was also retuned. For the first time, 17-inch aluminium alloy 'Cup-design' wheels were mounted as standard equipment. At the front, 7 J x 17 rims carried 205/50 ZR 17 rubber; at the rear, 9 J x 17 wheels were shod with 225/40 ZR 17 tyres.

The 911 turbo was even better equipped than the Carrera models. Its appointments included all-leather interior, air-conditioning, on-board computer, rear wiper and 'Symphony' cassette-radio as standard equipment.

In the process of model development, Carrera engines were fitted with a new, plastic two-stage resonance induction system, and new pistons. Cylinder-head sealing was also modified.

In the interior, all 911 models benefited from altered seat-back releases, with two round release push-buttons at the tops of the backrests.

Performance of the 911 turbo was slightly better than that of a good-running Carrera 2. In accelerating to 62mph (100kph) the turbo took all of 5.0 seconds. Maximum speed was about 168mph (270kph).

Model year 1992 (N Programme)

The model range was expanded with the addition of an extreme sports machine, the 911 Carrera RS, and the turbo-look 911 Carrera 2 Cabriolet.

Carrera models for the 1992 model year were recognizable by their standard 16-inch 'Cup-design' wheels and oval 'Cup' mirrors. As an option, the 911 turbo's 17-inch wheel and tyre combination was available, but with rear wheels only 8 inches wide, in keeping with the narrower Carrera bodywork. At about the middle of the model year, German-market models were fitted with a small metal tag with the vehicle identification number on the left inside A-pillar to enable police to check serial numbers more easily. (This had already been a requirement in the US market for many years).

The Tiptronic transmission was improved. The control unit now contained a special drive-off program for cold starts, and for better engine braking, change-downs to first gear were now possible at any speed below 34mph (55kph). 'Keylock' and 'Shiftlock' security features were introduced for the US and Canadian markets.

For the 911 turbo, the Porsche 'Exclusive' department offered a performance boost by means of sportier camshafts with altered timing, modified intake manifold and reworked cylinder heads, to provide 355hp (261kW). In addition, six examples of a high-output 911 turbo Cabriolet were built. Performance was well above that of the stock turbo, with 0-62mph (100kph) in 4.7 seconds and a top speed of more than 174mph (280kph).

The 911 Carrera RS was built around a lightened body. The bonnet lid was of aluminium, the side and unheated rear windows were of thin-gauge glass, undercoating was given a miss and weight was even saved on sound-insulation mats. For increased stiffness, key spot-welded joints were rewelded by hand. Instead of fog lamps, the Carrera RS had transparent covers at the front. The rear bumper carried a specially-shaped RS centre section.

The Carrera RS was powered by a modified 3.6-litre boxer engine. Pistons and cylinders were specially selected. Instead of hydraulic engine mounts, the RS used stiffer rubber mounts. The control unit was altered, and the engine tuned for 98 octane unleaded Super Plus petrol. The result: 260hp (191kW) at 6100rpm and peak torque increased to about 325Nm (240lb ft). The Carrera RS had a lightweight wiring harness, with fewer electrical load items, so the alternator and blower were driven by a single shaft. The transmission was given higher first and second gears. A ZF limited-slip differential, with 20 per cent lock-up under acceleration and 100 per cent in coasting, was installed as standard equipment. The dual-mass flywheel was deleted.

The Carrera RS rode on a very stiff 40mm lower suspension. While the front axle used cross-drilled rotors and four-piston fixed calliper brakes of the 911 turbo, the rear brake components were borrowed from the 'Cup' Carrera. ABS anti-lock brakes were included in the RS equipment package. The 17-inch 'Cup' wheels were of cast magnesium alloy on the RS; this alone reduced weight by 10 kg (22 lbs). Front wheels were 7.5 inches wide, with 205/50 ZR 17 tyres; rears were 255/40 ZR 17 on 9-inch rims. For weight reasons, even power steering was deleted on the RS.

Inside the Carrera RS, the driver could expect to forego all conceivable luxury items for the sake of sporting performance. The only 'luxury' in the lightweight interior was leather-upholstered bucket seats. The simple inside door panels each had a coloured pull-strap to open the door, a pull-handle, a twist knob for door locking or unlocking and a window winder. Luxurious trim parts and even rear seats were absent. The Carrera RS was only offered in coupé form, without airbags. There were, however, three different versions available. The base version offered no comfort, the touring version had a whiff of comfort with its sports seats and electric windows and the road-legal N/GT sports version, with its completely gutted interior and roll cage, was already 'prepped' for the race track.

The Carrera RS was significantly quicker than the stock Carrera 2, in both acceleration and across-the-board flexibility. In reaching 124mph (200kph) in 19.0 seconds, the RS beat a well-run-in stock Carrera by a good two seconds. Both had identical top speed, as the rev limiter cut in at 6720rpm and 162mph (260kph).

The comfortably-equipped, turbo-look Carrera 2 Cabriolet, with its wide turbo-derived body, suspension, brakes and wheels, represented the exact antithesis of the Carrera RS. Its engine compartment was filled with the familiar 3.6-litre normally-aspirated engine. Transmission choices were the five-speed manual or Tiptronic. In addition to the usual Carrera equipment list, the turbo-look Cabriolet was enhanced with a radio package including additional amplifier, automatic climate control, full power seats with seat heating, on-board computer and full leather upholstery. In acceleration and top speed, 158mph (255kph), the wide and relatively heavy turbo-look Cabriolet was slightly slower than its narrow-bodied siblings.

At the Geneva Auto Show in the spring of 1992, Porsche unveiled the 911 turbo S. Externally, its body was distinguished by side air inlets in the rear wings, a flatter, body-coloured rear wing, front brake-cooling air ducts in place of fog lamps and the RS rear centre section. Bonnet lid and doors were of lightweight plastic and the side and rear windows of lightweight thin-gauge glass. As on the Carrera RS, interior equipment was reduced and lightened. Consistent application of this lightweight design philosophy resulted in weight savings of 180kg (396lb). Output of the 3.3-litre turbo engine was raised to 381hp (280kW) by means of altered camshafts, ported intake tracts, 0.1bar higher boost pressure and optimized ignition and fuel-injection systems. Maximum torque rose to 490Nm (361lb ft) at 4800rpm. The suspension was stiffened and lowered by 40mm. Anti-roll bars were of the same dimensions as on the standard turbo. The turbo S was the first roadgoing Porsche to be delivered with

three-piece 18-inch Speedline aluminium-alloy wheels. These were 8 inches at the front, with 225/40 ZR 18 tyres, and 10 inches at the rear, with 265/35 ZR 18 rubber. Recognizable through the spokes of the Speedlines were red-painted four-piston brake callipers and cross-drilled, ventilated brake rotors. Acceleration was as impressive as its looks, reaching the 62mph (100kph) mark in just 4.6 seconds, 124mph (200kph) in 14.2 seconds, and 155mph (250kph) in 25.1 seconds. Top speed was about 180mph (290kph). Only 86 examples were built.

Model year 1993 (P Programme)

The Type 964 was about to be replaced. Its successor, the Type 993, would be presented at the Frankfurt International Automobile Show in the autumn. The 911 turbo 3.6 was now offered with a 3.6-litre engine. As an additional body variation, the Speedster re-entered the model line-up.
A special '30th Anniversary 911' was offered in the spring of 1993.

Because the 911 Carrera RS was not certified for sale in the US, a special model, the 911 RS America, was built for the US market. This was based on the production version of the Carrera 2, but fitted with 17-inch 'Cup' wheels, a fixed rear wing and sports-tuned suspension. Inside, the RS America had two fabric-covered sports seats and Carrera RS door panels, with electric windows, central locking, alarm system and rear package shelf.

The Speedster was offered in narrow-body form. The windscreen was rigidly attached to the body, i.e. no longer removable. The hood was improved compared to that of the earlier version of the 911 Speedster. The hardshell plastic cover over the stowed hood again had two fairings behind the seats. The 17-inch 'Cup' wheels were painted in body colour for standard colours; for metallic paint or black, the wheels were painted silver. The interior was equipped with Carrera RS bucket seats and door panels. Nearly all Speedsters had a three-spoke sports steering wheel fitted. Only a handful were built with dual front airbags, as it was first thought that the low-cut windscreen would not withstand the pressure of inflating bags. Electric windows and Carrera RS leather-covered bucket seats, with their shells painted in body colour, were standard; metallic or black cars had black seat shells. The Speedster was only available with rear drive and the 250hp (184kW) engine, but with a Tiptronic transmission option as of spring 1993. About 15 Speedsters were converted to the widebody turbo look by the Porsche Exclusive department. If desired, the 911 turbo brake system could be retrofitted.

Porsche had proven the reliability of its 3.6-litre engine in the Carrera Cup racing series, paving the way for installation of a turbocharged 3.6-litre engine in the 911 turbo. Cylinders and crank train were tuned with special pistons and the familiar turbo peripherals. The result: 360hp (265kW) at 5500rpm, and an increase in torque to 520Nm (384lb ft) at 4200rpm, giving it even more torque than the 5.4-litre 'big block' V8 of the 928 GTS. A five-speed manual transmission was standard, along with a limited-slip differential with a lock-up factor of 20 per cent under load and 100 per cent while coasting. The 911 turbo 3.6 had an improved brake system, with wider friction surfaces (extended inward) on the front rotors and with the red four-piston fixed callipers of the 911 turbo S. The suspension was lowered by 20mm and retuned. The 911 turbo 3.6 rolled on three-piece, 18-inch Speedline rims. At the front, 8-inch rims carried 225/40 ZR 18 tyres, while the rear 10-inch rims were fitted with 265/35 ZR 18 tyres. Except for the RS tail centre section and chromium 'turbo 3.6' script, 911 turbo 3.6 bodywork was identical to that of its predecessor. Inside, the 3.6-litre turbo could be recognized by a maximum speedometer marking of 320kph (198mph). Acceleration to 62mph (100kph) took only 4.8 seconds. Many testers could exceed

the factory's official top speed of 174mph (280kph).

As part of the model development process, Carrera 2 models were given the more robust dual-mass flywheel of the 911 turbo as well as its four-piston fixed rear brake callipers. Porsche was the world's first carmaker to make use of ozone-friendly R134a refrigerant in all of its air-conditioning systems. At the same time the paint shop converted nearly all of its colours to organic solvent-free, water-based formulations.

The anniversary model was only available as a Carrera 4 Coupé. Its wide turbo body was, however, combined with the small, electrically-deployed rear spoiler. A special colour, 'Viola Metallic', was reserved exclusively for this model. Alternative colours were 'Silver Metallic' and 'Amethyst Metallic'. The engine lid was graced by titanium '911' script. The anniversary model was equipped with the turbo's wide suspension and a modified brake system. Its 17-inch wheels put the finishing touch on a successful design. The normally-aspirated engine, five-speed manual transmission and all-wheel drive were taken from the Carrera 4. The full leather interior was trimmed with Rubicon Gray, including the steering wheel airbag cover. Gauge faces were also painted Rubicon Gray. The gear-change pattern atop the gear-lever knob was engraved into a titanium-coloured plate. A small titanium-coloured plaque with the special edition's

Phantom view of a 911 turbo, Type 964, with 3.3-litre engine

sequential number (limited to 911 examples) was affixed to the rear shelf.

Because of the wide body, top speed of the special '30th Anniversary 911' was 158mph (255kph). As well as this limited edition, other examples of the 911 Carrera 4 were built with the turbo's wide bodywork.

The racing department in Weissach-Flacht handbuilt a very limited run of the 911 Carrera RS 3.8. Visually, it was immediately recognizable by its wide turbo bodywork, unique front corner spoilers and rear biplane wing. The engine lid was made as a single piece with the six-position adjustable rear wing. To reduce weight, doors and bonnet lid were made of aluminium. Side and rear windows were of thin-gauge glass. The interior offered only the barest driving necessities: no airbags, no rear seats, no rear side-trim, but instead leather-covered, snugly-contoured sports bucket seats, a grippy three-spoke steering wheel and lightweight inner door panels. A quote from Ferry Porsche seemed to be tailored for this car in particular: 'Enjoyment is not the product of comfort; if anything, it results from its opposite.'

At the rear, appropriate propulsion was provided by a 3.8-litre boxer engine developing 300hp (221kW) at 6500rpm. Maximum torque of 360Nm (266lb ft) was available at 5250rpm. The crankshaft was fitted with a torsional vibration damper. The displacement increase was obtained by use of 102mm cylinder bores. Other powertrain changes included larger pistons, lightened rocker arms, an exhaust system with reduced back-pressure and a metal catalytic converter ahead of each silencer. The induction system was fitted with six individual throttle butterflies for instant response. The Motronic 2.10, with its hot-film mass-airflow sensor, anticipated the coming Type 993 generation. The suspension was tuned sportingly stiff, but with more comfort at the travel limit than the normal

Carrera RS. The front brakes, red callipers included, came from the 911 turbo S, while the rears were borrowed from the 'Cup' Carrera. The front axle mounted 235/40 ZR 18 tyres on three-piece Speedline rims, size 9 J x 18, while 285/35 ZR 18 tyres were carried by 11 J x 18 wheels at the rear.

Colour choices for the RS were reduced to only a handful of especially sporty hues: Guards Red, Grand Prix White, Maritime Blue, Black and Speed Yellow. Weighing only 1210kg (266 lb), the RS could catapult to 62mph (100kph) in 4.9 seconds. Engine power equalled drag at a top speed of 168mph (270kph).

For the 911 turbo 3.6, Porsche's Exclusive department offered a run of slant-nose conversions, limited to 76 examples. The flat-topped front wings used pop-up headlamps taken from the Porsche 968. Other body changes included the 'Exclusive 3.6 front spoiler' and front air ducts for the oil cooler. The air ducts in the rear wings recalled the Porsche 959. A modified, entirely body-coloured rear spoiler topped the engine lid. The package included the higher-output, 385hp (283kW) engine, with its larger turbocharger, altered camshaft timing, ported cylinder heads, modified intake manifold and flanges, an auxiliary oil cooler and a four-pipe exhaust system.

In the autumn of 1993, a visually and mechanically much-modified 911 was displayed on the Porsche stand at the Frankfurt International Auto Show. Internally, the new 911 Carrera was known as the Type 993. This model superseded the Type 964-based Carrera 2 and Carrera 4 model lines. By the end of 1993, the following 911 variants continued in production using the old 964 body: 911 turbo 3.6, 911 Carrera Cabriolet, 911 Carrera 2 Speedster, and Carrera 4 turbo look.

Porsche produced a total of 63,570 examples of the Type 964 911.

911 Carrera 4 Coupé
MY 1989–MY 1993
911 Carrera 4 Targa
911 Carrera 4 Cabriolet
MY 1990–MY 1993

Engine

Engine design:	6-cylinder horizontally-opposed
Installation:	Rear-engine
Cooling system:	Air-cooled
Number & form of blower blades:	12, curved
Blower outside diameter (mm):	253
Engine type:	M 64/01
Displacement (cc):	3600
Bore x stroke (mm):	100 x 76.4
Engine output DIN (kW/hp):	184/250 at 6100rpm
Maximum torque (Nm/lb ft):	310/229 at 4800rpm
Output per litre (kW/l / hp/l):	51.1 / 69.4
Compression ratio:	11.3 : 1
Valve operation & camshaft drive:	ohc, cams driven by double chain, 2 valves per cylinder
Carburation:	Bosch DME with sequential injection
Ignition system:	Bosch DME, dual ignition
Firing order:	1 - 6 - 2 - 4 - 3 - 5
Engine lubrication:	Dry sump
Engine oil total (l):	11.5

Transmission

Drive configuration:	Electronic controlled 4-wheel-drive, transaxle
Manual gearbox:	5-speed
Transmission type:	G 64/00
Transmission ratios:	
1st gear:	3.500
2nd gear:	2.118
3rd gear:	1.444
4th gear:	1.086
5the gear:	0.868
Reverse gear:	2.857
Drive ratio:	3.444
Limited-slip diff. locking value (%):	Variabel 0 - 100

Body, chassis, suspension, brakes, wheels

Body design:	Steel body, 2 doors, 2 + 2 seats, entirely hot-dip galvanized body, side-impact protection beams in doors, flexible polyurethane front- and rear bumpers with integrated aluminium beams, polyurethane side skirts, engine lid with integrated automatic rear spoiler, red non-reflecting valance with integrated reverse gear and rear fog lamps
MY 1992 - MY 1993:	Wing mirrors in Cup-Design
Coupé:	Fixed steel roof
Option:	Electric sunroof
Targa:	Removable, foldable Targa top, fixed black Targa roll bar, fixed glass rear window
Cabriolet:	Electrically-operated, fully-automatical hood with flexible plastic rear window
Suspension, front:	Individually suspended light-alloy lower wishbones, McPherson struts with coil springs, dual-tube gas-filled shock absorbers, anti-roll bar
Suspension, rear:	Individually suspended on tilted shafts, McPherson struts with coil springs, dual-tube gas-filled shock absorbers, anti-roll bar
Brakes, front/rear (Size (mm)):	Ventilated discs (298 x 28) Ventilated discs (299 x 24) Black 4-piston fixed aluminium callipers / Black 4-piston fixed aluminium callipers Bosch ABS
Wheels, front/rear:	6 J x 16 / 8 J x 16
Tyres, front/rear:	205/55 ZR 16 / 225/50 ZR 16
Option MY 1992 - MY 1993:	7 J x 17 / 8 J x 17 205/50 ZR 17 / 255/40 ZR 17

Electrical system

Alternator (W/A):	1610 / 115
Battery (V/Ah):	12 / 72
MY 1992 - MY 1993:	12 / 75

Dimensions and weight

Track, front/rear (mm):	1380 / 1374
7 J x 17 / 8 J x 17:	1374 / 1374
Wheelbase (mm):	2272
Length x width x height (mm):	4250 x 1652 x 1310
Kerb weight DIN (kg):	1450
Permissible gross weight (kg):	1790
Luggage compartment (VDA (l)):	88
Luggage volume interior*:	175
Fuel tank capacity (l):	77, including 10 reserve
Option MY 1993,	
Coupé and Cabriolet only:	92, including 12.5 reserve
C_w x A (m^2):	0.32 x 1.79 = 0.573
Power/weight ratio (kg/kW/kg/hp):	7.88 / 5.80
*on folded down rear seat-backs	

Fuel consumption

EG-Norm 80/1268 (mpg):	95 RON super unleaded
At constant 56mph/90kph:	35
At constant 74mph/120kph:	29.5
EG-emissions-urban cycle:	16
1/3 mix:	24

Performance, production, prices

Acceleration 0-62mph/100kph (s):	5.7
Maximum speed (mph / kph):	161 / 260
Production, total number:	
Coupé:	13,353
Targa:	1,329
Cabriolet:	4,802
Purchase prices:	
08/1988 Coupé:	DM 114,500
04/1989 Coupé:	DM 114,500
08/1989 Coupé:	DM 116,600
Targa:	DM 121,800
Cabriolet:	DM 131,100
02/1990 Coupé:	DM 120,550
Targa:	DM 125,900
Cabriolet:	DM 135,400
07/1990 Coupé:	DM 122,600
Targa:	DM 128,040
Cabriolet:	DM 137,705
02/1991 Coupé:	DM 126,100
Targa:	DM 131,540
Cabriolet:	DM 141,205
07/1991 Coupé:	DM 129,450
Targa:	DM 135,100
Cabriolet:	DM 145,100
03/1992 Coupé:	DM 131,985
Targa:	DM 137,740
Cabriolet:	DM 147,955
08/1992 Coupé:	DM 135,550
Targa:	DM 141,460
Cabriolet:	DM 151,950
01/1993 Coupé:	DM 136,739.04
Targa:	DM 142,700.88
Cabriolet:	DM 153,282.89
03/1993 Coupé:	DM 139,340
Targa:	DM 145,410
Cabriolet:	DM 156,200

911 Carrera 2 Coupé [Tiptronic]
911 Carrera 2 Targa [Tiptronic]
911 Carrera 2 Cabriolet [Tiptronic]
MY 1990–MY 1993

Engine
Engine design:	6-cylinder horizontally-opposed
Installation:	Rear-engine
Cooling system:	Air-cooled
Number & form of blower blades:	12, curved
Blower outside diameter (mm):	253
Engine type:	M 64/01 [M 64/02]
Displacement (cc):	3600
Bore x stroke (mm):	100 x 76.4
Engine output DIN (kW/hp):	184/250 at 6100rpm
Maximum torque (Nm/lb ft):	310/229 at 4800rpm
Output per litre (kW/l / hp/l):	51.1 / 69.4
Compression ratio:	11.3 : 1
Valve operation & camshaft drive:	ohc, cams driven by double chain, 2 valves per cylinder
Carburation:	Bosch DME with sequential injection
Ignition system:	Bosch DME, dual ignition
Firing order:	1 - 6 - 2 - 4 - 3 - 5
Engine lubrication:	Dry sump
Engine oil total (l):	11.5

Transmission
Drive configuration:	Rear-axle drive
Manual gearbox:	5-speed
Option Tiptronic:	[4-speed]
Transmission type:	G 50/03 [A 50/01]
MY 1992 - MY 1993:	[A 50/02]
Transmission ratios:	
1st gear:	3.500 [2.479]
2nd gear:	2.059 [1.479]
3rd gear:	1.407 [1.000]
4th gear:	1.086 [0.728]
5th gear:	0.868
Reverse gear:	2.857 [2.086]
Drive ratio:	3.444 [3.667]

Body, chassis, suspension, brakes, wheels
Body design:	Steel body, 2 doors, 2 + 2 seats, entirely hot-dip galvanized body, side-impact protection beams in doors, flexible polyurethane front- and rear bumpers with integrated aluminium beams, polyurethane side skirts, engine lid with integrated automatic rear spoiler, red non-reflecting valance with integrated reverse gear and rear fog lamps
MY 1992 - MY 1993:	Wing mirrors in Cup-Design
Coupé:	Fixed steel roof
Option:	Electric sunroof
Targa:	Removable, foldable Targa top, fixed black Targa roll bar, fixed glass rear window
Cabriolet:	Electrically-operated, fully-automatic hood with flexible plastic rear window
Suspension, front:	Individually suspended light-alloy lower wishbones, McPherson struts with coil springs, dual-tube gas-filled shock absorbers, anti-roll bar
Suspension, rear:	Individually suspended on tilted shafts, McPherson struts with coil springs, dual-tube gas-filled shock absorbers, anti-roll bar
Brakes, front/rear (Size (mm)):	Ventilated discs (298 x 28) Ventilated discs (299 x 24) Black 4-piston fixed aluminium callipers / Black 2-piston fixed aluminium callipers
MY 1993:	Black 4-piston fixed aluminium callipers / Black 4-piston fixed aluminium callipers Bosch ABS
Wheels, front/rear:	6 J x 16,/ 8 J x 16
Tyres, front/rear:	205/55 ZR 16 / 225/50 ZR 16
Option MY 1992 - MY 1993:	7 J x 17 / 8 J x 17 205/50 ZR 17 / 255/40 ZR 17

Electrical system
Alternator (W/A):	1610 / 115
Battery (V/Ah):	12 / 72
MY 1992 - MY 1993:	12 / 75

Dimensions and weight
Track, front/rear (mm):	1380 / 1374
7 J x 17 / 8 J x 17:	1374 / 1374
Wheelbase (mm):	2272
Length x width x height (mm):	4250 x 1652 x 1310
Kerb weight DIN (kg):	1350 [1380]
Permissible gross weight (kg):	1690 [1720]
Luggage compartment (VDA (l)):	88
Luggage volume interior*:	175
Fuel tank capacity (l):	77, including 10 reserve
Option MY 1993, Coupé and Cabriolet only:	92, including 12.5 reserve
c_W x A (m²):	0.32 x 1.79 = 0.573
Power/weigt ratio (kg/kW / kg/hp):	7.33 [7.50] / 5.40 [5.52]

*on folded down rear seat-backs

Fuel consumption
EG-Norm 80/1268 (mpg):	95 RON super unleaded
At constant 56mph/90kph:	36.25 [35.6]
At constant 74mph/120kph:	29 [29.5]
EG-emissions-urban cycle:	16.5 [16.8]
1/3 mix:	24.5 [24.8]

Performance, production, prices
Acceleration 0-62mph/100kph (s):	5.7 [6.6]
Maximum speed (mph / kph):	161 / 260 [159 / 256]
Production, total number:	
Coupé:	18,219
Targa:	3,534
Cabriolet:	11,013
Purchase prices:	
08/1989 Coupé:	DM 103,500 [DM 109,500]
Targa:	DM 108,700 [DM 114,700]
Cabriolet:	DM 118,000 [DM 124,000]
02/1990 Coupé:	DM 107,100 [DM 113,250]
Targa:	DM 112,450 [DM 118,600]
Cabriolet:	DM 121,950 [DM 128,100]
07/1990 Coupé:	DM 108,920 [DM 115,175]
Targa:	DM 114,360 [DM 120,615]
Cabriolet:	DM 124,025 [DM 130,280]
02/1991 Coupé:	DM 112,420 [DM 118,675]
Targa:	DM 117,860 [DM 124,115]
Cabriolet:	DM 127,525 [DM 133,780]
07/1991 Coupé:	DM 116,800 [DM 123,300]
Targa:	DM 122,450 [DM 128,950]
Cabriolet:	DM 132,450 [DM 138,950]
03/1992 Coupé:	DM 119,120 [DM 125,720]
Targa:	DM 124,875 [DM 131,475]
Cabriolet:	DM 135,090 [DM 141,690]
08/1992 Coupé:	DM 122,340 [DM 128,940]
Targa:	DM 128,250 [DM 134,850]
Cabriolet:	DM 138,740 [DM 145,340]
0/1993 Coupé:	DM 123,413.16 [DM 130,071.05]
Targa:	DM 129,375 [DM 126,032.89]
Cabriolet:	DM 139,957.01 [DM 146,614.90]
03/1993 Coupé:	DM 125,760 [DM 132,420]
Targa:	DM 131,530 [DM 138,480]
Cabriolet:	DM 142,620 [DM 149,280]
08/1993 Cabriolet:	DM 142,620 [DM 149,280]

911 turbo Coupé
MY 1991–MY 1992

Engine

Engine design:	6-cylinder horizontally-opposed, turbo charger, intercooler
Installation:	Rear-engine
Cooling system:	Air-cooled
Number & form of blower blades:	11, straight
Blower outside diameter (mm):	245
Engine type:	M 30/69
Displacement (cc):	3299
Bore x stroke (mm):	97 x 74.4
Engine output DIN (kW/hp):	235/320 at 5750rpm
Maximum torque (Nm/lb ft):	450/332 at 4500rpm
Output per litre (kW/l / hp/l):	71.2 / 97.0
Compression ratio:	7.0 : 1
Valve operation & camshaft drive:	ohc, cams driven by double chain, 2 valves per cylinder
Carburation:	Bosch K-Jetronic injection
Ignition system:	Battery, capacitive-discharge system, without contact
Firing order:	1 - 6 - 2 - 4 - 3 - 5
Engine lubrication:	Dry sump
Engine oil total (l):	13.0

Transmission

Drive configuration:	Rear-axle drive
Manual gearbox:	5-speed
Transmission type:	G 50/52
Transmission ratios:	
1st gear:	3.154
2nd gear:	1.789
3rd gear:	1.269
4th gear:	0.967
5th gear:	0.756
Reverse gear:	2.857
Drive ratio:	3.444
Ltd slip diff. load/deceleration (%):	20 / 100

Body, chassis, suspension, brakes, wheels

Body design:	Steel coupé body, 2 doors, 2 + 2 seats, entirely hot-dip galvanized body, side-impact protection beams in doors, wider front and rear wings, flexible polyurethane front and rear bumpers with integrated aluminium beams, polyurethane side skirts, rear wing with black polyurethane surround on engine lid, red non-reflecting valance with integrated reverse gear and rear fog lamps, wing mirrors in Cup-Design
Option:	Electric sunroof

Suspension, front:	Individually suspended light-alloy lower wishbones, McPherson struts with coil springs, dual-tube gas-filled shock absorbers, anti-roll bar
Suspension, rear:	Individually suspended on tilted shafts, McPherson struts with coil springs, dual-tube gas-filled shock absorbers, anti-roll bar
Brakes, front/rear (Size (mm)):	Ventilated and drilled discs (322 x 32) Ventilated and drilled discs (299 x 28) Black 4-piston fixed aluminium callipers / Black 4-piston fixed aluminium callipers Bosch ABS
Wheels, front/rear:	7 J x 17 / 9 J x 17
Tyres, front/rear:	205/50 ZR 17 / 255/40 ZR 17

Electrical system

Alternator (W/A):	1610 / 115
Battery (V/Ah):	12 / 72
MY 1992:	12 / 75

Dimensions and weight

Track, front/rear (mm):	1434 / 1493
Wheelbase (mm):	2272
Length x width x height (mm):	4250 x 1775 x 1310
Kerb weight DIN (kg):	1470
Permissible gross weight (kg):	1810
Luggage compartment (VDA (l)):	88
Luggage volume interior*:	175
Fuel tank capacity (l):	77, including 10 reserve
C_w x A (m^2):	0.36 x 1.89 = 0.680
Power/weight ratio (kg/kW / kg/hp):	6.25 / 4.59
*on folded down rear seat-backs	

Fuel consumption

EG-Norm 80/1268 (mpg):	95 RON super unleaded
At constant 56mph/90kph:	33
At constant 74mph/120kph:	27
EG-emissions-urban cycle:	13
1/3 mix:	21

Performance, production, prices

Acceleration 0-62mph/100kph (s):	5.0
Maximum speed (mph / kph):	167 / 270
Production, total number:	
Coupé:	3,660
Purchase prices:	
07/1990 Coupé:	DM 178,500
02/1991 Coupé:	DM 183,600
07/1991 Coupé:	DM 190,250
03/1992 Coupé:	DM 191,550

911 Carrera 2 Cabriolet Turbolook [Tiptronic]
MY 1992–MY 1993

Engine

Engine design:	6-cylinder horizontally-opposed
Installation:	Rear-engine
Cooling system:	Air-cooled
Number & form of blower blades:	12, curved
Blower outside diameter (mm):	253
Engine type:	M 64/01 [M 64/02]
Displacement (cc):	3600
Bore x stroke (mm):	100 x 76.4
Engine output DIN (kW/hp):	184/250 at 6100rpm
Maximum torque (Nm/lb ft):	310/229 at 4800rpm
Output per litre (kW/l / hp/l):	51.1 / 69.4
Compression ratio:	11.3 : 1
Valve operation & camshaft drive:	ohc, cams driven by double chain, 2 valves per cylinder
Carburation:	Bosch DME with sequential injection
Ignition system:	Bosch DME, dual ignition
Firing order:	1 - 6 - 2 - 4 - 3 - 5
Engine lubrication:	Dry sump
Engine oil total (l):	11.5

Transmission

Drive configuration:	Rear-axle drive
Manual gearbox:	5-speed
Option Tiptronic:	[4-speed]
Transmission type:	G 50/03 [A 50/02]
Transmission ratios:	
1st gear:	3.500 [2.479]
2nd gear:	2.059 [1.479]
3rd gear:	1.407 [1.000]
4th gear:	1.086 [0.728]
5th gear:	0.868
Reverse gear:	2.857 [2.086]
Drive ratio:	3.444 [3.667]

Body, chassis, suspension, brakes, wheels

Body design:	Steel cabriolet body, 2 doors, 2 + 2 seats, entirely hot-dip galvanized body, side-impact protection beams in doors, wider front and rear wings, flexible polyurethane front and rear bumpers with integrated aluminium beams, polyurethane side skirts, engine lid with integrated automatic rear spoiler, red non-reflecting valance with integrated reverse gear and rear fog lamps, wing mirrors in Cup-Design, electric hood with flexible rear window

Suspension, front:	Individually suspended light-alloy lower wishbones, McPherson struts with coil springs, dual-tube gas-filled shock absorbers, anti-roll bar
Suspension, rear:	Individually suspended on tilted shafts, McPherson struts with coil springs, dual-tube gas-filled shock absorbers, anti-roll bar
Brakes, front/rear (Size (mm)):	Ventilated and drilled discs (322 x 32) Ventilated and drilled discs (299 x 28) Black 4-piston fixed aluminium callipers / Black 4-piston fixed aluminium callipers Bosch ABS
Wheels, front/rear:	7 J x 17 / 9 J x 17
Tyres, front/rear:	205/50 ZR 17 / 255/40 ZR 17

Electrical system

Alternator (W/A):	1610 / 115
Battery (V/Ah):	12 / 75

Dimensions and weight

Track, front/rear (mm):	1434 / 1493
Wheelbase (mm):	2272
Length x width x height (mm):	4250 x 1775 x 1310
Kerb weight DIN (kg):	1420 [1450]
Permissible gross weight (kg):	1760 [1790]
Luggage compartment (VDA (l)):	88
Luggage volume interior*:	175
Fuel tank capacity (l):	77, including 10 reserve
Option MY 1993:	92, including 12.5 reserve
C_w x A (m^2):	0.36 x 1.89 = 0.680
Power/weight ratio (kg/kW/ kg/hp):	7.71 [7.88] / 5.68 [5.80]
*on folded down rear seat-backs	

Fuel consumption

EG-Norm 80/1268 (mpg):	95 RON super unleaded
At constant 56mph/90kph:	35 [34.4]
At constant 74mph/120kph:	28 [27.4]
EG-emission-urban cycle:	16.8 [16.8]
1/3 mix:	24 [24]

Performance, production, prices

Acceleration 0-62mph/100kph (s):	5.7 [6.6]
Maximum speed (mph / kph):	158 / 255 [156 / 251]
Production, total number:	702
Purchase prices:	
07/1991 Cabriolet:	DM 169,300 [DM 175,300]
08/1992 Cabriolet:	DM 173,870 [DM 179,870]
01/1993 Cabriolet:	DM 175,395.17 [DM 181,447.81]
03/1993 Cabriolet:	DM 175,395.17 [DM 181,447.81]

911 Carrera RS Coupé MY 1992

Engine

Engine design:	6-cylinder horizontally-opposed
Installation:	Rear-engine
Cooling system:	Air-cooled
Number & form of blower blades:	12, curved
Blower outside diameter (mm):	253
Engine type:	M 64/03
Displacement (cc):	3600
Bore x stroke (mm):	100 x 76.4
Engine output DIN (kW/hp):	191/260 at 6100rpm
Maximum torque (Nm/lb ft):	325/240 at 4800rpm
Output per litre (kW/l / hp/l):	53.0 / 72.2
Compression ratio:	11.3 : 1
Valve operation & camshaft drive:	ohc, cams driven by double chain, 2 valves per cylinder
Carburation:	Bosch DME with sequential injection
Ignition system:	Bosch DME, dual ignition
Firing order:	1 - 6 - 2 - 4 - 3 - 5
Engine lubrication:	Dry sump
Engine oil total (l):	11.5

Transmission

Drive configuration:	Rear-axle drive
Manual gearbox:	5-speed
Transmission type:	G 50/10
Transmission ratios:	
1st gear:	3.154
2nd gear:	1.895
3rd gear:	1.407
4th gear:	1.086
5th gear:	0.868
Reverse gear:	2.857
Drive ratio:	3.444
Ltd slip diff. load/deceleration (%):	20 / 100

Body, chassis, suspension, brakes, wheels

Body design:	Steel coupé body, 2 doors, 2 seats, entirely hot-dip galvanized body, side-impact protection beams in doors, flexible polyurethane front and rear bumpers with integrated aluminium beams, RS rear bumper, polyurethane side skirts, aluminium front lid, engine lid with integrated automatic rear spoiler, red non-reflecting valance with integrated reverse gear and rear fog lamps, thin-glass rear and side windows, wing mirrors in Cup-Design
Suspension, front:	Individually suspended light-alloy lower wishbones, McPherson struts with coil springs, dual-tube gas-filled shock absorbers, anti-roll bar
Suspension, rear:	Individually suspended on tilted shafts, McPherson struts with coil springs, dual-tube gas-filled shock absorbers, anti-roll bar
Brakes, front/rear (Size (mm)):	Ventilated and drilled discs (322 x 32) Ventilated and drilled discs (299 x 24) Black 4-piston fixed aluminium callipers / Black 4-piston fixed aluminium callipers Bosch ABS
Wheels, front/rear:	7.5 J x 17 / 9 J x 17
Tyres, front/rear:	205/50 ZR 17 / 255/40 ZR 17

Electrical system

Alternator (W/A):	1610 / 115
Battery (V/Ah):	12 / 36
Touring:	12 / 75

Dimensions and weight

Track, front/rear (mm):	1379 / 1380
Wheelbase (mm):	2272
Length x width x height (mm):	4275 x 1652 x 1270
Kerb weight DIN (kg):	1220
Touring:	1320
Permissible gross weight (kg):	1420
Touring:	1520
Luggage compartment (VDA (l)):	88
Fuel tank capacity (l):	77, including 10 reserve
Option:	92, including 12.5 reserve
C_w x A (m²):	0.32 X 1.79 = 0.573
Power/weight ratio (kg/kW/kg/hp):	6.38 / 4.69
Touring:	7.17 / 5.07

Fuel consumption

EG-Norm 80/1268 (mpg):	98 RON super plus unleaded
At constant 56mph/90kph:	37
At constant 74mph/120kph:	29.5
EG-emissions-urban cycle:	18
1/3 mix:	25.6

Performance, production, prices

Acceleration 0-62mph/100kph (s):	5.3
Touring:	5.3
Maximum speed (mph / kph):	161 / 260
Touring:	161 / 260
Production, total no. incl. M003:	2.282
Basic version:	1.916
Basic version RHD:	72
Touring version (M002):	76
Touring version RHD:	14
Purchase prices:	
08/1991 Coupé:	DM 145,450
03/1992 Coupé:	DM 145,450

911 Carrera RS Coupé N/GT
MY 1992

Engine

Engine design:	6-cylinder horizontally-opposed
Installation:	Rear-engine
Cooling system:	Air-cooled
Number & form of blower blades:	12, curved
Blower outside diameter (mm):	253
Engine type:	M 64/03
Displacement (cc):	3600
Bore x stroke (mm):	100 x 76.4
Engine output DIN (kW/hp):	191/260 at 6100rpm
Maximum torque (Nm/lb ft):	325/240 at 4800rpm
Output per litre (kW/l / hp/l):	53.0 / 72.2
Compression ratio:	11.3 : 1
Valve operation & camshaft drive:	ohc, cams driven by double chain, 2 valves per cylinder
Carburation:	Bosch DME with sequential injection
Ignition system:	Bosch DME, dual ignition
Firing order:	1 - 6 - 2 - 4 - 3 - 5
Engine lubrication:	Dry sump
Engine oil total (l):	11.5

Transmission

Drive configuration:	Rear-axle drive
Manual gearbox:	5-speed
Transmission type:	G 50/10
Transmission ratios:	
1st gear:	3.154
2nd gear:	1.895
3rd gear:	1.407
4th gear:	1.086
5th gear:	0.868
Reverse gear:	2.857
Drive ratio:	3.444
Ltd slip diff. load/deceleration (%):	20 / 100

Body, chassis, suspension, brakes, wheels

Body design:	Steel coupé body, 2 doors, 2 seats, entirely hot-dip galvanized body, side-impact protection beams in doors, flexible polyurethane front and rear bumpers with integrated aluminium beams, RS rear bumper, polyurethane side skirts, aluminium front lid, engine lid with integrated automatic rear spoiler, red non-reflecting valance with integrated reverse gear and rear fog lamps, thin-glass rear and side windows, wing mirrors in Cup-Design, roll cage

Suspension, front:	Individually suspended light-alloy lower wishbones, McPherson struts with coil springs, dual-tube gas-filled shock absorbers, anti-roll bar
Suspension, rear:	Individually suspended on tilted shafts, McPherson struts with coil springs, dual-tube gas-filled shock absorbers, anti-roll bar
Brakes, front/rear (Size (mm)):	Ventilated and drilled discs (322 x 32) Ventilated and drilled discs (299 x 24) Black 4-piston fixed aluminium callipers / Black 4-piston fixed aluminium callipers Bosch ABS
Wheels, front/rear:	7.5 J x 17 / 9 J x 17
Tyres, front/rear:	205/50 ZR 17 / 255/40 ZR 17

Electrical system

Alternator (W/A):	1610 / 115
Battery (V/Ah):	12 / 36

Dimensions and weight

Track, front/rear (mm):	1379 / 1380
Whelbase (mm):	2272
Length x width x height (mm):	4275 x 1652 x 1270
Kerb weight DIN (kg):	1220
Permissible gross weight (kg):	1420
Luggage compartment (VDA (l)):	88
Fuel tank capacity (l):	77, including 10 reserve
Option:	92, including 12.5 reserve
C_w x A (m^2):	0.32 x 1.79 = 0.573
Power/weight ratio (kg/kW/ kg/hp):	6.38 / 4.69

Fuel consumption

EG-Norm 80/1268 (mpg):	98 RON super plus unleaded
At constant 56mph/90kph:	37
At constant 74mph/120kph:	29.5
EG-emissions-urban cycle:	18
1/3 mix:	25.6

Performance, production, prices

Acceleration 0-62mph/100kph (s):	5.3
Maximum speed (mph / kph):	161 / 260
Production, total number:	
Sports version N/GT (M003):	290
Purchase price:	
08/1991 Coupé:	DM 160,000
03/1992 Coupé:	DM 160,000

911 turbo Coupé
911 turbo Cabriolet with performance kit
MY 1992–MY 1993

Engine

Engine design:	6-cylinder horizontally-opposed, turbo charger, intercooler
Installation:	Rear-engine
Cooling system:	Air-cooled
Number & form of blower blades:	11, straight
Blower outside diameter (mm):	245
Engine type:	M 30/69 S
Displacement (cc):	3299
Bore x stroke (mm):	97 x 74.4
Engine output DIN (kW/hp):	261/355 at 5750rpm
Maximum torque (Nm/lb ft):	471/347 at 5000rpm
Output per litre (kW/l / hp/l):	79.1 / 107.6
Compression ratio:	7.0 : 1
Valve operation & camshaft drive:	ohc, cams driven by double chain, 2 valves per cylinder
Carburation:	Bosch K-Jetronic injection
Ignition system:	Battery, capacitive-discharge system, without contact
Firing order:	1 - 6 - 2 - 4 - 3 - 5
Engine lubrication:	Dry sump
Engine oil total (l):	13.0

Transmission

Drive configuration:	Rear-axle drive
Manual gearbox:	5-speed
Transmission type:	G 50/52
Transmission ratios:	
1st gear:	3.154
2nd gear:	1.789
3rd gear:	1.269
4th gear:	0.967
5th gear:	0.756
Reverse gear:	2.857
Drive ratio:	3.444
Ltd slip diff. load/deceleration (%):	20 / 100

Body, chassis, suspension, brakes, wheels

Body design:	Steel body, 2 doors, 2 + 2 seats, entirely hot-dip galvanized body, side-impact protection beams in doors, wider front and rear wings, flexible polyurethane front and rear bumpers with integrated aluminium beams, polyurethane side skirts, rear wing with black polyurethane surround on engine lid, red non-reflecting valance with integrated reverse gear and rear fog lamps, wing mirrors in Cup-Design
Coupé:	Fixed steel roof
Option:	Electric sunroof
Cabriolet:	Electric hood with flexible plastic rear window
Suspension, front:	Individually suspended light-alloy lower wishbones, McPherson struts with coil springs, dual-tube gas-filled shock absorbers, anti-roll bar
Suspension, rear:	Individually suspended on tilted shafts, McPherson struts with coil springs, dual-tube gas-filled shock absorbers, anti-roll bar
Brakes, front/rear (Size (mm)):	Ventilated and drilled discs (322 x 32) Ventilated and drilled discs (299 x 28) Black 4-piston fixed aluminium callipers / Black 4-piston fixed aluminium callipers Bosch ABS
Wheels, front/rear:	7 J x 17 / 9 J x 17
Tyres, front/rear:	205/50 ZR 17 / 255/40 ZR 17

Electrical system

Alternator (W/A):	1610 / 115
Battery (V/Ah):	12 / 75

Dimensions and weight

Track, front/rear (mm):	1434 / 1493
Wheelbase (mm):	2272
Length x width x height (mm):	4250 x 1775 x 1310
Kerb weight DIN (kg):	1470
Permissible gross weight (kg):	1810
Luggage compartment (VDA (l)):	88
Luggage volume interior*:	175
Fuel tank capacity (l):	77, including 10 reserve
Option MY 1993:	92, including 12.5 reserve
C_w x A (m²):	0.36 x 1.89 = 0.680
Power/weight ratio (kg/kW/kg/hp):	5.63 / 4.14
*on folded down rear seat-backs	

Fuel consumption

EG-Norm 80/1268 (mpg):	95 RON super unleaded
At constant 56mph/90kph:	33
At constant 74mph/120kph:	27
EG-emissions-urban cycle:	13
1/3 mix:	21

Performance, production, prices

Acceleration 0-62mph/100kph (s):	4.7
Maximum speed (mph / kph):	174 / 280
Production, total number:	
Coupé:	n/a
Cabriolet:	6
Purchase prices:	
08/1991 Coupé:	DM 209,750
03/1992 Coupé:	DM 211,050
Cabriolet:	DM 254,150

911 turbo S Coupé - light weight
MY 1992

Engine

Engine design:	6-cylinder horizontally-opposed, turbo charger, intercooler
Installation:	Rear-engine
Cooling system:	Air-cooled
Number & form of blower blades:	11, straight
Blower outside diameter (mm):	245
Engine type:	M 30/69 SL
Displacement (cc):	3299
Bore x stroke (mm):	97 x 74.4
Engine output DIN (kW/hp):	280/381 at 5750rpm
Maximum torque (Nm/lb ft):	490/361 at 4800rpm
Output per litre (kW/l / hp/l):	84.9 / 115.5
Compression ratio:	7.0 : 1
Valve operation & camshaft drive:	ohc, cams driven by double chain, 2 valves per cylinder
Carburation:	Bosch K-Jetronic injection
Ignition system:	Battery, capacitive-discharge system, without contact
Firing order:	1 - 6 - 2 - 4 - 3 - 5
Engine lubrication:	Dry sump
Engine oil total (l):	13.0

Transmission

Drive configuration:	Rear-axle drive
Manual gearbox:	5-speed
Transmission type:	G 50/52
Transmission ratios:	
1st gear:	3.154
2nd gear:	1.789
3rd gear:	1.269
4th gear:	0.967
5th gear:	0.756
Reverse gear:	2.857
Drive ratio:	3.444
Ltd slip diff. load/deceleration (%):	20 / 100

Body, chassis, suspension, brakes, wheels

Body design:	Steel coupé body, 2 doors, 2 seats, entirely hot-dip galvanized body, side-impact protection beams in doors, wider front and rear wings, air intakes in rear wings, flexible polyurethane front and rear bumpers with integrated aluminium beams, air intakes in front bumper instead of fog lamps, RS rear bumper, polyurethane side skirts, rear wing without black polyurethane surround on engine lid, lightweight plastic bonnet lid and doors, red non-reflecting valance with integrated reverse gear and rear fog lamps, thin-glass rear and side windows, wing mirrors in Cup-Design
Suspension, front:	Individually suspended light-alloy lower wishbones, McPherson struts with coil springs, dual-tube gas-filled shock absorbers, anti-roll bar
Suspension, rear:	Individually suspended on tilted shafts, McPherson struts with coil springs, dual-tube gas-filled shock absorbers, anti-roll bar
Brakes, front/rear (Size (mm)):	Ventilated and drilled discs (322 x 32) Ventilated and drilled discs (299 x 28) Red 4-piston fixed aluminium callipers / Red 4-piston fixed aluminium callipers Bosch ABS
Wheels, front/rear:	8 J x 18 / 10 J x 18
Tyres, front/rear:	225/40 ZR 18 / 265/35 ZR 18

Electrical system

Alternator (W/A):	1610 / 115
Battery (V/Ah):	12 / 75

Dimensions and weight

Track, front/rear (mm):	1440 / 1481
Wheelbase (mm):	2272
Length x width x height (mm):	4275 x 1775 x 1270
Kerb weight DIN (kg):	1290
Permissible gross weight (kg):	1510
Luggage compartment (VDA (l)):	88
Fuel tank capacity (l):	92, including 12.5 reserve
C_w x A (m²):	0.35 x 1.89 = 0.662
Power/weight ratio (kg/kW/ kg/hp):	4.60 / 3.38

Fuel consumption

(mpg):	app. 14; 98 RON super plus unleaded

Performance, production, prices

Acceleration 0-62mph/100kph (s):	4.6
0-124mph/200kph (s):	14.2
0-155mph/250kph (s):	25.1
Maximum speed (mph / kph):	180 / 290
Production, total number:	
Coupé:	86
Purchase price:	
08/1991 Coupé:	DM 295,000

911 Carrera 2 Speedster [Tiptronic] MY 1993

Engine

Engine design:	6-cylinder horizontally-opposed
Installation:	Rear-engine
Cooling system:	Air-cooled
Number & form of blower blades:	12, curved
Blower outside diameter (mm):	253
Engine type:	M 64/01 [M 64/02]
Displacement (cc):	3600
Bore x stroke (mm):	100 x 76.4
Engine output DIN (kW/hp):	184/250 at 6100rpm
Maximum torque (Nm/lb ft):	310/229 at 4800rpm
Output per litre (kW/l / hp/l):	51.1 / 69.4
Compression ratio:	11.3 : 1
Valve operation & camshaft drive:	ohc, cams driven by double chain, 2 valves per cylinder
Carburation:	Bosch DME with sequential injection
Ignition system:	Bosch DME, dual ignition
Firing order:	1 - 6 - 2 - 4 - 3 - 5
Engine lubrication:	Dry sump
Engine oil total (l):	11.5

Transmission

Drive configuration:	Rear-axle drive
Manual gearbox:	5-speed
Option Tiptronic:	[4-speed]
Transmission type:	G 50/03 [A 50/02]
Transmission ratios:	
1st gear:	3.500 [2.479]
2nd gear:	2.059 [1.479]
3rd gear:	1.407 [1.000]
4th gear:	1.086 [0.728]
5th gear:	0.868
Reverse gear:	2.857 [2.086]
Drive ratio:	3.444 [3.667]

Body, chassis, suspension, brakes, wheels

Body design:	Steel Speedster body, 2 doors, 2 seats, entirely hot-dip galvanized body, small Speedster windscreen with black frame, side-impact protection beams in doors, flexible polyurethane front and rear bumpers with integrated aluminium beams, polyurethane side skirts, engine lid with integrated automatic rear spoiler, red non-reflecting valance with integrated reverse gear and rear fog lamps, thin-glass rear and side windows, wing mirrors in Cup-Design, manual hood with flexible plastic rear window, Speedster plastic hatch with two fairings
Suspension, front:	Individually suspended light-alloy lower wishbones, McPherson struts with coil springs, dual-tube gas-filled shock absorbers, anti-roll bar
Suspension, rear:	Individually suspended on tilted shafts, McPherson struts with coil springs, dual-tube gas-filled shock absorbers, anti-roll bar
Brakes, front/rear (Size (mm)):	Ventilated discs (298 x 28) Ventilated discs (299 x 24) Black 4-piston fixed aluminium callipers / Black 4-piston fixed aluminium callipers Bosch ABS
Wheels, front/rear:	7 J x 17 / 8 J x 17
Tyres, front/rear:	205/50 ZR 17 / 255/40 ZR 17

Electrical system

Alternator (W/A):	1610 / 115
Battery (V/Ah):	12 / 75

Dimensions and weight

Track, front/rear (mm):	1374 / 1374
Wheelbase (mm):	2272
Length x width x height (mm):	4250 x 1652 x 1280
Kerb weight DIN (kg):	1350 [1380]
Permissible gross weight (kg):	1600 [1630]
Luggage compartment (VDA (l)):	88
Fuel tank capacity (l):	77, including 10 reserve
Option:	92, including 12.5 reserve
C_w x A (m²):	n/a
Power/weight ratio (kg/kW/kg/hp):	7.33 [7.50] / 5.40 [5.52]

Fuel consumption

EG-Norm 80/1268 (mpg):	95 RON super unleaded
At constant 56mph/90kph:	36.25 [35.6]
At constant 74mph/120kph:	29 [29.5]
EG-emissions-urban cycle:	16.5 [16.8]
1/3 mix:	24.5 [24.8]

Performance, production, prices

Acceleration 0-62mph/100kph (s):	5.7 [6.6]
Maximum speed (mph / kph):	161 / 260 [158.7 / 256]
Production, total number:	930
Purchase prices:	
08/1992 Speedster:	DM 131,500
03/1993 Speedster:	DM 134,000 [DM 140,660]

147

911 Carrera 2 Speedster Turbolook
MY 1993

Engine

Engine design:	6-cylinder horizontally-opposed
Installation:	Rear-engine
Cooling system:	Air-cooled
Number & form of blower blades:	12, curved
Blower outside diameter (mm):	253
Engine type:	M 64/01 [M 64/02]
Displacement (cc):	3600
Bore x stroke (mm):	100 x 76.4
Engine output DIN (kW/hp):	184/250 at 6100rpm
Maximum torque (Nm/lb ft):	310/229 at 4800rpm
Output per litre (kW/l / hp/l):	51.1 / 69.4
Compression ratio:	11.3 : 1
Valve operation & camshaft drive:	ohc, cams driven by double chain, 2 valves per cylinder
Carburation:	Bosch DME with sequential injection
Ignition system:	Bosch DME, dual ignition
Firing order:	1 - 6 - 2 - 4 - 3 - 5
Engine lubrication:	Dry sump
Engine oil total (l):	11.5

Transmission

Drive configuration:	Rear-axle drive
Manual gearbox:	5-speed
Option Tiptronic:	[4-speed]
Transmission type:	G 50/03 [A 50/02]
Transmission ratios:	
1st gear:	3.500 [2.479]
2nd gear:	2.059 [1.479]
3rd gear:	1.407 [1.000]
4th gear:	1.086 [0.728]
5th gear:	0.868
Reverse gear:	2.857 [2.086]
Drive ratio:	3.444 [3.667]

Body, chassis, suspension, brakes, wheels

Body design:	Steel Speedster body, 2 doors, 2 seats, hot-dip galvanized body, wider front and rear wings, small windscreen with black frame, side-impact beams in doors, flexible polyurethane front and rear bumpers with integrated aluminium beams, polyurethane side skirts, engine lid with integral automatic rear spoiler, red non-reflecting valance with integrated reverse and rear fog lamps, thin-glass rear and side windows, wing mirrors in Cup-Design, manual hood with flexible plastic rear window, Speedster plastic hatch with 2 fairings

Suspension, front:	Individually suspended light-alloy lower wishbones, McPherson struts with coil springs, dual-tube gas-filled shock absorbers, anti-roll bar
Suspension, rear:	Individually suspended on tilted shafts, McPherson struts with coil springs, dual-tube gas-filled shock absorbers, anti-roll bar
Brakes, front/rear (Size (mm)):	Ventilated discs (298 x 28) / Ventilated discs (299 x 24) / Black 4-piston fixed aluminium callipers / Black 4-piston fixed aluminium callipers / Bosch ABS
Option:	Ventilated and drilled discs (322 x 32) / Ventilated and drilled discs (299 x 28) / Black 4-piston fixed aluminium callipers / Black 4-piston fixed aluminium callipers / Bosch ABS
Wheels, front/rear:	7 J x 17 / 9 J x 17
Tyres, front/rear:	205/50 ZR 17 / 255/40 ZR 17

Electrical system

Alternator (W/A):	1610 / 115
Battery (V/Ah):	12 / 75

Dimensions and weight

Track, front/rear (mm):	1434 / 1493
Wheelbase (mm):	2272
Length x width x height (mm):	4250 x 1775 x 1280
Kerb weight DIN (kg):	1420 [1450]
Permissible gross weight (kg):	1670 [1700]
Luggage compartment (VDA (l)):	88
Fuel tank capacity (l):	77, including 10 reserve
Option:	92, including 12.5 reserve
C_w x A (m^2):	n/a
Power/weight ratio (kg/kW/kg/hp):	7.71 [7.88] / 5.68 [5.80]

Fuel consumption

EG-Norm 80/1268 (mpg):	95 RON super unleaded
At constant 56mph/90kph:	35 [34.4]
At constant 74mph/120kph:	28.2 [27.4]
EG-emission-urban cycle:	16.8 [16.8]
1/3 mix:	24.3 [24]

Performance, production, prices

Acceleration 0-62mph/100kph (s):	5.7 [6.6]
Maximum speed (mph / kph):	158 / 255 [156 / 251]
Production, total number:	app. 15
Conversion price for Turbolook	
05/1993:	DM 16,410.52
09/1993:	DM 18,156.32
Turbo brakes:	DM 9,495.03

911 Carrera 4 Coupé Turbolook
'30 years 911'
911 Carrera 4 Coupé Turbolook
MY 1993–December 1993

Engine

Engine design:	6-cylinder horizontally-opposed
Installation:	Rear-engine
Cooling system:	Air-cooled
Number & form of blower blades:	12, curved
Blower outside diameter (mm):	253
Engine type:	M 64/01
Displacement (cc):	3600
Bore x stroke (mm):	100 x 76.4
Engine output DIN (kW/hp):	184/250 at 6100rpm
Maximum torque (Nm/lb ft):	310/229 at 4800rpm
Output per litre (kW/l / hp/l):	51.1 / 69.4
Compression ratio:	11.3 : 1
Valve operation & camshaft drive:	ohc, cams driven by double chain, 2 valves per cylinder
Carburation:	Bosch DME with sequential injection
Ignition system:	Bosch DME, dual ignition
Firing order:	1 - 6 - 2 - 4 - 3 - 5
Engine lubrication:	Dry sump
Engine oil total (l):	11.5

Transmission

Drive configuration:	Electronic controlled 4-wheel-drive, transaxle
Manual gearbox:	5-speed
Transmission type:	G 64/00
Transmission ratios:	
1st gear:	3.500
2nd gear:	2.118
3rd gear:	1.444
4th gear:	1.086
5the gear:	0.868
Reverse gear:	2.857
Drive ratio:	3.444
Limited-slip diff. locking value (%):	Variable 0 - 100

Body, chassis, suspension, brakes, wheels

Body design:	Steel coupé body, 2 doors, 2 + 2 seats, entirely hot-dip galvanized body, side-impact protection beams in doors, wider front and rear wings, flexible polyurethane front and rear bumpers with integrated aluminium beams, polyurethane side skirts, engine lid with integrated automatic rear spoiler, red non-reflecting valance with integrated reverse gear and rear fog lamps, wing mirrors in Cup-Design
Exclusive colour '30 Years 911':	Viola Metallic
Option:	Electric sunroof

Suspension, front:	Individually suspended light-alloy lower wishbones, McPherson struts with coil springs, dual-tube gas-filled shock absorbers, anti-roll bar
Suspension, rear:	Individually suspended on tilted shafts, McPherson struts with coil springs, dual-tube gas-filled shock absorbers, anti-roll bar
Brakes, front/rear (Size (mm)):	Ventilated discs (298 x 28) Ventilated discs (299 x 24) Black 4-piston fixed aluminium callipers / Black 4-piston fixed aluminium callipers Bosch ABS
Wheels, front/rear:	7 J x 17 / 9 J x 17
Tyres, front/rear:	205/50 ZR 17 / 255/40 ZR 17

Electrical system

Alternator (W/A):	1610 / 115
Battery (V/Ah):	12 / 75

Dimensions and weight

Track, front/rear (mm):	1434 / 1493
Wheelbase (mm):	2272
Length x width x height (mm):	4250 x 1775 x 1310
Kerb weight DIN (kg):	1500
Permissible gross weight (kg):	1810
Luggage compartment (VDA (l)):	88
Luggage volume interior*:	175
Fuel tank capacity (l):	77, including 10 reserve
Option:	92, including 12.5 reserve
C_w x A (m²):	0.36 x 1.89 = 0.680
Power/weight ratio (kg/kW/ kg/hp):	8.15 / 6.00
*on folded down rear seat-backs	

Fuel consumption

EG-Norm 80/1268 (mpg):	95 RON super unleaded
At constant 56mph/90kph:	35
At constant 74mph/120kph:	29.5
EG-emission-urban cycle:	15.8
1/3 mix:	24

Performance, production, prices

Acceleration 0-62mph/100kph (s):	5.7
Maximum speed (mph / kph):	158 / 255
Production, total number:	
Coupé '30 Years 911":	911
Coupé:	174
Purchase price:	
03/1993 Coupé:	DM 145,900
08/1993 Coupé:	DM 145,900

911 Carrera RS 3.8 Coupé 1993

Engine

Engine design:	6-cylinder horizontally-opposed
Installation:	Rear-engine
Cooling system:	Air-cooled
Number & form of blower blades:	12, curved
Blower outside diameter (mm):	253
Engine type:	M 64/04
Displacement (cc):	3746
Bore x stroke (mm):	102 x 76.4
Engine output DIN (kW/hp):	221/3000 at 6500rpm
Maximum torque (Nm/lb ft):	360/266 at 5250rpm
Output per litre (kW/l / hp/l):	59.0 / 80.1
Compression ratio:	11.0 : 1
Valve operation & camshaft drive:	ohc, cams driven by double chain, 2 valves per cylinder
Carburation:	Bosch DME with sequential injection
Ignition system:	Bosch DME, dual ignition
Firing order:	1 - 6 - 2 - 4 - 3 - 5
Engine lubrication:	Dry sump
Engine oil total (l):	11.5

Transmission

Drive configuration:	Rear-axle drive
Manual gearbox:	5-speed
Transmission type:	G 50/10
Transmission ratios:	
1st gear:	3.154
2nd gear:	1.895
3rd gear:	1.407
4th gear:	1.086
5th gear:	0.868
Reverse gear:	2.857
Drive ratio:	3.444
Ltd slip diff. load/deceleration (%):	20 / 100

Body, chassis, suspension, brakes, wheels

Body design:	Steel coupé body, 2 doors, 2 seats, entirely hot-dip galvanized body, side-impact protection beams in doors, wider front and rear wings, flexible polyurethane front and rear bumpers with integrated aluminium beams, air intakes in front bumper instead of fog lamps, RS rear bumper, polyurethane side skirts, adjustable rear wing on engine lid, aluminium bonnet lid and doors, red non-reflecting valance with integrated reverse gear and rear fog lamps, thin-glass rear and side windows, wing mirrors in Cup-Design

Suspension, front:	Individually suspended light-alloy lower wishbones, McPherson struts with coil springs, dual-tube gas-filled shock absorbers, anti-roll bar
Suspension, rear:	Individually suspended on tilted shafts, McPherson struts with coil springs, dual-tube gas-filled shock absorbers, anti-roll bar
Brakes, front/rear (Size (mm)):	Ventilated and drilled discs (322 x 32) Ventilated and drilled discs (299 x 28) Red 4-piston fixed aluminium callipers / Red 4-piston fixed aluminium callipers Bosch ABS
Wheels, front/rear:	9 J x 18 / 11 J x 18
Reifen v/h:	235/40 ZR 18 / 285/35 ZR 18

Electrical system

Alternator (W/A):	1610 / 115
Battery (V/Ah):	12 / 36

Dimensions and weight

Track, front/rear (mm):	1440 / 1481
Wheelbase (mm):	2272
Length x width x height (mm):	4275 x 1775 x 1270
Kerb weight DIN (kg):	1210
Permissible gross weight (kg):	1410
Luggage compartment (VDA (l)):	88
Fuel tank capacity (l):	92, including 12.5 reserve
C_w x A (m²):	0.35 x 1.89 = 0.662
Power/weight ratio (kg/kW/kg/hp):	5.47 / 4.03

Fuel consumption

80/1268/EWG (mpg):	98 RON super plus unleaded
At constant 56mph/90kph:	33.2
At constant 74mph/120kph:	26.6
EG-emissions-urban cycle:	20.3
1/3 mix:	25.6

Performance, production, prices

Acceleration 0-62mph/100kph (s):	4.9
0-124mph/200kph (s):	16.6
Maximum speed (mph / kph):	167 / 270
Production, total number incl. RSR:	90
purchase price:	
1993 Coupé:	DM 225,000

911 turbo 3.6 Coupé
MY 1993–December 1993

Engine

Engine design:	6-cylinder horizontally-opposed, turbo charger, intercooler
Installation:	Rear-engine
Cooling system:	Air-cooled
Number & form of blower blades:	11, straight
Blower outside diameter (mm):	245
Engine type:	M 64/50
Displacement (cc):	3600
Bore x stroke (mm):	100 x 76.4
Engine output DIN (kW/hp):	265/360 at 5500rpm
Maximum torque (Nm/lb ft):	520/384 at 4200rpm
Output per litre (kW/l / hp/l):	73.6 / 100
Compression ratio:	7.5 : 1
Valve operation & camshaft drive:	ohc, cams driven by double chain, 2 valves per cylinder
Carburation:	Bosch K-Jetronic injection
Ignition system:	Battery, capacitive-discharge system, without contact
Firing order:	1 - 6 - 2 - 4 - 3 - 5
Engine lubrication:	Dry sump
Engine oil total (l):	13.0

Transmission

Drive configuration:	Rear-axle drive
Manual gearbox:	5-speed
Transmission type:	G 50/52
Transmission ratios:	
1st gear:	3.154
2nd gear:	1.789
3rd gear:	1.269
4th gear:	0.967
5th gear:	0.756
Reverse gear:	2.857
Drive ratio:	3.444
Ltd slip diff. load/deceleration (%):	20 / 100

Body, chassis, suspension, brakes, wheels

Body design:	Steel coupé body, 2 doors, 2 + 2 seats, entirely hot-dip galvanized body, side-impact protection beams in doors, wider front and rear wings, flexible polyurethane front and rear bumpers with integrated aluminium beams, RS rear bumpers, polyurethane side skirts, rear wing with black polyurethane surround on engine lid, red non-reflecting valance with integrated reverse gear and rear fog lamps, wing mirrors in Cup-Design

Option:	Electric sunroof
Suspension, front:	Individually suspended light-alloy lower wishbones, McPherson struts with coil springs, dual-tube gas-filled shock absorbers, anti-roll bar
Suspension, rear:	Individually suspended on tilted shafts, McPherson struts with coil springs, dual-tube gas-filled shock absorbers, anti-roll bar
Brakes, front/rear (Size (mm)):	Ventilated and drilled discs (322 x 32) Ventilated and drilled discs (299 x 28) Red 4-piston fixed aluminium callipers / Red 4-piston fixed aluminium callipers Bosch ABS
Wheels, front/rear:	8 J x 18 / 10 J x 18
Tyres, front/rear:	225/40 ZR 18 / 265/35 ZR 18

Electrical system

Alternator (W/A):	1610 / 115
Battery (V/Ah):	12 / 75

Dimensions and weight

Track, front/rear (mm):	1442 / 1488
Wheelbase (mm):	2272
Length x width x height (mm):	4275 x 1775 x 1290
Kerb weight DIN (kg):	1470
Permissible gross weight (kg):	1810
Luggage compartment (VDA (l)):	88
Luggage volume interior*:	175
Fuel tank capacity (l):	77, including 10 reserve
Option:	92, including 12.5 reserve
C_w x A (m²):	0.35 x 1.89 = 0.662
Power/weight ratio (kg/kW / kg/hp):	5.54 / 4.08
*on folded down rear seat-backs	

Fuel consumption

80/1268/EWG (mpg):	95 RON super unleaded
At constant 56mph/90kph:	34
At constant 74mph/120kph:	27.4
EG-emissions-urban cycle:	13.25
1/3 mix:	21.2

Performance, production, prices

Acceleration 0-62mph/100kph (s):	4.8
Maximum speed (mph / kph):	174 / 280
Production, total number:	1,437
Purchase prices:	
08/1992 Coupé:	DM 204,000
03/1993 Coupé:	DM 207,880
08/1993 Coupé:	DM 207,880

911 Carrera RS America Coupé
(USA only) MY 1993–MY 1994

Engine
Engine design:	6-cylinder horizontally-opposed
Installation:	Rear-engine
Cooling system:	Air-cooled
Number & form of blower blades:	12, curved
Blower outside diameter (mm):	253
Engine type:	M 64/01
Displacement (cc):	3600
Bore x stroke (mm):	100 x 76.4
Engine output DIN (kW/hp):	182/247 at 6100rpm
Maximum torque (Nm/lb ft):	310/229 at 4800rpm
Output per litre (kW/l / hp/l):	50.6 / 68.6
Compression ratio:	11.3 : 1
Valve operation & camshaft drive:	ohc, cams driven by double chain, 2 valves per cylinder
Carburation:	Bosch DME with sequential injection
Ignition system:	Bosch DME, dual ignition
Firing order:	1 - 6 - 2 - 4 - 3 - 5
Engine lubrication:	Dry sump
Engine oil total (l):	11.5

Transmission
Drive configuration:	Rear-axle drive
Manual gearbox:	5-speed
Transmission type:	G 50/05
Transmission ratios:	
1st gear:	3.500
2nd gear:	2.059
3rd gear:	1.407
4th gear:	1.086
5th gear:	0.868
Reverse gear:	2.857
Drive ratio:	3.333

Body, chassis, suspension, brakes, wheels
Body design:	Steel body, 2 doors, 2 seats, entirely hot-dip galvanized body, side-impact protection beams in doors, flexible polyurethane front- and rear bumpers with integrated aluminium beams, polyurethane side skirts, engine lid with fixed 'Carrera 3.2' rear wing, red non-reflecting valance with integrated reverse gear and rear fog lamps, wing mirrors in Cup-Design

Suspension, front:	Individually suspended light-alloy lower wishbones, McPherson struts with coil springs, dual-tube gas-filled shock absorbers, anti-roll bar
Suspension, rear:	Individually suspended on tilted shafts, McPherson struts with coil springs, dual-tube gas-filled shock absorbers, anti-roll bar
Brakes, front/rear (Size (mm)):	Ventilated discs (298 x 28) Ventilated discs (299 x 24) Black 4-piston fixed aluminium callipers / Black 4-piston fixed aluminium callipers Bosch ABS
Wheels, front/rear:	7 J x 17 / 8 J x 17
Tyres, front/rear:	205/50 ZR 17 / 255/40 ZR 17

Electrical system
Alternator (W/A):	1610 / 115
Battery (V/Ah):	12 / 72

Dimensions and weight
Track, front/rear (mm):	1374 / 1368
Wheelbase (mm):	2272
Length x width x height (mm):	4275 x 1652 x 1310
Kerb weight DIN (kg):	1340
Permissible gross weight (kg):	1520
Luggage compartment (VDA (l)):	88
Luggage volume interior*:	175
Fuel tank capacity (l):	77, including 10 reserve
C_w x A (m^2):	032 X 1.79 = 0.573
Power/weight ratio (kg/kW/kg/hp):	7.36 / 5.42
*on rear luggage place	

Fuel capacity
80/1268 EWG (mpg):	95 RON super unleaded
At constant 56mph/90kph:	36.25
At constant 74mph/120kph:	29
EG-emissios-urban cycle:	16.5
1/3 mix:	24.5

Performance, production, prices
Acceleration 0-62mph/100kph (s):	5.6
Maximum speed (mph / kph):	161 / 260
Production, total number:	701
Purchase price:	US$ 53,900

911 turbo 3.6 Coupé 'slant nose' with performance kit MY 1994

Engine

Engine design:	6-cylinder horizontally-opposed, turbo charger, intercooler
Installation:	Rear-engine
Cooling system:	Air-cooled
Number & form of blower blades:	11, straight
Blower outside diameter (mm):	245
Engine type:	M 64/50 S
Displacement (cc):	3600
Bore x stroke (mm):	100 x 76.4
Engine output DIN (kW/hp):	283/385 at 5750rpm
Maximum torque (Nm/lb ft):	520/384 at 5000rpm
Output per litre (kW/l / hp/l):	78.6 / 106.9
Compression ratio:	7.5 : 1
Valve operation & camshaft drive:	ohc, cams driven by double chain, 2 valves per cylinder
Carburation:	Bosch K-Jetronic injection
Ignition system:	Battery, capacitive-discharge system, without contact
Firing order:	1 - 6 - 2 - 4 - 3 - 5
Engine lubrication:	Dry sump
Engine oil total (l):	13.0

Transmission

Drive configuration:	Rear-axle drive
Manual gearbox:	5-speed
Transmission type:	G 50/52
Transmission ratios:	
1st gear:	3.154
2nd gear:	1.789
3rd gear:	1.269
4th gear:	0.967
5th gear:	0.756
Reverse gear:	2.857
Drive ratio:	3.444
Ltd slip diff. load/deceleration (%):	20 / 100

Body, chassis, suspension, brakes, wheels

Body design:	Steel coupé body, 2 doors, 2 + 2 seats, entirely hot-dip galvanized body, side-impact protection beams in doors, wider front and rear wings, flat front wings with 968 head lamps, air intakes in rear wings, flexible polyurethane front and rear bumpers with integrated aluminium beams, air intakes in front bumper instead of fog lamps, RS rear bumper, polyurethane side skirts, Exclusive rear wing on engine lid, red non-reflecting valance with integrated reverse gear and rear fog lamps, wing mirrors in Cup-Design
Option:	Electric sunroof
Suspension, front:	Individually suspended light-alloy lower wishbones, McPherson struts with coil springs, dual-tube gas-filled shock absorbers, anti-roll bar
Suspension, rear:	Individually suspended on tilted shafts, McPherson struts with coil springs, dual-tube gas-filled shock absorbers, anti-roll bar
Brakes, front/rear (Size (mm)):	Ventilated and drilled discs (322 x 32) Ventilated and drilled discs (299 x 28) Red 4-piston fixed aluminium callipers / Red 4-piston fixed aluminium callipers Bosch ABS
Wheels, front/rear:	8 J x 18 / 10 J x 18
Tyres, front/rear:	225/40 ZR 18 / 265/35 ZR 18

Electrical system

Alternator (W/A):	1610 / 115
Battery (V/Ah):	12 / 75

Dimensions and weight

Track, front/rear (mm):	1442 / 1488
Wheel base (mm):	2272
Length x width x height (mm):	4275 x 1775 x 1290
Kerb weight DIN (kg):	1470
Permissible gross weight (kg):	1810
Luggage compartment (VDA (l)):	88
Luggage volume interior*:	175
Fuel tank capacity (l):	77, including 10 reserve
Option:	92, including 12.5 reserve
C_w x A (m²):	0.35 x 1.89 = 0.662
Power/weight ratio (kg/kW/kg/hp):	5.19 / 3.81
*on folded down rear seat-backs	

Fuel consumption

(mpg):	app. 14; 95 RON super unleaded

Performance, production, prices

Acceleration 0-62mph/100kph (s):	less than 4.8
Maximum speed (mph / kph):	more than 174 / 280
Production, total number:	76
Purchase price: 1994 Coupé.	DM 290,000

Porsche 911 (Type 993)

Model year 1994 (R Programme)

In the autumn of 1993, a visually and mechanically much modified 911 was displayed on the Porsche stand at the Frankfurt International Auto Show. Internally, the new 911 Carrera was known as the Type 993. This model superseded the Type 964-based Carrera 2 and Carrera 4 model lines.

The basic shape was changed for the first time in 911 history. The front wings were wider and flatter. The lenses of the new ellipsoid headlamps were mounted at a flatter angle. The bonnet lid was raised by 40mm, increasing luggage volume to 123 litres (4.34 cubic feet) with the standard fuel tank. The redesigned nose housed parking lamps, fog lamps and indicators. The rear wings were wider and blended into the tail in a more direct line. The tail lamps were mounted higher and included yellow indicators. The entire light band, including integrated rear fog lamps and back-up lamps, formed a slope between the engine lid and bumper. The plastic bumper included cut-outs on the left and right for oval tailpipes. The electrically raised rear spoiler was larger and reshaped. Windscreen-wiper pivots were located closer to the car centre line for a larger swept area. The exterior door handles were painted in body colour. At its introduction, the new 911 Carrera was available in coupé form only.

The 3.6-litre engine underwent thorough redevelopment. Mechanical changes included a torsionally stiffer crankshaft, lighter connecting rods, lighter pistons, expanded intake passages, larger valves and rocker arms with hydraulic valve-lash compensation. The 964 engine's familiar crankshaft torsional vibration damper was eliminated. The Motronic system was equipped with a hot-film mass-airflow meter. The exhaust system had lower back pressure. Exhaust was now fed to two small metal catalyst converters from a shared mixing chamber. Final exhaust silencers were fitted on the left and right sides behind the wheels, each with an oval tailpipe. With the same 11.3:1 compression ratio but tuned for 98 octane unleaded Super Plus, the engine developed 272hp (200kW) at 6100rpm. Maximum torque rose to 330Nm (243lb ft) at 5000rpm.

The so-called 'rest of world' configuration was given a short-geared six-speed manual transmission. For the United States, Austria and Switzerland, all gears from second onward were higher. New double-cone synchromesh reduced gear-change forces for the first two gears. As an option, an improved four-speed Tiptronic was available. One special option was a dynamic limited-slip system, consisting of an active brake differential (ABD) and a limited-slip differential. The ABD was intended as an aid to starting from rest on slippery surfaces, and for speeds below 43mph (70kph).

The front suspension was a further development of the previous model's hardware, including its negative steering offset. Wheels were independently sprung on struts. Hydraulic double-acting twin-tube gas-pressurized shock absorbers were surrounded by progressively wound coil springs. The power-steering system was modified for better straight-line stability and more precise feel. The multi-link rear suspension, mounted on a subframe, was dubbed the 'LSA axle' – LSA for lightweight, stable, agile. Here, too, each wheel was sprung by a progressively wound coil over a double-acting twin-tube gas-pressure damper. The brake system was greatly improved, with 1000kW (1360hp!) of braking power. Ventilated, cross-drilled brake rotors were combined with black four-piston fixed callipers. The new Bosch ABS 5 shortened braking distances, especially on uneven surfaces. Standard equipment included new 'Cup Design 93' 16-inch cast-aluminium wheels. At the front, 205/55 ZR 16 tyres were mounted on 7-inch rims, at the rear 245/45 ZR 16 tyres were carried on 9-inch wheels. Sports suspension, lowered 10mm at the front and 20mm at the rear, was available as an option.

Inside, obvious changes included the newly-designed, slimmer airbag steering wheel. Seats and door panels were also executed in a new design. The steering column stalks featured a grippier shape, and many switches were relocated for better visibility. Leather front seating surfaces were standard equipment.

The 993 Cabriolet, with reworked convertible top, became available in the spring of 1994. As an option, an integrated, self-deploying wind blocker was available. To open the power hood, it was no longer necessary to turn off the engine; rather, one only needed to apply the parking brake while the vehicle was stationary.

Equipped with a manual transmission, the new Carrera could reach 62mph (100kph) in 5.6 seconds; the Tiptronic version needed 6.6 seconds. Top speed with the six-speed manual was about 168mph (270kph); the Tiptronic topped out at 165mph (265kph).

The Porsche Exclusive department in Werk I offered a performance kit for the new 911 Carrera, boosting power to 285hp (210kW) at 6000rpm. Maximum torque of 350Nm (258lb ft) was achieved at 5000rpm. The added power was primarily obtained by increasing displacement to 3.8 litres with new 102mm pistons and cylinders. Two camshafts with altered valve timing, a modified fan pulley, and retuned engine management rounded out the system. This performance increase was available for vehicles with six-speed manual as well as Tiptronic transmissions.

Porsche Motorsport in Weissach offered its 'Motor Kit 2', an even more performance-oriented approach to higher output. The 3.8-litre engine was based on experience gained with the 911 Carrera RS 3.8 and other racing activities. Motor Kit 2 included a set of six 102mm pistons and cylinders, six cylinder heads with 51.5mm intake and 43.5mm exhaust valves, two camshafts with modified valve timing, one set of adjustable rocker arms with mechanical valve-lash adjustment and reprogramed engine electronics. The new rocker arms were capable of withstanding higher revs and eliminated the need for hydraulic valve-lash adjustment.

Porsche recommended checking valve lash every 6000 miles (10,000km) on these engines. The rated power was listed as 299hp (220kW) at 6100rpm, maximum torque as 365Nm (269lb ft) at 5250rpm. Conversion took about 50 hours, at a cost of 23,432 Deutschmarks. Porsche recommended checking rear wheel alignment after conversion. For the first 1250 miles (2000km) after conversion, engine revs were to be kept below 5000rpm.

Engine oil was to be changed, and valve lash checked, at 1250 miles (2000km). This engine was only available for vehicles with the six-speed transmission and 17-inch wheels. Maximum speed increased to 174mph (280kph).

Model year 1995 (S Programme)

In the autumn of 1994, the model range was expanded with the addition of the Carrera 4, available in Coupé and Cabriolet form. In the spring of 1995, the new 911 turbo, featuring twin-turbochargers, was introduced at the Geneva Show. Additional new models included the Carrera RS and the extremely performance-oriented 911 GT2. These three models were only available as coupés.

Porsche Exclusive built 14 Type 993 Cabriolets with turbocharged 3.6-litre boxer engines. The turbo engine, five-speed manual transmission, brake system and rigidly mounted rear wing were taken from the 964 turbo 3.6. The price for conversion of a 993 Cabriolet was 89,500 Deutschmarks.

Phantom view of a 911 Carrera Coupé, Type 993, with 3.6-litre engine

Bodywork of the 911 Carrera 4 visibly differed from that of the rear-drive 911 Carrera only in its white front indicator lenses and continuous red light band at the rear. The 'Carrera 4' script at the rear was titanium coloured. Under the engine lid of the Carrera 4 was the proven 3.6-litre engine, developing 272hp (200kW) at 6100rpm. As an option, customers could opt to have their new car modified by Porsche Exclusive, with a 3.8-litre engine making 285hp (310kW) at 6000rpm and a satisfying 350Nm (258lb ft) of torque at 5000rpm. The 3.8-litre engine was also available as a retrofit kit from Porsche Tequipment. Along with 102mm pistons and cylinders and special camshafts, the package included a modified fan belt.

The Carrera 4 was fitted with all-wheel drive and a six-speed manual transmission. All Porsche all-wheel-drive models had the dynamic limited-slip system, encompassing a limited-slip differential and ABD (active brake differential) as standard. All-wheel drive used a viscous multi-plate clutch at the transmission housing. This distributed tractive effort between the front and rear axles. At least 5 per cent of tractive force was sent to the front, in normal situations 35 per cent, and in extreme situations as much as 40 per cent. The entire all-wheel-drive system added only 50kg (110lb) to the car – about 50kg less than its predecessor's all-wheel-drive system. Handling was what one would expect of a rear-drive 911. The Carrera 4 was equipped with the same brake system as the Carrera, except that for visual identification, the brake callipers were painted titanium. Wheels and suspension were also shared with the rear-drive Carrera. The Carrera 4 was equipped like the normal Carrera, except that it was only available with a manual transmission. The plate on top of the gear lever, with the engraved gear-change pattern, was titanium-coloured on the Carrera 4. Performance of the Carrera 4 was comparable to that of the Carrera.

The Tiptronic transmission of rear-drive Carrera models was modified. Gear-change buttons were integrated in the upper left and right steering wheel spokes, enabling changes up or down without removing the hands from the wheel, thereby improving gear-change comfort and safety. The system was now called 'Tiptronic S' and could be retrofitted to 1994 model year Tiptronic models.

The 911 turbo had 60mm wider rear bodywork and was slightly broader in the sill area. The altered nose contained three air inlets, and the tail was matched to the wider wings. The turbo was fitted with a newly designed, fixed rear spoiler, painted entirely in body colour. The indicators were identical to those of the Carrera 4. The 'turbo' script was titanium coloured. The 3.6-litre twin-turbo engine was equipped with two KKK type K-16 turbochargers and dual-charge air intercoolers. Thanks to the two smaller turbochargers, throttle response at low revs was greatly improved, virtually eliminating turbo lag. With a compression ratio of 8.0:1, the engine developed 408hp (300kW) at 5750rpm. Maximum torque of 540Nm (398lb ft.) was developed at 4500rpm, but even at 2500rpm, 450Nm (332lb ft) was on call. The turbo's hydraulic lifters represented continued development beyond those found in the normally-aspirated engine. The hot-film mass-airflow sensor and Bosch Motronic M 5.2 were matched to the bi-turbo's characteristics. The exhaust system included two metal catalytic converters and four oxygen sensors. The On Board Diagnosis II System (OBD II) was a valuable contribution to environmental protection. This system was installed in nearly all 911 turbos worldwide. All emissions-relevant components were continuously monitored, and any faults were immediately recognized and communicated via a warning lamp in the cockpit. The 911 turbo had the world's cleanest exhaust emissions. The standard turbo drivetrain included the Carrera 4's all-wheel-drive system and six-speed manual transmission, although the 911 turbo transmission had higher gear ratios. The dynamic limited-slip system, with active brake differential (ABD) and limited-slip differential, was also standard equipment. The lowered 911 turbo suspension had firmer tuning. Brake components included red-painted callipers and 322mm brake rotors front and rear. The ABS system was modified to cope with the turbo's greater performance potential. A maximum-effort stop from 174mph (280kph) represents 1941hp (1427kW) of braking power; the turbo could come to a full stop from 124mph (200kph) in just 4.5 seconds, in only 130.3 metres (427ft) distance. The turbo was equipped with 18-inch hollow-spoke wheels. The rim and centre were cast separately, then the two components were friction welded by spinning them together under a load of 90 metric tons. This technology saved 11kg (24lb) per wheel set, for reduced unsprung weight and improved ride comfort and handling. At the front, the 8-inch wide rims carried 225/40 ZR 18 tyres, while the rear 10-inch wheels were equipped with 285/30 ZR 18 rubber. The standard-equipment list of the 911 turbo left little to be desired; features beyond those of the Carrera included Litronic (xenon) headlamps, metallic paint, air-conditioning, full leather upholstery, electrically-powered seats, rear wiper, on-board computer and a radio package and sound system. On the gear-lever knob was a titanium-coloured plate with an engraved gear-change pattern. Acceleration to 62mph (100kph) took 4.5

seconds. On an empty autobahn, the speedometer could be pushed beyond 180mph (290kph).

The 911 Carrera RS had front corner spoilers and a fixed, flat rear wing entirely in body colour. A small black polyurethane spoiler lip trimmed the sill and leading edge of the rear wheel arch. The Carrera RS could be ordered with the optional 'Club Sport' package, including larger front and rear spoilers. The RS's lightweight construction trimmed 100kg (220lb) off the kerb weight of the more comfortable Carrera. An aluminium bonnet lid saved 7.5kg (16.5lb), thinner rear and side window glass pared another 5kg (11lb). Even wiring for the heated rear window was deleted, as was insulation material and the headlamp-washer system. The 911 RS power unit was equipped with a larger 102mm cylinder bore, raising displacement to 3746cc and power to 300hp (221kW) at 6500rpm. Peak torque of 355Nm (262lb ft.) was reached at 5400rpm. The most important change was its variable-length induction runners – the 'Varioram' system, with vacuum-operated sliders to actively change induction runner length. At low and medium engine speeds, long runners provided a fuller torque curve, while short tracts at high engine speeds resulted in higher engine output. The valve train was also reworked; intake valve diameter was increased to 51.5mm, exhausts to 43mm. The RS engine used hydraulic lash adjusters. The Carrera RS could be ordered with either of two six-speed manual transmissions; in the Club Sport package, fifth and sixth were geared slightly shorter. Both versions used a limited-slip differential with 40 per cent lock-up under load and 65 per cent in coasting. For endurance racing, the Carrera RS could be fitted with a 92-litre (20-gallon) fuel tank. The 911 Carrera RS was fitted with the same brake system as the turbo, including its ABS system. It rode on a lowered, stiffer suspension system, although it was not quite as firm as the 3.6-litre Carrera RS of 1992. Power-steering was standard in both models. The Carrera RS rolled on three-piece 18-inch 'Cup' wheels by Speedline, 8 inches at the front with 225/40 ZR 18 tyres, 10 inches at the rear with 265/35 ZR 18 tyres. Because of motorsport-oriented weight-saving efforts, the Carrera RS had a spartan interior. Driver and passenger had lightweight, leather-covered bucket seats. For standard exterior colours, the rear of the plastic shell was painted in body colour. A grippy three-spoke leather-covered steering wheel and specially-contoured gear lever were part of the package. Door panels, covered with black leatherette, carried only a window winder, pull handle, and coloured door release strap. Rear seats and trim were deleted. Safety belts used brightly-coloured webbing to match the exterior colour. Options included air-conditioning, leather sports seats, a radio and two speakers, driver-side airbag or driver and passenger airbag system with electric windows. The Club Sport package for the Carrera RS included the following equipment alterations: roll cage, battery-kill switch, fire extinguisher, six-point harnesses, fabric-covered racing seats, sun visor on driver's side only, anti-theft immobilizer, suspension tower brace and emergency door-lock release. The gutted interior was painted in body colour. Carpets, headliner and A- and B-pillar trim were deleted. This equipment package was optimized for race-track applications, and this athlete among Carrera models sprinted to 62mph (100kph) in 5.0 seconds, and reached a top speed of 172mph (277kph).

The fastest, most sporty model in the line-up was the road-going version of the 911 GT2. Based on the 911 turbo body, the GT2 made no secret of its racing ambitions. Metal was pared away from the wing lips to make room for bolt-on plastic wing flares. This was not merely window dressing; this was modification born on the race track. Form follows function; plastic flares could be replaced cost-effectively in the event of the minor encounters that one might have in competition. A large spoiler, similar to that of the Carrera RS Club Sport model, was installed at the front. Additional air inlets were integrated in the side plates of the large rear wing. The 911 GT2 was built using the same lightweight practices found in the Carrera RS. The GT2 did, however, include the headlamp-washer system; to compensate, the doors were made of aluminium. The GT2 was fitted with the 92-litre (20-gallon) fuel tank. The GT2 engine was based on the 911 turbo power unit. A modified control unit and additional oil cooler raised power to 430hp (316kW) at 5750rpm. The torque curve was similar to that of the standard production turbo. Gear ratios of the six-speed manual transmission were identical to those of the 911 turbo. Rear 35-section tyres gave the GT2 slightly higher overall gearing. A limited-slip differential with asymmetrical lock-up factors (25 per cent under load, 40 per cent in coasting) was standard equipment. Deceleration was handled by the same ABS brake system found in the 911 turbo. The suspension was lowered and stiffened. Power-steering was standard. The GT2 rolled on three-piece Speedline wheels. While both rim sections were made of aluminium, the centres were of even lighter magnesium. The front axle mounted 235/40 ZR 18 tyres on 9 J x 18 rims; the rears were 285/35 ZR 18 on 11 J x 18 wheels. The weight-optimized interior of the 911 GT2 was identical to that of the 911 Carrera RS. The 911 GT2 accelerated to 62mph (100kph) in just 4.4 seconds; this fastest Porsche in the line-up topped out at 183mph (295kph).

The Exclusive Department built a custom Speedster for Ferdinand Alexander Porsche, based on the 911 Carrera. The car had 17-inch wheels and was fitted with a Tiptronic S transmission. This 993 Speedster remained a unique one-off.

Model year 1996 (T Programme)

The one-millionth Porsche rolled off the assembly line on 15 July 1996. Porsche donated this Carrera Coupé, fitted with a Tiptronic S transmission, to the autobahn police of its home state, Baden-Württemberg. For the new model year, the 3.6-litre normally-aspirated engines were given a power boost to 285hp (210kW). Additionally, the line-up saw two new creations: the 911 Targa, with its ingenious glass roof, and the 911 Carrera 4S Coupé with wide turbo bodywork.

All 911 models came with a folding ignition key which also permitted remote control of the alarm and central-locking systems. A Nokia hands-free cell-phone system with roof-mounted antenna was standard equipment, while a Motorola built-in cell-phone system was a no-cost alternative.

For the 1996 model year, the 3.6-litre normally-aspirated engine of all Carrera models underwent a thorough revamping. Displacement and compression-ratio remained unchanged, but the Varioram induction system pioneered on the Carrera RS was migrated to the 3.6-litre engines. Hydraulic valve-lash adjustment was improved by adopting the 911 turbo version. This improved version could also be retrofitted to the 272hp engines. Intake and exhaust ports in the cylinder head were enlarged, and valve diameters increased by 1mm; intake valve diameter was now 50mm, exhaust 43.5mm. Piston shape and cam profiles were modified. The Varioram system improved the torque curve at low and medium engine speeds; maximum torque of 340Nm (251lb ft) was achieved at 5250rpm. Output rose to 285hp (210kW) at 6100rpm. Externally, the 1996 models were recognizable by their different, slightly angular tailpipes.

For customers who wanted a little bit extra, Porsche Exclusive offered the epitome of normally-aspirated 911 engines: a 3.8-litre power unit with a brawny 355Nm (262lb ft) of torque at 5400rpm. Cylinder bore was increased to 102mm, raising displacement to 3746cc. Power output of 300hp (221kW) at 6600rpm was more than enough to satisfy most Carrera customers. This engine veritably doubled driving pleasure. The same engine kit was available from Porsche Tequipment for retrofitting to existing vehicles.

Porsche Exclusive also had a package for turbo customers, raising power to 430hp (316kW) at 5750rpm. Based on a modified electronic control unit and additional oil cooler, this reworked engine was essentially that of the 911 GT2 street version.

Externally, the 911 Carrera 4S resembled the 911 turbo. Instead of the rear wing, the Carrera 4S was fitted with the small electrically-extended spoiler, which retracted to maintain smooth, unbroken body lines when at rest. The Carrera 4S was only available with a six-speed manual transmission and all-wheel drive. Standard equipment included more powerful brakes from the 911 turbo, and turbo-design 18-inch wheels. Unlike the turbo's hollow-spoke wheels, however, the Carrera 4S used a monobloc design. The suspension was lowered by 10mm at the front, 20mm at the rear. Interior equipment of the 911 Carrera 4S was on the level of the turbo. The extensive standard-equipment list included air-conditioning, full leather interior, on-board computer, electrically-operated seats, rear wiper and a cassette radio with sound package. Because of its wide body, the Carrera 4S managed a top speed of 'only' 168mph (270kph).

The 911 Targa was based on a modified Cabriolet body. To this were attached additional mounting points for the glass roof. The roof was a pre-assembled unit, which was then bolted and bonded to the body in final assembly. The glass roof consisted of three glass elements: wind deflector, moving-roof section and rear window, as well as two body-coloured steel longitudinal members which provided rollover protection. The glass elements were made of green-tinted laminated safety glass. The small front element was raised to act as a wind deflector before the electrically-operated main roof opened and slid back under the rear window. With the roof closed or with the wind deflector raised, an electrically-operated shade could be extended for protection against cold draughts or hot sun. The shade stowed itself automatically if the glass roof was opened. A high-capacity air-conditioning system was installed as standard equipment. The 911 Targa was equipped with a six-speed manual or four-speed Tiptronic S transmission. An all-wheel-drive variant of the Targa was not offered. Bolted two-piece 17-inch wheels were a Targa exclusive.

Thanks to the more powerful engine, six-speed Carrera models could now reach 171mph (275kph); cars with the Tiptronic S topped out at 168mph (270kph). Compared to the previous model, acceleration was only marginally faster.

The GT1 racing rules required manufacture of at least one street-legal example of a model intended for racing. In 1996 Porsche built two road-licensed examples of its GT1 racer. Visually, their silhouette and details recalled the 993 model range. Their sheet-steel and carbon-fibre bodies included an integral roll bar. The water-cooled 3.2-litre twin-turbocharged six-cylinder boxer engine yielded 544hp (400kW) at 7200rpm. The double-wishbone pushrod front and rear suspension represented pure-bred racing technology. A year later, Porsche laid on a small run of roadgoing 911 GT1s.

Model year 1997 (V Programme)

The model range was extended to include the 911 Carrera S Coupé. This fulfilled the wish of many Tiptronic S customers for a car with wide turbo bodywork combined with the Tiptronic S transmission. The sports-oriented 911 Carrera RS, however, was dropped from the line-up.

In the course of product development, Porsche 911 models were fitted with smaller, visually more appealing roof aerials for the in-car telephone. All Carrera models were given a higher-geared six-speed manual transmission, formerly only installed for the United States, Switzerland and Austria. Inside, a small dashboard lamp illuminated the ignition switch.

The body of the 911 Carrera S Coupé was derived from the 911 turbo, as were its modified nose and tailpieces. Orange front and rear indicators came from the 911 Carrera. An obvious visual feature was the split, body-coloured inlet grille in the rear spoiler, installed only on the Carrera S. Another Carrera S exclusive was the colour 'Vesuvio Metallic', with outside door handles, wing-mirror housings, wheel centres, air-inlet grilles in the spoiler and 'Carrera S' script on the engine lid in steel grey. The 911 Carrera S was powered by the 3.6-litre Carrera engine, and only available in a rear-drive version. As an option, the Carrera S could be ordered with the Tiptronic S transmission. The Carrera S suspension was lowered by 10mm at the front and 20mm at the rear. Its brake system, with black callipers, was taken from the 911 Carrera. The Carrera S was fitted with 17-inch 'Cup' wheels as standard equipment. The central caps were adorned with a coloured Porsche crest. The rear hubs carried 31mm-thick spacers. Optionally, the 18-inch alloy wheels of the 911 turbo were available. Inside, several details, such as the instrument bezels, door sills, ball-shaped gear-lever knob and handbrake trim plate were painted steel grey. 'Carrera S' script was applied to the tachometer.

Acceleration of the Carrera S was comparable to that of the 911 Carrera. The wide body held top speed down to 168mph (270kph), 3mph (5kph) slower than the narrow bodies.

Model year 1998 (W Programme)

Porsche presented the successor to their air-cooled classic in the form of the Type 996, which would continue to be sold under the 911 Carrera name.

Porsche laid on a limited production run of 21 road-legal examples of the 911 GT1, at a price of 1,550,000 DM. The road version was a direct offshoot of the victorious Le Mans racer. Visually, the GT1 carried the headlamps, tail lamps and door handles of the new 996 Carrera generation. The coupé body was a composite construction of sheet-steel and carbon-fibre-reinforced plastics. Compared to the 1996 version, the front wings had different wheel cut-outs. A roof-mounted scoop fed air to the engine. The tail was topped by a full-width rear wing and terminated in a Gurney lip.

The water-cooled twin-turbo engine was based on the crankcase of the 964. The four-valve power unit produced 544hp (400kW) from a displacement of 3164cc. Maximum torque of 600Nm (443lb ft) was generated at 4250rpm. The six-speed manual transmission was teamed with a limited-slip differential providing 40 per cent lock-up under load and 60 per cent while coasting.

The suspension represented pure racing technology, with front and rear double wishbones and pushrods. The single-tube gas-pressure dampers were mounted within cylindrical coil springs. Front and rear anti-roll bars were adjustable. At the front, eight-piston monobloc brake callipers gripped 380mm ventilated, cross-drilled rotors; four-piston monobloc callipers were fitted at the rear. The multi-piece 18-inch alloy wheels featured a weight-optimized cross-spoke design. Front and rear tyres were 295/35 ZR 18 and 335/30 ZR 18, on 11-inch and 13-inch wide rims respectively.

Performance was on a par with race cars. The GT1 catapulted from zero to 62mph (100kph) in just 3.7 seconds, and passed through 124mph (200kph) in 10.5 seconds. Top speed was 193mph (310kph).

To give customers some time to become accustomed to the new 911 Carrera generation, the air-cooled classic remained in production, with a somewhat restricted model range. Deleted from the 1998 line-up were the 911 Carrera coupé, 911 Carrera 4 coupé, 911 Carrera Cabriolet and 911 Carrera 4 Cabriolet. Remaining in production were the 911 turbo Coupé, 911 Carrera 4S Coupé, 911 Carrera S Coupé and 911 Targa. The Tiptronic S transmission remained an option for the Carrera S and Targa. Beginning in April 1998, 21 street-legal examples of the reworked 911 GT2 were fitted with the 450hp engine.

Porsche Exclusive offered a long-awaited upgrade for the 911 turbo: a sports suspension package. The suspension could be installed at the factory on new cars, or retrofitted.

Also from the Works I Exclusive Department was a new performance-kit for the 911 turbo, giving 450hp (331kW) at 6000rpm. Torque was boosted too, rising by 45Nm to 585Nm (431lb ft) at 4500rpm. This kit could be installed directly in new cars, or retrofitted. The package included two larger turbochargers, an appropriately modified control unit and an additional oil cooler. With these modifications, a top speed of 186mph (300kph) was easily achieved.

The Exclusive Department built 345 examples of the 911 turbo S with the 450hp engine. Body modifications included the Aerokit II, with altered front and rear spoilers. At the front, additional small openings were added alongside the indicators for better brake cooling. An additional 959-style air-intake was added to each rear wing. The titanium 'turbo S' script on the tail was retained. Four tailpipes provided another obvious visual identifier. Suspension towers were reinforced to better withstand cornering forces generated by the 15mm lower sports suspension. Brake callipers were painted Speed Yellow. The 18-inch wheels included

central caps with 'turbo S' script. The front boot contained an aluminium and carbon-fibre suspension tower brace and silver 'turbo S' script embroidered in the carpet boot-liner. Inside, the headliner, three-spoke sports steering wheel and nearly all plastic parts were leather covered. Matching carbon-fibre parts were installed on the instrument panel, dashboard, wing mirrors, inside door release, gear-lever knob and, combined with aluminium, the handbrake. Instrument bezels were chromium-plated, and instrument faces painted silver. Silver 'turbo S' script was embroidered into the carpet behind the rear jump seats. Customers could choose between black, yellow, blue or red front safety belts.

For the American market, Porsche Exclusive built a single Speedster, based on the widebody 911 Carrera S. This was powered by a 3.6-litre engine, drove through a six-speed manual gearbox and rolled on 18-inch wheels.

The last air-cooled 911 – a 911 Carrera 4S Coupé destined for American comedian Jerry Seinfeld – rolled off the factory production line on 31 March 1998. The automotive world had lost one of its most enduring, endearing characters.

In all, Porsche built 68,839 examples of the Porsche 911 Type 993.

A total of 30,895 Porsche 912s were built, along with 2099 copies of the 912 E. A total of 409,081 examples of the air-cooled 911 rolled off the assembly lines.

911 Carrera Coupé [Tiptronic]
MY 1994–MY 1995
911 Carrera Cabriolet [Tiptronic]
March 1994–MY 1995

Engine

Engine design:	6-cylinder horizontally-opposed
Installation:	Rear-engine
Cooling system:	Air-cooled
Number & form of blower blades:	12, curved
Blower outside diameter (mm):	253
Engine type:	M 64/05 [M 64/06]
Displacement (cc):	3600
Bore x stroke (mm):	100 x 76.4
Engine output DIN (kW/hp):	200/272 at 6100rpm
Maximum torque (Nm/lb ft):	330/243 at 5000rpm
Output per litre (kW/l / hp/l):	55.6 / 75.6
Compression ratio:	11.3 : 1
Valve operation & camshaft drive:	ohc, cams driven by double chain, 2 valves per cylinder
Carburation:	Bosch DME, Motronic M 2.10, with sequential injection
Ignition system:	Bosch DME, dual ignition
Firing order:	1 - 6 - 2 - 4 - 3 - 5
Engine lubrication:	Dry sump
Engine oil total (l):	11.5

Transmission

Drive configuration:	Rear-axle drive
Manual gearbox:	6-speed
Option Tiptronic:	[4-speed]
Transmission type:	G 50/21 [A 50/04]
Transmission ratios:	
1st gear:	3.818 [2.479]
2nd gear:	2.150 [1.479]
3rd gear:	1.560 [1.000]
4th gear:	1.242 [0.728]
5th gear:	1.027
6th gear:	0.821
Reverse gear:	2.857 [2.086]
Drive ratio:	3.444 [3.667]
*MY 1995 Tiptronic S	

Body, chassis, suspension, brakes, wheels

Body design:	Steel body, 2 doors, 2 + 2 seats, entirely hot-dip galvanized body, side-impact protection beams in doors, flexible polyurethane front and rear bumpers with integrated aluminium beams, engine lid with integrated automatic rear spoiler, red non-reflecting valance with integrated reverse gear and rear fog lamps
Coupé:	Fixed steel roof
Option:	Electric sunroof
Cabriolet:	Electric hood with flexible plastic rear window
Option:	Automatic wind blocker
Suspension, front:	Individually suspended light-alloy lower wishbones, McPherson struts with coil springs, dual-tube gas-filled shock absorbers, anti-roll bar
Suspension, rear:	Individually suspended on light-alloy multi-wishbone axle with LSA system (Light weight, Stability, Agility) with progressive coil springs, dual-tube gas-filled shock absorbers, anti-roll bar
Brakes, front/rear (Size (mm)):	Ventilated and drilled discs (304 x 32) Ventilated and drilled discs (299 x 24) Black 4-piston fixed aluminium callipers / Black 4-piston fixed aluminium callipers Bosch ABS 5
Wheels, front/rear:	7 J x 16 / 9 J x 16
Tyres, front/rear:	205/55 ZR 16 / 245/45 ZR 16
Option:	7 J x 17 / 9 J x 17 205/50 ZR 17 / 255/40 ZR 17

Electrical system

Alternator (W/A):	1610 / 115
Battery (V/Ah):	12 / 75

Dimensions and weight

Track, front/rear (mm):	1405 / 1444
Wheelbase (mm):	2272
Length x width x height (mm):	4245 x 1735 x 1300
with sports suspension:	4245 x 1735 x 1285
Kerb weight DIN (kg):	1370 [1395]
Permissible gross weight (kg):	1710 [1735]
Luggage compartment (VDA (l)):	123
with 92 litre fuel tank:	100
Luggage volume interior*:	175
Fuel tank capacity (l):	73.5, including 10 reserve
Option:	92, including 12.5 reserve
C_w x A (m²):	0.33 x 1.86 = 0.614
Power/weight ratio (kg/kW/ kg/hp):	6.85 [6.97] / 5.03 [5.12]
*on folded-down rear seat-backs	

Fuel consumption

80/1268/EWG (mpg):	98 RON super plus unleaded
At constant 56mph/90kph:	37.6 [36.7]
At constant 74mph/120kph:	31 [29.5]
EG-emissions-urban cycle:	16.2 [16.8]
1/3 mix:	24.8 [25]

Performance, production, prices

Acceleration 0-62mph/100kph (s):	5.6 [6.6]
Maximum speed (mph / kph):	167 / 270 [164 / 265]
Production, total number:	
Coupé:	14,541
Cabriolet:	7,730
Purchase prices:	
08/1993 Coupé:	DM 125,760 [DM 132,420]
03/1994 Coupé:	DM 125,760 [DM 132,420]
Cabriolet:	DM 142,620 [DM 149,280]
08/1994 Coupé:	DM 125,760 [DM 132,420]
Cabriolet:	DM 142,620 [DM 149,280]
02/1995 Coupé:	DM 128,270 [DM 134,930]
Cabriolet:	DM 145,470 [DM 152,130]

911 Carrera Coupé with performance kit Exclusive [Tiptronic]
911 Carrera Cabriolet with performance kit Exclusive [Tiptronic]
MY 1994–MY 1995

Engine

Engine design:	6-cylinder horizontally-opposed
Installation:	Rear-engine
Cooling system:	Air-cooled
Number & form of blower blades:	12, curved
Blower outside diameter (mm):	253
Engine type:	M 64/05 S [M 64/06 S]
Displacement (cc):	3746
Bore x stroke (mm):	102 x 76.4
Engine output DIN (kW/hp):	210/285 at 6000rpm
Maximum torque (Nm/lb ft):	350/258 at 5000rpm
Output per litre (kW/l / hp/l):	56.1 / 76.1
Compression ratio:	11.3 : 1
Valve operation & camshaft drive:	ohc, cams driven by double chain, 2 valves per cylinder
Carburation:	Bosch DME, Motronic M 2.10, with sequential injection
Ignition system:	Bosch DME, dual ignition
Firing order:	1 - 6 - 2 - 4 - 3 - 5
Engine lubrication:	Dry sump
Engine oil total (l):	11.5

Transmission

Drive configuration:	Rear-axle drive
Manual gearbox:	6-speed
Option Tiptronic:	[4-speed]
Transmission type:	G 50/21 [A 50/04]
Transmission ratios:	
1st gear:	3.818 [2.479]
2nd gear:	2.150 [1.479]
3rd gear:	1.560 [1.000]
4th gear:	1.242 [0.728]
5th gear:	1.027
6th gear:	0.821
Reverse gear:	2.857 [2.086]
Drive ratio:	3.444 [3.667]
*MY 1995 Tiptronic S	

Body, chassis, suspension, brakes, wheels

Body design:	Steel body, 2 doors, 2 + 2 seats, entirely hot-dip galvanized body, side-impact protection beams in doors, flexible polyurethane front and rear bumpers with integrated aluminium beams, engine lid with integrated automatic rear spoiler, red non-reflecting valance with integrated reverse gear and rear fog lamps
Coupé:	Fixed steel roof
Option:	Electric sunroof
Cabriolet:	Electric hood with flexible plastic rear window

Option:	Automatic wind blocker
Suspension, front:	Individually suspended light-alloy lower wishbones, McPherson struts with coil springs, dual-tube gas-filled shock absorbers, anti-roll bar
Suspension, rear:	Individually suspended on light-alloy multi-wishbone axle with LSA system (Light weight, Stability, Agility) with progressive coil springs, dual-tube gas-filled shock absorbers, anti-roll bar
Brakes, front/rear (Size (mm)):	Ventilated and drilled discs (304 x 32) Ventilated and drilled discs (299 x 24) Black 4-piston fixed aluminium callipers / Black 4-piston fixed aluminium callipers Bosch ABS 5
Wheels, front/rear:	7 J x 16 / 9 J x 16
Tyres, front/rear:	205/55 ZR 16 / 245/45 ZR 16
Option:	7 J x 17 / 9 J x 17 205/50 ZR 17 / 255/40 ZR 17

Electrical system

Alternator (W/A):	1610 / 115
Battery (V/Ah):	12 / 75

Dimensions and weight

Track, front/rear (mm):	1405 / 1444
Wheelbase (mm):	2272
Length x width x height (mm):	4245 x 1735 x 1300
with sports suspension:	4245 x 1735 x 1285
Kerb weight DIN (kg):	1370 [1395]
Permissible gross weight (kg):	1710 [1735]
Luggage compartment (VDA (l)):	123
with 92 litre fuel tank:	100
Luggage volume interior*:	175
Fuel tank capacity (l):	73.5, including 10 reserve
Option:	92, including 12.5 reserve
C_w x A (m²):	0.33 x 1.86 = 0.614
Power/weight ratio (kg/kW/ kg/hp):	6.52 [6.64] / 4.80 [4.89]
*on folded-down rear seat-backs	

Fuel consumption

80/1268/EWG (mpg):	98 RON super plus unleaded
At constant 56mph/90kph:	37.6 [36.7]
At constant 74mph/120kph:	31 [29.5]
EG-emissions-urban cycle:	16.2 [16.8]
1/3 mix:	24.8 [25]

Performance, production, prices

Acceleration 0-62mph/100kph (s):	less than 5.6 [less than 6.6]
Maximum speed (mph / kph):	more than 167 / 270 [more than 164 / 265]
Production, total number:	n/a
Purchase price performance kit:	DM 12,850

911 Carrera Coupé with performance kit Porsche Motorsport Weissach
911 Carrera Cabriolet with performance kit Porsche Motorsport Weissach
MY 1994–MY 1995

Engine

Engine design:	6-cylinder horizontally-opposed
Installation:	Rear-engine
Cooling system:	Air-cooled
Number & form of blower blades:	12, curved
Blower outside diameter (mm):	253
Engine type:	M 64/05 R
Displacement (cc):	3746
Bore x stroke (mm):	102 x 76.4
Engine output DIN (kW/hp):	220/299 at 6100rpm
Maximum torque (Nm/lb ft):	365/269 at 5250rpm
Output per litre (kW/l / hp/l):	58.7 / 79.8
Compression ratio:	11.3 : 1
Valve operation & camshaft drive:	ohc, cams driven by double chain, 2 valves per cylinder
Carburation:	Bosch DME, Motronic M 2.10, with sequential injection
Ignition system:	Bosch DME, dual ignition
Firing order:	1 - 6 - 2 - 4 - 3 - 5
Engine lubrication:	Dry sump
Engine oil total (l):	11.5

Transmission

Drive configuration:	Rear-axle drive
Manual gearbox:	6-speed
Transmission type:	G 50/21
Transmission ratios:	
1st gear:	3.818
2nd gear:	2.150
3rd gear:	1.560
4th gear:	1.242
5th gear:	1.027
6th gear:	0.821
Reverse gear:	2.857
Drive ratio:	3.444

Body, chassis, suspension, brakes, wheels

Body design:	Steel body, 2 doors, 2 + 2 seats, entirely hot-dip galvanized body, side-impact protection beams in doors, flexible polyurethane front and rear bumpers with integrated aluminium beams, engine lid with integrated automatic rear spoiler, red non-reflecting valance with integrated reverse gear and rear fog lamps
Coupé:	Fixed steel roof
Option:	Electric sunroof
Cabriolet:	Electric hood with flexible plastic rear window
Option:	Automatic wind blocker
Suspension, front:	Individually suspended light-alloy lower wishbones, McPherson struts with coil springs, dual-tube gas-filled shock absorbers, anti-roll bar
Suspension, rear:	Individually suspended on light-alloy multi-wishbone axle with LSA system (Light weight, Stability, Agility) with progressive coil springs, dual-tube gas-filled shock absorbers, anti-roll bar
Brakes, front/rear (Size (mm)):	Ventilated and drilled discs (304 x 32) Ventilated and drilled discs (299 x 24) Black 4-piston fixed aluminium callipers / Black 4-piston fixed aluminium callipers Bosch ABS 5
Wheels, front/rear:	7 J x 17 / 9 J x 17*
Tyres, front/rear:	205/50 ZR 17 / 255/40 ZR 17*
	*Performance kit, only in combination with 17" wheels

Electrical system

Alternator (W/A):	1610 / 115
Battery (V/Ah):	12 / 75

Dimensions and weight

Track, front/rear (mm):	1405 / 1444
Wheelbase (mm):	2272
Length x width x height (mm):	4245 x 1735 x 1300
with sports suspension:	4245 x 1735 x 1285
Kerb weight DIN (kg):	1370
Permissible gross weight (kg):	1710
Luggage compartment (VDA (l)):	123
with 92 litre fuel tank:	100
Luggage volume interior*:	175
Fuel tank capacity (l):	73.5, including 10 reserve
Option:	92, including 12.5 reserve
C_w x A (m²):	0.33 x 1.86 = 0.614
Power/weight ratio (kg/kW / kg/hp):	6.22 / 4.58
*on folded-down rear seat-backs	

Fuel consumption

80/1268/EWG (mpg):	98 RON super plus unleaded
At constant 56mph/90kph:	37.6*
At constant 74mph/120kph:	31*
EG-emissions-urban cycle:	16.2*
1/3 mix:	24.8*
*Basic engine	

Performance, production, prices

Acceleration 0-62mph/100kph (s):	less than 5.6
Maximum speed (mph / kph):	174 / 280
Production, total number:	n/a
Purchase price performance kit:	DM 23,432

911 Carrera 4 Coupé
911 Carrera 4 Cabriolet MY 1995

Engine

Engine design:	6-cylinder horizontally-opposed
Installation:	Rear-engine
Cooling system:	Air-cooled
Number & form of blower blades:	12, curved
Blower outside diameter (mm):	253
Engine type:	M 64/05
Displacement (cc):	3600
Bore x stroke (mm):	100 x 76.4
Engine output DIN (kW/hp):	200/272 at 6100rpm
Maximum torque (Nm/lb ft):	330/243 at 5000rpm
Output per litre (kW/l / hp/l):	55.6 / 75.6
Compression ratio:	11.3 : 1
Valve operation & camshaft drive:	ohc, cams driven by double chain, 2 valves per cylinder
Carburation:	Bosch DME, Motronic M 2.10, with sequential injection
Ignition system:	Bosch DME, dual ignition
Firing order:	1 - 6 - 2 - 4 - 3 - 5
Engine lubrication:	Dry sump
Engine oil total (l):	11.5

Transmission

Drive configuration:	4-wheel-drive with visco-clutch, transaxle
Manual gearbox:	6-speed
Transmission type:	G 50/21
Transmission ratios:	
1st gear:	3.818
2nd gear:	2.150
3rd gear:	1.560
4th gear:	1.242
5th gear:	1.027
6th gear:	0.821
Reverse gear:	2.857
Drive ratio:	3.444
Ltd slip diff. laod/deceleration (%):	25 / 40

Body, chassis, suspension, brakes, wheels

Body design:	Steel body, 2 doors, 2 + 2 seats, entirely hot-dip galvanized body, side-impact protection beams in doors, flexible polyurethane front- and rear bumpers with integrated aluminium beams, engine lid with integrated automatic rear spoiler, red non-reflecting valance with integrated reverse gear and rear fog lamps
Coupé:	Fixed steel roof
Option:	Electric sunroof
Cabriolet:	Electric hood with flexible plastic rear window
Option:	Automatic wind blocker
Suspension, front:	Individually suspended light-alloy lower wishbones, McPherson struts with coil springs, dual-tube gas-filled shock absorbers, anti-roll bar
Suspension, rear:	Individually suspended on light-alloy multi-wishbone axle with LSA system (Light weight, Stability, Agility) with progressive coil springs, dual-tube gas-filled shock absorbers, anti-roll bar
Brakes, front/rear (Size (mm)):	Ventilated and drilled discs (304 x 32) Ventilated and drilled discs (299 x 24) Titanium colour 4-piston fixed aluminium callipers / Titanium colour 4-piston fixed aluminium callipers Bosch ABS
Wheels, front/rear:	7 J x 16 / 9 J x 16
Tyres, front/rear:	205/55 ZR 16 / 245/45 ZR 16
Option:	7 J x 17 / 9 J x 17 205/50 ZR 17 / 255/40 ZR 17

Electrical system

Alternator (W/A):	1610 / 115
Battery (V/Ah):	12 / 75

Dimensions and weight

Track, front/rear (mm):	1405 / 1444
Wheelbase (mm):	2272
Length x width x height (mm):	4245 x 1735 x 1300
with sports suspension:	4245 x 1735 x 1285
Kerb weight DIN (kg):	1420
Permissible gross weight (kg):	1760
Luggage compartment (VDA (l)):	123
with 92 litre fuel tank:	100
Luggage volume interior*:	175
Fuel tank capacity (l):	73.5, including 10 reserve
Option:	92, including 12.5 reserve
C_w x A (m²):	0.33 x 1.86 = 0.614
Power/weight ratio (kg/kW/kg/hp):	7.10 / 5.22
*on folded-down rear seat-backs	

Fuel consumption

80/1268/EWG (mpg):	98 RON super plus unleaded
At constant 56mph/90kph:	37.6
At constant 74mph/120kph:	31
EG-emissions-urban cycle:	16
1/3 mix:	24.8

Performance, production, prices

Acceleration 0-62mph/100kph (s):	5.6
Maximum speed (mph / kph):	167 / 270
Production, total number:	
Coupé:	2,884
Cabriolet:	1,284
Purchase prices:	
08/1994 Coupé:	DM 134,340
Cabriolet:	DM 151,190
02/1995 Coupé:	DM 137,030
Cabriolet:	DM 154,210

911 Carrera Speedster MY 1995

Engine

Engine design:	6-cylinder horizontally-opposed
Installation:	Rear-engine
Cooling system:	Air-cooled
Number & form of blower blades:	12, curved
Blower outside diameter (mm):	253
Engine type:	M 64/06
Displacement (cc):	3600
Bore x stroke (mm):	100 x 76.4
Engine output DIN (kW/hp):	200/272 at 6100rpm
Maximum torque (Nm/lb ft):	330/243 at 5000rpm
Output per litre (kW/l / hp/l):	55.6 / 75.6
Compression ratio:	11.3 : 1
Valve operation & camshaft drive:	ohc, cams driven by double chain, 2 valves per cylinder
Carburation:	Bosch DME, Motronic M 2.10, with sequential injection
Ignition system:	Bosch DME, dual ignition
Firing order:	1 - 6 - 2 - 4 - 3 - 5
Engine lubrication:	Dry sump
Engine oil total (l):	11.5

Transmission

Drive configuration:	Rear-axle drive
Tiptronic:	4-speed
Transmission type:	A 50/04
Transmission ratios:	
1st gear:	2.479
2nd gear:	1.479
3rd gear:	1.000
4th gear:	0.728
Reverse gear:	2.086
Drive ratio:	3.667

Body, chassis, suspension, brakes, wheels

Body design:	Steel Speedster body, 2 doors, 2 seats, entirely hot-dip galvanized body, wider rear wings, small Speedster windscreen with black frame, side-impact protection beams in doors, flexible polyurethane front and rear bumpers with integrated aluminium beams, engine lid with integrated automatic rear spoiler, red non-reflecting valance with integrated reverse gear and rear fog lamps, manual hood with flexible plastic rear window, Speedster plastic hatch with two fairings
Suspension, front:	Individually suspended light-alloy lower wishbones, McPherson struts with coil springs, dual-tube gas-filled shock absorbers, anti-roll bar
Suspension, rear:	Individually suspended on light-alloy multi-wishbone axle with LSA system (Light weight, Stability, Agility) with progressive coil springs, dual-tube gas-filled shock absorbers, anti-roll bar
Brakes, front/rear (Size (mm)):	Ventilated and drilled discs (304 x 32) Ventilated and drilled discs (299 x 24) Black 4-piston fixed aluminium callipers / Black 4-piston fixed aluminium callipers Bosch ABS 5
Wheels, front/rear:	7 J x 17 / 9 J x 17
Tyres, front/rear:	205/50 ZR 17 / 255/40 ZR 17

Electrical system

Alternator (W/A):	1610 / 115
Battery (V/Ah):	12 / 75

Dimensions and weight

Track, front/rear (mm):	1405 / 1444
Wheelbase (mm):	2272
Length x width x height (mm):	4245 x 1735 x 1280
Kerb weight (kg):	1395
Permissible gross weight (kg):	1650
Luggage compartment (VDA (l)):	123
Fuel tank capacity (l):	73.5, including 10 reserve
C_w x A (m²):	n/a
Power/weight ratio (kg/kW/kg/hp):	6.98 / 5.13

Fuel consumption

80/1268/EWG (mpg):	98 RON super unleaded
At constant 56mph/90kph:	36.7
At constant 74mph/120kph:	29.5
EG-emissions-urban cycle:	16.8
1/3 mix:	25

Performance, production, prices

Acceleration 0-62mph/100kph (s):	6.6
Maximum speed (mph / kph):	164 / 265
Production, total number:	1

911 Cabriolet turbo MY 1995

Engine

Engine design:	6-cylinder horizontally-opposed, turbo charger, intercooler
Installation:	Rear-engine
Cooling system:	Air-cooled
Number & form of blower blades:	11, straight
Blower outside diameter (mm):	245
Engine type:	M 64/50
Displacement (cc):	3600
Bore x stroke (mm):	100 x 76.4
Engine output DIN (kW/hp):	265/360 at 5500rpm
Maximum torque (Nm/lb ft):	520/384 at 4200rpm
Output per litre (kW/l / hp/l):	73.6 / 100
Compression ratio:	7.5 : 1
Valve operation & camshaft drive:	ohc, cams driven by double chain, 2 valves per cylinder
Carburation:	Bosch K-Jetronic injection
Ignition system:	Battery, capacitive-discharge system, without contact
Firing order:	1 - 6 - 2 - 4 - 3 - 5
Engine lubrication:	Dry sump
Engine oil total (l):	13.0

Transmission

Drive configuration:	Rear-axle drive
Manual gearbox:	5-speed
Transmission type:	G 50/52
Transmission ratios:	
1st gear:	3.154
2nd gear:	1.789
3rd gear:	1.269
4th gear:	0.967
5th gear:	0.756
Reverse gear:	2.857
Drive ratio:	3.444
Ltd slip diff. load/deceleration (%):	20 / 100

Body, chassis, suspension, brakes, wheels

Body design:	Steel Cabriolet body, 2 doors, 2 + 2 seats, entirely hot-dip galvanized body, side-impact protection beams in doors, flexible polyurethane front and rear bumpers with integrated aluminium beams, engine lid with fixed rear wing 'Turbo 3.6", red non-reflecting valance with integrated reverse gear and rear fog lamps, electric hood with flexible plastic rear window
Option:	Automatic wind blocker

Suspension, front:	Individually suspended light-alloy lower wishbones, McPherson struts with coil springs, dual-tube gas-filled shock absorbers, anti-roll bar
Suspension, rear:	Individually suspended on light-alloy multi-wishbone axle with LSA system (Light weight, Stability, Agility) with progressive coil springs, dual-tube gas-filled shock absorbers, anti-roll bar
Brakes, front/rear (Size (mm)):	Ventilated and drilled discs (332 x 32) Ventilated and drilled discs (299 x 28) Red 4-piston fixed aluminium callipers / Red 4-piston fixed aluminium callipers Bosch ABS 5
Wheels, front/rear:	7 J x 17 / 9 J x 17
Tyres, front/rear:	205/50 ZR 17 / 255/40 ZR 17

Electrical system

Alternator (W/A):	1610 / 115
Battery (V/Ah):	12 / 75

Dimensions and weight

Track, front/rear (mm):	1405 / 1444
Wheelbase (mm):	2272
Length x width x height (mm):	4245 x 1735 x 1300
Kerb weight DIN (kg):	1395
Permissible gross weight (kg):	1735
Luggage compartment (VDA (l)):	123
with 92 litre fuel tank:	100
Luggage volume interior*:	175
Fuel tank capacity (l):	73.5, including 10 reserve
Option:	92, including 12.5 reserve
C_w x A (m²):	0.33 x 1.86 = 0.614
Power/weight ratio (kg/kW/kg/hp):	5.26 / 3.87
*on folded-down rear seat-backs	

Fuel consumption

80/1268/EWG (mpg):	95 RON super unleaded
At constant 56mph/90kph:	34
At constant 74mph/120kph:	27.4
EG-emissions-urban cycle:	13.2
1/3 mix:	21.2

Performance, production, prices

Acceleration 0-62mph/100kph (s):	4.6
Maximum speed (mph / kph):	174 / 280
Production, total number:	14
Conversion price:	DM 89,500

911 Carrera RS Coupé
911 Carrera RS Coupé Clubsport
MY 1995–MY 1996

Engine

Engine design:	6-cylinder horizontally-opposed
Installation:	Rear-engine
Cooling system:	Air-cooled
Number & form of blower blades:	12, curved
Blower outside diameter (mm):	253
Engine type:	M 64/20
Displacement (cc):	3746
Bore x stroke (mm):	102 x 76.4
Engine output DIN (kW/hp):	221/300 at 6500rpm
Maximum torque (Nm/lb ft):	355/262 at 5400rpm
Output per litre (kW/l / hp/l):	60.0 / 80.1
Compression ratio:	11.3 : 1
Valve operation & camshaft drive:	ohc, cams driven by double chain, 2 valves per cylinder
Carburation:	Bosch DME, Motronic M 2.10, with sequential injection
Ignition system:	Bosch DME, dual ignition
Firing order:	1 - 6 - 2 - 4 - 3 - 5
Engine lubrication:	Dry sump
Engine oil total (l):	11.5

Transmission

Drive configuration:	Rear-axle drive
Manual gearbox:	6-speed
Transmission type:	G 50/31 (G 50/32)
Transmission ratios:	
1st gear:	3.154 (3.154)
2nd gear:	2.000 (2.000)
3rd gear:	1.522 (1.522)
4th gear:	1.242 (1.241)
5th gear:	1.024 (1.031)
6th gear:	0.821 (0.829)
Reverse gear:	2.857 (2.857)
Drive ratio:	3.444 (3.444)
Ltd slip diff. load/deceleration (%):	40 / 65
*Clubsport	

Body, chassis, suspension, brakes, wheels

Body design:	Steel coupé body, 2 doors, 2 seats, entirely hot-dip galvanized body, side-impact protection beams in doors, flexible polyurethane front and rear bumpers with integrated aluminium beams, front corner spoilers, black polyurethane spoiler edges at front end of rear wings, fixed rear wing on engine lid, aluminium front lid, red non-reflecting valance with integrated reverse gear and rear fog lamps, thin-glass rear and side windows
Clubsport:	Front bumper with bigger front spoiler, engine lid with fixed, adjustable rear wing with air intakes
Suspension, front:	Individually suspended light-alloy lower wishbones, McPherson struts with coil springs, dual-tube gas-filled shock absorbers, anti-roll bar
Suspension, rear:	Individually suspended on light-alloy multi-wishbone axle with LSA system (Light weight, Stability, Agility) with progressive coil springs, dual-tube gas-filled shock absorbers, anti-roll bar
Brakes, front/rear (Size (mm)):	Ventilated and drilled discs (322 x 32) Ventilated and drilled discs (322 x 28) Red 4-piston fixed aluminium callipers / Red 4-piston fixed aluminium callipers Bosch ABS 5
Wheels, front/rear:	8 J x 18 / 10 J x 18
Tyres, front/rear:	225/40 ZR 18 / 265/35 ZR 18

Electrical system

Alternator (W/A):	1610 / 115
Battery (V/Ah):	12 / 36

Dimensions and weight

Track, front/rear (mm):	1413 / 1452
Wheelbase (mm):	2272
Length x width x height (mm):	4245 x 1735 x 1270
Kerb weight DIN (kg):	1270
Permissible gross weight (kg):	1550
Luggage compartment (VDA (l)):	93
Fuel tank capacity (l):	92, including 12.5 reserve
C_w x A (m^2):	0.33 x 1.86 = 0.614
Clubsport rear wing at 0° angle:	0.34 x 1.86 = 0.632
Clubsport rear wing at 9° angle:	0.36 x 1.86 = 0.669
Power/weight ratio (kg/kW/kg/hp):	5.74 / 4.23

Fuel consumption

89/491/EWG (mpg):	98 RON super plus unleaded
At constant 56mph/90kph:	37
At constant 74mph/120kph:	29.5
EG-emissions-urban cyle:	14
1/3 mix:	22.7
93/116/EG (mpg):	98 RON super plus unleaded
Urban:	13.4
Extra urban:	29.5
Combined:	20.5
CO_2-emissions (g/km):	327

Performance, production, prices

Acceleration 0-62mph/100kph (s):	5.0
Maximum speed (mph / kph):	172 / 277
Production, total number:	1,014
Clubsport only:	227
Purchase prices:	
02/1995 Coupé:	DM 147,900
Coupé-Clubsport:	DM 164,700
08/1995 Coupé:	DM 153,350

911 turbo Coupé MY 1995–MY 1998

Engine

Engine design:	6-cylinder horizontally-opposed, twin-turbo charger, twin-intercooler
Installation:	Rear-engine
Cooling system:	Air-cooled
Number & form of blower blades:	11, straight
Blower outside diameter (mm):	245
Engine type:	M 64/60
Displacement (cc):	3600
Bore x stroke (mm):	100 x 76.4
Engine output DIN (kW/hp):	300/408 at 5750rpm
Maximum torque (Nm/lb ft):	540/398 at 4500rpm
Output per litre (kW/l / hp/l):	83.3 / 113.3
Compression ratio:	8.0 : 1
Valve operation & camshaft drive:	ohc, cams driven by double chain, 2 valves per cylinder
Carburation:	Bosch DME, Motronic M 5.2, with sequential injection
Ignition system:	Bosch DME
Firing order:	1 - 6 - 2 - 4 - 3 - 5
Engine lubrication:	Dry sump
Engine oil total (l):	11.5

Transmission

Drive configuration:	4-wheel-drive with visco-clutch, transaxle
Manual gearbox:	6-speed
Transmission type:	G 64/51
Übersetzungen:	
1st gear:	3.818
2nd gear:	2.150
3rd gear:	1.560
4th gear:	1.212
5th gear:	0.937
6th gear:	0.750
Reverse gear:	2.857
Drive ratio:	3.444
Ltd slip diff. load/deceleration (%):	25 / 40

Body, chassis, suspension, brakes, wheels

Body design:	Steel coupé body, 2 doors, 2 + 2 seats, entirely hot-dip galvanized body, wider rear wings and side skirts, side-impact protection beams in doors, flexible polyurethane front and rear bumpers with integrated aluminium beams, front bumpers with three air intakes, plastic engine lid with integrated rear wing, red non-reflecting valance with integrated reverse gear and rear fog lamps
Option:	Electric sunroof
Suspension, front:	Individually suspended light-alloy lower wishbones, McPherson struts with coil springs, dual-tube gas-filled shock absorbers, anti-roll bar
Suspension, rear:	Individually suspended on light-alloy multi-wishbone axle with LSA system (Light weight, Stability, Agility) with progressive coil springs, dual-tube gas-filled shock absorbers, anti-roll bar
Brakes, front/rear (Size (mm)):	Ventilated and drilled discs (322 x 32) Ventilated and drilled discs (322 x 28) Red 4-piston fixed aluminium callipers / Red 4-piston fixed aluminium callipers Bosch ABS 5
Wheels, front/rear:	8 J x 18 / 10 J x 18
Tyres, front/rear:	225/40 ZR 18 / 285/30 ZR 18

Electrical system

Alternator (W/A):	1610 / 115
Battery (V/Ah):	12 / 75

Dimensions and weight

Track, front/rear (mm):	1411 / 1504
Wheelbase (mm):	2272
Length x width x height (mm):	4245 x 1795 x 1285
Kerb weight DIN (kg):	1500
Permissible gross weight (kg):	1840
Luggage compartment (VDA (l)):	123
with 92 litre fuel tank:	100
Luggage volume interior*:	175
Fuel tank capacity (l):	73.5, including 15 reserve
Option:	92, including 15 reserve
C_w x A (m²):	0.34 x 1.93 = 0.656
Power/weight ratio (kg/kW/ kg/hp):	5.00 / 3.67
*on folded-down rear seat-backs	

Fuel consumption

89/491/EWG (mpg):	98 RON super plus unleaded
At constant 56mph/90kph:	34.4
At constant 74mph/120kph:	27.4
EG-urban cycle:	13.4
1/3 mix:	21.4
93/115/EG (mpg):	98 RON super plus unleaded
Urban:	12
Extra urban:	25.2
Combined:	18
CO_2-emissions (g/km):	376

Performance, production, prices

Acceleration 0-62mph/100kph (s):	4.5
Maximum speed (mph / kph):	180 / 290
Production, total number:	5,978
Purchase prices:	
02/1995 Coupé:	DM 212,040
08/1995 Coupé:	DM 219,850
08/1996 Coupé:	DM 222,500
08/1997 Coupé:	DM 222,500

911 GT 2 Coupé
MY 1995–MY 1997

Engine
Engine design:	6-cylinder horizontally-opposed, twin-turbo charger, twin-intercooler
Installation:	Rear-engine
Cooling system:	Air-cooled
Number & form of blower blades:	11, straight
Blower outside diameter (mm):	245
Engine type:	M 64/60 R
Displacement (cc):	3600
Bore x stroke (mm):	100 x 76.4
Engine output DIN (kW/hp):	316/430 at 5750rpm
Maximum torque (Nm/lb ft):	540/398 at 4500rpm
Output per litre (kW/l / hp/l):	87.8 / 119.4
Compression ratio:	8.0 : 1
Valve operation & camshaft drive:	ohc, cams driven by double chain, 2 valves per cylinder
Carburation:	Bosch DME, Motronic M 5.2, with sequential injection
Ignition system:	Bosch DME
Firing order:	1 - 6 - 2 - 4 - 3 - 5
Engine lubrication:	Dry sump
Engine oil total (l):	11.5

Transmission
Drive configuration:	Rear-axle drive
Manual gearbox:	6-speed
Transmission type:	G 64/51
Übersetzungen:	
1st gear:	3.818
2nd gear:	2.150
3rd gear:	1.560
4th gear:	1.212
5th gear:	0.937
6th gear:	0.750
Reverse gear:	2.857
Drive ratio:	3.444
Ltd-slip diff. load/deceleration (%):	25 / 40

Body, chassis, suspension, brakes, wheels
Body design:	Steel coupé body, 2 doors, 2 seats, entirely hot-dip galvanized body, wider rear wings and side skirts, side-impact protection beams in doors, flexible polyurethane front and rear bumpers with integrated aluminium beams, big front spoiler, polyurethane wing flares, plastic engine lid with integrated, adjustable rear wing with air intakes, aluminium bonnet lid and doors, red non-reflecting valance with integrated reverse gear and rear fog lamps, thin-glass rear and side windows

Suspension, front:	Individually suspended light-alloy lower wishbones, McPherson struts with coil springs, dual-tube gas-filled shock absorbers, anti-roll bar
Suspension, rear:	Individually suspended on light-alloy multi-wishbone axle with LSA system (Light weight, Stability, Agility) with progressive coil springs, dual-tube gas-filled shock absorbers, anti-roll bar
Brakes, front/rear (Size (mm)):	Ventilated and drilled discs (322 x 32) Ventilated and drilled discs (322 x 28) Red 4-piston fixed aluminium callipers / Red 4-piston fixed aluminium callipers Bosch ABS
Wheels, front/rear:	9 J x 18 / 11 J x 18
Tyres, front/rear:	235/40 ZR 18 / 285/35 ZR 18

Electrical system
Alternator (W/A):	1610 / 115
Battery (V/Ah):	12 / 36

Dimensions and weight
Track, front/rear (mm):	1475 / 1550
Wheelbase (mm):	2272
Length x width x height (mm):	4245 x 1855 x 1270
Kerb weight DIN (kg):	1295
Permissible gross weight (kg):	1575
Luggage compartment (VDA (l)):	100
Fuel tank capacity (l):	92, including 15 reserve
C_w x A (m^2):	0.34 x 2.04 = 0.694
Power/weight ratio (kg/kW/kg/hp):	4.09 / 3.01

Fuel consumption
89/491/EWG (mpg):	98 RON super plus unleaded
At constant 56mph/90kph:	33.5
At constant 74mph/120kph:	28.2
EG-urban cycle:	13.4
1/ 3 mix:	21.5
93/115/EG (mpg):	98 RON super plus unleaded
Urban:	12.1
Extra urban:	26
Combined:	18.3
CO_2-emissions (g/km):	368

Performance, production, prices
Acceleration 0-62mph/100kph (s):	4.4
Maximum speed (mph / kph):	183 / 295
Production, total number:	172
Purchase price:	
02/1995 Coupé:	DM 268,000
08/1995 Coupé:	DM 276,000
08/1996 Coupé:	DM 278,875
08/1997 Coupé:	DM 278,875

911 Carrera Coupé [Tiptronic S]
911 Carrera Cabriolet [Tiptronic S]
MY 1996–MY 1997

Engine

Engine design:	6-cylinder horizontally-opposed
Installation:	Rear-engine
Cooling system:	Air-cooled
Number & form of blower blades:	12, curved
Blower outside diameter (mm):	253
Engine type:	M 64/21 [M 64/22]
Displacement (cc):	3600
Bore x stroke (mm):	100 x 76.4
Engine output DIN (kW/hp):	210/285 at 6100rpm
Maximum torque (Nm/lb ft):	340/251 at 5250rpm
Output per litre (kW/l / hp/l):	58.3 / 79.2
Compression ratio:	11.3 : 1
Valve operation & camshaft drive:	ohc, cams driven by double chain, 2 valves per cylinder
Carburation:	Bosch DME, Motronic M 5.2, with sequential injection
Ignition system:	Bosch DME, dual ignition
Firing order:	1 - 6 - 2 - 4 - 3 - 5
Engine lubrication:	Dry sump
Engine oil total (l):	11.5

Transmission

Drive configuration:	Rear-axle drive
Manual gearbox:	6-speed (6-speed)
Option Tiptronic S:	[4-speed]
Transmission type:	G 50/21 (G 50/20)* [A 50/04]
Transmission ratios:	
1st gear:	3.818 (3.181) [2.479]
2nd gear:	2.150 (2.048) [1.479]
3rd gear:	1.560 (1.407) [1.000]
4th gear:	1.242 (1.118) [0.728]
5th gear:	1.027 (0.921)
6th gear:	0.821 (0.775)
Reverse gear:	2.857 (2.857) [2.086]
Drive ratio:	3.444 (3.444) [3.667]
*MY 1997	

Body, chassis, suspension, brakes, wheels

Body design:	Steel body, 2 doors, 2 + 2 seats, entirely hot-dip galvanized body, side-impact protection beams in doors, flexible polyurethane front and rear bumpers with integrated aluminium beams, engine lid with integrated automatic rear spoiler, red non-reflecting valance with integrated reverse gear and rear fog lamps
Coupé:	Fixed steel roof
Option:	Electric sunroof
Cabriolet:	Electric hood with flexible plastic rear window
Option:	Automatic wind blocker
Suspension, front:	Individually suspended light-alloy lower wishbones, McPherson struts with coil springs, dual-tube gas-filled shock absorbers, anti-roll bar
Suspension, rear:	Individually suspended on light-alloy multi-wishbone axle with LSA system (Light weight, Stability, Agility) with progressive coil springs, dual-tube gas-filled shock absorbers, anti-roll bar
Brakes, front/rear (Size (mm)):	Ventilated and drilled discs (304 x 32) Ventilated and drilled discs (299 x 24) Black 4-piston fixed aluminium callipers / Black 4-piston fixed aluminium callipers Bosch ABS 5
Wheels, front/rear:	7 J x 16 / 9 J x 16
Tyres, front/rear:	205/55 ZR 16 / 245/45 ZR 16
Option:	7 J x 17 / 9 J x 17 205/50 ZR 17 / 255/40 ZR 17

Electrical system

Alternator (W/A):	1610 / 115
Battery (V/Ah):	12 / 75

Dimensions and weight

Track, front/rear (mm):	1405 / 1444
Wheelbase (mm):	2272
Length x width x height (mm):	4245 x 1735 x 1300
with sports suspension:	4245 x 1735 x 1285
Kerb weight DIN (kg):	1370 [1395]
Permissible gross weight (kg):	1710 [1735]
Luggage compartment (VDA (l)):	123
with 92 litre fuel tank:	100
Luggage volume interior*:	175
Fuel tank capacity (l):	73.5, including 10 reserve
Option:	92, including 12.5 reserve
C_w x A (m^2):	0.33 x 1.86 = 0.614
Power/weight ratio (kg/kW/kg/hp):	6.85 [6.97] / 5.03 [5.12]
*on folded-down rear seat-backs	

Fuel consumption

89/491/EWG (mpg):	98 RON super plus unleaded
At constant 56mph/90kph:	37 [34.4]
At constant 74mph/120kph:	30.4 [28.8]
EG-urban cycle:	17.3 [17.9]
1/3 mix:	25.4 [25]
93/116/EG (mpg):	98 RON super plus unleaded
Urban:	15.8 [15.5]
Extra urban:	31.6 [32.5]
Combined:	23.1 [23.1]
CO_2-emissions (g/km):	289 [289]
MY 1997:	
89/491/EWG (mpg):	98 RON super plus unleaded
At constant 56mph/90kph:	37.6 [34.8]
At constant 74mph/120kph:	31 [29.5]
EG-urban cycle:	17.6 [17.9]
1/3 mix:	25.8 [25.2]
93/116/EG (mpg):	98 RON super plus unleaded
Urban:	16 [15.5]
Extra urban:	32.8 [32.5]
Combined:	23.7 [23.1]
CO_2-emissions (g/km):	295 [303]

Performance, production, prices

Acceleration 0-62mph/100kph (s):	5.4 [6.4]
Maximum speed (mph / kph):	171 / 275 [167 / 270]
Production, total number:	
Coupé:	8,586
Cabriolet:	7,769
Purchase prices:	
08/1995 Coupé:	DM 132,950 [DM 139,610]
Cabriolet:	DM 150,800 [DM 157,460]
08/1996 Coupé:	DM 132,950 [DM 139,610]
Cabriolet:	DM 150,800 [DM 157,460]
08/1997 Coupé:*	DM 132,950 [DM 139,610]
Cabriolet:*	DM 150,800 [DM 157,460]
*only a few cars at Porsche dealers available	

911 Carrera Coupé
with performance kit Exclusive
911 Carrera Cabriolet
with performance kit Exclusive
MY 1996–MY 1997

Engine

Engine design:	6-cylinder horizontally-opposed
Installation:	Rear-engine
Cooling system:	Air-cooled
Number & form of blower blades:	12, curved
Blower outside diameter (mm):	253
Engine type:	M 64/21 S
Displacement (cc):	3746
Bore x stroke (mm):	102 x 76.4
Engine output DIN (kW/hp):	221/300 at 6600rpm
Maximum torque (Nm/lb ft):	355/262 at 5400rpm
Output per litre (kW/l / hp/l):	59.0 / 80.1
Compression ratio:	11.3 : 1
Valve operation & camshaft drive:	ohc, cams driven by double chain, 2 valves per cylinder
Carburation:	Bosch DME, Motronic M 5.2, with sequential injection
Ignition system:	Bosch DME, dual ignition
Firing order:	1 - 6 - 2 - 4 - 3 - 5
Engine lubrication:	Dry sump
Engine oil total (l):	11.5

Transmission

Drive configuration:	Rear-axle drive
Manual gearbox:	6-speed (6-speed)
Transmission type:	G 50/21 (G 50/20)*
Transmission ratios:	
1st gear:	3.818 (3.181)
2nd gear:	2.150 (2.048)
3rd gear:	1.560 (1.407)
4th gear:	1.242 (1.118)
5th gear:	1.027 (0.921)
6th gear:	0.821 (0.775)
Reverse gear:	2.857 (2.857)
Drive ratio:	3.444 (3.444)
*MY 1997	

Body, chassis, suspension, brakes, wheels

Body design:	Steel body, 2 doors, 2 + 2 seats, entirely hot-dip galvanized body, side-impact protection beams in doors, flexible polyurethane front and rear bumpers with integrated aluminium beams, engine lid with integrated automatic rear spoiler, red non-reflecting valance with integrated reverse gear and rear fog lamps
Coupé:	Fixed steel roof
Option:	Electric sunroof
Cabriolet:	Electric hood with flexible plastic rear window
Option:	Automatic wind blocker
Suspension, front:	Individually suspended light-alloy lower wishbones, McPherson struts with coil springs, dual-tube gas-filled shock absorbers, anti-roll bar
Suspension, rear:	Individually suspended on light-alloy multi-wishbone axle with LSA system (Light weight, Stability, Agility) with progressive coil springs, dual-tube gas-filled shock absorbers, anti-roll bar
Brakes, front/rear (Size (mm)):	Ventilated and drilled discs (304 x 32) Ventilated and drilled discs (299 x 24) Black 4-piston fixed aluminium callipers / Black 4-piston fixed aluminium callipers Bosch ABS 5
Wheels, front/rear::	7 J x 17 / 9 J x 17*
Tyres, front/rear:	205/50 ZR 17 / 255/40 ZR 17*
*Performance kit only in combination with 17" wheels	

Electrical system

Alternator (W/A):	1610 / 115
Battery (V/Ah):	12 / 75

Dimensions and weight

Track, front/rear (mm):	1405 / 1444
Wheelbase (mm):	2272
Length x width x height (mm):	4245 x 1735 x 1300
with sports supension	4245 x 1735 x 1285
Kerb weight DIN (kg):	1370
Permissible gross weight (kg):	1710
Luggage compartment (VDA (l)):	123
with 92 litre fuel tank:	100
Luggage volume interior*:	175
Fuel tank capacity (l):	73.5, including 10 reserve
Option:	92, including 12.5 reserve
C_w x A (m²):	0.33 x 1.86 = 0.614
Power/weight ratio (kg/kW/ kg/hp):	6.19 / 4.56
*on folded-down rear seat-backs	

Fuel consumption

89/491/EWG (mpg):	98 RON super plus unleaded
At constant 56mph/90kph:	37*
At constant 74mph/120kph:	30.4*
EG-urban cyle:	17.3*
173 mix:	25.4*
93/116/EG (mpg):	98 RON super plus unleaded
Urban:	15.8*
Extra urban:	31.6*
Combined:	23.1*
CO_2-emissions (g/km):	289*
MY 1997:	
89/491/EWG (mpg):	98 RON super plus unleaded
At constant 56mph/90kph:	37.6*
At constant 74mph/120kph:	31*
EG-urban cycle:	17.6*
1/3 mix:	25.8*
93/116/EG (mpg):	98 RON super plus unleaded
Urban:	16*
Extra urban:	32.8*
Combined:	23.7*
CO_2-emissions (g/km)*:	295*
*Basic engine	

Performance, production, prices

Acceleration 0_100 km/h (s):	less than 5.4
Maximum speed (mph / kph):	more than 171 / 275
Production, total number:	
Coupé:	n/a
Cabriolet:	n/a
Purchase price performance kit:	DM 12,850

911 Carrera 4 Coupé
911 Carrera 4 Cabriolet
MY 1996–MY 1997

Engine

Engine design:	6-cylinder horizontally-opposed
Installation:	Rear-engine
Cooling system:	Air-cooled
Number & form of blower blades:	12, curved
Blower outside diameter (mm):	253
Engine type:	M 64/21
Displacement (cc):	3600
Bore x stroke (mm):	100 x 76.4
Engine output DIN (kW/hp):	210/285 at 6100rpm
Maximum torque (Nm/lb ft):	340/251 at 5250rpm
Output per litre (kW/l / hp/l):	58.3 / 79.2
Compression ratio:	11.3 : 1
Valve operation & camshaft drive:	ohc, cams driven by double chain, 2 valves per cylinder
Carburation:	Bosch DME, Motronic M 5.2, with sequential injection
Ignition system:	Bosch DME, dual ignition
Firing order:	1 - 6 - 2 - 4 - 3 - 5
Engine lubrication:	Dry sump
Engine oil total (l):	11.5

Transmission

Drive configuration:	4-wheel-drive with visco-clutch, transaxle
Manual gearbox:	6-speed (6-speed)
Transmission type:	G 50/21 (G 50/20)*
Transmission ratios:	
1st gear:	3.818 (3.181)
2nd gear:	2.150 (2.048)
3rd gear:	1.560 (1.407)
4th gear:	1.242 (1.118)
5th gear:	1.027 (0.921)
6th gear:	0.821 (0.775)
Reverse gear:	2.857 (2.857)
Drive ratio:	3.444 (3.444)
*MY 1997	

Body, chassis, suspension, brakes, wheels

Body design:	Steel body, 2 doors, 2 + 2 seats, entirely hot-dip galvanized body, side-impact protection beams in doors, flexible polyurethane front and rear bumpers with integrated aluminium beams, engine lid with integrated automatic rear spoiler, red non-reflecting valance with integrated reverse gear and rear fog lamps
Coupé:	Fixed steel roof
Option:	Electric sunroof
Cabriolet:	Electric hood with flexible plastic rear window
Option:	Automatic wind blocker
Suspension, front:	Individually suspended light-alloy lower wishbones, McPherson struts with coil springs, dual-tube gas-filled shock absorbers, anti-roll bar
Suspension, rear:	Individually suspended on light-alloy multi-wishbone axle with LSA system (Light weight, Stability, Agility) with progressive coil springs, dual-tube gas-filled shock absorbers, anti-roll bar
Brakes, front/rear (Size (mm)):	Ventilated and drilled discs (304 x 32) Ventilated and drilled discs (299 x 24) Titanium-colour 4-piston fixed aluminium callipers / Titanium-colour 4-piston fixed aluminium callipers Bosch ABS
Wheels, front/rear:	7 J x 16 / 9 J x 16
Tyres, front/rear:	205/55 ZR 16 / 245/45 ZR 16
Option:	7 J x 17 / 9 J x 17 205/50 ZR 17 / 255/40 ZR 17

Electrical system

Alternator (W/A):	1610 / 115
Battery (V/Ah):	12 / 75

Dimensions and weight

Track, front/rear (mm):	1405 / 1444
Wheelbase (mm):	2272
Length x width x height (mm):	4245 x 1735 x 1300
with sports suspension:	4245 x 1735 x 1285
Kerb weight DIN (kg):	1420
Permissible gross weight (kg):	1760
Luggage compartment (VDA (l)):	123
with 92 litre fuel tank:	100
Luggage volume interior*:	175
Fuel tank capacity (l):	73.5, including 10 reserve
Option:	92, including 12.5 reserve
C_w x A (m^2):	0.33 x 1.86 = 0.614
Power/weight ratio (kg/kW/kg/hp):	6.76 / 4.98
*on folded-down rear seat-backs	

Fuel consumption

89/491/EWG (mpg):	98 RON super plus unleaded
At constant 56mph/90kph:	36.3
At constant 74mph/120kph:	30.4
EG-urban cycle:	16.7
1/3 mix:	25
93/116/EG (mpg):	98 RON super plus unleaded
Urban:	15.3
Extra urban:	31
Combined:	22.4
CO_2-emissions (g/km):	289
MY 1997:	
89/491/EWG (mpg):	98 RON super plus unleaded
At constant 56mph/90kph:	36.7
At constant 74mph/120kph:	31
EG-urban cycle:	17
1/3 mix:	25.2
93/116/EG (mpg):	98 RON super plus unleaded
Urban:	15.8
Extra urban:	31.6
Combined:	23.1
CO_2-emissions (g/km):	299

Performance, production, prices

Acceleration 0-62mph/100kph (s):	5.3
Maximum speed (mph / kph):	171 / 275
Production, total number:	
Coupé:	1,860
Cabriolet:	1,138
Purchase prices:	
08/1995 Coupé:	DM 142,000
Cabriolet:	DM 159,850
08/1996 Coupé:	DM 143,500
Cabriolet:	DM 161,500
08/1997 Coupé:*	DM 143,500
Cabriolet:*	DM 161,500
*Only a few cars at Porsche dealers available	

911 Targa [Tiptronic S]
MY 1996–MY 1998

Engine

Engine design:	6-cylinder horizontally-opposed
Installation:	Rear-engine
Cooling system:	Air-cooled
Number & form of blower blades:	12, curved
Blower outside diameter (mm):	253
Engine type:	M 64/21 [M 64/22]
Displacement (cc):	3600
Bore x stroke (mm):	100 x 76.4
Engine output DIN (kW/hp):	210/285 at 6100rpm
Maximum torque (Nm/lb ft):	340/251 at 5250rpm
Output per litre (kW/l / hp/l):	58.3 / 79.2
Compression ratio:	11.3 : 1
Valve operation & camshaft drive:	ohc, cams driven by double chain, 2 valves per cylinder
Carburation:	Bosch DME, Motronic M 5.2, with sequential injection
Ignition system:	Bosch DME, dual ignition
Firing order:	1 - 6 - 2 - 4 - 3 - 5
Engine lubrication:	Dry sump
Engine oil total (l):	11.5

Transmission

Drive configuration:	Rear-axle drive
Manual gearbox:	6-speed (6-speed)
Option Tiptronic S:	[4-speed]
Transmission type:	G 50/21 (G 50/20)* [A 50/04]
Transmission ratios:	
1st gear:	3.818 (3.181) [2.479]
2nd gear:	2.150 (2.048) [1.479]
3rd gear:	1.560 (1.407) [1.000]
4th gear:	1.242 (1.118) [0.728]
5th gear:	1.027 (0.921)
6th gear:	0.821 (0.775)
Reverse gear:	2.857 (2.857) [2.086]
Drive ratio:	3.444 (3.444) [3.667]
*MY 1997	

Body, chassis, suspension, brakes, wheels

Body design:	Steel Targa body, 2 doors, 2 + 2 seats, entirely hot-dip galvanized body, side-impact protection beams in doors, electric Targa glass top with sliding glass element and wind deflector, flexible polyurethane front and rear bumpers with integrated aluminium beams, engine lid with integrated automatic rear spoiler, red non-reflecting valance with reverse gear and rear fog lamps
Suspension, front:	Individually suspended light-alloy lower wishbones, McPherson struts with coil springs, dual-tube gas-filled shock absorbers, anti-roll bar
Suspension, rear:	Individually suspended on light-alloy multi-wishbone axle with LSA system (Light weight, Stability, Agility) with progressive coil springs, dual-tube gas-filled shock absorbers, anti-roll bar
Brakes, front/rear (Size (mm)):	Ventilated and drilled discs (304 x 32) Ventilated and drilled discs (299 x 24) Black 4-piston fixed aluminium callipers / Black 4-piston fixed aluminium callipers Bosch ABS 5
Wheels, front/rear:	7 J x 17 / 9 J x 17
Tyres, front/rear:	205/50 ZR 17 / 255/40 ZR 17

Electrical system

Alternator (W/A):	1610 / 115
Battery (V/Ah):	12 / 75

Dimensions and weight

Track, front/rear (mm):	1405 / 1444
Wheelbase (mm):	2272
Length x width x height (mm):	4245 x 1735 x 1300
With sports suspension:	4245 x 1735 x 1285
Kerb weight DIN (kg):	1400 [1425]
Permissible gross weight (kg):	1740 [1765]
Luggage compartment (VDA (l)):	123
with 92 litre fuel tank:	100
Luggage volume interior*:	175
Fuel tank capacity (l):	73.5, including 10 reserve
Option:	92, including 12,5 reserve
C_w x A (m²):	0.33 x 1.86 = 0.614
Power/weight ratio (kg/kW / kg/hp):	6.66 [6.78] / 4.91 [5.00]
*on folded-down rear seat-backs	

Fuel consumption

89/491/EWG (mpg):	98 RON super plus unleaded
At constant 56mph/90kph:	37 [34.4]
At constant 74mph/120kph:	30.4 [28.8]
EG-urban cycle:	16.9 [17.9]
1/3 mix:	25.2 [25]
93/116/EG (mpg):	98 RON super plus unleaded
Urban:	15.5 [15.4]
Extra urban:	31 [31.6]
Combined:	22.7 [22.7]
CO_2-emissions (g/km):	289 [289]
MY 1997 - MY 1998:	
89/491/EWG (mpg):	98 RON super plus unleaded
At constant 56mph/90kph:	37.6 [34.8]
At constant 74mph/120kph:	31 [29.5]
EG-urban cycle:	17.2 [17.9]
1/3 mix:	25.6 [25.2]
93/116/EG (mpg):	98 RON super plus unleaded
Urban:	16 [15.5]
Extra urban:	32.8 [32.5]
Combined:	23.7 [23.1]
CO_2-emissions (g/km):	295 [303]

Performance, production, prices

Acceleration 0-62mph/100kph (s):	5.4 [6.4]
Maximum speed (mph / kph):	171 / 275 [167 / 270]
Production, total number:	4,583
Purchase price:	
08/1995 Targa:	DM 145,000 [DM 151,660]
08/1996 Targa:	DM 146,500 [DM 153,160]
08/1997 Targa:	DM 146,500 [DM 153,160]

911 Carrera 4S Coupé
MY 1996–MY 1998

Engine

Engine design:	6-cylinder horizontally-opposed
Installation:	Rear-engine
Cooling system:	Air-cooled
Number & form of blower blades:	12, curved
Blower outside diameter (mm):	253
Engine type:	M 64/21
Displacement (cc):	3600
Bore x stroke (mm):	100 x 76.4
Engine output DIN (kW/hp):	210/285 at 6100rpm
Maximum torque (Nm/lb ft):	340/251 at 5250rpm
Output per litre (kW/l / hp/l):	58.3 / 79.2
Compression ratio:	11.3 : 1
Valve operation & camshaft drive:	ohc, cams driven by double chain, 2 valves per cylinder
Carburation:	Bosch DME, Motronic M 5.2, with sequential injection
Ignition system:	Bosch DME, dual ignition
Firing order:	1 - 6 - 2 - 4 - 3 - 5
Engine lubrication:	Dry sump
Engine oil total (l):	11.5

Transmission

Drive configuration:	4-wheel-drive with visco-clutch, transaxle
Manual gearbox:	6-speed (6-speed)
Transmission type:	G 50/21 (G 50/20)*
Transmission ratios:	
1st gear:	3.818 (3.181)
2nd gear:	2.150 (2.048)
3rd gear:	1.560 (1.407)
4th gear:	1.242 (1.118)
5th gear:	1.027 (0.921)
6th gear:	0.821 (0.775)
Reverse gear:	2.857 (2.857)
Drive ratio:	3.444 (3.444)
*MY 1997	

Body, chassis, suspension, brakes, wheels

Body design:	Steel coupé body, 2 doors, 2 + 2 seats, entirely hot-dip galvanized body, wider rear wings and side skirts, side-impact protection beams in doors, flexible polyurethane front and rear bumpers with integrated aluminium beams, front bumpers with three air intakes, engine lid with integrated automatic rear spoiler, red non-reflecting valance with integrated reverse gear and rear fog lamps
Option:	Electric sunroof
Suspension, front:	Individually suspended light-alloy lower wishbones, McPherson struts with coil springs, dual-tube gas-filled shock absorbers, anti-roll bar
Suspension, rear:	Individually suspended on light-alloy multi-wishbone axle with LSA system (Light weight, Stability, Agility) with progressive coil springs, dual-tube gas-filled shock absorbers, anti-roll bar
Brakes, front/rear (Size (mm)):	Ventilated and drilled discs (322 x 32) Ventilated and drilled discs (322 x 28) Red 4-piston fixed aluminium callipers / Red 4-piston fixed aluminium callipers Bosch ABS 5
Wheels, front/rear:	8 J x 18 / 10 J x 18
Tyres, front/rear:	225/40 ZR 18 / 285/30 ZR 18

Electrical system

Alternator (W/A):	1610 / 115
Battery (V/Ah):	12 / 75

Dimensions and weight

Track, front/rear (mm):	1411 / 1504
Wheelbase (mm):	2272
Length x width x height (mm):	4245 x 1795 x 1285
Kerb weight DIN (kg):	1450
Permissible gross weight (kg):	1790
Luggage compartment (VDA (l)):	123
with 92 litre fuel tank:	100
Luggage volume interior*:	175
Fuel tank capacity (l):	73.5, including 10 reserve

Option:	92, including 12.5 reserve
C_w x A (m²):	0.34 x 1.93 = 0.656
Power/weight ratio (kg/kW/kg/hp):	6.90 / 5.08
*on folded-down rear seat-backs	

Fuel consumption

89/491/EWG (mpg):	98 RON super plus unleaded
At constant 56mph/90kph:	35
At constant 74mph/120kph:	29.5
EG-urban cycle:	16.7
1/3 mix:	24.5
93/116/EG (mpg):	98 RON super plus unleaded
Urban:	15.3
Extra urban:	29.5
Combined:	22.1
CO_2-emissions (g/km):	298
MY 1997 - MY 1998:	
89/491/EWG (mpg):	98 RON super plus unleaded
At constant 56mph/90kph:	36.3
At constant 74mph/120kph:	30
EG-urban cycle:	17
1/ 3 mix:	25
93/116/EG (mpg):	98 RON super plus unleaded
Urban:	15.7
Extra urban:	31
Combined:	23
CO_2-emissions (g/km):	301

Performance, production, prices

Acceleration 0-62mph/100kph (s):	5.3
Maximum speed (mph / kph):	168 / 270
Production, total number:	6,948
Purchase price:	
08/1995 Coupé:	DM 158,100
08/1996 Coupé:	DM 159,800
08/1997 Coupé:	DM 159,800

911 turbo Coupé with performance kit MY 1996–MY 1998

Engine

Engine design:	6-cylinder horizontally-opposed, twin-turbo charger, twin-intercooler
Installation:	Rear-engine
Cooling system:	Air-cooled
Number & form of blower blades:	11, straight
Blower outside diameter (mm):	245
Engine type:	M 64/60 R
Displacement (cc):	3600
Bore x stroke (mm):	100 x 76.4
Engine output DIN (kW/hp):	316/430 at 5750rpm
Maximum torque (Nm/lb ft):	540/398 at 4500rpm
Output per litre (kW/l / hp/l):	87.8 / 119.4
Compression ratio:	8.0 : 1
Valve operation & camshaft drive:	ohc, cams driven by double chain, 2 valves per cylinder
Carburation:	Bosch DME, Motronic M 5.2, with sequential injection
Ignition system:	Bosch DME
Firing order:	1 - 6 - 2 - 4 - 3 - 5
Engine lubrication:	Dry sump
Engine oil total (l):	11.5

Transmission

Drive configuration:	4-wheel-drive with visco-clutch, transaxle
Manual gearbox:	6-speed
Transmission type:	G 64/51
Transmission ratios:	
1st gear:	3.818
2nd gear:	2.150
3rd gear:	1.560
4th gear:	1.212
5th gear:	0.937
6th gear:	0.750
Reverse gear:	2.857
Drive ratio:	3.444
Ltd slip diff. load/deceleration (%):	25 / 40

Body, chassis, suspension, brakes, wheels

Body design:	Steel coupé body, 2 doors, 2 + 2 seats, entirely hot-dip galvanized body, wider rear wings and side skirts, side-impact protection beams in doors, flexible polyurethane front and rear bumpers with integrated aluminium beams, front bumpers with three air intakes, plastic engine lid with integrated rear wing, red non-reflecting valance with integrated reverse gear and rear fog lamps
Option:	Electric sunroof
Suspension, front:	Individually suspended light-alloy lower wishbones, McPherson struts with coil springs, dual-tube gas-filled shock absorbers, anti-roll bar
Suspension, rear:	Individually suspended on light-alloy multi-wishbone axle with LSA system (Light weight, Stability, Agility) with progressive coil springs, dual-tube gas-filled shock absorbers, anti-roll bar
Brakes, front/rear (Size (mm)):	Ventilated and drilled discs (322 x 32) Ventilated and drilled discs (322 x 28) Red 4-piston fixed aluminium callipers / Red 4-piston fixed aluminium callipers Bosch ABS 5
Wheels, front/rear:	8 J x 18 / 10 J x 18
Tyres, front/rear:	225/40 ZR 18 / 285/30 ZR 18

Electrical system

Alternator (W/A):	1610 / 115
Battery (V/Ah):	12 / 75

Dimensions and weight

Track, front/rear (mm):	1411 / 1504
Wheelbase (mm):	2272
Length x width x height (mm):	4245 x 1795 x 1285
Kerb weight DIN (kg):	1500
Permissible gross weight (kg):	1840
Luggage compartment (VDA (l)):	123
with 92 litre fuel tank:	100
Luggage volume interior*:	175
Fuel tank capacity (l):	73.5, including 15 reserve
Option:	92, including 15 reserve
C_w x A (m²):	0.34 x 1.93 = 0.656
Power/weight ratio (kg/kW/ kg/hp):	4.74 / 3.48
*on folded-down rear seat-backs	

Fuel consumption

89/491/EWG (mpg):	98 RON super plus unleaded
At constant 56mph/90kph:	33.5
At constant 74mph/120kph:	28.2
EG-urban cycle:	13.4
1/3 mix:	21.5
93/115/EG (mpg):	98 RON super plus unleaded
Urban:	12.1
Extra urban:	26
Combined:	18.3
CO_2-emissions (g/km):	368

Performance, production, prices

Acceleration 0-62mph/100kph (s):	less than 4.5
Maximum speed (mph / kph):	more than 180 / 290
Production, total number:	n/a
Purchase price:	
01/1996 performance kit new car:	DM 12,500
Conversion performance kit:	DM 13,150
Performance kit only:	DM 11,900

911 Carrera S Coupé [Tiptronic S]
MY 1997–MY 1998

Engine

Engine design:	6-cylinder horizontally-opposed
Installation:	Rear-engine
Cooling system:	Air-cooled
Number & form of blower blades:	12, curved
Blower outside diameter (mm):	253
Engine type:	M 64/21 [M 64/22]
Displacement (cc):	3600
Bore x stroke (mm):	100 x 76.4
Engine output DIN (kW/hp):	210/285 at 6100rpm
Maximum torque (Nm/lb ft):	340/251 at 5250rpm
Output per litre (kW/l / hp/l):	58.3 / 79.2
Compression ratio:	11.3 : 1
Valve operation & camshaft drive:	ohc, cams driven by double chain, 2 valves per cylinder
Carburation:	Bosch DME, Motronic M 5.2, with sequential injection
Ignition system:	Bosch DME, dual ignition
Firing order:	1 - 6 - 2 - 4 - 3 - 5
Engine lubrication:	Dry sump
Engine oil total (l):	11.5

Transmission

Drive configuration:	Rear-axle drive
Manual gearbox:	6-speed
Option Tiptronic S:	[4-speed]
Transmission type:	G 50/20 [A 50/04]
Transmission ratios:	
1st gear:	3.181 [2.479]
2nd gear:	2.048 [1.479]
3rd gear:	1.407 [1.000]
4th gear:	1.118 [0.728]
5th gear:	0.921
6th gear:	0.775
Reverse gear:	2.857 [2.086]
Drive ratio:	3.444 [3.667]

Body, chassis, suspension, brakes, wheels

Body design:	Steel coupé body, 2 doors, 2 + 2 seats, entirely hot-dip galvanized body, wider rear wings and side skirts, side-impact protection beams in doors, flexible polyurethane front and rear bumpers with integrated aluminium beams, front bumpers with three air-intakes, engine lid with integrated automatic rear spoiler with twin-grille, red non-reflecting valance with integrated reverse gear and rear fog lamps
Option:	Electric sunroof
Suspension, front:	Individually suspended light-alloy lower wishbones, McPherson struts with coil springs, dual-tube gas-filled shock absorbers, anti-roll bar
Suspension, rear:	Individually suspended on light-alloy multi-wishbone axle with LSA system (Light weight, Stability, Agility) with progressive coil springs, dual-tube gas-filled shock absorbers, anti-roll bar
Brakes, front/rear (Size (mm)):	Ventilated and drilled discs (304 x 32) Ventilated and drilled discs (299 x 24) Black 4-piston fixed aluminium callipers / Black 4-piston fixed aluminium callipers Bosch ABS 5
Wheels, front/rear:	7 J x 17 / 9 J x 17
Tyres, front/rear:	205/50 ZR 17 / 255/40 ZR 17
Option:	8 J x 18 / 10 J x 18 225/40 ZR 18 / 285/30 ZR 18

Electrical system

Alternator (W/A):	1610 / 115
Battery (V/Ah):	12 / 75

Dimensions and weight

Track, front/rear (mm):	1405 / 1536
Wheelbase (mm):	2272
Length x width x height (mm):	4245 x 1795 x 1285
Kerb weight DIN (kg):	1400 [1425]
Permissible gross weight (kg):	1740 [1765]
Luggage compartment (VDA (l)):	123
with 92 litre fuel tank:	100
Luggage volume interior*:	175
Fuel tank capacity (l):	73.5, including 10 reserve
Option:	92, including 12.5 reserve
C_w x A (m²):	0.34 x 1.93 = 0.656
Power/weight ratio (kg/kW/kg/hp):	6.66 [6.78] / 4.91 [5.00]
*on folded-down rear seat-backs	

Fuel consumption

89/491/EWG (mpg):	98 RON super plus unleaded
At constant 56mph/90kph:	37 [34.4]
At constant 74mph/120kph:	30.4 [28.8]
EG-urban cycle:	17.2 [17.9]
1/3 mix:	25.4 [25]
93/116/EG (mpg):	98 RON super plus unleaded
Urban:	15.9 [15.2]
Extra urban:	32.1 [32.5]
Combined:	23.5 [22.7]
CO_2-emissions (g/km):	296 [307]

Performance, production, prices

Acceleration 0-62mph/100kph (s):	5.4 [6.4]
Maximum speed (mph / kph):	167 / 270 [164 / 265]
Production, total number:	3,714
Purchase prices:	
08/1996 Coupé:	DM 137,500 [144,160]
08/1997 Coupé:	DM 137,500 [144,160]

911 turbo S Coupé MY 1998

Engine

Engine design:	6-cylinder horizontally-opposed, twin turbo charger, twin intercooler
Installation:	Rear-engine
Cooling system:	Air-cooled
Number & form of blower blades:	11, straight
Blower outside diameter (mm):	245
Engine type:	M 64/60 S
Displacement (cc):	3600
Bore x stroke (mm):	100 x 76.4
Engine output DIN (kW/hp):	331/450 at 6000rpm
Maximum torque (Nm/lb ft):	585/431 at 4500rpm
Output per litre (kW/l / hp/l):	91.9 / 125.0
Compression ratio:	8.0 : 1
Valve operation & camshaft drive:	ohc, cams driven by double chain, 2 valves per cylinder
Carburation:	Bosch DME, Motronic M 5.2, with sequential injection
Ignition system:	Bosch DME
Firing order:	1 - 6 - 2 - 4 - 3 - 5
Engine lubrication:	Dry sump
Engine oil total (l):	11.5

Transmission

Drive configuration:	4-wheel-drive with visco-clutch, transaxle
Manual gearbox:	6-speed
Transmission type:	G 64/51
Transmission ratios:	
1st gear:	3.818
2nd gear:	2.150
3rd gear:	1.560
4th gear:	1.212
5th gear:	0.937
6th gear:	0.750
Reverse gear:	2.857
Drive ratio:	3.444
Ltd slip diff. load/deceleration (%):	25 / 40

Body, chassis, suspension, brakes, wheels

Body design:	Steel Coupé body, 2 doors, 2 + 2 seats, entirely hot-dip galvanized body, wider rear wings with air intakes and side skirts, side-impact protection beams in doors, flexible polyurethane front and rear bumpers with integrated aluminium beams, front bumpers with three air intakes and additional air intakes for brake cooling, plastic engine lid with integrated rear wing (Aerokit II), red non-reflecting valance with integrated reverse gear and rear fog lamps
Option:	Electric sunroof
Suspension, front:	Individually suspended light-alloy lower wishbones, McPherson struts with coil springs, dual-tube gas-filled shock absorbers, anti-roll bar
Suspension, rear:	Individually suspended on light-alloy multi-wishbone axle with LSA system (Light weight, Stability, Agility) with progressive coil springs, dual-tube gas-filled shock absorbers, anti-roll bar
Brakes, front/rear (Size (mm)):	Ventilated and drilled discs (322 x 32) Ventilated and drilled discs (322 x 28) Red 4-piston fixed aluminium callipers / Red 4-piston fixed aluminium callipers Bosch ABS 5
Wheels, front/rear:	8 J x 18 / 10 J x 18
Tyres, front/rear:	225/40 ZR 18 / 285/30 ZR 18

Electrical system

Alternator (W/A):	1610 / 115
Battery (V/Ah):	12 / 75

Dimensions and weight

Track, front/rear (mm):	1411 / 1504
Wheelbase (mm):	2272
Length x width x height (mm):	4245 x 1795 x 1285
Kerb weight DIN (kg):	1500
Permissible gross weight (kg):	1840
Luggage compartment (VDA (l)):	123
with 92 litre fuel tank:	100
Luggage volume interior*:	175
Fuel tank capacity (l):	73.5, including 15 reserve
Option:	92, including 15 reserve
C_w x A (m²):	0.34 x 1.93 = 0.656
Power/weight ratio (kg/kW/kg/hp):	4.53 / 3.33
*on folded-down rear seat-backs	

Fuel consumption

89/491/EWG (mpg):	98 RON super plus unleaded
At constant 56mph/90kph:	33.5*
At constant 74mph/120kph:	28.2*
EG-urban cycle:	13.4*
1/3 mix:	21.5*
93/115/EG (mpg):	98 RON super plus unleaded
Urban:	12.1 *
Extra urban:	26.0*
Combined:	18.3*
CO_2-emissions (g/km):	368*
*Basic engine 430 hp	

Performance, production, prices

Acceleration 0-62mph/100kph (s):	app. 4.1
Maximum speed (mph / kph):	186 / 300
Production, total number:	345
Purchase prices:	
08/1997 Coupé:	DM 304,650
04/1998 Coupé:	DM 307,300

911 turbo Coupé
with performance kit MY 1998

Engine

Engine design:	6-cylinder horizontally-opposed, twin turbo charger, twin intercooler
Installation:	Rear-engine
Cooling system:	Air-cooled
Number & form of blower blades:	11, straight
Blower outside diameter (mm):	245
Engine type:	M 64/60 RS
Displacement (cc):	3600
Bore x stroke (mm):	100 x 76.4
Engine output DIN (kW/hp):	331/450 at 6000rpm
Maximum torque (Nm/lb ft):	585/431 at 4500rpm
Output per litre (kW/l / hp/l):	91.9 / 125.0
Compression ratio:	8.0 : 1
Valve operation & camshaft drive:	ohc, cams driven by double chain, 2 valves per cylinder
Carburation:	Bosch DME, Motronic M 5.2, with sequential injection
Ignition system:	Bosch DME
Firing order:	1 - 6 - 2 - 4 - 3 - 5
Engine lubrication:	Dry sump
Engine oil total (l):	11.5

Transmission

Drive configuration:	4-wheel-drive with visco-clutch, transaxle
Manual gearbox:	6-speed
Transmission type:	G 64/51
Transmission ratios:	
1st gear:	3.818
2nd gear:	2.150
3rd gear:	1.560
4th gear:	1.212
5th gear:	0.937
6th gear:	0.750
Reverse gear:	2.857
Drive ratio:	3.444
Ltd slip diff. load/deceleration (%):	25 / 40

Body, chassis, suspension, brakes, wheels

Body design:	Steel coupé body, 2 doors, 2 + 2 seats, hot-dip galvanized body, wider rear wings and side skirts, side-impact protection, flexible polyurethane front and rear bumpers with integral aluminium beams, front bumpers with 3 air-intakes, plastic engine lid with integral rear wing, red non-reflecting valance with integrated reverse and rear fog lamps
Option:	Electric sunroof
Suspension, front:	Individually suspended light-alloy lower wishbones, McPherson struts with coil springs, dual-tube gas-filled shock absorbers, anti-roll bar
Suspension, rear:	Individually suspended on light-alloy multi-wishbone axle with LSA system, with progressive coil springs, dual-tube gas-filled shock absorbers, anti-roll bar
Brakes, front/rear (Size (mm)):	Ventilated and drilled discs (322 x 32) Ventilated and drilled discs (322 x 28) Red 4-piston fixed aluminium callipers / Red 4-piston fixed aluminium callipers Bosch ABS 5
Wheels, front/rear:	8 J x 18 / 10 J x 18
Tyres, front/rear:	225/40 ZR 18 / 285/30 ZR 18

Electrical system

Alternator (W/A):	1610 / 115
Battery (V/Ah):	12 / 75

Dimensions and weight

Track, front/rear (mm):	1411 / 1504
Wheelbase (mm):	2272
Length x width x height (mm):	4245 x 1795 x 1285
Kerb weight DIN (kg):	1500
Permissible gross weight (kg):	1840
Luggage compartment (VDA (l)):	123
with 92 litre fuel tank:	100
Luggage volume interior*:	175
Fuel tank capacity (l):	73.5, including 15 reserve
Option:	92, including 15 reserve
C_w x A (m²):	0.34 x 1.93 = 0.656
Power/weight ratio (kg/kW/kg/hp):	4.53 / 3.33
*on folded-down rear seat-backs	

Fuel consumption

89/491/EWG (mpg):	98 RON super plus unleaded
At constant 56mph/90kph:	33.5*
At constant 74mph/120kph:	28.2*
EG-urban cycle:	13.4*
1/3 mix:	21.5*
93/115/EG (mpg):	98 RON super plus unleaded
Urban:	12.1 *
Extra urban:	26.0*
Combined:	18.3*
CO_2-emissions (g/km):	368*
*Basic engine 430 hp	

Performance, production, prices

Acceleration 0-62mph/100kph (s):	app. 4.1
Maximum speed (mph / kph):	186 / 300
Production, total number:	n/a
Purchase price for performance kit	
08/1997 Coupé:	DM 29,800
04/1998 Coupé:	DM 29,800

911 GT 2 Coupé
MY 1998

Engine

Engine design:	6-cylinder horizontally-opposed, twin-turbo charger, twin-intercooler
Installation:	Rear-engine
Cooling system:	Air-cooled
Number & form of blower blades:	11, straight
Blower outside diameter (mm):	245
Engine type:	M 64/60 S
Displacement (cc):	3600
Bore x stroke (mm):	100 x 76.4
Engine output DIN (kW/hp):	331/450 at 6000rpm
Maximum torque (Nm/lb ft):	585/431 at 4500rpm
Output per litre (kW/l / hp/l):	91.9 / 125.0
Compression ratio:	8.0 : 1
Valve operation & camshaft drive:	ohc, cams driven by double chain, 2 valves per cylinder
Carburation:	Bosch DME, Motronic M 5.2, with sequential injection
Ignition system:	Bosch DME
Firing order:	1 - 6 - 2 - 4 - 3 - 5
Engine lubrication:	Dry sump
Engine oil total (l):	11.5

Transmission

Drive configuration:	Rear-axle drive
Manual gearbox:	6-speed
Transmission type:	G 64/51
Transmission ratios:	
1st gear:	3.818
2nd gear:	2.150
3rd gear:	1.560
4th gear:	1.212
5th gear:	0.937
6th gear:	0.750
Reverse gear:	2.857
Drive ratio:	3.444
Ltd slip diff. load/deceleration (%):	25 / 40

Body, chassis, suspension, brakes, wheels

Body design:	Steel coupé body, 2 doors, 2 seats, entirely hot-dip galvanized body, wider rear wings and side skirts, side-impact protection beams in doors, flexible polyurethane front and rear bumpers with integrated aluminium beams, big front spoiler, polyurethane wing flares, plastic rear lid with integrated, adjustable rear wing with air-intakes, aluminium bonnet and doors, red non-reflecting valance with integrated reverse gear and rear fog lamps, thin-glass rear and side windows

Suspension, front:	Individually suspended light-alloy lower wishbones, McPherson struts with coil springs, dual-tube gas-filled shock absorbers, anti-roll bar
Suspension, rear:	Individually suspended on light-alloy multi-wishbone axle with LSA system (Light weight, Stability, Agility) with progressive coil springs, dual-tube gas-filled shock absorbers, anti-roll bar
Brakes, front/rear (Size (mm)):	Ventilated and drilled discs (322 x 32) Ventilated and drilled discs (322 x 28) Red 4-piston fixed aluminium callipers / Red 4-piston fixed aluminium callipers Bosch ABS 5
Wheels, front/rear:	9 J x 18 / 11 J x 18
Tyres, front/rear:	235/40 ZR 18 / 285/35 ZR 18

Electrical system

Alternator (W/A):	1610 / 115
Battery (V/Ah):	12 / 36

Dimensions and weight

Track, front/rear (mm):	1475 / 1550
Wheelbase (mm):	2272
Length x width x height (mm):	4245 x 1855 x 1270
Kerb weight DIN (kg):	1295
Permissible gross weight (kg):	1575
Luggage compartment (VDA (l)):	100
Fuel tank capacity (l):	92, including 15 reserve
C_w x A (m²):	0.34 x 2.04 = 0.694
Power/weight ratio (kg/kW/kg/hp):	3.91 / 2.87

Fuel consumption

89/491/EWG (mpg):	98 RON super plus unleaded
At constant 56mph/90kph:	33.5*
At constant 74mph/120kph:	28.2*
EG-urban cycle:	13.4*
1/3 mix:	21.5*
93/115/EG (mpg):	98 RON super plus unleaded
Urban:	12.1 *
Extra urban:	26*
Combined:	18.3*
CO_2-emissions (g/km):	368*
*Basic engine 430hp	

Performance, production, prices

Acceleration 0-62mph/100kph (s):	app. 4.1
Maximum speed (mph / kph):	186 / 300
Production, total number:	21
Purchase price:	
08/1997 Coupé:	DM 287,500

Porsche GT 1
1996

Engine

Engine design:	6-cylinder horizontally-opposed, twin-turbocharger, twin-intercooler
Installation:	Mid-engine
Cooling system:	Water-cooled
Engine type:	M 96/83
Displacement (cc):	3164
Bore x stroke (mm):	95 x 74.4
Engine output DIN (kW/hp):	400/544 at 7200rpm
Maximum torque (Nm/lb ft):	600/443 at 4250rpm
Output per litre (kW/l / hp/l):	126.4 / 171.9
Compression ratio:	9.0 : 1
Valve operation & camshaft drive:	dohc, cams diven by double chain, 4 valves per cylinder
Carburation:	Bosch DME, Motronic M 5.2, sequential ignition or TAG
Ignition system:	Bosch DME
Maximum boost (bar):	0,95 - 1,05
Firing order:	1 - 6 - 2 - 4 - 3 - 5
Engine oil total (l):	15

Transmission

Drive configuration:	Rear-axle drive
Manual gearbox:	6-speed
Transmission type:	G 96/82
Transmission ratios:	
1st gear:	3.153
2nd gear:	2.000
3rd gear:	1.440
4th gear:	1.133
5th gear:	0.941
6th gear:	0.829
Reverse gear:	2.857
Drive ratio:	3.444
Ltd slip diff. load/deceleration (%):	40 / 60

Body, chassis, suspension, brakes, wheels

Body design:	Steel coupé body, 2 doors, 2 seats, entirely hot-dip galvanized body, outside body parts made of carbon-fibre-reinforced plastic, fixed rear wing, red non-reflecting valance with integrated reverse gear and rear fog lamps

Suspension, front:	Individually suspended on double wishbones with pushrods, with coil springs, single-tube gas-filled shock absorbers, anti-roll bar
Suspension, rear:	Individually suspended on double wishbones with pushrods, with coil springs, single-tube gas-filled shock absorbers, anti-roll bar
Brakes, front/rear (Size (mm)):	Ventilated and drilled discs (380 x 32) / Ventilated and drilled discs (380 x 32) titanium colour 8-piston monobloc aluminium fixed callipers / titanium colour 4-piston monobloc aluminium fixed callipers Bosch ABS
Wheels, front/rear:	11 J x 18 / 13 J x 18
Tyres, front/rear:	295/35 ZR 18 / 335/30 ZR 18

Electrical system

Alternator (W/A):	1610 / 115
Battery (V/Ah):	12 / 50

Dimensions and weight

Track, front/rear (mm):	1502 / 1588
Wheelbase (mm):	2500
Lenght x width x height (mm):	4710 x 1980 x 1173
Kerb weight DIN (kg):	1120
Luggage compartment (l):	150
Fuel tank capacity (l):	73, including 10 reserve
C_w x A (m²):	n/a
Power/weight ratio (kg/kW/ kg/hp):	2.80 / 2.05

Fuel consumption

(mpg):	9.7–18.8; 98 RON super plus unleaded

Performance, production, prices

Acceleration 0-62mph/100kph (s):	3.7
0–100mph/160kph (s):	7.1
0–124mph/200kph (s):	10.5
Maximum speed (mph / kph):	192 / 310
Production, total number:	2

911 GT 1
1997–1998

Engine

Engine design:	6-cylinder horizontally-opposed, twin-turbo charger, twin-intercooler
Installation:	Mid-engine
Cooling system:	Water-cooled
Engine type:	M 96/83
Displacement (cc):	3164
Bore x stroke (mm):	95 x 74.4
Engine output DIN (kW/hp):	400/544 at 7200rpm
Maximum torque (Nm/lb ft):	600/443 at 4250rpm
Output per litre (kW/l / hp/l):	126.4 / 171.9
Compression ratio:	9.0 : 1
Valve operation & camshaft drive:	dohc, cams diven by double chain, 4 valves per cylinder
Carburation:	Bosch DME, Motronic M 5.2, sequential ignition or TAG
Ignition system:	Bosch DME
Maximum boost (bar):	0,95 - 1,05
Firing order:	1 - 6 - 2 - 4 - 3 - 5
Engine oil total (l):	15

Transmission

Drive configuration:	Rear-axle drive
Manual gearbox:	6-speed
Transmission type:	G 96/82
Transmission ratios:	
1st gear:	3.153
2nd gear:	2.000
3rd gear:	1.440
4th gear:	1.133
5th gear:	0.941
6th gear:	0.829
Reverse gear:	2.857
Drive ratio:	3.444
Ltd slip diff. load/deceleration (%):	40 / 60

Body, chassis, suspension, brakes, wheels

Body design:	Steel coupé body, 2 doors, 2 seats, entirely hot-dip galvanized body, outside body parts made of carbon-fibre-reinforced plastic, fixed rear wing
Suspension, front:	Individually suspended on double wishbones with pushrods, with coil springs, single-tube gas-filled shock absorbers, anti-roll bar
Suspension, rear:	Individually suspended on double wishbones with pushrods, with coil springs, single-tube gas-filled shock absorbers, anti-roll bar
Brakes, front/rear (Size (mm)):	Ventilated and drilled discs (380 x 32) / Ventilated and drilled discs (380 x 32) titanium-colour 8-piston monobloc aluminium fixed callipers / titanium-colour 4-piston monobloc aluminium fixed callipers Bosch ABS
Wheels, front/rear:	11 J x 18 / 13 J x 18
Tyres, front/rear:	295/35 ZR 18 / 335/30 ZR 18

Electrical system

Alternator (W/A):	1610 / 115
Battery (V/Ah):	12 / 50

Dimensions and weight

Track, front/rear (mm):	1502 / 1588
Wheelbase (mm):	2500
Lenght x width x height (mm):	4710 x 1980 x 1173
Kerb weight DIN (kg):	1120
Luggage compartment (l):	150
Fuel tank capacity (l):	73, including 10 reserve
C_w x A (m^2):	n/a
Power/weight ratio (kg/kW/kg/hp):	2.80 / 2.05

Fuel consumption

(mpg):	9.7–18.8; 98 RON super plus unleaded

Performance, production, prices

Acceleration 0-62mph/100kph (s):	3.7
0–100mph/160kph (s):	7.1
0–124mph/200kph (s):	10.5
Maximum speed (mph / kph):	192 / 310
Production, total number:	21
Purchase price:	
08/1997 Coupé:	DM 1,550,000

Porsche 911 (Type 996)

Model year 1998 (W Programme)

The new 911 Carrera, known within the factory as the Type 996, was Porsche's successor to its air-cooled classic. The 996 Carrera was developed completely from scratch. Other than its '911 Carrera' designation and a six-cylinder rear-mounted boxer engine, the 996 had nothing in common with the previous 911.

Its larger body offered noticeably more interior space, and the wheelbase grew to 2350mm. Because of a shared-parts concept, the new 911 Carrera and the Boxster had the same bonnet lid, front headlamps with their integral low beam, high beam, indicators and fog lamps and front wings and doors. Floorpans forward of the B-pillars were also identical. The nose of the 911 was, however, shaped differently. One special feature of the body was that the same basic body-shell could be built up as a right-hand or left-hand-drive car. Despite larger dimensions, the new 911 Carrera had a 50kg (110lb) lower DIN kerb weight than its predecessor, thanks to intelligent application of lightweight design. Along with two-side hot-dip galvanized sheet-steel, the body shell included high-strength steel to increase body stiffness. Side-impact beams in the doors were made of extremely strong boron steel. Also, the body structure consisted of so-called 'tailored blanks', made using a process which built up body parts of varying thicknesses by welding; heavier-gauge steel was used only where it was really needed. About an extra 10kg (22lb) was pared off the body weight by trimming the edges of steel sheets so that only the necessary weld tabs were retained. These specially-cut edges also provided added torsional stiffness. Overall, torsional stiffness of the new body was 45 per cent higher, and bending stiffness was even 50 per cent higher than its predecessor. At the rear of the car, large, higher-mounted tail lamps with orange indicators were an obvious change. The 911's trademark red tail-light band was missing entirely from the new Carrera. Wing mirrors were no longer attached to the doors, but ahead of the side windows. The drag coefficient of the new 911 Carrera was measured at 0.30cd. The boot, with a capacity of 130 litres (4.6cu ft) included a mini spare tyre mounted vertically ahead of the 64-litre (14-gall) fuel tank.

Like the Boxster's engine, that of the new 911 Carrera was water-cooled. Increasingly strict exhaust and noise emissions standards made this step i nevitable. Liquid cooling has the advantage of damping noise generated in the cylinders by the combustion process. Also, the introduction of multi-valve technology on high-performance engines offered exhaust quality benefits. Cylinder-cooling was in crossflow configuration, so that all cylinders were exposed to the same coolant temperature. Two coolant radiators were mounted in the nose of the car, ahead of the wheels. Displacement of the over-square engine (stroke dimension less than bore) was 3387cc. Its 96mm cylinder bore was less than that of its predecessor, while its 78mm stroke was somewhat longer. The compression ratio remained at 11.3:1, as did the 118mm cylinder spacing. The cylinder running surfaces were created by the Lokasil process. The desired microscopically rough cylinder surface had specific properties which resulted in better oil film retention. Oil was supplied by an integral dry-sump lubrication system with a capacity of 10.25 litres, without a separate oil tank. The two crankcase halves were made using a new 'squeeze casting' process, a special aluminium casting technique. The seven-bearing crankshaft was borne by an aluminium main bearing carrier, with embedded cast-iron inserts in the bearing areas. The exhaust camshafts were driven off the crankshaft by double chains and an intermediate shaft. The intake camshafts, in turn, were driven by simple chains from the exhaust shafts. Intake camshaft timing could be varied by as much as 25 degrees, independent of engine speed, by the VarioCam system. This reduced emissions and stabilized idle at low engine speeds, increased mid-range torque and produced more peak power at high engine speeds. Hydraulic valve-lash adjustment was, of course, standard in the new 911 engine. Engine management was handled by a Bosch Motronic M 5.2. This controlled the sequential fuel-injection system and six individual ignition coils of the distributorless ignition system. The two-stage resonance induction system modulated the induced air mass in the intake tract in response to engine speed, providing improved cylinder filling. For improved torque response, the resonance flap was closed at speeds between 2700rpm and 5100rpm. The exhaust system was made of stainless steel and consisted of two independent exhaust streams, one per cylinder bank, each with its own metal catalyst and oxygen sensor. Exhaust gases passed through an oval tailpipe on each side of the car. All these efforts showed in the new engine's performance data: the water-cooled boxer developed 300hp (221kW) at 6800rpm; the rev limiter cut in at 7300rpm. Maximum torque of 350Nm (258lb ft) was achieved at 4600rpm.

The six speeds of the manual transmission were selected by means of a newly-developed cable change. Clutch diameter was 240mm. As an option, buyers could choose a new 5-speed Tiptronic S.

For suspension, Porsche designed a front MacPherson-strut system with 'disconnected' aluminium locating links. A longitudinal link and transverse link were joined by means of elastic rubber bushing. The strut assemblies, front crossmember, anti-roll bar and steering box formed a single unit. The LSA axle was a weight-optimized multi-link suspension system with a subframe providing greatly improved handling properties. LSA was an acronym for 'lightweight, stable, agile'. Maximum lateral acceleration was in excess of 1.0g. The brake system consisted of black-painted monobloc fixed callipers and ventilated, cross-drilled discs. (Monobloc callipers were manufactured as a single piece). The new Carrera took advantage of Bosch's continued development of the ABS 5.3 anti-lock brake system.

Stock wheels for the new Carrera were 17-inch 'Carrera Design' rims. Front tyres were 205/50 ZR 17 on 7-inch wheels; rears were 255/40 ZR 17 on 9-inch alloys. As an option, customers could order turbo wheels, 7.5 J x 18 with 225/40 ZR 18 at the front, and 10 J x 18 with 265/35 ZR 18 at the rear.

The 911/Boxster shared-components concept continued in the interior. The instrument panel looked familiar, even though the 911 Carrera had five instruments to the Boxster's three. An analog tachometer took centre stage, with a selectable digital speed or on-board computer display integrated within its lower segment. The analog speedometer was mounted to its left, with a digital odometer display. A voltmeter was mounted on the far left. To the right of the tach, a combination instrument displayed analog coolant temperature and fuel level, as well as digital time and the new oil level monitor, readable when the engine was shut off. On vehicles equipped with the Tiptronic S, the combi instrument also included an LED display for the selected gear. On the far right was an oil-pressure gauge. As on the Boxster, brake and clutch

pedals were mounted in a 'hanging' configuration. Driver and passenger airbags were standard. As on the Boxster, the 911 Carrera had no glove compartment in the dashboard. As an option, 30-litre (1.1cu ft) side air-bags were available, as the Porsche Side-Impact Protection System (POSIP). These protected occupants' upper torso and head in the event of a side-impact. Their size and design also provided protection in the open Cabriolet. As was typical Porsche practice, headrests were integrated in the seat-backs. The partial-leather front seats were fitted with electric backrest rake adjustment, while lower cushion reach and height were manually adjustable. The steering wheel rim was axially adjustable over a range of 40mm on either side of centre; the wheel, shifter, handbrake handle and inner door handles were leather covered. Electric windows with automatic up/down function and electrically-adjustable and heatable wing mirrors were standard equipment. A new feature was a small storage space behind the rear seats, with a 65-litre (2.3cu ft) capacity, which could be expanded to 200 litres (7.1cu ft) by folding down the rear seat-backs. The Porsche Communication Management (PCM) system, with its large colour-monitor display in the centre console, was available as an option. PCM served as an information and navigation system, encompassing a cassette radio, GSM hands-free telephone, GPS navigation system with separate CD-ROM drive, and on-board computer. Another interesting option was Traction Control (TC), which combined Automatic Brake Differential (ABD) and Acceleration Slip Regulation (ASR), and, on manual-transmission cars, a torque-sensing limited-slip differential.

The 911 Carrera Cabriolet was available as of April 1998. The electrically-operated hood included a flexible plastic rear window and a sound-insulating headliner. With the vehicle parked, the hood could be raised or lowered in just 20 seconds. With its Z-folding design, even with the hood down, only its top side was exposed. When lowered, the hood's rear section automatically disappeared under a metal cover. Cumbersome unbuttoning, as on its predecessor, became a thing of the past. For better all-round visibility, the Cabriolet now had two small rear quarterlights. Two retracted roll bars were mounted behind the rear seats; in the event of an accident, these would deploy in a fraction of a second. A 33kg (73lb) aluminium hardtop, with electrically-heatable rear window, was included as Cabriolet standard equipment.

When equipped with a six-speed manual transmission, the 911 Carrera Coupé accelerated to 62mph (100kph) in just 5.2 seconds; the Tiptronic took 6.0 seconds. Because of its higher weight, the

911 Carrera Cabriolet took 0.2 seconds longer. For both body variants, top speed with a manual transmission was 174mph (280kph), and 171mph (275kph) with Tiptronic.

Model year 1999 (X Programme)

Beginning in October 1998, the model range was expanded by the 911 Carrera 4, with permanent all-wheel drive, available in Coupé or Cabriolet form. The extremely performance-oriented 911 GT3 Coupé became available in May 1999; its chassis numbers indicated that it was already considered part of the 2000 model year.

Beginning with the 1999 models, all 911 front and side indicators were white, with grey-white rear signals. Again using the Lokasil process, porous silicon inserts were placed in the moulds before casting the crankcase; the embedded silicon was subsequently exposed to form the hard-wearing cylinder surfaces. As part of the model development process, all Porsche 911s were equipped with dual side airbags (POSIP) as standard equipment. Two rotary control-knobs was an obvious change in the latest generation of Becker radios.

Externally, the body of the Carrera 4 was identical to that of the rear-drive Carrera; only the 'Carrera 4' script at the rear was titanium-coloured. Boot space was somewhat reduced, from 130 to 100 litres (4.6 to 3.5cu ft) to make room for the front differential. The Carrera 4 carried an inflatable space-saver spare wheel instead of the Carrera's small, inflated mini-spare. The new all-wheel drive system differed from previous transaxle designs by its open front driveshaft (instead of the earlier enclosed shaft). The viscous clutch was integrated in the front differential. Torque split to the front axle varied between 5 and 40 per cent. For the first time, Carrera 4 customers could choose between a six-speed manual or five-speed Tiptronic S transmission. Individual gear ratios were identical to those of the rear-drive Carrera. Standard equipment on the Carrera 4 included Porsche Stability Management (PSM). In critical situations, this vehicle dynamic control system would intervene in the ME 7.2 engine management system, and simultaneously stabilize the vehicle by means of wheel-specific brake application. This system necessitated a so-called 'E-Gas' or throttle-by-wire system, in effect an electronic throttle pedal. Throttle pedal position was read by a potentiometer and transmitted to the engine electronics. A servo motor opened or closed the throttle butterfly accordingly. On the rear-drive Carrera, however, the throttle was still mechanically actuated by a cable. The familiar Carrera suspension

was modified for all-wheel drive. Brake system configuration and dimensions were identical to those of the rear-drive Carrera, except that the four-piston monobloc callipers were painted titanium. The Carrera 4 rolled on specially styled 17-inch wheels, reminiscent of the classic Fuchs wheels. Wheel sizes were identical to those of the Carrera.

For brand-new manual-transmission Carreras and Carrera 4s, Porsche Exclusive offered a works performance increase to 320hp (235kW) at 6800rpm. Maximum torque remained largely unchanged, at 350Nm (258lb ft) at 4600rpm. The added horsepower was obtained through a modified induction system, cylinder heads and exhaust manifolds, altered camshafts and retuned engine electronics. This Carrera 'power kit' was available from Porsche Tequipment for retrofitting. Installation of the kit could be carried out by any Porsche dealership. Cars with the power kit treatment accelerated more quickly and gained about 3mph (5kph) in top speed.

The body of the 911 GT3 was based on a modified Carrera 4 bodyshell. Several modifications were needed to provide space for the GT3's separate dry-sump oil tank. Engine and transmission mounts were also modified for the GT3. Fuel tank volume was increased to 89 litres (20 gallons), but the spare wheel was left out; instead, the GT3 was delivered with a tyre repair system and inflator bottle. External changes included a modified nose and sills, and large fixed rear spoiler integrated in the engine lid. The GT3 engine was based on the crankcase of the Porsche 964, which was also installed in the GT1. Its dry-sump lubrication system used a separate oil tank. The eight-bearing crankshaft was plasma nitrided. Connecting rods were made of titanium. Reduced rotating masses made for a quicker-revving engine. Crankcase, cylinder heads and camshaft housing for each bank of three cylinders were joined into a single unit. Naturally, the GT3 power unit also employed water-cooling, four-valve cylinder heads and the VarioCam system for speed-independent timing adjustment of the inlet camshafts. An increase in compression ratio to 11.7:1 resulted in the engine's high specific output of 100hp per litre (73.6kW/l). Bore and stroke were identical to the earlier air-cooled 3.6-litre engines. Displacing 3600cc, the engine produced 360hp (265kW) at 7200rpm. Its peak torque of 370Nm (273lb ft) was generated at 5000rpm. Power was relayed to the rear wheels by a six-speed manual transmission and dual-mass flywheel, and a limited-slip differential with 40 per cent lock-up under load and 60 per cent in coasting. Compared to the Carrera, the GT3 suspension was lowered by 30mm and tuned more firmly. Anti-roll bars were adjustable. The cross-drilled, ventilated brake discs measured 330mm in diameter. Four-piston monobloc fixed callipers were machined from solid blocks of aluminium, and painted red to protect them against corrosion. The ABS 5.3 anti-lock brake system was adapted to the GT3. Ten-spoke, 18-inch wheels, 8in wide at the front and 10in at the rear, carried 225/40 ZR 18 and 285/30 ZR 18 tyres respectively. Additional track increase was obtained through 5mm-thick spacers. Inside, the GT3 had bucket seats for driver and passenger, with leather seating surfaces. For weight reasons, the rear seats and lower centre console were deleted. Front and side airbags and electric windows were retained as standard equipment. At no additional cost, the GT3 could be ordered with the Clubsport package for racing. Changes compared to the stock GT3 included a six-speed manual transmission with single-mass flywheel, bolt-in roll cage, racing seats with fire-resistant covering, three-point safety harness in red, a six-point racing harness for the driver's side (supplied ready to install), deleted side airbags, automatic passenger-side airbag cut-off (ready to install), fire extinguisher (ready to install) and a battery kill switch. The GT3's performance underscored its high sporting aspirations; weighing in at 1350kg (2974lb) the GT3 sprinted to 62mph (100kph) in 4.8 seconds. Its top speed of 188mph (302kph) broke the magic 300kph barrier.

Model year 2000 (Y Programme)

Introduced in May 1999, the 911 GT3 closed a gap in Porsche's line-up which had once been filled by the Carrera RS. It mixed a higher-performance normally-aspirated engine with a lightened body and sports-tuned suspension. At Porsche, this potent cocktail always represented the promise of pure driving enjoyment. For the 2000 model year, Porsche offered a millennium special-edition based on the Carrera 4 Coupé. The new 911 turbo Coupé was offered beginning in the spring of 2000; its chassis numbers were already allocated to the 2001 model year.

As of the 2000 model year, automatic climate control became a standard feature in all Carrera models. For a higher-quality feel, interior plastic items were given a soft finish coating. The more advanced ABS 5.7 system replaced the erstwhile ABS 5.3.

In the autumn of 1999, on the occasion of the impending millennium, Porsche presented a special model based on the Carrera 4 Coupé. Limited to a production run of 911 examples, this limited-edition was only available in a special colour, 'Violet Chromaflair'. Depending on the incident light, this colour appeared to shift from black to dark green to violet. Highly polished '911' script graced the engine lid. Exterior equipment of the millennium 911 included chrome stainless-steel tailpipes, rear wiper, green-tinted windscreen top, sunroof, Litronic headlamps with cleaning system and door sills with 911 script. The sports suspension was lowered by 10mm and retuned for its highly polished 18-inch monobloc alloy wheels, 7.5in at the front and 10in at the rear. Front and rear tyres were 225/40 ZR 18 and 265/35 ZR 18 respectively. A five-speed Tiptronic S transmission was optional. Inside, brown natural leather and dark maple trim satisfied the loftiest expectations. Natural leather also covered the front and rear seats, dashboard, door panels, pillars, steering column, centre console, passive microphone and hands-free telephone console and airbag module. Carpeting was keyed to leather colour. The headliner was done in black Alcantara, the sun visors with black leatherette. Plastic parts were given a soft-finish coating. Instrument faces had an aluminium look. Inside door handles, door pocket lids, and parts of the three-spoke steering wheel, gear lever and handbrake lever were trimmed with burled maple. A plaque with '911' and the sequential number was affixed to the centre console. The front seats were electrically fully adjustable and heatable. The driver's seat was equipped with a lumbar support and memory function for seat and wing-mirror settings. Standard equipment in the millennium model included the Porsche Communication Management (PCM) system with navigation, CD changer and Digital Sound Processing (DSP), as well as cruise control and on-board computer.

Porsche's turboless time ended in January 2000 with public introduction of the 911 turbo Coupé. The body of the 911 turbo differed only by a modified front valance, containing three large air inlets covered by decorative black grilles. The bi-xenon headlamps, with their rounded lower edges, were noticeably different from those of the Carrera models. The sills blended into the widened rear wings. Air inlets for the intercoolers were cut into the wings just behind the doors. Behind the rear wheels, three horizontal vent slits cut into each side of the rear valance. The rear light units were larger. A Gurney lip was integrated in the trailing edge of the rear spoiler. A secondary splitter wing was electrically extended at speeds above 75mph (120kph). The twin-turbo engine shared its basic engineering attributes with that of the 911 GT3, based on the crankcase of the 964 engine family and with a separate oil tank for its dry-sump lubrication system. Its 3.6-litre displacement and 9.4:1 compression ratio, relatively high for a turbocharged engine, produced 420hp (309kW) at 6000rpm. Maximum torque of 560Nm (413lb ft) was available across a broad rev range, from 2700rpm to 4600rpm. Maximum boost of 0.8bar was reached at 2700rpm. The 911 turbo was equipped with VarioCam Plus, a further development of the familiar VarioCam system. By not only changing intake valve timing but also intake valve lift, this system permitted optimization of power, torque and fuel economy across the entire engine speed range. Engine management was handled by Motronic ME 7.8 with E-Gas ('drive by wire'). The turbo's standard drivetrain included all-wheel drive and a six-speed manual transmission. For the first time on a 911 turbo, a five-speed Tiptronic S transmission was available as an option, making the turbo attractive to customers already familiar with powerful, automatic-equipped cars from other manufacturers. Suspension tuning was firmer in comparison to the Carrera 4.

The brake system included red-painted four-piston aluminium monobloc fixed callipers and ventilated, cross-drilled 330mm discs. Porsche Stability Management (PSM) with ABS 5.7, ASR and ABD was standard equipment. In conjunction with the introduction of the new 911 turbo, the Zuffenhausen company unveiled its Porsche Ceramic Composite Brake (PCCB), which would be available from the spring of 2001. The ventilated, cross-drilled ceramic brake discs were made of carbon-fibre impregnated with silicon carbide by means of a high-vacuum, high-temperature process at 1700°C (3100°F). Along with low disc wear and expected service life of up to 300,000km (186,000 miles), PCCB discs were also more than 50 per cent lighter: lower unsprung weight has a beneficial effect on handling. The brake system used yellow-painted six-piston monobloc fixed callipers at the front, four-piston at the rear. PCCB brakes were an added-cost option on new cars, and retrofit kits for certain models could be obtained from Porsche Tequipment.

The 18-inch cast wheels employed hollow-spoke technology. Front wheels were 8in wide, rears 11in. Tyres were 225/40 ZR 18 and 295/30 ZR 18 respectively. Obvious changes to the 911 turbo cockpit included its revised instruments. The analog speedometer ranged up to 320kph (200mph), with a digital speed display integrated in the same instrument. The on-board computer and boost-pressure gauge were integrated in the tachometer. A digital clock was included in the right-side combination instrument. A very complete standard equipment list included full-leather upholstery, air-conditioning and a cassette radio with Bose sound system. The turbo used an Alcantara headliner. Equipped with a manual transmission, the turbo accelerated to 62mph (100kph) in just 4.2 seconds; the Tiptronic S needed 4.9 seconds. Top speed for the manual-transmission turbo was about 190mph (305kph); the Tiptronic S topped out at 185mph (298kph).

Model year 2001 (1 Programme)

In the autumn of 2000, Porsche brought an extreme sports car, the 911 GT2, to market. Although the GT2 was based on the 911 turbo body, differences included an altered nose with three reshaped air inlets, and additional vent slits on the top side of the nose cap to extract radiator air. Compared to the turbo, the front lip spoiler was enlarged. Its rounded bi-xenon headlamps were also taken from the turbo. Sills blended into the rear wings. Air inlets for charge air intercoolers were cut into the rear wings. The sides of the rear valance also contained three horizontal vent slits. A large, fixed, manually-adjustable rear spoiler was mounted atop the engine lid, between turbo tail-light units.

The twin-turbo engine of the GT2 shared its technical basis with the 911 turbo power unit, but provided 10 per cent more power. Its 3.6 litres and 9.4:1 compression developed 463hp (340kW) at 5700rpm. Maximum torque of 620Nm (457lb ft) was available between 3500rpm and 4500rpm. Like the 911 turbo, the GT2 was equipped with VarioCam Plus. By adjusting intake cam timing as well as intake valve lift, this system permitted optimization of power, torque and fuel economy across the entire engine speed range. Engine management was by a Motronic ME 7.8 with E-gas.

In contrast to the 911, the GT2 was available only in rear-drive form, and only with a six-speed manual transmission and limited-slip differential. The suspension was lowered by 20mm and fitted with sports-tuned springs and shock absorbers. For racing, the suspension was adjustable for ride height, toe angle, camber and anti-roll bar stiffness. Weight-optimized monobloc wheels, in 'Turbo Look II' design, were 8.5 J x 18 at the front with 235/40 ZR 18 tyres, and 12 J x 18 at the rear with 315/30 ZR 18. Porsche Ceramic Composite Brakes (PCCB) were standard equipment on the 911 GT2. The ventilated, cross-drilled ceramic brake discs not only exhibited reduced wear and a life-expectancy of up to 300,000km (186,000 miles), but were also more than 50 per cent lighter. Front brakes used six-piston monobloc fixed callipers, with four-piston callipers at the rear. The callipers were painted yellow. Brake disc diameter was 350mm.

The GT2 cockpit was dominated by instrumentation adopted from the 911 turbo. The analog speedometer was marked to 320kph (200mph), with the digital speed display integrated in the same instrument. The tachometer included the on-board computer display and boost-pressure gauge. A digital clock was included in the rightmost combination instrument. Seating surfaces for the driver and passenger bucket seats were leather covered. Rear seats and lower centre console were deleted for weight reasons. Front and side airbags and power windows were retained as standard equipment in the GT2. The cabin was topped by an Alcantara headliner. Air-conditioning was standard, and a radio package was a no-cost option.

Porsche also offered the 911 GT2 with a Clubsport package for motorsports activities, at no added cost. Changes in comparison to the production GT2 included a bolt-on roll bar which could be expanded into a complete racing roll cage, racing seats with flame-resistant covering, three-point safety harness in red, a six-point racing harness for the driver's side (supplied ready to install), fire extinguisher (ready to install) and a battery kill switch retrofit kit.

Performance of the 911 GT2 was pegged at the highest levels. It took only 4.1 seconds to accelerate to 62mph (100kph) and 8.5 seconds to go from zero to just over 99mph (160kph). Top speed was 196mph (315kph).

Model year 2002 (2 Programme)

The Carrera line underwent a major facelift for the 2002 model year. Porsche also expanded its offerings with two attractive new models: the 911 Targa and 911 Carrera 4S Coupé.

To further distance the 911 from the Boxster, the 911 Carrera was given the headlamps of the 911 turbo. The nose was also redesigned, and the rear modified to match. Altered tailpipes rounded out the new rear aspect. Inside, 911 turbo instruments became standard on all Carrera models. All models had Alcantara headliners, and the surfaces of all switches had a matt-black finish. Interiors were further enhanced by aluminium appliqués. A glove compartment, its lid opening downward, was now fitted to the lower right of the dash. Cupholders extended from the centre console below the air vents. Air-conditioning was standard on all 911 Carreras.

Along with visual retouching, the most important change was the new 3.6-litre engine. A new crankshaft with 82.8mm stroke and unaltered bore of 96mm raised displacement to 3596cc. Power climbed to 320hp (235kW) at 6800rpm. Even more important than raw power was the more satisfying torque curve. Maximum torque of 370Nm (273lb ft) was available at 4250rpm. The reworked boxer engine was also equipped with the 911 turbo's familiar VarioCam system for intake valves and Motronic ME 7.8 engine management system.

Porsche positioned the new 911 Targa between two extremes: the Coupé, as a closed vehicle, and the Cabriolet, as an open vehicle. As with its predecessor, the 993 Targa, its roof panel was composed of three glass elements: a narrow strip of glass at the front, followed by the movable roof section, and finally the rear window. Two steel longitudinal members at the sides, welded to the body and painted body colour, offered rollover protection. The glass elements were made of green-tinted three-layer laminated safety glass. When opened, a small wind deflector was raised as soon as the electrically-actuated glass panel slid under the rear window. With the roof panel closed, a sunshade, also electrically actuated, could be extended as protection against cold or sun. The shade stowed itself automatically when the glass roof was opened. The Targa's opening rear hatch was a new feature never before seen on a 911. This could be electrically unlocked before loading or unloading the rear storage area. For safety reasons, the hatch could only be opened with the glass roof closed. Ferry Porsche would surely have been pleased with this glass hatch; even in the early 1960s, he wanted the original 911 to have a hatchback. At the time, there were doubts about the long-term sealing ability of such a hatch. The 911 Targa drivetrain consisted of the 3.6-litre normally-aspirated engine and six-speed manual transmission, with the five-speed Tiptronic S as an alternative. No all-wheel-drive Targa was offered.

The wide body of the Carrera 4S Coupé was borrowed from the 911 turbo. Front and rear ends, modified sills and widened rear wings with larger light units were as on the turbo, but the rear wings did not have air vents. The engine lid was equipped with the electrically extended rear spoiler used on the other Carrera models. Below the spoiler, a continuous red light band spanned the gap between the red parts of the rear light units. Standard powertrain for the Carrera 4S was the 320hp (235kW) 3.6-litre normally-aspirated engine, teamed with a six-speed manual transmission. As an option, the widebody Carrera 4S was also available with a five-speed Tiptronic S, providing a Porsche alternative for customers who in the past had owned other high-performance marques with automatic transmissions. Compared to the Carrera 4, the 4S sports suspension was lowered by 10mm and tuned more firmly. The brake system, taken from the 911 turbo, consisted of red-painted four-piston aluminium monobloc fixed callipers and cross-drilled, ventilated 330mm brake discs. The cast monobloc 18-inch 'Turbo Look II' wheels, 8in wide at the front and 10in at the rear, carried 225/40 ZR 18 and 295/30 ZR 18 tyres, respectively. Porsche Stability Management (PSR) with ABS 5.7, ASR and ABD were standard equipment on the 911 Carrera 4S. Also part of the very complete standard equipment list were metallic paint, full leather upholstery, electrically-powered seats (with memory for driver's seat) and wing mirrors, air-conditioning and a CD radio with a digital sound package. The manual transmission Carrera 4S accelerated to 62mph (100kph) in 5.1 seconds; the Tiptronic S took 5.6 seconds. Top speed for the manual was about 174mph (280kph), and 171mph (275kph) for the Tiptronic S.

Model year 2003 (3-Programme)

For 2003, Porsche offered increased power for all Carrera models. Porsche's top athletes, the 911 GT2

and 911 GT3, benefited from continued development and were offered as more powerful new editions. In the spring of 2003, the wide-body Carrera 4S was introduced to the market as a convertible.

The hoods of all Carrera Cabriolets could now be electrically opened or closed, while moving at speeds up to about 30mph (50 kph). The Targa's front seats had 10mm less padding, for increased headroom; the headrests were given extra padding.

For all brand-new manual-transmission Carrera and Carrera 4 models, Porsche Exclusive offered a power increase to 345hp (254kW) at 6800rpm. The package raised maximum torque to 370Nm (273lb ft), and also the maximum torque speed to 4800rpm. The power increase was achieved by means of an aluminium induction system, modified exhaust manifolds, altered camshafts, recalibrated engine electronics and an additional water radiator (except on the Carrera 4S). The 'Carrera Powerkit' was also available from Porsche Tequipment for retrofitting; installation of the kit could be carried out by any Porsche dealership. Powerkitted vehicles had slightly better acceleration and 3mph (5kph) higher top speed.

The body of the new 911 GT3 was also modified. Along with redesigned headlamps, the front and rear ends were reshaped. Most obvious was the new, fixed rear wing. The reworked engine produced even more power, and revved even higher.

Phantom view of a 911 Cabriolet, Type 996

Its 3600cc displacement now cranked out 381hp (280kW) at 7400rpm, and maximum torque of 385Nm (284lb ft) was achieved at 5000rpm. Power was directed to the rear wheels through a dual-mass flywheel, six-speed manual transmission and limited-slip differential. Compared to the Carrera, the suspension was stiffer and 30mm lower. Anti-roll bars were adjustable.

The brake system of the new GT3 was improved yet again; the cross-drilled, ventilated front brake discs were now 350mm in diameter, and 330mm at the rear. Front discs were gripped by six-piston monobloc fixed callipers. To prevent corrosion, the callipers, machined from a single piece of aluminium, were painted red. The ABS 5.7 system was matched to the GT3. As an added-cost option, customers could order the Porsche Ceramic Composite Brake (PCCB).

The 18-inch light-alloy rims, 8.5in wide at the front and 11in at the rear, sported a modified ten-spoke design. Front tyres were 235/40 ZR 18, rears 295/30 ZR 18. Inside, seating surfaces of the racing bucket seats were upholstered in leather. Rear seats and lower centre console were deleted for weight reasons. Front and side airbags, electric windows and upper centre-console cupholders from the basic version were retained for the GT3. Performance of the new 911 GT3 was improved yet again; with a kerb weight of 1380kg (3040lb), the GT3 accelerated to 62mph (100kph) in only 4.5 seconds. Zero to 124mph (200kph) took 14.3 seconds. Top speed was 190mph (306kph).

At no added cost, the GT3 was available with a Clubsport package for motorsports activities. Changes beyond the production GT3 included a roll cage (roll bar bolted on, front of cage packed loosely); racing bucket seats with flame-retardant upholstery, red three-point safety belts, driver's-side six-point racing harness (also red, packed separately), fire extinguisher (packed separately) and a battery kill switch installation kit.

The new 911 GT2 was also based on the 911 turbo body. Compared to its predecessor, there were no body changes. The new GT2's twin-turbo engine produced even more power; with a compression ratio of 9.4:1, the 3.6-litre engine produced 483hp (355kW) at 5700rpm. Maximum torque of 640Nm (472lb ft) was available between 3500rpm and 4500rpm. The GT2 was only available in rear-drive form, with a six-speed manual transmission and limited-slip differential. The suspension was lowered by 20mm and equipped with sports-tuned springs and shock absorbers. For motorsports applications, the suspension was adjustable for height, toe angle, camber and anti-roll bar stiffness. The ten-spoke, weight-optimized

18-inch alloy wheels were borrowed from the GT3. At the front, 8.5 J x 18 wheels carried 235/40 ZR 18 tyres; the rear 12 J x 18 rims mounted 315/30 ZR 18 rubber. The Porsche Ceramic Composite Brake (PCCB) was standard equipment in the 911 GT2. Front brakes used yellow-painted six-piston monobloc fixed callipers gripping 350mm discs.

The cockpit of the 911 GT2 featured leather-covered bucket seats. Sports seats were a no-cost option. The rear seats and lower centre console were deleted for weight reasons. Front and side airbags, electric windows and upper centre-console cupholders from the basic version were also retained for the GT2. Air-conditioning was standard equipment on the 911 GT2, and a radio package was available at no additional cost. Customers could choose between Guards Red, Speed Yellow and Maritime Blue safety belts. Another no-cost option was the 'Carbon' exterior package, with a visible carbon-fibre rear wing, two carbon-look wing mirrors and carbon-look front radiator exhaust duct framing.

Performance of the new 911 GT2 was further improved; acceleration to 62mph (100kph) was achieved in just 4.0 seconds, while zero to just over 99mph (160kph) took 8.3 seconds. Top speed was 198mph (319kph).

Porsche also offered the 911 GT2 with a Clubsport package at no additional cost. Changes compared to the production GT2 included: visible carbon rear wing, carbon-look wing mirrors and front exhaust duct framing, roll cage (roll bar bolted on, front of cage packed loosely); racing bucket seats with flame-retardant upholstery, red three-point safety belts, driver's side six-point racing harness (also red, packed separately), fire extinguisher (packed separately) and a battery kill switch installation kit.

The 911 Carrera 4S Cabriolet was built on the wide turbo body, with the added special features of the Carrera 4S Coupé. The windscreen had a green-tinted top. A wind blocker was included as standard equipment. The standard drivetrain consisted of the 320hp (235kW) 3.6-litre normally-aspirated engine, all-wheel drive and six-speed manual transmission. Optionally, a five-speed Tiptronic was available. The firmer sports suspension was lowered 10mm.

The brake system, with its red-painted four-piston aluminium monobloc fixed callipers and cross-drilled discs, was taken from the 911 turbo. The 18-inch 'Turbo Look II' monobloc wheels, 8in wide at the front and 11in at the rear, carried 225/40 ZR 18 and 295/30 ZR 18 tyres, respectively. Porsche Stability Management (PSM) with ABS 5.7, ASR and ABD was also standard on the Carrera 4S Cabriolet. The remaining equipment was identical to

Phantom view of a 911 Coupé, Type 996

that of the Carrera 4S Coupé. With a manual transmission, the Carrera 4S Cabriolet accelerated to 62mph (100kph) in 5.3 seconds; the Tiptronic S took 5.9 seconds. Top speed with the six-speed was about 174mph (280kph), while the Tiptronic reached 171mph (275kph).

Model year 2004 (4-Programme)

For the 2004 model year, Porsche expanded the 911 model line-up again, with the 911 turbo Cabriolet, the 911 GT3 RS and a special edition '40th anniversary 911'. Never before had the 911 been available in so many variations. These were: 911 Carrera Coupé, 40th Anniversary 911 Carrera Coupé, 911 Carrera Cabriolet, 911 Targa, 911 Carrera 4 Coupé, 911 Carrera 4 Cabriolet, 911 Carrera 4S Coupé, 911 Carrera 4S Cabriolet, 911 turbo Coupé, 911 turbo Cabriolet, 911 GT3, 911 GT3 Clubsport, 911 GT3 RS, 911 GT2, and 911 GT2 Clubsport. In addition, Porsche offered increased-performance packages for all production 911 Carrera and 911 turbo models.

In the summer of 2003, a 911 turbo Cabriolet rejoined the model range for the first time since 1989. The Cabriolet was based on the wide body,

with the mechanicals and equipment of the 911 turbo. Added reinforcement made the drop-top turbo 70kg (154lb) heavier than its metal-roofed stablemate. Naturally, the cloth top of the 911 turbo included a heatable glass rear window. The hood could be raised or closed in about 20 seconds, even while rolling at speeds up to about 30mph (50kph). An aluminium hardtop was included as standard equipment. In the engine department, customers could choose between the stock 420hp (309kW) engine, or the tuned Exclusive version with 450hp (331kW) and 60Nm (44lb ft) added torque. Either engine could be teamed with the six-speed manual or five-speed Tiptronic S transmission. Sports suspension was not offered for the Cabriolet. With manual transmission and stock engine, the turbo Cabriolet accelerated to 62mph (100kph) in 4.3 seconds; the Tiptronic S needed 4.9 seconds. With the top up, the manual Cabriolet maxed out at 190mph (305kph); with the top down, a breezy 180mph (290kph).

For the 911 GT3 RS, Porsche laid on a limited production run of 200 units for homologation. The 911 GT3 RS was conceived as a street-legal pure-bred race car, meeting the FIA N-GT and ACO (Automobile Club de l'Ouest, the Le Mans organizers) rules. Bodywork of the 911 GT3 RS was painted Carrera White. Buyers had a choice of red or blue '911 GT3 RS' decals on the vehicle flanks and at the rear. Wheel centres were painted to match; wheel rims were polished. The nose was fitted with a chin spoiler and additional top exhaust vents for radiator air. The bonnet was made of lightweight carbon-fibre-reinforced plastic. At the rear, a spoiler and ram air-intake sprouted from the engine lid. Wing mirrors maintained the carbon-fibre look. A plastic rear window saved a few more kilograms. The 381hp (280kW) normally-aspirated engine, six-speed manual transmission and brakes were identical to those of the 'normal' 911 GT3. The suspension was tuned for the race track. For racing set-up, toe angle, camber and anti-roll bar stiffness were adjustable.

The racing seats were padded with fire-resistant fabric. Steering wheel rim, gear lever and handbrake handle were covered with Alcantara. The three-point belts were available in red or blue. Additionally, a six-point driver harness was included with the car. The roll bar was bolted in place, the remainder of the roll cage packed separately. A fire extinguisher was also packed with the car. At 1360kg (2996lb) the 911 GT3 RS weighed 20 kilos less than the normal GT3.

Acceleration to 62mph (100kph) took just 4.4 seconds; and zero to 124mph (200kph) took 14.0 seconds. Top speed was in the neighbourhood of 190mph (306kph).

In the summer of 2003, Porsche presented its 40th Anniversary 911, based on the 911 Carrera Coupé, powered by a normally-aspirated tuned engine developing 345hp (254kW) and driving through a six-speed manual gearbox. Standard equipment included a limited-slip differential with 22 per cent lock-up under power and 27 per cent in coasting, as well as Porsche Stability Management (PSM) with ABS, ASR, and ABD. The sport suspension was lowered by 10mm. Eighteen-inch Carrera wheels, 8in at the front and 10in at the rear, were polished by bead blasting and carried 225/40 ZR 18 tyres at the front and 285/30 ZR 18 at the rear. All anniversary models were painted 'GT Silver Metallic'. The nose had larger radiator air inlets, and body-coloured side inlet grilles. At the sides, fairings were installed over the sills. Aluminium '911' script was affixed to the rear lid. The two tailpipes were polished. Bi-xenon headlamps, with dynamic range adjustment and headlamp washer system, were standard, along with an electric sunroof. The cabin was trimmed with dark grey natural leather and included heated sports seats. Seat centres, door handles, handbrake handle, gear lever and the grip area of the steering wheel were covered in specially

Water-cooled six-cylinder boxer engine as used in the Type 996 Carrera

embossed leather. The plastic rear shells of the sports seats, centre console and handbrake lever were painted in the 'GT Silver Metallic' exterior colour. Instrument trim rings and dashboard trim strip were painted aluminium colour. A numbered '911 40th Anniversary' plaque was affixed to the centre console. '911' script also graced the door thresholds. Additional goodies included several exclusive accessories: one medium and one large suitcase, a key fob and a briefcase, all in the same hand-tooled dark grey natural leather with special embossing as found in the car's interior. Production of the special edition was limited to 1963 examples. Acceleration to 62mph (100kph) took 4.9 seconds; to 124mph (200kph) it took 16.5 seconds. Top speed was about 180mph (290kph).

Phantom view of a 911 GT2 Coupé, Type 996

911 Carrera Coupé [Tiptronic S]
MY 1998–MY 2001
911 Carrera Cabriolet [Tiptronic S]
April 1998–MY 2001

Engine

Engine design:	6-cylinder horizontally-opposed
Installation:	Rear-engine
Cooling system:	Water-cooled
Engine type:	M 96/01 [M 96/01]
Displacement (cc):	3387
Bore x stroke (mm):	96 x 78
Engine output DIN (kW/hp):	221/300 at 6800rpm
Maximum torque (Nm/lb ft):	350/258 at 4600rpm
Output per litre (kW/l / hp/l):	65.2 / 88.6
Compression ratio:	11.3 : 1
Valve operation & camshaft drive:	dohc, cams driven by double chain, 4 valves per cylinder, VarioCam, intake camshaft timing varies 25°
Carburation:	Bosch DME, Motronic M 5.2, sequential multi-point manifold injection
MY 2000 - MY 2001:	Bosch DME, Motronic M 7.2, sequential multi-point manifold injection
Ignition system:	Bosch DME, distributorless ignition system with six individual ignition coils
Firing order:	1 - 6 - 2 - 4 - 3 - 5
Engine lubrication:	Integrated dry sump
Engine oil total (l):	10.25

Transmission

Drive configuration:	Rear-axle drive
Manual gearbox:	6-speed
Option Tiptronic S:	[5-speed]
Transmission type:	G 96/00 [A 96/00]
Transmission ratios:	
1st gear:	3.82 [3.66]
2nd gear:	2.20 [2.00]
3rd gear:	1.52 [1.41]
4th gear:	1.22 [1.00]
5th gear:	1.02 [0.74]
6th gear:	0.84
Reverse gear:	3.55 [4.10]
Drive ratio:	3.44 [3.68]
Option:	
Ltd-slip diff. load/deceleration (%):	25 / 40

Body, chassis, suspension, brakes, wheels

Body design:	Steel body, 2 doors, 2 + 2 seats, entirely hot-dip galvanized body, side-impact protection beams in doors, flexible polyurethane front and rear bumpers with integrated aluminium beams, engine lid with integrated automatic rear spoiler
Coupé:	Fixed steel roof
Option:	Electric sunroof
Cabriolet:	Electric hood with flexible plastic rear window, two retracted roll bars
Standard:	Aluminium hardtop with electrically-heatable rear window
Suspension, front:	Individually suspended with 'disconnected' light-alloy wishbones, McPherson struts with coil springs, dual-tube gas-filled shock absorbers, anti-roll bar
Suspension, rear:	Individually suspended on five wishbones per side on light-alloy multi-wishbone axle with LSA system (Light weight, Stability, Agility) with coil springs, single-tube gas-filled shock absorbers, anti-roll bar
Brakes, front/rear (Size (mm)):	Ventilated and drilled discs (318 x 28) Ventilated and drilled discs (299 x 24) Black 4-piston fixed aluminium monobloc callipers / Black 4-piston fixed aluminium monobloc callipers Bosch ABS 5.3
Wheels, front/rear:	7 J x 17 / 9 J x 17
Tyres, front/rear:	205/50 ZR 17 / 255/40 ZR 17
Option:	7.5 J x 18 / 10 J x 18 225/40 ZR 18 / 265/35 ZR 18

Electrical system

Alternator (W/A):	1680 / 120
Battery (V/Ah):	12 / 70

Dimensions and weight

Track, front/rear (mm):	1455 / 1500
7.5 J x 18 / 10 J x 18:	1465 / 1480
Wheelbase (mm):	2350
Length x width x height (mm):	4430 x 1765 x 1305
Kerb weight DIN (kg):	1320 [1365]
Cabriolet:	1395 [1440]
Permissible gross weight (kg):	1720 [1765]
Cabriolet:	1795 [1840]
Luggage compartment (VDA (l)):	130
Luggage volume interior*:	200 / 210**
Fuel tank capacity (l):	64, including 10 reserve
C_w x A (m²):	0.30 x 1.94 = 0.582
Power/weight ratio (kg/kW / kg/hp):	5.97 [6.31] / 4.40 [4.65]
Cabriolet:	6.31 [6.51] / 4.65 [4.80]
*with folded-down rear seat-backs	
**Cabriolet with closed hood	

Fuel consumption

89/491/EWG (mpg):	98 RON super plus unleaded
At constant 56mph/90kph:	41.6 [38.75]
At constant 74mph/120kph:	32.5 [32.5]
Urban cycle:	19 [17.8]
1/3 mix:	27.9 [26.6]
93/116/EG (mpg):	98 RON super plus unleaded
Urban:	16.4 [15.4]
Extra urban:	33.2 [33.2]
Combined:	24 [23.5]
CO_2-emissions (g/km):	285 [290]

Performance, production, prices

Acceleration 0-62mph/100kph (s):	5.2 [6.0]
Cabriolet:	5.4 [6.2]
0–100mph/160kph (s):	11.5 [13.0]
Cabriolet:	11.9 [13.4]
Maximum speed (mph / kph):	174 / 280 [171 / 275]
Cabriolet:	174 / 280 [171 / 275]
Production, total number:	
Coupé:	31,135
Cabriolet:	23,598
Purchase price:	
08/1997 Coupé:	DM 135,610 [DM 141,170]
04/1998 Coupé:	DM 136,790 [DM 142,400]
Cabriolet:	DM 155,160 [DM 160,770]
08/1998 Coupé:	DM 136,790 [DM 142,400]
Cabriolet:	DM 155,160 [DM 160,770]
08/1999 Coupé:	DM 139,530 [DM 145,140]
Cabriolet:	DM 158,340 [DM 163,950]
08/2000 Coupé:	DM 140,940 [DM 146,550]
Cabriolet:	DM 159,940 [DM 165,550]

911 Carrera 4 Coupé [Tiptronic S]
911 Carrera 4 Cabriolet [Tiptronic S]
MY 1999–MY 2001

Engine

Engine design:	6-cylinder horizontally-opposed
Installation:	Rear-engine
Cooling system:	Water-cooled
Engine type:	M 96/02 [M 96/02]
Displacement (cc):	3387
Bore x stroke (mm):	96 x 78
Engine output DIN (kW/hp):	221/300 at 6800rpm
Maximum torque (Nm/lb ft):	350/258 at 4600rpm
Output per litre (kW/l / hp/l):	65.2 / 88.6
Compression ratio:	11.3 : 1
Valve operation & camshaft drive:	dohc, cams driven by double chain, 4 valves per cylinder, VarioCam, intake camshaft timing varies 25°
Carburation:	Bosch DME, Motronic M 7.2, sequential multi-point manifold injection
Ignition system:	Bosch DME, distributorless ignition system with six individual ignition coils
Firing order:	1 - 6 - 2 - 4 - 3 - 5
Engine lubrication:	Integrated dry sump
Engine oil total (l):	10.25

Transmission

Drive configuration:	4-wheel-drive with visco-clutch, cardan shaft
Manual gearbox:	6-speed
Option Tiptronic S:	[5-speed]
Transmission type:	G 96/30 [A 96/30]
Transmission ratios:	
1st gear:	3.82 [3.66]
2nd gear:	2.20 [2.00]
3rd gear:	1.52 [1.41]
4th gear:	1.22 [1.00]
5th gear:	1.02 [0.74]
6th gear:	0.84
Reverse gear:	3.55 [4.10]
Drive ratio:	3.44 [3.68]
Option:	
Ltd-slip diff. load/deceleration (%):	25 / 40

Body, chassis, suspension, brakes, wheels

Body design:	Steel body, 2 doors, 2 + 2 seats, entirely hot-dip galvanized body, side-impact protection beams in doors, flexible polyurethane front and rear bumpers with integrated aluminium beams, engine lid with integrated automatic rear spoiler
Coupé:	Fixed steel roof
Option:	Electric sunroof
Cabriolet:	Electric hood with flexible plastic rear window, two retracted roll bars
Standard:	Aluminium hardtop with electrically-heatable rear window
Suspension, front:	Individually suspended with 'disconnected' light-alloy wishbones, McPherson struts with coil springs, dual-tube gas-filled shock absorbers, anti-roll bar
Suspension, rear:	Individually suspended on five wishbones per side on light-alloy multi-wishbone axle with LSA system (Light weight, Stability, Agility) with coil springs, single-tube gas-filled shock absorbers, anti-roll bar
Brakes, front/rear (Size (mm)):	Ventilated and drilled discs (318 x 28) Ventilated and drilled discs (299 x 24) Titanium-colour 4-piston fixed aluminium monobloc callipers / Titanium-colour 4-piston fixed aluminium monobloc callipers Bosch ABS 5.3
Wheels, front/rear:	7 J x 17 / 9 J x 17
Tyres, front/rear:	205/50 ZR 17 / 255/40 ZR 17
Option:	7.5 J x 18 / 10 J x 18 225/40 ZR 18 / 265/35 ZR 18

Electrical system

Alternator (W/A):	1680 / 120
Battery (V/Ah):	12 / 70

Dimensions and weight

Track, front/rear (mm):	1455 / 1500
7.5 J x 18 / 10 J x 18:	1465 / 1480
Wheelbase (mm):	2350
Length x width x height (mm):	4430 x 1765 x 1305
Kerb weight DIN (kg):	1375 [1420]
Cabriolet:	1450 [1495]
Permissible gross weight (kg):	1775 [1820]
Cabriolet:	1850 [1895]
Luggage compartment (VDA (l)):	110
Luggage volume interior*:	200 / 210**
Fuel tank capacity (l):	64, including 10 reserve
C_w x A (m²):	0.30 x 1.94 = 0.582
Power/weight ratio (kg/kW/ kg/hp):	6.22 [6.42] / 4.58 [4.73]
Cabriolet:	6.56 [6.76] / 4.83 [4.98]

*with folded-down rear seat-backs
**Cabriolet with closed hood

Fuel consumption

89/491/EWG (mpg):	98 RON super plus unleaded
At constant 56mph/90kph:	40.8 [38]
At constant 74mph/120kph:	31.6 [31.6]
Urban cycle:	18.2 [17.1]
1/3 mix:	27 [25.8]
93/116/EG (mpg):	98 RON super plus unleaded
Urban:	16.2 [15.1]
Extra urban:	32.1 [32.1]
Combined:	23.5 [22.7]
CO_2-emissions (g/km):	295 [304]

Performance, production, prices

Acceleration 0-62mph/100kph (s):	5.2 [6.0]
Cabriolet:	5.4 [6.2]
0–100mph/160kph (s):	11.6 [13.1]
Cabriolet:	12.0 [13.5]
Maximum speed (mph / kph):	174 / 280 [171 / 275]
Cabriolet:	174 / 280 [171 / 275]
Production, total number:	
Coupé:	12,643
Cabriolet:	9,411
Purchase prices:	
08/1998 Coupé:	DM 147,640 [DM 153,250]
Cabriolet:	DM 166,160 [DM 171,770]
08/1999 Coupé:	DM 150,590 [DM 156,200]
Cabriolet:	DM 169,400 [DM 175,010]
08/2000 Coupé:	DM 152,100 [DM 157,710]
Cabriolet:	DM 171,100 [DM 176,710]

911 GT 3 Coupé
911 GT 3 Clubsport Coupé
MY 1999–MY 2001

Engine

Engine design:	6-cylinder horizontally-opposed
Installation:	Rear-engine
Cooling system:	Water-cooled
Engine type:	M 96/76
Displacement (cc):	3600
Bore x stroke (mm):	100 x 76.4
Engine output DIN (kW/hp):	265/360 at 7200rpm
Maximum torque (Nm/lb ft):	370/273 at 5000rpm
Output per litre (kW/l / hp/l):	73.6 / 100.0
Compression ratio:	11.7 : 1
Valve operation & camshaft drive:	dohc, cams driven by double chain, 4 valves per cylinder, VarioCam, intake camshaft timing varies 25°
Carburation:	Bosch DME, Motronic M 5.2.2, sequential multi-point manifold injection
Ignition system:	Bosch DME, distributorless ignition system with six individual ignition coils
Firing order:	1 - 6 - 2 - 4 - 3 - 5
Engine lubrication:	Dry sump
Engine oil total (l):	12.5

Transmission

Drive configuration:	Rear-axle drive
Manual gearbox:	6-speed
Transmission type:	G 96/90
Transmission ratios:	
1st gear:	3.82
2nd gear:	2.15
3rd gear:	1.56
4th gear:	1.21
5th gear:	0.97
6th gear:	0.83
Reverse gear:	2.86
Drive ratio:	3.44
Ltd-slip diff. load/deceleration (%)	40 / 60

Body, chassis, suspension, brakes, wheels

Body design:	Steel body, 2 doors, 2 seats, entirely hot-dip galvanized body, side-impact protection beams in doors, flexible polyurethane front and rear bumpers with integrated aluminium beams, front bumper with spoiler, side skirts, engine lid with spoiler lip and fixed rear wing
Clubsport:	Roll cage (fixed by screws)
Suspension, front:	Individually suspended on 'disconnected' light-alloy wishbones, McPherson struts with coil springs, dual-tube gas-filled shock absorbers, anti-roll bar
Suspension, rear:	Individually suspended on five wishbones per side on light-alloy multi-wishbone axle with LSA system (Light weight, Stability, Agility) with coil springs, single-tube gas-filled shock absorbers, anti-roll bar
Brakes, front/rear (Size (mm)):	Ventilated and drilled discs (330 x 34) Ventilated and drilled discs (330 x 28) Red 4-piston fixed aluminium monobloc callipers / Red 4-piston fixed aluminium monobloc callipers Bosch ABS 5.3
Wheels, front/rear:	8 J x 18* / 10 J x 18*
Tyres, front/rear:	225/40 ZR 18 / 285/30 ZR 18
*plus spacers 5 mm	

Electrical system

Alternator (W/A):	1680 / 120
Battery (V/Ah):	12 / 36
with air-conditioning:	12 / 46

Dimensions and weight

Track, front/rear (mm):	1475 / 1495
Wheelbase (mm):	2350
Length x width x height (mm):	4430 x 1765 x 1270
Kerb weight DIN (kg):	1350
Permissible gross weight (kg):	1630
Luggage compartment (VDA (l)):	110
Fuel tank capacity (l):	89, including 12.5 reserve
C_w x A (m^2):	0.30 x 1.95 = 0.585
Power/weight ratio (kg/kW/kg/hp):	5.09 / 3.75

Fuel consumption

93/116/EG (mpg):	98 RON super plus unleaded
Urban:	14
Extra urban:	31.6
Combined:	21.8
CO_2-emissions (g/km):	320

Performance, production, prices

Acceleration 0-62mph/100kph (s):	4.8
0–100mph/160kph (s):	10.2
Maximum speed (mph / kph):	188 / 302
Production, total number:	1,868
Purchase prices:	
03/1999 Coupé:	DM 179,500
Coupé-Clubsport:	DM 179,500
08/2000 Coupé:	DM 181,295
Coupé-Clubsport:	DM 181,295

911 Carrera Coupé
with performance kit
911 Carrera Cabriolet
with performance kit
MY 1999–December 2000

Engine

Engine design:	6-cylinder horizontally-opposed
Installation:	Rear-engine
Cooling system:	Water-cooled
Engine type:	M 96/01 S
Displacement (cc):	3387
Bore x stroke (mm):	96 x 78
Engine output DIN (kW/hp):	235/320 at 6800rpm
Maximum torque (Nm/lb ft):	350/258 at 4600rpm
Output per litre (kW/l / hp/l):	69.4 / 94.5
Compression ratio:	11.3 : 1
Valve operation & camshaft drive:	dohc, cams driven by double chain, 4 valves per cylinder, VarioCam, intake camshaft timing varies 25°
Carburation:	Bosch DME, Motronic M 5.2, sequential multi-point monifold injection
MY 2000 - Dec. 2002:	Bosch DME, Motronic M 7.2, sequential multi-point manifold injection
Ignition system:	Bosch DME, distributorless ignition system with six individual ignition coils
Firing order:	1 - 6 - 2 - 4 - 3 - 5
Engine lubrication:	Integrated dry sump
Engine oil total (l):	10.25

Transmission

Drive configuration:	Rear-axle drive
Manual gearbox:	6-speed
Transmission type:	G 96/00
Transmission ratios:	
1st gear:	3.82
2nd gear:	2.20
3rd gear:	1.52
4th gear:	1.22
5th gear:	1.02
6th gear:	0.84
Reverse gear:	3.55
Drive ratio:	3.44

Body, chassis, suspension, brakes, wheels

Body design:	Steel body, 2 doors, 2 + 2 seats, entirely hot-dip galvanized body, side-impact protection beams in doors, flexible polyurethane front and rear bumpers with integrated aluminium beams, engine lid with integrated automatic rear spoiler
Coupé:	Fixed steel roof
Option:	Electric sunroof
Cabriolet:	Electric hood with flexible plastic rear window, two retracted roll bars
Standard:	Aluminium hardtop with electrically-heatable rear window
Suspension, front:	Individually suspended with 'disconnected' light-alloy wishbones, McPherson struts with

	coil springs, dual-tube gas-filled shock absorbers, anti-roll bar
Suspension, rear:	Individually suspended on five wishbones per side on light-alloy multi-wishbone axle with LSA system (Light weight, Stability, Agility) with coil springs, single-tube gas-filled shock absorbers, anti-roll bar
Brakes, front/rear (Size (mm)):	Ventilated and drilled discs (318 x 28) Ventilated and drilled discs (299 x 24) Black 4-piston fixed aluminium monobloc callipers / Black 4-piston fixed aluminium monobloc callipers Bosch ABS 5.3
Wheels, front/rear:	7 J x 17 / 9 J x 17
Tyres, front/rear:	205/50 ZR 17 / 255/40 ZR 17
Option:	7.5 J x 18 / 10 J x 18 225/40 ZR 18 / 265/35 ZR 18

Electrical system

Alternator (W/A):	1680 / 120
Battery (V/Ah):	12 / 80

Dimensions and weight

Track, front/rear (mm):	1455 / 1500
7.5 J x 18 / 10 J x 18:	1465 / 1480
Wheelbase (mm):	2350
Length x width x height (mm):	4430 x 1765 x 1305
Kerb weight DIN (kg):	1320
Cabriolet:	1395
Permissible gross weight (kg):	1720
Cabriolet:	1795
Luggage compartment (VDA (l)):	130
Luggage volume interior*:	200 / 210**
Fuel tank capacity (l):	64, including 10 reserve
C_w x A (m²):	0.30 x 1.94 = 0.582
Power/weight ratio (kg/kW/ kg/hp):	5.61 / 4.12
Cabriolet:	5.93 / 4.35
*with folded-down rear seat-backs	
**Cabriolet with closed hood	

Fuel consumption

93/116/EG (mpg):	98 RON super plus unleaded
Urban:	16.2
Extra urban:	32.1
Combined:	23.5
CO_2-emissions (g/km):	295

Performance, production, prices

Acceleration 0-62mph/100kph (s):	less than 5.2
Cabriolet:	less than 5.4
0–100mph/160kph (s):	less than 11.5
Cabriolet:	less than 12.0
Maximum speed (mph / kph):	177 / 285
Production, total number:	n/a
Purchase price for option:	
08/2000 Tequipment:	DM 14,500
08/2001 Tequipment:	DM 14,997

911 Carrera 4 Coupé Millenium [Tiptronic S] MY 2000

Engine
Engine design:	6-cylinder horizontally-opposed
Installation:	Rear-engine
Cooling system:	Water-cooled
Engine type:	M 96/02 [M 96/02]
Displacement (cc):	3387
Bore x stroke (mm):	96 x 78
Engine output DIN (kW/hp):	221/300 at 6800rpm
Maximum torque (Nm/lb ft):	350/258 at 4600rpm
Output per litre (kW/l / hp/l):	65.2 / 88.6
Compression ratio:	11.3 : 1
Valve operation & camshaft drive:	dohc, cams driven by double chain, 4 valves per cylinder, VarioCam, intake camshaft timing varies 25°
Carburation:	Bosch DME, Motronic M 7.2, sequential multi-point manifold injection
Ignition system:	Bosch DME, distributorless ignition system with six individual ignition coils
Firing order:	1 - 6 - 2 - 4 - 3 - 5
Engine lubrication:	Integrated dry sump
Engine oil total (l):	10.25

Transmission
Drive configuration:	4-wheel-drive with visco-clutch, cardan shaft
Manual gearbox:	6-speed
Option Tiptronic S:	[5-speed]
Transmission type:	G 96/30 [A 96/30]
Transmission ratios:	
1st gear:	3.82 [3.66]
2nd gear:	2.20 [2.00]
3rd gear:	1.52 [1.41]
4th gear:	1.22 [1.00]
5th gear:	1.02 [0.74]
6th gear:	0.84
Reverse gear:	3.55 [4.10]
Drive ratio:	3.44 [3.68]
Option:	
Ltd-slip diff. load/deceleration (%):	25 / 40

Body, chassis, suspension, brakes, wheels
Body design:	Steel body, 2 doors, 2 + 2 seats, entirely hot-dip galvanized body, side-impact protection beams in doors, flexible polyurethane front and rear bumpers with integrated aluminium beams, engine lid with integrated automatic rear spoiler
Exclusive colour:	Violet Chromaflair
Standard:	Electric sunroof
Suspension, front:	Individually suspended with 'disconnected' light-alloy wishbones, McPherson struts with coil springs, dual-tube gas-filled shock absorbers, anti-roll bar
Suspension, rear:	Individually suspended on five wishbones per side on light-alloy multi-wishbone axle with LSA system (Light weight, Stability, Agility) with coil springs, single-tube gas-filled shock absorbers, anti-roll bar
Brakes, front/rear (Size (mm)):	Ventilated and drilled discs (318 x 28) Ventilated and drilled discs (299 x 24) Titanium-colour 4-piston fixed aluminium monobloc callipers / Titanium-colour 4-piston fixed aluminium monobloc callipers Bosch ABS 5.3
Wheels, front/rear:	7.5 J x 18 / 10 J x 18
Tyres, front/rear:	225/40 ZR 18 / 265/35 ZR 18

Electrical system
Alternator (W/A):	1680 / 120
Battery (V/Ah):	12 / 80

Dimensions and weight
Track, front/rear (mm):	1465 / 1480
Wheelbase (mm):	2350
Length x width x height (mm):	4430 x 1765 x 1305
Kerb weight DIN (kg):	1375 [1420]
Permissible gross weight (kg):	1775 [1820]
Luggage compartment (VDA (l)):	130
Luggage volume interior*:	200
Fuel tank capacity (l):	64, including 10 reserve
C_w x A (m²):	0.30 x 1.94 = 0.582
Power/weight ratio (kg/kW/kg/hp):	6.22 [6.42] / 4.58 [4.73]

*with folded-down rear seat-backs

Fuel consumption
93/116/EG (mpg):	98 RON super plus unleaded
Urban:	16.2 [15.1]
Extra urban:	32.1 [32.1]
Combined:	23.5 [22.7]
CO_2-emissions (g/km):	295 [304]

Performance, production, prices
Acceleration 0-62mph/100kph (s):	5.2 [6.0]
0–100mph/160kph (s):	11.6 [13.1]
Maximum speed (mph / kph):	174 / 280 [171 / 275]
Production, total number:	911
Purchase price:	
09/1999 Coupé:	DM 185,000 [DM 190,610]

911 turbo Coupé [Tiptronic S]
January 2000–MY 2005

Engine

Engine design:	6-cylinder horizontally-opposed, twin turbo charger, twin intercooler
Installation:	Rear-engine
Cooling system:	Water-cooled
Engine type:	M 96/70 [M 96/70]
Displacement (cc):	3600
Bore x stroke (mm):	100 x 76.4
Engine output DIN (kW/hp):	309/420 at 6000rpm
Maximum torque (Nm/lb ft):	560/413 at 2700-4600rpm
Output per litre (kW/l / hp/l):	85.8 / 116.7
Compression ratio:	9.4 : 1
Valve operation & camshaft drive:	dohc, cams driven by double chain, 4 valves per cylinder, VarioCam Plus, intake camshaft timing varies 25°, intake valve lift
Carburation:	Bosch DME, Motronic M 7.8, sequential multi-point manifold injection
Ignition system:	Bosch DME, distributorless ignition system with six individual ignition coils
Firing order:	1 - 6 - 2 - 4 - 3 - 5
Engine lubrication:	Dry sump
Engine oil total (l):	11.0

Transmission

Drive configuration:	4-wheel-drive with visco-clutch, cardan shaft
Manual gearbox:	6-speed
Option Tiptronic S:	[5-speed]
Transmission type:	G 96/50 [A 96/59]
Transmission ratios:	
1st gear:	3.82 [3.59]
2nd gear:	2.05 [2.19]
3rd gear:	1.41 [1.41]
4th gear:	1.12 [1.00]
5th gear:	0.92 [0.83]
6th gear:	0.75
Reverse gear:	2.86 [1.99/3.16]
Drive ratio:	3.44 [2.89]

Body, chassis, suspension, brakes, wheels

Body design:	Steel body, 2 doors, 2 + 2 seats, entirely hot-dip galvanized body, side-impact protection beams in doors, wider rear wings with air intakes and side skirts, flexible polyurethane front and rear bumpers with integrated aluminium beams, front bumper with bigger air intakes, rear bumper with air outlets, engine lid with integrated spoiler lip and automatic rear wing
Option:	Electric sunroof
Suspension, front:	Individually suspended with 'disconnected' light-alloy wishbones, McPherson struts with coil springs, dual-tube gas-filled shock absorbers, anti-roll bar
Suspension, rear:	Individually suspended on five wishbones per side on light-alloy multi-wishbone axle with LSA system (Light weight, Stability, Agility) with coil springs, single-tube gas-filled shock absorbers, anti-roll bar
Brakes, front/rear (Size (mm)):	Ventilated and drilled discs (330 x 34) Ventilated and drilled discs (330 x 28) Red 4-piston fixed aluminium monobloc callipers / Red 4-piston fixed aluminium monobloc callipers Bosch ABS 5.7
Option MY 2003–MY 2005:	Porsche Ceramic Composite Brake (PCCB) Ventilated and drilled ceramic composite discs (350 x 34) / Ventilated and drilled ceramic composite discs (350 x 28) Yellow 6-piston fixed aluminium monobloc callipers / Yellow 4-piston fixed aluminium monobloc callipers Bosch ABS 5.7
Wheels, front/rear:	8 J x 18 / 11 J x 18
Tyres, front/rear:	225/40 ZR 18 / 295/30 ZR 18

Electrical system

Alternator (W/A):	1680 / 120
Battery (V/Ah):	12 / 80

Dimensions and weight

Track, front/rear (mm):	1465 / 1522
MY 2003 - 2005:	1472 / 1528
Wheelbase (mm):	2350
Length x width x height (mm):	4435 x 1830 x 1295
Kerb weight DIN (kg):	1540 [1585]
MY 2004 - 2005:	1590 [1630]
Permissible gross weight (kg):	1885 [1930]
MY 2004 - 2005:	1935 [1975]
Luggage compartment (VDA (l)):	130
Luggage volume interior*:	200
Fuel tank capacity (l):	64, including 10 reserve
C_w x A (m²):	0.31 x 2.00 = 0.62
Power/weight ratio (kg/kW/ kg/hp):	4.98 [5.12] / 3.66 [3.77]
*with folded-down rear seat-backs	

Fuel consumption

1999/100/EG (mpg):	98 RON super plus unleaded
Urban:	14.9 [12.9]
Extra urban:	31 [29.5]
Combined:	21.8 [20.3]
CO_2-emissions (g/km):	309 [339]

Performance, production, prices

Acceleration 0-62mph/100kph (s):	4.2 [4.9]
MY 2004 - MY 2005:	4.2 [4.8]
0–100mph/160kph (s):	9.2 [10.6]
MY 2004 - MY 2005:	9.3 [10.4]
Maximum speed (mph / kph):	190 / 305 [185 / 298]
Production, total number:	*
*Production until MY 2002:	11,248
Purchase prices:	
01/2000 Coupé:	DM 234,900 [DM 240,510]
08/2001 Coupé:	DM 244,346 [DM 249,961]
08/2002 Coupé:	Euro 126,208 [Euro 129,079]
08/2003 Coupé:	Euro 128,676 [Euro 131,547]

911 GT 2 Coupé
911 GT 2 Clubsport Coupé
MY 2001–December 2002

Engine

Engine design:	6-cylinder horizontally-opposed, twin turbo charger, twin intercooler
Installation:	Rear-engine
Cooling system:	Water-cooled
Engine type:	M 96/70 S
Displacement (cc):	3600
Bore x stroke (mm):	100 x 76.4
Engine output DIN (kW/hp):	340/462 at 5700rpm
Maximum torque (Nm/lb ft):	620/457 at 3500-4500rpm
Output per litre (kW/l / hp/l):	94.4 / 128.3
Compression ratio:	9.4 : 1
Valve operation & camshaft drive:	dohc, cams driven by double chain, 4 valves per cylinder, VarioCam Plus, intake camshaft timing varies 30°, intake valve lift
Carburation:	Bosch DME, Motronic M 7.8, sequential multi-point manifold injection
Ignition system:	Bosch DME, distributorless ignition system with six individual ignition coils
Firing order:	1 - 6 - 2 - 4 - 3 - 5
Engine lubrication:	Dry sump
Engine oil total (l):	11.0

Transmission

Drive configuration:	Rear-axle drive
Manual gearbox:	6-speed
Transmission type:	G 96/88
Transmission ratios:	
1st gear:	3.82
2nd gear:	2.05
3rd gear:	1.41
4th gear:	1.12
5th gear:	0.92
6th gear:	0.75
Reverse gear:	2.86
Drive ratio:	3.44
Ltd-slip diff. load/deceleration (%):	40 / 60

Body, chassis, suspension, brakes, wheels

Body design:	Steel body, 2 doors, 2 seats, entirely hot-dip galvanized body, side-impact protection beams in doors, wider rear wings with air intakes and side skirts, flexible polyurethane front and rear bumpers with integrated aluminium beams, front bumper with bigger air intakes and additional air outlets, rear bumper with air outlets, engine lid with integrated spoiler lip and fixed rear wing
Clubsport:	Roll cage (roll bar fixed by screws, front part enclosed)
Suspension, front:	Individually suspended with 'disconnected' light-alloy wishbones, McPherson struts with coil springs, dual-tube gas-filled shock absorbers, anti-roll bar
Suspension, rear:	Individually suspended on five wishbones per side on light-alloy multi-wishbone axle with LSA system (Light weight, Stability, Agility) with coil springs, single-tube gas-filled shock absorbers, anti-roll bar
Brakes, front/rear (Size (mm)):	Porsche Ceramic Composite Brake (PCCB) Ventilated and drilled ceramic composite discs (350 x 34) / Ventilated and drilled ceramic composite discs (350 x 28) Yellow 6-piston fixed aluminium monobloc callipers / Yellow 4-piston fixed aluminium monobloc callipers Bosch ABS 5.7
Wheels, front/rear:	8.5 J x 18 / 12 J x 18
Tyres, front/rear:	235/40 ZR 18 / 315/30 ZR 18

Electrical system

Alternator (W/A):	1680 / 120
Battery (V/Ah):	12 / 80

Dimensions and weight

Track, front/rear (mm):	1495 / 1520
Wheelbase (mm):	2355
Length x width x height (mm):	4450 x 1830 x 1275
Kerb weight DIN (kg):	1440
MY 2003:	1420
Permissible gross weight (kg):	1730
Luggage compartment (VDA (l)):	110
Fuel tank capacity (l):	89, including 12.5 reserve
C_w x A (m^2):	0.34 x 1.96 = 0.666
Power/weight ratio (kg/kW/kg/hp):	4.23 / 3.11
MY 2003:	4.17 / 3.07

Fuel consumption

1999/100/EG (mpg):	98 RON super plus unleaded
Urban:	14.9
Extra urban:	30.4
Combined:	21.8
CO_2-emissions (g/km):	309

Performance, production, prices

Acceleration 0-62mph/100kph (s):	4.1
0–100mph/160kph (s):	8.5
Maximum speed (mph / kph):	196 / 315
Production, total no. until MY 2002:	963
Purchase prices:	
08/2000 Coupé:	DM 339,000
Coupé-Clubsport:	DM 339,000
07/2001 Coupé:	Euro 173,328
Coupé-Clubsport:	Euro 173,328
08/2002 Coupé:	Euro 175,044
Coupé-Clubsport:	Euro 175,044

911 Carrera Coupé [Tiptronic S]
911 Carrera Cabriolet [Tiptronic S]
MY 2002–MY 2004
MY 2002–MY 2005

Engine

Engine design:	6-cylinder horizontally-opposed
Installation:	Rear-engine
Cooling system:	Water-cooled
Engine type:	M 96/03 [M 96/03]
Displacement (cc):	3596
Bore x stroke (mm):	96 x 82.8
Engine output DIN (kW/hp):	235/320 at 6800rpm
Maximum torque (Nm/lb ft):	370/273 at 4250rpm
Output per litre (kW/l / hp/l):	65.4 / 89.0
Compression ratio:	11.3 : 1
Valve operation & camshaft drive:	dohc, cams driven by double chain, 4 valves per cylinder, VarioCam Plus, intake camshaft timing varies 40°, intake valve lift
Carburation:	Bosch DME, Motronic M 7.8, sequential multi-point manifold injection
Ignition system:	Bosch DME, distributorless ignition system with six individual ignition coils
Firing order:	1 - 6 - 2 - 4 - 3 - 5
Engine lubrication:	Integrated dry sump
Engine oil total (l):	8.75

Transmission

Drive configuration:	Rear-axle drive
Manual gearbox:	6-speed
Option Tiptronic S:	[5-speed]
Transmission type:	G 96/01 [A 96/50]
Transmission ratios:	
1st gear:	3.82 [3.60]
2nd gear:	2.20 [2.19]
3rd gear:	1.52 [1.41]
4th gear:	1.22 [1.00]
5th gear:	1.02 [0.83]
6th gear:	0.84
Reverse gear:	3.55 [3.17]
Drive ratio:	3.44 [3.37]

Body, chassis, suspension, brakes, wheels

Body design:	Steel body, 2 doors, 2 + 2 seats, entirely hot-dip galvanized body, side-impact protection beams in doors, flexible polyurethane front and rear bumpers with integrated aluminium beams, engine lid with integrated automatic rear spoiler
Coupé:	Fixed steel roof
Option:	Electric sunroof
Cabriolet:	Electric hood with electrically-heatable rear window, two retracted roll bars
Standard:	Aluminium hardtop with electrically-heatable rear window
Suspension, front:	Individually suspended with 'disconnected' light-alloy wishbones, McPherson struts with coil springs, dual-tube gas-filled shock absorbers, anti-roll bar
Suspension, rear:	Individually suspended on five wishbones per side on light-alloy multi-wishbone axle with LSA system (Light weight, Stability, Agility) with coil springs, single-tube gas-filled shock absorbers, anti-roll bar
Brakes, front/rear (Size (mm)):	Ventilated and drilled discs (318 x 28) Ventilated and drilled discs (299 x 24) Black 4-piston fixed aluminium monobloc callipers / Black 4-piston fixed aluminium monobloc callipers Bosch ABS 5.7
Wheels, front/rear:	7 J x 17 / 9 J x 17
Tyres, front/rear:	205/50 ZR 17 / 255/40 ZR 17
Option:	8 J x 18 / 10 J x 18 225/40 ZR 18 / 285/30 ZR 18

Electrical system

Alternator (W/A):	1680 / 120
Battery (V/Ah):	12 / 80

Dimensions and weight

Track, front/rear (mm):	1465 / 1500
8 J x 18 / 10 J x 18:	1465 / 1480
Wheelbase (mm):	2350
Length x width x height (mm):	4430 x 1770 x 1305
Kerb weight DIN (kg):	1345 [1400]
Cabriolet:	1425 [1480]
MY 2003–MY 2004:	1370 [1425]
Cabriolet:	1450 [1505]
Permissible gross weight (kg):	1790 [1845]
Cabriolet:	1855 [1910]
Luggage compartment (VDA (l)):	130
Luggage volume interior*:	200 / 210**
Fuel tank capacity (l):	64, including 10 reserve
C_w x A (m²):	0.30 x 1.94 = 0.582
Power/weight ratio (kg/kW/ kg/hp):	5.72 [5.95] / 4.20 [4.37]
Cabriolet:	6.06 [6.29] / 4.45 [4.62]
MY 2003 - MY 2004:	5.82 [6.06] / 4.28 [4.45]
Cabriolet:	6.17 [6.40] / 4.53 [4.70]

*with folded-down rear seat-backs
**Cabriolet with closed hood

Fuel consumption

1999/100/EG (mpg):	98 RON super plus unleaded
Urban:	17.5 [16.7]
Extra urban:	34.8 [34.8]
Combined:	25.4 [25]
CO_2-emissions (g/km):	269 [274]

Performance, production, prices

Acceleration 0-62mph/100kph (s):	5.0 [5.5]
Cabriolet:	5.2 [5.7]
0–100mph/160kph (s):	11.0 [12.0]
Cabriolet:	11.4 [12.4]
Maximum speed (mph / kph):	177 / 285 [174 / 280]
Cabriolet:	177 / 285 [174 / 280]
Production, total number:	*
*Production MY 2002:	Coupé 6,621
*Production MY 2002:	Cabriolet 7,254
Purchase prices:	
08/2001 Coupé:	DM 143,840 [DM 149,455]
Cabriolet:	DM 163,125 [DM 168,740]
08/2002 Coupé:	Euro 74,356 [Euro 77,227]
Cabriolet:	Euro 84,322 [Euro 87,193]
08/2003 Coupé:	Euro 74,504 [Euro 77,375]
Cabriolet:	Euro 84,480 [Euro 87,351]

911 Carrera 4 Coupé [Tiptronic S]
911 Carrera 4 Cabriolet [Tiptronic S]
MY 2002–MY 2004
MY 2002–MY 2005

Engine

Engine design:	6-cylinder horizontally-opposed
Installation:	Rear-engine
Cooling system:	Water-cooled
Engine type:	M 96/03 [M 96/03]
Displacement (cc):	3596
Bore x stroke (mm):	96 x 82.8
Engine output DIN (kW/hp):	235/320 at 6800rpm
Maximum torque (Nm/lb ft):	370/273 at 4250rpm
Output per litre (kW/l / hp/l):	65.4 / 89.0
Compression ratio:	11.3 : 1
Valve operation & camshaft drive:	dohc, cams driven by double chain, 4 valves per cylinder, VarioCam Plus, intake camshaft timing varies 40°, intake valve lift
Carburation:	Bosch DME, Motronic M 7.8, sequential multi-point manifold injection
Ignition system:	Bosch DME, distributorless ignition system with six individual ignition coils
Firing order:	1 - 6 - 2 - 4 - 3 - 5
Engine lubrication:	Integrated dry sump
Engine oil total (l):	8.75

Transmission

Drive configuration:	4-wheel-drive with visco-clutch, cardan shaft
Manual gearbox:	6-speed
Option Tiptronic S:	[5-speed]
Transmission type:	G 96/31 [A 96/50]
Transmission ratios:	
1st gear:	3.82 [3.60]
2nd gear:	2.20 [2.19]
3rd gear:	1.52 [1.41]
4th gear:	1.22 [1.00]
5th gear:	1.02 [0.83]
6th gear:	0.84
Reverse gear:	3.55 [3.17]
Drive ratio:	3.44 [3.37]

Body, chassis, suspension, brakes, wheels

Body design:	Steel body, 2 doors, 2 + 2 seats, entirely hot-dip galvanized body, side-impact protection beams in doors, flexible polyurethane front and rear bumpers with integrated aluminium beams, engine lid with integrated automatic rear spoiler
Coupé:	Fixed steel roof
Option:	Electric sunroof
Cabriolet:	Electric hood with electrically-heatable rear window, two retracted roll bars
Standard:	Aluminium hardtop with electrically-heatable rear window
Suspension, front:	Individually suspended with 'disconnected' light-alloy wishbones, McPherson struts with coil springs, dual-tube gas-filled shock absorbers, anti-roll bar
Suspension, rear:	Individually suspended on five wishbones per side on light-alloy multi-wishbone axle with LSA system (Light weight, Stability, Agility) with coil springs, single-tube gas-filled shock absorbers, anti-roll bar
Brakes, front/rear (Size (mm)):	Ventilated and drilled discs (318 x 28) Ventilated and drilled discs (299 x 24) Titanium-colour 4-piston fixed aluminium monobloc callipers / Titanium-colour 4-piston fixed aluminium monobloc callipers Bosch ABS 5.7
Wheels, front/rear:	7 J x 17 / 9 J x 17
Tyres, front/rear:	205/50 ZR 17 / 255/40 ZR 17
Option:	8 J x 18 / 10 J x 18 225/40 ZR 18 / 285/30 ZR 18

Electrical system

Alternator (W/A):	1680 / 120
Battery (V/Ah):	12 / 80

Dimensions and weight

Track, front/rear (mm):	1465 / 1500
8 J x 18 / 10 J x 18:	1465 / 1480
Wheelbase (mm):	2350
Length x width x height (mm):	4430 x 1770 x 1305
Kerb weight DIN (kg):	1405 [1460]
Cabriolet:	1485 [1540]
MY 2003–MY 2005:	1430 [1485]
Cabriolet:	1510 [1565]
Permissible gross weight (kg):	1850 [1905]
Cabriolet:	1915 [1970]
Luggage compartment (VDA (l)):	100
Luggage volume interior*:	200 / 210**
Fuel tank capacity (l):	64, including 10 reserve
C_w x A (m²):	0.30 x 1.94 = 0.582
Power/weight ratio (kg/kW/kg/hp):	5.97 [6.21] / 4.39 [4.56]
Cabriolet:	6.31 [6.55] / 4.64 [4.81]
MY 2003–MY 2005:	6.08 [6.31] / 4.46 [4.64]
Cabriolet:	6.42 [6.65] / 4.71 [4.89]

*with folded-down rear seat-backs
**Cabriolet with closed hood

Fuel consumption

1999/100/EG (mpg):	98 RON super plus unleaded
Urban:	17.3 [15.6]
Extra urban:	34.1 [32.5]
Combined:	25 [23.7]
CO_2-emissions (g/km):	274 [289]

Performance, production, prices

Acceleration 0-62mph/100kph (s):	5.0 [5.5]
Cabriolet:	5.2 [5.7]
0–100mph/160kph (s):	11.1 [12.1]
Cabriolet:	11.5 [12.5]
Maximum speed (mph / kph):	177 / 285 [174 / 280]
Cabriolet:	177 / 285 [174 / 280]
Production, total number:	*
*Production MY 2002:	Coupé 6,621
*Production MY 2002:	Cabriolet 7,254
Purchase prices:	
08/2001 Coupé:	DM 155,184 [DM 160,799]
Cabriolet:	DM 174,468 [DM 180,083]
08/2002 Coupé:	Euro 80,156 [Euro 83,027]
Cabriolet:	Euro 90,132 [Euro 93,003]
08/2003 Coupé:	Euro 80,304 [Euro 83,175]
Cabriolet:	Euro 90,280 [Euro 93,151]

911 Targa [Tiptronic S]
December 2001–MY 2005

Engine

Engine design:	6-cylinder horizontally-opposed
Installation:	Rear-engine
Cooling system:	Water-cooled
Engine type:	M 96/03 [M 96/03]
Displacement (cc):	3596
Bore x stroke (mm):	96 x 82.8
Engine output DIN (kW/hp):	235/320 at 6800rpm
Maximum torque (Nm/lb ft):	370/273 at 4250rpm
Output per litre (kW/l / hp/l):	65.4 / 89.0
Compression ratio:	11.3 : 1
Valve operation & camshaft drive:	dohc, cams driven by double chain, 4 valves per cylinder, VarioCam Plus, intake camshaft timing varies 40°, intake valve lift
Carburation:	Bosch DME, Motronic M 7.8, sequential multi-point manifold injection
Ignition system:	Bosch DME, distributorless ignition system with six individual ignition coils
Firing order:	1 - 6 - 2 - 4 - 3 - 5
Engine lubrication:	Integrated dry sump
Engine oil total (l):	8.75

Transmission

Drive configuration:	Rear-axle drive
Manual gearbox:	6-speed
Option Tiptronic S:	[5-speed]
Transmission type:	G 96/01 [A 96/50]
Transmission ratios:	
1st gear:	3.82 [3.60]
2nd gear:	2.20 [2.19]
3rd gear:	1.52 [1.41]
4th gear:	1.22 [1.00]
5th gear:	1.02 [0.83]
6th gear:	0.84
Reverse gear:	3.55 [3.17]
Drive ratio:	3.44 [3.37]

Body, chassis, suspension, brakes, wheels

Body design:	Steel body, 2 doors, 2 + 2 seats, entirely hot-dip galvanized body, side-impact protection beams in doors, electric glass top, openable rear window, flexible polyurethane front and rear bumpers with integrated aluminium beams, engine lid with integrated automatic rear spoiler
Suspension, front:	Individually suspended with 'disconnected' light-alloy wishbones, McPherson struts with coil springs, dual-tube gas-filled shock absorbers, anti-roll bar
Suspension, rear:	Individually suspended on five wishbones per side on light-alloy multi-wishbone axle with LSA system (Light weight, Stability, Agility) with coil springs, single-tube gas-filled shock absorbers, anti-roll bar

Brakes, front/rear (Size (mm)):	Ventilated and drilled discs (318 x 28) Ventilated and drilled discs (299 x 24) Black 4-piston fixed aluminium monobloc callipers / Black 4-piston fixed aluminium monobloc callipers Bosch ABS 5.7
Wheels, front/rear:	7 J x 17 / 9 J x 17
Tyres, front/rear:	205/50 ZR 17 / 255/40 ZR 17
Option:	8 J x 18 / 10 J x 18 225/40 ZR 18 / 285/30 ZR 18

Electrical system

Alternator (W/A):	1680 / 120
Battery (V/Ah):	12 / 80

Dimensions and weight

Track, front/rear (mm):	1465 / 1500
8 J x 18 / 10 J x 18:	1465 / 1480
Wheelbase (mm):	2350
Length x width x height (mm):	4430 x 1770 x 1305
Kerb weight DIN (kg):	1415 [1470]
MY 2003–MY 2005:	1440 [1495]
Permissible gross weight (kg):	1845 [1900]
Luggage compartment (VDA (l)):	130
Luggage volume interior*:	230
Fuel tank capacity (l):	64, including 10 reserve
C_w x A (m²):	0.30 x 1.94 = 0.582
Power/weight ratio (kg/kW / kg/hp):	6.02 [6.25] / 4.42 [4.59]
MY 2003–MY 2005:	6.12 [6.36] / 4.50 [4.67]
*with folded-down rear seat-backs	

Fuel consumption

1999/100/EG (mpg):	98 RON super plus unleaded
Urban:	17.5 [16.7]
Extra urban:	34.8 [34.8]
Combined:	25.4 [25]
CO_2-emissions (g/km):	269 [274]

Performance, production, prices

Acceleration 0-62mph/100kph (s):	5.2 [5.7]
0–100mph/160kph (s):	11.4 [12.4]
Maximum speed (mph / kph):	177 / 285 [174 / 280]
Production, total number:	*
*Production MY 2002:	Targa 2,693
Purchase prices:	
08/2001 Targa:	DM 159,041 [DM 164,656]
08/2002 Targa:	Euro 82,128 [Euro 84,999]
08/2003 Targa:	Euro 82,276 [Euro 85,147]

911 Carrera 4S Coupé [Tiptronic S]
December 2001–2005

Engine

Engine design:	6-cylinder horizontally-opposed
Installation:	Rear-engine
Cooling system:	Water-cooled
Engine type:	M 96/03 [M 96/03]
Displacement (cc):	3596
Bore x stroke (mm):	96 x 82.8
Engine output DIN (kW/hp):	235/320 at 6800rpm
Maximum torque (Nm/lb ft):	370/273 at 4250rpm
Output per litre (kW/l / hp/l):	65.4 / 89.0
Compression ratio:	11.3 : 1
Valve operation & camshaft drive:	dohc, cams driven by double chain, 4 valves per cylinder, VarioCam Plus, intake camshaft timing varies 40°, intake valve lift
Carburation:	Bosch DME, Motronic M 7.8, sequential multi-point manifold injection
Ignition system:	Bosch DME, distributorless ignition system with six individual ignition coils
Firing order:	1 - 6 - 2 - 4 - 3 - 5
Engine lubrication:	Integrated dry sump
Engine oil total (l):	8.75

Transmission

Drive configuration:	4-wheel-drive with visco-clutch, cardan shaft
Manual gearbox:	6-speed
Option Tiptronic S:	[5-speed]
Transmission type:	G 96/31 [A 96/50]
Transmission ratios:	
1st gear:	3.82 [3.60]
2nd gear:	2.20 [2.19]
3rd gear:	1.52 [1.41]
4th gear:	1.22 [1.00]
5th gear:	1.02 [0.83]
6th gear:	0.84
Reverse gear:	3.55 [3.17]
Drive ratio:	3.44 [3.37]

Body, chassis, suspension, brakes, wheels

Body design:	Steel coupé body, 2 doors, 2 + 2 seats, entirely hot-dip galvanized body, side-impact protection beams in doors, wider rear wings and side skirts, flexible polyurethane front and rear bumpers with integrated aluminium beams, front bumper with bigger air intakes, rear bumper with air outlets, engine lid with integrated automatic rear spoiler and red non-reflecting valance
Option:	Electric sunroof
Suspension, front:	Individually suspended with 'disconnected' light-alloy wishbones, McPherson struts with coil springs, dual-tube gas-filled shock bsorbers, anti-roll bar
Suspension, rear:	Individually suspended on five wishbones per side on light-alloy multi-wishbone axle with LSA system (Light weight, Stability, Agility) with coil springs, single-tube gas-filled shock absorbers, anti-roll bar
Brakes, front/rear (Size (mm)):	Ventilated and drilled discs (330 x 34) Ventilated and drilled discs (330 x 28) Red 4-piston fixed aluminium monobloc callipers / Red 4-piston fixed aluminium monobloc callipers Bosch ABS 5.7
Option MY 2003–2005:	Porsche Ceramic Composite Brake (PCCB) Ventilated and drilled ceramic composite discs (350 x 34) / Ventilated and drilled ceramic composite discs (350 x 28) Yellow 6-piston fixed aluminium monobloc callipers / Yellow 4-piston fixed aluminium monobloc callipers Bosch ABS 5.7
Wheels, front/rear:	8 J x 18 / 11 J x 18
Tyres, front/rear:	225/40 ZR 18 / 295/30 ZR 18

Electrical system

Alternator (W/A):	1680 / 120
Battery (V/Ah):	12 / 80

Dimensions and weight

Track, front/rear (mm):	1472 / 1528
Wheelbase (mm):	2350
Length x width x height (mm):	4435 x 1830 x 1295
Kerb weight DIN (kg):	1470 [1525]
MY 2003–2005:	1495 [1550]
Permissible gross weight (kg):	1870 [1925]
Luggage compartment (VDA (l)):	100
Luggage volume interior*:	200
Fuel tank capacity (l):	64, including 10 reserve
C_w x A (m^2):	0.30 x 2.00 = 0.60
Power/weight ratio (kg/kW/kg/hp):	6.25 [6.48] / 4.59 [4.76]
MY 2003–2005:	6.36 [6.59] / 4.67 [4.84]
*with folded-down rear seat-backs	

Fuel consumption

1999/100/EG (mpg):	98 RON super plus unleaded
Urban:	17.3 [15.5]
Extra urban:	33.2 [31.6]
Combined:	24.8 [23.3]
CO_2-emissions (g/km):	277 [294]

Performance, production, prices

Acceleration 0-62mph/100kph (s):	5.1 [5.6]
0–100mph/160kph (s):	11.3 [12.3]
Maximum speed (mph / kph):	174 / 280 [171 / 275]
Production, total number:	*
*Production MY 2002:	Coupé 4,817
Purchase prices:	
08/2001 Coupé:	DM 170,158 [DM 175,773]
08/2002 Coupé:	Euro 88,740 [Euro 91,611]
08/2003 Coupé:	Euro 89,816 [Euro 92,687]

911 Carrera Coupé with performance kit
911 Carrera Cabriolet with porformance kit
MY 2003–MY 2004

Engine

Engine design:	6-cylinder horizontally-opposed
Installation:	Rear-engine
Cooling system:	Water-cooled
Engine type:	M 96/03 S
Displacement (cc):	3596
Bore x stroke (mm):	96 x 82.8
Engine output DIN (kW/hp):	254/345 at 6800rpm
Maximum torque (Nm/lb ft):	370/273 at 4800rpm
Output per litre (kW/l / hp/l):	70.6 / 95.9
Compression ratio:	11.3 : 1
Valve operation & camshaft drive:	dohc, cams driven by double chain, 4 valves per cylinder, VarioCam Plus, intake camshaft timing varies 40°, intake valve lift
Carburation:	Bosch DME, Motronic M 7.8, sequential multi-point manifold injection
Ignition system:	Bosch DME, distributorless ignition system with six individual ignition coils
Firing order:	1 - 6 - 2 - 4 - 3 - 5
Engine lubrication:	Integrated dry sump
Engine oil total (l):	8.75

Transmission

Drive configuration:	Rear-axle drive
Manual gearbox:	6-speed
Transmission type:	G 96/01
Transmission ratios:	
1st gear:	3.82
2nd gear:	2.20
3rd gear:	1.52
4th gear:	1.22
5th gear:	1.02
6th gear:	0.84
Reverse gear:	3.55
Drive ratio:	3.44

Body, chassis, suspension, brakes, wheels

Body design:	Steel body, 2 doors, 2 + 2 seats, entirely hot-dip galvanized body, side-impact protection beams in doors, flexible polyurethane front and rear bumpers with integrated aluminium beams, engine lid with integrated automatic rear spoiler
Coupé:	Fixed steel roof
Option:	Electric sunroof
Cabriolet:	Electric hood with electrically-heatable rear window, two retracted roll bars
Standard:	Aluminium hardtop with electrically-heatable rear window
Suspension, front:	Individually suspended with 'disconnected' light-alloy wishbones, McPherson struts with coil springs, dual-tube gas-filled shock absorbers, anti-roll bar
Suspension, rear:	Individually suspended on five wishbones per side on light-alloy multi-wishbone axle with LSA system (Light weight, Stability, Agility) with coil springs, single-tube gas-filled shock absorbers, anti-roll bar
Brakes, front/rear (Size (mm)):	Ventilated and drilled discs (318 x 28) Ventilated and drilled discs (299 x 24) Black 4-piston fixed aluminium monobloc callipers / Black 4-piston fixed aluminium monobloc callipers Bosch ABS 5.7
Wheels, front/rear:	7 J x 17 / 9 J x 17
Tyres, front/rear:	205/50 ZR 17 / 255/40 ZR 17
Option:	8 J x 18 / 10 J x 18 225/40 ZR 18 / 285/30 ZR 18

Electrical system

Alternator (W/A):	1680 / 120
Battery (V/Ah):	12 / 80

Dimensions and weight

Track, front/rear (mm):	1465 / 1500
8 J x 18 / 10 J x 18:	1465/ 1480
Wheelbase (mm):	2350
Length x width x height (mm):	4430 x 1770 x 1305
Kerb weight (kg):	1345
MY 2003–MY 2005:	1370
Cabriolet:	1425
MY 2003–MY 2005:	1450
Permissible gross weight (kg):	1790
Cabriolet:	1855
Luggage compartment (VDA (l)):	130
Luggage volume interior*:	200 / 210**
Fuel tank capacity (l):	64, including 10 reserve
C_w x A (m^2):	0.30 x 1.94 = 0.582
Power/weight ratio (kg/kW/kg/hp):	5.29 / 3.89
MY 2003–MY 2005:	5.39 / 3.97
Cabriolet:	5.61 / 4.13
MY 2003–MY 2005:	5.70 / 4.20

*with folded-down rear seat-backs
**Cabriolet with closed hood

Fuel consumption

1999/100/EG (mpg):	98 RON super plus unleaded
Urban:	17.1
Extra urban:	34.1
Combined:	25
CO_2-emissions (g/km):	274

Performance, production, prices

Acceleration 0-62mph/100kph (s):	4.9
Cabriolet:	5.1
0–124mph/200kph (s):	16.5
Cabriolet:	n/a
Maximum speed (mph / kph):	180 / 290
Cabriolet:	180 / 290
Production, total number:	
Purchase price for option:	
08/2002 performance kit X51:	Euro 9,727
as Tequipment Carrera Powerkit:	Euro 7,946
08/2003 performance kit X51:	Euro 9,727
as Tequipment Carrera Powerkit:	Euro 7,946

911 turbo Coupé
with performance kit [Tiptronic S]
November 2001–2005
911 turbo Cabriolet
with performance kit [Tiptronic S]
MY 2004–2005

Engine

Engine design:	6-cylinder horizontally-opposed, twin-turbo charger, twin-intercooler
Installation:	Rear-engine
Cooling system:	Water-cooled
Engine type:	M 96/70 E (M 96/70 E)
Displacement (cc):	3600
Bore x stroke (mm):	100 x 76.4
Engine output DIN (kW/hp):	331/450 at 5700rpm
Maximum torque (Nm/lb ft):	620/457 at 3500-4500rpm
Output per litre (kW/l / hp/l):	91.4 / 125.0
Compression ratio:	9.4 : 1
Valve operation & camshaft drive:	dohc, cams driven by double chain, 4 valves per cylinder, VarioCam Plus, intake camshaft timing varies 25°, intake valve lift
Carburation:	Bosch DME, Motronic M 7.8, sequential multi-point manifold injection
Ignition system:	Bosch DME, distributorless ignition system with six individual ignition coils
Firing order:	1 - 6 - 2 - 4 - 3 - 5
Engine lubrication:	Dry sump
Engine oil total (l):	11.0

Transmission

Drive configuration:	4-wheel-drive with visco-clutch, cardan shaft
Manual gearbox:	6-speed*
Option Tiptronic S:	[5-speed]
Transmission type:	G 96/50 [A 96/50]
Transmission ratios:	
1st gear:	3.82 [3.59]
2nd gear:	2.15 [2.19]
3rd gear:	1.41 [1.41]
4th gear:	1.12 [1.00]
5th gear:	0.92 [0.83]
6th gear:	0.75
Reverse gear:	2.86 [1.99/3.16]
Drive ratio:	3.44 [2.89]
*modifiziertes Schaltgetriebe	

Body, chassis, suspension, brakes, wheels

Body design:	Steel body, 2 doors, 2 + 2 seats, entirely hot-dip galvanized body, side-impact protection beams in doors, wider rear wings with air intakes and side skirts, flexible polyurethane front and rear bumpers with integrated aluminium beams, front bumper with bigger air intakes, rear bumper with air outlets, engine lid with integrated spoiler lip and automatic rear wing
Coupé:	Fixed steel roof
Option:	Electric sunroof
Cabriolet:	Electric hood with electrically-heatable rear window, two retracted roll bars
Standard:	Aluminium hardtop with electrically-heatable rear window
Suspension, front:	Individually suspended with 'disconnected' light-alloy wishbones, McPherson struts with coil springs, dual-tube gas-filled shock absorbers, anti-roll bar
Suspension, rear:	Individually suspended on five wishbones per side on light-alloy multi-wishbone axle with LSA system (Light weight, Stability, Agility) with coil springs, single-tube gas-filled shock absorbers, anti-roll bar
Brakes, front/rear (Size (mm)):	Ventilated and drilled discs (330 x 34) Ventilated and drilled discs (330 x 28) Red 4-piston fixed aluminium monobloc callipers / Red 4-piston fixed aluminium monobloc callipers Bosch ABS 5.7
Option MY 2003–2005:	Porsche Ceramic Composite Brake (PCCB) Ventilated and drilled ceramic composite discs (350 x 34) / Ventilated and drilled ceramic composite discs (350 x 28) Yellow 6-piston fixed aluminium monobloc callipers / Yellow 4-piston fixed aluminium monobloc callipers Bosch ABS 5.7
Wheels, front/rear:	8 J x 18 / 11 J x 18
Tyres, front/rear:	225/40 ZR 18 / 295/30 ZR 18

Electrical system

Alternator (W/A):	1680 / 120
Battery (V/Ah):	12 / 80

Dimensions and weight

Track, front/rear (mm):	1465 / 1522
MY 2003–2005:	1472 / 1528
Wheelbase (mm):	2350
Length x width x height (mm):	4435 x 1830 x 1295
Kerb weight DIN (kg):	1540 [1585]
MY 2004–2005:	1590 [1630]
Cabriolet:	1660 [1700]
Permissible gross weight (kg):	1885 [1930]
MY 2004–2005:	1935 [1975]
Cabriolet:	1980 [2020]
Luggage compartment (VDA (l)):	100
Luggage volume interior*:	200 / 210**
Fuel tank capacity (l):	64, including 10 reserve
C_w x A (m²):	0.31 x 2.00 = 0.62
Power/weight ratio (kg/kW/ kg/hp/):	4.65 [4.78] / 3.42 [3.52]
MY 2004–2005:	4.80 [4.92] / 3.53 [3.62]
Cabriolet:	5.01 [5.13] / 3.68 [3.77]
*with folded-down rear seat-backs	
**Cabriolet with closed hood	

Fuel consumption

1999/100/EG (mpg):	98 RON super plus unleaded
Urban:	14.4 [12.7]
Extra urban:	29.1 [28.8]
Combined:	21.2 [19.9]
CO_2-emissions (g/km):	324 [345]

Performance, production, prices

Acceleration 0-62mph/100kph (s):	4.2 [4.5]
MY 2004–MY 2005:	4.2 [4.5]
Cabriolet.	4.3 [4.6]
Maximum speed (mph / kph):	190 / 307 [186 / 300]
Cabriolet:	190 / 307 [186 / 300]
Production, total number:	
Purchase prices for option:	
08/2001 performance kit X50:	DM 24,730
08/2002 performance kit X50:	Euro 12,748
08/2003 performance kit X50:	Euro 12,748

911 GT 3 Coupé
911 GT 3 Clubsport Coupé
January 2003–MY 2005

Engine

Engine design:	6-cylinder horizontally-opposed
Installation:	Rear-engine
Cooling system:	Water-cooled
Engine type:	M 96/79
Displacement (cc):	3600
Bore x stroke (mm):	100 x 76.4
Engine output DIN (kW/hp):	280/381 at 7400rpm
Maximum torque (Nm/lb ft):	385/284 at 5000rpm
Output per litre (kW/l / hp/l):	77.8 / 105.8
Compression ratio:	11.7 : 1
Valve operation & camshaft drive:	dohc, cams driven by double chain, 4 valves per cylinder, VarioCam, intake camshaft timing varies 45°
Carburation:	Bosch DME, Motronic M 7.8, sequential multi-point manifold injection
Ignition system:	Bosch DME, distributorless ignition system with six individual ignition coils
Firing order:	1 - 6 - 2 - 4 - 3 - 5
Engine lubrication:	Dry sump
Engine oil total (l):	12.5

Transmission

Drive configuration:	Rear-axle drive
Manual gearbox:	6-speed
Transmission type:	G 96/96
Transmission ratios:	
1st gear:	3.82
2nd gear:	2.15
3rd gear:	1.56
4th gear:	1.21
5th gear:	1.00
6th gear:	0.85
Reverse gear:	2.86
Drive ratio:	3.44
Ltd-slip diff. load/deceleration (%):	40 / 60

Body, chassis, suspension, brakes, wheels

Body design:	Steel body, 2 doors, 2 seats, entirely hot-dip galvanized body, side-impact protection beams in doors, flexible polyurethane front and rear bumpers with integrated aluminium beams, front bumper with spoiler, side skirts, engine lid with spoiler lip and fixed rear spoiler
Clubsport:	Roll cage (roll bar fixed by screws, front part enclosed)
Suspension, front:	Individually suspended with 'disconnected' light-alloy wishbones, McPherson struts with coil springs, dual-tube gas-filled shock absorbers, anti-roll bar
Suspension, rear:	Individually suspended on five wishbones per side on light-alloy multi-wishbone axle with LSA system (Light weight, Stability, Agility) with coil springs, single-tube gas-filled shock absorbers, anti-roll bar
Brakes, front/rear (Size (mm)):	Ventilated and drilled discs (350 x 34) Ventilated and drilled discs (330 x 28) Red 4-piston fixed aluminium monobloc callipers / Red 4-piston fixed aluminium monobloc callipers Bosch ABS 5.7
Option:	Porsche Ceramic Composite Brake (PCCB) Ventilated and drilled ceramic composite discs (350 x 34) / Ventilated and drilled ceramic composite discs (350 x 28) Yellow 6-piston fixed aluminium monobloc callipers / Yellow 4-piston fixed aluminium monobloc callipers Bosch ABS 5.7
Wheels, front/rear:	8.5 J x 18 / 11 J x 18
Tyres, front/rear:	235/40 ZR 18 / 295/30 ZR 18

Electrical system

Alternator (W/A):	1680 / 120
Battery (V/Ah):	12 / 80

Dimensions and weight

Track, front/rear (mm):	1485 / 1495
Wheelbase (mm):	2355
Length x width x height (mm):	4435 x 1770 x 1275
Kerb weight DIN (kg):	1380
Permissible gross weight (kg):	1660
Luggage compartment (VDA (l)):	110
Fuel tank capacity (l):	89, including 12.5 reserve
C_w x A (m²):	0.30 x 1.95 = 0.585
Power/weight ratio (kg/kW / kg/hp):	4.92 / 3.62

Fuel consumption

1999/100/EG (mpg):	98 RON super plus unleaded
Urban:	13.9
Extra urban:	32.1
Combined:	21.8
CO_2-emissions (g/km):	328

Performance, production, prices

Acceleration 0-62mph/100kph (s):	4.5
0–124mph/200kph (s):	14.3
Maximum speed (mph / kph):	190 / 306
Production, total number:	
Purchase prices:	
01/2003 Coupé:	Euro 102,112
Coupé-Clubsport:	Euro 102,112

911 GT 2 Coupé
911 GT 2 Clubsport Coupé
April 2003–MY 2005

Engine

Engine design:	6-cylinder horizontally-opposed, twin-turbocharger, twin-intercooler
Installation:	Rear-engine
Cooling system:	Water-cooled
Engine type:	M 96/70 SL
Displacement (cc):	3600
Bore x stroke (mm):	100 x 76.4
Engine output DIN (kW/hp):	355/483 at 5700rpm
Maximum torque (Nm/lb ft):	640/472 at 3500-4500rpm
Output per litre (kW/l / hp/l):	98.6 / 134.2
Compression ratio:	9.4 : 1
Valve operation & camshaft drive:	dohc, cams driven by double chain, 4 valves per cylinder, VarioCam Plus, intake camshaft timing varies 30°, intake valve lift
Carburation:	Bosch DME, Motronic M 7.8, sequential multi-point manifold injection
Ignition system:	Bosch DME, distributorless ignition system with six individual ignition coils
Firing order:	1 - 6 - 2 - 4 - 3 - 5
Engine lubrication:	Dry sump
Engine oil total (l):	11.0

Transmission

Drive configuration:	Rear-axle drive
Manual gearbox:	6-speed
Transmission type:	G 96/88
Transmission ratios:	
1st gear:	3.82
2nd gear:	2.05
3rd gear:	1.41
4th gear:	1.12
5th gear:	0.92
6th gear:	0.75
Reverse gear:	2.86
Drive ratio:	3.44
Ltd-slip diff. load/deceleration (%):	40 / 60

Body, chassis, suspension, brakes, wheels

Body design:	Steel body, 2 doors, 2 seats, entirely hot-dip galvanized body, side-impact protection beams in doors, wider rear wings with air intakes and side skirts, flexible polyurethane front and rear bumpers with integrated aluminium beams, front bumper with bigger air intakes and additional air outlets, rear bumper with air outlets, engine lid with integrated spoiler lip and fixed rear spoiler
Clubsport:	Air outlet in front bumper in carbon-look, fixed carbon rear spoiler, manually adjustable, wing mirrors in carbon-look, roll cage (roll bar fixed by screws, front part enclosed)

Suspension, front:	Individually suspended with 'disconnected' light-alloy wishbones, McPherson struts with coil springs, dual-tube gas-filled shock absorbers, anti-roll bar
Suspension, rear:	Individually suspended on five wishbones per side on light-alloy multi-wishbone axle with LSA system (Light weight, Stability, Agility) with coil springs, single-tube gas-filled shock absorbers, anti-roll bar
Brakes, front/rear (Size (mm)):	Porsche Ceramic Composite Brake (PCCB) Ventilated and drilled ceramic composite discs (350 x 34) / Ventilated and drilled ceramic composite discs (350 x 28) Yellow 6-piston fixed aluminium monobloc callipers / Yellow 4-piston fixed aluminium monobloc callipers Bosch ABS 5.7
Wheels, front/rear:	8.5 J x 18 / 12 J x 18
Tyres, front/rear:	235/40 ZR 18 / 315/30 ZR 18

Electrical system

Alternator (W/A):	1680 / 120
Battery (V/Ah):	12 / 80

Dimensions and weight

Track, front/rear (mm):	1495 / 1520
Wheelbase (mm):	2355
Length x width x height (mm):	4450 x 1830 x 1275
Kerb weight DIN (kg):	1420
Permissible gross weight (kg):	1730
Luggage compartment (VDA (l)):	110
Fuel tank capacity (l):	89, including 12.5 reserve
C_w x A (m^2):	0.34 x 1.96 = 0.666
Power/weight ratio (kg/kW/kg/hp):	4.00 / 2.93

Fuel consumption

1999/100/EG (mpg):	98 RON super plus unleaded
Urban:	14.9
Extra urban:	30.4
Combined:	21.8
CO_2-emissions (g/km):	309

Performance, production, prices

Acceleration 0-62mph/100kph (s):	4.0
0-100mph/160kph (s):	8.3
Maximum speed (mph / kph):	198 / 319
Production, total number:	
Purchase prices:	
04/2003 Coupé:	Euro 184,674
Coupé-Clubsport:	Euro 184,674

911 Carrera 4S Cabriolet [Tiptronic S]
Spring 2003–MY 2005

Engine

Engine design:	6-cylinder horizontally-opposed
Installation:	Rear-engine
Cooling system:	Water-cooled
Engine type:	M 96/03 [M 96/03]
Displacement (cc):	3596
Bore x stroke (mm):	96 x 82.8
Engine output DIN (kW/hp):	235/320 at 6800rpm
Maximum torque (Nm/lb ft):	370/273 at 4250rpm
Output per litre (kW/l / hp/l):	65.4 / 89.0
Compression ratio:	11.3 : 1
Valve operation & camshaft drive:	dohc, cams driven by double chain, 4 valves per cylinder, VarioCam Plus, intake camshaft timing varies 40°, intake valve lift
Carburation:	Bosch DME, Motronic M 7.8, sequential multi-point manifold injection
Ignition system:	Bosch DME, distributorless ignition system with six individual ignition coils
Firing order:	1 - 6 - 2 - 4 - 3 - 5
Engine lubrication:	Integrated dry sump
Engine oil total (l):	8.75

Transmission

Drive configuration:	4-wheel-drive with visco-clutch, cardan shaft
Manual gearbox:	6-speed
Option Tiptronic S:	[5-speed]
Transmission type:	G 96/31 [A 96/50]
Transmission ratios:	
1st gear:	3.82 [3.60]
2nd gear:	2.20 [2.19]
3rd gear:	1.52 [1.41]
4th gear:	1.22 [1.00]
5th gear:	1.02 [0.83]
6th gear:	0.84
Reverse gear:	3.55 [3.17]
Drive ratio:	3.44 [3.37]

Body, chassis, suspension, brakes, wheels

Body design:	Steel cabriolet body, 2 doors, 2 + 2 seats, entirely hot-dip galvanized body, side-impact protection beams in doors, wider rear wings and side skirts, flexible polyurethane front and rear bumpers with integrated aluminium beams, front bumper with bigger air intakes, rear bumper with air outlets, engine lid with integrated automatic rear spoiler and red non-reflecting valance, electric hood with electrically-heatable rear window, two retracted roll bars
Standard:	Aluminium hardtop with electrically-heatable rear window
Suspension, front:	Individually suspended with 'disconnected' light-alloy wishbones, McPherson struts with coil springs, dual-tube gas-filled shock absorbers, anti-roll bar
Suspension, rear:	Individually suspended on five wishbones per side on light-alloy multi-wishbone axle with LSA system (Light weight, Stability, Agility) with coil springs, single-tube gas-filled shock absorbers, anti-roll bar
Brakes, front/rear (Size (mm)):	Ventilated and drilled discs (330 x 34) Ventilated and drilled discs (330 x 28) Red 4-piston fixed aluminium monobloc callipers / Red 4-piston fixed aluminium monobloc callipers Bosch ABS 5.7
Option:	Porsche Ceramic Composite Brake (PCCB) Ventilated and drilled ceramic composite discs (350 x 34) / Ventilated and drilled ceramic composite discs (350 x 28) Yellow 6-piston fixed aluminium monobloc callipers / Yellow 4-piston fixed aluminium monobloc callipers Bosch ABS 5.7

Wheels, front/rear:	8 J x 18 / 11 J x 18
Tyres, front/rear:	225/40 ZR 18 / 295/30 ZR 18

Electrical system

Alternator (W/A):	1680 / 120
Battery (V/Ah):	12 / 80

Dimensions and weight

Track, front/rear (mm):	1472 / 1528
Wheelbase (mm):	2350
Length x width x height (mm):	4435 x 1830 x 1295
Kerb weight DIN (kg):	1565 [1620]
Permissible gross weight (kg):	1965 [2020]
Luggage compartment (VDA (l)):	100
Luggage volume interior*:	210**
Fuel tank capacity (l):	64, including 10 reserve
C_w x A (m²):	0.30 x 2.00 = 0.60
Power/weight ratio (kg/kW/ kg/hp):	6.65 [6.89] / 4.89 [5.06]

*with folded-down rear seat-backs
**Cabriolet with closed hood

Fuel consumption

1999/100/EG (mpg):	98 RON super plus unleaded
Urban:	17.3 [15.4]
Extra urban:	33.2 [31.6]
Combined:	24.8 [23.1]
CO_2-emissions (g/km):	277 [299]

Performance, production, prices

Acceleration 0-62mph/100kph (s):	5.3 [5.9]
0–100mph/160kph (s):	11.8 [13.4]
Maximum speed (mph / kph):	174 / 280 [171 / 275]
Production, total number:	
Purchase price:	
08/2003 Cabriolet:	Euro 99,792 [Euro 102,663]

911 turbo Cabriolet [Tiptronic S]
MY 2004–MY 2005

Engine

Engine design:	6-cylinder horizontally-opposed, twin-turbocharger, twin-intercooler
Installation:	Rear-engine
Cooling system:	Water-cooled
Engine type:	M 96/70 [M 96/70]
Displacement (cc):	3600
Bore x stroke (mm):	100 x 76.4
Engine output DIN (kW/hp):	309/420 at 6000rpm
Maximum torque (Nm/lb ft):	560/413 at 2700-4600rpm
Output per litre (kW/l / hp/l):	85.8 / 116.7
Compression ratio:	9.4 : 1
Valve operation & camshaft drive:	dohc, cams driven by double chain, 4 valves per cylinder, VarioCam Plus, intake camshaft timing varies 25°, intake valve lift
Carburation:	Bosch DME, Motronic M 7.8, sequential multi-point manifold injection
Ignition system:	Bosch DME, distributorless ignition system with six individual ignition coils
Firing order:	1 - 6 - 2 - 4 - 3 - 5
Engine lubrication:	Dry sump
Engine oil total (l):	11.0

Transmission

Drive configuration:	4-wheel-drive with visco-clutch, cardan shaft
Manual gearbox:	6-speed
Option Tiptronic S:	[5-speed]
Transmission type:	G 96/50 [A 96/50]
Transmission ratios:	
1st gear:	3.82 [3.59]
2nd gear:	2.05 [2.19]
3rd gear:	1.41 [1.41]
4th gear:	1.12 [1.00]
5th gear:	0.92 [0.83]
6th gear:	0.75
Reverse gear:	2.86 [1.99/3.16]
Drive ratio:	3.44 [2.89]

Body, chassis, suspension, brakes, wheels

Body design:	Steel cabriolet body, 2 doors, 2 + 2 seats, entirely hot-dip galvanized body, side-impact protection beams in doors, wider rear wings with air intakes and side skirts, flexible polyurethane front and rear bumpers with integrated aluminium beams, front bumper with bigger air intakes, rear bumper with air outlets, engine lid with integrated spoiler lip and automatic rear spoiler, electric hood with electrically-heatable rear window, two retracted roll bars
Standard:	Aluminium hardtop with electrically-heatable rear window
Suspension, front:	Individually suspended with 'disconnected' light-alloy wishbones, McPherson struts with coil springs, dual-tube gas-filled shock absorbers, anti-roll bar
Suspension, rear:	Individually suspended on five wishbones per side on light-alloy multi-wishbone axle with LSA system (Light weight, Stability, Agility) with coil springs, single-tube gas-filled shock absorbers, anti-roll bar
Brakes, front/rear (Size (mm)):	Ventilated and drilled discs (330 x 34) Ventilated and drilled discs (330 x 28) Red 4-piston fixed aluminium monobloc callipers / Red 4-piston fixed aluminium monobloc callipers Bosch ABS 5.7
Option:	Porsche Ceramic Composite Brake (PCCB) Ventilated and drilled ceramic composite discs (350 x 34) / Ventilated and drilled ceramic composite discs (350 x 28) Yellow 6-piston fixed aluminium monobloc callipers / Yellow 4-piston fixed aluminium monobloc callipers Bosch ABS 5.7

Wheels, front/rear:	8 J x 18 / 11 J x 18
Tyres, front/rear:	225/40 ZR 18 / 295/30 ZR 18

Electrical system

Alternator (W/A):	1680 / 120
Battery (V/Ah):	12 / 80

Dimensions and weight

Track, front/rear (mm):	1465 / 1522
Wheelbase (mm):	2350
Length x width x height (mm):	4435 x 1830 x 1295
Kerb weight DIN (kg):	1660 [1700]
Permissible gross weight (kg):	1980 [2020]
Luggage compartment (VDA (l)):	100
Luggage volume interior*:	210**
Fuel tank capacity (l):	64, including 10 reserve
C_w x A (m²):	0.31 x 2.00 = 0.62
Power/weight ratio (kg/kW/ hp/kg):	5.37 [5.50] / 3.95 [4.04]

*with folded-down rear seat-backs
**Cabriolet with closed hood

Fuel consumption

1999/100/EG (mpg):	98 RON super plus unleaded
Urban:	14.9 [12.9]
Extra urban:	31 [29.5]
Combined:	21.8 [20.3]
CO_2-emissions (g/kg):	309 [339]

Performance, production, prices

Acceleration 0-62mph/100kph (s):	4.3 [4.9]
0–100mph/160kph (s):	9.5 [10.7]
Maximum speed (mph / kph):	190 / 305 [185 / 298]
Production, total number:	
Purchase price:	
08/2003 Cabriolet:	Euro 138,652 [Euro 141,523]

911 GT 3 RS Coupé
MY 2004–MY 2005

Engine

Engine design:	6-cylinder horizontally-opposed
Installation:	Rear-engine
Cooling system:	Water-cooled
Engine type:	M 96/79
Displacement (cc):	3600
Bore x stroke (mm):	100 x 76.4
Engine output DIN (kW/hp):	280/381 at 7400rpm
Maximum torque (Nm/lb ft):	385/284 at 5000rpm
Output per litre (kW/l / hp/l):	77.8 / 105.8
Compression ratio:	11.7 : 1
Valve operation & camshaft drive:	dohc, cams driven by double chain, 4 valves per cylinder, VarioCam, intake camshaft timing varies 45°
Carburation:	Bosch DME, Motronic M 7.8, sequential multi-point manifold injection
Ignition system:	Bosch DME, distributorless ignition system with six individual ignition coils
Firing order:	1 - 6 - 2 - 4 - 3 - 5
Engine lubrication:	Dry sump
Engine oil total (l):	12.5

Transmission

Drive configuration:	Rear-axle drive
Manual gearbox:	6-speed
Transmission type:	G 96/96
Transmission ratios:	
1st gear:	3.82
2nd gear:	2.15
3rd gear:	1.56
4th gear:	1.21
5th gear:	1.00
6th gear:	0.85
Reverse gear:	2.86
Drive ratio:	3.44
Ltd-slip diff. load/deceleration (%):	40 / 60

Body, chassis, suspension, brakes, wheels

Body design:	Steel body, 2 doors, 2 seats, entirely hot-dip galvanized body, side-impact protection beams in doors, flexible polyurethane front and rear bumpers with integrated aluminium beams, front bumper with spoiler and additional air outlets, side skirts, carbon-fibre-reinforced plastic engine lid with spoiler lip and fixed carbon rear spoiler, carbon wing mirrors, lightweight plastic rear window
Exclusive colour:	Carrera white, red or blue 'GT 3 RS' stickers at doors and engine lid
Suspension, front:	Individually suspended with 'disconnected' light-alloy wishbones, McPherson struts with coil springs, dual-tube gas-filled shock absorbers, anti-roll bar
Suspension, rear:	Individually suspended on five wishbones per side on light-alloy multi-wishbone axle with LSA system (Light weight, Stability, Agility) with coil springs, single-tube gas-filled shock absorbers, anti-roll bar
Brakes, front/rear (Size (mm)):	Ventilated and drilled discs (350 x 34) Ventilated and drilled discs (330 x 28) Red 4-piston fixed aluminium monobloc callipers / Red 4-piston fixed aluminium monobloc callipers Bosch ABS 5.7
Option:	Porsche Ceramic Composite Brake (PCCB) Ventilated and drilled ceramic composite discs (350 x 34) / Ventilated and drilled ceramic composite discs (350 x 28) Yellow 6-piston fixed aluminium monobloc callipers / Yellow 4-piston fixed aluminium monobloc callipers Bosch ABS 5.7
Wheels, front/rear:	8.5 J x 18 / 11 J x 18
Tyres, front/rear:	235/40 ZR 18 / 295/30 ZR 18

Electrical system

Alternator (W/A):	1680 / 120
Battery (V/Ah):	12 / 80

Dimensions and weight

Track, front/rear (mm):	1485 / 1495
Wheelbase (mm):	2355
Length x width x height (mm):	4435 x 1770 x 1275
Kerb weight DIN (kg):	1360
Permissible gross weight (kg):	1660
Luggage compartment (VDA (l)):	110
Fuel tank capacity (l):	89, including 12.5 reserve
C_w x A (m^2):	0.30 x 1.95 = 0.585
Power/weight ratio (kg/kW/ kg/hp):	4.85 / 3.56

Fuel consumption

80/1268/EWG (mpg):	98 RON super plus unleaded
Urban:	14.2
Extra urban:	31.3
Combined:	21.8
CO_2-emissions (g/km):	315

Performance, production, prices

Acceleration 0-62mph/100kph (s):	4.4
0–124mph/200kph (s):	14.0
Maximum speed (mph / kph):	190 / 306
Production, total number limited:	200
Purchase price:	
08/2003 Coupé:	Euro 120,788

911 Carrera Coupé
'40th Anniversary 911'
MY 2004

Engine
Engine design:	6-cylinder horizontally-opposed
Installation:	Rear-engine
Cooling system:	Water-cooled
Engine type:	M 96/03 S
Displacement (cc):	3596
Bore x stroke (mm):	96 x 82.8
Engine output DIN (kW/hp):	254/345 at 6800rpm
Maximum torque (Nm/lb ft):	370/273 at 4800rpm
Output per litre (kW/l / hp/l):	70.6 / 95.9
Compression ratio:	11.3 : 1
Valve operation & camshaft drive:	dohc, cams driven by double chain, 4 valves per cylinder, VarioCam Plus, intake camshaft timing varies 40°, intake valve lift
Carburation:	Bosch DME, Motronic M 7.8, sequential multi-point manifold injection
Ignition system:	Bosch DME, distributorless ignition system with six individual ignition coils
Firing order:	1 - 6 - 2 - 4 - 3 - 5
Engine lubrication:	Integrated dry sump
Engine oil total (l):	8.75

Transmission
Drive configuration:	Rear-axle drive
Manual gearbox:	6-speed
Transmission type:	G 96/01
Transmission ratios:	
1st gear:	3.82
2nd gear:	2.20
3rd gear:	1.52
4th gear:	1.22
5th gear:	1.02
6th gear:	0.84
Reverse gear:	3.55
Drive ratio:	3.44
Ltd-slip diff. load/deceleration (%):	22 / 27

Body, chassis, suspension, brakes, wheels
Body design:	Steel body, 2 doors, 2 + 2 seats, entirely hot-dip galvanized body, side-impact protection beams in doors, flexible polyurethane front and rear bumpers with integrated aluminium beams, front bumper with bigger air intakes, front grilles left and right painted, side skirts, engine lid with integrated automatic rear spoiler
Exclusive colour:	GT Silver Metallic

Standard:	Electric sunroof
Suspension, front:	Individually suspended with 'disconnected' light-alloy wishbones, McPherson struts with coil springs, dual-tube gas-filled shock absorbers, anti-roll bar
Suspension, rear:	Individually suspended on five wishbones per side on light-alloy multi-wishbone axle with LSA system (Light weight, Stability, Agility) with coil springs, single-tube gas-filled shock absorbers, anti-roll bar
Brakes, front/rear (Size (mm)):	Ventilated and drilled discs (318 x 28) Ventilated and drilled discs (299 x 24) Black 4-piston fixed aluminium monobloc callipers / Black 4-piston fixed aluminium monobloc callipers Bosch ABS 5.7
Wheels, front/rear:	8 J x 18 / 10 J x 18
Tyres, front/rear:	225/40 ZR 18 / 285/30 ZR 18

Electrical system
Alternator (W/A):	1680 / 120
Battery (V/Ah):	12 / 80

Dimensions and weight
Track, front/rear (mm):	1455 / 1480
Wheelbase (mm):	2350
Length x width x height (mm):	4430 x 1770 x 1295
Kerb weight DIN (kg):	1370
Permissible gross weight (kg):	1790
Luggage compartment (VDA (l)):	130
Luggage volume interior*:	200
Fuel tank capacity (l):	64, including 10 reserve
C_w x A (m²):	0.30 x 1.94 = 0.582
Power/weight ratio (kg/kW/kg/hp):	5.29 / 3.89
*with folded-down rear seat-backs	

Fuel consumption
1999/100/EG (mpg):	98 RON super plus unleaded
Urban:	17.1
Extra urban:	34.1
Combined:	25
CO_2-emissions (g/km):	274

Performance, production, prices
Acceleration 0-62mph/100kph (s):	4.9
0–124mph/200kph (s):	16.5
Maximum speed (mph / kph):	180 / 290
Production, total number limited:	1,963
Purchase price:	
08/2003 Coupé:	Euro 95,616

Porsche 914

Porsche 914 and 914/6

In 1969, Porsche and Volkswagen presented a joint venture – the Porsche 914, often dubbed the 'VW Porsche'. The 914 resulted from studies in which both firms, independently of one another, recognized that a mid-engine layout represented a promising future design trend. In this arrangement the engine was placed behind the driver, but ahead of the rear axle. Porsche and Volkswagen already had a longstanding agreement for co-operative work, and as usual Porsche assumed the design and engineering duties. Mid-engined vehicles are especially noted for their precise handling. For a vehicle of its overall length, the 914 had a remarkably long wheelbase and very short front and rear overhang.

The 914 was first shown at the Frankfurt International Automobile Exhibition (IAA). Two different versions were offered: the base 914, with a 1.7-litre, 80hp (59kW) four-cylinder boxer engine borrowed from the VW 411 E, and the 914/6, powered by the 2-litre six-cylinder engine of the Porsche 911 T, developing 110hp (81kW). Porsche built the 914/6 in Zuffenhausen; the 914 was built by Karmann in Osnabrück.

Model year 1970 (C Series)

The two-door all-metal body incorporated a roll bar and chromium-plated bumpers with integrated round auxiliary lamps. Weighing only 7.9kg (17.4lb), the fibreglass roof could be removed and stowed in the rear boot. In total, the 914 had 370 litres (13.1cu ft) of boot space, 160 litres (5.7cu ft) in the front boot and 210 litres (7.4cu ft) in the rear boot. The corners of the bonnet were notched for flip-up headlamps, which were actuated by two electric motors. A 62-litre (13.5-gallon) fuel tank was located in a well-protected area, behind a bulkhead. For the body shape of the low-slung sports car (only 123 centimetres – 48.4 inches – tall), emphasis was placed on good aerodynamics. For this reason, the windscreen was fixed flush to the bodywork. The body structure was divided and reinforced by four transverse bulkheads.

Every 914 was equipped with a rack-and-pinion safety steering system. At the front, double-acting shock absorbers were attached to the body through a built-in tower brace. A crossmember served as a mounting point for lower A-arms and steering rack. The A-arms carried the ends of the torsion bars and the shock absorber's lower ball joint. Progressively-acting hollow rubber bump-stops limited upward suspension travel. Rear wheels were located by semi-trailing arms. Suspension characteristics were tuned by means of camber and toe angle adjustment to provide good handling. Springing was by means of coil springs and shock absorbers. The 914 was braked by a dual-circuit system with four discs and a small handbrake drum. The handbrake handle was mounted to the left of the driver's seat. The 914/6 had ventilated discs at the front. The 914 was equipped with stock wheels from the VW 411 E: 4.5 J x 15 steel wheels fitted with 155 SR 15 tyres. As an option, 165 SR 15 tyres were available. The 914/6 had 5.5 J x 15 steel wheels and 165 HR 15 tyres as standard equipment. While wheels of the four-cylinder models were held by only four wheelnuts, Porsche used five wheelnuts on the six-cylinder models.

The 914 was designed as a two-seater, but the interior was wide enough for two passengers to squeeze in side-by-side for short distances. For the first time, seats were equipped with integral headrests. The driver's seat was adjustable for reach, but the passenger seat was not; adjustment for different-sized passengers was accomplished by means of a footrest, dubbed the 'dog bone'. The left door panel included a storage pocket, the right panel an armrest and grab handle. Windscreen frame and roll bar were padded, and the cabin and boot were lined with needle felt carpeting. Interior air exhausted through two ducts behind the seats. The padded dashboard housed three round gauges: a combination instrument at the left, with fuel level and oil temperature, a tachometer in the centre, and a speedometer at the right. Other interior items included continuously variable heating and ventilation controls, glove compartment, ashtray and cigarette lighter. Levers for heating and manual throttle were placed on the centre tunnel. In keeping with familiar Porsche practice, the 914/6 ignition lock was located to the left of the steering column; on the 914, it was on the right.

The 914 was offered with two different engines. The 914 was delivered with the 1.7-litre four-cylinder fuel-injected engine of the VW 411 E, which developed 80hp (59kW) at 4900rpm. The 914/6 had the 2-litre six-cylinder of the 911 T. Developing 110hp (81kW), the boxer engine was fitted with cast-iron cylinders and achieved its rated power at 5800rpm. Compression was lowered to 8.6:1. The torque peak of 157Nm (116lb ft) was at 4200rpm. Fuel mixture was supplied by two Weber triple-choke carburettors. As on the 911, oil was supplied by a dry-sump lubrication system.

On the air-cooled four-cylinder boxer engine, cylinders and cooling fins were of cast iron, topped by aluminium-alloy cylinder heads. The central camshaft was gear driven off the crankshaft. Overhead valves were actuated by rocker arms. With a compression ratio of only 8.2:1, the engine was pressure-lubricated. Cooling was provided by a radial blower mounted directly on the crankshaft.

Both models used a Porsche five-speed manual transmission. As of early 1970, the Sportomatic transmission was available as an option. The single-plate clutch was cable actuated. Engine output was transferred to the rear wheels through double-jointed halfshafts.

Porsche's official performance figures for the 914 claimed a 0-62mph (0-100kph) time of 13 seconds, with a top speed of 110mph (177kph). The 914/6 was listed at 9.9 seconds and 125mph (201kph) respectively. Well run-in sixes have been known to sprint to 62mph (100kph) in just 8.5 seconds, and reach 129mph (207kph) with the roof in place.

Model year 1971 (D Series)

Vertical slits were cut in the shortened rear skirt for better ventilation of the hot air around the silencer.

Replicas of the 'Marathon de la Route' car could be ordered as option M471. Welded-on steel wing flares provided space for 7-inch wide Fuchs wheels, carrying 185/70 HR 15 tyres. Anti-roll bars were fitted front and rear.

Wheel choices for the 914 were 5.5 J x 15 steel, or aluminium alloys. The alloys were sourced from an Italian manufacturer, Pedrini.

Inside changes included a central windscreen defroster vent and an additional coathook on the right side of the roll bar. Other detail changes included new ignition locks and changes to the headlight controls, allowing them to be retracted only when completely turned off.

Several European countries had tightened-up their emissions regulations. In response, Porsche changed several emissions components on the four-cylinder engines: control unit, ignition distributor,

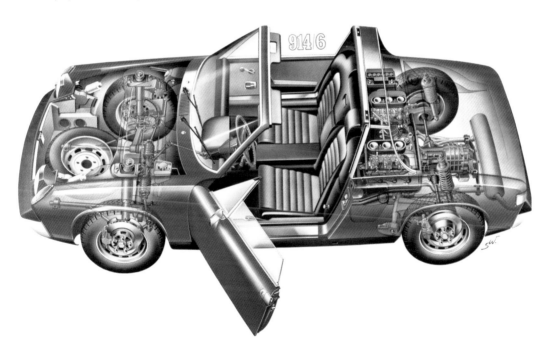

Phantom view of the 914/6, powered by the 2-litre-six-cylinder boxer engine of the 911 T

manifold pressure sensor and throttle body were modified. Fuel cut-off while coasting was eliminated, as customers had complained about backfiring. The US version of the 1.7-litre engine included an activated charcoal filter for the fuel tank vent system.

Model year 1972 (E Series)

Although the 914/6 was no longer included in Porsche's price lists, remaining examples were sold into 1972.

The interior benefited from several detail improvements. For better ventilation, additional vents were placed at the left and right ends of the dashboard. The inner door panels had a woven texture. The passenger seat was now adjustable. Windscreen wiper and washer switches were combined into a single switch unit on the steering wheel, and the steering column was altered. The bulkhead between engine and interior was modified to permit installation of automatic safety belts.

The four-cylinder injection system and engine were retuned.

Model year 1973 (F Series)

Visually, the new 914 for 1973 was recognizable by its matt-black bumpers and black engine lid script. The rear skirt was shortened to prevent bottoming on rough roads, and a sound insulation mat behind the cabin was intended to reduce interior noise. Additional insulation helped prevent overheating of the rear luggage compartment. The inside of the removable plastic top was finished with fabric matching the seat upholstery.

For improved comfort, the suspension was modified to give a softer ride.

The new interior style was reflected in matt-black window winders and door release escutcheons. The newly-introduced 2-litre model included a speedometer calibrated to 250kph (155mph). A comfort package included a vinyl roll bar cover with chromium-plated trim strips, durable velour carpeting, a leather gear-lever boot, centre console with clock, oil temperature gauge, voltmeter and dual-tone horns. A sports package added Fuchs forged-alloy wheels, front and rear anti-roll bars and halogen headlamps.

The most important new item for 1973 was the 2-litre four-cylinder engine, which was based on the 1.7-litre. Fitted with D-Jetronic fuel injection, the engine developed 100hp (74kW) at 5000rpm, and maximum torque of 157Nm (116lb ft) at only 3500rpm. A new dry-element air cleaner and new engine mounts reduced engine noise.

A more precise gear change and shorter gear lever added more enjoyment to sporty driving.

The 914 2.0 accelerated to 62mph (100kph) in just 10.5 seconds. Top speed was in excess of 118mph (190kph), and overtaking could be accomplished more quickly and more safely.

Model year 1974 (G Series)

The front bulkhead included a hole for an additional towing eye. Cars destined for overseas markets had large rubber over-riders at the rear.

All 914 models were fitted with newly-styled wheels as standard equipment.

Inside, the instrument panel and door panels were restyled. Some symbols on the dashboard were changed. Cars fitted with the new 1.8-litre engine were equipped with the speedometer of the 2-litre model, calibrated to 250kph (155mph). For added safety, the forward seat adjustment range was limited. Safety equipment included a pair of three-point automatic safety belts as standard.

The 1.7-litre engine was replaced by a 1.8-litre unit. For the European market, the engine was topped by two downdraught carburettors. Power output was 85hp (63kW) at 5000rpm; maximum torque of 138Nm (102lb ft) was achieved at 3400rpm. Cylinder bore was increased from 90mm to 93mm. Further modifications included reshaped combustion chambers, intake and exhaust ports, valve-head diameter and rocker arms. For the American and Canadian markets, the engine was fitted with new Bosch L-Jetronic injection. So equipped, the engine produced 76hp (56kW) at 4800rpm, with maximum torque of 128Nm (94lb ft) available at 3400rpm.

The clutch pressure plate was reinforced.

The 2-litre engine was slightly modified. Technical specifications remained unchanged.

Performance testing of the 1.8-litre carburated 914 saw a top speed of 110mph (178kph) and acceleration to 62mph (100kph) in 12.0 seconds.

Model year 1975 (H Series)

1975 model year cars were recognizable by their newly designed safety bumpers. A rubber-like cover hid a sturdy steel beam which could withstand an impact of up to 5mph (8kph). Driving lights set in the front bumper were now rectangular. At the rear, the number plate was illuminated from the side, as on the 911. Horns were mounted at the left and right front of the boot floor. A plastic front spoiler was available as an option.

The Comfort Package included sports steering wheel, centre console with clock, oil-temperature gauge and voltmeter, leather gear-lever boot, two-tone horns and H4 halogen headlamps. The GT Package included a front spoiler, Mahle alloy wheels and front and rear anti-roll bars. The 914 2.0 was also available in a 'GT' special edition.

Engines for the European market continued without changes. Engines for California and the rest of the United States were modified to meet new exhaust emissions standards. Exhaust systems for California included a thermal reactor, heat exchanger, pre-silencer, catalytic converter and silencer. Cars destined for California were also unique in being fitted with exhaust-gas recirculation. For the 49-state version, the catalytic converter was replaced by a section of exhaust tubing. The fuel pump was now mounted directly below the fuel tank; the expansion tank was reshaped and made of a new material.

Production of the 914 ended in the spring of 1976. The last examples were all shipped to the United States. A total of 115,646 four-cylinder 914s were built; of the 914/6, only 3338 left the factory.

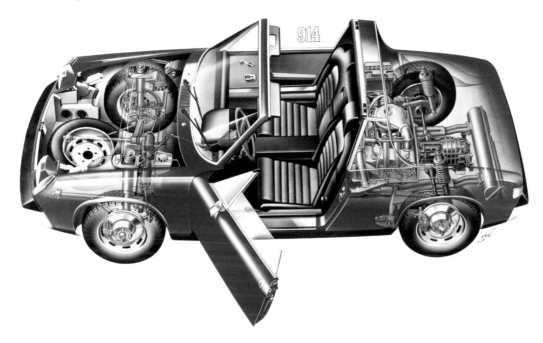

Phantom view of the 914/4, with the Volkswagen four-cylinder boxer engine

914-1.7 [Sportomatic]
MY 1970–MY 1973

Engine

Engine design:	4-cylinder horizontally-opposed
Installation:	Mid-engine
Cooling system:	Air-cooled
Engine type*:	W
Displacement (cc):	1679
Bore x stroke (mm):	90 x 66
Engine output DIN (kW/hp):	59/80 at 4900rpm
Maximum torque (Nm/lb ft):	133/98 at 2700rpm
Output per litre (kW/l / hp/l):	35.1 / 47.6
Compression ratio:	8.2 : 1
Valve operation & camshaft drive:	ohv, cam driven by gears, 2 valves per cylinder
Carburation:	Bosch D-Jetronic injection
Ignition system:	Battery coil ignition
Firing order:	1 - 4 - 3 - 2
Engine lubrication:	Full pressure oil lubrication
Engine oil total (l):	3.5
*Volkswagen engine	

Transmission

Drive configuration:	Rear-axle drive
Manual gearbox:	5-speed
Option Sportomatic:	[4-speed]*
Transmission type:	914/11 [914/15]
MY 1973:	914/12
Transmission ratios:	
1st gear:	3.091 [2.400]
2nd gear:	1.889 [1.476]
3rd gear:	1.261 [1.040]
4th gear:	0.926 [0.793]
5th gear:	0.710
Reverse gear:	3.127 [2.533]
Drive ratio:	4.429 [3.857]
*until MY 1971	

Body, chassis, suspension, brakes, wheels

Body design:	Steel roadster body, 2 doors, 2 (+ 1) seats, integrated roll-over bar, removable fibreglass roof, chromium-plated front and rear bumpers integrated in body form, flip-up headlamps, front bumper with integrated round auxiliary lamps
MY 1973:	Matt-black bumpers, front bumper with integrated round auxiliary lamps

Suspension, front:	Independent suspension struts with track control arms, one round-section longitudinal torsion bar per wheel, hydraulic double-action shock absorbers
Suspension, rear:	Independent suspension with semi-trailing arms, coil springs, hydraulic double-action shock absorbers and progressive-rate hollow rubber springs
Brakes, front/rear (Size (mm)):	Discs (282.5 x 12.7) / Discs (286 x 12.7) 2-piston fixed cast-iron callipers / 2-piston fixed cast-iron callipers
Wheels, front/rear:	4.5 J x 15 / 4.5 J x 15
Tyres, front/rear:	155 SR 15 / 155 SR 15
Option,	5.5 J x 15 / 5.5 J x 15
MY 1973 standard:	165 SR 15 / 165 SR 15

Electrical system

Alternator (W/A):	700 / 50
Battery (V/Ah):	12 / 45

Dimensions and weight

Track, front/rear (mm):	1337 / 1374
MY 1973:	1343 / 1383
Wheelbase (mm):	2450
Length x width x height (mm):	3985 x 1650 x 1230
Kerb weight DIN (kg):	900
MY 1973:	950
Permissible gross weight (kg):	1220
Luggage com., front/rear (VDA (l)):	160 / 210
Fuel tank capacity (l):	62, including 6 reserve
C_w x A (m²):	0.38 x 1.60 = 0.608
Power/weight ratio (kg/kW/kg/hp):	15.25 / 11.25
MY 1973:	16.10 / 11.87

Fuel consumption

DIN 70 030 (mpg):	35; 98 RON super leaded

Performance, production, prices

Acceleration 0-62mph/100kph (s):	13.0
Maximum speed (mph / kph):	110 / 177 [105 / 170]
Production, total number:	65,351
Purchase prices:	
12/1969:	DM 11,954.70
09/1970:	DM 11,955
09/1971:	DM 12,250
08/1972:	DM 13,360
02/1973:	DM 13,990

914/6 [Sportomatic]
MY 1970–MY 1972

Engine

Engine design:	6-cylinder horizontally-opposed
Installation:	Mid-engine
Cooling system:	Air-cooled
Engine type:	901/36 [901/37]
Displacement (cc):	1991
Bore x stroke (mm):	80 x 66
Engine output DIN (kW/hp):	81/110 at 5800rpm
Maximum torque (Nm/lb ft):	157/116 at 4200rpm
Output per litre (kW/l / hp/l):	40.7 / 55.2
Compression ratio:	8.6 : 1
Valve operation & camshaft drive:	ohc, cams driven by double chains, 2 valves per cylinder
Carburation:	2 triple-choke carburettors Weber IDT 3 C/3 C 1 also IDT-PS 4
Ignition system:	Battery, capacitive-discharge system
Firing order:	1 - 6 - 2 - 4 - 3 - 5
Engine lubrication:	Dry sump
Engine oil total (l):	9.0

Transmission

Drive configuration:	Rear-axle drive
Manual gearbox:	5-speed
Option Sportomatic:	[4-speed]*
Transmission type:	914/01 [914/05]
Transmission ratios:	
1st gear:	3.091 [2.400]
2nd gear:	1.778 [1.550]
3rd gear:	1.217 [1.125]
4th gear:	0.926 [0.857]
5th gear:	0.759
Reverse gear:	3.127 [2.533]
Drive ratio:	4.429 [3.857]
*until MY 1971	

Body, chassis, suspension, brakes, wheels

Body design:	Steel roadster body, 2 doors, 2 (+ 1) seats, integrated roll-over bar, removable fibreglass roof, chromium-plated front and rear bumpers integrated in body form, flip-up headlamps, front bumper with integrated round auxiliary lamps
Option (M 471):	Wider wing flares
Suspension, front:	Independent suspension struts with track control arms, one round-section longitudinal torsion bar per wheel, hydraulic double-action shock absorbers
Option (M 471):	Anti-roll bar
Suspension, rear:	Independent suspension with semi-trailing arms, coil springs, hydraulic double-action shock absorbers and progressive-rate hollow rubber springs
Option (M 471):	Anti-roll bar
Brakes, front/rear (Size (mm)):	Ventilated discs (282.5 x 20) / Discs (286 x 12,7) 2-piston fixed cast-iron callipers / 2-piston fixed cast-iron callipers
Wheels, front/rear:	5.5 J x 15 / 5.5 J x 15
Tyres, front/rear:	165 HR 15 / 165 HR 15
Option:	5.5 J x 14 / 5.5 J x 14 185 HR 14 / 185 HR 14
Option (M 471):	7 J x 15 / 7 J x 15 185/70 HR 15 / 185/70 / HR 15

Electrical system

Alternator (W/A):	770 / 55
Battery (V/Ah):	12 / 45

Dimensions and weight

Track, front/rear (mm):	1361 / 1382
Wheelbase (mm):	2450
Length x width x height (mm):	3985 x 1650 x 1240
Kerb weight DIN (kg):	940
Permissible gross weight (kg):	1260
Luggage com., front/rear (VDA (l)):	160 / 210
Fuel tank capacity (l):	62, including 6 reserve
C_w x A (m²):	0.38 x 1.60 = 0.608
Power/weight ratio (kg/kW/kg/hp):	11.60 / 8.54

Fuel consumption

DIN 70 030 (mpg):	31.3; 96 RON super leaded

Performance, production, prices

Acceleration 0-62mph/100kph (s):	9.9
Maximum speed (mph / kph):	125 / 201 [122 / 197]
Production, total number:	3,338
Purchase prices:	
12/1969:	DM 19,980
09/1970:	DM 19,980
09/1971:	DM 19,980
08/1972:	DM 19,980

914-2.0
MY 1973–MY 1976

Engine

Engine design:	4-cylinder horizontally-opposed
Installation:	Mid-engine
Cooling system:	Air-cooled
Engine type*:	GB
Displacement (cc):	1971
Bore x stroke (mm):	94 x 71
Engine output DIN (kW/hp):	74/100 at 5000rpm
Maximum torque (Nm/lb ft):	157/116 at 3500rpm
Output per litre (kW/l / hp/l):	37.5 / 50.7
Compression ratio:	8.0 : 1
Valve operation & camshaft drive:	ohv, cam driven by gears, 2 valves per cylinder
Carburation:	Bosch D-Jetronic injection
Ignition system:	Battery coil ignition
Firing order:	1 - 4 - 3 - 2
Engine lubrication:	Full-pressure oil lubrication
Engine oil total (l):	3.5
*Volkswagen engine	

Transmission

Drive configuration:	Rear-axle drive
Manual gearbox:	5-speed
Transmission type:	914/12
Transmission ratios:	
1st gear:	3.091
2nd gear:	1.889
3rd gear:	1.261
4th gear:	0.926
5th gear:	0.710
Reverse gear:	3.127
Drive ratio:	4.429

Body, chassis, suspension, brakes, wheels

Body design:	Steel roadster body, 2 doors, 2 (+ 1) seats, integrated roll-over bar, removable fibreglass roof, matt-black front and rear bumpers integrated in body form, flip-up headlamps, front bumper with integrated round auxiliary lamps
MY 1975 - MY 1976:	Black safety bumpers, front bumper with integrated square auxiliary lamps
Suspension, front:	Independent suspension struts with track-control arms, one round-section longitudinal

Suspension, rear:	torsion bar per wheel, hydraulic double-action shock absorbers Independent suspension with semi-trailing arms, coil springs, hydraulic double-action shock absorbers and progressive-rate hollow rubber springs
Brakes, front/rear (Size (mm)):	Discs (282.5 x 12.7) / Discs (286 x 12.7) 2-piston fixed cast-iron callipers / 2-piston fixed cast-iron callipers
Wheels, front/rear:	5.5 J x 15 / 5.5 J x 15
Tyres, front/rear:	165 HR 15 / 165 HR 15

Electrical system

Alternator (W/A):	700 / 50
Battery (V/Ah):	12 / 45

Dimensions and weight

Track, front/rear (mm):	1343 / 1383
Wheelbase (mm):	2450
Length x width x height (mm):	3985 x 1650 x 1230
MY 1975 - MY 1976:	4114 x 1650 x 1230
Kerb weight DIN (kg):	950
MY 1975 - MY 1976:	965
Permissible gross weight (kg):	1220
Luggage com., front/rear (VDA (l)):	160 / 210
Fuel tank capacity (l):	62, including 6 reserve
C_w x A (m²):	0.38 x 1.60 = 0.608
MY 1975 - MY 1976:	0.377 x 1.60 = 0.603
Power/weight ratio (kg/kW/kg/hp):	12.83 / 9.50
MY 1975 - MY 1976:	13.04 / 9.65

Fuel consumption

DIN 70 030 (mpg):	36.25; 95 RON super leaded

Performance, production, prices

Acceleration 0-62mph/100kph (s):	10.5
Maximum speed (mph / kph):	118 / 190
Production, total number:	32,522
Purchase prices:	
08/1972:	DM 13,360
02/1973:	DM 14,450
08/1973:	DM 14,990
05/1974:	DM 16,870
01/1975:	DM 17,460
04/1975:	DM 18,335

914-1.8
MY 1974–MY 1976

Engine

Engine design:	4-cylinder horizontally-opposed
Installation:	Mid-engine
Cooling system:	Air-cooled
Engine type*:	AN
Displacement (cc):	1795
Bore x stroke (mm):	93 x 66
Engine output DIN (kW/hp):	63/85 at 5000rpm
Maximum torque (Nm/lb ft):	138/102 at 3400rpm
Output per litre (kW/l / hp/l):	35.1 / 47.4
Compression ratio:	8.6 : 1
Valve operation & camshaft drive:	ohv, cam driven by gears, 2 valves per cylinder
Carburation:	2 downdraught carburettors Solex 40 PDSIT
Ignition system:	Battery coil ignition
Firing order:	1 - 4 - 3 - 2
Engine lubrication:	Full-pressure oil lubrication
Engine oil total (l):	3.5
*Volkswagen engine	

Transmission

Drive configuration:	Rear-axle drive
Manual gearbox:	5-speed
Transmission type:	914/12
Transmission ratios:	
1st gear:	3.091
2nd gear:	1.889
3rd gear:	1.261
4th gear:	0.926
5th gear:	0.710
Reverse gear:	3.127
Drive ratio:	4.429

Body, chassis, suspension, brakes, wheels

Body design:	Steel roadster body, 2 doors, 2 (+ 1) seats, integrated roll-over bar, removable fibreglass roof, matt-black front and rear bumpers integrated in body form, flip-up headlamps, front bumper with integrated round auxiliary lamps
MY 1975 - MY 1976:	Black safety bumpers, front bumper with integrated square auxiliary lamps
Suspension, front:	Independent suspension struts with track control arms, one round-section longitudinal

	torsion bar per wheel, hydraulic double-action shock absorbers
Option with sports package:	Anti-roll bar
Suspension, rear:	Independent suspension with semi-trailing arms, coil springs, hydraulic double-action shock absorbers and progressive-rate hollow rubber springs
Option with sports package:	Anti-roll bar
Brakes, front/rear (Size (mm)):	Discs (282.5 x 12.7) / Discs (286 x 12.7) 2-piston fixed cast-iron callipers / 2-piston fixed cast-iron callipers
Wheels, front/rear:	5.5 J x 15 / 5.5 J x 15
Tyres, front/rear:	165 SR 15 / 165 SR 15

Electrical system

Alternator (W/A):	700 / 50
Battery (V/Ah):	12 / 45

Dimensions and weight

Track, front/rear (mm):	1343 / 1383
Wheelbase (mm):	2450
Length x width x height (mm):	3985 x 1650 x 1230
MY 1975 - MY 1976:	4114 x 1650 x 1230
Kerb weight DIN (kg):	950
MY 1975 - MY 1976:	965
Permissible gross weight (kg):	1220
Luggage com., front/rear (VDA (l)):	160 / 210
Fuel tank capacity (l):	62, including 6 reserve
C_w x A (m²):	0.38 x 1.60 = 0.608
MY 1975 - MY 1976:	0.377 x 1.60 = 0.603
Power/weight ratio (kg/kW/kg/hp):	15.97 / 11.17
MY 1975 - MY 1976:	15.31 / 11.35

Fuel consumption

DIN 70 030 (mpg):	40; 98 RON super leaded

Performance, production, prices

Acceleration 0-62mph/100kph (s):	12.0
Maximum speed (mph / kph):	110 / 178
Production, total number:	17,773
Purchase prices:	
08/1973:	DM 13,990
05/1974:	DM 15,750
01/1975:	DM 16,300
04/1974:	DM 17,115

Porsche 914/8

Only two examples of this very special 914 were built, one red, the other silver. They were powered by the eight-cylinder engine of Porsche's 908 race car. Externally, these two cars were virtually indistinguishable from regular production versions.

The flip-up headlights of the red car were somewhat wider and fitted with two round lamps. The fuel tank had an external filler. The nose had an oil-cooler duct, and auxiliary driving lights were deleted. The wings were slightly flared to provide space for wider wheels. The suspension used titanium coil springs and stiffer shock absorbers. The engine remained as it was in the race car, with mechanical fuel injection. A single silencer was installed to reduce noise. The engine yielded 300hp (221kW) at 8200rpm. Capable of speeds in excess of 155mph (250kph), this car was not street-legal but could be driven on temporary plates.

The second car, the 914/8 S-II, was painted silver and fitted with the usual 914 flip-up headlamps. The front bumper housed stock driving lights and an oil-cooler duct. The engine was converted to four twin-choke carburettors and an air-filter. The result: 260hp (191kW) in a street-legal car. Instead of the removable top, the car had a steel top welded in place, with a sliding sunroof. On 19 September 1969, on the occasion of his 60th birthday, this car was given to Dr Ferry Porsche by Porsche employees. He proceeded to drive it for more than 10,000km (6200 miles).

Porsche 916

This 914 derivative was a rarity. Only eleven prototypes were built. Originally the 916 was intended as an answer to the Ferrari Dino, but when the costing department calculated a price of 40,000 Deutschmarks in 1972, the project was cancelled. Five examples remained in the hands of the Porsche and Piëch families. Another five examples were sold in Germany to loyal Porsche customers, and one was exported to the United States.

The body was based on the 914/6 bodyshell. Instead of a removable plastic roof, the 916 used a welded-in steel roof, rigidly attached to the windscreen header and safety roll bar. The floorpan longitudinals were reinforced. The front bumper carried a spoiler, oil cooler and two auxiliary driving lamps. Bumpers were painted body colour. Wings were widened by 9cm to fit 185/70 tyres on 7-inch wide alloy rims. The suspension was derived from that of the 1971 914/6. Anti-roll bars and Bilstein shock absorbers were mounted front and rear. The brake system, with four ventilated discs, came from the 911 S. Customers could choose interiors to suit their own tastes.

Originally it was planned to use a 2.6-litre six-cylinder engine developing 210hp (154kW) on premium-grade petrol. Because of spare-part supply difficulties, the actual engine was a 190hp (140kW) 2.4-litre, derived from the 911 S and tuned to run on regular petrol.

The 916 could accelerate to 62mph (100kph) in just under seven seconds. Top speed was measured at about 143mph (230kph). Although the 916 was never officially offered for sale, it nevertheless represents a piece of Porsche history.

914/8 S-I (test car of Ferdinand Piëch) 1969

Engine

Engine design:	8-cylinder horizontally-opposed
Installation:	Mid-engine
Cooling system:	Air-cooled
Engine type:	918
Displacement (cc):	2996
Bore x stroke (mm):	85 x 66
Engine output DIN (kW/hp):	221/300 at 8200rpm
Maximum torque (Nm/lb ft):	319/235 at 6700rpm
Output per litre (kW/l / hp/l):	73.7 / 100.1
Compression ratio:	10.5 : 1
Valve operation & camshaft drive:	ohc, cams driven by double chain, 2 valves per cylinder
Carburation:	8-plunger, twin-row, mechanical Bosch injection pump, manifold injection
Ignition system:	Transistor dual ignition
Firing order:	1 - 5 - 2 - 7 - 4 - 8 - 3 - 6
Engine lubrication:	Dry sump
Engine oil total (l):	15.0

Transmission

Drive configuration:	Rear-axle drive
Manual gearbox:	5-speed
Transmission type:	916
Transmission ratios:	
1st gear:	2.82
2nd gear:	1.76
3rd gear:	1.32
4th gear:	1.04
5th gear:	0.82
Reverse gear:	2.29
Drive ratio:	4.429
Standard:	Limited-slip differential

Body, chassis, suspension, brakes, wheels

Body design:	Steel roadster body, 2 doors, 2 seats, integrated roll-over bar, fixed steel roof, slightly flared wings, chromium-plated front and rear bumpers integrated in body form, flip-up twin headlamps, front bumper with integrated oil cooler
Suspension, front:	Independent suspension struts with track-control arms, one round-section longitudinal torsion bar per wheel, double-action shock absorbers
Suspension, rear:	Independent suspension with semi-trailing arms, titanium coil springs, double-action shock absorbers
Brakes, front/rear (Size (mm)):	Ventilated discs (282.5 x 20) / Ventilated discs (290 x 20) 2-piston fixed aluminium callipers / 2-piston fixed cast-iron callipers
Wheels, front/rear:	7 J x 15 / 7 J x 15
Tyres, front/rear:	185/70 VR 15 / 185/70 VR 15

Electrical system

Alternator (W/A):	770 / 55
Battery (V/Ah):	12 / 45

Dimensions and weight

Track, front/rear (mm):	1261 / 1337
Wheelbase (mm):	2450
Length x width x height (mm):	3985 x 1650 x 1240
Kerb weight DIN (kg):	1150
Permissible gross weight (kg):	1350
Luggage com., front/rear (VDA (l)):	160 / 210*
Fuel tank capacity (l):	117, including 10 reserve
C_w x A (m^2):	0.38 x 1.60 = 0.608
Power/weight ratio (kg/kW/ kg/hp):	4.75 / 3.50
*additional aggregates reduce volume	

Fuel

	98 RON super leaded

Performance, production

Acceleration 0-62mph/100kph (s):	app. 6,0
Maximum speed (mph / kph):	more than 155 / 250
Production, total number:	1

914/8 S-II
(Present for Ferry Porsche's 60th birthday) 1969

Engine

Engine design:	8-cylinder horizontally-opposed
Installation:	Mid-engine
Cooling system:	Air-cooled
Engine type:	918
Displacement (cc):	2996
Bore x stroke (mm):	85 x 66
Engine output DIN (kW/hp):	191/260 at 7700rpm
Maximum torque (Nm/lb ft):	260/192 at 6200rpm
Output per litre (kW/l / hp/l):	63.7 / 86.8
Compression ratio:	10.2 : 1
Valve operation & camshaft drive:	ohc, cams driven by double chain, 2 valves per cylinder
Carburation:	4 twin-choke carburettors Weber 46 IDA 2/3
Ignition system:	Battery dual ignition
Firing order:	1 - 5 - 2 - 7 - 4 - 8 - 3 - 6
Engine lubrication:	Dry sump
Engine oil total (l):	15.0

Transmission

Drive configuration:	Rear-axle drive
Manual gearbox:	5-speed
Transmission type:	916
Transmission ratios:	
1st gear:	2.82
2nd gear:	1.76
3rd gear:	1.32
4th gear:	1.04
5th gear:	0.82
Reverse gear:	2.29
Drive ratio:	4.429
Limited slip differential	

Body, chassis, suspension, brakes, wheels

Body design:	Steel roadster body, 2 doors, 2 seats, integrated roll-over bar, fixed steel roof with integrated sunroof, chromium-plated front

	and rear bumpers integrated in body form, flip-up headlamps, front bumper with integrated round auxiliary lamps and oil cooler
Suspension, front:	Independent suspension struts with track-control arms, one round-section longitudinal torsion bar per wheel, double-action shock absorbers
Suspension, rear:	Independent suspension with semi-trailing arms, titanium coil springs, double-action shock absorbers
Brakes, front/rear (Size (mm)):	Ventilated discs (282.5 x 20) / Ventilated discs (290 x 20) 2-piston fixed aluminium callipers / 2-piston fixed cast-iron callipers
Wheels, front/rear:	6 J x 15 / 6 J x 15
Tyres, front/rear:	185/70 VR 15 / 185/70 VR 15

Electrical system

Alternator (W/A):	770 / 55
Battery (V/Ah):	12 / 45

Dimensions and weight

Track, front/rear (mm):	1380 / 1403
Wheelbase (mm):	2450
Length x width x height (mm):	3985 x 1650 x 1240
Kerb weight DIN (kg):	1150
Permissible gross weight (kg):	1350
Luggage com., front/rear (VDA (l)):	160 / 210*
Fuel tank capacity (l):	117, including 10 reserve
C_w x A (m²):	0.38 x 1.60 = 0.608
Power/weight ratio (kg/kW/ kg/hp):	6.02 / 4.42
*additional aggregates reduce volume	

Fuel

	98 RON super leaded

Performance, production

Acceleration 0-62mph/100kph (s):	app. 6.0
Maximum speed (mph / kph):	156 / 252
Production, total number:	1

916
MY 1972

Engine

Engine design:	6-cylinder horizontally-opposed
Installation:	Mid-engine
Cooling system:	Air-cooled
Engine type:	911/56
planned for Europe:	911/86
Displacement (cc):	2341
911/86:	2538
Bore x stroke (mm):	84 x 70.4
911/86:	87.5 x 70.4
Engine output DIN (kW/hp):	140/190 at 6500rpm
911/86:	154/210 at 6800rpm
Maximum torque (Nm/lb ft):	216/159 at 5200rpm
911/86:	240/177 at 5200rpm
Output per litre (kW/l / hp/l):	59.8 / 81.2
911/86:	60.7 / 82.7
Compression ratio:	8.5 : 1
911/86:	9.8 : 1
Valve operation & camshaft drive:	ohc, cams driven by double chain, 2 valves per cylinder
Carburation:	6-plunger, twin-row, mechanical Bosch injection pump, manifold injection
Ignition system:	Battery coil ignition
Firing order:	1 - 6 - 2 - 4 - 3 - 5
Engine lubrication:	Dry sump
Engine oil total (l):	12.0

Transmission

Drive configuration:	Rear-axle drive
Manual gearbox:	5-speed
Transmission type:	915/20
Transmission ratios:	
1st gear:	3.182
2nd gear:	1.833
3rd gear:	1.261
4th gear:	0.962
5th gear:	0.759
Reverse gear:	3.325
Drive ratio:	4.429
Limited slip differential	

Body, chassis, suspension, brakes, wheels

Body design:	Steel roadster body, 2 doors, 2 seats, integrated roll-over bar, fixed steel roof, wider wing flares front and rear, painted plastic front and rear bumpers integrated in body form, flip-up headlamps, front bumper with spoiler and integrated round auxiliary lamps and oil cooler
Suspension, front:	Independent suspension struts with track-control arms, one round-section longitudinal torsion bar per wheel, hydraulic double-action shock absorbers, anti-roll bar
Suspension, rear:	Independent suspension with semi-trailing arms, coil springs, hydraulic double-action shock absorbers and progressive-rate hollow rubber springs, anti-roll bar
Brakes, front/rear (Size (mm)):	Ventilated discs (282.5 x 20) / Ventilated discs (290 x 20) 2-piston fixed aluminium callipers / 2-piston fixed cast-iron callipers
Wheels, front/rear:	7 J x 15 / 7 J x 15
Tyres, front/rear:	185/70 VR 15 / 185/70 VR 15

Electrical system

Alternator (W/A):	770 / 55
Battery (V/Ah):	12 / 45

Dimensions and weight

Track, front/rear (mm):	1392 / 1445
Wheelbase (mm):	2450
Length x width x height (mm):	4010 x 1740 x 1230
Kerb weight DIN (kg):	1000
Permissible gross weight (kg):	1260
Luggage com., front/rear (VDA (l)):	160 / 210
Fuel tank capacity (l):	62, including 6 reserve
C_w x A (m²):	n. a.
Power/weight ratio (kg/kW/kg/hp):	7.14 / 5.26
911/86:	6.49 / 4.76

Fuel consumption

DIN 70 030/1 (mpg):	app. 27, 91 RON normal leaded

Performance, production, prices

Acceleration 0-62mph/100kph (s):	7.0
911/86:	less than 7.0
Maximum speed (mph / kph):	app. 143 / 230
911/86:	app. 146 / 235
Production, total number:	11*
*delivery only with engine 911/56	
Purchase price:	DM 39,980

Porsche 924

Porsche 924, 924 turbo and 924 Carrera GT

Volkswagen contracted Porsche to develop a new sports car, a project begun in 1970 as Entwicklungsauftrag ('Development Project') EA 425. The Porsche 924 was originally intended as the successor to the VW-Porsche 914. Volkswagen first intended to build the car itself, as a VW, but eventually dropped the sports car project from its plans. Yet the design of the 924 was simply too good to disappear into a filing cabinet. Porsche bought back its own design from Volkswagen, and had the sports car built under its own direction by Audi in Neckarsulm. The Porsche 924 was positioned as a second model line below the Porsche 911, and served as the firm's entry-level model. Production for the 1976 model year started in the autumn of 1975.

Model year 1976 (J Series)

The coupé body was a completely new design, with an emphasis on good aerodynamics. A flat bonnet and flip-up headlamps helped in achieving an aerodynamic drag coefficient of 0.36. Low drag not only reduced fuel consumption, but also high-speed wind noise. Indicators and long-range driving lamps were integrated in the front bumper. An air inlet for the engine coolant radiator was located in the valance panel below the front bumper. One striking feature was the 924's large glass rear hatch. The floorpan was hot-dip galvanized; like the 911, the 924 carried a six-year anti-corrosion warranty. In countless crash tests at Porsche's own research and development centre in Weissach, the body structure achieved a level of passive safety that was state of the art.

In handling, the 924 was largely neutral; straight-line stability at high speeds was impeccable. The front spring/shock absorber units were individually located by transverse links in a MacPherson strut design. Springing was by coaxial coil springs over hydraulic shock absorbers. The design was very similar to that of the first-generation VW Golf. The rear suspension consisted of individual semi-trailing arms, transverse torsion bars and hydraulic shock absorbers. This configuration was well known from the VW Beetle 1302 and 1303. The brake system was laid out in a dual-diagonal configuration, with floating-calliper front disc brakes and drums at the rear. A brake booster was installed for reduced pedal effort. Steel disc wheels, size 5.5 J x 14, were shod with 165 HR 14 tyres. As an option, 6 J x 14 aluminium-alloy wheels were available, with 185/70 HR 14 steel-belted radial tyres. Rack-and-pinion steering ensured good handling, light steering feel and good road grip.

The interior layout of the 924 was entirely functional. The instrument panel carried three individual round gauges behind a two-spoke steering wheel. At the left, a combination instrument contained fuel-level and coolant-temperature gauges, as well as several warning lights; in the centre, the 250kph (155mph) speedometer, marked in 50kph steps; and at the right, the tachometer. Auxiliary instruments in the centre console consisted of a clock and, as an option, oil-pressure gauge and voltmeter. The radio, and controls for the oversized heating and air ventilation system, were placed below these three instruments. Behind this, a short gear lever sprouted from the centre console, ahead of an ashtray. Seats, with their integral headrests, were taken over from the 911. The dashboard included a lockable glove compartment and four air vents directed at the cabin interior. The handbrake lever was mounted to the left of the driver's seat. The rear seat-backs could be folded forward to increase luggage capacity from 318 litres to 514 litres (11.2-18.2 cu ft). Other equipment details included halogen headlamps, multi-speed windscreen wipers and a heated rear window.

Porsche broke new ground in the engine department. For the first time in company history, the engine was mounted at the front. Also new for Porsche were water-cooling and in-line cylinders. The 1834cc engine was derived from the Audi 100 power unit, but fitted with K-Jetronic fuel injection. Exhaust was routed through twin pipes to a final silencer, from which it escaped through a single round tailpipe. With a compression ratio of 9.3:1, the engine developed 125hp (92kW) at 5800rpm.

Maximum torque of 165Nm (122lb ft) was available at 3500rpm. A forged crankshaft spun in five journal bearings, and its overhead camshaft was driven by a timing belt. The 2-litre engine was oiled by a pressure lubrication system. A single-plate dry clutch was bolted to the flywheel.

The four-speed manual transmission was located at the rear suspension. Power was transmitted between the clutch and transmission by a transaxle system: a torsionally elastic 20mm diameter driveshaft was located by four bearings in a rigid tube bolted between engine and transmission. Power flowed from the transmission, through the differential, via two double-jointed halfshafts to the rear wheels.

The Porsche 924 topped out at 124mph (200kph). Acceleration to 62mph (100kph) took 9.9 seconds.

Model year 1977 (K Series)

In January 1977 Porsche laid on a limited edition, the '924 Martini', to commemorate two racing world championships, which were also recalled by a dash plaque.

The '924 Martini' special edition was painted white, with red and blue side deco stripes, the colours of the Porsche-Martini factory racing team. The suspension, with its front and rear anti-roll bars, white 6 J x 14 aluminium-alloy wheels, and wide 185/70 HR 14 tyres, was well-equipped for performance driving. Front and rear seats had red centre sections and blue welting. Carpeting and boot lining were also red. The steering wheel rim was leather covered.

All 924s carried a rubber side-trim strip.

The wide tyre/wheel combination was available as an optional extra on the standard model, as were front 20mm and rear 18mm anti-roll bars. Aluminium wheels for the standard model were painted silver.

An easily operated retracting shade could be pulled out to hide any luggage compartment contents from prying eyes. Lashing-eyes were also provided to keep luggage from sliding, even when the car was driven briskly. Voltmeter and oil-pressure gauges were fitted in the centre console as standard equipment. Available options included headlamp washers, rear wiper, air-conditioning and a removable top which could be placed in a bag and stored in the luggage compartment.

From the beginning of October 1976 the 924 was available with an optional three-speed automatic transmission.

Model year 1978 (L Series)

The 50,000th Porsche 924 rolled off the factory assembly line on 24 April 1978, after only 26 months of production.

Interior trim and luggage cover were now available in three colours: black, brown or beige. Electric windows were added to the options list.

The exhaust system was modified; a larger oval tailpipe added visual appeal at the rear and improved engine sound. A five-speed transmission was available as an option.

Model year 1979 (M Series)

The introduction of the 924 turbo, with 170hp (125kW) filled the performance gap between the 924 and 911 SC.

The body of the 924 turbo was based on the normally-aspirated 924 production body. An obvious recognition feature was the row of additional openings at the front. Vertical slits in the front apron provided fresh air to the brakes and oil-cooler. The four cooling air openings between the flip-up headlamps and a duct on the right side of the bonnet helped cool the engine compartment. Body modifications were strictly for engineering and functional reasons, and not for visual effect. At the rear, a black polyurethane spoiler served to lower the drag coefficient to 0.33. Other differences were black window frames and sills. As on the normally-aspirated 924, luggage compartment volume could be increased from 318 litres to 514 litres (11.2-18.2cu ft) by folding down the rear seat-backs. The 924 turbo carried a collapsible space-saver spare tyre.

The suspension was designed for higher loads. Because the turbocharged engine and its accessories weighed about 30kg (66lb) more, the suspension was stiffened, and front and rear anti-roll bars installed. Sports shock absorbers were available as an option. In contrast to the 924's four-bolt wheels, the reinforced hubs of the turbo carried five-bolt spoke design aluminium wheels, 6 J x 15, with 185/70 VR 15 tyres. The larger wheels provided space for an upgraded dual-circuit brake system, with four ventilated discs, supported by a 9-inch brake booster. The handbrake acted on separate rear brake drums, which added 20mm to rear track.

Inside, the 924 turbo borrowed the leather-rimmed steering wheel of the 911 turbo; a four-spoke wheel was also available. The gear lever was leather covered, the sides of the centre console were carpeted. Seats were upholstered in a plaid fabric exclusive to the turbo. Gauge markings were light green in colour. The speedometer was marked in 20kph increments up to 260kph (161mph).

Compression ratio of the 2-litre engine was reduced to 7.5:1. The turbocharger, spinning at up to 90,000rpm, forced air at a maximum boost of 0.7bar into the combustion chambers. The result was a maximum of 170hp (125kW) at 5500rpm. Maximum torque rose to 245Nm (181lb ft) at 3500rpm. The K-Jetronic system was modified in keeping with the power increase, and fed by two fuel pumps. An auxiliary oil-cooler, breakerless transistorized ignition and platinum spark plugs rounded out the list of modifications. Despite considerably higher performance, the turbo generated less exhaust noise than the normally-aspirated car, thanks to the exhaust turbine's sound absorbing properties.

The five-speed manual transmission and halfshafts were modified in keeping with the higher engine output. Transaxle shaft diameter increased from 20mm to 25mm, and the hydraulic clutch grew to 225mm in diameter.

In the performance department, the 924 turbo's top speed was 140mph (225kph). Acceleration to 62mph (100kph) took just 7.8 seconds.

Standard equipment on the base 924 now included silver-painted 6 J x 14 aluminium-alloy wheels with 185/70 HR 14 tyres. As an option, customers could choose sports shock absorbers or black-painted wheel centres. Inside, instrument markings were white, and the speedometer was calibrated in 20kph steps to 240kph (149mph).

Model year 1980 (A Programme)

Along with new colours, two-tone schemes and new interior appointments were available. The normally-aspirated 924 now had black window frames like the turbo. The outside rear-view mirror was manually adjustable by the driver. The fuel filler cap was covered by a body-colour flap. These modifications were also applied to the 924 turbo.

The brake booster of the base model was enlarged from 7 inches to 9 inches for lower brake pedal effort.

Opening the glass hatchback automatically turned on a luggage-compartment lamp. The 924 turbo was fitted with electric windows and a rear fog lamp.

The base model in the 924 line-up was now equipped with a five-speed manual transmission as standard equipment. The gear pattern matched that of the 911 SC: first and second gears shared a single gear-change plane, as did third and fourth. Fifth was right and forward, reverse was right and back. Acceleration performance improved slightly with the five-speed.

Model year 1981 (B Programme)

With the use of hot-dip galvanized steel for the entire body, Porsche's rust-through warranty was extended to seven years. The 924 turbo was given a reworked, more fuel-economical power unit, even

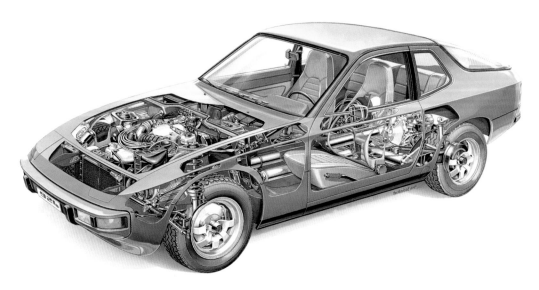

Phantom view of the 924 Coupé with 2-litre fuel-injected engine

as output increased by 7hp (5kW). The special edition '924 Le Mans' remained in the model line-up until late autumn. The 100,000th Porsche 924 rolled off the assembly line on 4 February 1981.

The '924 Le Mans' was painted Alpine White and was externally identified by its three-colour stripes and 'Le Mans' script. A 924 turbo rear spoiler graced its rear. Black-spoke aluminium 6 J x 15 wheels had matt-finished bright rims and were shod with 205/60 HR 15 low-profile tyres. Firmer shock absorbers and two anti-roll bars provided a sports-tuned suspension. The interior combined black leatherette upholstery and black fabric with white pinstripes and white welting. The small, 36cm (14-inch) steering wheel, normally an option, was part of the Le Mans edition standard package.

All 924 models had side indicators on the front wings. The 924 now also had a standard rear fog lamp and the same horns as the 924 turbo. Added insulation reduced interior noise.

For reduced roll in hard cornering, the 924 was fitted with a 21mm front anti-roll bar and stiffer rear torsion bars. Additionally, the aluminium spoked wheels of the 924 turbo were made available in a four-bolt version with 60-series tyres as an option for the normal 924.

New paint colours, new interior equipment and new door panels with Porsche script distinguished 1981 models from the previous year. Extras included new 'Berber' seat fabric, centre-console cassette storage, and a new digital-display radio generation.

The 924 turbo power unit was completely reworked. A new electronic ignition system permitted more efficient engine layout. Compression was raised from 7.5 to 8.5:1, which also reduced fuel consumption by 13 per cent. Power output rose to 177hp (130kW), and torque to 250Nm (184lb ft). No changes were made to the engine rev range. The new engine pulled even more strongly at lower engine speeds. For the German market, fuel tank volume was increased to 84 litres (18.5 gallons).

The power boost also improved the 924 turbo's road performance. Acceleration to 62mph (100kph) was achieved in 7.7 seconds, and the car's top speed was 143mph (230kph).

Porsche 924 Carrera GT

At the Frankfurt International Automobile Exhibition (the IAA), Porsche presented the 924 Carrera GT, a sports car equally suited for racing or use on public roads. In the following 12 months Porsche built 406 examples to qualify for Group 4 racing. Vehicle weight was kept very low through use of lightweight components and reduced interior equipment. Visually, the 924 Carrera GT appeared much brawnier than its stock sibling. The front apron, wide front wings fitted with 928 side indicators, and rear wing flares were made of fibreglass. Four air inlets between the headlamps and an intercooler air scoop on the right side of the aluminium bonnet characterized its unique appearance. The doors were also made of aluminium. Although the hand-wound door windows retained their normal thickness, tinted thin-gauge glazing elsewhere shaved a few more kilograms. A larger rear spoiler was attached to the glass rear hatch. Despite weight-saving measures, the interior appeared downright comfortable, with its three-spoke steering wheel, black and red pinstriped sports seats with red welting and matching door panels.

With a displacement of 1984cc, the engine benefited from a compression increase to 8.5:1, modified electronic ignition system and a charge air intercooler placed immediately below the bonnet scoop. These modifications raised the turbocharged engine's power output to 210hp (154kW) at 6000rpm. The five-speed manual transmission was matched to the increased power and top speed.

Standard wheels and tyres for the 924 Carrera GT were forged Fuchs 7 J x 15 aluminium alloys with 215/60 VR 15 tyres. Optionally, owners could order 16-inch wheels, with 205/55 VR 16 tyres on 7-inch rims at the front and 225/50 VR 16 on 8-inch wheels at the rear.

From a standstill, the 924 Carrera GT accelerated to 62mph (100kph) in just 6.9 seconds; top speed was 149mph (240kph).

Model year 1982 (C Programme)

The 924 turbo was removed from the product line at the end of the 1982 model year, since the newly-introduced Porsche 944 supplanted the 924 turbo in many markets. The only exception was Italy, because of its much lower tax on vehicles under 2 litres. The 924 turbo held on in the Italian market until 1984.

Porsche increased the permissible roof load from 35kg to 75kg (77-165lb), permitting two surfboards or several bicycles to be carried on the roof. Fuel-tank venting and air-filter installation were altered. At the front, a slimmer 20mm anti-roll bar was fitted, and front caster settings were modified.

The 924 was now fitted with the 924 turbo steering wheel design. Storage bins in the doors were carpet lined. A small, swing-away Porsche crest covered the glove-compartment lock. Static lap belts were installed for rear seat occupant protection.

The heating system moved more air, and an improved air-conditioning system better matched to the heating system was available as an option.

Detail improvements were made to the automatic transmission. The manual transmission was fitted with improved synchronizer rings and an air deflector for transmission venting. As an option, a limited-slip differential with a 40 per cent lock-up factor was available.

Model year 1983 (D Programme)

The 1983 model line-up saw deletion of the 924 for the United States, Canada and Japan, as well as automatic transmission and two-tone paint options.

The 924 turbo rear spoiler was now standard on the 924 as well, which improved aerodynamic drag coefficient from 0.36 to 0.33. Top speed also increased slightly thanks to the aerodynamic improvements. The 924 now included the improved cabin sound-insulation of the 924 turbo. Gas-pressure springs made the engine lid easier to open.

Front seats were available in partial leather. Improved speakers, two in the doors and two more in the rear side-panels, were matched to new stereo cassette radios.

Model year 1984 (E Programme)

To date, more than 130,000 sports cars of the 924 model line had been sold, making it one of the most successful Porsche models of all time.

The rear of the optional removable roof could now be raised electrically while underway. The glass rear hatch could be released and opened electrically from the driver's position. Make-up mirrors were integrated in both sunvisors. Cruise control was also available as an option.

Model year 1985 (F Programme)

The 2-litre 924 entered its final year of production. Porsche improved occupant protection with the fitting of standard door impact beams. Model improvements also included standard green-tinted windows all round and heated windscreen washer nozzles. New choices included Blaupunkt 'Hamburg' and 'Boston' radios.

Of the 2-litre Porsche 924s, a total of 121,510 base-model 924s were built, along with 12,427 924 turbos and only 406 924 Carrera GTs.

924 Coupé [Automatic]
MY 1976–MY 1985

Engine

Engine design:	4-cylinder in-line
Installation:	Front engine
Cooling system:	Water-cooled
Engine type:	047/8 [047/9]
Engine type:	XK
Displacement (cc):	1984
Bore x stroke (mm):	86.5 x 84.4
Engine output (kW/hp):	92/125 at 5800rpm
Maximum torque (Nm/lb ft):	165/122 at 3500rpm
Output per litre (kW/l / hp/l):	46.4 / 63.0
Compression ratio:	9.3 : 1
Valve operation camshaft drive:	ohc, cam driven by synchronous belt drive, 2 valves per cylinder
Carburation:	Bosch K-Jetronic fuel injection
Ignition system:	Battery coil ignition
MY 1980–MJ 1985:	Transistorized coil ignition (TCI)
Firing order:	1- 3 - 4 - 2
Engine lubrication:	Full-pressure oil lubrication
Engine oil total (l):	5.0

Transmission

Drive configuration:	Rear-axle drive, transaxle system
Manual gearbox:	4-speed (5-speed)
Option Automatic:	[3-speed]³
Transmission type:	088/6 (016Z)* (016/8)² [087/3]³
Transmission ratios:	
1st gear:	3.600 (2.786)* (3.600)² [2.551]³
2nd gear:	2.125 (1.722)* (2.125)² [1.448]³
3rd gear:	1.360 (1.217)* (1.458)²[1.000]³
4th gear:	0.966 (0.931)* (1.107)²
5th gear:	(0.706)* (0.857)²
Reverse gear:	3.500 (2.503)* (3.500)² [2.461]³
Drive ratio:	3.444 (4.714)* (3.889)² [3.454]³

*Option MY 1978–MY 1979
²MY 1980 standard
³Option MY 1977–MY 1982

Body, chassis, suspension, brakes, wheels

Body design:	Steel coupé body, 2 doors, 2 + 2 seats, hot-dip galvanized floor panel, front and rear bumpers integrated in body form, flip-up headlamps, glass rear lid
Option MY 1977–MY 1983:	Removable roof
MY 1981–MY 1985:	Entirely hot-dip galvanized body, side indicators on front wings
MY 1983–MY 1985:	Glass rear lid with black polyurethane rear spoiler
MY 1984–MY 1985:	Removable roof with electric lift feature
MY 1985:	Side-impact protection beams in doors
Suspension, front:	Independent suspension, wishbones, McPherson struts, coil springs, dual-tube hydraulic shock absorbers
Option MY 1977–MY 1980, MY 1981 standard:	Anti-roll bar
Suspension, rear:	Individually suspended on driveshafts, transverse torsion bars on each side in transaxle tube, light alloy transverse tube suspension, dual-tube hydraulic shock absorbers
Option MY 1977–MY 1980, MY 1981 standard:	Anti-roll bar
Brakes, front/rear (Size (mm)):	Dics (257 x 13) / Drums Simplex (230 x 38.6) Floating callipers, front
Wheels, front/rear:	5.5 J x 14 / 5.5 J x 14
Tyres, front/rear:	165 HR 14 / 165 HR 14
Option,	6 J x 14 / 6 J x 14
MY 1979 standard:	185/70 HR 14 / 185/70 HR 14
Option MY 1981–MY 1985:	6 J x 15 / 6 J x 15
	205/60 HR 15 / 205/60 HR 15

Electrical system

Alternator (W/A):	1050 / 75
Battery (V/Ah):	12 / 45 [12 / 63]
Option:	12 / 63

Dimensions and weight

Track, front/rear (mm):	1418 / 1372
Wheel base (mm):	2400
Length x width x height (mm):	4212 x 1685 x 1270
Kerb weight DIN (kg):	1080
MY 1979–MY 1985:	1130
Permissible gross weight (kg):	1400
MY 1979–MY 1985:	1450
Luggage compartment (VDA (l)):	318
with folded down rear seat-backs:	514
Fuel tank capacity (l):	62, including 5 reserve
MY 1980–MY 1985:	66, including 6 reserve
C_w x A (m²):	0.36 x 1.76 = 0.634
MY 1983–MY 1985:	0.33 x 1.79 = 0.591
Power/weight ratio (kg/kW/kg/hp):	11.73 / 8.64
MY 1979–MY 1985:	12.28 / 9.04

Fuel consumption

DIN 70 030/1 (mpg):	98 RON super leaded
At constant 56mph/90kph:	42.8 [38]
At constant 74mph/120kph:	34.8 [31]
EG-emissions-urban cycle:	22.7 [22.1]

Performance, production, prices

Acceleration 0-62mph/100kph (s):	10.5
MY 1977–MY 1979:	9.9 [11.4]
5-speed:	9.6
0-100mph/160kph (s):	26.5 [31.4]
Maximum speed (mph / kph):	124 / 200 [121 / 195]
MY 1980–MY 1985:	126 / 204
Production, total number:	121,510
Purchase prices:	
01/1976:	DM 23,240
08/1976:	DM 23,450 [DM 24,940]
02/1977:	DM 24,300 [DM 25,790]
06/1977:	DM 24,980 [DM 26,530]
01/1978:	DM 25,960 [DM 27,510]
08/1978:	DM 26,850 [DM 28,400]
01/1979:	DM 26,850 [DM 28,400]
08/1979:	DM 27,980 [DM 29,430]
04/1980:	DM 28,980 [DM 30,480]
08/1980:	DM 28,980 [DM 30,480]
02/1981:	DM 29,530 [DM 31,030]
08/1981:	DM 29,980 [DM 31,480]
01/1982:	DM 30,980 [DM 32,480]
08/1982:	DM 31,480
03/1983:	DM 32,350
08/1983:	DM 32,950
02/1984:	DM 33,250
10/1984:	DM 33,950
02/1985:	DM 34,650

924 turbo Coupé (Typ 931)
January 1979–MY 1980

Engine
Engine design:	4-cylinder in-line, turbocharger
Installation:	Front-engine
Cooling system:	Water-cooled
Engine type:	M 31/01
Displacement (cc):	1984
Bore x stroke (mm):	86.5 x 84.4
Engine output (kW/hp):	125/170 at 5500rpm
Maximum torque (Nm/lb ft):	245/181 at 3500rpm
Output per litre (kW/l / hp/l):	63.0 / 85.7
Compression ratio:	7.5 : 1
Valve operation camshaft drive:	ohc, cam driven by synchronous belt drive, 2 valves per cylinder
Carburation:	Bosch K-Jetronic fuel injection
Ignition system:	Breakerless transistorized coil ignition (TCI)
Firing order:	1 - 3 - 4 - 2
Engine lubrication:	Full-pressure oil lubrication
Engine oil total (l):	5.5

Transmission
Drive configuration:	Rear-axle drive, transaxle system
Manual gearbox:	5-speed
Transmission type:	G 31/01
Transmission ratios:	
1th gear:	3.166
2nd gear:	1.777
3rd gear:	1.217
4th gear:	0.931
5th gear:	0.706
Reverse gear:	2.909
Drive ratio:	4.125
Option:	Limited-slip differential 40%

Body, chassis, suspension, brakes, wheels
Body design:	Steel coupé body, 2 doors, 2 + 2 seats, entirely hot-dip galvanized body, front and rear bumpers integrated in body form, flip-up headlamps, additional slots under front bumper, front with four black grilles, air intake in bonnet, glass rear lid with black polyurethane rear spoiler, painted electric outside mirror
Option:	Removable roof
Suspension, front:	Independent suspension, wishbones, McPherson struts, coil springs, dual-tube hydraulic shock absorbers, anti-roll bar
Suspension, rear:	Individually suspended on driveshafts, transverse torsion bars on each side in transaxle tube, light alloy transverse tube suspension, dual-tube hydraulic shock absorbers, anti-roll bar
Brakes, front/rear (Size (mm)):	Ventilated discs (282.5 x 20.5) / Ventilated discs (289 x 20) Floating callipers / Floating callipers
Wheels, front/rear:	6 J x 15 / 6 J x 15
Tyres, front/rear:	185/70 VR 15 / 185/70 VR 15
Option:	6 J x 16 / 6 J x 16 205/55 VR 16 / 205/55 VR 16

Electrical system
Alternator (W/A):	1050 / 75
Battery (V/Ah):	12 / 45
Option:	12 / 63

Dimensions and weight
Track, front/rear (mm):	1418 / 1392
Wheelbase (mm):	2400
Length x width x height (mm):	4212 x 1685 x 1270
Kerb weight DIN (kg):	1180
Permissible gross weight (kg):	1500
Luggage compartment (VDA (l)):	318
with folded down rear seatbacks:	514
Fuel tank capacity (l):	66, including 6 reserve
C_w x A (m^2):	0.34 x 1.79 = 0.609
Power/weight ratio (kg/kW/ kg/hp):	9.44 / 6.94

Fuel consumption
DIN 70 030/1 (mpg):	98 RON super leaded
At constant 56mph/90kph:	36.25
At constant 74mph/120kph:	26.8
EG-emissions-urban cycle:	18.5

Performance, production, prices
Acceleration 0-62mph/100kph (s):	7.8
0-100mph/160kph (s):	17.8
Maximum speed (mph / kph):	140 / 225
Production, total number:	7,136
Purchase price:	
01/1979:	DM 39,480
08/1979:	DM 39,980
04/1980:	DM 41,480

924 turbo Coupé (Type 931)
MY 1981–MY 1982
(Italy–MY 1984)

Engine

Engine design:	4-cylinder in-line, turbocharger
Installation:	Front-engine
Cooling system:	Water-cooled
Engine type:	M 31/03
Displacement (cc):	1984
Bore x stroke (mm):	86.5 x 84.4
Engine output (kW/hp):	130/177 at 5500rpm
Maximum torque (Nm/lb ft):	250/184 at 3500rpm
Output per litre (kW/l / hp/l):	65.5/ 89.2
Compression ratio:	8.5 : 1
Valve operation camshaft drive:	ohc, cam driven by synchronous belt drive, 2 valves per cylinder
Carburation:	Bosch K-Jetronic fuel injection
Ignition system:	Transistorized ignition with digital ignition angle
Firing order:	1- 3 - 4 - 2
Engine lubrication:	Full-pressure oil lubrication
Engine oil total (l):	5.5

Transmission

Drive configuration:	Rear-axle drive, transaxle system
Manual gearbox:	5-speed
Transmission type:	G 31/01
Transmission ratios:	
1th gear:	3.166
2nd gear:	1.777
3rd gear:	1.217
4th gear:	0.931
5th gear:	0.706
Reverse gear:	2.909
Drive ratio:	4.125
Option:	Limited-slip differential 40%

Body, chassis, suspension, brakes, wheels

Body design:	Steel coupé body, 2 doors, 2 + 2 seats, entirely hot-dip galvanized body, front and rear bumpers integrated in body form, flip-up headlamps, additional slots under front bumper, front with four black grilles, air intake in bonnet, glass rear lid with black polyurethane rear spoiler, side indicators on front wings, painted electric outside mirror
Option:	Removable roof
Suspension, front:	Independent suspension, wishbones, McPherson struts, coil springs, dual-tube hydraulic shock absorbers, anti-roll bar
Suspension, rear:	Individually suspended on driveshafts, transverse torsion bars on each side in transaxle tube, light alloy transverse tube suspension, dual-tube hydraulic shock absorbers, anti-roll bar
Brakes, front/rear (Size (mm)):	Ventilated discs (282.5 x 20.5) / Ventilated discs (289 x 20) Floating callipers / Floating callipers
Wheels, front/rear:	6 J x 15 / 6 J x 15
Tyres, front/rear:	185/70 VR 15 / 185/70 VR 15
Option:	6 J x 16 / 6 J x 16 205/55 VR 16 / 205/55 VR 16

Electrical system

Alternator (W/A):	1050 / 75
Battery (V/Ah):	12 / 45
Option:	12 / 63

Dimensions and weight

Track, front/rear (mm):	1418 / 1392
Wheelbase (mm):	2400
Length x width x height (mm):	4212 x 1685 x 1270
Kerb weight DIN (kg):	1180
Permissible gross weight (kg):	1500
Luggage compartment (VDA (l)):	318
with folded down rear seatbacks:	514
Fuel tank capacity (l):	84, including 7 reserve
C_w x A (m^2):	0.34 x 1.79 = 0.609
Power/weight ratio (kg/kW/kg/hp):	9.07 / 6.66

Fuel consumption

DIN 70 030/1 (mpg):	98 RON super leaded
At constant 56mph/90kph:	42.2
At constant 74mph/120kph:	32.8
im EG-emissions-urban cycle:	25

Performance, production, prices

Acceleration 0-62mph/100kph (s):	7.7
Maximum speed (mph / kph):	143 / 230
Production, total number:	5,291
Purchase price:	
08/1980:	DM 41,980
02/1981:	DM 42,780
08/1981:	DM 42,780
01/1982:	DM 44,200

924 Carrera GT Coupé MY 1981

Engine
Engine design:	4-cylinder in-line, turbocharger, intercooler
Installation:	Front-engine
Cooling system:	Water-cooled
Engine type:	M 31/50
Displacement (cc):	1984
Bore x stroke (mm):	86.5 x 84.4
Engine output (kW/hp):	154/210 at 6000rpm
Maximum torque (Nm/lb ft):	280/207 at 3500rpm
Output per litre (kW/l / ph/l):	77.6 / 105.8
Compression ratio:	8.5 : 1
Valve operation camshaft drive:	ohc, cam driven by synchronous belt drive, 2 valves per cylinder
Carburation:	Bosch K-Jetronic fuel injection
Ignition system:	Transistorized ignition with digital ignition angle
Firing order:	1- 3 - 4 - 2
Engine lubrication:	Full-pressure oil lubrication
Engine oil total (l):	5.5

Transmission
Drive configuration:	Rear-axle drive, transaxle system
Manual gearbox:	5-speed
Transmission type:	G 31/03
Transmission ratios:	
1th gear:	3.166
2nd gear:	1.777
3rd gear:	1.217
4th gear:	0.931
5th gear:	0.706
Reverse gear:	2.909
Drive ratio:	3.889
Option:	Limited-slip differential 40%

Body, chassis, suspension, brakes, wheels
Body design:	Steel coupé body, 2 doors, 2 seats, entirely hot-dip galvanized body, wider plastic front and rear wings, aluminium bonnet and doors, front spoiler bumper and rear bumper integrated in body form, front with four black grilles, intercooler air scoop in engine lid, flip-up headlamps, glass rear lid with big black polyurethane rear spoiler, thin glass windows, door windows in normal glass, 928 side indicators on front wings, black outside mirror
Suspension, front:	Independent suspension, wishbones, McPherson struts, coil springs, dual-tube hydraulic shock absorbers, anti-roll bar
Suspension, rear:	Individually suspended on driveshafts, transverse torsion bars on each side in transaxle tube, light alloy transverse tube suspension, dual-tube hydraulic shock absorbers, anti-roll bar
Brakes, front/rear (Size (mm)):	Ventilated discs (282.5 x 20.5) / Ventilated discs (289 x 20) Floating callipers / Floating callipers
Wheels, front/rear:	7 J x 15 / 7 J x 15*
Tyres, front/rear:	215/60 VR 15 / 215/60 VR 15
Option:	7 J x 15 / 8 J x 15
	215/60 VR 15 / 215/60 VR 15
Option:	7 J x 16 / 8 J x 16
	205/55 VR 16 / 225/50 VR 16

*spacer 21 mm per wheel, rear

Electrical system
Alternator (W/A):	1050 / 75
Battery (V/Ah):	12 / 45

Dimensions and weight
Track, front/rear (mm):	1477 / 1451
7 J x 15 / 8 J x 15:	1477 / 1476
7 J x 16 / 8 J x 16:	1477 / 1476
Wheelbase (mm):	2400
Length x width x height (mm):	4320 x 1735 x 1275
Kerb weight DIN (kg):	1180
Permissible gross weight (kg):	1500
Luggage compartment (VDA (l)):	
without rear seats:	514
Fuel tank capacity (l):	84, including 7 reserve
C_w x A (m²):	0.34 x 1.82 = 0.619
Power/weight ratio (kg/kW/kg/hp):	7.66 / 5.61

Fuel consumption
DIN 70 030/1 (mpg):	98 RON super leaded
At constant 56mph/90kph:	44.9
At constant 74mph/120kph:	33.2
EG-emissions-urban cycle:	22.7

Performance, production, prices
Acceleration 0-62mph/100kph (s):	6.9
Maximum speed (mph / kph):	149 / 240
Production, total number:	406
Purchase price:	DM 60,000

Porsche 924 S

Model year 1986 (G Programme)

The 924 model line was technically revamped with the introduction of the 924 S, the body of which carried on from the 924 without external changes. Like all Porsches, the 924 S was fitted with massive side-impact beams integrated within its doors.

Brakes and suspension components were taken from the 944, giving the 924 S the same aluminium-alloy chassis pieces as the larger four-cylinder models. The brake system consisted of four ventilated discs and floating callipers. Standard equipment included 195/65 VR 15 tyres mounted on 'Telephone Design' 6 J x 15 aluminium wheels. Forged 6 J x 16 disc-style alloys with 205/55 VR 16 tyres were optional.

Interior equipment, carried over from the 924, was supplemented with some 944 production parts such as window-winders and door-locking buttons. Options included air-conditioning, sports seats, cruise control, power steering, electric windows and the removable roof whose trailing edge could be raised electrically while the vehicle was in motion.

The engine installed in the 924 S was identical to that of the 944, although the 924 S version only offered 9.7:1 compression and could therefore be operated on regular-grade petrol. Power dropped slightly to 150hp (110kW) at 5800rpm. Maximum torque was also somewhat lower: 190Nm (140lb ft) at 3000rpm. Identical output figures were achieved by catalyst-equipped examples, which were also offered in the model line. These were tuned to run on unleaded regular petrol.

Five-speed manual transmission was standard in the 924 S. A three-speed automatic was an option.

Performance was significantly better than that of its predecessor. Top speed was about 134mph (215kph). Weighing 1210kg (2665lb), the 924 S could accelerate to 62mph (100kph) in just 8.5 seconds. The 2.5-litre engine also exhibited better engine elasticity and pulled better across the rev range.

924 S Coupé with the 2.5-litre engine of the 944

Model year 1987 (H Programme)

For 1987, the 924 S underwent only minor modification. The ignition keys included tiny lamps to make the door locks easier to find at night. The cassette radios were now encoded to make them useless in the event of theft.

Model year 1988 (J Programme)

The 924 model line entered its last year of production. The 924 S had a reworked engine, and Porsche offered two 'Exclusive' models based on the 924 S. The 924 S body now included two electrically-adjustable and heatable outside mirrors and a rear wiper.

The special editions were available in black or white. Side rub-strips were painted body colour. Additional features included spray guards and the electrically lifting, removable roof.

A rear anti-roll bar was now standard on the 924 S. For the Exclusive models, standard tyres,

195/65 VR 15, were mounted on front 6-inch and rear 7-inch aluminium alloy wheels, painted body colour. On the black special edition, the edges of the rims were painted turquoise; on the white cars, ochre. Additionally, the special edition cars had sports suspensions and thicker anti-roll bars.

The standard equipment list of the 924 S was expanded with the addition of an aerial, four speakers, cassette and coin-holder, electric windows, three-spoke leather steering wheel and a leather gear lever knob.

The exclusive model added sports seats and a 36cm (14-inch) sports steering wheel. Seats and door panels were covered with a special flannel fabric, grey/turquoise or grey/ochre yellow to match the exterior colour. Interior leatherette trim was black over turquoise or ochre leatherette.

Higher compression ratio (10.2:1) and tuning the engine to run on 95 octane Euro-Super petrol increased power output to 160hp (118kW), regardless of whether a catalyst was fitted or not. Performance improved to a top speed of 137mph 220kph) and a 0-62mph (0-100kph) sprint in 8.2 seconds. Porsche produced a total of 16,274 examples of the 924 S.

The 924 S is the last evolutionary step of the 924-generation

924 S Coupé [Automatic]
MY 1986–MY 1987

Engine

Engine design:	4-cylinder in-line
Installation:	Front-engine
Cooling system:	Water-cooled
Engine type:	M 44/07 [M 44/08]
Displacement (cc):	2479
Bore x stroke (mm):	100 x 78.9
Engine output DIN (kW/hp):	110/150 at 5800rpm
Maximum torque (Nm/lb ft):	190/140 at 3000rpm
Output per litre (kW/l / hp/l):	44.4 / 60.5
Compression ratio:	9.7 : 1
Valve operation camshaft drive:	ohc, cam driven by synchronous belt drive, 2 valves per cylinder
Carburation:	DME, Bosch L-Jetronic fuel injection
Ignition system:	DME, breakerless
Firing order:	1- 3 - 4 - 2
Engine lubrication:	Full-pressure oil lubrication
Engine oil total (l):	6.0

Transmission

Drive configuration:	Rear-axle drive, transaxle system
Manual gearbox:	5-speed
Option Automatic:	[3-speed]
Transmission type:	016J [087M]
Transmission ratios:	
1st gear:	3.600 [2.714]
2nd gear:	2.125 [1.500]
3rd gear:	1.458 [1.000]
4th gear:	1.107
5th gear:	0.829
Reverse gear:	3.500 [2.429]
Drive ratio:	3.889 [3.083]
Option for manual gearbox:	Limited-slip differential 40%

Body, chassis, suspension, brakes, wheels

Body design:	Steel coupé body, 2 doors, 2 + 2 seats, entirely hot-dip galvanized body, side-impact protection beams in doors, front and rear bumpers integrated in body form, flip-up headlamps, glass rear lid with black polyurethane rear spoiler, side indicators on front wings, painted electric outside mirror
Option:	Removable roof with electric lift feature
Suspension, front:	Independent suspension, wishbones, McPherson struts, coil springs, dual-tube hydraulic shock absorbers, anti-roll bar
Suspension, rear:	Individually suspended on driveshafts, transverse torsion bars on each side in transaxle tube, light alloy transverse tube suspension, dual-tube hydraulic shock absorbers, anti-roll bar

Brakes, front/rear (Size (mm)):	Ventilated discs (282.5 x 20.5) / Ventilated discs (289 x 20) Floating callipers / Floating callipers
Option MY 1987:	ABS
Wheels, front/rear:	6 J x 15 / 6 J x 15
Tyres, fron/rear:	195/65 VR 15 / 195/65 VR 15
Option:	6 J x 16 / 6 J x 16 205/55 VR 16 / 205/55 VR 16

Electrical system

Alternator (W/A):	1260 / 90
Battery (V/Ah):	12 / 50 [12 / 63]
Option:	12 / 63

Dimensions and weight

Track, front/rear (mm):	1419 / 1393
Wheelbase (mm):	2400
Length x width x height (mm):	4212 x 1685 x 1275
Kerb weight DIN (kg):	1210
Permissible gross weight (kg):	1530
Luggage compartment (VDA (l)):	318
with folded down rear seatbacks:	514
Fuel tank capacity (l):	66, including 6 reserve
C_w x A (m^2):	0.33 x 1.81 = 0.597
Power/weight ratio (kg/kW/kg/hp):	11.00 / 8.06

Fuel consumption

Without catalytic converter:	91 RON normal leaded or unleaded
EG-Norm 80/1268 (mpg):	46.3 [39.2]
At constant 56mph/90kph:	34.8 [32.5]
At constant 74mph/120kph:	23 [22.7]
EG-emissions-urban cycle:	
With catalytic converter:	91 RON normal unleaded
EG-Norm 80/1268 (mpg):	44.9 [38.75]
At constant 56mph/90kph:	34.1 [31.6]
At constant 74mph/120kph:	22.4 [22.4]
EG-emissions-urban cycle:	

Performance, production, prices

Acceleration 0-62mph/100kph (s):	8.5 [10.0]
Maximum speed (mph / kph):	133 / 215 [133 / 215]
Production, total number:	12,195
Purchase price:	
08/1985:	DM 41,950 [DM 44,250]
with catalytic converter:	DM 44,140 [DM 46,440]
08/1986:	DM 43,750 [DM 46,230]
with catalytic converter:	DM 45,115 [DM 47,595]
03/1987:	DM 44,590 [DM 47,090]
with catalytic converter:	DM 45,955 [DM 48,455]

924 S Coupé [Automatic] MY 1988

Engine

Engine design:	4-cylinder in-line
Installation:	Front-engine
Cooling system:	Water-cooled
Engine type:	M 44/09 [M 44/10]
Displacement (cc):	2479
Bore x stroke (mm):	100 x 78.9
Engine output DIN (kW/hp):	118/160 at 5900rpm
Maximum torque (Nm/lb ft):	210/155 at 4500rpm
Output per litre (kW/l / hp/l):	47.6 / 64.5
Compression ratio:	10.2 : 1
Valve operation camshaft drive:	ohc, cam driven by synchronous belt drive, 2 valves per cylinder
Carburation:	DME, Bosch L-Jetronic fuel injection
Ignition system:	DME, breakerless
Firing order:	1- 3 - 4 - 2
Engine lubrication:	Full-pressure oil lubrication
Engine oil total (l):	6.5

Transmission

Drive configuration:	Rear-axle drive, transaxle system
Manual gearbox:	5-speed
Option Automatic:	[3-speed]
Transmission type:	016J [087M]
Transmission ratios:	
1st gear:	3.600 [2.714]
2nd gear:	2.125 [1.500]
3rd gear:	1.458 [1.000]
4th gear:	1.107
5th gear:	0.829
Reverse gear:	3.500 [2.429]
Drive ratio:	3.889 [3.083]
Option for manual gearbox:	Limited-slip differential 40%

Body, chassis, suspension, brakes, wheels

Body design:	Steel coupé body, 2 doors, 2 + 2 seats, entirely hot-dip galvanized body, side-impact protection beams in doors, front and rear bumpers integrated in body form, flip-up headlamps, glass rear lid with black polyurethane rear spoiler, side indicators on front wings, painted electric outside mirror
Option:	Removable roof with electric lift feature
Suspension, front:	Independent suspension, wishbones, McPherson struts, coil springs, dual-tube hydraulic shock absorbers, anti-roll bar
Suspension, rear:	Individually suspended on driveshafts, transverse torsion bars on each side in transaxle tube, light alloy transverse tube suspension, dual-tube hydraulic shock absorbers, anti-roll bar

Brakes, front/rear (Size (mm)):	Ventilated discs (282.5 x 20.5) / Ventilated discs (289 x 20) Floating callipers / Floating callipers
Option:	ABS
Wheels, front/rear:	6 J x 15 / 6 J x 15
Tyres, front/rear:	195/65 VR 15 / 195/65 VR 15
Option:	6 J x 16 / 6 J x 16 205/55 VR 16 / 205/55 VR 16

Electrical system

Alternator (W/A):	1260 / 90
Battery (V/Ah):	12 / 50 [12 / 63]
Option:	12 / 63

Dimensions and weight

Track, front/rear (mm):	1419 / 1393
Wheelbase (mm):	2400
Length x width x height (mm):	4212 x 1685 x 1275
Kerb weight DIN (kg):	1240
Permissible gross weight (kg):	1560
Luggage compartment (VDA (l)):	318
with folded down rear seatbacks:	514
Fuel tank capacity (l):	66, including 6 reserve
C_w x A (m²):	0.33 x 1.81 = 0.597
Power/weight ratio (kg/kW/kg/hp):	10.50 / 7.75

Fuel consumption

Without catalytic converter:	
EG-Norm 80/1268 (mpg):	95 RON super leaded or unleaded
At constant 56mph/90kph:	42.2 [38.75]
At constant 74mph/120kph:	34.1 [32.1]
EG-emissions-urban cycle:	22.4 [23.3]
With catalytic converter:	
EG-Norm 80/1268 (mpg):	95 RON super unleaded
At constant 56mph/90kph:	42.2 [38.75]
At constant 74mph/120kph:	34.1 [31.6]
EG-emissions-urban cycle:	22.4 [22.4]

Performance, production, prices

Acceleration 0-62mph/100kph (s):	8.2 [9.5]
Maximum speed (mph / kph):	136 / 220 [135 / 218]
Production, total number:	4,079
Purchase prices:	
07/1987:	DM 47,900 [DM 50,400]
with catalytic converter:	DM 49,265 [DM 51,765]
04/1988:	DM 48,800 [DM 51,300]
with catalytic converter:	DM 50,165 [DM 52,665]

Porsche 928

Porsche 928 and 928 S

As early as 1968, Porsche's design and styling departments turned their thoughts to a new model line. In 1971 a concept for a front-mounted engine joined to a rear-mounted transmission by means of a central tube was approved. The engine concept was based on an especially low-profile water-cooled, 90° V8, expected to develop about 300hp (221kW) from just under 5 litres.

The first 1/5-scale models were wind-tunnel tested in mid-February 1972. In June a full-scale mock-up of the interior was completed. For powertrain testing, five test mules were built: a Mercedes-Benz 350 SL, known internally as V1, served to test the transaxle system which conveyed power from the front-mounted engine to the rear-mounted transmission. An Opel Admiral (V2) was primarily used to test suspension components. The entire drivetrain, consisting of engine, central tube and transaxle transmission with differential, was implanted in V3, an Audi 100 coupé. This was followed by V4 and V5, two additional Audi 100 coupés. An additional test mule was a DKW 'Munga' for engine testing. A dozen actual 928 prototypes, designated W1 to W12, were also built; the last one actually represented the pre-production series, which was already being built by that time.

Model year 1978 (L Series)

The 928 body was the epitome of modern lightweight design. The bodyshell unit was made of two-side hot-dip galvanized steel. Doors, front wings and bonnet were made of aluminium, with a weight-saving of 50 per cent compared to equivalent steel parts. A large glass rear hatch covered the luggage area. Two gas struts supported the hatch for easy opening. The luggage space had a capacity of 200 litres (7.1 cubic feet); folding down the two rear seat-backs doubled this volume. The rear hatch could only be opened with a key. An emergency tool-kit, jack and warning triangle were stowed in the rear bulkhead behind a trim panel. Transmission, battery, collapsible space-saver spare tyre and 86-litre (19-gallon) polyethylene fuel tank

were located below the luggage area. Plastic bumpers, integrated in the body lines, covered sturdy aluminium beams which could withstand impacts up to 5mph (8kph) without deformation. At the front, indicators, driving lamps and fog lamps were integrated in the bumper; the rear end housed tail-light units. Flip-up headlamps were electrically deployed from their stowage spaces in the wings; retracted, the headlamp lenses remained visible on the wing tops. A headlamp washer system and remote headlamp adjustment were standard equipment, as was a hatch-mounted rear wiper. The outside rear-view mirror, painted in body colour, was electrically adjustable and heatable. Depending on equipment, the 928 tipped the scales at 1450kg to 1540kg (3197lb to 3395lb). Maximum kerb weight was 1870kg (4123lb).

The transverse-link front suspension employed negative steering offset, extremely rigid cast-aluminium upper and lower A-arms, and coil springs over shock absorbers. Anti-dive geometry provided a 30 per cent reduction in front-end dive under braking. The rear suspension, the so-called 'Weissach axle', represented a completely new concept. One of the key features of this double transverse-link suspension was its ability to generate stabilizing toe-in. The lower suspension arm, consisting of a semi-trailing link and flexible toe control link, was designed to eliminate dangerous oversteer. This was a trailblazing contribution to active vehicle safety. As at the front, the rear suspension also employed coil springs over shock absorbers. The camber characteristics of the rear suspension also helped keep tyre wear at a minimum. Anti-squat geometry reduced rear-end squat on acceleration by about 60 per cent.

The dual-diagonal brake system employed floating brake callipers at both ends, gripping ventilated brake discs. Small handbrake drums were integrated in the rear discs.

The standard cast five-hole aluminium-alloy wheels, in so-called 'Telephone Design', measured 7 J x 16. These carried 225/50 VR 16 rubber. Optionally, customers could choose 7 J x 15 rims with 215/60 VR 15 tyres, offering slightly greater comfort.

The 2+2 coupé offered a very complete equipment list. Its interior was characterized by functionality and passive safety. The instrument

Phantom view of a 928 Coupé with 4.5-litre V8 engine

binnacle and three-spoke steering wheel were
height-adjustable as a complete unit. Instruments
comprised a speedometer, tachometer, voltmeter,
petrol, coolant-temperature and oil-pressure
gauges. The most important switches were arrayed
on the left and right sides within the binnacle. The
centre console housed two air ducts, sliding controls
for the heater, the radio, several switches and a
round analog clock. Adjustable vents were mounted
in the door panels. Pulling out the armrests revealed
side storage pockets. Electrically-powered front
seats were offered as an option. Electric windows
were standard. The doors locked by means of a
vacuum-actuated central-locking system. The
passenger side sun visor included a lighted vanity
mirror. Cruise control was also standard equipment.
Two automatic lap belts provided added protection
for rear-seat passengers. A net in the boot kept
luggage from sliding, while a retractable shade
protected it from prying eyes. The optional air-
conditioning system also cooled the glove
compartment. A cassette radio stereo system, also
optional, included two door speakers and two rear
side-panel speakers. The 928 was the first Porsche
with power steering as standard equipment. It had
been intended to offer an optional electrically-
operated sliding sunroof, but this was not ready at
the time production got underway.

A water-cooled V8 engine was installed at the
front of the car. Tuned for regular-grade petrol, its
4474cc displacement and 8.5:1 compression ratio
yielded 240hp (176kW) at 5500rpm. Maximum
torque of 350Nm (258lb ft) was produced at
3600rpm. A forged crankshaft spun in five sintered
steel journal bearings. The camshafts were driven by
a timing belt.

Intake and exhaust valves were actuated by
hydraulic bucket tappets, obviating the need for
periodic valve adjustment. Oil was supplied by a
pressure lubrication system and a crescent pump.
Service and maintenance were scheduled for every
20,000km (12,000 miles). Fuel was supplied by an
electric feed pump and K-Jetronic fuel-injection
system. The breakerless transistorized coil ignition,
known by its German acronym TSZ, fired the
cylinders in the order 1-3-7-2-6-5-4-8.

A twin-disc clutch was bolted to the engine
flywheel. The five-speed manual transmission was
installed at the rear suspension. A transaxle tube
containing a rotating solid shaft carried power from
the engine to the transmission. A three-speed
automatic transmission, made by Daimler-Benz and
given sportier tuning for the 928, was available as
an option.

With a manual transmission, the 928 sprinted to
62mph (100kph) in 7.2 seconds. Top speed was in
excess of 143mph (230kph). The automatic
transmission needed 7.8 seconds to reach 62mph
(100kph), and topped out at 140mph (225kph).

In 1978, the 928 was the first and, to date, only
sports car to be named 'Car of the Year' by the
European motoring press.

Model year 1979 (M Series)

For 1979, the Porsche 928 continued without any
significant changes compared to the previous year.

Model year 1980 (A Programme)

Porsche introduced the 928 S, the top of the 928 model line. With a 300hp (221kW) 4.7-litre V8 engine, it produced as much power as the 911 turbo. The non-S 928 also benefited from detail development, with its engine revamped in the interest of reduced fuel consumption.

The 928 S was primarily recognizable by its black polyurethane front and rear spoilers and body-colour side mouldings. The spoilers reduced its aerodynamic drag coefficient to 0.38. The 928 S included a rear wiper as standard equipment.

The unaltered suspension of the 928 S offered the same level of ride comfort as the 928. To match the increased engine output, brakes were uprated, with larger pads and thicker discs. The anodized finish of its forged-aluminium disc wheels imparted an even more exclusive look to the 928 S. Tyres, size 225/50 VR 16, were mounted on 7 J x 16 rims.

The 928 S had a very extensive list of standard features. These included, for example, cruise control, electronic central warning system, headlamp-cleaning system, rear sunshades, four stereo speakers and a cassette and coin holder. Also standard were partial leather interior and a four-spoke steering wheel. New features included improved radios with optional auxiliary amplifiers. One new development was the electronically-controlled climate-control system, which maintained a preset temperature.

Cylinder bore on the 928 S was increased from 95mm to 97mm, raising displacement to 4664cc. With a compression ratio of 10:1, the engine demanded premium-grade petrol. Induction tract and exhaust system were optimized to improve engine gas flow. At an engine speed of 5900rpm, the 928 S developed 300hp (221kW). The V8 engine of the 928 S had a sportier state of tune than the base 928, and did not develop its peak torque of 385Nm (284lb ft) until revs had risen to 4500rpm.

The 928 S could be ordered with a five-speed manual transmission or an optional three-speed automatic. With the manual, it could reach 62mph (100kph) in 6.6 seconds, and a top speed of 155mph (250kph).

The engine of the base 928 was reworked for better fuel economy. Compression was raised to 10:1 and the engine retuned for premium-grade fuel. Output remained unchanged at 240hp (176kW), but at lower engine speed (5250rpm instead of 5500rpm). Torque, however, increased, from 350Nm (258lb ft) to 380Nm (280lb ft), still at 3600rpm. Performance remained unchanged.

On the base 928, the rear wiper and headlamp-cleaning system were deleted from the standard equipment roster.

Model year 1981 (B Programme)

Porsche extended its anti-corrosion warranty from six to seven years, and expanded it to cover not just the floorpan but the entire body.

The 928 was equipped with a rear wiper, headlamp-cleaning system, and rear fog lamp as standard equipment. The 928 S also received a rear fog lamp. As an option, the standard seats could be upholstered in 'Berber' fabric, or, alternatively, customers could order full-leather sports seats. Instead of Porsche radios, Blaupunkt QTS radios were available.

Model year 1982 (C Programme)

The base model 928, with its 4.5-litre engine, entered its final model year. Permissible roof load for the 928 line was increased from 35kg to 75kg (77lb to 165lb).

As a theft-proofing measure, locking wheelnuts were available as an option.

The 928 equipment list was extended by a precise fuel consumption gauge, improved ventilation with ten per cent greater air flow, cassette and coin holder on the centre tunnel, rear sun visors, boot illumination, four-spoke steering wheel, intensive windscreen-washer system, four speakers, fade/balance control and electric aerial. The 928 S got improved ventilation, a fuel consumption gauge and an electrically-operated driver's seat.

A reverse gear lock-out was added to vehicles with five-speed manual transmissions.

The 928 ended its production run with a total of 17,669 examples built.

Model year 1983 (D Programme)

For 1983, the 928 S was the only model in the eight-cylinder line. For the United States and Canada, automatic transmission, dual outside mirrors, and forged 16-inch wheels were standard equipment. In these markets, side mouldings and rear '928 S' badging were deleted.

Five new metallic colours were introduced, and

green-tinted solar-heat-blocking glass was fitted as standard equipment.

The 928 S was now equipped with cast-aluminium 16-inch 'Telephone Design' wheels and 225/50 VR 16 tyres as standard equipment. Anodized forged wheels continued to be offered as an option.

The instrument binnacle and steering wheel were now coloured to match the rest of the interior. The round analog clock was replaced by a digital clock. Other equipment details included entry lamps and automatic climate control.

A new timing-belt tensioner and hydraulic engine mounts helped to reduce noise levels.

Model year 1984 (E Programme)

Within the framework of model development, the V8 engine was subjected to a thorough revamping. The 928 S was the first Porsche to be offered with an anti-lock brake system (ABS) as an option.

A Sekuriflex windscreen was installed for better occupant protection. Heated windscreen-washer nozzles were an effective means to prevent frozen, clogged nozzles in winter driving conditions. The rear hatch could be opened electrically from the driver's position.

Modified front seat design provided even more headroom for tall occupants. A locking button on the centre console kept uninvited visitors from opening the doors.

The engine was retuned for better fuel economy by means of a Bosch LH Jetronic fuel-injection system with hot-wire mass air-flow sensor, overrun fuel cut-off and transistorized map ignition. Compression ratio was raised to 10.4:1. A happy byproduct was a 10hp (7kW) power increase to 310hp (228kW) at 5900rpm. Torque also benefited, with 400Nm (295lb ft) available at 4100rpm. Also new was the four-speed automatic transmission supplied by Mercedes-Benz.

Performance of the manual-transmission 928 S improved, with a top speed of about 158mph (255kph) and acceleration to 62mph (100kph) in 6.2 seconds.

Model year 1985 (F Programme)

In September 1984 Dr Ferry Porsche received a four-seat 928, the 'Doktorwagen', on the occasion of his 75th birthday. This car would remain a unique one-off.

The 928 S was equipped with side-impact protection in the doors for all markets worldwide. This measure further improved the 928's passive safety features.

The radio aerial was unobtrusively integrated in the windscreen. Electrically-adjustable comfort

Phantom view of a 928 S Coupé with 4.7-litre V8 engine

928 S Coupé, USA version

seats, matching the style of the new 911 seat generation, markedly improved seating comfort and side support. Safety-belt latches were integrated in the seat structure, and heated seats were an available option. The instrument cluster included a gear selector display on automatic transmission cars, and a warning light for timing-belt tension. The steering wheel pad, like the redesigned automatic transmission gear selector, was covered with leather. A complete radio installation kit was pre-installed. For especially warm climates, a second, rear air-conditioning system was available, taking the place of the lockable storage bin between the rear seats.

The alternator was more powerful, now delivering 115 amps.

Synchronizers of the five-speed manual transmission were revised, for faster, more precise gear changes. This also resulted in a somewhat shorter gear lever.

Model year 1986 (G Programme)

The 928 S entered its final model year. For a cleaner environment, the 928 S could be ordered with an optional catalytic converter. Anti-lock brakes were now standard equipment.

Cast-aluminium 'Telephone Design' wheels were no longer available. Forged-disc wheels now measured 7 J x 16 and included locking wheelnuts. The newly-developed, powerful four-piston fixed-calliper brakes were combined with ABS as standard equipment.

For the first time, the 928 S was available with a controlled three-way catalytic converter and oxygen sensor. For this application, Porsche drew on the four-valve engine developed for the American market. This 5-litre V8 was tuned for regular-grade petrol and developed 288hp (212kW) at 5750rpm. Maximum torque of 400Nm (295lb ft) matched that of the non-catalyst 4.7-litre engine, but was produced at a much lower engine speed, 2700rpm. Performance of the 5-litre V8 was roughly equivalent to that of the 4.7-litre engine. A modified exhaust system was fitted to help minimize noise levels.

An interesting fact is that worldwide, 70 per cent of 928 S buyers opted for an automatic transmission.

A total number of 22,662 examples of the 928 S were built.

928 Coupé [Automatic]
MY 1978–MY 1982

Engine

Engine design:	8-cylinder V-engine, 90°
Installation:	Front engine
Cooling system:	Water-cooled
Engine type:	M 28/01 [M 28/02]
MY 1980–MY 1982:	M 28/09 [M 28/10]
Displacement (cc):	4474
Bore x stroke (mm):	95 x 78,9
Engine output DIN (kW/hp):	177/240 at 5500rpm
MY 1980–MY 1982:	177/240 at 5250rpm
Maximum torque (Nm/lb ft):	350/258 at 3600rpm
MY 1980–MY 1982:	380/280 at 3600rpm
Output per litre (kW/l / hp/l):	39.6 / 53.6
Compression ratio:	8.5 : 1
MY 1980–MY 1982:	10.0 : 1
Valve operation camshaft drive:	ohc, cam driven by synchronous belt drive, 2 valves per cylinder
Carburation:	Bosch K-Jetronic fuel injection
Ignition system:	Transistorized coil ignition (TCI)
Firing order:	1- 3 - 7 - 2 - 6 - 5 - 4 - 8
Engine lubrication:	Full-pressure oil lubrication
Engine oil total (l):	7.5

Transmission

Drive configuration:	Rear-axle drive, transaxle system
Manual gearbox:	5-speed
Option Automatic:	[3-speed]
Transmission type:	G 28/03 [A 22/01]
MY 1981– MY 1982:	G 28/05
Transmission ratios:	
1st gear:	3.601 [2.306]
2nd gear:	2.465 [1.460]
3rd gear:	1.819 [1.000]
4th gear:	1.343
5th gear:	1.000
Reverse gear:	3.162 [1.836]
Drive ratio:	2.750 [2.750]
January 1981–MY 1982:	2.727
Option with manual gearbox:	Limited-slip differential 40%

Body, chassis, suspension, brakes, wheels

Body design:	Steel coupé body, 2 doors, 2 + 2 seats, entirely hot-dip galvanized body, aluminium engine lid, front wings and doors, flexible front and rear bumpers integrated in body form with integrated aluminium beams, flip-up headlamps, rear lid with glass window, painted electric outside mirrors
Option:	Electric sunroof
Suspension, front:	Independent suspension, dual transverse arms with coil springs enclosing shock absorbers, one coil spring per wheel, dual-action hydraulic shock absorbers, anti-roll bar
Suspension, rear:	Independent suspension, dual transverse arms with toe-in stabilization by control link (Weissach axle), one coil spring per wheel, dual-action hydraulic shock absorbers, anti-roll bar
Brakes, front/rear (Size (mm)):	Ventilated discs (282 x 32) / Ventilated discs (289 x 20) Fixed callipers / Floating callipers

Wheels, front/rear:	7 J x 16 / 7 J x 16
Tyres, front/rear:	225/50 VR 16 / 225/50 VR 16
Option,	7 J x 15 / 7 J x 15
MY 1980–MY 1982 standard:	215/60 VR 15 / 215/60 VR 15

Electrical system

Alternator (W/A):	1260 / 90
Battery (V/Ah):	12 / 66
Option:	12 / 88

Dimensions and weight

Track, front/rear (mm):	1551 / 1530
MY 1980–MY 1982:	1552 / 1529
Wheelbase (mm):	2500
Lenght x width x height (mm):	4447 x 1836 x 1313
MY 1980–MY 1982:	4447 x 1836 x 1282
Kerb weight DIN (kg):	1450
Permissible gross weight (kg):	1870
Luggage compartment (VDA (l)):	200
with folded down rear seatbacks:	400
Fuel tank capacity (l):	86, including 8 reserve
C_w x A (m^2):	0.41 x 1.95 = 0.799
Power/weight ratio (kg/kW / kg/hp):	8.19 / 6.04

Fuel consumption

DIN 70 030 (mpg):	91 RON normal leaded
At constant 56mph/90kph:	25 [29.1]
At constant 74mph/120kph:	21.7 [16.7]
Urban cycle:	10.6 [13.2]
MY 1980:	
DIN 70 030 (mpg):	98 RON Super leaded
At constant 56mph/90kph:	29.5 [26.6]
At constant 74mph/120kph:	23.7 [21.2]
Urban cycle:	16 [17.2]
MY 1981–MY 1982:	
DIN 70 030 (mpg):	98 RON Super leaded
At constant 56mph/90kph:	30 [29.1]
At constant 74mph/120kph:	24.5 [23]
Urban cycle:	15.3 [18.8]

Performance, production, prices

Acceleration 0-62mph/100kph (s):	6.8 [8.0]
MY 1980–MY 1982:	7.2 [7.7]
Maximum speed (mph / kph):	143 / 230 [140 / 225]
Production, total number:	17,669
Purchase prices:	
06/1977:	DM 55,000 [DM 56,890]
01/1978:	DM 58,800 [DM 60,707]
08/1978:	DM 58,800 [DM 60,780]
01/1979:	DM 58,800 [DM 60,780]
08/1979:	DM 56,900 [DM 59,000]
04/1980:	DM 59,100 [DM 61,200]
08/1980:	DM 59,900 [DM 62,280]
02/1981:	DM 61,650 [DM 64,030]
08/1981:	DM 62,750 [DM 65,540]
01/1982:	DM 64,900 [DM 67,690]

928 S Coupé [Automatic]
MY 1980–MY 1983

Engine
Engine design:	8-cylinder V-engine, 90°
Installation:	Front-engine
Cooling system:	Water-cooled
Engine type:	M 28/11 [M 28/12]
Displacement (cc):	4664
Bore x stroke (mm):	97 x 78.9
Engine output DIN (kW/hp):	221/300 at 5900rpm
Maximum torque (Nm/lb ft):	385/284 at 4500rpm
Output per litre (kW/l / hp/l):	45.2 / 64.3
Compression ratio:	10.0 : 1
Valve operation camshaft drive:	ohc, cam driven by synchronous belt drive, 2 valves per cylinder
Carburation:	Bosch K-Jetronic fuel injection
Ignition system:	Transistorized coil ignition (TCI)
Firing order:	1- 3 - 7 - 2 - 6 - 5 - 4 - 8
Engine lubrication:	Full-pressure oil lubrication
Engine oil total (l):	7.5

Transmission
Drive configuration:	Rear-axle drive, transaxle system
Manual gearbox:	5-speed
Option Automatic:	[3-speed]
Transmission type:	G 28/05 (G 28/07)* [A 22/04]
Transmission ratios:	
1st gear:	3.601 (3.765) [2.306]
2nd gear:	2.465 (2.512) [1.460]
3rd gear:	1.819 (1.790) [1.000]
4th gear:	1.343 (1.354)
5th gear:	1.000 (1.000)
Reverse gear:	3.162 (3.306) [1.836]
Drive ratio:	2.750 [2.750]
14.01.1981–MY 1983:	2.727 (2.727)
Option with manual gearbox:	Limited-slip differential 40%
*MY 1983	

Body, chassis, suspension, brakes, wheels
Body design:	Steel coupé body, 2 doors, 2 + 2 seats, entirely hot-dip galvanized body, aluminium engine lid, front wings and doors, flexible front and rear bumpers integrated in body form with integrated aluminium beams, flip-up headlamps, rear lid with glass window, black polyurethane front and rear spoiler, painted electric outside mirrors
Option:	Electric sunroof
Suspension, front:	Independent suspension, dual transverse arms with coil springs enclosing shock absorbers, one coil spring per wheel, dual-action hydraulic shock absorbers, anti-roll bar
Suspension, rear:	Independent suspension, dual transverse arms with toe-in stabilization by control link (Weissach axle), one coil spring per wheel, dual-action hydraulic shock absorbers, anti-roll bar
Brakes, front/rear (Size (mm)):	Ventilated discs (282 x 32) / Ventilated discs (289 x 20) Fixed callipers / Floating callipers
Wheels, front/rear:	7 J x 16 / 7 J x 16
Tyres, front/rear:	225/50 VR 16 / 225/50 VR 16

Electrical system
Alternator (W/A):	1260 / 90
Battery (V/Ah):	12 / 66
Option, MY 1983 standard:	12 / 88

Dimensions and weight
Track, front/rear (mm):	1552 / 1529
Wheelbase (mm):	2500
Length x width x height (mm):	4447 x 1836 x 1282
Kerb weight DIN (kg):	1450
Permissible gross weight (kg):	1870
Luggage compartment (VDA (l)):	200
with folded down rear seatbacks:	400
Fuel tank capacity (l):	86, including 8 reserve
C_w x A (m²):	0.38 x 1.95 = 0.741
Power/weight ratio (kg/kW/ kg/hp):	6.56 / 4.83

Fuel consumption
DIN 70 030/1 (mpg):	98 RON super leaded
At constant 56mph/90kph:	28.4 [27.4]
At constant 74mph/120kph:	22.5 [21.4]
Urban cycle:	14.3 [15.9]
MY 1981–MY 1983:	
DIN 70 030/1 (mpg):	98 RON super leaded
At constant 56mph/90kph:	29.1 [28.2]
At constant 74mph/120kph:	22.1 [22.4]
Urban cycle:	14.3 [15.5]

Performance, production, prices
Acceleration 0-62mph/100kph (s):	6.6 [7.2]
Maximum speed (mph / kph):	155 / 250 [152 / 245]
Production, total number:	8,315
Purchase prices:	
04/1980:	DM 75,750 [DM 77,850]
08/1980:	DM 75,750 [DM 78,130]
02/1981:	DM 77,950 [DM 80,330]
08/1981:	DM 79,100 [DM 81,890]
01/1982:	DM 81,800 [DM 84,590]
08/1982:	DM 79,950 [DM 82,940]
03/1983:	DM 81,950 [DM 84,940]

928 S Coupé [Automatic]
MY 1984–MY 1986

Engine

Engine design:	8-cylinder V-engine, 90°
Installation:	Front-engine
Cooling system:	Water-cooled
Engine type:	M 28/21 [M 28/22]
Displacement (cc):	4664
Bore x stroke (mm):	97 x 78.9
Engine output DIN (kW/hp):	228/310 at 5900rpm
Maximum torque (Nm/lb ft):	400/295 at 4100rpm
Output per litre (kW/l / hp/l):	48.9 / 66.5
Compression ratio:	10.4 : 1
Valve operation camshaft drive:	ohc, cam driven by synchronous belt drive, 2 valves per cylinder
Carburation:	Bosch LH-Jetronic fuel injection
Ignition system:	Breakerless electronic ignition (ESA)
Firing order:	1 - 3 - 7 - 2 - 6 - 5 - 4 - 8
Engine lubrication:	Full-pressure oil lubrication
Engine oil total (l):	7.5

Transmission

Drive configuration:	Rear-axle drive, transaxle system
Manual gearbox:	5-speed
Option Automatic:	[4-speed]
Transmission type:	G 28/07 [A 28/02] [A 28/04]* [A 28/08][2]
Transmission ratios:	
1st gear:	3.765 [3.676] [3.676]* [3.676][2]
2nd gear:	2.512 [2.412] [2.412]* [2.412][2]
3rd gear:	1.790 [1.436] [1.436]* [1.436][2]
4th gear:	1.354 [1.000] [1.000]* [1.000][2]
5th gear:	1.000
Reverse gear:	3.306 [5.139] [5.139]* [5.139][2]
Drive ratio:	2.727 [2.357] [2.200]* [2.357][2]
Option:	[2.538]
Option with manual gearbox:	Limited-slip differential 40%
*Option MY 1985	
[2]Option MY 1986	

Body, chassis, suspension, brakes, wheels

Body design:	Steel coupé body, 2 doors, 2 + 2 seats, entirely hot-dip galvanized body, aluminium engine lid, front wings and doors, flexible front and rear bumpers integrated in body form with integrated aluminium beams, flip-up headlamps, rear lid with glass window, black polyurethane front and rear spoiler, painted electric outside mirrors
MY 1985–MY 1986:	Side-impact protection beams in doors
Option:	Electric sunroof
Suspension, front:	Independent suspension, dual transverse arms with coil springs enclosing shock absorbers, one coil spring per wheel, dual-action hydraulic shock absorbers, anti-roll bar
Suspension, rear:	Independent suspension, dual transverse arms with toe-in stabilization by control link (Weissach axle), one coil spring per wheel, dual-action hydraulic shock absorbers, anti-roll bar
Brakes, front/rear (Size (mm)):	Ventilated discs (282 x 32) / Ventilated discs (289 x 20) Fixed callipers / Floating callipers
MY 1986:	Ventilated discs (304 x 32) / Ventilated discs (299 x 24) Black 4-piston fixed aluminium callipers / Black 4-piston fixed aluminium callipers
Option MY 1986:	ABS
Wheels, front/rear:	7 J x 16 / 7 J x 16
Tyres, front/rear:	225/50 VR 16 / 225/50 VR 16

Electrical system

Alternator (W/A):	1260 / 90
MY 1985–MY 1986:	1610 / 115
Battery (V/Ah):	12 / 88
MY 1986:	12 / 72

Dimensions and weight

Track, front/rear (mm):	1552 / 1529
MY 1985–MY 1986:	1549 / 1521
Wheelbase (mm):	2500

Length x width x height (mm):	4447 x 1836 x 1282
Kerb weight DIN (kg):	1500 [1520]
MY 1985–MY 1986:	1530 [1550]
Permissible gross weight (kg):	1870 [1870]
MY 1985–MY 1986:	1890 [1890]
Luggage compartment (VDA (l)):	200
with folded down rear seatbacks:	400
Fuel tank capacity (l):	86, including 8 reserve
C_w x A (m²):	0.38 x 1.95 = 0.741
Power/weight ratio (kg/kW/ kg/hp):	6.57 [6.66] / 4.83 [4.90]
MY 1985–MY 1986:	6.71 [6.79] / 4.93 [5.00]

Fuel consumption

DIN 70 030/1 (mpg):	98 RON super leaded
At constant 56mph/90kph:	32.5 [32.8]
At constant 74mph/120kph:	27.5 [26.8]
EG-emissions-urban cycle:	14.8 [16.9]
MY 1985–MY 1987:	
EG-Norm 80/1268 (mpg):	98 RON super leaded
At constant 56mph/90kph:	32.5 [32.8]
At constant 74mph/120kph:	27.5 [26.8]
EG-emissions-urban cycle:	14.8 [16.9]

Performance, production, prices

Acceleration 0-62mph/100kph (s):	6,2 [6,7]
Maximum speed (mph / kph):	158 / 255 [155 / 250]
Production, total number:	
(incl. veh. with catalytic converter):	14,347
Purchase prices:	
08/1983:	DM 84,950 [DM 88,240]
02/1984:	DM 87,650 [DM 90,940]
10/1984:	DM 90,950 [DM 94,900]
02/1985:	DM 93,000 [DM 96,950]
08/1985:	DM 100,000 [DM 103,990]

928 S Coupé with catalytic converter [Automatic] MY 1986

Engine
Engine design:	8-cylinder V-engine, 90°
Installation:	Front-engine
Cooling system:	Water-cooled
Engine type:	M 28/45 [M 28/46]
Displacement (cc):	4957
Bore x stroke (mm):	100 x 78.9
Engine output DIN (kW/hp):	212/288 at 5750rpm
Maximum torque (Nm/lb ft):	400/295 at 2700rpm
Output per litre (kW/l / hp/l):	42.8 / 58.1
Compression ratio:	9.3 : 1
Valve operation camshaft drive:	dohc, cam driven by synchronous belt drive, 4 valves per cylinder
Carburation:	Bosch LH-Jetronic fuel injection
Ignition system:	Breakerless electronic ignition (ESA)
Firing order:	1 - 3 - 7 - 2 - 6 - 5 - 4 - 8
Engine lubrication:	Full-pressure oil lubrication
Engine oil total (l):	7.5

Transmission
Drive configuration:	Rear-axle drive, transaxle system
Manual gearbox:	5-speed
Option Automatic:	[4-speed]
Transmission type:	G 28/10 [A 28/11]
Transmission ratios:	
1st gear:	3.764 [3.676]
2nd gear:	2.512 [2.412]
3rd gear:	1.790 [1.436]
4th gear:	1.354 [1.000]
5th gear:	1.000
Reverse gear:	3.305 [5.139]
Drive ratio:	2.727 [2.538]
Option with manual gearbox:	Limited-slip differential 40%

Body, chassis, suspension, brakes, wheels
Body design:	Steel coupé body, 2 doors, 2 + 2 seats, entirely hot-dip galvanized body, aluminium engine lid, front wings and doors, side-impact protection beams in doors, flexible front and rear bumpers integrated in body form with integrated aluminium beams, flip-up headlamps, rear lid with glass window, black polyurethane front and rear spoiler, painted electric outside mirrors
Option:	Electric sunroof
Suspension, front:	Independent suspension, dual transverse arms with coil springs enclosing shock absorbers, one coil spring per wheel, dual-action hydraulic shock absorbers, anti-roll bar
Suspension, rear:	Independent suspension, dual transverse arms with toe-in stabilization by control link (Weissach axle), one coil spring per wheel, dual-action hydraulic shock absorbers, anti-roll bar
Brakes, front/rear (Size (mm)):	Ventilated discs (304 x 32) / Ventilated discs (299 x 24) Black 4-piston fixed aluminium callipers / Black 4-piston fixed aluminium callipers
Option:	ABS
Wheels, front/rear:	7 J x 16 / 7 J x 16
Tyres, front/rear:	225/50 VR 16 / 225/50 VR 16

Electrical system
Alternator (W/A):	1610 / 115
Battery (V/Ah):	12 / 72

Dimensions and weight
Track, front/rear (mm):	1549 / 1521
Wheel base (mm):	2500
Length x width x height (mm):	4447 x 1836 x 1282
Kerb weight DIN (kg):	1530 [1550]
Permissible gross weight (kg):	1890 [1890]
Luggage compartment (VDA (l)):	200
with folded down rear seatbacks:	400
Fuel tank capacity (l):	86, including 8 reserve
C_w x A (m²):	0.38 x 1.95 = 0.741
Power/weight ratio (kg/kW/kg/hp):	7.21 [7.31] / 5.31 [5.38]

Fuel consumption
EG-Norm 80/1268 (mpg):	91 RON normal unleaded
At constant 56mph/90kph:	30 [29.5]
At constant 74mph/120kph:	24.8 [22.1]
EG-emissions-urban cycle:	14.25 [16.4]

Performance, production, prices
Acceleration 0-62mph/100kph (s):	6.2 [6.7]
Maximum speed (mph / kph):	156 / 252 [153 / 247]
Production, total number: (incl. veh. w/o catalytic converter):	14,347
Purchase prices: 08/1985:	DM 109,000 [DM 112,990]

Porsche 928 S4, 928 S4 Clubsport, 928 GT and 928 GTS

Porsche 928 S4, 928 S4 Clubsport and 928 GT

Porsche subjected the 928 to a major programme of model development. The 928 S4 presented a new, aerodynamically-improved body and a new 5-litre four-valve-per-cylinder engine.

Model year 1987 (H Programme)

Because of its considerably reworked body and improved aerodynamics, the 928 S4 was immediately recognizable as different from its predecessors. The more rounded nose, with modified front spoiler, incorporated indicators, driving and fog lamps, and air inlets for brake cooling. The car's modified tail carried larger tail-light units with integrated rear fog lamps. A particularly obvious change was the larger, black polyurethane rear spoiler, mounted away from the body. Sill mouldings and an undertray rounded out the list of modifications. The results were impressive: the aerodynamic drag coefficient dropped from 0.38 to 0.34.

The drivetrain also underwent major modification. Without a catalytic converter, the V8 engine, tuned for unleaded 95 Research Octane Number Euro-Super petrol, developed 320hp (235kW) at 6000rpm. With a compression ratio of 10:1, the engine also pulled much more strongly through the gears. Maximum torque rose to 430Nm (317lb ft) at 3000rpm.

A cylinder bore increase from 97mm to 100mm raised displacement to 4957cc, and four valves per cylinder ensured better gas flow. Intake valves had 37mm heads, exhausts 34mm. The proven LH-Jetronic fuel-injection system was retained. Knock

sensors enabled the electronics to detect low-quality fuel and dial back ignition timing accordingly. The V-belt-driven, viscous-clutch engine cooling fan was replaced by two electric fans. Also new was the closed, controlled fuel tank vent system.

The five-speed manual transmission, now teamed with a single-plate dry clutch, as well as the four-speed automatic, received slightly modified final drive ratios. The limited-slip differential continued to be available as an option.

At the rear, 245/45 VR 16 tyres on 8-inch forged rims improved handling.

A new option was seat memory, which stored seat and outside mirror settings for three different drivers. At the touch of a button, these could be recalled from memory and the driver's seat and mirrors automatically set to the driver's preferences.

Performance of the 928 S4 was appreciably better than that of its predecessor. Top speed was 168mph (270kph) with the manual transmission, and 165mph (265kph) with the automatic, making the 928 S4 the fastest production Porsche to date. This Grand Touring car accelerated to 62mph (100kph) in 5.9 seconds, or 6.3 seconds with automatic transmission.

Model year 1988 (J Programme)

Weighing about 130kg (286lb) less than the stock version, Porsche offered an extremely sporty 928 S4 in the form of a Clubsport model. Weight reduction was achieved by carefully considered deletion of equipment and features. The 928 S4 Clubsport was delivered without PVC undercoating, saving 15kg (33lb). Other eliminated equipment included the air-conditioning system, rear wiper and rear sun visors. Electric seats were replaced by mechanically-adjustable seats. Exhaust system, starter motor,

Phantom view of a 928 S4 Coupé with 5-litre V8 engine

battery and alternator were all replaced by lighter parts. The final drive ratio of the lightweight 928 was geared 3 per cent lower.

Suspension of the lightweight 928 was lowered 20mm and more firmly tuned. The forged-alloy wheels were of a new design, saving an additional 1.2kg (2.6lb). Tyres were 225/50 VR 16 and 245/45 VR 16 on 8-inch and 9-inch wide rims front and rear, respectively.

In acceleration and engine elasticity, the lightweight was notably superior to its regular production counterpart, but the top speed of the 928 S4 Clubsport was identical to that of the normal version.

The regular production 928 S4 was equipped with precise electronic cruise control. Moreover, interior appointments were upgraded by improving the driver's seat controls and adding a speaker sound package. Other options included special crushed leather and preparation for later installation of a cell-net telephone.

Model year 1989 (K Programme)

The Porsche 928 S4 was the world's first car to be fitted with a tyre-pressure monitor and a cockpit-mounted information and diagnostic system, and the autumn of 1989 saw the introduction of the even more sporty 928 GT.

The 928 GT power unit's output characteristics were designed to be more high-stepping. The 5-litre engine developed 330hp (243kW) at 6200rpm.

This additional power was obtained through a modified control unit, more aggressive camshaft layout with altered cam timing and one millimetre greater valve lift, as well as induction tract modifications. Maximum torque of 430Nm (317lb ft) was produced at 4100rpm. The rev limiter cut in at 6800rpm.

Because the 928 GT assumed the sporting role in the eight-cylinder line, its suspension could be ordered with firmer Boge gas-pressure shock absorbers. The GT rolled on forged 'Cup Design' aluminium-alloy wheels, 8 J x 16 at the front with 225/50 ZR 16 tyres, and 9 J x 16 at the rear with 245/45 ZR 16 rubber. The 928 S4 continued to be equipped with the familiar forged disc wheels. All 928s were equipped with a tyre pressure monitoring system. Each wheel was fitted with two sensors, which reliably kept track of tyre pressure and signalled pressure loss by means of a visual indicator in the dash-mounted combination instrument.

The redesigned combination instrument contained an information and diagnostic system. Depending on vehicle equipment level, its LCD displays could convey up to 21 different items of information, as text or symbols. Porsche dealership service personnel could also call up the built-in on-board diagnostic system through these displays. A new alarm system, activated by locking the door, indicated its armed status with blinking LEDs in the door-lock buttons. The central-locking system was

Phantom view of a 928 GT Coupé with an even more performance-oriented 5-litre V8 engine

adapted to the new alarm system. A ten-speaker sound package with amplifier was included as standard equipment. It could be combined with a radio and CD player.

The flanks of the 928 GT body were devoid of any trim strips, but customers could order these as a no-cost option.

The only remaining transmission choice for the 928 S4 was the automatic, whose layout was made even sportier. By contrast, the 928 GT could only be ordered with a five-speed manual transmission and stock limited-slip differential with a 40 per cent lock-up factor. Top speed of the sporty 928 GT was in the vicinity of 171mph (275kph).

The 5-litre V8 engine of a 928 S4

Model year 1990 (L Programme)

Beginning with the 1990 model year, all Porsche 928s were equipped with a controlled three-way catalyst and oxygen sensor as standard equipment. The 928 S4 was only available with a four-speed automatic transmission, the 928 GT only with a five-speed manual. Porsche's electronically-controlled limited-slip differential (PSD) was phased in on both models. On the 928 GT, new 'Design 90' cast-aluminium wheels were phased in, 7.5 inches wide at the front and 9 inches at the rear. The 928 S4 was available with the wider cast-alloy wheels and tyres of the 928 GT at no additional cost.

A single-piece defroster vent provided better windscreen air distribution. An analog clock once again took its place in the centre console, displacing the digital clock. Rear seat three-point automatic safety belts were installed as standard equipment.

Engine compartment of a 928 S4 Coupé

Model year 1991 (M Programme)

Both 5-litre models, the 928 S4 and 928 GT, entered their last year of production. Interior noise levels were reduced by installation of more effective insulation material, particularly at the rear.

As of February 1991, the 928 S4 was fitted with the same wheel and tyre combination as the 928 GT as standard equipment. The leather-covered handbrake handle was rounded off to make entry easier. The steering wheel rim had thicker padding. The reworked power steering system provided more feedback to the driver, for more agile handling. As of 1 February 1991, all left-hand-drive Porsche vehicles, worldwide, were equipped with driver and front-passenger airbags.

Porsche built a total of 17,894 examples of the 928 S4, 928 GT and 928 S4 Clubsport.

Model year 1992 (N Programme)

The 928 GTS marked the final evolutionary phase of Porsche's V8 supercar. The body of the new 928 GTS was recognizable by its wider rear wings, continuous red light band at the rear, body-colour rear spoiler and new 'Cup Design' outside mirrors. Side mouldings were deleted entirely.

For the first time, the big eight-cylinder sports car was equipped with 17-inch 'Cup Design' alloy wheels. At the front these carried 225/45 ZR 17 tyres on 7.5-inch wide rims; rear 255/40 ZR 17

rubber was mounted on 9-inchers. The tyre pressure monitoring system was retained. Larger 332mm ventilated brake discs were installed at the front. The especially powerful four-piston fixed-calliper brake system included ABS.

A comprehensive list of comfort features made the 928 GTS an ideal long-distance sports car. New to these was the 'Symphony' model radio, with its RDS traffic report system and station identification.

The heart of the 928 GTS was doubtless its redesigned V8 engine. A new crankshaft with 85.9mm stroke increased displacement to 5397cc. Technical details included four-valve cylinder heads, LH Jetronic fuel injection, resonance induction system and electronic map ignition. This engine produced 350hp (257kW) at 5700rpm. Even more impressive than its output was its torque characteristic: peak torque of 500Nm (369lb ft) was available at 4250rpm, and at least 400Nm (295lb ft) was available across a broad swath of engine speed, from 1000rpm to 6000rpm.

The 928 GTS was teamed with a five-speed manual transmission or, at no additional cost, a four-speed automatic. PSD was standard equipment in either case. The five-speed version accelerated to 62mph (100kph) in 5.7 seconds; the automatic needed only 0.2 seconds longer. Maximum speed for both versions was about 171mph (275kph).

Model year 1993 (P Programme)

For the 1993 model year, Porsche introduced several environmentally-friendly changes to its production

Phantom view of a 928 GTS Coupé with a 5.4-litre V8 engine

methods and its vehicles. Most colours used in the paint shop had been switched over to water-based paints, resulting in greatly reduced use of organic solvents in the paint process. Also, the brake system now used a new brake fluid, meeting DOT 4 Type 200 specs, with a higher wet boiling point, and a change interval increased to three years.

The air-conditioning system was switched over to environmentally-friendly CFC-free R134a refrigerant. This required modification to all seals and components of the air-conditioning system. For right-hand-drive 928 GTS models, a driver airbag in the steering wheel was now standard. Additionally, Porsche offered new radio units with CD players and code cards to deter theft.

Model year 1994 (R Programme)

To improve interior air quality, the heating and ventilation system was equipped with a pollen filter capable of capturing airborne dust and pollen particles larger than 1/1000th of a millimetre. The filter change interval was 20,000km (12,000 miles).

'Cup Design 93' aluminium wheels were standard. Wheel and tyre sizes remained unchanged. The tyre-pressure monitoring system was deleted with introduction of the new wheels.

Dynamic kickdown was introduced on the automatic transmission, which changed down in reaction to rapid accelerator pedal application. It was no longer necessary to floor the pedal.

Model year 1995 (S Programme)

1995 marked the end of the 928 model line. The 928 GTS finished its final year without changes compared to the previous year.

A total of 2,831 examples of the 928 GTS were built. In all, Porsche built 61,056 examples of the 928 model line.

928 S4 Coupé [Automatic]
MY 1987–MY 1991

Engine

Engine design:	8-cylinder V-engine, 90°
Installation:	Front-engine
Cooling system:	Water-cooled
Engine type:	M 28/41 [M 28/42]
Displacement (cc):	4957
Bore x stroke (mm):	100 x 78.9
Engine output DIN (kW/hp):	235/320 at 6000rpm
Maximum torque (Nm/lb ft):	430/317 at 3000rpm
Output per litre (kW/l / hp/l):	47.4 / 64.6
Compression ratio:	10.0 : 1
Valve operation camshaft drive:	dohc, cams driven by synchronous belt drive, 4 valves per cylinder
Carburation:	Bosch LH-Jetronic fuel injection
Ignition system:	Breakerless electronic ignition (ESA)
Firing order:	1 - 3 - 7 - 2 - 6 - 5 - 4 - 8
Engine lubrication:	Full-pressure oil lubrication
Engine oil total (l):	7.5

Transmission

Drive configuration:	Rear-axle drive, transaxle system
Manual gearbox (until MY 1989):	5-speed
Option Automatic:	[4-speed]
Transmission type:	G 28/12 [A 22/14] [A 22/16]*
Transmission ratios:	
1st gear:	3.765 [3.676] [3.870]*
2nd gear:	2.512 [2.412] [2.250]*
3rd gear:	1.790 [1.436] [1.440]*
4th gear:	1.354 [1.000] [1.000]*
5th gear:	1.000*
Reverse gear:	3.306 [5.139] [5.590]*
Drive ratio:	2.636 [2.538] [2.538]*
Option with manual gearbox:	Limited-slip differential 40%
MY 1990–MY 1991 standard:	Porsche-limited slip differential (PDS)
*MY 1989–MY 1991	

Body, chassis, suspension, brakes, wheels

Body design:	Steel coupé body, 2 doors, 2 + 2 seats, entirely hot-dip galvanized body, aluminium engine lid, front wings and doors, side-impact protection beams in doors, flexible front and rear bumpers with integrated aluminium beams, flip-up headlamps, big rear lamps, rear lid with glass window, black polyurethane rear wing, painted electric outside mirrors
Option:	Electric sunroof
Suspension, front:	Independent suspension, dual transverse arms with coil springs enclosing shock absorbers, one coil spring per wheel, dual-action hydraulic shock absorbers, anti-roll bar
Suspension, rear:	Independent suspension, dual transverse arms with toe-in stabilization by control link (Weissach axle), one coil spring per wheel, dual-action hydraulic shock absorbers, anti-roll bar
Brakes, front/rear (Size (mm)):	Ventilated discs (304 x 32) / Ventilated discs (299 x 24) Black 4-piston fixed aluminium callipers / Black 4-piston fixed aluminium callipers
Option, MY 1989 standard:	ABS
Wheels, front/rear:	7 J x 16 / 8 J x 16
Tyres, front/rear:	225/50 VR 16 / 245/45 VR 16
MY 1989 - MY 1991:	225/50 ZR 16 / 245/45 ZR 16

Electrical system

Alternator (W/A):	1610 / 115
Battery (V/Ah):	12 / 72

Dimensions and weight

Track, front/rear (mm):	1551 / 1546
Wheelbase (mm):	2500
Lenght x width x height (mm):	4520 x 1836 x 1282
Kerb weight DIN (kg):	1580 [1600]
Permissible gross weight (kg):	1920 [1920]
Luggage compartment (VDA (l)):	200
with folded down rear seatbacks:	400

Fuel tank capacity (l):	86, including 8 reserve
MY 1991:	86, including 12 reserve
C_w x A (m²):	0.34 x 1.98 = 0.673
Power/weight ratio (kg/kW/kg/hp):	6.72 [6.80] / 4.93 [5.00]

Fuel consumption

Without catalytic converter:	
EG-Norm 80/1268 (mpg):	95 RON super leaded or unleaded
At constant 56mph/90kph:	30 [31.3]
At constant 74mph/120kph:	26 [25.8]
EG-emissions-urban cycle:	14.4 [16.5]
With catalytic converter:	
EG-Norm 80/1268 (mpg):	95 RON super unleaded
At constant 56mph/90kph:	28.8 [30]
At constant 74mph/120kph:	25.2 [25]
EG-emissions-urban cycle:	14.25 [16.1]
MY 1989–MY 1991:	
With catalytic converter:	
EG-Norm 80/1268 (mpg):	95 RON super unleaded
At constant 56mph/90kph:	[28.2]
At constant 74mph/120kph:	[24]
EG-emissions-urban cycle:	[17]

Performance, production, prices

Acceleration 0-62mph/100kph (s):	5.9 [6.3]
Maximum speed (mph / kph):	168 / 270 [165 / 265]
Production, total number:	
(S4, GT, Clubsport):	17,894
Purchase prices:	
08/1986:	DM 119,500 [DM 123,790]
with catalytic converter:	DM 121,365 [DM 125,655]
03/1987:	DM 121,950 [DM 126,240]
with catalytic converter:	DM 123,815 [DM 128,105]
07/1987:	DM 126,000 [DM 130,590]
with catalytic converter:	DM 127,865 [DM 132,455]
04/1988:	DM 128,500 [DM 133,090]
with catalytic converter:	DM 130,365 [DM 134,955]
08/1988:	DM 133,000 [DM 137,900]
with catalytic converter:	DM 134,865 [DM 139,765]
04/1989:	DM 133,000 [DM 137,900]
with catalytic converter:	DM 134,865 [DM 139,765]
08/1989:	[DM 143,000]
02/1990:	[DM 145,900]
07/1990:	[DM 148,380]
02/1991:	[DM 151,880]

928 S4 Clubsport Coupé
MY 1988

Engine

Engine design:	8-cylinder V-engine, 90°
Installation:	Front-engine
Cooling system:	Water-cooled
Engine type:	M 28/41 Club Sport
Displacement (cc):	4957
Bore x stroke (mm):	100 x 78.9
Engine output DIN (kW/hp):	235/320 at 6000rpm
Maximum torque (Nm/lb ft):	430/317 at 3000rpm
Output per litre (kW/l / hp/l):	47.4 / 64.6
Compression ratio:	10.0 : 1
Valve operation camshaft drive:	dohc, cams driven by synchronous belt drive, 4 valves per cylinder
Carburation:	Bosch LH-Jetronic fuel injection
Ignition system:	Breakerless electronic ignition (ESA)
Firing order:	1 - 3 - 7 - 2 - 6 - 5 - 4 - 8
Engine lubrication:	Full-pressure oil lubrication
Engine oil total (l):	7.5

Transmission

Drive configuration:	Rear-axle drive, transaxle system
Manual gearbox:	5-speed
Transmission type:	G 28/55
Transmission ratios:	
1st gear:	3.765
2nd gear:	2.512
3rd gear:	1.790
4th gear:	1.354
5th gear:	1.000
Reverse gear:	3.306
Drive ratio:	2.727
Standard:	Limited-slip differential 40%

Body, chassis, suspension, brakes, wheels

Body design:	Steel coupé body, 2 doors, 2 + 2 seats, entirely hot-dip galvanized body, aluminium engine lid, front wings and doors, side-impact protection beams in doors, flexible front and rear bumpers with integrated aluminium beams, flip-up headlamps, big rear lamps, rear lid with glass window, black polyurethane rear wing, painted electric outside mirrors
Suspension, front:	Independent suspension, dual transverse arms with coil springs enclosing shock absorbers, one coil spring per wheel, dual-action hydraulic shock absorbers, anti-roll bar
Suspension, rear:	Independent suspension, dual transverse arms with toe-in stabilization by control link (Weissach axle), one coil spring per wheel, dual-action hydraulic shock absorbers, anti-roll bar
Brakes, front/rear (Size (mm)):	Ventilated discs (304 x 32) / Ventilated discs (299 x 24) Black 4-piston fixed aluminium callipers / Black 4-piston fixed aluminium callipers ABS
Wheels, front/rear:	8 J x 16 / 9 J x 16
Tyres, front/rear:	225/50 VR 16 / 245/45 VR 16

Electrical system

Alternator (W/A):	1610 / 115
Battery (V/Ah):	12 / 72

Dimensions and weight

Track, front/rear (mm):	1561 / 1565
Wheelbase (mm):	2500
Maße (L x B x H (mm)):	4520 x 1836 x 1282
Kerb weight DIN (kg):	1450
Permissible gross weight (kg):	1920
Luggage compartment (VDA (l)):	200
with folded down rear seatbacks:	400
Fuel tank capacity (l):	86, including 8 reserve
C_w x A (m²):	0.34 x 1.98 = 0.673
Power/weight ratio (kg/kW/ kg/hp):	6.17 / 4.53

Fuel consumption

Without catalytic converter:	
EG-Norm 80/1268 (mpg):	95 RON super leaded or unleaded
At constant 56mph/90kph:	30
At constant 74mph/120kph:	26
EG-emissions-urban cycle:	14.4
With catalytic converter:	
EG-Norm 80/1268 (mpg):	95 RON super unleaded
At constant 56mph/90kph:	28.8
At constant 74mph/120kph:	25.2
EG-emissions-urban cycle:	14.25

Performance, production, prices

Acceleration 0-62mph/100kph (s):	5.7
Maximum speed (mph / kph):	168 / 270
Production, total number:	
(S4, GT, Clubsport):	17,894
Purchase price:	
04/1988:	DM 128,500
with catalytic converter:	DM 130,365

928 GT Coupé
Spring 1989–MY 1991

Engine
Engine design:	8-cylinder V-engine, 90°
Installation:	Front-engine
Cooling system:	Water-cooled
Engine type:	M 28/47
Displacement (cc):	4957
Bore x stroke (mm):	100 x 78.9
Engine output DIN (kW/hp):	243/330 at 6200rpm
Maximum torque (Nm/lb ft):	430/317 at 4100rpm
Output per litre (kW/l / hp/l):	49.0 / 66.6
Compression ratio:	10.0 : 1
Valve operation camshaft drive:	dohc, cams driven by synchronous belt drive, 4 valves per cylinder
Carburation:	Bosch LH-Jetronic fuel injection
Ignition system:	Breakerless electronic ignition (ESA)
Firing order:	1- 3 - 7 - 2 - 6 - 5 - 4 - 8
Engine lubrication:	Full-pressure oil lubrication
Engine oil total (l):	7.5

Transmission
Drive configuration:	Rear-axle drive, transaxle system
Manual gearbox:	5-speed
Transmission ratio:	G 28/55
Transmission ratios:	
1st gear:	3.765
2nd gear:	2.512
3rd gear:	1.790
4th gear:	1.354
5th gear:	1.000
Reverse gear:	3.306
Drive ratio:	2.727
Standard:	Limited-slip differential 40%
MY 1990–MY 1991:	Porsche limited slip differential (PDS)

Body, chassis, suspension, brakes, wheels
Body design:	Steel coupé body, 2 doors, 2 + 2 seats, entirely hot-dip galvanized body, aluminium engine lid, front wings and doors, side-impact protection beams in doors, flexible front and rear bumpers with integrated aluminium beams, flip-up headlamps, big rear lamps, rear lid with glass window, black polyurethane rear wing, painted electric outside mirrors
Option:	Electric sunroof
Suspension, front:	Independent suspension, dual transverse arms with coil springs enclosing shock absorbers, one coil spring per wheel, dual-action hydraulic shock absorbers, anti-roll bar
Suspension, rear:	Independent suspension, dual transverse arms with toe-in stabilization by control link (Weissach axle), one coil spring per wheel, dual-action hydraulic shock absorbers, anti-roll bar

(Brakes, wheels continued)
Brakes, front/rear (Size (mm)):	Ventilated discs (304 x 32) Ventilated discs (299 x 24) Black 4-piston fixed aluminium callipers / Black 4-piston fixed aluminium callipers ABS
Wheels, front/rear:	8 J x 16 / 9 J x 16
MY 1990–MY 1991:	7.5 J x 16 / 9 J x 16
Tyres, front/rear:	225/50 ZR 16 / 245/45 ZR 16

Electrical system
Alternator (W/A):	1610 / 115
Battery (V/Ah):	12 / 72

Dimensions and weight
Track, front/rear (mm):	1561 / 1565
MY 1990–MY 1991:	1551 / 1546
Wheelbase (mm):	2500
Length x width x height (mm):	4520 x 1836 x 1282
Kerb weight DIN (kg):	1580
Permissible gross weight (kg):	1920
Luggage compartment (VDA (l)):	200
with folded down rear seatbacks:	400
Fuel tank capacity (l):	86, including 8 reserve
MY 1991:	86, including 12 reserve
C_w x A (m²):	0.34 x 1.98 = 0.673
Power/weight ratio (kg/kW/kg/hp):	6.50 / 4.78

Fuel consumption
Without catalytic converter:	
EG-Norm 80/1268 (mpg):	95 RON Super leaded or unleaded
At constant 56mph/90kph:	28.2
At constant 74mph/120kph:	24
EG-emissions-urban cycle:	12.9
With catalytic converter:	
EG-Norm 80/1268 (mpg):	95 RON Super unleaded
At constant 56mph/90kph:	29.1
At constant 74mph/120kph:	23.5
EG-emissions-urban cycle:	12.9

Performance, production, prices
Acceleration 0-62mph/100kph (s):	5.8
Maximum speed (mph / kph):	171 / 275
Production, total number:	
(S4, GT, Clubsport):	17,894
Purchase prices:	
04/1989:	DM 137,900
with catalytic converter:	DM 139,765
08/1989:	DM 143,000
02/1990:	DM 145,900
07/1990:	DM 148,380
02/1991:	DM 151,880

928 GTS Coupé [Automatic]
MY1992–MY 1995

Engine

Engine design:	8-cylinder V-engine, 90°
Installation:	Front-engine
Cooling system:	Water-cooled
Engine type:	M 28/49 [M 28/50]
Displacement (cc):	5397
Bore x stroke (mm):	100 x 85.9
Engine output DIN (kW/hp):	257/350 at 5700rpm
Maximum torque (Nm/lb ft):	500/369 at 4250rpm
Output per litre (kW/l / hp/l):	47.6 / 64.9
Compression ratio:	10.4 : 1
Valve operation camshaft drive:	dohc, cams driven by synchronous belt drive, 4 valves per cylinder
Carburation:	Bosch LH-Jetronic fuel injection
Ignition system:	Breakerless electronic ignition (ESA)
Firing order:	1 - 3 - 7 - 2 - 6 - 5 - 4 - 8
Engine lubrication:	Full-pressure oil lubrication
Engine oil total (l):	7.5

Transmission

Drive configuration:	Rear-axle drive, transaxle system
Manual gearbox:	5-speed
Option Automatic:	[4-speed]
Transmission type:	G 28/57 [A 22/18]
Transmission ratios:	
1st gear:	3.775 [3.870]
2nd gear:	2.519 [2.250]
3trd gear:	1.795 [1.440]
4th gear:	1.358 [1.000]
5th gear:	1.000
Reverse gear:	3.314 [5.590]
Drive ratio:	2.727 [2.538]
Standard:	Porsche-Limited-slip differential (PDS)

Body, chassis, suspension, brakes, wheels

Body design:	Steel coupé body, 2 doors, 2 + 2 seats, entirely hot-dip galvanized body with wider rear wings, aluminium engine lid, front wings and doors, side-impact protection beams in doors, flexible front and rear bumpers with integrated aluminium beams, flip-up headlamps, big rear lamps, red non-reflecting valance, rear lid with glass window, painted polyurethane rear wing, painted electric outside mirrors in Cup design
Option:	Electric sunroof
Suspension, front:	Independent suspension, dual transverse arms with coil springs enclosing shock absorbers, one coil spring per wheel, dual-action hydraulic shock absorbers, anti-roll bar
Suspension, rear:	Independent suspension, dual transverse arms with toe-in stabilization by control link (Weissach axle), one coil spring per wheel, dual-action hydraulic shock absorbers, anti-roll bar
Brakes, front/rear (Size (mm)):	Ventilated discs (322 x 32) Ventilated discs (299 x 24) Black 4-piston fixed aluminium callipers / Black 4-piston fixed aluminium callipers ABS
Wheels, front/rear:	7.5 J x 17 / 9 J x 17
Tyres, front/rear:	225/45 ZR 17 / 255/40 ZR 17

Electrical system

Alternator (W/A):	1610 / 115
Battery (V/Ah):	12 / 72

Dimensions and weight

Track, front/rear (mm):	1551 / 1616
Wheelbase (mm):	2500
Length x width x height (mm):	4520 x 1890 x 1282
Kerb weight DIN (kg):	1620 [1640]
Permissible gross weight (kg):	1960 [1960]
Luggage compartment (VDA (l)):	200
with folded down rear seatbacks:	400
Fuel tank capacity (l):	86, including 12 reserve
C_w x A (m²):	0.35 x 2.02 = 0.707
Power/weight ratio (kg/kW/kg/hp):	6.30 [6.38] / 4.62 [4.68]

Fuel consumption

EG-Norm 80/1268 (mpg):	98 RON super plus unleaded
At constant 56mph/90kph:	28.8 [28.8]
At constant 74mph/120kph:	23.5 [23.7]
EG-emissions-urban cycle:	13.6 [15]

Performance, production, prices

Acceleration 0-62mph/100kph (s):	5.7 [5.9]
Maximum speed (mph / kph):	171 / 275 [171 / 275]
Production, total number:	2,831
Purchase prices:	
07/1991:	DM 156,050 [DM 156,050]
03/1992:	DM 158,860 [DM 158,860]
08/1992:	DM 163,140 [DM 163,140]
01/1993:	DM 164,571 [DM 164,571]
08/1993:	DM 164,600 [DM 164,600]
08/1994:	DM 164,600 [DM 164,600]
02/1995:	DM 167,890 [DM 167,890]

Porsche 944

Porsche 944, 944 S, 944 turbo and 944 turbo S

An especially affordable car in terms of both purchase price and operating costs, the 924 served as the entry-level model in Porsche's product range. For many Porsche fans, the Audi 100-derived engine of the 924 represented an image problem: simply not enough Porsche. And for many, its shape was not masculine enough. The gap between the 924 and the classic 911 SC provided enough room for another model. In price and performance, the new 944 was aimed precisely between these two models. It was a true Porsche, in shape as well as motive force – powerful styling teamed with 100 per cent Porsche power in the engine room. Like the 924, the 944 was built at Audi's Neckarsulm plant.

Model year 1982 (C Programme)

The Porsche 944 was presented in the autumn of 1981. Although its body was based on the 924 design, the 944's wider wings were immediately obvious. Other changes included a body-colour front spoiler and a black polyurethane spoiler around the glass rear hatch. Appearance of the 944 recalled the brawny 924 Carrera GT. In the case of the 944, the entire body, including its wide wings, was made of hot-dip galvanized steel. Bonnet, pop-up headlamps, roof structure, doors, glass rear hatch and the tail section, including light units, were identical to those of the Porsche 924 series. Aerodynamics were further optimized compared to the 924. With an aerodynamic drag coefficient of 0.35, the 944 had about the same total drag as the 924 of the same model year, despite its wider bodywork. As an option, impact-resistant plastic body-colour side moulding was available. The 944 options list also included air-conditioning and a removable roof which could be stowed in a bag in the boot.

The independent front suspension consisted of transverse arms and MacPherson struts, with coil springs over telescopic shock absorbers. Additionally, the 944 used an aluminium crossmember and 20mm front anti-roll bar. The rear independent suspension used semi-trailing arms, sprung by one transverse

torsion bar per side mounted in a transverse tube.

The hydraulic dual-circuit brake system was split between front and rear axles. Its four ventilated discs were gripped by floating callipers. The handbrake acted on a separate drum on the rear axle. Tyres, size 185/70 VR 15, were mounted on 7 J x 15 ATS cast-aluminium wheels with black centres. The 911's familiar Fuchs forged-alloy wheels, 7 J x 16 with 205/55 VR 16 rubber, could be ordered as an option. This wheel and tyre combination gave the 944 an even more attractive appearance.

As befitting a proper sports car, the 944 was conceived as a 2+2. The backs of the rear jump seats could be folded down for increased luggage space. The newly-developed heating and ventilation system could be combined with an optional air-conditioning system. The interior, too, was derived from the 924. One difference from the 924 was the use of metallic fascias around the instruments and on the centre console. Instrument markings were white. The 944's very complete instrumentation package consisted of a combination gauge with fuel-level and coolant-temperature on the left, speedometer in the centre, a tachometer on the right (with a fuel economy gauge integrated in its upper arc) and three round dials in the centre console: oil-pressure gauge, voltmeter and clock. The voltmeter was deleted in vehicles with air-conditioning to make room for the a/c rotary knob in the central gauge position. Standard equipment included a retractable luggage cover under the tinted-glass rear hatch to shield items from inquisitive eyes. The optional equipment list was rather extensive; a few of the available options for personalizing the 944 included electric windows, tinted windscreen and side glass, alarm system, various radio packages, sports seats in leather or Berber, different steering wheels and front and rear anti-roll bars, as well as sports shock absorbers.

The 944 engine was a completely new design: a true Porsche engine, derived from the V8 of the 928. It was based on a cast-aluminium four-cylinder block. The cylinder head was also borrowed from the 928. The in-line four developed 163hp (120kW) at 5800rpm from 2479cc, making it one of the largest fours on the market. With a 10.6:1 compression ratio, it achieved its maximum torque of 205Nm (151lb ft) at just 3000rpm. The two-valve-per-cylinder engine was equipped with balance shafts turning at twice crankshaft speed to

Cutaway of a 2.5-litre four-cylinder two-valve 944 engine

compensate for secondary inertia forces. The resulting engine smoothness was comparable to that of a six-cylinder engine. Its fat torque curve enabled very economical motoring. Mixture control was by means of a Bosch L-Jetronic system, while Digital Motor Electronics (DME) provided optimum ignition timing.

The 944 could be ordered with a five-speed manual or three-speed automatic transmission. With a manual, the 1180kg (2600lb.) coupé could accelerate to 62mph (100kph) in 8.4 seconds; Porsche listed top speed at 137mph (220kph). An optional limited-slip differential with 40 per cent lock-up was available. Like the 924, the 944 employed a transaxle principle: in the manual transmission version, engine and clutch were at the front, the transmission at the rear, joined by a rigid tube housing a rotating driveshaft. Advantages of the transaxle design included good road manners, favourable weight distribution and good traction in unloaded as well as loaded condition.

Model year 1983 (D Programme)

The 944 was well-received by both the motoring press and the buying public.

An obvious exterior change was body-colour outside mirrors. These were now electrically adjustable and heatable. In addition, fog lamps built into the front apron were available as options. New paint colours were added to the range.

At added cost, customers could order wider 215/60 VR 15 tyres on the stock rims.

Choices included new interior colours and upholstery materials. A new Blaupunkt 'Köln' audio system included four speakers, aerial, electronic noise suppression and fader. Headlamp-washers and power-steering were added-cost options.

For the United States and Canadian markets, the standard equipment list included air-conditioning, removable roof, tinted glass all round, two electrically-actuated outside mirrors, 215/60 VR 15 tyres, radio installation kit with four speakers, electric aerial and fader, three-spoke steering wheel, 63Ah battery and fog lamps in the front apron with a flash-to-pass function.

Model year 1984 (E Programme)

A switch for electrically unlatching the rear hatch was located at the left side of the driver's footwell. Vanity mirrors were added to both sun visors. Added safety was provided by a brake pad wear indicator. As an option, the 944 was available with cruise control. The removable roof was equipped with an electric lift feature; its rear edge could be raised while driving.

Optionally, Fuchs forged-alloy wheels could be supplied with their centres painted Grand Prix White or Platinum Metallic.

Model year 1985 (F programme)

In its first three years Porsche sold more than 60,000 examples of the 944. As part of an intensive model development programme, Porsche unveiled the 944 turbo in February 1985.

The windscreen was mounted flush to the body for improved aerodynamics and reduced wind noise. An active radio aerial and active amplifier were integrated in the windscreen. An optional Sekuriflex windscreen was available, offering added protection

in the event of stone impact or an accident. Standard equipment now included tinted glass all round and heated washer-nozzles. All Porsche models worldwide were fitted with side-impact beams, which reinforced the doors and increased passive safety in the event of an accident. Fuel tank capacity was increased from 66 litres to 80 litres (14.5 gallons to 17.6 gallons) for greater range. The fuel system was also fitted with an active charcoal filter to reliably prevent fuel evaporation.

The new 944 turbo could be recognized by its new, aerodynamically-improved nose with integrated fog and driving lamps, black sill appliqués and body-colour diffuser below the rear bumper. The 944's drag coefficient was a low 0.33.

The 944 and 944 turbo suspension now used cast-aluminium front and rear suspension arms. Their 7 J x 15 aluminium-alloy wheels echoed the five-hole ('Telephone Design') styling of the 928's wheels.

The 944 turbo was given firmer chassis tuning, with two anti-roll bars – 24mm at the front and 18mm at the rear. The brake system was even more powerful than that of the normally-aspirated 944; its four ventilated discs were teamed with black four-piston fixed aluminium callipers. The five-hole 16-inch cast aluminium-alloy wheels measured 7 inches and 8 inches wide, front and rear, carrying 205/55 VR 16 and 225/50 VR 16 tyres respectively. The turbo had power steering as standard equipment.

The biggest changes were found in the interior. Where the 944 once had a slightly modified 924

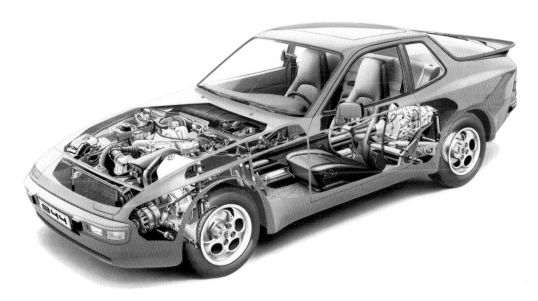

Phantom view of a 944 Coupé with 2.5-litre four-cylinder engine

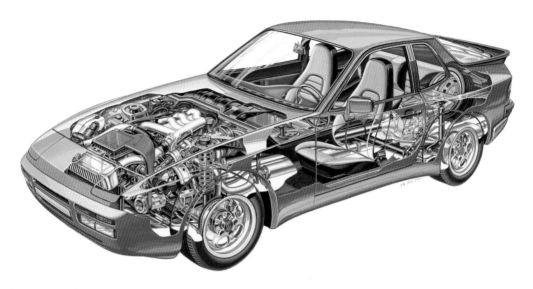

Phantom view of a 944 turbo Coupé with 2.5-litre four-cylinder turbocharged engine

interior, it now had its own unique design. An obvious change was the redesigned dashboard with large air vents and four round central instruments. At the left, an instrument housed coolant-temperature and fuel-level indicators. Next, the speedometer, followed by the tachometer including a fuel-economy gauge and, on automatic transmission cars, a gear-indicator; turbos replaced the economy gauge with a turbo-boost gauge. Finally, on the right, a combination instrument with voltmeter and oil-pressure gauges. The digital clock with stopwatch function was inset in the dashboard. All switches and heating controls were redesigned, as were the centre console and door panels. The new 911 seat generation also found its way into the 944 line. The driver's seat was now electrically adjustable for height and rake. A four-spoke steering wheel with 'Porsche' script on its central pad completed the interior equipment list. The steering column was mounted 12mm higher to provide more space for the driver's thighs.

The 944 turbo was given an expanded array of standard equipment: four speakers with electronic amplifier, windscreen aerial, electric windows, automatic heater-control, headlamp-washer system, leather-rimmed steering wheel and leather gear-lever knob.

The normally-aspirated 944 engine was fitted with redesigned combustion chambers, and the engine now operated on 96 octane premium-grade petrol. Cam profiles and the idle-stabilization system were modified. A more powerful alternator generated 115 amps instead of the previous 90 amps. The engine could easily be retrofitted with a catalytic converter.

On the 944 turbo engine, Porsche drew on its many years of turbocharging experience. At its introduction, the motoring press heaped praises on the new power unit, calling it the most highly developed turbocharged engine on the market. Although modified, the engine remained unchanged in configuration and displacement. Fitted with a turbocharger made by KKK, its compression ratio was 8.0:1. At 5800rpm, the turbo engine produced 220hp (162kW), with maximum torque of 330Nm (243lb ft) at only 3500rpm. One special feature of the 944 turbo was that from the very beginning it was offered with a controlled three-way catalytic converter and oxygen sensor. This was the first German production vehicle to offer identical power output with or without a catalytic converter. As expected in a nation with unlimited-speed highways, the converter was perfectly capable of withstanding continuous full-throttle operation.

While the 944 continued to be available with an optional three-speed automatic transmission, the 944 turbo was only offered with a five-speed manual transmission driving through the rear wheels. A limited-slip differential with 40 per cent lock-up was optional on the turbo.

Porsche listed the 944 turbo's performance as 6.3 seconds to 62mph (100kph), with a top speed of 152mph (245kph).

Model year 1986 (G Programme)

Porsche continued to improve the environmental compatibility of its vehicles. The 944 was available with a catalytic converter, at added cost. Because regular-grade unleaded fuel enjoyed better distribution in Europe than premium unleaded, Porsche reduced compression ratio to 9.7:1 and tuned the engine for operation on 91 octane fuel. Power output was 150hp (110kW) at 5800rpm, with maximum torque of 190Nm (140lb ft) available as low as 3000rpm. Lower power reduced top speed to 130mph (210kph). The 944 now rolled on 195/65 VR 15 tyres. As an option, forged Fuchs alloy-wheels were available, 7 J and 8 J x 15 front and rear, with 215/60 VR 15 rubber. For both the 944 and 944 turbo, the 16-inch wheel and tyre combination found on the 911 turbo were available, on Fuchs wheels: 7 J x 16 with 205/55 VR 16 at the front, 8 J x 16 with 225/50 VR 16 at the rear. As an option, all 944 models could be equipped with central-locking.

Model year 1987 (H Programme)

The 944 S was introduced, powered by a four-valve-per-cylinder engine. Simultaneously, Porsche introduced ABS brakes throughout the 944 model range. Catalyst-equipped models were now listed as distinctly separate types in the product line-up.

As far as bodywork and equipment was concerned, the new 944 S was identical to the basic 944. The only visible difference was the '944 S' script at the rear, and the optional side moulding with '16 Ventiler' ('16 Valve') script.

ABS anti-lock brakes were available as an option for all 944 models. The front suspension and its negative steering offset were revised to meet the needs of the ABS installation, and for this reason Fuchs wheels could no longer be used. Instead, the familiar 16-inch 'Telephone' wheels of the 928 S were available, front 7 J x 16 and rear 8 J x 16 with 205/55 and 225/50 VR 16 tyres, respectively. Customers could order an optional sports suspension for any 944 model.

New items on the options menu included electrically-adjustable seats, if desired with electrically-adjustable lumbar supports. Dual airbags were available on US models; these were standard on the US 944 turbo and optional on the US market 944 and 944 S. Porsche was the first European carmaker to offer a vehicle in the American market with airbags as standard equipment.

A ten-speaker sound package and Blaupunkt equalizer/amplifier offered even greater musical enjoyment on the road.

Phantom view of a 944 S Coupé with 2.5-litre four-cylinder four-valve engine

The four-valve engine of the 944 S was equipped with double overhead camshafts and spark plugs centrally located in the combustion chambers. In addition, the camshaft drive was beefed up, and modifications made to the magnesium induction system, exhaust system, oil pan and Digital Motor Electronics (DME). The engine block was taken from the 944, the cylinder head borrowed from the 928 S4. Compression was raised to 10.9:1 and the engine tuned to run on 95 octane unleaded premium fuel. Maximum power output of 190hp (140kW) was developed at 6000rpm; maximum torque of 230Nm (170lb ft) was available at 4300rpm. Power output of the catalyst-equipped model was identical. The four-valve-per-cylinder engine was notably more agile at high engine speeds. The 944 S was only available with a five-speed manual transmission driving through the rear wheels; a limited-slip differential with 40 per cent lock-up was optional. The 944 S accelerated to 62mph (100kph) in 7.9 seconds, and top speed was listed by Porsche at 142mph (228kph).

Model year 1988 (J Programme)

1988 was the last model year in which the 944 and 944 S were offered with 2.5-litre four-cylinder engines. Porsche offered a special edition in the form of the 944 turbo S, at a price of 99,800 Deutschmarks. The 1988 model year witnessed the 100,000th Porsche 944 rolling off the assembly line.

The 2.5-litre catalyst-equipped engine was retuned for unleaded premium petrol. This resulted in 160hp (118kW) at 5900rpm and increased torque, 210Nm (155lb ft) at 4500rpm. The 944 power unit now produced 160hp, regardless of whether or not it had a catalyst, and was tuned for 95 octane premium fuel. Road performance was roughly equal to the earlier non-catalyst 163hp version. Except for the rear wiper, now standard, there were no bodywork changes. A rear anti-roll bar was phased in as standard equipment for the 944 and 944 S.

The standard equipment list for the 944 and 944 S was upgraded to include power steering, central locking, electrically-adjustable and heatable driver

side outside mirror, four speakers, windscreen aerial, coin and cassette holder, four-spoke 36cm (14-inch) leather steering wheel and leather-covered gear lever and handbrake handle. On the 944 turbo, central-locking, passenger-side outside mirror and 36cm steering wheel became standard equipment.

944 turbo S

The new top-of-the-line 944 model was the 944 turbo S; its engine was a direct descendant of the 944 turbo 'Cup' racing power unit. It produced 250hp (184kW) at 6000rpm. Maximum torque, too, rose to 350Nm (258lb ft) at a slightly higher speed of 4000rpm. A larger turbocharger and boost increase to 0.7bar provided the performance increase. Standard equipment included a five-speed manual transmission, with transmission oil cooler and a reinforced limited-slip differential with 40 per cent lock-up, as well as an uprated clutch to handle the increased torque.

The 944 turbo S rolled on 16-inch alloy disc wheels and Goodyear Eagle tyres, 225/50 VR 16 on 7-inch wide rims at the front, and 245/45 VR 16 on 9-inchers at the rear. The larger brakes were taken from the 928 S4, combined with an anti-lock system as standard equipment. Specially-tuned sports suspension rounded out the package.

The equipment list of the 944 turbo S left absolutely nothing to be desired. 'Silver Rose Metallic' exterior colour and 'multicolour burgundy' interior fabric hinted at its very exclusive character. Other elements of the very complete equipment package included, among other things, power-steering, central-locking, electric windows, automatic climate-control, comfort seats, split rear seats, headlamp-cleaning system, 'Berlin' radio, side mouldings and Sekuriflex windscreen.

Performance was pegged at a very high level. The 62mph (100kph) mark was reached in 5.9 seconds, and top speed was in the vicinity of 162mph (260kph).

In all, a total of 111,500 examples of the 2.5-litre 944 were built, along with 7,524 examples of the 944 S, 19,627 944 turbos with the 220hp engine and 1,635 examples of the 944 turbo S.

944 Coupé (Series I) [Automatic]
MY 1982–December 1984

Engine
Engine design:	4-cylinder in-line
Installation:	Front-engine
Cooling system:	Water-cooled
Engine type:	M 44/01 [M 44/03]
MY 1985:	M 44/05 [M 44/06]
Displacement (cc):	2479
Bore x stroke (mm):	100 x 78.9
Engine output (kW/hp):	120/163 at 5800rpm
Maximum torque (Nm/lb ft):	205/151 at 3000rpm
Output per litre (kW/l / hp/l):	48.4 / 65.7
Compression ratio:	10.6 : 1
Valve operation camshaft drive:	ohc, cam driven by synchronous belt drive, 2 valves per cylinder
Carburation:	DME, Bosch L-Jetronic fuel injection
Ignition system:	DME; breakerless
Firing order:	1 - 3 - 4 - 2
Engine lubrication:	Full-pressure oil lubrication
Engine oil total (l):	5.5

Transmission
Drive configuration:	Rear-axle drive, transaxle system
Manual gearbox:	5-speed
Option Automatic:	[3-speed]
Transmission type:	016J [087M] [087M]
Transmission ratios:	
1st gear:	3.600 [2.551] [2.714]*
2nd gear:	2.125 [1.448] [1.500]*
3rd gear:	1.458 [1.000] [1.000]*
4th gear:	1.071
5th gear:	0.829
Reverse gear:	3.500 [2.461] [2.429]*
Drive ratio:	3.889 [3.083] [3.083]*
Option with manual gearbox:	Limited-slip differential 40%
*MY 1983–MY 1985	

Body, chassis, suspension, brakes, wheels
Body design:	Steel coupé body, 2 doors, 2 + 2 seats, entirely hot-dip galvanized body with wider wings, front bumper integrated in body form, polyurethane front spoiler, rear bumper integrated in body form, flip-up headlamps, glass rear lid with black polyurethane rear spoiler, black outside mirror
MY 1983–December 1984:	Painted electric outside mirror
MY 1985:	Side-impact protection beams in doors
Option:	Removable roof
MY 1984–December 1984:	Removable roof with electric lift feature
Suspension, front:	Independent suspension, wishbones, McPherson struts, coil springs, dual-tube hydraulic shock absorbers, anti-roll bar
Suspension, rear:	Individually suspended on driveshafts, transverse torsion bars on each side in transaxle tube, light alloy transverse tube suspension, dual-tube hydraulic shock absorbers, anti-roll bar

Brakes, front/rear (Size (mm)):	Ventilated discs (282.5 x 20.5) / Ventilated discs (289 x 20) Floating callipers / Floating callipers
Wheels, front/rear:	7 J x 15 / 7 J x 15
Tyres, front/rear:	185/70 VR 15 / 185/70 VR 15
Option:	215/60 VR 15 / 215/60 VR 15 7 J x 15 / 8 J x 15 185/70 VR 15 / 215/60 VR 15
Option:	7 J x 16 / 7 J x 16 205/55 VR 16 / 205/55 VR 16

Electrical system
Alternator (W/A):	1260 / 90
MY 1984:	1610 / 115
Battery (V/Ah):	12 / 50 [12 / 63]

Dimensions and weight
Track, front/rear (mm):	1477 / 1451
7 J x 15 / 8 J x 15:	1477 / 1476
Wheelbase (mm):	2400
Length x width x height (mm):	4200 x 1735 x 1275
Kerb weight DIN (kg):	1180 [1210]
Permissible gross weight (kg):	1500 [1530]
Luggage compartment (VDA (l)):	318
with folded down rear seatbacks:	514
Fuel tank capacity (l):	66, including 9 reserve
C_w x A (m²):	0.35 x 1.82 = 0.637
Powerweight ratio (kg/kW / kg/hp):	9.83 [10.08] / 7.23 [7.42]

Fuel consumption
DIN 70 030/01 (mpg):	98 RON super leaded
At constant 56mph/90kph:	40 [35.6]
At constant 74mph/120kph:	32.5 [30]
EG-emissions-urban cycle:	24.8 [25.2]
MY 1985:	
EG-Norm 80/1268 (mpg):	98 RON super leaded
At constant 56mph/90kph:	44 [43.4]
At constant 74mph/120kph:	35 [34.8]
EG-emissions-urban cycle:	24.5 [25]

Performance, production, prices
Acceleration 0-62mph/100kph (s):	8.4 [9.6]
Maximum speed (mph / kph):	137 / 220 [137 / 220]
Production, total number:	64,486
Purchase prices:	
08/1981:	DM 38,900 [DM 40,400]
01/1982:	DM 38,900 [DM 40,400]
08/1982:	DM 40,430 [DM 42,030]
03/1983:	DM 41,850 [DM 43,450]
08/1983:	DM 42,950 [DM 44,800]
02/1984:	DM 43,950 [DM 45,830]
10/1984:	DM 45,350 [DM 47,350]

944 Coupé (Series II) [Automatic]
January 1985–MJ 1987

Engine

Engine design:	4-cylinder in-line
Installation:	Front-engine
Cooling system:	Water-cooled
Engine type:	M 44/05 [M 44/06]
Displacement (cc):	2479
Bore x stroke (mm):	100 x 78.9
Engine output (kW/hp):	120/163 at 5800rpm
Maximum torque (Nm/lb ft):	205/151 at 3000rpm
Output per litre (kW/l / hp/l):	48.4 / 65.7
Compression ratio:	10.6 : 1
Valve operation camshaft drive:	ohc, cam driven by synchronous belt drive, 2 valves per cylinder
Carburation:	DME, Bosch L-Jetronic fuel injection
Ignition system:	DME; breakerless
Firing order:	1- 3 - 4 - 2
Engine lubrication:	Full-pressure oil lubrication
Engine oil total (l):	6.0
MY 1988:	6.5

Transmission

Drive configuration:	Rear-axle drive, transaxle system
Manual gearbox:	5-speed
Option Automatic:	[3-speed]
Transmission type:	016J [087M]
Transmission ratios:	
1st gear:	3.600 [2.714]
2nd gear:	2.125 [1.500]
3rd gear:	1.458 [1.000]
4th gear:	1.071
5th gear:	0.829
Reverse gear:	3.500 [2.429]
Drive ratio:	3.889 [3.083]
Option with manual gearbox:	Limited-slip differential 40%

Body, chassis, suspension, brakes, wheels

Body design:	Steel coupé body, 2 doors, 2 + 2 seats, entirely hot-dip galvanized body with wider wings, side-impact protection beams in doors, front bumper integrated in body form, polyurethane front spoiler, rear bumper integrated in body form, flip-up headlamps, glass rear lid with black polyurethane rear spoiler, painted electric outside mirrors
Option:	Removable roof with electric lift feature
Suspension, front:	Independent suspension, aluminium wishbones, McPherson struts, coil springs, dual-tube hydraulic shock absorbers, anti-roll bar
Suspension, rear:	Individually suspended on driveshafts, transverse torsion bars on each side in transaxle tube, light alloy transverse tube suspension, dual-tube hydraulic shock absorbers, anti-roll bar

Brakes, front/rear (Size (mm)):	Ventilated discs (282.5 x 20.5) / Ventilated discs (289 x 20) Floating callipers / Floating callipers
Option MY 1987:	ABS
Wheels, front/rear:	7 J x 15 / 7 J x 15
Tyres, front/rear:	195/65 VR 15 / 195/65 VR 15
Option:	215/60 VR 15 / 215/60 VR 15 7 J x 15 / 8 J x 15 195/65 VR 15 / 215/60 VR 15
Option:	7 J x 16 / 7 J x 16 205/55 VR 16 / 205/55 VR 16

Electrical system

Alternator (W/A):	1610 / 115
Battery (V/Ah):	12 / 50 [12 / 63]

Dimensions and weight

Track, front/rear (mm):	1477 / 1451
7 J x 15 / 8 J x 15:	1477 / 1476
Wheelbase (mm):	2400
Length x width x height (mm):	4200 x 1735 x 1275
Kerb weight DIN (kg):	1210
MY 1987:	1240
Permissible gross weight (kg):	1530
MY 1987:	1560
Luggage compartment (VDA (l)):	318
with folded down rear seatbacks:	514
Fuel tank capacity (l):	80, including 8 reserve
C_w x A (m²):	0.35 x 1.82 = 0.637
Power/weight ratio (kg/kW / kg/hp):	10.08 / 7.42
MY 1987:	10.33 / 7.60

Fuel consumption

DIN 70 030/01 (mpg):	98 RON super leaded
At constant 56mph/90kph:	40 [35.6]
At constant 74mph/120kph:	32.5 [30]
EG-emissions-urban cycle:	24.8 [25.2]
EG-Norm 80/1268 (mpg):	96 RON super leaded
At constant 56mph/90kph:	44 [37.6]
At constant 74mph/120kph:	35 [31.3]
EG-emissions-urban cycle:	24.5 [25]

Performance, production, prices

Acceleration 0-62mph/100kph (s):	8.4 [9.6]
Maximum speed (mph / kph):	137 / 220 [137 / 220]
Production, total number 944 total Jan. 1985–MY 1987:	41,174
Purchase price:	
02/1985:	DM 48,950 [DM 50,950]
08/1985:	DM 50,950 [DM 53,250]
08/1986:	DM 52,950 [DM 55,430]
03/1987:	DM 53,950 [DM 56,450]

944 turbo Coupé
January 1985–MY 1988

Engine

Engine design:	4-cylinder in-line, turbo charger, intercooler
Installation:	Front-engine
Cooling system:	Water-cooled
Engine type:	M 44/51
Displacement (cc):	2479
Bore x stroke (mm):	100 x 78.9
Engine output (kW/hp):	162/220 at 5800rpm
Maximum torque (Nm/lb ft):	330/243 at 3500rpm
Output per litre (kW/l / hp/l):	65.3 / 88.7
Compression ratio:	8.0 : 1
Valve operation camshaft drive:	ohc, cam driven by synchronous belt drive, 2 valves per cylinder
Carburation:	DME, Bosch L-Jetronic fuel injection
Ignition system:	DME; breakerless
Firing order:	1- 3 - 4 - 2
Engine lubrication:	Full-pressure oil lubrication
Engine oil total (l):	6.5
MY 1988:	7.0

Transmission

Drive configuration:	Rear-axle drive, transaxle system
Manual gearbox:	5-speed
Transmission type:	016R
MY 1988:	016S/R
Transmission ratios:	
1st gear:	3.500
2nd gear:	2.059
3rd gear:	1.400
4th gear:	1.034
5th gear:	0.829
Reverse gear:	3.500
Drive ratio:	3.375
Option:	Limited-slip differential 40%

Body, chassis, suspension, brakes, wheels

Body design:	Steel coupé body, 2 doors, 2 + 2 seats, entirely hot-dip galvanized body with wider wings, side-impact protection beams in doors, front bumper integrated in body form, polyurethane front spoiler, rear bumper integrated in body form, flip-up headlamps, glass rear lid with black polyurethane rear spoiler, rear diffuser, painted electric outside mirrors
Option:	Removable roof with electric lift feature
Suspension, front:	Independent suspension, aluminium wishbones, McPherson struts, coil springs, dual-tube hydraulic shock absorbers, anti-roll bar
Suspension, rear:	Individually suspended on driveshafts, transverse torsion bars on each side in transaxle tube, light alloy transverse tube suspension, dual-tube hydraulic shock absorbers, anti-roll bar
Brakes, front/rear (Size (mm)):	Ventilated discs (298 x 28) Ventilated discs (299 x 24) Black 4-piston fixed aluminium callipers / Black 4-piston fixed aluminium callipers
Option MY 1987–MY 1988:	ABS
Wheels, front/rear:	7 J x 16 / 8 J x 16
Tyres, front/rear:	205/55 VR 16 / 225/50 VR 16

Electrical system

Alternator (W/A):	1610 / 115
Battery (V/Ah):	12 / 50

Dimensions and weight

Track, front/rear (mm):	1477 / 1451
Wheelbase (mm):	2400
Length x width x height (mm):	4230 x 1735 x 1275
Kerb weight DIN (kg):	1280
MY 1987–MY 1988:	1350
Permissible gross weight (kg):	1600
MY 1987–MY 1988:	1670
Luggage compartment (VDA (l)):	318
with folded down rear seatbacks:	514
Fuel tank capacity (l):	80, including 8 reserve

C_w x A (m²):	0.33 x 1.89 = 0.624
Power/weight ratio (kg/kW/kg/hp):	7.90 / 5.81
MY 1987–MY 1988:	8.33 / 6.13

Fuel consumption

DIN 70 030 (mpg):	96 RON super leaded
At constant 56mph/90kph:	41.6
At constant 74mph/120kph:	33.2
EG-emissions-urban cycle:	23
MY 1986–MY 1988 EG-Norm	
Without catalytic converter:	
EG-Norm 80/1268 (mpg):	95 RON super leaded or unleaded
At constant 56mph/90kph:	44
At constant 74mph/120kph:	32.1
EG-emissions-urban cycle:	22.7
With catalytic converter:	
EG-Norm 80/1268 (mpg):	95 RON super unleaded
At constant 56mph/90kph:	42.2
At constant 74mph/120kph:	31
EG-emissions-urban cycle:	22.2

Performance, production, prices

Acceleration 0-62mph/100kph (s):	6.3
Maximum speed (mph / kph):	152 / 245
Production, total number:	17,627
Purchase price:	
02/1985:	DM 72,500
with catalytic converter:	DM 74,550
08/1985:	DM 72,500
with catalytic converter:	DM 74,690
08/1986:	DM 74,980
with catalytic converter:	DM 76,555
03/1987:	DM 75,790
with catalytic converter:	DM 77,365
07/1987:	DM 77,800
with catalytic converter:	DM 79,375
04/1988:	DM 80,000
with catalytic converter:	DM 81,575

944 Coupé with catalytic converter [Automatic] MY 1986–MY 1987

Engine
Engine design:	4-cylinder in-line
Installation:	Front-engine
Cooling system:	Water-cooled
Engine type:	M 44/07 [M 44/08]
Displacement (cc):	2479
Bore x stroke (mm):	100 x 78.9
Engine output (kW/hp):	110/150 at 5800rpm
Maximum torque (Nm/lb ft):	195/144 at 3000rpm
Output per litre (kW/l / hp/l):	44.4 / 60.5
Compression ratio:	9.7 : 1
Valve operation camshaft drive:	ohc, cam driven by synchronous belt drive, 2 valves per cylinder
Carburation:	DME, Bosch L-Jetronic fuel injection
Ignition system:	DME; breakerless
Firing order:	1- 3 - 4 - 2
Engine lubrication:	Full-pressure oil lubrication
Engine oil total (l):	6.0

Transmission
Drive configuration:	Rear-axle drive, transaxle system
Manual gearbox:	5-speed
Option Automatic:	[3-speed]
Transmission type:	016J [087M]
Transmission ratios:	
1st gear:	3.600 [2.714]
2nd gear:	2.125 [1.500]
3rd gear:	1.458 [1.000]
4th gear:	1.071
5th gear:	0.829
Reverse gear:	3.500 [2.429]
Drive ratio:	3.889 [3.083]
Option with manual gearbox:	Limited-slip differential 40%

Body, chassis, suspension, brakes, wheels
Body design:	Steel coupé body, 2 doors, 2 + 2 seats, entirely hot-dip galvanized body with wider wings, side-impact protection beams in doors, front bumper integrated in body form, polyurethane front spoiler, rear bumper integrated in body form, flip-up headlamps, glass rear lid with black polyurethane rear spoiler, painted electric outside mirrors
Option:	Removable roof with electric lift feature
Suspension, front:	Independent suspension, aluminium wishbones, McPherson struts, coil springs, dual-tube hydraulic shock absorbers, anti-roll bar
Suspension, rear:	Individually suspended on driveshafts, transverse torsion bars on each side in transaxle tube, light alloy transverse tube suspension, dual-tube hydraulic shock absorbers, anti-roll bar
Brakes, front/rear (Size (mm)):	Ventilated discs (282.5 x 20.5) / Ventilated discs (289 x 20) Floating callipers / Floating callipers
Option MY 1987:	ABS
Wheels, front/rear:	7 J x 15 / 7 J x 15
Tyres, front/rear:	195/65 VR 15 / 195/65 VR 15
Option:	205/60 VR 15 / 205/60 VR 15
Option:	7 J x 16 / 7 J x 16
	205/55 VR 16 / 205/55 VR 16

Electrical system
Alternator (W/A):	1610 / 115
Battery (V/Ah):	12 / 50 [12 / 63]

Dimensions and weight
Track, front/rear (mm):	1477 / 1451
Wheelbase (mm):	2400
Length x width x height (mm):	4200 x 1735 x 1275
Kerb weight DIN (kg):	1210
MY 1987:	1240
Permissible gross weight (kg):	1530
MY 1987:	1560
Luggage compartment (VDA (l)):	318
with folded down rear seatbacks:	514
Fuel tank capacity (l):	80, including 8 reserve
C_w x A (m²):	0.35 x 1.82 = 0.637
Power/weight ratio (kg/kW/ kg/hp):	11.00 / 8.06
MY 1987:	11.27 / 8.26

Fuel consumption
EG-Norm 80/1268 (mpg):	91 RON normal unleaded
At constant 56mph/90kph:	44 [37.6]
At constant 74mph/120kph:	33.5 [31.3]
EG-emissions-urban cycle:	22.4 [22.4]

Performance, production, prices
Acceleration 0-62mph/100kph (s):	8.5 [10.0]
Maximum speed (mph / kph):	130 / 210 [130 / 210]
Production, total number	
944 total Jan. 1985–MY 1987:	41,174
Purchase prices:	
08/1985:	DM 53,140 [DM 55,440]
08/1986:	DM 54,315 [DM 56,795]
03/1987:	DM 55,315 [DM 57,815]

944 S Coupé
MY 1987–MY 1988

Engine
Engine design:	4-cylinder in-line
Installation:	Front-engine
Cooling system:	Water-cooled
Engine type:	M 44/40
Displacement (cc):	2479
Bore x stroke (mm):	100 x 78.9
Engine output (kW/hp):	140/190 at 6000rpm
Maximum torque (Nm/lb ft):	230/170 at 4300rpm
Output per litre (kW/l / hp/l):	56.5 / 76.6
Compression ratio:	10.9 : 1
Valve operation camshaft drive:	dohc, cams driven by synchronous belt drive, 4 valves per cylinder
Carburation:	DME, Bosch L-Jetronic fuel injection
Ignition system:	DME; DME; breakerless
Firing order:	1 - 3 - 4 - 2
Engine lubrication:	Full-pressure oil lubrication
Engine oil total (l):	6.5

Transmission
Drive configuration:	Rear-axle drive, transaxle system
Manual gearbox:	5-speed
Transmission type:	083D
Transmission ratios:	
1st gear:	3.500
2nd gear:	2.059
3rd gear:	1.400
4th gear:	1.034
5th gear:	0.829
Reverse gear:	3.500
Drive ratio:	3.889
Option:	Limited-slip differential 40%

Body, chassis, suspension, brakes, wheels
Body design:	Steel coupé body, 2 doors, 2 + 2 seats, entirely hot-dip galvanized body with wider wings, side-impact protection beams in doors, front bumper integrated in body form, polyurethane front spoiler, rear bumper integrated in body form, flip-up headlamps, glass rear lid with black polyurethane rear spoiler, painted electric outside mirrors
Option:	Removable roof with electric lift feature
Suspension, front:	Independent suspension, aluminium wishbones, McPherson struts, coil springs, dual-tube hydraulic shock absorbers, anti-roll bar
Suspension, rear:	Individually suspended on driveshafts, transverse torsion bars on each side in transaxle tube, light alloy transverse tube suspension, dual-tube hydraulic shock absorbers, anti-roll bar

Brakes, front/rear (Size (mm)):	Ventilated discs (282.5 x 20.5) / Ventilated discs (289 x 20) Floating callipers / Floating callipers
Option:	ABS
Wheels, front/rear:	7 J x 15 / 7 J x 15
Tyres, front/rear:	195/65 VR 15 / 195/65 VR 15
Option:	205/60 VR 15 / 205/60 VR 15
Option:	7 J x 16 / 7 J x 16
	205/55 VR 16 / 205/55 VR 16

Electrical system
Alternator (W/A):	1610 / 115
Battery (V/Ah):	12 / 50

Dimensions and weight
Track, front/rear (mm):	1477 / 1451
Wheelbase (mm):	2400
Lenght x width x height (mm):	4200 x 1735 x 1275
Kerb weight DIN (kg):	1280
Permissible gross weight (kg):	1600
Luggage compartment (VDA (l)):	318
with folded down rear seatbacks:	514
Fuel tank capacity (l):	80, including 8 reserve
C_w x A (m²):	0.35 x 1.82 = 0.637
Power/weight ratio (kg/kW/kg/hp):	9.14 / 6.74

Fuel consumption
Without catalytic converter:	
EG-Norm 80/1268 (mpg):	95 RON super leaded or unleaded
At constant 56mph/90kph:	42.8
At constant 74mph/120kph:	34.1
EG-emissions-urban cycle:	22.5
With catalytic converter:	
EG-Norm 80/1268 (mpg):	95 RON super unleaded
At constant 56mph/90kph:	42.2
At constant 74mph/120kph:	32.8
EG-emissions-urban cycle:	22.4

Performance, production, prices
Acceleration 0-62mph/100kph (s):	7.9
Maximum speed (mph / kph):	142 / 228
Production, total number:	7,324
Purchase prices:	
08/1986:	DM 58,950
with catalytic converter:	DM 60,315
03/1987:	DM 59,990
with catalytic converter:	DM 61,355
07/1987:	DM 64,800
with catalytic converter:	DM 66,165
04/1988:	DM 66,000
with catalytic converter:	DM 67,365

944 Coupé [Automatic] MY1988

Engine
Engine design:	4-cylinder in-line
Installation:	Front-engine
Cooling system:	Water-cooled
Engine type:	M 44/09 [M 44/10]
Displacement (cc):	2479
Bore x stroke (mm):	100 x 78.9
Engine output (kW/hp):	118/160 at 5900rpm
Maximum torque (Nm/lb ft):	210/155 at 4500rpm
Output per litre (kW/l / hp/l):	47.6 / 64.5
Compression ratio:	10.2 : 1
Valve operation camshaft drive:	ohc, cam driven by synchronous belt drive, 2 valves per cylinder
Carburation:	DME, Bosch L-Jetronic fuel injection
Ignition system:	DME; breakerless
Firing order:	1- 3 - 4 - 2
Engine lubrication:	Full-pressure oil lubrication
Engine oil total (l):	6.5

Transmission
Drive configuration:	Rear-axle drive, transaxle system
Manual gearbox:	5-speed
Option Automatic:	[3-speed]
Transmission type:	016J [087M]
Transmission ratios:	
1st gear:	3.600 [2.714]
2nd gear:	2.125 [1.500]
3rd gear:	1.458 [1.000]
4th gear:	1.071
5th gear:	0.829
Reverse gear:	3.500 [2.429]
Drive ratio:	3.889 [3.083]
Option with manual gearbox:	Limited-slip differential 40%

Body, chassis, suspension, brakes, wheels
Body design:	Steel coupé body, 2 doors, 2 + 2 seats, entirely hot-dip galvanized body with wider wings, side-impact protection beams in doors, front bumper integrated in body form, polyurethane front spoiler, rear bumper integrated in body form, flip-up headlamps, glass rear lid with black polyurethane rear spoiler, painted electric outside mirrors
Option:	Removable roof with electric lift feature
Suspension, front:	Independent suspension, aluminium wishbones, McPherson struts, coil springs, dual-tube hydraulic dampers, anti-roll bar
Suspension, rear:	Individually suspended on driveshafts, transverse torsion bars on each side in transaxle tube, light alloy transverse tube suspension, dual-tube hydraulic shock absorbers, anti-roll bar

Brakes, front/rear (Size (mm)):	Ventilated discs (282.5 x 20.5) / Ventilated discs (289 x 20) Floating callipers / Floating callipers
Option:	ABS
Wheels, front/rear:	7 J x 15 / 7 J x 15
Tyres, front/rear:	195/65 VR 15 / 195/65 VR 15
Option:	205/60 VR 15 / 205/60 VR 15
Option:	7 J x 16 / 7 J x 16
	205/55 VR 16 / 205/55 VR 16

Electrical system
Alternator (W/A):	1610 / 115
Battery (V/Ah):	12 / 50 [12 / 63]

Dimensions and weight
Track, front/rear (mm):	1477 / 1451
Wheelbase (mm):	2400
Length x width x height (mm):	4200 x 1735 x 1275
Kerb weight DIN (kg):	1260
Permissible gross weight (kg):	1580
Luggage compartment (VDA (l)):	318
with folded down rear seatbacks:	514
Fuel tank capacity (l):	80, including 8 reserve
C_w x A (m²):	0.35 x 1.82 = 0.637
Power/weight ratio (kg/kW/kg/hp):	10.68 / 7.88

Fuel consumption
Without catalytic converter:	
EG-Norm 80/1268 (mpg):	95 RON super leaded or unleaded
At constant 56mph/90kph:	41.6 [37.6]
At constant 74mph/120kph:	32.8 [31]
EG-emissions-urban cycle:	22.4 [23.3]
With catalytic converter:	
EG-Norm 80/1268 (mpg):	95 RON super unleaded
At constant 56mph/90kph:	41.6 [37.6]
At constant 74mph/120kph:	32.8 [31.3]
EG-emissions-urban cycle:	22.4 [22.4]

Performance, production, prices
Acceleration 0-62mph/100kph (s):	8.4 [9.6]
Maximum speed (mph / kph):	135 / 218 [133 / 215]
Production, total number:	5,840
Purchase prices:	
07/1987:	DM 58,900 [DM 61,400]
with catalytic converter:	DM 60,265 [DM 62,765]
04/1988:	DM 60,000 [DM 62,500]
with catalytic converter:	DM 61,365 [DM 63,865]

944 turbo S Coupé MY 1988

Engine

Engine design:	4-cylinder in-line, turbo charger, intercooler
Installation:	Front-engine
Cooling system:	Water-cooled
Engine type:	M 44/52
Displacement (cc):	2479
Bore x stroke (mm):	100 x 78.9
Engine output (kW/hp):	184/250 at 6000rpm
Maximum torque (Nm/lb ft):	350/258 at 4000rpm
Output per litre (kW/l / hp/l):	74.2 / 100.4
Compression ratio:	8.0 : 1
Valve operation camshaft drive:	ohc, cam driven by synchronous belt drive, 2 valves per cylinder
Carburation:	DME, Bosch L-Jetronic fuel injection
Ignition system:	DME; breakerless
Firing order:	1- 3 - 4 - 2
Engine lubrication:	Full-pressure oil lubrication
Engine oil total (l):	7.0

Transmission

Drive configuration:	Rear-axle drive, transaxle system
Manual gearbox:	5-speed
Transmission type:	016R
Transmission ratios:	
1st gear:	3.500
2nd gear:	2.059
3rd gear:	1.400
4th gear:	1.034
5th gear:	0.829
Reverse gear:	3.500
Drive ratio:	3.375
Standard:	Limited-slip differential 40%

Body, chassis, suspension, brakes, wheels

Body design:	Steel coupé body, 2 doors, 2 + 2 seats, entirely hot-dip galvanized body with wider wings, side-impact protection beams in doors, flexible polyurethane front bumper with integrated aluminium beams, rear bumper integrated in body form, flip-up headlamps, glass rear lid with black polyurethane rear spoiler, rear diffuser, painted electric outside mirrors
Option:	Removable roof with electric lift feature
Suspension, front:	Independent suspension, aluminium wishbones, McPherson struts, coil springs, dual-tube hydraulic shock absorbers, anti-roll bar
Suspension, rear:	Individually suspended on driveshafts, transverse torsion bars on each side in

	transaxle tube, light alloy transverse tube suspension, dual-tube hydraulic shock absorbers, anti-roll bar
Brakes, front/rear (Size (mm)):	Ventilated discs (304 x 32) Ventilated discs (299 x 24) Black 4-piston fixed aluminium callipers / Black 4-piston fixed aluminium callipers ABS
Wheels, front/rear:	7 J x 16 / 9 J x 16
Tyres, front/rear:	225/50 VR 16 / 245/45 VR 16

Electrical system

Alternator (W/A):	1610 / 115
Battery (V/Ah):	12 / 50

Dimensions and weight

Track, front/rear (mm):	1477 / 1442
Wheelbase (mm):	2400
Length x width x height (mm):	4230 x 1735 x 1275
Kerb weight DIN (kg):	1400
Permissible gross weight (kg):	1740
Luggage compartment (VDA (l)):	318
with folded down rear seatbacks:	514
Fuel tank capacity (l):	80, including 8 reserve
C_w x A (m^2):	0.33 x 1.89 = 0.624
Power/weight ratio (kg/kW/kg/hp):	7.60 / 5.60

Fuel consumption

Without catalytic converter:	
EG-Norm 80/1268 (mpg):	95 RON super leaded or unleaded
At constant 56mph/90kph:	40.8
At constant 74mph/120kph:	31.3
EG-emissions-urban cycle:	21.5
With catalytic converter:	
EG-Norm 80/1268 (mpg):	95 RON super unleaded
At constant 56mph/90kph:	39.7
At constant 74mph/120kph:	30.4
EG-emissions-urban cycle:	21.2

Performance, production, prices

Acceleration 0-62mph/100kph (s):	5.9
Maximum speed (mph / kph):	162 / 260
Production, total number:	1,635
Purchase prices:	
07/1987:	DM 99,800
04/1988:	DM 99,800

Porsche 944, 944 S2, 944 S2 Cabriolet, 944 turbo and 944 turbo Cabriolet

Model year 1989 (K Programme)

In its last year of production, the base 944 left the assembly line with a larger 2.7-litre engine. The 944 S was replaced by the 944 S2, with a muscular 3-litre four-cylinder engine, available in both Coupé and Cabriolet form. The 944 turbo was now equipped with the more powerful engine of the special-edition 944 turbo S.

While the body of the base model continued unchanged, the 944 S2 was given the body of the turbo model, which also remained in the programme without modifications.

The 944 S2 Cabriolet was based on the body of the 944 S2 Coupé. ASC (American Sunroof Corporation) in Weinsberg, north of Zuffenhausen, converted coupé body shells into Cabriolets by first cutting off the roof and cutting down the windscreen frame. A second floorpan was welded in for reinforcement, and a metal boot-lid fitted. Luggage volume could be enlarged by folding down the rear seat-backs. A vibration damper, intended to reduce body vibrations, was built into the right-hand side of the boot. With the top down, the mechanical hood mechanism could be covered by a fabric tonneau. An electric hood was optional, needing only manual latching of the hood to the

Phantom view of a 944 S2 Coupé with 3.0-litre four-cylinder four-valve engine

944 S2 Cabriolet

windscreen header. The 944 S2 Cabriolet was very attractive, in open or closed configuration.

The 944 S2 was equipped with four ventilated brake discs and four-piston fixed brake callipers. Its 16-inch 'Design 90' cast-aluminium wheels, 7 inches and 8 inches wide, carried 205/55 ZR 16 and 225/50 ZR 16 tyres front and rear, respectively. The 944 turbo was fitted with the wheels of the 944 turbo S, along with sports suspension and ABS brakes. All 944 models were now equipped with power-steering as standard equipment.

Interior equipment of the 944 S2 was derived from the base model, while the body was taken from the turbo. As well as new exterior colours and fabrics, all models were fitted with a higher-capacity 63Ah battery, automatic heater control and electrically-operated height adjustment for the passenger seat. The 944 turbo was also fitted with an automatic climate-control system, integrated alarm system and body-colour side mouldings. A radio/CD player was available as an option.

The two-valve engine was re-engineered, with cylinder bore increased to 104mm. The resulting displacement of 2681cc provided a respectable peak torque of 225Nm (166lb ft) at 4200rpm. With or without catalyst, power rose slightly to 165hp (121kW) at 5800rpm. Top speed was about 137mph (220kph), and acceleration to 62mph (100kph) took 8.2 seconds. A three-speed automatic transmission was an optional extra.

A torquey 2990cc four-cylinder four-valve engine was installed in the 944 S2. This power unit was the world's largest-displacement four-cylinder automobile engine. With or without catalytic converter, power output was 211hp (155kW) at 5800rpm; maximum torque was 280Nm (207lb ft) at 4000rpm. Forged pistons, redesigned induction system, modified Digital Motor Electronics and an external aluminium oil-cooler represented only a few of its engineering upgrades. Road performance nearly matched that of the 944 turbo: acceleration to 62mph (100kph) took just 6.9 seconds, and top speed was a respectable 149mph (240kph).

The 944 turbo was fitted with the engine of the 944 turbo S, producing 250hp (184kW) at 6000rpm. Maximum torque of 350Nm (258lb ft) was available at 4000rpm. The source of this power increase over its 220hp predecessor was a larger turbocharger delivering 0.7bar of boost. Standard equipment included a five-speed manual transmission and limited-slip differential with 40 per cent lock-up.

Road performance of the 944 turbo was identical to that of the 944 turbo S.

Model year 1990 (L Programme)

The base model 944, with its 2.7-litre engine, was no longer available; only the 944 S2 and 944 turbo remained in the model line.

At the rear, the 944 turbo sported a new hoop-shaped rear spoiler. An electric hood was now standard on the 944 S2 Cabriolet. Three-point automatic rear seatbelts were installed in all 944 Coupé models.

Anti-lock brakes were now standard on the 944 S2. The 944 turbo had 'Design 90' cast-aluminium wheels, which were now 7.5 inches wide at the front. The tyres used and the rear wheel width were carried over unchanged.

Model year 1991 (M Programme)

The entire 944 model range entered its last year of production. As of the autumn of 1990, dual front airbags were available as an option on left-hand-drive examples of the 944 S2. As of 1 February 1991, all 944 S2 models were equipped with dual airbags as standard equipment. A limited series of 944 turbo Cabriolets was built, with an electric hood mechanism which only needed manual latching to the windscreen header. Equipment and performance were identical to those of the 944 turbo coupé. Porsche's contract with Audi's plant in Neckarsulm ended in April 1991, and with it production of the 944 turbo. The last examples of the 944 S2 left Porsche's own Zuffenhausen assembly line in May 1991.

The 944 S2 Coupé was fitted with the same rear wing as the 944 turbo Coupé. For drivers with sporting aspirations, Porsche offered an optional suspension package for the 944 S2, with firmer tuning and the wider wheels of the 944 turbo.

A total of 4,246 examples of the 944 powered by the 2.7-litre engine were built, along with 9,352 944 S2 Coupés, 6,980 S2 Cabriolets, 3,738 of the 250hp 944 turbo Coupé and 528 944 turbo Cabriolets. In all, a total of 163,302 examples of the 944 model range were produced, including 172 944 turbo 'Cup' cars.

944 Coupé [Automatic] MY 1989

Engine

Engine design:	4-cylinder in-line
Installation:	Front-engine
Cooling system:	Water-cooled
Engine type:	M 44/11 [M 44/12]
Displacement (cc):	2681
Bore x stroke (mm):	104 x 78.9
Engine output (kW/hp):	121/165 at 5800rpm
Maximum torque (Nm/lb ft):	225/166 at 4200rpm
Output per litre (kW/l / hp/l):	45.1 / 61.5
Compression ratio:	10.9 : 1
Valve operation camshaft drive:	ohc, cam driven by synchronous belt drive, 2 valves per cylinder
Carburation:	DME, Bosch L-Jetronic fuel injection
Ignition system:	DME; breakerless
Firing order:	1- 3 - 4 - 2
Engine lubrication:	Full-pressure oil lubrication
Engine oil total (l):	6.0

Transmission

Drive configuration:	Rear-axle drive, transaxle system
Manual gearbox:	5-speed
Option Automatic:	[3-speed]
Transmission type:	016J [087M]
Transmission ratios:	
1st gear:	3.600 [2.714]
2nd gear:	2.125 [1.500]
3rd gear:	1.458 [1.000]
4th gear:	1.071
5th gear:	0.829
Reverse gear:	3.500 [2.429]
Drive ratio:	3.889 [3.083]
Option with manual gearbox:	Limited-slip differential 40%

Body, chassis, suspension, brakes, wheels

Body design:	Steel coupé body, 2 doors, 2 + 2 seats, entirely hot-dip galvanized body with wider wings, side-impact protection beams in doors, front bumper integrated in body form, polyurethane front spoiler, rear bumper integrated in body form, flip-up headlamps, glass rear lid with black polyurethane rear spoiler, painted electric outside mirrors
Option:	Removable roof with electric lift feature
Suspension, front:	Independent suspension, aluminium wishbones, McPherson struts, coil springs, dual-tube hydraulic shock absorbers, anti-roll bar
Suspension, rear:	Individually suspended on driveshafts, transverse torsion bars on each side in transaxle tube, light alloy transverse tube suspension, dual-tube hydraulic shock absorbers, anti-roll bar

Brakes, front/rear (Size (mm)):	Ventilated discs (282.5 x 20.5) / Ventilated discs (289 x 20) Floating callipers / Floating callipers
Option:	ABS
Wheels, front/rear:	7 J x 15 / 7 J x 15
Tyres, front/rear:	195/65 VR 15 / 195/65 VR 15
Option:	205/60 VR 15 / 205/60 VR 15
Option:	7 J x 16 / 7 J x 16
	205/55 VR 16 / 205/55 VR 16

Electrical system

Alternator (W/A):	1610 / 115
Battery (V/Ah):	12 / 63

Dimensions and weight

Track, front/rear (mm):	1477 / 1451
Wheelbase (mm):	2400
Length x width x height (mm):	4200 x 1735 x 1275
Kerb weight DIN (kg):	1290
Permissible gross weight (kg):	1630
Luggage compartment (VDA (l)):	318
with folded down rear seatbacks:	514
Fuel tank capacity (l):	80, including 8 reserve
C_w x A (m²):	0.35 x 1.82 = 0.637
Power/weight ratio (kg/kW/hp/hp):	10.66 / 7.82

Fuel consumption

Without catalytic converter:	
EG-Norm 80/1268 (mpg):	95 RON super leaded or unleaded
At constant 56mph/90kph:	40.8 [37]
At constant 74mph/120kph:	33.2 [31.3]
EG-emissions-urban cycle:	21.4 [23.7]
With catalytic converter:	
EG-Norm 80/1268 (mpg):	95 RON super unleaded
At constant 56mph/90kph:	40 [36.7]
At constant 74mph/120kph:	33.5 [31]
EG-emissions-urban cycle:	20.9 [23.7]

Performance, production, prices

Acceleration 0-62mph/100kph (s):	8.2 [9.4]
Maximum speed (mph / kph):	137 / 220 [135 / 218]
Production, total number:	4,426
Purchase prices:	
08/1988:	DM 61,900 [DM 64,500]
with catalytic converter:	DM 63,265 [DM 65,865]

944 S2 Coupé
MY 1989–MY 1991

Engine

Engine design:	4-cylinder in-line
Installation:	Front-engine
Cooling system:	Water-cooled
Engine type:	M 44/41
Displacement (cc):	2990
Bore x stroke (mm):	104 x 88
Engine output (kW/hp):	155/211 at 5800rpm
Maximum torque (Nm/lb ft):	280/207 at 4000rpm
Output per litre (kW/l / hp/l):	51.8 / 70.6
Compression ratio:	10.9 : 1
Valve operation camshaft drive:	dohc, cams driven by synchronous belt drive, 4 valves per cylinder
Carburation:	DME, Bosch L-Jetronic fuel injection
Ignition system:	DME; breakerless
Firing order:	1- 3 - 4 - 2
Engine lubrication:	Full-pressure oil lubrication
Engine oil total (l):	6.5

Transmission

Drive configuration:	Rear-axle drive, transaxle system
Manual gearbox:	5-speed
Transmission type:	083F
Transmission ratios:	
1st gear:	3.500
2nd gear:	2.059
3rd gear:	1.400
4th gear:	1.034
5th gear:	0.778
Reverse gear:	3.500
Drive ratio:	3.875
Option:	Limited-slip differential 40%

Body, chassis, suspension, brakes, wheels

Body design:	Steel coupé body, 2 doors, 2 + 2 seats, entirely hot-dip galvanized body with wider wings, side-impact protection beams in doors, flexible polyurethane front bumper with integrated aluminium beams, rear bumper integrated in body form, flip-up headlamps, glass rear lid with black polyurethane rear spoiler, rear diffuser, painted electric outside mirrors
MY 1991:	Rear wing
Option:	Removable roof with electric lift feature
Suspension, front:	Independent suspension, aluminium wishbones, McPherson struts, coil springs, dual-tube hydraulic shock absorbers, anti-roll bar
Suspension, rear:	Individually suspended on driveshafts, transverse torsion bars on each side in transaxle tube, light alloy transverse tube suspension, dual-tube hydraulic shock absorbers, anti-roll bar

Brakes, front/rear (Size (mm)):	Ventilated discs (298 x 28) Ventilated discs (299 x 24) Black 4-piston fixed aluminium callipers / Black 4-piston fixed aluminium callipers
Option, MY 1990–MY 1991 stand.:	ABS
Wheels, front/rear:	7 J x 16 / 8 J x 16
Tyres, front/rear:	205/55 ZR 16 / 225/50 ZR 16

Electrical system

Alternator (W/A):	1610 / 115
Battery (V/Ah):	12 / 63

Dimensions and weight

Track, front/rear (mm):	1477 / 1451
Wheelbase (mm):	2400
Length x width x height (mm):	4230 x 1735 x 1275
Kerb weight DIN (kg):	1310
MY 1990–MY 1991:	1340
Permissible gross weight (kg):	1650
MY 1990–MY 1991:	1680
Luggage compartment (VDA (l)):	318
with folded down rear seatbacks:	514
Fuel tank capacity (l):	80, including 8 reserve
C_w x A (m²):	0.33 x 1.89 = 0.624
Power/weight ratio (kg/kW/ kg/hp):	8.45 / 6.21
MY 1990–MY 1991:	8.65 / 6.35

Fuel consumption
MY 1989
Without catalytic converter:

EG-Norm 80/1268 (mpg):	95 RON super leaded or unleaded
At constant 56mph/90kph:	41.6
At constant 74mph/120kph:	33.5
EG-emissions-urban cycle:	20.1

With catalytic converter:

EG-Norm 80/1268 (mpg):	95 RON super unleaded
At constant 56mph/90kph:	38
At constant 74mph/120kph:	31
EG-emissions-urban cycle:	19.7

Performance, production, prices

Acceleration 0-62mph/100kph (s):	7.1
Maximum speed (mph / kph):	149 / 240
Production, total number:	9,352

Purchase prices:

08/1988:	DM 73,600
with catalytic converter:	DM 74,965
08/1989:	DM 78,100
02/1990:	DM 79,700
07/1990:	DM 81,055
02/1991:	DM 84,555

944 S2 Cabriolet
MY 1989–MY 1991

Engine

Engine design:	4-cylinder in-line
Installation:	Front-engine
Cooling system:	Water-cooled
Engine type:	M 44/41
Displacement (cc):	2990
Bore x stroke (mm):	104 x 88
Engine output (kW/hp):	155/211 at 5800rpm
Maximum torque (Nm/lb ft):	280/207 at 4000rpm
Output per litre (kW/l / hp/l):	51.8 / 70.6
Compression ratio:	10.9 : 1
Valve operation camshaft drive:	dohc, cams driven by synchronous belt drive, 4 valves per cylinder
Carburation:	DME, Bosch L-Jetronic fuel injection
Ignition system:	DME; breakerless
Firing order:	1- 3 - 4 - 2
Engine lubrication:	Full-pressure oil lubrication
Engine oil total (l):	6.5

Transmission

Drive configuration:	Rear-axle drive, transaxle system
Manual gearbox:	5-speed
Transmission type:	083F
Transmission ratios:	
1st gear:	3.500
2nd gear:	2.059
3rd gear:	1.400
4th gear:	1.034
5th gear:	0.778
Reverse gear:	3.500
Drive ratio:	3.875
Option:	Limited-slip differential 40%

Body, chassis, suspension, brakes, wheels

Body design:	Steel cabriolet body, 2 doors, 2 + 2 seats, entirely hot-dip galvanized body with wider wings, side-impact protection beams in doors, flexible polyurethane front bumper with integrated aluminium beams, rear bumper integrated in body form, flip-up headlamps, steel rear lid, rear diffuser, painted electric outside mirrors, manual hood with flexible plastic rear window
Option, MY 1990–MY 1991 stand.:	Electric hood with flexible plastic rear window
Suspension, front:	Independent suspension, aluminium wishbones, McPherson struts, coil springs, dual-tube hydraulic shock absorbers, anti-roll bar
Suspension, rear:	Individually suspended on driveshafts, transverse torsion bars on each side in transaxle tube, light alloy transverse tube suspension, dual-tube hydraulic shock absorbers, anti-roll bar

Brakes, front/rear (Size (mm)):	Ventilated discs (298 x 28) Ventilated discs (299 x 24) Black 4-piston fixed aluminium callipers / Black 4-piston fixed aluminium callipers
Option, MY 1990–MY 1991 stand.:	ABS
Wheels, front/rear:	7 J x 16 / 8 J x 16
Tyres, front/rear:	205/55 ZR 16 / 225/50 ZR 16

Electrical system

Alternator (W/A):	1610 / 115
Battery (V/Ah):	12 / 63

Dimensions and weight

Track, front/rear (mm):	1477 / 1451
Wheelbase (mm):	2400
Length x width x height (mm):	4230 x 1735 x 1275
Kerb weight DIN (kg):	1340
MY 1990–MY 1991:	1390
Permissible gross weight (kg):	1650
MY 1990–MY 1991:	1710
Luggage compartment (VDA (l)):	162
Fuel tank capacity (l):	80, including 8 reserve
C_w x A (m²):	0.36 x 1.87 = 0.673
Power/weight ratio (kg/kW/kg/hp):	8.64 / 6.35
MY 1990 - MY 1991:	8.96 / 6.58

Fuel consumption

MY 1989
Without catalytic converter:

EG-Norm 80/1268 (mpg):	95 RON super leaded or unleaded
At constant 56mph/90kph:	41.6
At constant 74mph/120kph:	33.5
EG-emissions-urban cycle:	20.1

With catalytic converter:

EG-Norm 80/1268 (mpg):	95 RON super unleaded
At constant 56mph/90kph:	38
At constant 74mph/120kph:	31
EG-emissions-urban cycle:	19.7

Performance, production, prices

Acceleration 0-62mph/100kph (s):	7.1
Maximum speed (mph / kph):	149 / 240
Production, total number:	6,980

Purchase prices:

08/1988:	DM 84,900
with catalytic converter:	DM 86,265
08/1989:	DM 89,900
02/1990:	DM 91,700
07/1990:	DM 93,260
02/1991:	DM 96,760

944 turbo Coupé MY 1989–MY 1991

Engine

Engine design:	4-cylinder in-line, turbo charger, intercooler
Installation:	Front-engine
Cooling system:	Water-cooled
Engine type:	M 44/52
Displacement (cc):	2479
Bore x stroke (mm):	100 x 78.9
Engine output (kW/hp):	184/250 at 6000rpm
Maximum torque (Nm/lb ft):	350/258 at 4000rpm
Output per litre (kW/l / hp/l):	74.2 / 100.4
Compression ratio:	8.0 : 1
Valve operation camshaft drive:	ohc, cam driven by synchronous belt drive, 2 valves per cylinder
Carburation:	DME, Bosch L-Jetronic fuel-injection
Ignition system:	DME; breakerless
Firing order:	1- 3 - 4 - 2
Engine lubrication:	Full-pressure oil lubrication
Engine oil total (l):	7.0

Transmission

Drive configuration:	Rear-axle drive, transaxle system
Manual gearbox:	5-speed
Transmission type:	016S/R
MY 1990–MY 1991:	016R
Transmission ratios:	
1st gear:	3.500
2nd gear:	2.059
3rd gear:	1.400
4th gear:	1.034
5th gear:	0.829
Reverse gear:	3.500
Drive ratio:	3.375
Standard:	Limited-slip differential 40%

Body, chassis, suspension, brakes, wheels

Body design:	Steel coupé body, 2 doors, 2 + 2 seats, entirely hot-dip galvanized body with wider wings, side-impact protection beams in doors, flexible polyurethane front bumper with integrated aluminium beams, rear bumper integrated in body form, flip-up headlamps, glass rear lid with black polyurethane rear spoiler, rear diffuser, painted electric outside mirrors
MY 1990–MY 1991:	Rear spoiler
Option:	Removable roof with electric lift feature
Suspension, front:	Independent suspension, aluminium wishbones, McPherson struts, coil springs, dual-tube hydraulic shock absorbers, anti-roll bar
Suspension, rear:	Individually suspended on driveshafts, transverse torsion bars on each side in transaxle tube, light alloy transverse tube suspension, dual-tube hydraulic shock absorbers, anti-roll bar
Brakes, front/rear (Size (mm)):	Ventilated discs (304 x 32) Ventilated discs (299 x 24) Black 4-piston fixed aluminium callipers / Black 4-piston fixed aluminium callipers ABS
Wheels, front/rear:	7 J x 16 / 9 J x 16
MY 1990–MY 1991:	7.5 J x 16 / 9 J x 16
Tyres, front/rear:	225/50 VR 16 / 245/45 VR 16

Electrical system

Alternator (W/A):	1610 / 115
Battery (V/Ah):	12 / 63

Dimensions and weight

Track, front/rear (mm):	1457 / 1436
MY 1990–MY 1991:	1457 / 1451
Wheelbase (mm):	2400
Length x width x height (mm):	4230 x 1735 x 1275
Kerb weight DIN (kg):	1350
MY 1990–MY 1991:	1400
Permissible gross weight (kg):	1670
MY 1990–MY 1991:	1740
Luggage compartment (VDA (l)):	318
with folded down rear seatbacks:	514

Fuel tank capacity (l):	80, including 8 reserve
C_w x A (m²):	0.33 x 1.89 = 0.624
Power/weight ratio (kg/kW/kg/hp):	7.33 / 5.40
MY 1990–MY 1991:	7.60 / 5.60

Fuel consumption

MY 1989	
Without catalytic converter:	
EG-Norm 80/1268 (mpg):	95 RON super leaded or unleaded
At constant 56mph/90kph:	40.8
At constant 74mph/120kph:	31.3
EG-emissions-urban cycle:	21.5
With catalytic converter:	
EG-Norm 80/1268 (mpg):	95 RON super unleaded
At constant 56mph/90kph:	39.7
At constant 74mph/120kph:	30.4
EG-emissions-urban cycle:	21.2

Performance, production, prices

Acceleration 0-62mph/100kph (s):	5.9
Maximum speed (mph / kph):	162 / 260
Production, number total:	3,738
Purchase prices:	
08/1988:	DM 93,500
with catalytic converter:	DM 95,075
08/1989:	DM 97,175
02/1990:	DM 97,175
07/1990:	DM 97,175
02/1991:	DM 97,175

944 turbo Cabriolet MY 1991

Engine

Engine design:	4-cylinder in-line, turbo charger, intercooler
Installation:	Front-engine
Cooling system:	Water-cooled
Engine type:	M 44/52
Displacement (cc):	2479
Bore x stroke (mm):	100 x 78.9
Engine output (kW/hp):	184/250 at 6000rpm
Maximum torque (Nm/lb ft):	350/258 at 4000rpm
Output per litre (kW/l / hp/l):	74.2 / 100.4
Compression ratio:	8.0 : 1
Valve operation camshaft drive:	ohc, cam driven by synchronous belt drive, 2 valves per cylinder
Carburation:	DME, Bosch L-Jetronic fuel injection
Ignition system:	DME; breakerless
Firing order:	1- 3 - 4 - 2
Engine lubrication:	Full-pressure oil lubrication
Engine oil total (l):	7.0

Transmission

Drive configuration:	Rear-axle drive, transaxle system
Manual gearbox:	5-speed
Transmission type:	016R
Transmission ratios:	
1st gear:	3.500
2nd gear:	2.059
3rd gear:	1.400
4th gear:	1.034
5th gear:	0.829
Reverse gear:	3.500
Drive ratio:	3.375
Standard:	Limited-slip differential 40%

Body, chassis, suspension, brakes, wheels

Body design:	Steel cabriolet body, 2 doors, 2 + 2 seats, entirely hot-dip galvanized body with wider wings, side-impact protection beams in doors, flexible polyurethane front bumper with integrated aluminium beams, rear bumper integrated in body form, flip-up headlamps, steel rear lid, rear diffuser, painted electric outside mirrors, electric hood with flexible plastic rear window
Suspension, front:	Independent suspension, aluminium wishbones, McPherson struts, coil springs, dual-tube hydraulic shock absorbers, anti-roll bar
Suspension, rear:	Individually suspended on driveshafts, transverse torsion bars on each side in transaxle tube, light alloy transverse tube suspension, dual-tube hydraulic shock absorbers, anti-roll bar
Brakes, front/rear (Size (mm)):	Ventilated discs (304 x 32) Ventilated discs (299 x 24) Black 4-piston fixed aluminium callipers / Black 4-piston fixed aluminium callipers ABS
Wheels, front/rear:	7 J x 16 / 9 J x 16
Tyres, front/rear:	225/50 VR 16 / 245/45 VR 16

Electrical system

Alternator (W/A):	1610 / 115
Battery (V/Ah):	12 / 63

Dimensions and weight

Track, front/rear (mm):	1457 / 1451
Wheelbase (mm):	2400
Length x width x height (mm):	4230 x 1735 x 1275
Kerb weight DIN (kg):	1400
Permissible gross weight (kg):	1740
Luggage compartment (VDA (l)):	162
Fuel tank capacity (l):	80, including 8 reserve
C_w x A (m²):	0.36 x 1.87 = 0.673
Power/weight ratio (kg/kW/ kg/hp):	7.60 / 5.60

Fuel consumption

EG-Norm 80/1268 (mpg):	95 RON super unleaded
At constant 56mph/90kph:	39.7
At constant 74mph/120kph:	30.4
EG-emissions-urban cycle:	21.2

Performance, production, prices

Acceleration 0-62mph/100kph (s):	5.9
Maximum speed (mph / kph):	162 / 260
Production, total number:	528
Purchase price:	DM 103,725

Porsche 959

At the 1983 IAA (the Frankfurt International Auto Show) Porsche displayed its 'Group B' design study, intended for racing competition in FIA Group B. Class homologation rules required production of at least 200 examples. The finished car, shown at the IAA two years later, differed in only a few details from the Porsche 959 in the form delivered to customers between 1986 and 1988.

The 959 was a high-end sports car which could be driven on public roads but also entered in racing events. Design of the 959 incorporated a multitude of extraordinary engineering solutions. It also employed many 911 production parts in order to keep costs at a level that could still be considered economically justifiable.

Body shape was determined by the specific demands of aerodynamics. Apart from an extremely low drag coefficient of 0.31, it exhibited nearly zero aerodynamic lift even at its exceptional high top speed. Its design included a rear spoiler integrated in the body shape. Bumpers were also integrated in the body. The floorpan was capped by a flat undertray to give air as little grip as possible. For weight savings, the body structure itself was of mixed construction: the safety cell was made of hot-dip galvanized sheet-steel, doors and front lid of a heat-treated aluminium alloy, front apron of polyurethane foam, rear body section and roof skin of aramid and fibreglass-reinforced epoxy resin.

Porsche also broke new ground in the chassis department. The 959 was equipped with adjustable, speed-dependent shock absorber valving. A twist knob on the centre console permitted manual setting of the shock absorber stiffness. In the interests of safety, at high speeds the shock valving was set automatically. Another twist knob adjusted the 959's ground clearance, in three stages – 120mm, 150mm and 180mm. This ride height adjustment also operated automatically to lower the body at high speeds for reduced aerodynamic drag and improved vehicle handling. A special anti-lock brake system was developed for the 959, capable of delivering optimum braking even from speeds in excess of 186mph (300kph). The brake system itself consisted of four ventilated, cross-drilled discs and four-piston aluminium fixed callipers. A tyre-pressure monitoring system provided an added piece of safety technology, reporting pressure loss in the event of tyre damage or cracked wheels. The

magnesium wheels had hollow-cast spokes. A Dunlop Denloc safety system gave the tyres the ability to generate enough side force, even with loss of air pressure, to provide directional stability. Wheels were attached by means of centre-lock hubs. Front tyres were 235/45 ZR 17 on 8 x 17 rims; rears were 255/40 ZR 17 on 9 x 17 wheels. Optionally, customers could order 275/35 ZR 17 rear tyres on 10-inch wide wheels. The 959 was available in two equipment levels: a comfort version was available alongside the sports version. The sports version offered heat-blocking glass, a stereo radio/cassette player, power-steering and electric seat-height adjustment. The more comfortable variant added a second electrically-adjustable outside mirror, electric windows, automatic climate-control, full leather upholstery, electrically powered seats and central-locking. Ride-height adjustment was only available on the comfort version. With such a concentration of technology, the sports version weighed in at 1350kg (2974lb); the comfort model weighed 100kg (220lb) more.

The turbocharged engine of the 959 was derived from the racing Type 962 C, which was dominating Group C racing at the time. For use on public roads, the racing power unit was taught more civilized manners. Fed by twin turbochargers, the engine extracted all of 450hp (331kW) out of 2.85 litres – a phenomenal 158hp per litre. The engine concept was unusual: crankcase and all six cylinder barrels were air-cooled, while the cylinder heads and turbochargers were water-cooled. Each of the two four-valve cylinder heads was equipped with hydraulic valve-lash adjustment and dual overhead camshafts. Connecting rods were made of lightweight, extremely strong titanium. Dry-sump lubrication provided optimum lubrication even in high-speed turns. One unusual feature was sequential turbocharging; at low engine speeds, both cylinder banks were fed only from the smaller, faster-responding turbocharger. At 4300rpm, the larger turbocharger was brought on-line to unleash the engine's full output potential. This boost strategy combined best possible response with highest possible power output. A Bosch Motronic unit provided optimum fuel/air mixture. The engine was tuned to operate on 95 octane unleaded fuel. If desired, catalytic converters could be installed.

Power was transmitted through a single-plate dry

Phantom view of a 959

clutch, six-speed manual transmission and permanent all-wheel drive with electronic power-distribution management. The all-wheel drive system was configured as a transaxle layout. One special feature was its four different driving programs, driver-selectable from the cockpit. The 'traction' program was for difficult starting in deep snow or mud; the other choices were 'dry', 'wet' and 'snow and ice'. This system provided drivers with the right program for any conceivable traction situation.

The 959 set new standards in terms of performance and safe handling characteristics. Accelerating to 62mph (100kph), the super sports car set a new benchmark at only 3.9 seconds. Top speed was in excess of 196mph (315kph). In all, Porsche built 292 examples. Twenty-nine of these were sold ex-works in an increased-performance version. Known internally as the 959 S, this special model produced 515hp (379kW) and topped out at 211mph (339kph). In view of the revolutionary technology packed into the car, its retail price of 420,000 Deutschmarks was not out of line. Even today there is hardly a vehicle available anywhere in the world which offers such a concentration of cutting-edge engineering. To this day, the Porsche 959 remains a technological milestone in automobile history.

959 Coupé MY 1987–MY 1988

Engine
Engine design:	6-cylinder horizontally-opposed, twin turbocharger, twin intercoolers
Installation:	Rear-engine
Cooling system:	Air/Water-cooled
Number & form of blower blades:	10, straight
Engine type:	959/50
Displacement (cc):	2849
Bore x stroke (mm):	95 x 67
Engine output (kW/hp):	331/450 at 6500rpm
Maximum torque (Nm/lb ft):	500/369 at 5000rpm
Output per litre (kW/l / hp/l):	116.2 / 158.0
Compression ratio:	8.3 : 1
Valve operation & camshaft drive:	dohc, cams driven by double chain, 4 valves per cylinder
Carburation:	Bosch DME
Ignition system:	DME
Firing order:	1- 6 - 2 - 4 - 3 - 5
Engine lubrication:	Dry oil sump
Engine oil total (l):	18.0

Transmission
Drive configuration:	Four-wheel drive with drive-programs, transaxle system
Manual gearbox:	6-speed
Transmission type:	959
Transmission ratios:	
1st gear:	3.500
2nd gear:	2.059
3rd gear:	1.409
4th gear:	1.036
5th gear:	0.813
6th gear:	0.639
Reverse gear:	2.860
Drive ratio:	4.125

Body, chassis, suspension, brakes, wheels
Body design:	Steel coupé body, 2 doors, 2 + 2 seats, hot-dip galvanized body parts with wider wings, aluminium bonnet and doors, side-impact protection beams in doors, flexible polyurethane front bumper, wings, rear body with integrated rear spoiler and roof skin made of aramid and fibreglass-reinforced epoxy resin, electric outside mirror(s) in Cup-Design

Suspension, front:	Individually suspended on double wishbones, twin coil spring per wheel with a variable and a lift-regulating shock absorber, anti-roll bar
Suspension, rear:	Individually suspended on double wishbones, twin coil spring per wheel with a variable and a lift-regulating shock absorber, anti-roll bar
Brakes, front/rear (Size (mm)):	Ventilated and drilled discs (322 x 32) Ventilated and drilled discs (304 x 28) Black 4-piston fixed aluminium callipers / Black 4-piston fixed aluminium callipers ABS
Wheels, front/rear:	8 J x 17 / 9 J x 17
Tyres, front/rear:	235/45 ZR 17 / 255/40 ZR 17
Option:	8 J x 17 / 10 J x 17 235/45 ZR 17 / 275/35 ZR 17

Electrical system
Alternator (W/A):	1610 / 115
Battery (V/Ah):	12 / 66
Sports version:	12 / 50

Dimensions and weight
Track, front/rear (mm):	1504 / 1550
Wheelbase (mm):	2300
Length x width x height (mm):	4260 x 1840 x 1280
Kerb weight DIN (kg):	1450–1590
Sports version:	1350–1550
Permissible gross weight (kg):	1770
Sports version:	1690
Fuel tank capacity (l):	84, including 15 reserve
C_w x A (m^2):	0.31 x 1.92 = 0.595
Power/weight ratio (kg/kW/ kg/hp):	4.38–4.80 / 3.22–3.53
Sports version:	4.07–4.68 / 3.00–3.44

Fuel consumption
EG-Norm 80/1268 (mpg):	95 RON super unleaded
At constant 56mph/90kph:	30.4
At constant 74mph/120kph:	26.4
EG-emissions-urban cycle:	16.1

Performance, production, price
Acceleration 0-62mph/100kph (s):	3.9
0-124mph/200kph (s):	14.3
Maximum speed (mph / kph):	196 / 315
Production, total number:	292
Purchase price:	DM 420,000

278

Porsche 968

Porsche 968 Coupé, 968 Cabriolet, 968 CS Coupé and 968 turbo S Coupé

Development of Porsche's four-cylinder transaxle models culminated in the autumn of 1991, with the introduction of the 968. This final evolutionary stage was offered in coupé and cabriolet form. From a styling standpoint, the Porsche 968 was more closely allied to the other Porsche models, the 911 and 928, although visually and technically, it represented a further development of its direct ancestor, the 944 S2.

Model year 1992 (N Programme)

The Porsche 968 was available as a coupé or cabriolet. Most of its body parts were taken over from the final 944 S2 version. Overall, its body contours did appear rounder and better-harmonized. From the front, the 968 resembled the 928. The bonnet was narrower and longer, reaching all the way to the front bumper. The lenses of the flip-up headlamps remained visible when retracted, just as on the 928. The tops of the front wings were convex. The nose moulding was also more rounded, and fitted with indicators, driving lamps and fog lamps. The combustion air intake was just above the number plate, with two longer air inlets below. At the sides, the sills were capped with plastic fairings which drew up just ahead of the rear wheel arches and so served as rock impact protection. The rear ends were pulled forward to the wheel arches. The tail lamp assemblies were entirely red. 'PORSCHE' script graced the rear bumper between the lamp assemblies. Redesigned door handles were painted body colour. The aerodynamic drag coefficient of the 968 Coupé was 0.34, with overall drag (frontal area x coefficient) of 0.639.

The 968's sports-oriented suspension tuning was matched to the car's performance capabilities, and provided a high level of driving enjoyment as well as safety. Its MacPherson front suspension employed light-alloy transverse links, coil springs, and gas-pressure shock absorbers; the semi-trailing arm rear

suspension took advantage of elastokinematic design, with a subframe, transverse torsion bars and gas-pressure shock absorbers. Naturally, the brake system was equipped with ABS, four aluminium four-piston fixed callipers, and ventilated brake discs. The standard version used 'Cup Design' alloy wheels, front 7 J x 16 with 205/55 ZR 16 tyres, rear 8 J x 16 with 225/50 ZR 16. As an option, customers could order a sports suspension with 17-inch 'Cup' wheels, 7.5-inches wide at the front with 225/45 ZR 17 tyres, and 9-inches wide at the back with 255/40 ZR 17 tyres.

The equipment list of the regular production 968 left little to be desired: green-tinted glass, six-speaker radio installation kit, power-steering, electric windows, dual front airbags for driver and front passenger for all left-hand-drive vehicles, electric seat height adjustment, electrically-adjustable and heatable outside mirrors and central-locking with alarm system. Steering wheel, gear lever and handbrake were leather-covered. Inner door panels were pleated, as on the 911. The instrument package was also very complete; the instrument panel housed a speedometer, tachometer, oil-pressure gauge, coolant gauge, fuel-level gauge and voltmeter. Vehicles equipped with a Tiptronic transmission included a gear indicator in the speedometer's bottom sector. An analog clock was mounted in the centre console, and an outside-temperature gauge was located to the right of the heater controls. The Coupé was equipped with a rear wiper, the Cabriolet with an electric hood mechanism. The hood was manually unlatched from the windscreen header, and then electrically stowed by holding down a push-button. A cover could be snapped onto the stowed top for protection. Options included air-conditioning, headlamp-cleaning system, a choice of several stereo radio/cassette units, heated seats, cruise-control and leather interior. A removable, electric tilting roof was available for the Coupé.

A 3-litre, four-cylinder, four-valve engine was installed longitudinally at the front. This generated 240hp (176kW) at 6200rpm, with a peak torque of 305Nm (225lb ft) at 4100rpm, more than any other normally-aspirated engine of similar size. Two counter-rotating balance shafts compensated for secondary inertia forces and moments, imparting the four with a level of smoothness that compared

Phantom view of a 968 Coupé

favourably to six-cylinder engines. A hot-wire mass air-flow-meter sensed the quantity of induced air, while a Motronic system metered the exact amount of fuel to be delivered by the sequential injection system. The VarioCam system provided a fuller torque curve at low engine speeds, with increased valve overlap between 1500rpm and 5000rpm. For the cleanest possible combustion, the engine, with its 11.0:1 compression ratio, was tuned for 98 octane premium unleaded fuel. The metal catalyst had especially low exhaust back-pressure.

Porsche offered the 968 with two different transmissions: a six-speed manual or a four-speed Tiptronic. The Tiptronic was an automatic transmission in which gears could be selected fully automatically, or by moving the gear lever to the 'manual' gate and 'tipping' it forward to change up, or back to change down. All gear changes were carried out without interruption of power flow to the wheels.

Like its predecessor, the 968 was equipped with a transaxle system. The engine was installed at the front, the transmission and final drive at the rear. The clutch for manual-transmission versions was coupled to a dual-mass flywheel. A limited-slip differential with 40 pe rcent lock-up was offered as an option.

Performance of the manual-transmission 968 nearly matched the high standards of the 911 Carrera models. The car needed only 6.5 seconds to

reach 62mph (100kph), and top speed was 157mph (252kph). With Tiptronic, the car accelerated to the 62mph (100kph) mark in 7.9 seconds, and top speed was listed as 153mph (247kph).

Model year 1993 (P Programme)

The prime beneficiary of 968 Coupé and Cabriolet model development was the environment. Conversion to CFC-free air-conditioning refrigerant helped preserve the ozone layer. Water-based paints used significantly less solvent. Along with marking the vehicle's various plastic components for recycling, environmental considerations also led to introduction of improved brake fluid with a higher wet boiling point. All right-hand-drive vehicles were now equipped with a driver's-side airbag.

In early 1993 the 968 CS (Clubsport) rounded out the four-cylinder model line. This lightened model represented an affordable entry point into the Porsche product range. 50kg (110lb) were saved by leaving out weight-intensive extras. The 968 CS was only available in coupé form.

The CS's suspension was lowered by 20mm, and the car was given a firmer ride. It rolled on 17-inch 'Cup' wheels, 7.5 J x 17 rims with 225/45 ZR 17 tyres at the front and 9 J x 17 rims with 255/40 ZR 17 tyres at the rear.

Even stiffer chassis tuning was available with a sports package which included a limited-slip differential. Wheels and rear spoiler were painted body colour. Black cars and special-order colours had silver-painted wheels.

Inside, an obvious change was the familiar 911 Carrera RS bucket seats. In the 968 CS these were covered with black fabric. The shells were painted body colour, or black in the case of special-order colours. Rear seats were deleted, but this made for a longer luggage area. A smaller three-spoke sports steering wheel was installed. Driver and passenger airbags were deleted from the standard equipment list but remained available as an option. Elimination of many electrical items made for a lighter wiring harness. Deleted items included central-locking, electric windows, electrically-adjustable outside mirrors, electric hatchback release, engine compartment illumination and rear audio speakers. To save weight, even the engine compartment did without some trim pieces. The hatch could be opened by means of a cable release, and a net for tying down luggage was standard equipment. Elimination of electrical load items permitted installation of a smaller 36Ah battery. Available options included air-conditioning (but only in conjunction with a more powerful battery), tilt roof,

Blaupunkt 'Paris' radio with two speakers and regular-production manually-adjustable front seats.

The entire powertrain of the 968 CS was identical to that of the normal 968 version. Thanks to its lower weight, however, the car was more agile in acceleration, handling and braking.

Porsche 968 turbo S

Porsche offered its most performance-oriented 968 model in the form of the 968 turbo S Coupé, based on the lightweight 968 CS. Externally, the 968 turbo variant was recognizable by an additional pair of ducts on the bonnet, an additional chin spoiler at the front and a somewhat larger, adjustable rear spoiler. Compared to the 968, its suspension was 20mm lower and with firmer tuning. Three-piece 'Cup Design' Speedline wheels, 8 J x 18 at the front and 10 J x 18 at the rear, carried 235/40 ZR 18 and 265/35 ZR 18 tyres, respectively. Visible through these wheels were red-painted four-piston fixed brake callipers and cross-drilled discs of the brake system, borrowed from the 911 turbo S. The ABS system was matched to the car's higher performance potential.

The 968 3-litre four-cylinder four-valve engine

Compared to the regular-production 968, the 3-litre turbocharged engine had only a two-valve cylinder head. Its KKK turbocharger raised power output to 305hp (224kW) at just 5400rpm, and maximum torque of 500Nm (369lb ft) was available as low as 3000rpm. With this much power on tap, the 1300kg (2863lb) 968 turbo S sprinted to 62mph (100kph) in 5.0 seconds, and could climb to a top speed of 174mph (280kph).

The final drive ratio, fifth and sixth gears were higher. Its limited-slip differential had up to 75 per cent lock-up both under load and while coasting. The interior recalled the 968 CS, with its freedom from luxury features. Electric windows, central-locking and rear seats fell victim to the weight reduction regimen. Instead, it was fitted with front bucket seats and a rear parcel-shelf with embroidered 'turbo S' script.

Model year 1994 (R Programme)

Porsche's 968 models entered the new model year with almost no mechanical or visual changes. Stock equipment now included a pollen filter for cleaner cabin air.

The aluminium-alloy wheels had a new 'Cup Design 93' look. Some equipment items were combined into option packages. A seating package included leather seats, along with driver and passenger seat heating. The special suspension package encompassed stiffer chassis tuning, 17-inch wheels and a more powerful brake system.

Special packages were offered with the 968 CS. The sports package included firmer suspension, limited-slip differential and more powerful brakes. The comfort package offered electric windows and electrically-adjustable outside mirrors. Central-locking, alarm system and locking wheelnuts were combined in the safety package. Manually-adjustable regular production seats and rear seating, along with an electric hatch release, were offered as no-cost options.

Model year 1995 (S Programme)

There were no changes for the last year of the 968 model line.

In total, Porsche built 5,731 examples of the 968 Coupé, 3,959 968 Cabriolets, 1,538 968 CS Coupés, and only 14 of the 968 turbo S Coupé. In addition, three competition cars were built as 968 turbo RS Coupés.

Production of the 968 came to an end after only 11,245 cars had been built. The last 968 marked the end of Porsche's successful era of four-cylinder transaxle models.

968 turbo S Coupé

968 Coupé [Tiptronic]
MY 1992–MY 1995

Engine

Engine design:	4-cylinder in-line
Installation:	Front-engine
Cooling system:	Water-cooled
Engine type:	M 44/43 [M 44/44]
Displacement (cc):	2990
Bore x stroke (mm):	104 x 88
Engine output (kW/hp):	176/240 at 6200rpm
Maximum torque (Nm/lb ft):	305/225 at 4100rpm
Output per litre (kW/l / hp/l):	58.9 / 80.3
Compression ratio:	11.0 : 1
Valve operation camshaft drive:	dohc, cams driven by synchronous belt drive, 4 valves per cylinder, VarioCam
Carburation:	Bosch DME fuel injection
Ignition system:	DME
Firing order:	1- 3 - 4 - 2
Engine lubrication:	Full-pressure oil lubrication
Engine oil total (l):	7.0

Transmission

Drive configuration:	Rear-axle drive, transaxle system
Manual gearbox:	6-speed
Option Tiptronic:	[4-speed]
Transmission type:	G 44/00 [A 44/00]
Transmission ratios:	
1st gear:	3.182 [2.579]
2nd gear:	2.000 [1.407]
3rd gear:	1.435 [1.000]
4th gear:	1.111 [0.742]
5th gear:	0.912
6th gear:	0.778
Reverse gear:	3.455 [2.882]
Drive ratio:	3.778 [3.250]
Option:	Limited-slip differential 40%

Body, chassis, suspension, brakes, wheels

Body design:	Steel coupé body, 2 doors, 2 + 2 seats, entirely hot-dip galvanized body with wider wings, side-impact protection beams in doors, flexible polyurethane front and rear bumpers with integrated aluminium beams, flip-up headlamps, polyurethane side skirts, glass rear lid with painted rear wing, painted door handles, electric outside mirrors in Cup-Design
Option:	Removable roof with electric lift feature
Suspension, front:	Independent suspension, aluminium wishbones, McPherson struts, coil springs, dual-tube shock absorbers, anti-roll bar
Suspension, rear:	Individually suspended on driveshafts, transverse torsion bars on each side in transaxle tube, light alloy transverse tube suspension, dual-tube shock absorbers, anti-roll bar

Brakes, front/rear (Size (mm)):	Ventilated discs (298 x 28) Ventilated discs (299 x 24) Black 4-piston fixed aluminium callipers / Black 4-piston fixed aluminium callipers ABS
with sports suspension M 030:	Ventilated and drilled discs (304 x 32) Ventilated and drilled discs (299 x 24) Black 4-piston fixed aluminium callipers / Black 4-piston fixed aluminium callipers ABS
Wheels, front/rear:	7 J x 16 / 8 J x 16
Tyres, front/rear:	205/55 ZR 16 / 225/50 ZR 16
Option:	7.5 J x 17 / 9 J x 17 225/45 ZR 17 / 255/40 ZR 17

Electrical system

Alternator (W/A):	1610 / 115
Battery (V/Ah):	12 / 63 [12 / 65]

Dimensions and weight

Track, front/rear (mm):	1477 / 1451
7.5 J x 17 / 9 J x 17:	1457 / 1445
Wheelbase (mm):	2400
Length x width x height (mm):	4320 x 1735 x 1275
with sports suspension M 030:	4320 x 1735 x 1255
Kerb weight DIN (kg):	1370 [1400]
Permissible gross weight (kg):	1700 [1730]
MY 1993–MY 1995:	1730 [1760]
Luggage compartment (VDA (l)):	318
with folded down rear seatbacks:	514
Fuel tank capacity (l):	74, including 8 reserve
C_w x A (m^2):	0.34 x 1.88 = 0.639
Power/weight ratio (kg/kW/kg/hp):	7.78 [7.95] / 5.70 [5.83]

Fuel consumption

EG-Norm 80/1268 (mpg):	98 RON super plus unleaded
At constant 56mph/90kph:	39.2 [39.7]
At constant 74mph/120kph:	32.1 [32.5]
EG-emissions-urban cycle:	19.1 [19.3]

Performance, production, prices

Acceleration 0-62mph/100kph (s):	6.5 [7.9]
Maximum speed (mph / kph):	157 / 252 [153 / 247]
Production, total number:	5,731

Purchase prices:	
07/1991:	DM 89,800 [DM 95,650]
03/1992:	DM 92,300 [DM 98,300]
08/1992:	DM 94,790 [DM 100,790]
01/1993:	DM 95,621 [DM 101,674]
08/1993:	DM 97,440 [DM 103,490]
03/1994:	DM 97,440 [DM 103,490]
08/1994:	DM 97,440 [DM 103,490]
02/1995:	DM 99,390 [DM 105,440]

968 Cabriolet [Tiptronic]
MY 1992–MY 1995

Engine

Engine design:	4-cylinder in-line
Installation:	Front-engine
Cooling system:	Water-cooled
Engine type:	M 44/43 [M 44/44]
Displacement (cc):	2990
Bore x stroke (mm):	104 x 88
Engine output (kW/hp):	176/240 at 6200rpm
Maximum torque (Nm/lb ft):	305/225 at 4100rpm
Output per litre (kW/l / hp/l):	58.9 / 80.3
Compression ratio:	11.0 : 1
Valve operation camshaft drive:	dohc, cams driven by synchronous belt drive, 4 valves per cylinder, VarioCam
Carburation:	Bosch DME fuel injection
Ignition system:	DME
Firing order:	1 - 3 - 4 - 2
Engine lubrication:	Full-pressure oil lubrication
Engine oil total (l):	7.0

Transmission

Drive configuration:	Rear-axle drive, transaxle system
Manual gearbox:	6-speed
Option Tiptronic:	[4-speed]
Transmission type:	G 44/00 [A 44/00]
Transmission ratios:	
1st gear:	3.182 [2.579]
2nd gear:	2.000 [1.407]
3rd gear:	1.435 [1.000]
4th gear:	1.111 [0.742]
5th gear:	0.912
6th gear:	0.778
Reverse gear:	3.455 [2.882]
Drive ratio:	3.778 [3.250]
Option:	Limited-slip differential 40%

Body, chassis, suspension, brakes, wheels

Body design:	Steel cabriolet body, 2 doors, 2 + 2 seats, entirely hot-dip galvanized body with wider wings, side-impact protection beams in doors, flexible polyurethane front and rear bumpers with integrated aluminium beams, flip-up headlamps, polyurethane side skirts, steel rear lid, painted door handles, electric outside mirrors in Cup-Design, electric hood with flexible plastic rear window
Suspension, front:	Independent suspension, aluminium wishbones, McPherson struts, coil springs, dual-tube shock absorbers, anti-roll bar
Suspension, rear:	Individually suspended on driveshafts, transverse torsion bars on each side in transaxle tube, light alloy transverse tube suspension, dual-tube shock absorbers, anti-roll bar
Brakes, front/rear (Size (mm)):	Ventilated discs (298 x 28) Ventilated discs (299 x 24) Black 4-piston fixed aluminium callipers / Black 4-piston fixed aluminium callipers ABS
Wheels, front/rear:	7 J x 16 / 8 J x 16
Tyres, front/rear:	205/55 ZR 16 / 225/50 ZR 16
Option:	7.5 J x 17 / 9 J x 17
	225/45 ZR 17 / 255/40 ZR 17

Electrical system

Alternator (W/A):	1610 / 115
Battery (V/Ah):	12 / 63 [12 / 65]

Dimensions and weight

Track, front/rear (mm):	1477 / 1451
7.5 J x 17 / 9 J x 17:	1457 / 1445
Wheelbase (mm):	2400
Length x width x height (mm):	4320 x 1735 x 1275
Kerb weight DIN (kg):	1440 [1470]
Permissible gross weight (kg):	1760 [1790]
MY 1993–MY 1995:	1790 [1820]
Luggage compartment (VDA (l)):	162
Fuel tank capacity (l):	74, including 8 reserve
C_w x A (m²):	0.34 x 1.88 = 0.639
Power/weight ratio (kg/kW/ kg/hp):	8.18 [8.35] / 6.00 [6.12]

Fuel consumption

EG-Norm 80/1268 (mpg):	98 RON super plus unleaded
At constant 56mph/90kph:	39.2 [39.7]
At constant 74mph/120kph:	32.1 [32.5]
EG-emissions-urban cycle:	19.1 [19.3]

Performance, production, prices

Acceleration 0-62mph/100kph (s):	6.5 [7.9]
Maximum speed (mph / kph):	157 / 252 [153 / 247]
Production, total number:	3,959

Purchase prices:

07/1991:	DM 99,800 [DM 105,650]
03/1992:	DM 104,800 [DM 110,800]
08/1992:	DM 107,630 [DM 113,630]
01/1993:	DM 108,574 [DM 114,627]
08/1993:	DM 110,640 [DM 116,690]
03/1994:	DM 110,640 [DM 116,690]
08/1994:	DM 110,640 [DM 116,690]
02/1995:	DM 112,850 [DM 118,900]

968 CS Coupé
January 1993–MY 1995

Engine
Engine design:	4-cylinder in-line
Installation:	Front-engine
Cooling system:	Water-cooled
Engine type:	M 44/43 [M 44/44]
Displacement (cc):	2990
Bore x stroke (mm):	104 x 88
Engine output (kW/hp):	176/240 at 6200rpm
Maximum torque (Nm/lb ft):	305/225 at 4100rpm
Output per litre (kW/l / hp/l):	58.9 / 80.3
Compression ratio:	11.0 : 1
Valve operation camshaft drive:	dohc, cams driven by synchronous belt drive, 4 valves per cylinder, VarioCam
Carburation:	Bosch DME fuel injection
Ignition system:	DME
Firing order:	1- 3 - 4 - 2
Engine lubrication:	Full-pressure oil lubrication
Engine oil total (l):	7.0

Transmission
Drive configuration:	Rear-axle drive, transaxle system
Manual gearbox:	6-speed
Transmission type:	G 44/00
Transmission ratios:	
1st gear:	3.182
2nd gear:	2.000
3rd gear:	1.435
4th gear:	1.111
5th gear:	0.912
6th gear:	0.778
Reverse gear:	3.455
Drive ratio:	3.778
Option:	Limited-slip differential 40%

Body, chassis, suspension, brakes, wheels
Body design:	Steel coupé body, 2 doors, 2 (+ 2) seats, entirely hot-dip galvanized body with wider wings, side-impact protection beams in doors, flexible polyurethane front and rear bumpers with integrated aluminium beams, flip-up headlamps, polyurethane side skirts, glass rear lid with painted rear wing, painted door handles, manual outside mirrors in Cup-Design
Suspension, front:	Independent suspension, aluminium wishbones, McPherson struts, coil springs, dual-tube shock absorbers, anti-roll bar
Suspension, rear:	Individually suspended on driveshafts, transverse torsion bars on each side in transaxle tube, light alloy transverse tube suspension, dual-tube shock absorbers, anti-roll bar
Brakes, front/rear (Size (mm)):	Ventilated discs (298 x 28) Ventilated discs (299 x 24) Black 4-piston fixed aluminium callipers / Black 4-piston fixed aluminium callipers ABS
with sports suspension M 030:	Ventilated and drilled discs (304 x 32) Ventilated and drilled discs (299 x 24) Black 4-piston fixed aluminium callipers / Black 4-piston fixed aluminium callipers ABS
Wheels, front/rear:	7.5 J x 17 / 9 J x 17
Tyres, front/rear:	225/45 ZR 17 / 255/40 ZR 17

Electrical system
Alternator (W/A):	1260 / 90
Battery (V/Ah):	12 / 50

Dimensions and weight
Track, front/rear (mm):	1457 / 1445
Wheelbase (mm):	2400
Length x width x height (mm):	4320 x 1735 x 1255
Kerb weight DIN (kg):	1320
Permissible gross weight (kg):	1570
Luggage compartment (VDA (l)):	318
with folded down rear setbacks:	514
Fuel tank capacity (l):	74, including 8 reserve
C_w x A (m²):	0.34 x 1.88 = 0.639
Power/weight ratio (kg/kW/kg/hp):	7.50 / 5.50

Fuel consumption
EG-Norm 80/1268 (mpg):	98 RON super plus unleaded
At constant 56mph/90kph:	39.2
At constant 74mph/120kph:	32.1
EG-emissions-urban cycle:	19.1

Performance, production, prices
Acceleration 0-62mph/100kph (s):	6.5
Maximum speed (mph / kph):	157 / 252
Production, total number:	1,538
Purchase prices:	
01/1993:	DM 77,500
08/1993:	DM 79,300
03/1994:	DM 79,300
08/1994:	DM 79,300
02/1995:	DM 80,890

968 turbo S Coupé
MY 1993–MY 1994

Engine

Engine design:	4-cylinder in-line, turbo charger, intercooler
Installation:	Front-engine
Cooling system:	Water-cooled
Engine type:	M 44/60
Displacement (cc):	2990
Bore x stroke (mm):	104 x 88
Engine output (kW/hp):	224/305 at 5400rpm
Maximum torque (Nm/lb ft):	500/369 at 3000rpm
Output per litre (kW/l / hp/l):	74.9 / 102.0
Compression ratio:	8.0 : 1
Valve operation camshaft drive:	ohc, cam driven by synchronous belt drive, 2 valves per cylinder
Carburation:	Bosch DME fuel injection
Ignition system:	DME
Firing order:	1- 3 - 4 - 2
Engine lubrication:	Full-pressure oil lubrication
Engine oil total (l):	7.0

Transmission

Drive configuration:	Rear-axle drive, transaxle system
Manual gearbox:	6-speed
Transmission type:	G 44/00
Transmission ratios:	
1st gear:	3.182
2nd gear:	2.000
3rd gear:	1.435
4th gear:	1.111
5th gear:	0.882
6th gear:	0.711
Reverse gear:	3.455
Drive ratio:	3.400
Ltd slip diff. load/deceleration (%):	75 / 75

Body, chassis, suspension, brakes, wheels

Body design:	Steel coupé body, 2 doors, 2 (+ 2) seats, entirely hot-dip galvanized body with wider wings, side-impact protection beams in doors, NACA-air intake in bonnet, flexible polyurethane front and rear bumpers with integrated aluminium beams, front spoiler lip, flip-up headlamps, polyurethane side skirts, glass rear lid with big adjustable painted rear wing, painted door handles, manual outside mirrors in Cup-Design

Suspension, front:	Independent suspension, aluminium wishbones, McPherson struts, coil springs, dual-tube shock absorbers, anti-roll bar
Suspension, rear:	Individually suspended on driveshafts, transverse torsion bars on each side in transaxle tube, light alloy transverse tube suspension, dual-tube shock absorbers, anti-roll bar
Brakes, front/rear (Size (mm)):	Ventilated and drilled discs (322 x 32) Ventilated and drilled discs (299 x 28) Red 4-piston fixed aluminium callipers / Red 4-piston fixed aluminium callipers Bosch ABS
Wheels, front/rear:	8 J x 18 / 10 J x 18
Tyres, front/rear:	235/40 ZR 18 / 265/35 ZR 18

Electrical system

Alternator (W/A):	1260 / 90
Battery (V/Ah):	12 / 50

Dimensions and weight

Track, front/rear (mm):	1522 / 1500
Wheelbase (mm):	2400
Length x width x height (mm):	4320 x 1735 x 1255
Kerb weight DIN (kg):	1300
Permissible gross weight (kg):	1550
Luggage compartment (VDA (l)) without rear seats:	514
Fuel tank capacity (l):	74, including 8 reserve
C_w x A (m²):	0.34 x 1.88 = 0.639
Power/weight ratio (kg/kW/ kg/hp):	5.80 / 4.26

Fuel consumption

(mpg):	app. 18; 98 RON super plus unleaded

Performance, production, price

Acceleration 0-62mph/100kph (s):	5.0
0-124mph/200kph (s):	16.4
Maximum speed (mph / kph):	174 / 280
Production, total number: incl. 968 turbo RS:	14
Purchase price:	DM 175,000

Porsche Boxster (Type 986)

At the Detroit Motor Show in January 1993, Porsche presented a show car concept dubbed the 'Boxster'. This artificially created word combined the first syllable of 'boxer' and second syllable of 'roadster'. The 'Boxster' was a two-seat mid-engined roadster. In its vocabulary of form, it continued the old Porsche Spyder tradition of the Type 550 and Type 718. Public response to the show car was overwhelming, and Porsche promised to consider realizing the Boxster as a production vehicle.

Model year 1997 (V Programme)

In the autumn of 1996, Porsche's Boxster went into series production. For technical reasons, the production model deviated from the styling study in several respects, but it remained a two-seat mid-engined roadster.

The body of the Boxster anticipated several styling and design features of the new 911 generation, which would follow a year later. As the Boxster and new 911 Carrera were designed with a shared-parts concept, their front hoods, front headlamp units with integrated fog lamps and indicators, front wings and doors were identical. The nose of the Boxster was, however, shaped differently. The floorpan was identical as well, as far back as the B pillar. The Boxster stood on a 2315mm wheelbase.

One special feature of the body was that the same body-in-white could be built up as either a left- or right-hand drive model.

Along with two-side hot-dip galvanized steel, Porsche employed high strength steels for reinforcement. Side-impact door beams were made of extremely strong boron steel. Additionally, the body structure employed so-called 'tailored blanks', a process which built up body parts of varying thickness by laser welding additional thicknesses of steel; heavier-gauge steel was used only where it was really needed. Additional weight was pared off the body weight by trimming the edges of steel sheets so that only the necessary weld tabs were retained. These specially-cut edges also provided extra torsional stiffness. At the rear, one unusual feature was the automatically extending aerodynamic 'fence' spoiler between the two large tail lamp units with their orange indicators. Air inlets for combustion air and engine compartment ventilation were cut into the rear wings just behind the doors. Outside mirrors were attached ahead of the side windows. The Boxster's aerodynamic drag coefficient was about 0.31.

Its 130-litre (4.6cu ft) front boot included a small mini-spare mounted vertically ahead of the 60-litre (13-gallon) fuel tank. The rear boot capacity also measured 130 litres. An oil and coolant fill and monitoring unit was mounted on the right-hand side of the boot. The engine was mounted below the hood stowage box. For service, the engine could be accessed through a hatch from above, from below, or from the front through a cover in the cabin. The unpadded, power-operated fabric hood included a plastic rear window. With the vehicle stationary, it could be opened or closed in just 12 seconds. Latching or unlatching to the windscreen header was done manually. Even when lowered, the Z-folding hood kept its outside surface turned to the elements. When lowered, the rear of the hood was covered by an automatically-actuated metal lid. Two roll bars were firmly mounted behind the seats to protect the occupants in the event of a rollover. An optional wind blocker could be mounted between these; this consisted of two black plastic grilles which fit exactly into each roll bar, and a Plexiglas screen stretched between the roll bars. A 25kg (55lb) aluminium hardtop with electrically-heatable rear window was available as an option.

The Boxster was powered by a new, water-cooled generation of boxer engine. Ever more stringent exhaust and noise emissions standards made this step inevitable. Liquid cooling has the advantage of damping noise generated in the cylinders by the combustion process. Additionally, the introduction of multi-valve technology on high-performance engines offered exhaust quality benefits. Cylinder cooling was configured as crossflow cooling, so that all cylinders were exposed to the same coolant temperature. Two coolant radiators were mounted in the nose of the car ahead of the wheels. Displacement of the oversquare engine (stroke dimension less than bore) was 2480cc. Cylinder bore was 85.5mm, stroke was 72mm, with an 11.0:1 compression ratio. The cylinder running surfaces were created by the Lokasil process; its desired microscopically rough cylinder surface had certain properties which resulted in better oil film retention. Oil was supplied by an integral dry-sump lubrication system with a capacity of 8.75 litres, without a separate oil tank.

The two crankcase halves were made using a new 'squeeze casting' process, a special aluminium casting technique. The seven-bearing crankshaft was carried by an aluminium main bearing carrier, with embedded cast-iron inserts in the bearing areas. The connecting rods were 'cracked', i.e. the rod caps were deliberately broken off the finished rod along the desired parting line. The resulting fracture surfaces could be precisely matched and bolted together again during engine assembly. The exhaust camshafts were driven off the crankshaft by double chains and an intermediate shaft. The intake camshafts in turn were driven by simple chains from the exhaust shafts. Intake cam timing could be varied, independently of engine speed, by the VarioCam system. This reduced emissions and stabilized idle at low engine speeds, increased mid-range torque and produced more peak power at high engine speed. Hydraulic valve-lash adjustment was, of course, standard in the new 911 engine.

Engine management was handled by a Bosch Motronic M5.2. This controlled the sequential fuel injection system and six individual ignition coils of the distributorless ignition system. A two-stage resonance induction system modulated induced air mass in the intake tract in response to engine speed, providing improved cylinder filling and improved torque response.

The stainless steel exhaust system consisted of two independent exhaust streams, one per cylinder bank, each with its own metal catalyst and oxygen sensor. Exhaust gases passed through a shared silencer and out through a large oval tailpipe on the car's centre line.

The water-cooled boxer engine developed 204hp (150kW) at 6000rpm, and maximum torque of 345Nm (254 lb ft) was achieved at 4500rpm.

The five-speed manual transmission was actuated by a newly-developed cable gear change. A 240mm clutch disc was coupled to a dual-mass flywheel. As an option, customers could choose a new five-speed Tiptronic S transmission.

For the Boxster's front suspension, Porsche chose a MacPherson strut system with aluminium suspension links. A longitudinal link and transverse link were joined by means of an elastic rubber bushing. The strut assemblies, front crossmember, anti-roll bar and steering box formed a single unit.

Rear wheels were independently suspended by lateral and trailing links, toe control rods and MacPherson struts.

The brake system consisted of black-painted monobloc fixed callipers and ventilated discs, 298mm at the front and 292mm at the rear. For better heat transfer, the monobloc callipers were each machined from a solid billet. The Boxster took advantage of Bosch's continued development of the ABS 5.3 anti-lock brake system. For improved handling safety, traction control (TC) was available as an option; TC combined an automatic brake differential (ABD) and Acceleration Slip Regulation (ASR).

Stock wheels were 16-inch 'Boxster Design' rims, 6 inches wide at the front and carrying 205/55 ZR 16 tyres, 8 inches at the rear with 225/50 ZR 16 tyres. An optional sport suspension lowered the car by 10mm, and added newly designed 17-inch wheels, 7 J x 17 with 205/50 ZR 17 at the front and 8.5 J x 17 with 255/40 ZR 17 tyres at the rear.

Inside, too, the Boxster's shared parts concept anticipated the coming 911, although the Boxster instrument panel only held three round instruments. An analog tachometer was centrally located, its lower segment containing a digital speed read-out or on-board computer display. To the left of the tach was an analog speedometer with digital odometer display. To the right of the tach was a combination instrument with analog displays for coolant-temperature and fuel-tank level, as well as a digital clock and the new oil-level monitor, readable when the engine was shut off. On vehicles equipped with the Tiptronic S, the combi instrument also included an LED gear selection display. Brake and clutch pedals were mounted in a 'hanging' configuration. Driver and passenger airbags were standard. The Boxster had no glove compartment in the dashboard. As was typical Porsche practice, headrests were integrated in the seat-backs. The fabric- and leather-covered front seats were fitted with electric backrest rake adjustment, while lower cushion reach and height were manually adjustable. The steering wheel rim was axially adjustable over a 20mm range; the steering wheel, gear lever, handbrake handle and inner door handles were covered with black leather. Electric windows with automatic up/down function and electrically-adjustable and heatable outside mirrors were standard equipment. Air-conditioning was available as an option.

Fitted with a five-speed manual transmission, the Boxster accelerated from zero to 62mph (100kph) in just 6.9 seconds; the Tiptronic S version needed 7.6 seconds. Top speed for the manual was 149mph (240kph), and 146mph (235kph) for the Tiptronic S.

Model year 1998 (W Programme)

Porsche expanded its Boxster accessory programme. The Porsche Communication Management (PCM) system, with its large colour monitor display in the centre console, was available as an option. PCM served as an information and navigation system, encompassing a cassette radio, GSM hands-free telephone, GPS navigation system with separate CD-ROM drive and on-board computer. Another interesting option was Digital Sound Processing with an included sound package for the stereo systems, and a storage shelf on the engine lid.

For the first time, 30-litre (1.1cu ft) side airbags were available as an option, as the Porsche Side-Impact Protection System (POSIP). Integrated in the doors, these protected occupants' upper torso and head in the event of a side-impact. Their size and design also provided protection even with the hood down.

Also new was a three-spoke sports steering wheel with airbag, and two equipment packages: 'Sport Design' and 'Trend'. The 'Sport Design' package included black leather upholstery, sports seats and two-spoke leather-covered steering wheel. Matched to these were Metal Grey painted trim items and black lozenge-pattern surfaces. The 'Trend' package was available with either of two exterior colours, Zenith Blue Metallic or Ocean Jade Metallic. The hood was Graphite Grey in either case. Seats were covered with Graphite Grey and Anthracite 'Trend' fabric. Several trim details were also painted in the same colour as the body.

Model year 1999 (X Programme)

Fuel tank volume was increased from 60 litres to 64 litres (13 to 14 gallons), giving the Boxster greater cruising range.

A new addition to the Boxster line was the Boxster Classic Package, consisting of leather seats, metallic paint, amber-look interior components and Granite Grey interior trim panels. Two rotary control knobs represented an obvious change in the latest generation of Becker radios. Along with cassette or CD radios, choices included a minidisc radio and a six-disc CD changer.

18-inch turbo alloy wheels were now available for the Boxster. At the front, 7.5 J x 18 rims carried 225/40 ZR 18 tyres; at the rear, 9 J x 18 carried 265/35 ZR 18 rubber.

Model year 2000 (Y Programme)

In the autumn of 1999, Porsche presented the new pinnacle of the Boxster model line, the Boxster S, powered by a 3.2-litre engine. The base model was uprated with a 2.7-litre power unit offering more torque. Plastic interior parts were covered with black soft-finish coatings for a higher-quality surface feel. Seat centres were covered with Alcantara. Driver and passenger side airbags of the Porsche Side-Impact Protection System (POSIP) were standard equipment as of the 2000 model year. The steering wheel now had a 40mm axial adjustment range.

A new crankshaft with 78mm stroke increased Boxster engine displacement to 2687cc. The new power unit was teamed with the further developed Bosch M 7.2 digital engine-management system and a two-stage resonant induction system for improved torque. The revamped boxer engine produced 220hp (162kW) at 6400rpm. Even more important than the added 16hp was the noticeably greater torque at low engine speeds. Maximum torque of 260Nm (192lb ft) was produced at 4750rpm. Acceleration from standstill to 62mph (100kph) took 6.6 seconds with the manual transmission, or 7.4 seconds with the Tiptronic S. Top speed with the manual was 155mph (250kph), or 3mph (5kph) slower with Tiptronic S.

Visually, the top-of-the-line Boxster S differed from the 2.7-litre Boxster in only a few details. At the front, the Boxster S was recognizable by its grey air inlet grilles. An auxiliary radiator was mounted behind the centre air duct. 'Boxster S' script graced the door sills, and a matt-silver 'Boxster S' emblem adorned the rear lid. Two tailpipes poked through the centre of the rear valance.

The 3.2-litre Boxster S engine developed 252hp (185kW) at 6250rpm. The increase in displacement was achieved by a 93mm bore and 78mm stroke. Maximum torque of 305Nm (225lb ft) was reached at 4500rpm. Compression ratio was 11.0:1. Like the 2.7-litre engine, the S engine was equipped with advanced Bosch M 7.2 digital engine-management and a two-stage resonant induction system.

The standard version of this car was a six-speed manual transmission coupled to a dual-mass flywheel, but a five-speed Tiptronic S was also available as an option.

The Boxster S suspension had more sports-oriented tuning. The package included 17-inch light alloy 'Boxster S Design' wheels, 7 inches at the front with 205/50 ZR 17 tyres, and 255/40 ZR 17 at the rear on 8.5-inch wheels. The brake system included ventilated, cross-drilled discs and red four-piston monobloc callipers.

The Boxster S hood was fitted with a headliner. Variable interval windscreen wipers and remote radio-operated alarm system with interior monitoring were standard equipment on the Boxster S.

The manual gear-change Boxster S sprinted to 62mph (100kph) in 5.9 seconds; the Tiptronic S transmission added another 0.6 seconds. Power and drag finally balanced each other at a top speed of 162mph (260kph) with the manual, or 158mph (255kph) with the Tiptronic S.

Model year 2001 (1 Programme)

Both Boxster and Boxster S engines were equipped with Motronic ME 7.2 and an electronic throttle pedal ('throttle by wire'), also known as 'E Gas'. This was necessitated by the migration of Porsche Stability Management (PSM) from the 911 to the Boxster line, with its ABS, ASR and ABD vehicle-stabilization systems. Only an electronically-modulated throttle, actuated by E Gas, enabled these systems to react in a fraction of a second.

Model development resulted in a padded interior headliner under the fabric hood, for improved comfort and a quieter ride.

Model year 2002 (2 Programme)

The 2002 model year saw no significant changes. Porsche's Exclusive Department offered nearly every conceivable means for individualizing the Boxster. Customers could order nearly any exterior colour they desired, as well as 17-inch and 18-inch wheels in a variety of designs. Several different interior and exterior equipment packages were available.

Model year 2003 (3 Programme)

For the 2003 model year, the entire model line benefited from a thorough facelift. The bodywork treatment included a new nose and tail, reshaped side air-inlets with body-colour grilles and a modified rear spoiler. All indicators were now mounted behind quartz-coloured lenses. Even the tailpipes of all Boxster models were redesigned. The aerodynamic drag coefficient (cd) was about 0.31. The Boxster S had an additional duct in its nose for an auxiliary radiator, which raised cd to 0.32.

Both Boxster engines were slightly reworked and tuned for the new Motronic ME 7.8. The power of the base engine rose to 228hp (168kW) at

Phantom view of a Type 986 Boxster

6300rpm; Peak torque was 260Nm (192lb ft) at 4600rpm. Road performance of both models improved only slightly.

The Boxster hood underwent a basic revamping. Closed, its more rounded contours resembled those of the optional hardtop. The rear window was now made of safety glass and could be heated for better visibility in rainy and wintry conditions. Inside, changes included a three-spoke steering wheel and restyled instruments taken from the 911 Carrera.

The analog speedometer ranged to 300kph (186mph); a digital speed display was integrated in the same instrument. The combination instrument on the right included a digital clock. Instrument lettering was still the typical rounded Boxster script.

Readily apparent changes in the reworked interior included a locking glovebox on the passenger side, opening downward below the dashboard. Also new were two integrated cupholders which could be extended from below the centre air ducts. Porsche introduced the next radio generation on the Boxster, ranging from a simple two-speaker CD radio to a digital sound package or CD changer, all the way up to the Porsche Communication Management system with its Bose sound system.

Model year 2004 (4 Programme)

Porsche celebrated the 50th anniversary of the 550 Spyder with a special edition '50 Years of the 550 Spyder' model, limited to 1953 examples. This was available in only one colour – GT Silver Metallic, previously offered only on the Carrera GT and the '40th anniversary 911'. Rear grilles were painted silver. Chromium 'Boxster S' script was affixed to the tail. A special dark brown interior colour, 'Cocoa', was also reserved exclusively for this model. The convertible top was available in 'Cocoa' or black.

Power output of the 3.2-litre engine was raised by 6hp to 266hp (196kW) at 6200rpm; maximum torque of 310Nm (229lb ft) was available at 4600rpm. The specially-styled tailpipe provided the typically Porsche sound. Standard transmission was a six-speed manual with 15 per cent shorter gear-change travel. A Tiptronic S transmission with gear-change buttons on the steering wheel was available as an option. The sports-tuned suspension was lowered by 10mm. Porsche Stability Management (PSM) was standard issue. The aluminium monobloc brake callipers of the special edition were painted aluminium colour. Centres of the 18-inch Carrera wheels were painted Seal Grey. Coloured Porsche crests decorated the wheel centre-caps, and between wheels and hubs were 5mm-wide spacers.

Inside, dark grey natural leather was available as an alternative to 'Cocoa' (with black carpets and hood). The centres of the heated sports seats, the steering wheel rim, gear lever, handbrake handle and interior door handles were covered with a specially-embossed leather. The ball gear-lever knob design combined leather and aluminium. Instruments were rimmed by chromium bezels. The seat-back shells, rear centre console, handbrake handle, dashboard deco strip, instrument panel and backs of the roll bars were painted GT Silver Metallic for contrast. Brightly polished 'Boxster S' script graced the black door sills.

A plaque with the sequential number of the special edition was attached to the centre console. Standard equipment included automatic climate-control, a CDR 23 radio with sound package, on-board computer, wind blocker and Litronic headlamps with dynamic beam-adjustment and a headlamp-cleaning system.

Top speed with the six-speed manual transmission was 165mph (266kph); the Tiptronic S reached 162mph (260kph). With manual gearbox the sprint to 62mph (100kph) took 5.7 seconds, while the Tiptronic S needed 6.4 seconds.

986 Boxster [Tiptronic S]
MY 1997–MY 1999

Engine

Engine design:	6-cylinder horizontally-opposed
Installation:	Mid-engine
Cooling system:	Water-cooled
Engine type:	M 96/20
Displacement (cc):	2480
Bore x stroke (mm):	85.5 x 72
Engine output DIN (kW/hp):	150/204 at 6000rpm
Maximum torque (Nm/lb ft):	245/181 at 4500rpm
Output per litre (kW/l / hp/l):	60.5 / 82.3
Compression ratio:	11.0 : 1
Valve operation & camshaft drive:	dohc, cams driven by double chain, 4 valves per cylinder, VarioCam
Carburation:	Bosch DME, Motronic M 5.2
Ignition system:	DME, distributorless ignition system with six individual ignition coils
Firing order:	1 - 6 - 2 - 4 - 3 - 5
Engine lubrication:	Integrated dry oil sump
Engine oil total (l):	8.75

Transmission

Drive configuration:	Rear-axle drive
Manual gearbox:	5-speed
Option Tiptronic S:	[5-speed]
Transmission type:	G 86/00 [A 86/00]
Transmission ratios:	
1st gear:	3.50 [3.67]
2nd gear:	2.12 [2.00]
3rd gear:	1.43 [1.41]
4th gear:	1.03 [1.00]
5th gear:	0.79 [0.74]
Reverse gear:	3.44 [4.10]
Drive ratio:	3.89 [4.21]

Body, chassis, suspension, brakes, wheels

Body design:	Steel roadster body, 2 doors, 2 seats, entirely hot-dip galvanized body, side-impact protection beams in doors, flexible polyurethane front and rear bumpers with integrated aluminium beams, automatic rear spoiler, electric hood with flexible plastic rear window, two fixed roll bars
Option:	Aluminium hardtop with electrically-heatable rear window
Suspension, front:	Individually suspended, McPherson struts with aluminium suspension links, longitudinal and transverse link, coil springs, dual-tube gas-filled shock absorbers, anti-roll bar
Suspension, rear:	Individually suspended, McPherson struts with aluminium suspension links, lateral and trailing links, coil springs, dual-tube gas-filled shock absorbers, anti-roll bar

Brakes, front/rear (Size (mm)):	Ventilated discs (298 x 24) / Ventilated discs (292 x 20) Black 4-piston fixed aluminium monobloc callipers / Black 4-piston fixed aluminium monobloc callipers Bosch ABS 5.3
Wheels, front/rear:	6 J x 16 / 7 J x 16
Tyres, front/rear:	205/55 ZR 16 / 225/50 ZR 16
Option:	7 J x 17 / 8.5 J x 17 205/50 ZR 17 / 255/40 ZR 17
Option MY 1999:	7.5 J x 18 / 9 J x 18 225/40 ZR 18 / 265/35 ZR 18

Electrical system

Alternator (W/A):	1680 / 120
Battery (V/Ah):	12 / 60 [12 / 70]

Dimensions and weight

Track, front/rear (mm):	1465 / 1528
7 J x 17 / 8.5 J x 17:	1455 / 1508
7.5 J x 18 / 9 J x 18:	1465 / 1504
Wheelbase (mm):	2415
Length x width x height (mm):	4315 x 1780 x 1290
Kerb weight (kg):	1250 [1300]
Permissible gross weight (kg):	1560 [1610]
Luggage com. front/rear (VDA (l)):	130 / 130
Fuel tank capacity (l):	60, including 9 reserve
MY 1999:	64, including 9 reserve
C_w x A (m²):	0.31 x 1.93 = 0.598
Power/weight ratio (kg/kW/ kg/hp):	8.33 [8.66] / 6.12 [6.37]

Fuel consumption

ECE (mpg)	98 RON super plus unleaded
At constant 56mph/90kph:	44.9 [42.2]
At constant 74mph/120kph:	34.8 [33.5]
Urban cycle:	23.3 [21.7]
1/3 mix:	31.6 [30]
EWG (mpg)	
Urban:	19.7 [17.9]
Extra urban:	39.7 [34.8]
Combined:	29.1 [25.8]
CO_2-emissions (g/km):	239 [263]

Performance, production, prices

Acceleration 0-62mph/100kph (s):	6.9 [7.6]
0-100mph/160kph (s):	16.5 [18.9]
Maximum speed (mph / kph):	149 / 240 [146 / 235]
Production, total number:	55,705
Purchase prices:	
08/1996:	DM 76,500 [DM 81,400]
08/1997:	DM 78,030 [DM 83,030]
08/1998:	DM 79,210 [DM 84,250]

986 Boxster [Tiptronic S]
MY 2000–MY 2002

Engine

Engine design:	6-cylinder horizontally-opposed
Installation:	Mid-engine
Cooling system:	Water-cooled
Engine type:	M 96/22
Displacement (cc):	2687
Bore x stroke (mm):	85.5 x 78
Engine output DIN (kW/hp):	162/220 at 6400rpm
Maximum torque (Nm/lb ft):	260/192 at 4750rpm
Output per litre (kW/l / hp/l):	60.3 / 81.9
Compression ratio:	11.0 : 1
Valve operation & camshaft drive:	dohc, cams driven by double chain, 4 valves per cylinder, VarioCam
Carburation:	Bosch DME, Motronic M 7.2
MY 2001–MY 2002:	Bosch DME, Motronic ME 7.2
Ignition system:	DME, distributorless ignition system with six individual ignition coils
Firing order:	1 - 6 - 2 - 4 - 3 - 5
Engine lubrication:	Integrated dry sump
Engine oil total (l):	8.75

Transmission

Drive configuration:	Rear-axle drive
Manual gearbox:	5-speed
Option Tiptronic S:	[5-speed]
Transmission type:	G 86/01 [A 86/01]
Transmission ratios:	
1st gear:	3.50 [3.66]
2nd gear:	2.12 [2.00]
3rd gear:	1.43 [1.41]
4th gear:	1.09 [1.00]
5th gear:	0.84 [0.74]
Reverse gear:	3.44 [4.10]
Drive ratio:	3.56 [4.02]

Body, chassis, suspension, brakes, wheels

Body design:	Steel roadster body, 2 doors, 2 seats, entirely hot-dip galvanized body, side-impact protection beams in doors, flexible polyurethane front and rear bumpers with integrated aluminium beams, automatic rear spoiler, electric hood with flexible plastic rear window, two fixed roll bars
Option:	Aluminium hardtop with electrically-heatable rear window
Suspension, front:	Individually suspended, McPherson struts with aluminium suspension links, longitudinal and transverse link, coil springs, dual-tube gas-filled shock absorbers, anti-roll bar
Suspension, rear:	Individually suspended, McPherson struts with aluminium suspension links, lateral and trailing links, coil springs, dual-tube gas-filled shock absorbers, anti-roll bar
Brakes, front/rear (Size (mm)):	Ventilated discs (298 x 24) / Ventilated discs (292 x 20) Black 4-piston fixed aluminium monobloc callipers / Black 4-piston fixed aluminium monobloc callipers Bosch ABS 5.3
Wheels, front/rear:	6 J x 16 / 7 J x 16
Tyres, front/rear:	205/55 ZR 16 / 225/50 ZR 16
Option:	7 J x 17 / 8.5 J x 17
	205/50 ZR 17 / 255/40 ZR 17
Option:	7.5 J x 18 / 9 J x 18
	225/40 ZR 18 / 265/35 ZR 18

Electrical system

Alternator (W/A):	1680 / 120
Battery (V/Ah):	12 / 60 [12 / 70]

Dimensions and weight

Track, front/rear (mm):	1465 / 1528
7 J x 17 / 8.5 J x 17:	1455 / 1508
7.5 J x 18 / 9 J x 18:	1465 / 1504
Wheelbase (mm):	2415
Length x width x height (mm):	4315 x 1780 x 1290
Kerb weight DIN (kg):	1260 [1310]
Permissible gross weight (kg):	1570 [1620]
Luggage com. front/rear (VDA (l)):	130 / 130
Fuel tank capacity (l):	64, including 9 reserve
C_w x A (m²):	0.31 x 1.93 = 0.598
Power/weight ratio (kg/kW / kg/hp):	7.77 [8.08] / 5.72 [5.95]

Fuel consumption

93/116/EG (mpg):	98 RON super plus unleaded
Urban:	19.3 [17.8]
Extra urban:	38 [35]
Combined:	28.4 [25.8]
CO_2-emissions (g/km):	245 [250]

Performance, production, prices

Acceleration 0-62mph/100kph (s):	6.6 [7.4]
0-100mph/160kph (s):	15.9 [17.4]
Maximum speed (mph / kph):	155 / 250 [152 / 245]
Production, total number:	27,990
plus Boxster/Boxster S Valmet*:	23,294

*not possible to assign if Boxster or Boxster S

Purchase prices:

08/1999:	DM 80,790 [DM 85,830]
08/2000:	DM 80,790 [DM 85,830]
08/2001:	DM 82,356 [DM 87,393]

986 Boxster S [Tiptronic S]
MY 2000–MY 2002

Engine
Engine design:	6-cylinder horizontally-opposed
Installation:	Mid-engine
Cooling system:	Water-cooled
Engine type:	M 96/21
Displacement (cc):	3179
Bore x stroke (mm):	93 x 78
Engine output DIN (kW/PS):	185/252 at 6250rpm
Maximum torque (Nm/lb ft):	305/225 at 4500rpm
Output per litre (kW/l / hp/l):	58.2 / 79.3
Compression ratio:	11.0 : 1
Valve operation & camshaft drive:	dohc, cams driven by double chain, 4 valves per cylinder, VarioCam
Carburation:	Bosch DME, Motronic M 7.2
MY 2001–MY 2002:	Bosch DME, Motronic ME 7.2
Ignition system:	DME, distributorless ignition system with six individual ignition coils
Firing order:	1 - 6 - 2 - 4 - 3 - 5
Engine lubrication:	Integrated dry oil sump
Engine oil total (l):	8.75

Transmission
Drive configuration:	Rear-axle drive
Manual gearbox:	6-speed
Option Tiptronic S:	[5-speed]
Transmission type:	G 86/20 [A 86/20]
Transmission ratios:	
1st gear:	3.82 [3.66]
2nd gear:	2.20 [2.00]
3rd gear:	1.52 [1.41]
4th gear:	1.22 [1.00]
5th gear:	1.02 [0.74]
6th gear:	0.84
Reverse gear:	3.55 [4.10]
Drive ratio:	3.44 [3.73]

Body, chassis, suspension, brakes, wheels
Body design:	Steel roadster body, 2 doors, 2 seats, entirely hot-dip galvanized body, side-impact protection beams in doors, flexible polyurethane front and rear bumpers with integrated aluminium beams, automatic rear spoiler, electric hood with flexible plastic rear window, two fixed roll bars
Option:	Aluminium hardtop with electrically-heatable rear window
Suspension, front:	Individually suspended, McPherson struts with aluminium suspension links, longitudinal and transverse link, coil springs, dual-tube gas-filled shock absorbers, anti-roll bar

Suspension, rear:	Individually suspended, McPherson struts with aluminium suspension links, lateral and trailing links, coil springs, dual-tube gas-filled shock absorbers, anti-roll bar
Brakes, front/rear (Size (mm)):	Ventilated discs (318 x 28) / Ventilated discs (299 x 24) Red 4-piston fixed aluminium monobloc callipers / Red 4-piston fixed aluminium monobloc callipers Bosch ABS 5.3
Wheels, front/rear:	7 J x 17 / 8.5 J x 17
Tyres, front/rear:	205/50 ZR 17 / 255/40 ZR 17
Option:	7.5 J x 18 / 9 J x 18 225/40 ZR 18 / 265/35 ZR 18

Electrical system
Alternator (W/A):	1680 / 120
Battery (V/Ah):	12 / 60 [12 / 70]

Dimensions and weight
Track, front/rear (mm):	1455 / 1508
7.5 J x 18 / 9 J x 18:	1465 / 1508
Wheelbase (mm):	2415
Length x width x height (mm):	4315 x 1780 x 1290
Kerb weight DIN (kg):	1295 [1335]
Permissible gross weight (kg):	1615 [1655]
Luggage com. front/rear (VDA (l)):	130 / 130
Fuel tank capacity (l):	64, including 9 reserve
C_w x A (m²):	0.32 x 1.93 = 0.617
Power/weight ratio (kg/kW/kg/hp):	7.00 [7.21] / 5.13 [5.29]

Fuel consumption
93/116/EG (mpg):	98 RON super plus unleaded
Urban:	18 [16.4]
Extra urban:	35 [34.4]
Combined:	26.4 [25]
CO_2-emissions (g/km):	265 [280]

Performance, production, prices
Acceleration 0-62mph/100kph (s):	5.9 [6.5]
0-100mph/160kph (s):	13.8 [15.1]
Maximum speed (mph / kph):	162 / 260 [158 / 255]
Production, total number:	23,651
plus Boxster/Boxster S Valmet*:	23,294

*not possible to assign if Boxster or Boxster S

Purchase prices:	
08/1999:	DM 94,900 [DM 99,940]
08/2000:	DM 94,900 [DM 99,940]
08/2001:	DM 97,330 [DM 102,367]

986 Boxster [Tiptronic S]
MY 2003–MY 2005

Engine

Engine design:	6-cylinder horizontally-opposed
Installation:	Mid-engine
Cooling system:	Water-cooled
Engine type:	M 96/23
Displacement (cc):	2687
Bore x stroke (mm):	85.5 x 78
Engine output DIN (kW/hp):	168/228 at 6300rpm
Maximum torque (Nm/lb ft):	260/192 at 4700rpm
Output per litre (kW/l / hp/l):	62.5 / 84.9
Compression ratio:	11.0 : 1
Valve operation & camshaft drive:	dohc, cams driven by double chain, 4 valves per cylinder, VarioCam
Carburation:	Bosch DME, Motronic ME 7.8
Ignition system:	DME, distributorless ignition system with six individual ignition coils
Firing order:	1 - 6 - 2 - 4 - 3 - 5
Engine lubrication:	Integrated dry sump
Engine oil total (l):	8.75

Transmission

Drive configuration:	Rear-axle drive
Manual gearbox:	5-speed
Option Tiptronic S:	[5-speed]
Transmission type:	G 86/01 [A 86/01]
Transmission ratios:	
1st gear:	3.50 [3.66]
2nd gear:	2.12 [2.00]
3rd gear:	1.43 [1.41]
4th gear:	1.09 [1.00]
5th gear:	0.84 [0.74]
Reverse gear:	3.44 [4.10]
Drive ratio:	3.56 [3.33]

Body, chassis, suspension, brakes, wheels

Body design:	Steel roadster body, 2 doors, 2 seats, entirely hot-dip galvanized body, side-impact protection beams in doors, flexible polyurethane front and rear bumpers with integrated aluminium beams, automatic rear spoiler, electric hood with electrically-heatable rear window, two fixed roll bars
Option:	Aluminium hardtop with electrically-heatable rear window
Suspension, front:	Individually suspended, McPherson struts with aluminium suspension links, longitudinal and transverse link, coil springs, dual-tube gas-filled shock absorbers, anti-roll bar
Suspension, rear:	Individually suspended, McPherson struts with aluminium suspension links, lateral and trailing links, coil springs, dual-tube gas-filled shock absorbers, anti-roll bar
Brakes, front/rear (Size (mm)):	Ventilated discs (298 x 24) / Ventilated discs (292 x 20) Black 4-piston fixed aluminium monobloc callipers / Black 4-piston fixed aluminium monobloc callipers Bosch ABS 5.7
Wheels, front/rear:	6 J x 16 / 7 J x 16
Tyres, front/rear:	205/55 ZR 16 / 225/50 ZR 16
Option:	7 J x 17 / 8.5 J x 17 205/50 ZR 17 / 255/40 ZR 17
Option:	7.5 J x 18 / 9 J x 18 225/40 ZR 18 / 265/35 ZR 18

Electrical system

Alternator (W/A):	1680 / 120
Battery (V/Ah):	12 / 60 [12 / 70]

Dimensions and weight

Track, front/rear (mm):	1465 / 1528
7 J x 17 / 8.5 J x 17:	1455 / 1514
Wheelbase (mm):	2415
Length x width x height (mm):	4320 x 1780 x 1290
Kerb weight DIN (kg):	1275 [1330]
Permissible gross weight (kg):	1600 [1655]
Luggage com. front/rear (VDA (l)):	130 / 130
Fuel tank capacity (l):	64, including 9 reserve
C_w x A (m^2):	0.31 x 1.93 = 0.598
Power/weight ratio (kg/kW/kg/hp):	7.58 [7.91] / 5.59 [5.83]

Fuel consumption

1999/100/EG (mpg):	98 RON super plus unleaded
Urban:	19.9 [18.5]
Extra urban:	39.7 [35.6]
Combined:	29.1 [26.4]
CO_2-emissions (g/km):	233 [259]

Performance, production, prices

Acceleration 0-62mph/100kph (s):	6.4 [7.3]
0-100mph/160kph (s):	15.0 [17.2]
Maximum speed (mph / kph):	157 / 253 [154 / 248]
Production, total number:	
Purchase prices:	
08/2002:	Euro 42,108 [Euro 44,683]
04/2003:	Euro 42,912 [Euro 44,831]

295

986 Boxster S [Tiptronic S]
MY 2003–MY 2005

Engine

Engine design:	6-cylinder horizontally-opposed
Installation:	Mid-engine
Cooling system:	Water-cooled
Engine type:	M 96/24
Displacement (cc):	3179
Bore x stroke (mm):	93 x 78
Engine output DIN (kW/PS):	191/260 at 6200rpm
Maximum torque (Nm/lb ft):	310/229 at 4600rpm
Output per litre (kW/l / hp/l):	60.1 / 81.8
Compression ratio:	11.0 : 1
Valve operation & camshaft drive:	dohc, cams driven by double chain, 4 valves per cylinder, VarioCam
Carburation:	Bosch DME, Motronic ME 7.8
Ignition system:	DME, distributorless ignition system with six individual ignition coils
Firing order:	1 - 6 - 2 - 4 - 3 - 5
Engine lubrication:	Integrated dry sump
Engine oil total (l):	8.75

Transmission

Drive configuration:	Rear-axle drive
Manual gearbox:	6-speed
Option Tiptronic S:	[5-speed]
Transmission type:	G 86/20 [A 86/20]
Transmission ratios:	
1st gear:	3.82 [3.66]
2nd gear:	2.20 [2.00]
3rd gear:	1.52 [1.41]
4th gear:	1.22 [1.00]
5th gear:	1.02 [0.74]
6th gear:	0.84
Reverse gear:	3.55 [4.10]
Drive ratio:	3.44 [3.09]

Body, chassis, suspension, brakes, wheels

Body design:	Steel roadster body, 2 doors, 2 seats, entirely hot-dip galvanized body, side-impact protection beams in doors, flexible polyurethane front and rear bumpers with integrated aluminium beams, automatic rear spoiler, electric hood with electrically-heatable rear window, two fixed roll bars
Option:	Aluminium hardtop with electrically-heatable rear window
Suspension, front:	Individually suspended, McPherson struts with aluminium suspension links,
Suspension, rear:	longitudinal and transverse link, coil springs, dual-tube gas-filled shock absorbers, anti-roll bar Individually suspended, McPherson struts with aluminium suspension links, lateral and trailing links, coil springs, dual-tube gas-filled shock absorbers, anti-roll bar
Brakes, front/rear (Size (mm)):	Ventilated discs (318 x 28) / Ventilated discs (299 x 24) Red 4-piston fixed aluminium monobloc callipers / Red 4-piston fixed aluminium monobloc callipers Bosch ABS 5.7
Wheels, front/rear:	7 J x 17 / 8.5 J x 17
Tyres, front/rear:	205/50 ZR 17 / 255/40 ZR 17
Option:	7.5 J x 18 / 9 J x 18 225/40 ZR 18 / 265/35 ZR 18

Electrical system

Alternator (W/A):	1680 / 120
Battery (V/Ah):	12 / 60 [12 / 70]

Dimensions and weight

Track, front/rear (mm):	1455 / 1514
Wheelbase (mm):	2415
Length x width x height (mm):	4320 x 1780 x 1290
Kerb weight DIN (kg):	1320 [1360]
Permissible gross weight (kg):	1630 [1670]
Luggage com. front/rear (VDA (l)):	130 / 130
Fuel tank capacity (l):	64, including 9 reserve
C_w x A (m²):	0.32 x 1.93 = 0.617
Power/weight ratio (kg/kW/ kg/hp):	6.91 [7.12] / 5.07 [5.23]

Fuel consumption

1999/100/EG (mpg):	98 RON super plus unleaded
Urban:	18.5 [17.2]
Extra urban:	36.25 [35]
Combined:	26.8 [25.4]
CO_2-emissions (g/km):	255 [268]

Performance, production, prices

Acceleration 0-62mph/100kph (s):	5.7 [6.4]
0-100mph/160kph (s):	13.2 [14.9]
Maximum speed (mph / kph):	164 / 264 [160 / 258]
Production, total number:	
Purchase prices:	
08/2002:	Euro 49,764 [Euro 52,339]
04/2003:	Euro 49,912 [Euro 52,487]

986 Boxster S '50 Years 550 Spyder' [Tiptronic S] MY 2004–MY 2005

Engine

Engine design:	6-cylinder horizontally-opposed
Installation:	Mid-engine
Cooling system:	Water-cooled
Engine type:	M 96/24
Displacement (cc):	3179
Bore x stroke (mm):	93 x 78
Engine output DIN (kW/PS):	196/266 at 6200rpm
Maximum torque (Nm/lb ft):	310/229 at 4600rpm
Output per litre (kW/l / hp/l):	61.7 / 83.7
Compression ratio:	11.0 : 1
Valve operation & camshaft drive:	dohc, cams driven by double chain, 4 valves per cylinder, VarioCam
Carburation:	Bosch DME, Motronic ME 7.8
Ignition system:	DME, distributorless ignition system with six individual ignition coils
Firing order:	1 - 6 - 2 - 4 - 3 - 5
Engine lubrication:	Integrated dry sump
Engine oil total (l):	8.75

Transmission

Drive configuration:	Rear-axle drive
Manual gearbox:	6-speed
Option Tiptronic S:	[5-speed]
Transmission type:	G 86/20 [A 86/20]
Transmission ratios:	
1st gear:	3.82 [3.66]
2nd gear:	2.20 [2.00]
3rd gear:	1.52 [1.41]
4th gear:	1.22 [1.00]
5th gear:	1.02 [0.74]
6th gear:	0.84
Reverse gear:	3.55 [4.10]
Drive ratio:	3.44 [3.09]

Body, chassis, suspension, brakes, wheels

Body design:	Steel roadster body, 2 doors, 2 seats, entirely hot-dip galvanized body, side-impact protection beams in doors, flexible polyurethane front and rear bumpers with integrated aluminium beams, automatic rear spoiler, electric hood with electrically-heatable rear window, two fixed roll bars
Exclusive colour:	GT Silver Metallic
Option:	Aluminium hardtop with electrically-heatable rear window

Suspension, front:	Individually suspended, McPherson struts with aluminium suspension links, longitudinal and transverse link, coil springs, dual-tube gas-filled shock absorbers, anti-roll bar
Suspension, rear:	Individually suspended, McPherson struts with aluminium suspension links, lateral and trailing links, coil springs, dual-tube gas-filled shock absorbers, anti-roll bar
Brakes, front/rear (Size (mm)):	Ventilated discs (318 x 28) / Ventilated discs (299 x 24) Red 4-piston fixed aluminium monobloc callipers / Red 4-piston fixed aluminium monobloc callipers Bosch ABS 5.7
Wheels, front/rear:	7.5 J x 18* / 9 J x 18*
Tyres, front/rear:	225/40 ZR 18 / 265/35 ZR 18
*5 mm spacers	

Electrical system

Alternator (W/A):	1680 / 120
Battery (V/Ah):	12 / 60 [12 / 70]

Dimensions and weight

Track, front/rear (mm):	1455 / 1514
Wheelbase (mm):	2415
Length x width x height (mm):	4320 x 1780 x 1290
Kerb weight DIN (kg):	1320 [1360]
Permissible gross weight (kg):	1630 [1670]
Luggage com. front/rear (VDA (l)):	130 / 130
Fuel tank capacity (l):	64, including 9 reserve
C_w x A (m²):	0.32 x 1.93 = 0.617
Power/weight ratio (kg/kW/kg/hp):	6.73 [6.93] / 4.96 [5.11]

Fuel consumption

1999/100/EG (mpg):	98 RON super plus unleaded
Urban:	18.5 [17.2]
Extra urban:	36.25 [35]
Combined:	26.8 [25.4]
CO_2-emissions (g/km):	255 [268]

Performance, production, prices

Acceleration 0-62mph/100kph (s):	5.7 [6.4]
0-100mph/160kph (s):	13.2 [14.9]
Maximum speed (mph / kph):	165 / 266 [162 / 260]
Production, total number:	Limited on 1,953
Purchase prices:	
11/2003:	Euro 59,192 [Euro 61,767]

Porsche Cayenne

With the Porsche Cayenne, the Stuttgart sports car maker ventured forth, literally, into unexplored territory. This fully-off-road-capable vehicle staked Porsche's claim in the steadily growing sports utility vehicle (SUV) market segment.

Model year 2003 (3 Programme)

The 'third Porsche', as the company called its new vehicle in advertising campaigns, entered the market in the autumn of 2002. From the very beginning two versions were available: the Cayenne S and Cayenne turbo.

The SUV unit body of the Porsche Cayenne was made of two-side hot-dip galvanized steel. It was approximately 4.80 metres (15.75ft) long, nearly 2 metres (6.5ft) wide and 1.7 meters (5.5ft) tall. The design of its front 'face' emphasized a family resemblance to the 911. Four large doors allowed passengers easy access to five seats. The wide-opening rear hatch could swallow up to 540 litres (19cu ft) of cargo; folding down the rear seats increased this to 1770 litres (62.5cu ft). The front and rear valances consisted largely of flexible plastic. The Cayenne turbo was recognizable from the front by its larger air inlets and the two power domes on the engine hood, as well as bi-xenon headlights with dynamically-controlled static sidelights. At the rear, exhaust escaped through a pair of twin tailpipes. The Cayenne S, by contrast, had only two single exhausts. A roof-rail system was standard equipment on both models, black on the Cayenne S, silver on the Cayenne turbo.

Under the bonnet of both models was a water-cooled V8 engine displacing 4511cc, topped by four-valve cylinder heads. With a 93mm bore and 83mm stroke, the engine enjoyed a performance-oriented, oversquare layout. Both engines were equipped with hydraulic valve-lash adjusters, VarioCam variable valve-timing, and a high-performance Motronic ME 7.1.1

Phantom view of a Cayenne turbo

Cayenne turbo 4.5-litre V8 twin-turbocharged engine

engine management system. Additionally, the normally-aspirated Cayenne S engine, with 11.5:1 compression ratio, employed a resonant induction system. Power output was 340hp (250kW) at 6000rpm, with 420Nm (310lb ft) of torque available in a broad swath from 2500rpm to 5500rpm. With a compression of 9.5:1, the Cayenne turbo engine was fed by two turbochargers operating in parallel. Its output was 450hp (331kW) at 6000rpm; the driver could call on 620Nm (457lb ft) of torque between 2250rpm and 4750 rpm.

Both models were delivered with a six-speed Tiptronic transmission. A six-speed manual was under development for the Cayenne S, to be available no sooner than the end of 2003. The Cayenne drive system was dubbed 'Porsche Traction Management' (PTM). Permanent all-wheel drive, with a torque split of 38 per cent front and 62 per cent rear, was combined with an electronically-controlled locking centre differential, reduction gearbox ('low range') and automatic brake differential (ABD) for even more refinement.

Standard equipment included Porsche Stability Management (PSM), an electronic control system to stabilize the vehicle at the handling limit for improved safety. ABS was part of PSM.

At the front, wheels were suspended by wide-based aluminium and steel upper and lower A-arms. At the rear, a multi-link suspension employed steel and aluminium links. Both ends of the Cayenne S employed coil springs over tubular shock absorbers. Ground clearance at the vehicle centre line was 217mm (8.5in). As an option, the Cayenne S could be ordered with load-levelling, height-adjustable air suspension (a standard feature on the Cayenne turbo), with six selectable ride heights: Loading Level, 157mm (6.2in); Special Low Level, 179mm (7.0in); Low, 190mm (7.5in); Normal, 217mm (8.5in); Off-Road, 243mm (9.6in); and Special Off-Road Level, 273mm (10.7in). When fording streams, the all-important wading depth for the Cayenne S with steel springs was 500mm (20in) and with air suspension set at Special Off-Road, as much as 555mm (22in).

At the front, six-piston aluminium monobloc fixed callipers clamped 350mm ventilated discs. At the rear, four-piston aluminium monobloc fixed callipers were mounted over 330mm discs. Cross-drilled discs were deliberately ruled out because of off-road considerations. Cayenne S callipers were titanium-coloured, while the turbo had red callipers. Both models rolled on 8 J x 18 wheels with 255/55 R18 tyres, with different wheel designs.

The Cayenne interior recalled the classic Porsche design line, with its use of metal-look or aluminium-and-leather high-tech. As is customary at Porsche, the ignition lock was located to the left of the steering column. Between the two large round gauges (tachometer on the left, speedometer on the right), a multi-function display took centre stage. On the turbo, this took the form of a 5-inch colour monitor. The centre console was wide enough to mount the 6.5-inch, 16:9 aspect ratio colour display for the Porsche Communication Management (PCM) system. PCM was standard on the Cayenne turbo, optional on the Cayenne S. It combined navigation, radio and optional telephone functions. Standard equipment included leather interior, four electric windows, automatic climate-control, on-board computer and radio. The turbo added front and rear heated seats, power steering wheel adjustment and heated steering wheel, park assist, PCM with Bose sound system, bi-xenon headlamps, smooth leather, comfort seat package with power adjusts and memory, Alcantara headliner and aluminium trim.

Performance of the Cayenne S left nothing to be desired. With the Tiptronic S, it could accelerate to 62mph (100kph) in 7.2 seconds. Top speed was measured at 150mph (242kph). The Cayenne turbo topped out at 165mph (266 kph), with 0-62mph (100kph) in 5.6 seconds, making it the fastest production SUV of its time.

Model year 2004 (4 Programme)

Porsche expanded the Cayenne line to include an entry-level model, powered by a six-cylinder engine. With three variants – Cayenne, Cayenne S and Cayenne turbo, the model line was quite complete.

The new base model was powered by a longitudinally-mounted, normally-aspirated 24-valve V6 engine, displacing 3189cc, with an 11.5:1 compression ratio. This produced 250hp (184kW) at 6000rpm, with maximum torque of 310Nm (229lb ft) available between 2500rpm and 5500rpm. In contrast to the two V8 engines, the V6 power unit, with an 84mm bore and 95.9mm stroke, was decidedly undersquare. The reason for this was that components of the V6 engine were adopted from Volkswagen's 3.2-litre engine. Porsche, however, did expend considerable engineering effort on the six-cylinder, adding continuous variable valve-timing for both intake and exhaust camshafts, two-stage resonant induction system, electronic throttle pedal and Motronic ME 7.1.1.

At the time of its market introduction, the only available transmission for the V6 Cayenne was the six-speed Tiptronic S. The six-speed manual became available as of early 2004.

Body and chassis of the Cayenne were largely identical to those of the Cayenne S. The Cayenne employed a steel-spring suspension, with air suspension available as an option. Standard wheels were 7.5 J x 17, carrying 235/65 R 17 tyres. Front brake discs were 330mm in diameter and 32mm thick, somewhat smaller than those of the V8 models. Brake callipers were painted black.

Inside, the Cayenne differed from the Cayenne S in only a few details. Black instrument bezels and gear lever surround replaced silver, and the climate-control system was manually controlled instead of the automatic system of the Cayenne S. Tuft velour carpeting replaced pearl velour. Door sills and pedal pads were plastic instead of stainless steel, and the centre armrest was not leather covered.

Even with the six-cylinder engine, the Cayenne offered more than satisfactory performance for an SUV. With the six-speed transmission available from early 2004, it took 9.1 seconds to reach 62mph (100kph); Tiptronic S added 0.6 seconds to this time. Top speed for either transmission variant was listed at 133mph (214 kph).

From early 2004 the Cayenne S became available with a six-speed manual transmission, which needed only 6.8 seconds to reach 62mph (100kph).

Cayenne S [Tiptronic S] MY 2003–

Engine

Engine design:	8-cylinder V-engine, 90°
Installation:	Front-engine
Cooling system:	Water-cooled
Engine type:	M 48/00
Displacement (cc):	4511
Bore x stroke (mm):	93 x 83
Engine output DIN (kW/hp):	250/340 at 6000rpm
Maximum torque (Nm/lb ft):	420/310 at 2500-5500rpm
Output per litre (kW/l / hp/l):	55.4 / 75.4
Compression ratio:	11.5 : 1
Valve operation & camshaft drive:	dohc, cams driven by double chain, 4 valves per cylinder, VarioCam
Carburation:	Bosch DME, Motronic ME 7.1.1
Ignition system:	DME
Firing order:	1 - 3 - 7 - 2 - 6 - 5 - 4 - 8
Engine lubrication:	Integrated dry sump
Engine oil total (l):	9.5

Transmission

Drive configuration:	Permanent four wheel drive 38% / 62%
Manual gearbox:	6-speed
Option Tiptronic S:	[6-speed]
Transmission type:	G 48/00 [A 48/00]
Transmission ratios:	
1st gear:	4.68 [4.15]
2nd gear:	2.53 [2.37]
3rd gear:	1.69 [1.56]
4th gear:	1.22 [1.16]
5th gear:	1.00 [0.86]
6th gear:	0.84 [0.69]
Reverse gear:	4.27 [3.39]
Drive ratio:	3.70 [4.10]

Body, chassis, suspension, brakes, wheels

Body design:	Steel SUV body, 4 doors, 5 seats, entirely hot-dip galvanized body, side-impact protection beams in doors, flexible polyurethane front and rear bumpers with integrated aluminium beams
Option:	Electric sunroof
Suspension, front:	Individually suspended, wide-based aluminium and steel upper and lower A-arms, steel and aluminium links, coil springs over tubular shock absorbers, anti-roll bar
Option:	Air suspension
Suspension, rear:	Individually suspended, multi-link-axle employed steel and aluminium links, coil springs over tubular shock absorbers, anti-roll bar
Option:	Air suspension
Brakes, front/rear (Size (mm)):	Ventilated discs (350 x 34) / Ventilated discs (330 x 28)

	Titanium-colour 6-piston fixed aluminium monobloc callipers / Titanium-colour 4-piston fixed aluminium monobloc callipers ABS
Wheels, front/rear:	8 J x 18 / 8 J x 18
Tyres, front/rear:	255/55 R 18 109 Y / 255/55 R 18 109 Y
Option:	9 J x 19 / 9 J x 19
	275/45 R 19 108 Y / 275/45 R 19 108 Y
Option:	9 J x 20 / 9 J x 20
	275/40 R 20 106 Y / 275/40 R 20 106 Y

Electrical system

Alternator (W):	2660
Battery (V/Ah):	12 / 95 or 12 / 110*
*dependent on equipment	

Dimensions and weight

Track, front/rear (mm):	1647 / 1662
9 J x 19 / 9 J x 19:	1641 / 1656
9 J x 20 / 9 J x 20:	1641 / 1656
Wheelbase (mm):	2855
Length x width x height (mm):	4782* x 1928 x 1699
Kerb weight DIN (kg):	2225 [2245]
Permissible gross weight (kg):	3060 [3060]
MY 2004 -:	3080 [3080]
Luggage compartment (VDA (l)):	540
with folded down rear seatbacks:	1770
Fuel tank capacity (l):	100, including 12 reserve
MY 2004 -:	100, including 15 reserve
C_w x A (m²):	0.39 x 2.78 = 1.084
Power/weight ratio (kg/kW/kg/hp):	8.90 [8.98] / 6.54 [6.60]
*with outdoor spare wheel: 5018	

Fuel consumption

80/1268/EWG (mpg):	98 RON super plus unleaded
Urban:	12.4 [13.5]
Extra urban:	24 [25.2]
Combined:	17.9 [19]
CO_2-emissions (g/km):	380 [361]

Performance, production, prices

Acceleration 0-62mph/100kph (s):	6.8 [7.2]
0-100mph/160kph (s):	16.4 [16.8]
Maximum speed (mph / kph):	150 / 242 [150 / 242]
Production, total number:	still in production
Purchase prices:	
08/2002:	[Euro 60,204]
08/2003:	Euro 60,352 [Euro 62,927]

Cayenne turbo Tiptronic S MY 2003–

Engine

Engine design:	8-cylinder-V-engine, 90°
Installation:	Front-engine, twin turbo charger, twin intercooler
Cooling system:	Water-cooled
Engine type:	M 48/50
Displacement (cc):	4511
Bore x stroke (mm):	93 x 83
Engine output DIN (kW/hp):	331/450 at 6000rpm
Maximum torque (Nm/lb ft):	620/457 at 2250-4750rpm
Output per litre (kW/l / hp/l):	73.4 / 99.8
Compression ratio:	9.5 : 1
Valve operation & camshaft drive:	dohc, cams driven by double chain, 4 valves per cylinder, VarioCam
Carburation:	Bosch DME, Motronic ME 7.1.1
Ignition system:	DME
Firing order:	1- 3 - 7 - 2 - 6 - 5 - 4 - 8
Boost (bar):	0.6
Engine lubrication:	Intrgrated dry sump
Engine oil total (l):	9.5

Transmission

Drive configuration:	Permanent four wheel drive 38% / 62%
Tiptronic S:	6-speed
Transmission type:	A 48/50
Transmission ratios:	
1st gear:	4.15
2nd gear:	2.37
3rd gear:	1.56
4th gear:	1.16
5th gear:	0.86
6th gear:	0.69
Reverse gear:	3.39
Drive ratio:	3.70

Body, chassis, suspension, brakes, wheels

Body design:	Steel SUV body, 4 doors, 5 seats, entirely hot-dip galvanized body, side-impact protection beams in doors, flexible polyurethane front and rear bumpers with integrated aluminium beams, big air intakes in front bumpers, engine lid with two power domes
Option:	Electric sunroof
Suspension, front:	Individually suspended, wide-based aluminium and steel upper and lower A-arms, steel and aluminium links, air suspension, anti-rollbar
Suspension, rear:	Individually suspended, multi-link-axle employed steel and aluminium links, air suspension, anti-roll bar

Brakes, front/rear (Size (mm)):	Ventilated discs (350 x 34) / Ventilated discs (330 x 28) Red 6-piston fixed aluminium monobloc callipers / Red 4-piston fixed aluminium monobloc callipers ABS
Wheels, front/rear:	8 J x 18 / 8 J x 18
Tyres, front/rear:	255/55 R 18 109 Y / 255/55 R 18 109 Y
Option:	9 J x 19 / 9 J x 19
	275/45 R 19 108 Y / 275/45 R 19 108 Y
Option:	9 J x 20 / 9 J x 20
	275/40 R 20 106 Y / 275/40 R 20 106 Y

Electrical system

Alternator (W):	2660
Battery (V/Ah):	12 / 110

Dimensions and weight

Track, front/rear (mm):	1647 / 1662
9 J x 19 / 9 J x 19:	1641 / 1656
9 J x 20 / 9 J x 20:	1641 / 1656
Wheelbase (mm):	2855
Length x width x height (mm):	4786* x 1928 x 1699
Kerb weight DIN (kg):	2355
Permissible gross weight (kg):	3080
Luggage compartment (VDA (l)):	540
with folded down rear seatbacks:	1770
Fuel tank capacity (l):	100, including 12 reserve
MY 2004 - :	100, including 15 reserve
C_w x A (m²):	0.39 x 2.78 = 1.084
Power/weight ratio (kg/kW/ kg/hp):	7.11 / 5.23
*with outdoor spare wheel: 5021	

Fuel consumption

80/1268/EWG (mpg):	98 RON super plus unleaded
Urban:	12.9
Extra urban:	23.7
Combined:	18
CO_2-emissions (g/km):	378

Performance, production, prices

Acceleration 0-62mph/100kph (s):	5.6
0-100mph/160kph (s):	12.9
Maximum speed (mph / kph):	165 / 266
Production, total number:	still in production
Purchase prices:	
08/2002:	Euro 99,876
08/2003:	Euro 100,024

Cayenne [Tiptronic S] MY 2004–

Engine

Engine design:	6-cylinder V-engine, 15°
Installation:	Front-engine
Cooling system:	Water-cooled
Engine type:	BFD
Displacement (cc):	3189
Bore x stroke (mm):	84 x 95.9
Engine output DIN (kW/hp):	184/250 at 6000rpm
Maximum torque (Nm/lb ft):	310/229 at 2500-5500rpm
Output per litre (kW/l / hp/l):	57.7 / 78.4
Compression ratio:	11.5 : 1
Valve operation & camshaft drive:	dohc, cams driven by synchronous belt drive, 4 valves per cylinder, continuous variable valve timing for intake and exhaust camshafts
Carburation:	Bosch DME, Motronic ME 7.1.1
Ignition system:	DME
Firing order:	1- 5 - 3 - 6 - 2 - 4
Engine lubrication:	Full preasure oil lubrication
Engine oil total (l):	6.3

Transmission

Drive configuration:	Permanent four wheel drive 38% / 62%
Manual gearbox:	6-speed
Option Tiptronic S:	[6-speed]
Transmission type:	G 48/20 [A 48/20]
Transmission ratios:	
1st gear:	4.68 [4.15]
2nd gear:	2.53 [2.37]
3rd gear:	1.69 [1.56]
4th gear:	1.22 [1.16]
5th gear:	1.00 [0.86]
6th gear:	0.84 [0.69]
Reverse gear:	4.27 [3.39]
Drive ratio:	4.10 [4.56]

Body, chassis, suspension, brakes, wheels

Body design:	Steel SUV body, 4 doors, 5 seats, entirely hot-dip galvanized body, side-impact protection beams in doors, flexible polyurethane front and rear bumpers with integrated aluminium beams
Option:	Electric sunroof
Suspension, front:	Individually suspended, wide-based aluminium and steel upper and lower A-arms, steel and aluminium links, coil springs over tubular shock absorbers, anti-roll bar
Option:	Air suspension
Suspension, rear:	Individually suspended, multi-link-axle employed steel and aluminium links, coil springs over tubular shock absorbers, anti-roll bar
Option:	Air suspension

Brakes, front/rear (Size (mm)):	Ventilated discs (330 x 32) / Ventilated discs (330 x 28) Black 6-piston fixed aluminium monobloc callipers / Black 4-piston fixed aluminium monobloc callipers ABS
Wheels, front/rear:	7.5 J x 17 / 7.5 J x 17
Tyres, front/rear:	235/65 R 17 108 V / 235/65 R 17 108 V
Option:	8 J x 18 / 8 J x 18 255/55 R 18 109 Y / 255/55 R 18 109 Y
Option:	9 J x 19 / 9 J x 19 275/45 R 19 108 Y / 275/45 R 19 108 Y
Option:	9 J x 20 / 9 J x 20 275/40 R 20 106 Y / 275/40 R 20 106 Y

Electrical system

Alternator (W):	2100 or 2660*
Battery (V/Ah):	12 / 70 or 12 / 95*
*dependent on equipment	

Dimensions and weight

Track, front/rear (mm):	1655 / 1670
8 J x 18 / 8 J x 18:	1647 / 1662
9 J x 19 / 9 J x 19:	1641 / 1656
9 J x 20 / 9 J x 20:	1641 / 1656
Wheelbase (mm):	2855
Length x width x height (mm):	4782* x 1928 x 1699
Kerb weight DIN (kg):	2160 [2170]
Permissible gross weight (kg):	2945 [2945]
Luggage compartment (VDA (l)):	540
with folded down rear seatbacks:	1770
Fuel tank capacity (l):	100, including 15 reserve
C_w x A (m²):	0.38 x 2.78 = 1.056
Power/weight ratio (kg/kW/ kg/hp):	11.73 [11.79] / 8.64 [8.68]
*with outside spare wheel: 5018	

Fuel consumption

80/1268/EWG (mpg):	98 RON super plus unleaded
Urban:	15.9 [184]
Extra urban:	26.6 [26.4]
Combined:	21.4 [20.9]
CO_2-emissions (g/km):	317 [324]

Performance, production, prices

Acceleration 0-62mph/100kph (s):	9.1 [9.7]
0-100mph/160kph (s):	23.8 [25.0]
Maximum speed (mph / kph):	133 / 214 [133 / 214]
Production, total number:	still in production
Purchase price:	
08/2003:	Euro 47,592 [Euro 50,167]

Porsche Carrera GT

The starting gun for development of the Carrera GT was fired as early as February 1999. Only 18 months would pass before the show car was completed. On 28 September 2000 Porsche presented, to great acclaim, an almost production-ready study of an open high-performance sports car.

The Carrera GT's engineering was based on pure racing technology; this applied to the chassis and suspension, as well as its ten-cylinder normally-aspirated engine, which was directly descended from a racing power unit originally conceived for Le Mans. This engine would extract 558hp (410kW) and 600Nm (443lb ft) of torque from 5.5 litres – enough to accelerate to 124mph (200kph) in less than 10 seconds, and reach a top speed of 205mph (330kph).

Of course, the Carrera GT shown at Paris was entirely capable of being driven; rally champion Walter Röhrl drove the car down the Champs Elysées to the Louvre. At the Detroit Motor Show in early January 2002, Dr Wendelin Wiedeking, Porsche's chairman, announced that about one thousand Carrera GTs would be built, with market introduction planned for autumn 2003.

Porsche applied the most modern, race-car specific design and manufacturing methods to the Carrera GT. The vehicle concept's goal was to cultivate the pure, unadulterated character of a race car to achieve maximum motoring pleasure in a street-legal car. Design of the vehicle concentrated on low weight, high torsional stiffness and the lowest possible vehicle centre of gravity.

Exterior design of the open two-seater showed unmistakable Porsche elements. At the front, the Carrera GT recalled the legendary Porsche 718 RSK Spyder of the late 1950s. Three large cooling openings were cut into the nose. Bi-xenon headlamp modules, containing high and low beams as well as indicators, were mounted behind clear plastic lenses. From the side, the long wheelbase (necessitated by its mid-engine layout) and short rear overhang were apparent. Its doors were inset from the car's flanks towards the centre line, to provide space for the front wheel arch air extractors and rear cooling air openings. Oval outside mirrors were mounted on V-shaped stalks. Behind the seats were two roll bars, joined by a crossmember. A three-section lightweight polycarbonate rear

Phantom view of a Carrera GT

Carrera GT 5.7-litre V10 engine

window stretched between the roll bars; with the top removed, this acted as a wind blocker. For open-air driving, two lightweight roof halves of carbon fibre-reinforced honeycomb could be removed and stowed in the front boot. The longitudinally-mounted engine lived under two fairings and a cover which stretched back from the roll bars. The rear was punctuated by a remarkable spoiler profile. Actuated by electronically-controlled hydraulics, at speeds above 75mph (120kph) the spoiler's centre section was raised by 160mm in less than five seconds, and retracted as soon as speed dropped below 50mph (80kph). A black carbon-fibre valance was mounted above the rear diffuser. Left and right tailpipes exited through this valance on either side of the number plate. Outboard of the exhausts, a rear fog lamp was mounted on the left, and a reversing lamp on the right. The tail lamps consisted of LEDs; the advantage of LEDs is that they offer faster response and longer life.

Porsche also rose to the engineering challenge in its choice of materials. The monocoque body, a form favoured in racing, was made of carbon fibre sandwich material. The Carrera GT marked the first time that a vehicle's tub was also made using this technology. The carbon-fibre-reinforced plastic

(CFRP) chassis, consisting of monocoque, windscreen frame and roll bars, was bolted to the tub to form a single load-bearing structure. Front and rear lids, rear wings, sills and doors with integral side-impact protection were made of carbon-fibre-reinforced plastic. Front and rear ends were made of deformable plastic.

The normally-aspirated V10 engine of the Carrera GT was originally developed to contest the Le Mans 24 Hours race. For the Carrera GT, its displacement was increased from 5.5 litres to 5.7 litres by enlarging cylinder bore, and the cylinder bank angle optimized at 68°. Compression ratio was very high at 12.0:1. The V10 developed its maximum power output of 612hp (450kW) at 8000rpm; maximum torque of 590Nm (435lb ft) was available at 5750rpm. Cylinder surfaces were Nikasil coated, and connecting rods made of titanium. Its dry sump lubrication system used ten oil pumps: one pressure pump and nine scavenge pumps. VarioCam provided continuously-variable intake camshaft timing over a 40° range. Two Motronic ME 7.1.1 control units operated in a master/slave configuration.

While the engine was installed longitudinally, the transmission, developed especially for the Carrera

GT, was installed transversely in order to be as close to the rear axle as possible. The compact six-speed manual transmission had a low centre of gravity and was capable of handling extremely high power levels. The Carrera GT was the world's first application of a two-disc ceramic clutch; the Porsche Ceramic Composite Clutch (PCCC) had a diameter of only 169mm (6.7in).

Because of its uncompromising suspension, designed to achieve ultimate vehicle dynamics, all Carrera GTs worldwide were given the exact same chassis tuning. Front independent suspension was by upper and lower aluminium A-arms and pushrods. Progressively-wound coil springs on threaded spring perches over gas-pressure shock absorbers formed lightweight spring/damper units. Rear suspension, too, used upper and lower A-arms and pushrods. As at the front, lightweight gas-pressure shock absorbers were combined with progressive coil springs into spring/damper assemblies. Anti-roll bar actuation through pushrods and cranks permitted direct translation of wheel travel to stabilizer bar movement, resulting in a more weight-efficient anti-roll bar layout.

The Carrera GT was equipped with an even more highly developed version of the Porsche Ceramic Composite Brake (PCCB). Its perforated ceramic fibre brake discs contained internal, spiral cooling channels. Compared to cast iron, ceramic fibre discs offered about 50 per cent less weight and longer disc service life. Both front and rear axles used six-piston aluminium monobloc fixed callipers. The handbrake acted on the rear discs through additional callipers. A four-channel ABS 5.7 system reliably prevented wheel lock-up in instances of maximum-effort stops.

The five-spoke wheels were made of lightweight forged magnesium. The centre-lock hubs and multi-point nuts were derived from racing practice. On the left side, wheels were attached by red central nuts using conventional right-hand thread, while the right side of the car used blue nuts (to avoid confusion with the left-side hardware) and left-hand thread. The front axle carried 9.5 J x 19 wheels with 265/35 ZR 19 tyres; rears were 12.5 J x 20 mounting 335/30 ZR 20 rubber.

The interior, too, was dominated by lightweight materials: carbon fibre, magnesium and aluminium, combined with leather. The seats, with lightweight carbon fibre – Kevlar composite shells were covered in leather and available in two different widths. The dashboard fascia consisted of titanium-painted carbon fibre. The centre console trim and inside door latches were magnesium, the pedals aluminium. A short aluminium gear lever topped by a wooden knob sprouted from the tall centre console, with the most important switches arrayed in plain sight forward of and above the gear lever. Five instruments were arranged as in the 911. The three-spoke leather-rimmed steering wheel was manually adjustable over a 40mm range. Driver and passenger front and side airbags were, of course, standard equipment. Additionally, each Carrera GT included a set of custom-made luggage, with travel bag, garment bag, briefcase, shoulder bag and a centre console bag which fitted into the space behind the console. At no additional cost, customers could order manual air-conditioning and the Porsche Online Pro CD radio with navigation, telephone and six-speaker Bose sound system. Tweeters and mid-range speakers were mounted in the doors, with bass speakers in the footwells.

Road performance of the Carrera GT was in the realm of pure race cars. Acceleration to 62mph (100kph) took only 3.9 seconds; 124mph (200kph) was reached in a breathtaking 9.9 seconds. Engine power matched total drag at a top speed of 205mph (330kph).

Beginning in autumn 2003, the first Carrera GTs were hand-built in Leipzig and sold at a price of 452,690 Euros. Production was limited to 1,500 examples, and most were quickly spoken for.

Carrera GT MY 2004–

Engine

Engine design:	10-cylinder V-engine, 68°
Installation:	Mid-engine
Cooling system:	Water-cooled
Engine type:	M 80
Displacement (cc):	5733
Bore x stroke (mm):	98 x 76
Engine output DIN (kW/hp):	450/612 at 8000rpm
Maximum torque (Nm/lb ft):	590/435 at 5750rpm
Output per litre (kW/l / hp/l):	78.5 / 106.7
Compression ratio:	12.0 : 1
Valve operation & camshaft drive:	dohc, cams driven by gears and double chains, 4 valves per cylinder, VarioCam with 40°
Carburation:	Bosch DME, 2 x Motronic ME 7.1.1
Ignition system:	DME
Firing order:	1 - 6 - 3 - 8 - 5 - 10 - 4 - 9 - 2 - 7
Engine lubrication:	Dry sump
Engine oil total (l):	10.5

Transmission

Drive configuration:	Rear-axle drive
Manual gearbox:	6-speed
Transmission type:	G 80
Transmission ratios:	
1st gear:	3.20
2nd gear:	1.87
3rd gear:	1.36
4th gear:	1.07
5th gear:	0.90
6th gear:	0.75
Reverse gear:	2.19
Drive ratio:	4.44
Ltd slip diff. load/deceleration (%):	25% / 25%

Body, chassis, suspension, brakes, wheels

Body design:	Roadster body, 2 doors, 2 seats, two-piece detachable hardtop in carbon fibre, carbon-fibre chassis (consisting of monocoque, windscreen surround and supplemental safety system), carbon-fibre carrier for engine, gearbox and rear suspension with a honeycomb core, engine carrier bolted to rear of monocoque as second fully-stressed member, frameless doors in carbon fibre with integrated side-impact protection, front and rear lids, rear side panels and sill panels in carbon fibre, front and rear aprons in plastic, automatically extending rear spoiler, underbody panelling with rear diffuser

Suspension, front:	Individually suspended on aluminium double wishbones with pushrod actuated spring-and-shock absorber units, progressive coil springs, anti-roll bar
Suspension, rear:	Individually suspended on aluminium double wishbones with pushrod actuated spring-and-shock absorber units, progressive coil springs, anti-roll bar
Brakes, front/rear (Size (mm)):	Porsche Ceramic Composite Brake (PCCB) Ventilated and drilled ceramic composite discs (380 x 34) / Ventilated and drilled ceramic composite discs (380 x 34) Yellow 6-piston fixed aluminium monobloc callipers / Yellow 6-piston fixed aluminium monobloc callipers Bosch ABS 5.7
Wheels, front/rear:	9.5 J x 19 / 12.5 J x 20
Tyres, front/rear:	265/35 ZR 19 / 335/30 ZR 20

Electrical system

Alternator (W/A):	2100 / 150
Battery (V/Ah):	12 / 60
with air condition/radio:	12 / 80

Dimensions and weight

Track, front/rear (mm):	1612 / 1587
Wheelbase (mm):	2730
Length x width x height (mm):	4613 x 1921 x 1166
Kerb weight DIN (kg):	1380–1445
Permissible gross weight (kg):	1635
Luggage compartment (VDA (l)):	76
Fuel tank capacity (l):	92, including 13.5 reserve
C_w x A (m²):	0.396 x 1.94 = 0.768
Power/weight ratio (kg/kW/kg/hp):	3.06 / 2.25

Fuel consumption

80/1268/EWG (mpg):	98 RON super plus unleaded
Urban:	10
Extra urban:	22.7
Combined:	15.8
CO_2-emissions (g/km):	432

Performance, production, prices

Acceleration 0-62mph/100kph (s):	3.9
0-100mph/160kph (s):	6.9
0-124mph/200kph (s):	9.9
Maximum speed (mph / kph):	205 / 330
Production, total number:	Limited to 1,500 (new limit 1,250)
Purchase Price: 08/2003:	Euro 452,690

RUF cars based on Porsche

RUF Automobile GmbH cars

'You can hardly see the difference, but you can really feel it!'

Since 1948 the Porsche name has stood for high-quality, very special sports cars built with sophisticated technology for everyday use by sports car fans throughout the world. Pfaffenhausen, a small Swabian village in the Allgäu region near Mindelheim, west of Munich, is the home of RUF Automobile GmbH, a small company that, in conjunction with Porsche, has written a sports car history of its own.

RUF's competency in things automotive is based on a tradition dating back to the late 1930s. In 1939 Alois Ruf, Snr founded his firm, 'Auto RUF', a general automotive and mechanical repair shop in Pfaffenhausen's Mindelheimer Strasse, where it remains to this day. A petrol station was added in 1949. In January 1950, son Alois entered the world. Five years later the company built its own tour bus and added a bus charter service to its businesses. The timing was perfect as it catered for the growing wanderlust in that era of the 'German economic miracle'. Another RUF development was Volkswagen engines with displacement reduced to 700cc, which found favour for their low tax rate and exceptional fuel economy. Despite modest power output, the RUF Beetles were a market success. In 1958 FIAT automobiles could be ordered and serviced through RUF of Pfaffenhausen.

In 1963 the company became a representative of a Bavarian brand: BMW. While Alois Ruf, Snr continued to expand his company, Alois, Jnr discovered a passion for sports cars. In that same year, RUF serviced its first Porsche 356. Today, RUF remains one of the world's pre-eminent providers of first-class, authentic restoration services for all types of Porsche vehicles.

After the death of Alois Ruf, Snr in the spring of 1974, his son Alois, now 24, took the reins of the company. His interest in the sports cars from Zuffenhausen, especially the Porsche 911, a sports car endowed by its makers with the best genetic heritage, continued unabated, and as early as 1975, he built his first car, a 911 Carrera RS 3.0, to his own design. The car attracted attention with its special interior equipment, headlamp-washer system and roof aerial.

In 1977, RUF presented its first modified Porsche 911 turbo, with an engine enlarged from 3.0 litres to 3.3 litres. Output of the turbocharged engine was increased by 43hp (32kW), from 260hp (191kW) to 303hp (223kW). RUF teamed the uprated turbo power unit with a five-speed Getrag manual transmission.

Just a year later, RUF presented the 911 SCR, a more powerful normally-aspirated 911. While the Porsche factory throttled output of the 911 SC to 180hp (132kW) for marketing reasons, RUF offered a 3.2-litre engine developing 217hp (160kW). Combined with weight-optimized equipment, the RUF 911 SCR achieved performance levels comparable to the 930 turbo. At the front, the 911 SCR carried a large RUF front spoiler, with its integrated oil cooler and round brake-cooling ducts. Beginning in 1978, RUF offered driver training courses on race tracks.

In 1980, RUF presented a turbo-bodied 911 SCR Targa with a so-called T-roof, i.e. two removable roof halves. A rigidly-welded longitudinal member stretched between the windscreen header and Targa bar. Its purpose was to provide improved torsional stiffness even when the car was driven with roof panels removed.

In 1981, RUF presented a five-speed manual transmission, developed in-house, for the 930 turbo, which made driving the turbo even more fascinating and pleasurable, as engine speed could more easily be kept in the optimum boost range. In that same year the company received an important recognition: the German Federal Bureau of Motor Vehicles certified RUF Automobile GmbH as an automobile manufacturer.

In 1982, a 930 RUF turbo, painted NATO olive drab, made headlines in the automotive press.

The first vehicle to bear a RUF chassis number was the RUF BTR of 1983. The core of this car was a 3.4-litre RUF turbo engine of 374hp (275kW) and the RUF-developed five-speed manual transmission. The car was hand-built from the body shell up. Along with the wide turbo bodywork, RUF also offered the BTR in the narrow 911 Carrera body.

In its engineering development programmes, RUF concentrates not only on engine, transmission and body, but also on wheels and brakes. Beginning in 1985, RUF 17-inch Speedline wheels complemented the model range. Seventeen-inch tyres, originally developed for the Porsche 959, resulted from close co-operation with tyre manufacturer Dunlop. Along with run-flat capability, the Dunlop Denloc system offered maximum safety at extremely high speeds.

In 1987, the company presented the RUF CTR, a lightweight coupé powered by a 469hp (345kW) 3.4-litre twin-turbo engine and Motronic engine management in a narrow, aerodynamically-optimized body. In performance, the CTR, which the international motoring press dubbed the 'Yellow Bird', set new benchmarks for street-legal sports cars. In comparison tests on the high-speed track at Nardo in southern Italy the CTR, with its top speed of 213mph (342kph) left even such pedigreed high-end sports cars like the Ferrari F40, an AMG Mercedes and a works-tuned Porsche 959 in its dust. In that same year, the United States Environmental Protection Agency (EPA) and Department of Transportation (DOT) certified RUF as an automobile manufacturer.

A year later, a RUF-developed six-speed manual transmission was available for the BTR and CTR models. The BTR III, with its 408hp (300kW) 3.4-litre turbocharged engine, was the first single-turbo engine to be fitted with the Motronic engine management system.

In 1991, RUF offered 18-inch wheels, in effect an evolution of the 17-inch idea. The RUF BR, based on the 964 turbo 2, developed 360hp (265kW), a 40hp improvement over stock.

RUF also reported new developments in the drivetrain department. The EKS electronic clutch system, a joint development of RUF and Fichtel & Sachs, became available in 1992. EKS combined the comfort of an automatic transmission in city stop-and-go traffic, with the sports car pleasure of a manual transmission. In addition, EKS reliably prevented engine over-revving in the event of a missed gear. At worst, such an error might require a new clutch, but not a new engine.

The year 1993 saw the introduction of two new turbo engines with Motronic management. Both were characterized by excellent fuel economy and clean exhaust emissions. The BTR 3.8 generated 415hp (305kW). The RCT engine, based on the dual-ignition 964 Carrera power unit, produced 370hp (272kW). The motoring press repeatedly praised this engine for its driving feel, which resembled that of a large-displacement normally-aspirated engine.

In the spring of 1994, shortly after introduction

Alois Ruf with a RUF turbo 3.3 Cabriolet in front of his firm's showroom in Pfaffenhausen, 1983

of the Porsche 993 Carrera, RUF presented the BTR 2, with a 3.6-litre turbocharged engine and 964 rear spoiler. The RUF-modified front valance was marked by larger air inlets and two additional top vent slots.

In 1996, the Porsche 993-based CTR II was introduced as a worthy modern successor to the legendary CTR 'Yellow Bird'. It included innovations such as 19-inch wheels and carbon brake system. Top speed of the 520hp (382kW) CTR II was in excess of 211mph (340kph). Shortly thereafter it was followed by a lightweight version, the RUF CTR II Sport.

Based on the 993 turbo, RUF offered the turbo R, with a 490hp (360kW) twin-turbo engine. In comparison tests with the world's finest high-end sports cars, the turbo R often came out on top in handling, performance and top speed.

At the 1999 Essen Motor Show, RUF presented its first water-cooled vehicle. Based on the Porsche Boxster, the Pfaffenhausen company built the RUF 3400 S, powered by a 310hp (228kW) 3.4-litre Carrera engine. With this model, RUF filled a gap which Porsche had imposed on itself for reasons of model politics.

In the new millennium, RUF continued to explore market niches which the Stuttgart sportscar-maker had left open. The RUF RGT was based on the 996 Carrera and powered by a 3.6-litre engine derived from the 911 GT3 power unit. With 385hp (283kW), the RGT had 25hp more than the limited-edition 911 GT3. The RGT was intended for all Porsche customers who missed the opportunity to get a GT3. Also, in contrast to the GT3, the RGT was approved for sale in the United States.

For 2001, RUF presented the R turbo, based on the 996 turbo. RUF customers could order the 520hp (382kW) car with rear- or all-wheel drive, and choose between narrow Carrera bodywork or turbo wide-body. The R turbo was also available in Cabriolet form. Porsche would not offer a 911 turbo Cabriolet until 2003.

For the 2002 model year, RUF presented its 3600 S, a development of the 3400 S. Built on a Boxster body, the roadster was powered by the new 3.6-litre normally-aspirated engine of the 996 Carrera. This yielded 325hp (239kW) and propelled the visually modified car to a top speed of 173mph (278kph). Optionally, an even more powerful model was available, with 345hp (254kW).

At almost the same time, RUF launched the next performance level for the R turbo. Power level was initially pegged at 550hp (404kW). At Nardo, Italy, the German magazine *Auto Motor und Sport* measured the turbo R's top speed at 218mph (351kph), making it the fastest-ever street-legal 911 tested to date by the German press.

In all, by early 2004, RUF had built or converted about 400 complete cars, and about 200 optimized 964 Carrera 3.6-litre engines. Sports car fans throughout the world have come to value RUF's reputation for performance and quality.

RUF turbo 3.3

In 1977 RUF introduced its first performance-tuned car, based on the Porsche 911 turbo 3.0 Coupé. Obvious visual changes included a front air dam in the style of the 911 Carrera RS 3.0, with air ducts feeding engine and transmission oil-coolers and air-conditioning system. Ductwork took the place of Porsche's standard fog lamps. The larger rear spoiler appeared to have been taken directly from racing practice.

Engine displacement was increased to 3243cc, with new, 98.9mm pistons and cylinders. Power increased from 260hp (191kW) to 303hp (223kW) at 5500rpm. Maximum torque of 412Nm (304lb ft) was available at 4000rpm. These performance numbers are even more impressive when one considers that the engine did not have an intercooler. Exhaust was vented by a modified system with two tailpipes. Instead of the standard four speeds, the RUF turbo 3.3 used a five-speed Getrag transmission whose gearing and configuration were matched to the engine's boost characteristics and torque curve.

The suspension was lowered and tuned more firmly with Bilstein gas-pressure shock absorbers. The brake system was uprated with special discs and pads to match the increased engine power.

The car's exclusivity continued to the custom leather interior. This was done in a shade complementing the chosen exterior colour. Even the headliner was made of perforated leather. The sports seat centres and door panels were upholstered in matching plaid fabric.

Customers were pampered by an extensive equipment list featuring many comfort features. The car was equipped with air-conditioning, stereo cassette radio and four speakers, headlamp-cleaning system, electric windows, power central-locking, a second electrically-adjustable outside mirror, automatic heat control and an electronic delay relay for interior and footwell lighting.

Weighing 1280kg (2819lb), the RUF turbo 3.3 accelerated to 62mph (100kph) in only 5.1 seconds; the 124mph (200kph) mark was passed in 20.8 seconds. Top speed was 163mph (263kph).

RUF SCR

While the 911 SC of 1978 had to content itself with a power output of 180hp (132kW) for marketing reasons, RUF offered an agile 911 in the form of its SCR (the 'R' was for RUF). Installation of 98mm pistons and cylinders increased displacement to 3185cc. Compression ratio was raised to 9.8:1 to take advantage of premium-grade petrol. The SC's air-injection pump was deleted. The exhaust system was modified and a second tailpipe fitted. These measures raised engine output to 217hp (160kW) at 5700rpm. Maximum torque increased to 280Nm (207lb ft) at 4100rpm. Fifth gear was made higher for greater top speed. At the front, the 911 SCR carried the large RUF front spoiler with integral oil-cooler and round brake-cooling ducts; at the rear, an engine lid with integral flat rear spoiler was fitted. Combined with weight-optimized equipment, the RUF SCR nearly approached the 911 turbo in performance. Acceleration to 62mph (100kph) was achieved in only 5.7 seconds, on its way to a top speed of 158mph (255kph).

RUF BTR 3.4

The first vehicle to carry a RUF chassis number was the RUF BTR 3.4 of 1983. 'BTR' stood for Group B, Turbo, RUF. The heart of this car was a 3.4-litre RUF turbocharged engine developing 374hp (275kW) at 6000rpm. Maximum torque of 480Nm (354lb ft) was reached at 4800rpm. Displacement was increased with 98mm pistons and cylinders. Other power-boosting modifications included a different turbocharger and larger intercooler. A RUF-developed five-speed manual transmission was matched to the more powerful engine and geared to keep engine speed in the optimum boost range. The vehicle was hand-built, beginning with a bare body shell. Along with the wide turbo bodywork, RUF also offered the BTR in narrow Carrera body form. For equipment, customers could choose between a comfort version, with all imaginable luxury features, and an extreme lightweight version, offering low weight and even better performance. An oil-cooler mounted behind the RUF front spoiler ensured low oil temperatures. The suspension was lowered and given firmer tuning to match the power increase. Brakes consisted of ventilated, cross-drilled discs and four-piston fixed callipers. Initially, RUF used only the forged 16-inch Fuchs wheels, but as of 1985 17-inch Ruf Speedline wheels were available as an alternative.

Depending on equipment and weight, a BTR 3.4 could accelerate from a standstill to 124mph (200kph) in 15.5 to 16.7 seconds. The wide turbo body limited top speed to 174mph (280kph), while the slimmer, more aerodynamic Carrera body enabled the car to break the 186mph (300kph) barrier, logging a speed of 190mph (306kph) at the Ehra-Lessien high-speed test track.

RUF Carrera 3.4

RUF offered a larger-displacement alternative to the 3.2-litre 911 Carrera engines. Displacement was increased to exactly 3366cc by fitting 98mm pistons and cylinders. Minus catalytic converter and with a 10.3:1 compression ratio, this engine produced 250hp (184kW) at 5900rpm and offered a maximum torque of 304Nm (224lb ft) at 4800rpm. Adding a three-way catalytic converter reduced power by 5hp to 245hp (180kW) at 5900rpm. Maximum torque of the catalyst-equipped version matched that of the non-catalyst 3.2-litre stock engine – 285Nm (210lb ft) at 4800rpm. Carrera models equipped with the 3.4-litre engine could reach 3mph (5kph) higher top speeds.

RUF CTR

The RUF CTR was a lightweight coupé based on the Carrera body, with each rear wing widened about 2.5cm (1 inch). Hand-applied welds provided additional body stiffening. Rain gutters were removed for improved aerodynamics and reduced wind noise at high speed. At the front, the CTR was fitted with a lightweight, aerodynamically-shaped nose containing an integral oil-cooler, fitted fog lamps and indicators which wrapped around to the sides. Another lightweight plastic moulding was mounted at the rear. The rear wings included d ucting for two charge-air intercoolers. A small, aerodynamic rear-view mirror was mounted on the driver's side. The 3.4-litre engine was equipped with a Motronic engine-management system and two KKK Type K26 turbochargers. Compression ratio was 7.5:1. RUF's official power output for the CTR was listed as 496hp (345kW) at 5950rpm. The biturbo's maximum torque was 554Nm (409lb ft) at 5100rpm, with at least 400Nm (295lb ft) available in a broad band between 3500rpm and 6800rpm. The five-speed manual transmission was high geared for high top speed. The suspension was lowered 40mm and equipped with specially tuned Bilstein gas-pressure shock absorbers. 17-inch RUF Speedline wheels carried Dunlop Denloc tyres, specially developed for the RUF CTR. In laboratory high-speed testing, these tyres were required to survive at 217mph (350kph) while running with 2.5° of camber. The brake system, with 330mm discs, was taken from the Group C race cars; 'CTR' stood for Group C, Turbo, RUF. Weight reduction was a prime consideration for the interior. Driver and passenger sat in two lightweight shell seats. A roll cage provided extra body stiffening of the CTR, which weighed only 1150kg (2533lb). Performance of the CTR spoke for itself; the 'Yellow Bird', as it was lovingly dubbed by the English-speaking motoring press on account of its body colour, could accelerate from a standstill to 124mph (200kph) in only 11.4 seconds. The standing kilometre was covered in 20.9 seconds. Officially, top speed was listed as 211mph (339kph), but in comparison testing against the world's fastest sports cars in Nardo, Italy, the CTR was fastest of all, at 213mph (342kph).

RUF BTR III

The BTR III was the first RUF single-turbo engine to be equipped with Motronic engine-management. The turbocharged 3.4-litre engine produced 408hp

(300kW) at 6000rpm. Maximum torque of 480Nm (354lb ft) was available at 4800rpm. Its torque curve was characterized by a smooth transition into the turbocharger boost range; in addition, the engine was more flexible at low revs. Motronic also provided significant fuel economy benefits. RUF offered customers a slant-nose version of the BTR III, with flip-up headlamps. This was built with the same hand-crafted quality and attention to detail as could be found in Porsche's own shops. Customers could choose between the familiar RUF five-speed manual transmission or the new RUF six-speed manual. The BTR III could accelerate to 62mph (100kph) in a mere 4.6 seconds. Aerodynamic drag finally matched available power to hold the wide turbo bodywork to a top speed of 180mph (290kph).

RUF CR 2 and CR 4

RUF offered the rear-drive CR 2 and all-wheel-drive CR 4, based on the 964 Carrera 2 and Carrera 4 models respectively. 'CR' stood for Carrera RUF. The CR 2 and CR 4 were available in Coupé, Targa and Cabriolet form. Soon after the appearance of the 3.6-litre normally-aspirated engines, RUF's engineers recognized the engine's untapped potential. A

Alois Ruf with his team and the RUF-models CTR, BTR 3.4 and BTR III slant-nose, 1988

programme of engine optimization raised power output to 280hp (206kW) at 6000rpm, and torque to 325Nm (240lb ft) at 5800rpm. Compression ratio was raised slightly to 11.5:1. Connecting rod weights were matched to a tolerance of less than one gram. Timing of the standard camshafts was precisely adjusted. Intake ports were enlarged, polished and joined to larger intake runners. In addition, a sports air-filter was installed in the Cup induction system. The Motronic system was tuned for unleaded premium fuel, and the rev limiter bumped 200rpm higher. The suspension was retuned and fitted with 17-inch RUF Speedline wheels. A short-throw gearbox provided even quicker gear changes.

The CR 2 accelerated to 62mph (100kph) in about 5.3 seconds. From a standing start, it could reach 124mph (200kph) in about 19 seconds. Acceleration finally ended at a top speed of 168mph (270 kph).

RUF BR 2 and BR 4

Based on the rear-drive 964 turbo II, the RUF BR 2 engine developed 360hp (265kW) at 5750rpm. Maximum torque of 465Nm (343lb ft) was available at 5000rpm. The turbocharged engine was equipped with K-Jetronic fuel-injection, charge-air intercooling and a controlled three-way catalytic converter with oxygen sensor. For this car, RUF chose the narrow Carrera body, which allowed about 12mph (20kph) higher top speed. RUF installed a front air dam which provided even more stability at high speeds. To reduce wind noise, RUF offered an A-pillar fairing, painted body colour, which was cemented into the gutters at the windscreen edges. To house the intercooler, a 911 turbo rear spoiler was mounted on the engine lid. The left side of the rear fascia had a cut-out for a second tailpipe; this was the outlet for the turbocharger wastegate, which vented through an uncontrolled catalytic converter. The RUF six-speed manual transmission was fitted with the EKS electronic clutch system, and so operated without a clutch pedal. This system was a joint development of RUF and Fichtel & Sachs. When the gear lever was moved, an electric actuator operated the clutch automatically. EKS combined the comfort of an automatic transmission in city stop-and-go traffic, with the sports car pleasure of a manual transmission. The EKS control unit was located at the left front of the luggage compartment. The RUF sports suspension was sports tuned with shorter, firmer springs, Bilstein gas-pressure shock absorbers,

and modified anti-roll bars. For the brake system, RUF selected ventilated, cross-drilled discs and large four-piston aluminium fixed callipers. The newly-developed RUF 18-inch Speedline wheels provided an ideal match for the transmission gearing. Inside, lightweight appointments were immediately apparent: simply covered door panels, lightweight shell seats, deleted rear seats and rear trim. The result of these measures was an empty weight of 1355kg (2985lb). With EKS, the BR 2 accelerated to 62mph (100kph) in just 4.4 seconds. Top speed was 188mph (303kph).

RUF BTR 3.8

In the year of the 911's 30th anniversary, RUF presented the BTR 3.8, a lightweight, narrow-bodied 911. The new turbo engine displaced 3746cc, achieved through larger 102mm pistons and cylinders. Motronic sequential fuel-injection fed fuel to each cylinder, individually, at the exact time it was needed. This made a noticeable improvement in fuel economy over turbocharged engines with K-Jetronic continuous fuel-injection. Thanks to its cleaner combustion, Motronic engine-control also improved exhaust emissions. The high-geared RUF six-speed manual transmission was combined with EKS. Firmer suspension tuning and a high-performance brake system offered adequate reserves, even with the enhanced performance of the BTR 3.8.

In keeping with its lightweight concept, the interior retained only the most necessary equipment. A leather-rimmed steering wheel and two thinly-padded, leather-covered shell seats were its only luxury features. Weighing only 1260kg (2775lb), the Coupé accelerated to 62mph (100kph) in just 3.9 seconds, and to 124mph (200kph) in 12.9 seconds. Top speed was 198mph (319kph).

RUF RCT

Based on the 964 Carrera engine with twin-plug ignition and Motronic engine-management, RUF built the RCT turbo engine, with 370hp (272kW) at 5500rpm and maximum torque of 535Nm (395lb ft) at 4500rpm. This power unit was characterized by its smooth power development and high degree of engine flexibility; in terms of smoothness, the engine felt almost like a 5-litre normally-aspirated engine. Use of Motronic and twin-plug ignition made the RCT engine very fuel efficient. The engine could be used in a rear-wheel-drive or all-wheel-drive configuration, in narrow or wide coupé bodywork, or in a cabriolet or Targa body. The RUF six-speed manual transmission was well matched to the engine, and could be combined with EKS. The suspension and brake system were modified in keeping with the higher engine output. Customers could choose between 17-inch and 18-inch RUF Speedline wheels. In narrow-body Carrera form, the RCT could accelerate to 62mph (100kph) in about 4.5 seconds, and reach a maximum speed of 190mph (305kph).

RUF RCT EVO

The RCT EVO was equipped with a further development of the RCT engine. Initially, the reworked engine developed 405hp (298kW); but after additional optimization, it produced 425hp (313kW) at 5800rpm. Maximum torque was 570Nm (420lb ft) at 4500rpm. The RCT EVO was also based on the 3.6-litre normally-aspirated engine, with Motronic and twin-plug ignition. Cylinder heads with larger valves were taken from the Varioram-equipped 993 engine. Like the RUF RCT, the RCT EVO engine could be combined with all body and drivetrain variations. Fitted to the narrow Carrera body and with a high-geared six-speed manual gearbox, it could accelerate to 62mph (100kph) in about four seconds, and reach a top speed of 199mph (320kph).

RUF BTR 2

Shortly after introduction of the 993 Carrera, RUF presented the 993-based BTR 2, with a turbocharged engine and fixed rear spoiler. The RUF-modified nose included larger air inlets and two additional top vent slits. Based on the Carrera engine, the 3.6-litre turbo generated 420hp (309kW) at only 5000rpm. Maximum torque of 590Nm (435lb ft) was available at 4800rpm.

The power increase over the normally-aspirated Carrera was achieved with a turbocharger, intercooler, altered camshafts, an auxiliary oil-cooler, new exhaust system and Motronic modifications. The RUF six-speed manual transmission was combined with a limited-slip differential with 60 per cent lock-up.

The suspension was retuned by RUF. To match the horsepower increase, the brake system carried larger discs and callipers. RUF 18-inch aluminium

alloy wheels were a good match for the revised gearing. The BTR could accelerate from a standstill to 62mph (100kph) in 4.1 seconds, and reach a top speed of 191mph (308kph).

RUF CTR II

Based on the 993 Carrera, the RUF CTR II represented a modern successor to the CTR 'Yellow Bird', with a number of innovations. It was built on a narrow coupé body, the gutters of which had been removed for improved aerodynamics. Its nose was reshaped for more front downforce and to pass more cooling air, the sills were shrouded and the rear valance had a central cut-out for two tailpipes and additional side-vents for the charge-air intercoolers. The engine lid was completely reshaped, extending across the entire width of the car, and the integral rear spoiler was hollow and had openings that ducted air through the spoiler to the intercoolers.

The rear lid also had an opening for the engine induction airbox. The air-cooled 3.6-litre twin-turbo engine was fed by a pair of KKK turbochargers. With an 8.0:1 compression ratio, the power unit developed 520hp (382kW) at 5800rpm, and maximum torque of 685Nm (505lb ft) at 4800rpm. Standard equipment included a six-speed manual transmission and a limited-slip differential with a 60 per cent lock-up factor.

As an alternative to the CTR II's standard rear-wheel drive, customers could opt for all-wheel drive at added cost. The suspension was given firmer, sports-oriented tuning, and benefited from RUF's pioneering work on carbon brakes. For the first time it was possible to tune a carbon brake system (a facility usually found only in racing) for satisfactory cold response. Carbon brakes combined light weight and extremely good braking effect even under continuous high loads.

Forged magnesium wheels, 19-inches in diameter, were made by OZ Racing; weight saved over aluminium wheels was about 6kg (13lb) per wheel. The integral roll cage (IRC) was unobtrusively welded to the body and provided additional structural reinforcement.

In rear-drive form, the CTR II weighed only 1380kg (3040lb). Acceleration from zero to 62mph (100kph) took just 3.6 seconds, and the 124mph (200kph) mark was passed in 11.4 seconds. Depending on gearing, a top speed of up to 211mph (340kph) was possible.

The CTR II was soon followed by a wide-body lightweight version, the RUF CTR II Sport.

RUF turbo R

Based on the 993 turbo, RUF built a twin-turbo engine that produced 490hp (360kW) at 5500rpm and 650Nm (479lb ft) at 4800rpm. When combined with the turbo wide-body, actively controlled all-wheel drive and one of the world's finest brake systems, this power unit was teamed with the ideal equipment for achieving ultimate automotive performance. The turbo R suspension was tuned with firmer springs, altered shock absorber damping curves and larger anti-roll bars.

Suspension modifications were complemented by 18-inch RUF five-spoke alloy wheels and Bridgestone Potenza S-02 tyres. Aerodynamics were optimized with RUF outside mirrors. The BTR interior could be supplied with RUF instruments and their green markings, RUF sports steering wheel with airbag, and specially-contoured sports seats. Another option was the unobtrusive, integrated roll cage. Acceleration to 62mph (100kph) took only 3.6 seconds; 124mph (200kph) took 11.8 seconds. With a suitably high sixth gear, top speed was 204mph (329kph).

RUF RGT

As with the air-cooled cars before them, RUF conquered new market niches with water-cooled models. The RUF RGT was based on the 996 Carrera in Coupé or Cabriolet form, but powered by a 3.6-litre engine based on the GT3 power unit, with the crankcase of the air-cooled 3.6-litre engines. Power output was 385hp (283kW) at 7700rpm.

Maximum torque of 375Nm (277lb ft.) was available at 5200rpm. The power increase was achieved using four modified camshafts, a high-performance exhaust system, sports air-filter and retuned engine-control system. The RGT was intended for the many customers who missed out on the GT3. And in contrast to the GT3, the RGT was certified for sale in the United States. Aerodynamics of the narrow RGT body were optimized by a front spoiler, sill extensions, a large fixed rear spoiler and electrically-adjustable and heatable aero exterior mirrors.

The interior was entirely trimmed in leather, and, in the Coupé, fitted with a very unobtrusive, integrated roll cage. The brake system used six-piston callipers at the front and four-piston callipers at the rear. Ventilated, cross-drilled discs measured 330mm in diameter. Its sports suspension was tuned for agile handling. The RGT rolled on 18-inch RUF

alloy wheels. Acceleration from zero to 62mph (100kph) took 4.6 seconds, and top speed was recorded at 191mph (307kph).

RUF R turbo

RUF presented the R turbo on the mechanical basis of the 996 turbo. RUF customers could order their R turbo with all-wheel drive or, at added cost, choose a rear-drive version. Buyers also had a choice between the narrow Carrera body and the turbo wide-body. The R turbo was available in Coupé or Cabriolet form. The body was fitted with a modified nose with vent slots on top and RUF air dam below, aerodynamically optimized RUF outside mirrors, and a modified, electrically-adjustable rear spoiler. Side air inlets for the intercoolers were inset above the wheel arches, putting them closer to the intercoolers. Output of the water-cooled 3.6-litre twin-turbo engine was raised to a reliable 520hp (383kW) at 6000rpm by altered turbochargers, modified engine control unit, sports air-filter, special intake runners and a RUF exhaust system. To safely extract its maximum torque of 740Nm (546lb ft) at 3500rpm, vehicles with six-speed manual transmissions were equipped with a reinforced clutch. Alternatively, a five-speed Tiptronic S was available. The sports suspension included specially tuned Bilstein gas-pressure shock absorbers and stiffer springs. In place of the turbo brake system, customers could choose extremely durable ceramic brakes as an extra-cost option. Wheel choices were 18-inch RUF modular rims and 19-inch RUF aluminium alloys. Inside, the instrument panel housed special RUF instruments with green markings, a special sports steering wheel, and shell seats. The R turbo accelerated to 62mph (100kph) in just 3.7 seconds, and, depending on gearing, could reach a top speed between 205mph and 214mph (330kph and 345kph).

RUF soon launched the next performance level of the R turbo, with output set at 550hp (404kW) at 6000rpm. Maximum torque increased to 780Nm (575lb ft) at 4000rpm. The improved R turbo reached a top speed of 218mph (351kph).

RUF 3400 S

The RUF 3400 S was conceived for customers wanting an extremely powerful, open mid-engined car with abundant torque. A 3.4-litre 996 Carrera engine with an extra 10hp proved to be an ideal power source. The water-cooled boxer engine developed 310hp (228kW) at 6800rpm, with maximum torque of 360Nm (266lb ft) available at 4750rpm. A six-speed manual transmission was standard. The car's sports suspension was lowered and retuned with Bilstein gas-pressure shock absorbers. Instead of the Boxster S brake system, customers could opt for the even more powerful 911 turbo brake system, with 330mm brake discs.

Instead of the standard 18-inch RUF modular wheels, 19-inch alloy wheels were available as an added-cost option. Body aerodynamics were optimized with the Aero front spoiler, sills, RGT panels, modified air inlets and Aero outside mirrors. The tailpipe of the high-performance exhaust system exited through the centre of the rear valance. Customers could configure the interior to satisfy their individual tastes. Acceleration to 62mph (100kph) took 5.2 seconds, and top speed was 173mph (278kph).

RUF 3600 S

The RUF 3600 S represents the logical development of the 3400 S. The water-cooled 3.6-litre engine,

introduced with the 2002 model year 996 Carrera, proved to be the ideal power unit for installation in the Boxster. The engine developed 325hp (239kW) at 6800rpm, with maximum torque of 370Nm (273lb ft) available at 4250rpm. As an option, output could be uprated to 345hp (254kW).

Power was transmitted to the rear wheels through a six-speed manual transmission. The sports suspension was decently lowered and fitted with Bilstein gas-pressure shock absorbers for firmer tuning. Instead of the standard Boxster S brake system, with its ventilated, cross-drilled discs, customers could opt for the larger turbo brake system with 330mm discs. Buyers could substitute 19-inch RUF alloy rims for the standard 18-inch RUF modular wheels.

The 3600 S was fitted with the round-bottomed turbo headlamp units, Aero front spoiler, sills and RGT panels. At the rear, obvious changes included a diffuser and tailpipes exiting through the rear valance on either side of the number plate. Customers were free to configure the interior to suit their individual tastes; five gauges instead of three, special sports seats or selected leather colours – nearly anything was possible. Acceleration to 62mph (100kph) took 5.1 seconds, with a top speed of 173mph (278kph).

RUF turbo 3.3 Coupé 1977

Engine

Engine design:	6-cylinder horizontally-opposed, turbo charger
Installation:	Rear-engine
Cooling system:	Air-cooled
Displacement (cc):	3243
Bore x stroke (mm):	98.9 x 70.4
Engine output DIN (kW/hp):	223/303 at 5500rpm
Maximum torque (Nm/lb ft):	412/304 at 4000rpm
Output per litre (kW/l / hp/l):	68.8 / 93.4
Compression ratio:	6.5 : 1
Valve operation & camshaft drive:	ohc, cams driven by double chain, 2 valves per cylinder
Carburation:	Bosch K-Jetronic injection
Ignition system:	Battery, capacitive discharge system, breakerless
Firing order:	1 - 6 - 2 - 4 - 3 - 5
Turbo boost (bar):	0.8
Engine lubrication:	Dry sump
Engine oil total (l):	13.0

Transmission

Drive configuration:	Rear-axle drive
Manual gearbox:	5-speed (Getrag)
Transmission ratios:	
1st gear:	3.182
2nd gear:	1.833
3rd gear:	1.261
4th gear:	0.960
5th gear:	0.720
Reverse gear:	3.325
Drive ratio:	3.875
Option:	Limited-slip differential 40%

Body, chassis, suspension, brakes, wheels

Body design:	Steel coupé body, 2 doors, 2 + 2 seats, welded assembly, sheet metal box-section, unitized with body with wider front and rear wings, galvanized floorpanel, RUF plastic front and rear bumpers, black polyurethane front spoiler lip, fibreglass engine lid with flat rear wing with black polyurethane surround, red non-reflecting valance, painted outside mirror
Suspension, front:	Independent suspension with wishbones and McPherson struts, one round, longitudinal torsion bar per wheel, Bilstein gas-filled shock absorbers, anti-roll bar
Suspension, rear:	Independent suspension with semi-trailing arms, one round, transverse torsion bar per wheel, Bilstein gas-filled shock absorbers, anti-roll bar
Brakes, front/rear (Size (mm)):	Ventilated discs (282.5 x 20.5) / Ventilated discs (290 x 20) 2-piston fixed aluminium callipers / 2-piston fixed cast-iron callipers
Wheels, front/rear:	7 J x 16 / 8 J x 16
Tyres, front/rear:	205/55 VR 16 / 225/50 VR 16

Electrical system

Alternator (W/A):	980 / 70
Battery (V/Ah):	12 / 66

Dimensions and weight

Track, front/rear (mm):	1432 / 1530
Wheelbase (mm):	2272
Length x width x height (mm):	4235 x 1778 x 1260
Kerb weight (kg):	1280
Permissible gross weight (kg):	1470
Fuel tank capacity (l):	80, including 8 reserve
Power/weight ratio (kg/kW/kg/hp):	5.74 / 4.22

Fuel

	98 RON super leaded

Performance, prices

Acceleration 0-62mph/100kph (s):	5.1
0-124mph/200kph (s):	20.8
Maximum speed (mph / kph):	163 / 263
Purchase prices:	
1977:	DM 98,000

RUF SCR Coupé
RUF SCR Targa
1978–1983

Engine

Engine design:	6-cylinder horizontally-opposed
Installation:	Rear-engine
Cooling system:	Air-cooled
Displacement (cc):	3185
Bore x stroke (mm):	98 x 70.4
Engine output DIN (kW/hp):	160/217 at 5700rpm
Maximum torque (Nm/lb ft):	280/207 at 4100rpm
Output per litre (kW/l / hp/l):	50.2 / 68.1
Compression ratio:	9.8 : 1
Valve operation & camshaft drive:	ohc, cams driven by double chain, 2 valves per cylinder
Carburation:	Bosch K-Jetronic injection
Ignition system:	Battery, capacitive discharge system
Firing order:	1 - 6 - 2 - 4 - 3 - 5
Engine lubrication:	Dry sump
Engine oil total (l):	13.0

Transmission

Drive configuration:	Rear-axle drive
Manual gearbox:	5-speed
Transmission ratios:	
1st gear:	3.182
2nd gear:	1.833
3rd gear:	1.261
4th gear:	1.000
5th gear:	0.759
Reverse gear:	3.325
Drive ratio:	3.875
Limited-slip differential:	80%

Body, chassis, suspension, brakes, wheels

Body design:	Steel body, 2 doors, 2 + 2 seats, welded assembly, sheet metal box-section, unitized with body, hot-dip galvanized body panels, wider rear wings, boxy bumpers with black bellows, RUF front spoiler with engine oil cooler, engine lid with integrated rear spoiler, red non-reflecting valance, painted electric outside mirror

1981–1983:	Entirely hot-dip galvanized body, side indicators on front wings
Coupé:	Fixed steel roof
Option:	Electric sunroof
Targa:	Removable, foldable Targa top, fixed stainless steel Targa roll bar, fixed glass rear window
1979–1983:	Black Targa roll bar
Suspension, front:	Independent suspension with wishbones and McPherson struts, one round, longitudinal torsion bar per wheel, Bilstein gas-filled shock absorbers, anti-roll bar
Suspension, rear:	Independent suspension with semi-trailing arms, one round, transverse torsion bar per wheel, Bilstein gas-filled shock absorbers, anti-roll bar
Brakes, front/rear (Size (mm)):	Ventilated discs (282.5 x 20.5) / Ventilated discs (290 x 20) 2-piston fixed aluminium callipers / 2-piston fixed cast-iron callipers
Wheels, front/rear:	6 J x 16 / 7 J x 16
Tyres, front/rear:	205/55 VR 16 / 225/50 VR 16

Electrical system

Alternator (W/A):	980 / 70
Battery (V/Ah):	12 / 66

Dimensions and weight

Track, front/rear (mm):	1369 / 1379
Wheelbase (mm):	2272
Length x width x height (mm):	4291 x 1652 x 1320
Kerb weight DIN (kg):	1110
Permissible gross weight (kg):	1400
Fuel tank capacity (l):	80, including 8 reserve
Power/weight ratio (kg/kW/kg/hp):	6.94 / 5.12

Fuel

	98 RON super leaded

Performance, prices

Acceleration 0-62mph/100kph (s):	5.7
0-124mph/200kph (s):	23.7
Maximum speed (mph / kph):	158 / 255
Purchase prices:	
1978:	DM 65,000

RUF BTR 3.4 Coupé – Lightweight – 1983–1989

Engine

Engine design:	6-cylinder horizontally-opposed, turbocharger, intercooler
Installation:	Rear-engine
Cooling system:	Air-cooled
Displacement (cc):	3366
Bore x stroke (mm):	98 x 74.4
Engine output DIN (kW/hp):	275/374 at 6000rpm
Maximum torque (Nm/lb ft):	480/354 at 4800rpm
Output per litre (kW/l / hp/l):	81.7 / 111.1
Compression ratio:	7.0 : 1
Valve operation & camshaft drive:	ohc, cams driven by double chain, 2 valves per cylinder
Carburation:	Bosch K-Jetronic injection
Ignition system:	Battery, capacitive discharge system, breakerless
Firing order:	1 - 6 - 2 - 4 - 3 - 5
Turbo boost (bar):	0.8
Engine lubrication:	Dry sump
Engine oil total (l):	13.0

Transmission

Drive configuration:	Rear-axle drive
Manual gearbox:	5-speed (RUF)
Transmission ratios:	
1st gear:	2.786
2nd gear:	1.600
3rd gear:	1.120
4th gear:	0.828
5th gear:	0.625
Reverse gear:	2.909
Drive ratio:	4.000

Body, chassis, suspension, brakes, wheels

Body design:	Steel body, 2 doors, 2 + 2 seats, welded assembly, sheet metal box-section, unitized with body, entirely hot-dip galvanized body, wider front and rear wings, side-impact protection beams in doors, RUF front spoiler with engine oil cooler, RUF rear bumper, turbo rear wing with black polyurethane surround on engine lid, red non-reflecting valance, painted electric outside mirror, side indicators on front wings
1987–1989	Red non-reflecting valance with two integrated rear fog lamps
Suspension, front:	Independent suspension with wishbones and McPherson struts, one round, longitudinal torsion bar per wheel, Bilstein gas-filled shock absorbers, anti-roll bar
Suspension, rear:	Independent suspension with semi-trailing arms, one round, transverse torsion bar per wheel, Bilstein gas-filled shock absorbers, anti-roll bar
Brakes, front/rear (Size (mm)):	Ventilated and drilled discs (304 x 32) / Ventilated and drilled discs (309 x 28) 4-piston fixed aluminium callipers / 4-piston fixed aluminium callipers
Wheels, front/rear:	7 J x 16 / 8 J x 16
1986–1989:	9 J x 17 / 10 J x 17
Tyres, front/rear:	205/55 VR 16 / 225/50 VR 16
1986–1989:	235/40 VR 17 / 255/40 VR 17

Electrical system

Alternator (W/A):	1260 / 90
Battery (V/Ah):	12 / 36

Dimensions and weight

Track, front/rear (mm):	1432 / 1501
Wheelbase (mm):	2272
Length x width x height (mm):	4251 x 1775 x 1270
Kerb weight DIN (kg):	1169
Permissible gross weight (kg):	1580
Fuel tank capacity (l):	80, including 8 reserve
Power/weight ratio (kg/kW / kg/hp):	4.25 / 3.12

Fuel

	98 RON super leaded

Performance, prices

Acceleration 0-62mph/100kph (s):	4.6
0-124mph/200kph (s):	15.5
Maximum speed (mph / kph):	175 / 281
Purchase prices:	
1984:	DM 168,000
1986:	DM 196,000

RUF BTR 3.4 Coupé
1987–1989

Engine

Engine design:	6-cylinder horizontally-opposed, turbo charger, intercooler
Installation:	Rear-engine
Cooling system:	Air-cooled
Displacement (cc):	3366
Bore x stroke (mm):	98 x 74.4
Engine output DIN (kW/hp):	275/374 at 6000rpm
Maximum torque (Nm/lb ft):	480/354 at 4800rpm
Output per litre (kW/l / hp/l):	81.7 / 111.1
Compression ratio:	7.0 : 1
Valve operation & camshaft drive:	ohc, cams driven by double chain, 2 valves per cylinder
Carburation:	Bosch K-Jetronic injection
Ignition system:	Battery, capacitive discharge system, breakerless
Firing order:	1 - 6 - 2 - 4 - 3 - 5
Turbo boost (bar):	0.8
Engine lubrication:	Dry sump
Engine oil total (l):	13.0

Transmission

Drive configuration:	Rear-axle drive
Manual gearbox:	5-speed (RUF)
Transmission ratios:	
1st gear:	2.786
2nd gear:	1.600
3rd gear:	1.120
4th gear:	0.828
5th gear:	0.625
Reverse gear:	2.909
Drive ratio:	4.000
1989:	6-speed (RUF)
Transmission ratios:	
1st gear:	3.500
2nd gear:	2.059
3rd gear:	1.409
4th gear:	1.074
5th gear:	0.861
6th gear:	0.718
Reverse gear:	2.857
Drive ratio:	3.444

Body, chassis, suspension, brakes, wheels

Body design:	Steel body, 2 doors, 2 + 2 seats, welded assembly, sheet metal box-section, unitized with body, entirely hot-dip galvanized body, wider rear wings, side-impact protection beams in doors, RUF front spoiler with engine oil cooler and intregrated fog lamps, RUF rear bumper, turbo rear wing with black polyurethane surround on engine lid, red non-reflecting valance with two integrated rear fog lamps, painted electric outside mirror, side indicators on front wings
Suspension, front:	Independent suspension with wishbones and McPherson struts, one round, longitudinal torsion bar per wheel, Bilstein gas-filled shock absorbers, anti-roll bar
Suspension, rear:	Independent suspension with semi-trailing arms, one round, transverse torsion bar per wheel, Bilstein gas-filled shock absorbers, anti-roll bar
Brakes, front/rear (Size (mm)):	Ventilated and drilled discs (304 x 32) / Ventilated and drilled discs (309 x 28) 4-piston fixed aluminium callipers / 4-piston fixed aluminium callipers
Wheels, front/rear:	7 J x 16 / 8 J x 16
1988–1989:	8 J x 17 / 9 J x 17
Tyres, front/rear:	205/55 VR 16 / 225/50 VR 16
1988–1989:	215/45 VR 17 / 235/40 VR 17

Electrical system

Alternator (W/A):	1260 / 90
Battery (V/Ah):	12 / 66

Dimensions and weight

Track, front/rear (mm):	1398 / 1405
Wheelbase (mm):	2272
Length x width x height (mm):	4251 x 1652 x 1270
Kerb weight DIN (kg):	1256
Permissible gross weight (kg):	1680
Fuel tank capacity (l):	80, including 8 reserve
Power/weight ratio (kg/kW / kg/hp):	4.56 / 3.35

Fuel

	98 RON super leaded

Performance, prices

Acceleration 0-62mph/100kph (s):	4.8
0-124mph/200kph (s):	16.7
Maximum speed (mph / kph):	190 / 305
Purchase price 1987:	DM 188,000
1989 (6-speed and 17"):	DM 214,320

RUF Carrera 3.4 Coupé
[Catalytic converter]
RUF Carrera 3.4 Targa
[Catalytic converter]
RUF Carrera 3.4 Cabriolet
[Catalytic converter]
MY 1984–MY 1989
[MY 1986–MY 1989]

Engine

Engine design:	6-cylinder horizontally-opposed
Installation:	Rear-engine
Cooling system:	Air-cooled
Displacement (cc):	3366
Bore x stroke (mm):	98 x 74.4
Engine output DIN (kW/hp):	184/250 at 5900rpm
with catalytic converter:	[180/245 at 5900rpm]
Maximum torque (Nm/lb ft):	304/224 at 4800rpm
with catalytic converter:	[284/209 at 4800rpm]
Output per litre (kW/l / hp/l):	54.7 / 74.3
with catalytic converter:	[53.5 / 72.8]
Compression ratio:	10.3 : 1
with catalytic converter:	[10.3 : 1]
Valve operation & camshaft drive:	ohc, cams driven by double chain, 2 valves per cylinder
Carburation:	Bosch DME with L-Jetronic injection
Ignition system:	Bosch DME
Firing order:	1 - 6 - 2 - 4 - 3 - 5
Engine lubrication:	Dry sump
Engine oil total (l):	13.0

Transmission

Drive configuration:	Rear-axle drive
Manual gearbox:	5-speed
Transmission ratios:	
1st gear:	3.182 (3.500)*
2nd gear:	1.833 (2.059)*
3rd gear:	1.261 (1.409)*
4th gaer:	0.965 (1.074)*
5th gear:	0.763 (0.861)*
Reverse gear:	3.325 (2.857)*
Drive ratio:	3.875 (3.444)*
Option:	Limited-slip differential 40%

*From MY 1987 gearbox type G 50

Body, chassis, suspension, brakes, wheels

Body design:	Steel body, 2 doors, 2 + 2 seats, welded assembly, sheet metal box-section, unitized with body, entirely hot-dip galvanized body, wider rear wings, boxy bumpers with black bellows, intregrated front fog lamps, engine lid with black grille, red non-reflecting valance, painted electric outside mirror, side indicators on front wings
MY 1985–MY 1989:	Side-impact protection beams in doors
MY 1987–MY 1989:	Red non-reflecting valance with two integrated rear fog lamps

Option:	Black polyurethane front spoiler lip, rear spoiler with black polyurethane surround on engine lid
Coupé:	Fixed steel roof
Option:	Electric sunroof
Targa:	Removable, foldable Targa top, fixed black Targa roll bar, fixed glass rear window
Cabriolet:	Manual soft top with flexible plastic rear window
Option MY 1987–MY 1989:	Electric soft top with flexible plastic rear window
Suspension, front:	Independent suspension with wishbones and McPherson struts, one round, longitudinal torsion bar per wheel, Bilstein gas-filled shock absorbers, anti-roll bar
Suspension, rear:	Independent suspension with semi-trailing arms, one round, transverse torsion bar per wheel, Bilstein gas-filled shock absorbers, anti-roll bar
Brakes, front/rear (Size (mm)):	Ventilated discs (282,5 x 24) / Ventilated discs (290 x 24) 2-piston fixed cast-iron callipers/ 2-piston fixed cast-iron callipers
Wheels, front/rear:	6 J x 15 / 7 J x 15
Tyres, front/rear:	185/70 VR 15 / 215/60 VR 15
Option, 1988–1989 standard:	7 J x 15 / 8 J x 15 195/65 VR 15 / 215/60 VR 15
Option–1988:	6 J x 16 / 7 J x 16 205/55 VR 16 / 225/50 VR 16
1989 standard:	6 J x 16 / 8 J x 16 205/55 VR 16 / 225/50 VR 16

Electrical system

Alternator (W/A):	1260 / 90
Battery (V/Ah):	12 / 66
Option:	12 / 88

Dimensions and weight

Track, front/rear (mm):	1372 / 1380
7 J x 15 / 8 J x 15:	1398 / 1405
6 J x 16 / 8 J x 16:	1372 / 1405
Wheelbase (mm):	2272
Length x width x height (mm):	4291 x 1652 x 1320
Kerb weight DIN (kg):	1160
MY 1986–MY 1989:	1210
Permissible gross weight (kg):	1500
MY 1986–MY 1989:	1530
Fuel tank capacity (l):	80, including 8 reserve
Power/weight ratio (kg/kW / kg/hp):	6.30 [6.44] / 4.64 [4.73]
MY 1986–MY 1989:	6.58 [6.72] / 4.84 [4.94]

Fuel

	98 RON super leaded

Performance, prices

Acceleration 0-62mph/100kph (s):	app. 5.7 [app. 5.9]
Maximum speed (mph / kph):	155 / 250 [152 / 245]
Conversion prices:	
1999 conversion w/o catalytic con.:	DM 16,820
1999 conversion w. catalytic con.:	DM 19,140

RUF CTR
1987

Engine

Engine design:	6-cylinder horizontally-opposed, twin-turbo charger, twin-intercooler
Installation:	Rear-engine
Cooling system:	Air-cooled
Displacement (cc):	3366
Bore x stroke (mm):	98 x 74.4
Engine output DIN (kW/hp):	345/469 at 5950rpm
Maximum torque (Nm/lb ft):	553/408 at 5100rpm
Output per litre (kW/l / hp/l):	102.5 / 139.3
Compression ratio:	7.5 : 1
Valve operation & camshaft drive:	ohc, cams driven by double chain, 2 valves per cylinder
Carburation:	Bosch Motronic 1.2
Ignition system:	Bosch Motronic 1.2
Firing order:	1 - 6 - 2 - 4 - 3 - 5
Turbo boost (bar):	1.1
Engine lubrication:	Dry sump
Engine oil total (l):	13.0

Transmission

Drive configuration:	Rear-axle drive
Manual gearbox:	5-speed (RUF)
Transmission ratios:	
1st gear:	2.786
2nd gear:	1.600
3rd gear:	1.120
4th gear:	0.828
5th gear:	0.625
Reverse gear:	2.909
Drive ratio:	4.000
1989:	6-speed (RUF)
Transmission ratios:	
1st gear:	3.500
2nd gear:	2.059
3rd gear:	1.409
4th gear:	1.074
5th gear:	0.861
6th gear:	0.718
Reverse gear:	2.857
Drive ratio:	3.444

Body, chassis, suspension, brakes, wheels

Body design:	Steel body, 2 doors, 2 seats, welded assembly, sheet metal box-section, unitized with body, entirely hot-dip galvanized body, rear wings on each side 2.5 centimetres wider, side-impact protection beams in doors, aluminium front lid and doors, no rain gutters, RUF front spoiler with engine oil cooler and intregrated fog lamps, RUF rear bumper, 'Carrera' rear spoiler with black polyurethane surround on engine lid, red non-reflecting valance with two integrated rear fog lamps, RUF sports outside mirrors
Suspension, front:	Independent suspension with wishbones and McPherson struts, one round, longitudinal torsion bar per wheel, Bilstein gas-filled shock absorbers, anti-roll bar
Suspension, rear:	Independent suspension with semi-trailing arms, one round, transverse torsion bar per wheel, Bilstein gas-filled shock absorbers, anti-roll bar
Brakes, front/rear (Size (mm)):	Ventilated and drilled discs (330 x 30) / Ventilated and drilled discs (330 x 30) 4-piston fixed aluminium callipers / 4-piston fixed aluminium callipers
Wheels, front/rear:	8 J x 17 / 10 J x 17
Wheels, type:	RUF 5-spoke, Speedline
Tyres, front/rear:	215/45 VR 17 / 255/40 VR 17
Tyres, type:	Dunlop-Denloc

Electrical system

Alternator (W/A):	1260 / 90
Battery (V/Ah):	12 / 66

Dimensions and weight

Track, front/rear (mm):	1384 / 1417
Wheelbase (mm):	2272
Length x width x height (mm):	4251 x 1652 x 1270
Kerb weight DIN (kg):	1150
Permissible gross weight (kg):	1530
Fueltank capacity (l):	105, including 8 reserve
Power/weight ratio (kg/kW/kg/hp):	3.33 / 2.45

Fuel

	98 RON super leaded

Performance, prices

Acceleration 0-62mph/100kph (s):	4.8
0-124mph/200 kph (s):	11.3
Maximum speed (mph / kph):	211 / 339
In Nardo:	213 / 342
Purchase price:	
1988:	DM 288,000

RUF BTR III
1988–1989

Engine

Engine design:	6-cylinder horizontally-opposed, turbo charger, intercooler
Installation:	Rear-engine
Cooling system:	Air-cooled
Displacement (cc):	3366
Bore x stroke (mm):	98 x 74.4
Engine output DIN (kW/hp):	300/408 at 6000rpm
Maximum torque (Nm/lb ft):	480/354 at 4800rpm
Output per litre (kW/l / hp/l):	81.7 / 111.1
Compression ratio:	7.0 : 1
Valve operation & camshaft drive:	ohc, cams driven by double chain, 2 valves per cylinder
Carburation:	Bosch Motronic
Ignition system:	Bosch Motronic
Firing order:	1 - 6 - 2 - 4 - 3 - 5
Turbo boost (bar):	1.0
Engine lubrication:	Dry sump
Engine oil total (l):	13.0

Transmission

Drive configuration:	Rear-axle drive
Manual gearbox:	5-speed (RUF)
Transmission ratios:	
1st gear:	2.786
2nd gear:	1.600
3rd gear:	1.120
4th gear:	0.828
5th gear:	0.625
Reverse gear:	2.909
Drive ratio:	4.000
1989:	6-speed (RUF)
Transmission ratios:	
1st gear:	3.500
2nd gear:	2.059
3rd gear:	1.409
4th gear:	1.074
5th gear:	0.861
6th gear:	0.718
Reverse gear:	2.857
Drive ratio:	3.444

Body, chassis, suspension, brakes, wheels

Body design:	Steel body, 2 doors, 2 + 2 seats, welded assembly, sheet metal box-section, unitized with body, entirely hot-dip galvanized body, wider front and rear wings, side-impact protection beams in doors, RUF front spoiler with engine oil cooler and integrated fog lamps, RUF rear bumper, intregrated front fog

lamps, turbo rear spoiler with black polyure-thane surround on engine lid, red non-reflecting valance with two integrated rear fog lamps, painted electric outside mirror, side indicators on front wings

Suspension, front:	Independent suspension with wishbones and McPherson struts, one round, longitudinal torsion bar per wheel, Bilstein gas-filled shock absorbers, anti-roll bar
Suspension, rear:	Independent suspension with semi-trailing arms, one round, transverse torsion bar per wheel, Bilstein gas-filled shock absorbers, anti-roll bar
Brakes, front/rear (Size (mm)):	Ventilated and drilled discs (304 x 32) / Ventilated and drilled discs (309 x 28) 4-piston fixed aluminium callipers / 4-piston fixed aluminium callipers
Wheels, front/rear:	7 J x 16 / 8 J x 16
17 inch:	9 J x 17 / 10 J x 17
Tyres, front/rear:	205/55 VR 16 / 225/50 VR 16
17 inch:	235/40 VR 17 / 255/40 VR 17

Electrical system

Alternator (W/A):	1260 / 90
Battery (V/Ah):	12 / 36

Dimensions and weight

Track, front/rear (mm):	1432 / 1501
9 J x 17 / 10 J x 17:	1443 / 1512
Wheelbase (mm):	2272
Length x width x height (mm):	4251 x 1775 x 1270
Kerb weight DIN (kg):	1169
Permissible gross weight (kg):	1580
Fuel tank capacity (l):	80, including 8 reserve
Power/weight ratio (kg/kW / kg/hp):	4.17 / 3.06

Fuel

	98 RON super leaded

Performance, prices

Acceleration 0-62mph/100kph (s):	4.6
0-124mph/200 kph (s):	15.5
Maximum speed (mph / kph):	180 / 290

Purchase and conversion prices:

1992 conversion engine:	DM 38,190
RUF 6-speed gearbox 1987:	DM 22,230
RUF turbo brakes:	DM 10,248.60
RUF suspension:	DM 4,332
RUF 17 inch wheels:	DM 6,783
930 turbo rear wing:	DM 3,363

RUF CR 2
RUF CR 4
1990–1993

Engine
Engine design:	6-cylinder horizontally-opposed
Installation:	Rear-engine
Cooling system:	Air-cooled
Displacement (cc):	3600
Bore x stroke (mm):	100 x 76.4
Engine output DIN (kW/hp):	206/280 at 6000rpm
Maximum torque (Nm/lb ft):	325/240 at 5800rpm
Output per litre (kW/l / hp/l):	57.2 / 77.8
Compression ratio:	11.4 : 1
Valve operation & camshaft drive:	ohc, cams driven by double chain, 2 valves per cylinder
Carburation:	Bosch DME with sequential injection
Ignition system:	Bosch DME, dual-ignition
Firing order:	1 - 6 - 2 - 4 - 3 - 5
Engine lubrication:	Dry sump
Engine oil total (l):	11.5

Transmission
Drive configuration:	Rear-axle drive
CR 4:	[Electronic-controlled 4-wheel-drive, transaxle]
Manual gearbox:	5-speed
Transmission ratios:	
1st gear:	3.500 [3,500]
2nd gear:	2.059 [2.118]
3rd gear:	1.407 [1.444]
4th gear:	1.086 [1.086]
5th gear:	0.868 [0.868]
Reverse gear:	2.857 [2.857]
Drive ratio:	3.444 [3.444]

Body, chassis, suspension, brakes, wheels
Body design:	Steel body, 2 doors, 2 + 2 seats, entirely hot-dip galvanized body, side-impact protection beams in doors, flexible polyurethane front and rear bumpers with integrated aluminium beams, RUF front spoiler lip polyurethane side skirts, engine lid with integrated automatic rear spoiler, red non-reflecting valance with integrated reversing and rear fog lamps
1992–1993:	Outside mirrors in Cup-Design
Coupé:	Fixed steel roof
Option:	Electric sunroof
Targa:	Removable, foldable Targa top, fixed black Targa roll bar, fixed glass rear window
Cabriolet:	Electric hood with flexible plastic rear window
Suspension, front:	Individually suspended light alloy lower wishbones, McPherson struts with coil springs, Bilstein gas-filled shock absorbers, anti-roll bar
Suspension, rear:	Individually suspended on tilted shafts, McPherson struts with coil springs, Bilstein gas-filled shock absorbers, anti-roll bar
Brakes, front/rear (Size (mm)):	Ventilated discs (298 x 28) / Ventilated discs (299 x 24) 4-piston fixed aluminium callipers / 2-piston fixed aluminium callipers
CR 2 1993, CR 4:	4-piston fixed aluminium callipers / 4-piston fixed aluminium callipers Bosch ABS
Wheels, front/rear:	8.5 J x 18 / 9.5 J x 18
Wheels, type:	RUF 5-spoke, Speedline
Tyres, front/rear:	235/40 ZR 18 / 265/35 ZR 18
Tyres, type:	Dunlop SP Sport 8000

Electrical system
Alternator (W/A):	1610 / 115
Battery (V/Ah):	12 / 72
1992–1993:	12 / 75

Dimensions and weight
Track, front/rear (mm):	1363 / 1382
Wheelbase (mm):	2272
Length x width x height (mm):	4250 x 1652 x 1310
Kerb weight DIN (kg):	1350
CR 4:	1450
Permissible gross weight (kg):	1690
Fuel tank capacity (l):	77, including 10 reserve
Power/weight ratio (kg/kW / kg/hp):	6.55 / 4.82
CR 4:	4.04 / 5.18

Fuel
	98 RON super plus unleaded

Performance, prices
Acceleration 0-62mph/100kph (s):	app. 5.3*
0-124mph/200 kph (s):	app. 19.0*
Maximum speed (mph / kph):	app. 168 / 270*
*CR 2 with 5-speed gearbox	
Conversion price:	
Engine conversion 1993:	DM 8,970

RUF BR 2
RUF BR 4
1991–1992

Engine

Engine design:	6-cylinder horizontally-opposed, turbo charger, intercooler
Installation:	Rear-engine
Cooling system:	Air-cooled
Displacement (cc):	3299
Bore x stroke (mm):	97 x 74.4
Engine output DIN (kW/hp):	265/360 at 5750rpm
Maximum torque (Nm/lb ft):	465/343 at 5000rpm
Output per litre (kW/l / hp/l):	80.3 / 109.1
Compression ratio:	7.0 : 1
Valve operation & camshaft drive:	ohc, cams driven by double chain, 2 valves per cylinder
Carburation:	Bosch K-Jetronic injection
Ignition system:	Battery, capacitive discharge system, breakerless
Firing order:	1 - 6 - 2 - 4 - 3 - 5
Turbo boost (bar):	0.8
Engine lubrication:	Dry sump
Engine oil total (l):	13.0

Transmission

Drive configuration:	Rear-axle drive
Option BR 4:	Electronic-controlled 4-wheel-drive, transaxle
Manual gearbox:	6-speed (RUF)
Transmission ratios:	
1st gear:	3.500
2nd gear:	2.059
3rd gear:	1.409
4th gear:	1.074
5th gear:	0.861
6th gear:	0.718
Reverse gear:	2.812
Drive ratio:	3.444
Limited-slip differential:	60%
Option:	Electronic clutch system (EKS)

Body, chassis, suspension, brakes, wheels

Body design:	Steel body, 2 doors, 2 seats, entirely hot-dip galvanized body, side-impact protection beams in doors, flexible polyurethane front and rear bumpers with integrated aluminium beams, RUF front spoiler lip, polyurethane side skirts, engine lid with fixed turbo rear spoiler, red non-reflecting valance with integrated reversing and rear fog lamps, RUF sports outside mirrors
Suspension, front:	Individually suspended light alloy lower wishbones, McPherson struts with coil springs, Bilstein gas-filled shock absorbers, anti-roll bar
Suspension, rear:	Individually suspended on tilted shafts, McPherson struts with coil springs, Bilstein gas-filled shock absorbers, anti-roll bar
Brakes, front/rear (Size (mm)):	Ventilated and drilled discs (322 x 32) / Ventilated and drilled discs (299 x 28) 4-piston fixed aluminium callipers / 4-piston fixed aluminium callipers Bosch ABS
Wheels, front/rear:	8.5 J x 18 / 9.5 J x 18
Wheels, type:	RUF 5-spoke, Speedline
Tyres, front/rear:	235/40 ZR 18 / 265/35 ZR 18
Tyres, type:	Dunlop SP Sport 8000

Electrical system

Alternator (W/A):	1610 / 115
Battery (V/Ah):	12 / 72

Dimensions and weight

Track, front/rear (mm):	1363 / 1382
Wheelbase (mm):	2272
Length x width x height (mm):	4250 x 1652 x 1295
Kerb weight DIN (kg):	1355
Permissible gross weight (kg):	1810
Fuel tank capacity (l):	77, including 15 reserve
Power/weight ratio (kg/kW/kg/hp):	5.11 / 3.76

Fuel

	98 RON super plus unleaded

Performance, prices

Acceleration 0–62mph/100kph (s):	4.4
0–124mph/200 kph (s):	15.5
Maximum speed (mph / kph):	188 / 303
Purchase prices:	
1992:	DM 226,000
with EKS:	DM 238,000

RUF BTR 3.8
1992–1994

Engine

Engine design:	6-cylinder horizontally-opposed, turbocharger, intercooler
Installation:	Rear-engine
Cooling system:	Air-cooled
Displacement (cc):	3746
Bore x stroke (mm):	102 x 76.4
Engine output DIN (kW/hp):	305/415 at 6000rpm
Maximum torque (Nm/lb ft):	550/406 at 4800rpm
Output per litre (kW/l / hp/l):	81.4 / 110.7
Compression ratio:	8.5 : 1
Valve operation & camshaft drive:	ohc, cams driven by double chain, 2 valves per cylinder
Carburation:	Bosch Motronic with sequential injection
Ignition system:	Bosch Motronic
Firing order:	1 - 6 - 2 - 4 - 3 - 5
Turbo boost (bar):	0.8
Engine lubrication:	Dry sump
Engine oil total (l):	14.0

Transmission

Drive configuration:	Rear-axle drive
Option:	Electronic-controlled 4-wheel-drive, transaxle
Manual gearbox:	6-speed (RUF)
Transmission ratios:	
1st gear:	3.500
2nd gear:	2.059
3rd gear:	1.409
4th gear:	1.074
5th gear:	0.861
6th gear:	0.718
Reverse gear:	2.812
Drive ratio:	3.444
Limited-slip differential:	60%
Option:	Electronic clutch system (EKS)

Body, chassis, suspension, brakes, wheels

Body design:	Steel body, 2 doors, 2 seats, entirely hot-dip galvanized body, side-impact protection beams in doors, flexible polyurethane front and rear bumpers with integrated aluminium beams, RUF front spoiler lip, polyurethane side skirts, RS rear bumper, engine lid with fixed turbo rear spoiler, red non-reflecting
Suspension, front:	valance with integrated reversing and rear fog lamps, RUF sports outside mirrors Individually suspended light alloy lower wishbones, McPherson struts with coil springs, Bilstein gas-filled shock absorbers, anti-roll bar
Suspension, rear:	Individually suspended on tilted shafts, McPherson struts with coil springs, Bilstein gas-filled shock absorbers, anti-roll bar
Brakes, front/rear (Size (mm)):	Ventilated and drilled discs (322 x 32) / Ventilated and drilled discs (299 x 28) 4-piston fixed aluminium callipers / 4-piston fixed aluminium callipers Bosch ABS
Wheels, front/rear:	8.5 J x 18 / 9.5 J x 18
Wheels, type:	RUF 5-spoke, Speedline
Tyres, front/rear:	235/40 ZR 18 / 265/35 ZR 18
Tyres, type:	Dunlop SP Sport 8000

Electrical system

Alternator (W/A):	1610 / 115
Battery (V/Ah):	12 / 72
1993–1994:	12 / 75

Dimensions and weight

Track, front/rear (mm):	1379 / 1380
Wheelbase (mm):	2272
Length x width x height (mm):	4275 x 1652 x 1270
Kerb weight DIN (kg):	1260
Permissible gross weight (kg):	1810
Fuel tank capacity (l):	77, including 15 reserve
Power/weight ratio (kg/kW/kg/hp):	4.13 / 3.04

Fuel

	98 RON super plus unleaded

Performance, prices

Acceleration 0-62mph/100kph (s):	3.9
0-124mph/200 kph (s):	12.9
Maximum speed (mph / kph):	198 / 319
Purchase prices:	
1993:	DM 249,148

RUF RCT
1992–1994

Engine

Engine design:	6-cylinder horizontally-opposed, turbo charger, intercooler
Installation:	Rear-engine
Cooling system:	Air-cooled
Displacement (cc):	3600
Bore x stroke (mm):	100 x 76.4
Engine output DIN (kW/hp):	272/370 at 5500rpm
Maximum torque (Nm/lb ft):	535/395 at 4500rpm
Output per litre (kW/l / hp/l):	75.5 / 102.8
Compression ratio:	8.4 : 1
Valve operation & camshaft drive:	ohc, cams driven by double chain, 2 valves per cylinder
Carburation:	Bosch Motronic with sequential injection
Ignition system:	Bosch Motronic, dual-ignition
Firing order:	1 - 6 - 2 - 4 - 3 - 5
Turbo boost (bar):	0.8
Engine lubrication:	Dry sump
Engine oil total (l):	14.0

Transmission

Drive configuration:	Rear-axle drive
Option:	Electronic controlled 4-wheel-drive, transaxle
Manual gearbox:	6-speed (RUF)
Transmission ratios:	
1st gear:	3.500
2nd gear:	2.059
3rd gear:	1.409
4th gear:	1.074
5th gear:	0.861
6th gear:	0.718
Reverse gear:	2.812
Drive ratio:	3.444
Limited-slip differential:	60%
Option:	Electronic clutch system (EKS)

Body, chassis, suspension, brakes, wheels

Body design:	Steel body, 2 doors, 2 seats, entirely hot-dip galvanized body, side-impact protection beams in doors, flexible polyurethane front and rear bumpers with integrated aluminium beams, RUF front spoiler lip, polyurethane side skirts, engine lid with fixed turbo rear spoiler, red non-reflecting valance with

	integrated reversing and rear fog lamps, outside mirrors in Cup-Design
Option:	RUF sports outside mirrors
Suspension, front:	Individually suspended light alloy lower wishbones, McPherson struts with coil springs, Bilstein gas-filled shock absorbers, anti-roll bar
Suspension, rear:	Individually suspended on tilted shafts, McPherson struts with coil springs, Bilstein gas-filled shock absorbers, anti-roll bar
Brakes, front/rear (Size (mm)):	Ventilated and drilled discs (322 x 32) / Ventilated and drilled discs (299 x 28) 4-piston fixed aluminium callipers / 4-piston fixed aluminium callipers Bosch ABS
Wheels, front/rear:	8.5 J x 18 / 9.5 J x 18
Wheels, type:	RUF 5-spoke, Speedline
Tyres, front/rear:	235/40 ZR 18 / 265/35 ZR 18
Tyres, type:	Dunlop SP Sport 8000

Electrical system

Alternator (W/A):	1610 / 115
Battery (V/Ah):	12 / 75

Dimensions and weight

Track, front/rear (mm):	1363 / 1382
Wheel base (mm):	2272
Length x width x height (mm):	4250 x 1652 x 1270
Kerb weight DIN (kg):	1350
Permissible gross weight (kg):	1690
Fuel tank capacity (l):	77, including 15 reserve
Power/weight ratio (kg/kW/kg/hp):	5.04 / 3.65

Fuel

	98 RON super plus unleaded

Performance, prices

Acceleration 0-62mph/100kph (s):	app. 4.4
Maximum speed (mph / kph):	app. 190 / 305

Purchase and conversion prices 1994:

RCT engine conversion:	DM 33,350
6-speed gearbox conversion:	DM 13,085.85
BTR brakes:	DM 8,582.80
RUF 18 inch wheels:	DM 7,992.50
Turbo rear wing:	DM 4,025

RUF RCT EVO
1992–1994

Engine

Engine design:	6-cylinder horizontally-opposed, turbo charger, intercooler
Installation:	Rear-engine
Cooling system:	Air-cooled
Displacement (cc):	3600
Bore x stroke (mm):	100 x 76.4
Engine output DIN (kW/hp):	313/425 at 5800rpm
Maximum torque (Nm/lb ft):	570/420 at 4500rpm
Output per litre (kW/l / hp/l):	86.9 / 118.1
Compression ratio:	9.0 : 1
Valve operation & camshaft drive:	ohc, cams driven by double chain, 2 valves per cylinder
Carburation:	Bosch Motronic with sequential injection
Ignition system:	Bosch Motronic, dual-ignition
Firing order:	1 - 6 - 2 - 4 - 3 - 5
Turbo boost (bar):	0.8
Engine lubrication:	Dry sump
Engine oil total (l):	14.0

Transmission

Drive configuration:	Rear-axle drive
Option:	Electronic-controlled 4-wheel-drive, transaxle
Manual gearbox:	6-speed (RUF)
Transmission ratios:	
1st gear:	3.500
2nd gear:	2.059
3rd gear:	1.409
4th gear:	1.074
5th gear:	0.861
6th gear:	0.718
Reverse gear:	2.812
Drive ratio:	3.444
Limited-slip differential:	60%
Option:	Electronic clutch system (EKS)

Body, chassis, suspension, brakes, wheels

Body design:	Steel body, 2 doors, 2 seats, entirely hot-dip galvanized body, side-impact protection beams in doors, flexible polyurethane front and rear bumpers with integrated aluminium beams, RUF front spoiler lip, polyurethane side skirts, engine lid with fixed turbo rear spoiler, red non-reflecting valance with integrated reversing and rear fog lamps, outside mirrors in Cup-Design

Option:	RUF sports outside mirrors
Suspension, front:	Individually suspended light alloy lower wishbones, McPherson struts with coil springs, Bilstein gas-filled shock absorbers, anti-roll bar
Suspension, rear:	Individually suspended on tilted shafts, McPherson struts with coil springs, Bilstein gas-filled shock absorbers, anti-roll bar
Brakes, front/rear (Size (mm)):	Ventilated and drilled discs (322 x 32) / Ventilated and drilled discs (299 x 28) 4-piston fixed aluminium callipers / 4-piston fixed aluminium callipers Bosch ABS
Wheels, front/rear:	8.5 J x 18 / 9.5 J x 18
Wheels, type:	RUF 5-spoke, Speedline
Tyres, front/rear:	225/40 ZR 18 / 265/35 ZR 18
Tyres, type:	Dunlop SP Sport 8000

Electrical system

Alternator (W/A):	1610 / 115
Battery (V/Ah):	12 / 75
Dimensions and weight	
Track, front/rear (mm):	1363 / 1382
Wheelbase (mm):	2272
Length x width x height (mm):	4250 x 1652 x 1270
Kerb weight DIN (kg):	1400
Permissible gross weight (kg):	1690
Fuel tank capacity (l):	77, including 15 reserve
Power/weight ratio (kg/kW/kg/hp):	4.47 / 3.29

Fuel

	98 RON super plus unleaded

Performance, prices

Acceleration 0-62mph/100kph (s):	app. 3.9
0-124mph/200 kph (s):	app. 12.9
Maximum speed (mph / kph):	app. 200 / 320

Purchase and conversion prices:

2003 engine conversion RCT:	Euro 25,520
6-speed gearbox conversion C2:	Euro 5,568
6-speed gearbox conversion C4:	Euro 6,844
RUF 18 inch wheels:	Euro 3,584.40
BTR brakes C2 MY 92/C 4:	Euro 4,268.80
Auxiliary oil cooler with oil cooler:	Euro 1,119.40
Auxiliary oil cooler w/o oil cooler:	Euro 1,363
Turbo rear wing:	Euro 2,842*
*plus painting	

RUF BTR 2 Coupé
RUF BTR 2 Cabriolet
1994–1997

Engine

Engine design:	6-cylinder horizontally-opposed, turbo charger, intercooler
Installation:	Rear-engine
Cooling system:	Air-cooled
Displacement (cc):	3600
Bore x stroke (mm):	100 x 76.4
Engine output DIN (kW/hp):	309/420 at 5000rpm
Maximum torque (Nm/lb ft):	580/428 at 4800rpm
Output per litre (kW/l / hp/l):	83.3 / 113.3
Compression ratio:	8.4 : 1
Valve operation & camshaft drive:	ohc, cams driven by double chain, 2 valves per cylinder
Carburation:	Bosch DME, Motronic
Ignition system:	Bosch DME
Firing order:	1 - 6 - 2 - 4 - 3 - 5
Turbo boost (bar):	0.8
Engine lubrication:	Dry sump
Engine oil total (l):	13.5

Transmission

Drive configuration:	Rear-axle drive
Option:	4-wheel-drive with visco-clutch, transaxle
Manual gearbox:	6-speed
Transmission ratios:	
1st gear:	3.818
2nd gear:	2.150
3rd gear:	1.560
4th gear:	1.242
5th gear:	1.027
6th gear:	0.750
Reverse gear:	2.857
Drive ratio:	3.444
Limited-slip differential:	60%
Option:	Electronic clutch system (EKS)

Body, chassis, suspension, brakes, wheels

Body design:	Steel body, 2 doors, 2 seats, entirely hot-dip galvanized body, side-impact protection beams in doors, flexible polyurethane front and rear bumpers with integrated aluminium beams, RUF front bumper with three

additional air outlets, engine lid with fixed rear spoiler 'Turbo 3.6', red non-reflecting valance with integrated reversing and rear fog lamps, electric hood with flexible plastic rear window

Coupé:	Fixed steel roof
Option:	Electric sunroof
Cabriolet:	Electric hood with flexible plastic rear window
Option:	Automatic wind blocker
Suspension, front:	Individually suspended light alloy lower wishbones, McPherson struts with coil springs, Bilstein gas-filled shock absorbers, anti-roll bar
Suspension, rear:	Individually suspended on light alloy multi wishbone axle with LSA system (Lightweight, Stability, Agility) with progressive coil springs, Bilstein gas-filled shock absorbers, anti-roll bar
Brakes, front/rear (Size (mm)):	Ventilated and drilled discs (322 x 32) / Ventilated and drilled discs (299 x 24) 4-piston fixed aluminium callipers / 4-piston fixed aluminium callipers Bosch ABS 5
Wheels, front/rear:	8,5 J x 18 / 10 J x 18
Tyres, front/rear:	225/40 ZR 18 / 285/30 ZR 18

Electrical system

Alternator (W/A):	1610 / 115
Battery (V/Ah):	12 / 75

Dimensions and weight

Track, front/rear (mm):	1405 / 1444
Wheelbase (mm):	2272
Length x width x height (mm):	4245 x 1735 x 1285
Kerb weight DIN (kg):	1250
Permissible gross weight (kg):	1710
Fuel tank capacity (l):	73.5, including 15 reserve
Power/weight ratio (kg/kW/kg/hp):	4.05 / 2.98

Fuel

	98 RON super plus unleaded

Performance, prices

Acceleration 0-62mph/100kph (s):	4.1
Maximum speed (mph / kph):	191 / 308
Purchase price:	
1996:	DM 210,697

RUF CTR II [CTR II sport]
1996–2000

Engine

Engine design:	6-cylinder horizontally-opposed, twin-turbo charger, twin-intercooler
Installation:	Rear-engine
Cooling system:	Air-cooled
Displacement (cc):	3600
Bore x stroke (mm):	100 x 76.4
Engine output DIN (kW/hp):	382/520 [426/580] at 5800rpm
Maximum torque (Nm/lb ft):	685/505 [780/575] at 4800rpm
Output per litre (kW/l / hp/l):	106.1 [118.3] / 144.4 [161.1]
Compression ratio:	8.0 : 1
Valve operation & camshaft drive:	ohc, cams driven by double chain, 2 valves per cylinder
Carburation:	TAGtronic
Ignition system:	TAGtronic
Firing order:	1 - 6 - 2 - 4 - 3 - 5
Turbo boost (bar):	1.1
Engine lubrication:	Dry sump
Engine oil total (l):	13.5

Transmission

Drive configuration:	Rear-axle drive
Option:	4-wheel-drive with visco-clutch, transaxle
Manual gearbox:	6-speed
Transmission ratios:	
1st gear:	3.15
2nd gear:	1.79
3rd gear:	1.27
4th gear:	0.97
5th gear:	0.76
6th gear:	0.60
Reverse gear:	2.857
Drive ratio:	3.444
Limited-slip differential:	60%

Body, chassis, suspension, brakes, wheels

Body design:	Steel coupé body, 2 doors, 2 seats, entirely hot-dip galvanized body without rain gutters, integrated roll cage (IRC), wider rear wings and side skirts, side-impact protection beams in doors, integrated roll cage (IRC), flexible polyurethane front and rear bumpers with integrated aluminium beams, RUF front bumpers with three air intakes and air outlets at the sides, plastic engine lid with

	integrated rear spoiler with integrated air intakes for intercoolers and air intake for central airbox, RUF rear wings with centre exhaust pipes, red non-reflecting valance with integrated reversing and rear fog lamps, RUF sports outside mirrors
CTR II sport:	Wider kevlar carbon front wings, side skirts and rear wings
Suspension, front:	Individually suspended light alloy lower wishbones, McPherson struts with coil springs, Bilstein gas-filled shock absorbers, anti-roll bar
Suspension, rear:	Individually suspended on light alloy multi wishbone axle with LSA system (Lightweight, Stability, Agility) with progressive coil springs, Bilstein gas-filled shock absorbers, anti-roll bar
Brakes, front/rear (Size (mm)):	Carbon discs (360 x 25) / Carbon discs (360 x 25) 4-piston fixed aluminium callipers / 4-piston fixed aluminium callipers
Wheels, front/rear:	8.5 J x 19 / 10 J x 19 [10 J x 18 / 12 J x 18]
Tyres, front/rear:	245/35 ZR 19 / 285/30 ZR 19 [285/35 ZR 18 / 325/30 ZR 18]

Electrical system

Alternator (W/A):	1610 / 115
Battery (V/Ah):	12 / 75

Dimensions and weight

Track, front/rear (mm):	1405 [1565] / 1453 [1578]
Wheelbase (mm):	2272
Length x width x height (mm):	4290 x 1735 [1920] x 1275
Kerb weight DIN (kg):	1380
Permissible gross weight (kg):	1835
Fuel tank capacity (l):	73.5, including 15 reserve
Power/weight ratio (kg/kW/ kg/hp):	3.61 [3.23] / 2.65 [2.38]

Fuel

	98 RON super plus unleaded

Performance, prices

Acceleration 0-62mph/100kph (s):	3.6
0-124mph/200 kph (s):	11.4 [10.5]
Maximum speed (mph / kph):	over 211 / 340
Purchase and conversion prices:	
1997:	DM 425,500 [DM 520,000]
Fou wheel drive:	DM 20,700
Kevlar carbon light weight parts:	DM 27,600

RUF turbo R Coupé
1994–1997

Engine

Engine design:	6-cylinder horizontally-opposed, twin-turbo charger, twin-intercooler
Installation:	Rear-engine
Cooling system:	Air-cooled
Displacement (cc):	3600
Bore x stroke (mm):	100 x 76.4
Engine output DIN (kW/hp):	360/490 at 5500rpm
Maximum torque (Nm/lb ft):	650/479 at 4800rpm
Output per litre (kW/l / hp/l):	100.0 / 136.1
Compression ratio:	8.0 : 1
Valve operation & camshaft drive:	ohc, cams driven by double chain, 2 valves per cylinder
Carburation:	Bosch DME, Motronic M 5.2
Ignition system:	Bosch DME
Firing order:	1 - 6 - 2 - 4 - 3 - 5
Turbo boost (bar):	1.0
Engine lubrication:	Dry sump
Engine oil total (l):	13.5

Transmission

Drive configuration:	4-wheel-drive with visco-clutch, transaxle
Manual gearbox:	6-speed
Transmission ratios:	
1st gear:	3.818
2nd gear:	2.150
3rd gear:	1.560
4th gear:	1.212
5th gear:	0.937
6th gear:	0.710
Reverse gear:	2.857
Drive ratio:	3.444
Ltd slip diff. load/deceleration (%):	25 / 40
Option:	Electronic clutch system (EKS)

Body, chassis, suspension, brakes, wheels

Body design:	Steel coupé body, 2 doors, 2 + 2 seats, entirely hot-dip galvanized body, wider rear wings and side skirts, side-impact protection beams in doors, integrated roll cage (IRC), flexible polyurethane front and rear bumpers with integrated aluminium beams, front bumpers with three air intakes, plastic engine lid with integrated rear spoiler, red non-reflecting valance with integrated reversing and rear fog lamps
Option:	RUF sports outside mirrors
Suspension, front:	Individually suspended light alloy lower wishbones, McPherson struts with coil springs, Bilstein gas-filled shock absorbers, anti-roll bar
Suspension, rear:	Individually suspended on light alloy multi wishbone axle with LSA system (Lightweight, Stability, Agility) with progressive coil springs, Bilstein gas-filled shock absorbers, anti-roll bar
Brakes, front/rear (Size (mm)):	Ventilated and drilled discs (322 x 32) / Ventilated and drilled discs (322 x 28) 4-piston fixed aluminium callipers / 4-piston fixed aluminium callipers Bosch ABS 5
Wheels, front/rear:	8.5 J x 18 / 10 J x 18
Wheels, type:	RUF 5-spoke aluminium
Tyres, front/rear:	225/40 ZR 18 / 285/30 ZR 18

Electrical system

Alternator (W/A):	1610 / 115
Battery (V/Ah):	12 / 75

Dimensions and weight

Track, front/rear (mm):	1411 / 1504
Wheelbase (mm):	2272
Length x width x height (mm):	4245 x 1795 x 1285
Kerb weight DIN (kg):	1491
Permissible gross weight (kg):	1840
Fuel tank capacity (l):	73.5, including 15 reserve
Option:	92, including 15 reserve
Power/weight ratio (kg/kW / kg/hp):	4.14 / 3.04

Fuel

	98 RON super plus unleaded

Performance, prices

Acceleration 0-62mph/100 kph (s):	3.6
0-124mph/200 kph (s):	11.8
Maximum speed (mph / kph):	204 / 329
Purchase price:	
2000:	DM 298,000

RUF RGT Coupé
RUF RGT Cabriolet
2000–2005

Engine

Engine design:	6-cylinder horizontally-opposed
Installation:	Rear-engine
Cooling system:	Water-cooled
Displacement (cc):	3600
Bore x stroke (mm):	100 x 76.4
Engine output DIN (kW/hp):	283/385 at 7700rpm
Maximum torque (Nm/lb ft):	375/277 at 5200rpm
Output per litre (kW/l / hp/l):	78.3 / 106.9
Compression ratio:	11.7 : 1
Valve operation & camshaft drive:	dohc, cams driven by double chain, 4 valves per cylinder, VarioCam, intake camshaft timing varies 25°
Carburation:	Bosch DME, Motronic M 5.2.2, sequential multi-point manifold injection
Ignition system:	Bosch DME, distributorless ignition system with six individual ignition coils
Firing order:	1 - 6 - 2 - 4 - 3 - 5
Engine lubrication:	Dry sump
Engine oil total (l):	12,5

Transmission

Drive configuration:	Rear-axle drive
Option:	4-wheel-drive with visco-clutch, cardan shaft
Manual gearbox:	6-speed
Transmision ratios:	
1st gear:	3.82
2nd gear:	2.15
3rd gear:	1.56
4th gear:	1.21
5th gear:	0.97
6th gear:	0.83
Reverse gear:	2.86
Drive ratio:	3.44
Ltd slip diff. load/deceleration (%):	40 / 60

Body, chassis, suspension, brakes, wheels

Body design:	Steel body, 2 doors, 2 + 2 seats, entirely hot-dip galvanized body, side-impact protection beams in doors, RUF side skirts, flexible polyurethane front and rear bumpers with integrated aluminium beams, RUF front bumper, engine lid with fixed RUF rear spoiler, RUF sports outside mirrors
Coupé:	Fixed steel roof, integrated roll cage (IRC)
Option:	Electric sunroof
Cabriolet:	Electric hood with flexible plastic rear window, two retracted roll bars
Standard:	Aluminium hardtop with electrically-heatable rear window
Suspension, front:	Individually suspended with 'disconnected' light alloy wishbones, McPherson struts with coil springs, Bilstein gas-filled shock absorbers, anti-roll bar
Suspension, rear:	Individually suspended on five wishbones per side on light alloy multi-wishbone axle with LSA system (Lightweight, Stability, Agility) with coil springs, Bilstein gas-filled shock absorbers, anti-roll bar
Brakes, front/rear (Size (mm)):	Ventilated and drilled discs (350 x 34) / Ventilated and drilled discs (330 x 28) 6-piston fixed aluminium monobloc callipers / 4-piston fixed aluminium monobloc callipers Bosch ABS 5.3
Wheels, front/rear:	8.5 J x 18 / 11 J x 18
Tyres, front/rear:	225/40 ZR 18 / 285/30 ZR 18

Electrical system

Alternator (W/A):	1680 / 120
Battery (V/Ah):	12 / 36
with air condition:	12 / 46

Dimensions and weight

Track, front/rear (mm):	1475 / 1495
Wheelbase (mm):	2350
Length x width x height (mm):	4430 x 1765 x 1270
Kerb weight DIN (kg):	1350
Permissible gross weight (kg):	1630
Fuel tank capacity (l):	89, including 12.5 reserve
Power/weight ratio (kg/kW/kg/hp):	4.77 / 3.51

Fuel

	98 RON super plus unleaded

Performance, prices

Acceleration 0-62mph/100kph (s):	4.6
Maximum speed (mph / kph):	191 / 307
Purchase price:	
2000:	US$ 135,000

RUF R turbo Coupé
RUF R turbo Cabriolet
2001–2005

Engine

Engine design:	6-cylinder horizontally-opposed, twin-turbo charger, twin-intercooler
Installation:	Rear-engine
Cooling system:	Water-cooled
Displacement (cc):	3600
Bore x stroke (mm):	100 x 76.4
Engine output DIN (kW/hp):	382/520 at 6000rpm
Maximum torque (Nm/lb ft):	740/546 at 3500rpm
Output per litre (kW/l / hp/l):	106.1 / 144.4
Compression ratio:	9.4 : 1
Valve operation & camshaft drive:	dohc, cams driven by double chain, 4 valves per cylinder, VarioCam Plus, intake camshaft timing varies 25°, intake valve lift
Carburation:	Bosch DME, Motronic M 7.8, sequential multi-point manifold injection
Ignition system:	Bosch DME, distributorless ignition system with six individual ignition coils
Firing order:	1 - 6 - 2 - 4 - 3 - 5
Turbo boost (bar):	1.1
Engine lubrication:	Dry sump
Engine oil total (l):	12.0

Transmission

Drive configuration:	4-wheel-drive with visco-clutch, cardan shaft
Option:	Rear-axle drive
Manual gearbox:	6-speed
Transmission ratios:	
1st gear:	3.82
2nd gear:	2.05
3rd gear:	1.41
4th gear:	1.12
5th gear:	0.92
6th gear:	0.71
Reverse gear:	2.86
Drive ratio:	3.44

Body, chassis, suspension, brakes, wheels

Body design:	Steel body, 2 doors, 2 + 2 seats, entirely hot-dip galvanized body, side-impact protection beams in doors, wider rear wings with RUF air intakes and side skirts, flexible polyurethane front and rear bumpers with integrated aluminium beams, RUF front bumper with bigger air intakes and additional air outlet, rear bumper with air outlets, engine lid with integrated spoiler lip and automatic RUF rear spoiler, RUF sports outside mirrors
Coupé:	Fixed steel roof, integrated roll cage (IRC)
Option:	Electric sunroof, narrow body
Cabriolet:	Electric hood with electrically-heatable rear window, two retracted roll bars
Standard:	Aluminium hardtop with electrically-heatable rear window

Suspension, front:	Individually suspended with 'disconnected' light alloy wishbones, McPherson struts with coil springs, Bilstein gas-filled shock absorbers, anti-roll bar
Suspension, rear:	Individually suspended on five wishbones per side on light alloy multi wishbone axle with LSA system (Light weight, Stability, Agility) with coil springs, Bilstein gas-filled shock absorbers, anti-roll bar
Brakes, front/rear (Size (mm)):	Ventilated and drilled discs (350 x 34) / Ventilated and drilled discs (330 x 28) 6-piston fixed aluminium monobloc callipers / 4-piston fixed aluminium monobloc callipers Bosch ABS 5.7
Option:	Porsche Ceramic Composite Brake (PCCB) Ventilated and drilled ceramic composite discs (350 x 34) / Ventilated and drilled ceramic composite discs (330 x 28) 6-piston fixed aluminium monobloc callipers / 4-piston fixed aluminium monobloc callipers Bosch ABS 5.7
Wheels, front/rear:	8.5 J x 18 / 11.5 J x 18
Wheels, type:	RUF Modular wheels
Tyres, front/rear:	225/40 ZR 18 / 295/30 ZR 18
Tyres, type:	Pirelli P Zero Asimmetrico
Option:	8.5 J x 19 / 11 J x 19 RUF 5-spoke Magnesium 225/35 ZR 19 / 305/25 ZR 19

Electrical system

Alternator (W/A):	1680 / 120
Battery (V/Ah):	12 / 80

Dimensions and weight

Track, front/rear (mm):	1465 / 1522
With narrow body:	1465 / 1500
Wheelbase (mm):	2350
Length x width x height (mm):	4435 x 1830 x 1275 - 1295*
Kerb weight DIN (kg):	1540
With narrow body:	1530
Permissible gross weight (kg):	1885
Fuel tank capacity (l):	64, including 10 reserve
Power/weight ratio (kg/kW/kg/hp):	4.03 / 2.96
With narrow body	4.00 / 2.94
*dependent on suspension	

Fuel

	98 RON super plus unleaded

Performance, prices

Acceleration 0-62mph/100kph (s):	3.7
0-124mph/200 kph (s):	11.5
Maximum speed (mph / kph):	213 / 343
Purchase and conversion prices:	
2002 Coupé wide body 4WD:	Euro 219,588
Narrow body:	Euro 14,848
Cabriolet:	Euro 20,764
Hardtop:	Euro 2,204
Rear-axle drive & 89 l fuel tank:	Euro 14,848
Integrated roll cage (IRC):	Euro 9,048

RUF R turbo Coupé
RUF R turbo Cabriolet
2002–2005

Engine

Engine design:	6-cylinder horizontally-opposed, twin-turbo charger, twin-intercooler
Installation:	Rear-engine
Cooling system:	Water-cooled
Displacement (cc):	3600
Bore x stroke (mm):	100 x 76.4
Engine output DIN (kW/hp):	404/550 at 6000rpm
Maximum torque (Nm/lb ft):	780/575 at 4000rpm
Output per litre (kW/l / hp/l):	112.2 / 152.8
Compression ratio:	9.4 : 1
Valve operation & camshaft drive:	dohc, cams driven by double chain, 4 valves per cylinder, VarioCam Plus, intake camshaft timing varies 25°, intake valve lift
Carburation:	Bosch DME, Motronic M 7.8, sequential multi-point manifold injection
Ignition system:	Bosch DME, distributorless ignition system with six individual ignition coils
Firing order:	1 - 6 - 2 - 4 - 3 - 5
Turbo boost (bar):	1.1
Engine lubrication:	Dry sump
Engine oil total (l):	12.0

Transmission

Drive configuration:	4-wheel-drive with visco-clutch, cardan shaft
Option:	Rear-axle drive
Manual gearbox:	6-speed
Transmission ratios:	
1st gear:	3.82
2nd gear:	2.05
3rd gear:	1.41
4th gear:	1.12
5th gear:	0.92
6th gear:	0.71
Reverse gear:	2.86
Drive ratio:	3.44

Body, chassis, suspension, brakes, wheels

Body design:	Steel body, 2 doors, 2 + 2 seats, entirely hot-dip galvanized body, side-impact protection beams in doors, wider rear wings with RUF air intakes and side skirts, flexible polyurethane front and rear bumpers with integrated aluminium beams, RUF front bumper with bigger air intakes and additional air outlet, rear bumper with air outlets, engine lid with integrated spoiler lip and automatic RUF rear spoiler, RUF sports outside mirrors
Coupé:	Fixed steel roof, integrated roll cage (IRC)
Option:	Electric sunroof, narrow body
Cabriolet:	Electric hood with electrically-heatable rear window, two retracted roll bars
Standard:	Aluminium hardtop with electrically-heatable rear window
Suspension, front:	Individually suspended with 'disconnected' light alloy wishbones, McPherson struts with coil springs, Bilstein gas-filled shock absorbers, anti-roll bar
Suspension, rear:	Individually suspended on five wishbones per side on light alloy multi wishbone axle with LSA system (Light weight, Stability, Agility) with coil springs, Bilstein gas-filled shock absorbers, anti-roll bar
Brakes, front/rear (Size (mm)):	Ventilated and drilled discs (350 x 34) / Ventilated and drilled discs (330 x 28) 6-piston fixed aluminium monobloc callipers / 4-piston fixed aluminium monobloc callipers Bosch ABS 5.7
Option:	Porsche Ceramic Composite Brake (PCCB) Ventilated and drilled ceramic composite discs (350 x 34) / Ventilated and drilled ceramic composite discs (350 x 28) 6-piston fixed aluminium monobloc callipers / 4-piston fixed aluminium monobloc callipers Bosch ABS 5.7
Wheels, front/rear:	8.5 J x 18 / 11.5 J x 18
Wheels, type:	RUF Modular wheels
Tyres, front/rear:	225/40 ZR 18 / 295/30 ZR 18
Tyres, type:	Pirelli P Zero Asimmetrico
Option:	8.5 J x 19 / 11 J x 19 RUF 5-spoke Magnesium 225/35 ZR 19 / 305/25 ZR 19

Electrical system

Alternator (W/A):	1680 / 120
Battery (V/Ah):	12 / 80

Dimensions and weight

Track, front/rear (mm):	1465 / 1522
With narrow body:	1465 / 1500
Wheelbase (mm):	2350
Length x width x height (mm):	4435 x 1830 x 1275 - 1295*
Kerb weight DIN (kg):	1540
With narrow body:	1530
Permissible gross weight (kg):	1885
Fuel tank capacity (l):	64, including 10 reserve
Power/weight ratio (kg/kW/kg/hp):	3.81 / 2.80
With narrow body	3.79 / 2.78
*dependent on suspension	

Fuel

	98 RON super plus unleaded

Performance, prices

Acceleration 0-62mph/100kph (s):	3.7
0-124mph/200 kph (s):	10.8
Maximum speed (mph / kph):	218 / 351
Purchase and conversion prices:	
2002 Coupé wide body 4WD:	Euro 226,548
Narrow body:	Euro 14,848
Cabriolet:	Euro 20,764
Hardtop:	Euro 2,204
Rear-axle drive & 89 l fuel tank:	Euro 14,848
Integrated roll cage (IRC):	Euro 9,048

RUF 3400 S
1997–2005

Engine

Engine design:	6-cylinder horizontally-opposed
Installation:	Rear-engine
Cooling system:	Water-cooled
Displacement (cc):	3387
Bore x stroke (mm):	96 x 78
Engine output DIN (kW/hp):	228/310 at 6800rpm
Maximum torque (Nm/lb ft):	360/266 at 4750rpm
Output per litre (kW/l / hp/l):	67.3 / 91.5
Compression ratio:	11.3 : 1
Valve operation & camshaft drive:	dohc, cams driven by double chain, 4 valves per cylinder, VarioCam, intake camshaft timing varies 25°
Carburation:	Bosch DME, Motronic M 5.2, sequential mult point manifold injection
2000 - 2005:	Bosch DME, Motronic M 7.2, sequential multi point manifold injection
Ignition system:	Bosch DME, distributorless ignition system with six individual ignition coils
Firing order:	1 - 6 - 2 - 4 - 3 - 5
Engine lubrication:	Integrated dry sump
Engine oil total (l):	10.25

Transmission

Drive configuration:	Rear-axle drive
Manual gearbox:	6-speed
Transmission ratios:	
1st gear:	3.82
2nd gear:	2.20
3rd gear:	1.52
4th gear:	1.22
5th gear:	1.02
6th gear:	0.84
Reverse gear:	3.55
Drive ratio:	3.44

Body, chassis, suspension, brakes, wheels

Body design:	Steel roadster body, 2 doors, 2 seats, entirely hot-dip galvanized body, side-impact protection beams in doors, flexible polyurethane front and rear bumpers with integrated aluminium beams, RUF front bumper, RUF air intakes, automatic rear spoiler, electric hood with electrically-heatable rear window, two fixed roll bars, RUF sports outside mirrors
Option:	Aluminium hardtop with electrically-heatable rear window

Suspension, front:	Individually suspended, McPherson struts with aluminium suspension links, longitudinal and transverse link, coil springs, Bilstein gas-filled shock absorbers, anti-roll bar
Suspension, rear:	Individually suspended, McPherson struts with aluminium suspension links, lateral and trailing links, coil springs, Bilstein gas-filled shock absorbers, anti-roll bar
Brakes, front/rear (Size (mm)):	Ventilated and drilled discs (318 x 28) / Ventilated and drilled discs (299 x 24)
Option:	Ventilated and drilled discs (330 x 34) / Ventilated and drilled discs (330 x 28) 4-piston fixed aluminium monobloc callipers / 4-piston fixed aluminium monobloc callipers Bosch ABS 5.3
2003–2005:	Bosch ABS 5.7
Wheels, front/rear:	8.5 J x 18 / 10 J x 18
Wheels, type:	RUF Modular wheels
Tyres, front/rear:	225/40 ZR 18 / 265/35 ZR 18
Tyres, type:	Pirelli P Zero Asimmetrico
Option:	8.5 J x 19 / 10 J x 19 RUF 5-spoke Magnesium 235/35 ZR 19 / 275/30 ZR 19 Pirelli P Zero Asimmetrico

Electrical system

Alternator (W/A):	1680 / 120
Battery (V/Ah):	12 / 60

Dimensions and weight

Track, front/rear (mm):	1455 / 1514
Wheelbase (mm):	2415
Length x width x height (mm):	4315 x 1780 x 1265
Kerb weight DIN (kg):	1410
Permissible gross weight (kg):	1615
Fuel tank capacity (l):	58, including 9 reserve
1999 - 2005:	64, including 9 reserve
Power/weight ratio (kg/kW/kg/hp):	6.18 / 4.59

Fuel

	98 RON super plus unleaded

Performance, prices

Acceleration 0-62mph/100kph (s):	5.2
0-124mph/200 kph (s):	11.5
Maximum speed (mph / kph):	173 / 278
Purchase and conversion prices:	
2003 conversion basis Boxster S:	Euro 31,320
2003 conversion basis Boxster:	Euro 39,556
GT 3 front spoiler:	Euro 1,624
Side skirts:	Euro 1,044
RUF 19' wheels:	Euro 9,628

RUF 3600 S
2002–2005

Engine

Engine design:	6-cylinder horizontally-opposed
Installation:	Rear-engine
Cooling system:	Water-cooled
Displacement (cc):	3596
Bore x stroke (mm):	96 x 82.8
Engine output DIN (kW/hp):	239/325 at 6800rpm
with performance kit:	254/345 at 6800rpm
Maximum torque (Nm/lb ft):	370/273 at 4250rpm
with performance kit:	370/273 at 4800rpm
Output per litre (kW/l / hp/l):	66.5 / 90.4
with performance kit:	70.6 / 95.8
Compression ration:	11.3 : 1
Valve operation & camshaft drive:	dohc, cams driven by double chain, 4 valves per cylinder, VarioCam Plus, intake camshaft timing varies 40°, intake valve lift
Carburation:	Bosch DME, Motronic M 7.8, sequential multi-point manifold injection
Ignition system:	Bosch DME, distributorless ignition system with six individual ignition coils
Firing order:	1 - 6 - 2 - 4 - 3 - 5
Engine lubrication:	Integrated dry sump
Engine oil total (l):	8.75

Transmission

Drive configuration:	Rear-axle drive
Manual gearbox:	6-speed
Transmission ratios:	
1st gear:	3.82
2nd gear:	2.20
3rd gear:	1.52
4th gear:	1.22
5th gear:	1.02
6th gear:	0.84
Reverse gear:	3.55
Drive ratio:	3.44

Body, chassis, suspension, brakes, wheels

Body design:	Steel roadster body, 2 doors, 2 seats, entirely hot-dip galvanized body, side-impact protection beams in doors, flexible polyurethane front and rear bumpers with integrated aluminium beams, RUF front bumper, side skirts and rear diffuser, exhaust through rear bumper left and right, automatic rear spoiler, electric hood with electrically-heatable rear window, two fixed roll bars, RUF sports outside mirrors
Option:	Aluminium hardtop with electrically-heatable rear window, 'R turbo look' front wings and front spoiler

Suspension, front:

Suspension, front:	Individually suspended, McPherson struts with aluminium suspension links, longitudinal and transverse link, coil springs, Bilstein gas-filled shock absorbers, anti-roll bar
Suspension, rear:	Individually suspended, McPherson struts with aluminium suspension links, lateral and trailing links, coil springs, Bilstein gas-filled shock absorbers, anti-roll bar
Brakes, front/rear (Size (mm)):	Ventilated and drilled discs (318 x 28) / Ventilated and drilled discs (299 x 24)
Option:	Ventilated and drilled discs (330 x 34) / Ventilated and drilled discs (330 x 28) 4-piston fixed aluminium monobloc callipers / 4-piston fixed aluminium monobloc callipers Bosch ABS 5.3
2003–2005:	Bosch ABS 5.7
Wheels, front /rear:	8,5 J x 18 / 10 J x 18
Wheels, type:	RUF Modular wheels
Tyres, front/rear:	225/40 ZR 18 / 265/35 ZR 18
Tyres, type:	Pirelli P Zero Asimmetrico
Option:	8,5 J x 19 / 10 J x 19 RUF 5-spoke Magnesium 235/35 ZR 19 / 275/30 ZR 19 Pirelli P Zero Asimmetrico

Electrical system

Alternator (W/A):	1680 / 120
Battery (V/Ah):	12 / 60

Dimensions and weight

Track, front/rear (mm):	1455 / 1514
Wheelbase (mm):	2415
Length x width x height (mm):	4320 x 1780 x 1265
Kerb weight DIN (kg):	1410
Permissible gross weight (kg):	1630
Fuel tank capacity (l):	64, including 9 reserve
Power/weight ratio (kg/kW/kg/hp):	5.90 / 4.34
with performance kit:	5.55 / 4.09

Fuel

	98 RON super plus unleaded

Performance, prices

Acceleration 0-62mph/100kph (s):	5.1
with performance kit:	4.9
Maximum speed (mph / kph):	173 / 278
Purchase and conversion prices:	
2002:	Euro 109,040
Performance kit 345 hp:	Euro 15,196
RGT front spoiler:	Euro 1,508
Side skirts:	Euro 1,044
RUF 19 inch wheels:	Euro 9,060